Poverty and Social Impact Analysis of Reforms

*Lessons and Examples
from Implementation*

Poverty and Social Impact Analysis of Reforms

Lessons and Examples from Implementation

EDITED BY
Aline Coudouel
Anis A. Dani
Stefano Paternostro

 THE WORLD BANK

ISBN-10: 0-8213-6486-3
ISBN-13: 978-0-8213-6486-4
eISBN: 0-8213-6487-1
DOI: 10.1596/978-0-8213-6486-4

Cover design and typesetting by Circle Graphics.

Library of Congress Cataloging-in-Publication Data

Poverty and social impact analysis of reforms : lessons and examples from
    implementation / edited by Aline Coudouel, Anis A. Dani, Stefano Paternostro.
       p. cm.
    Includes bibliographical references and index.
    ISBN-13: 978-0-8213-6486-4
    ISBN-10: 0-8213-6486-3
    1. Developing countries—Economic policy. 2. Poverty—Developing countries. I.
Coudouel, Aline. II. Dani, Anis A. (Anis Ahmad) III. Paternostro, Stefano. IV. World
Bank.

HC59.7.P66 2006
339.4'6091724—dc22   2006044704

Contents

BOXES

FIGURES

TABLES

Foreword

Following the adoption of the Poverty Reduction Strategy (PRS) approach, the World Bank and International Monetary Fund committed, in 2001, to a systematic assessment of the poverty and social impacts of policy reforms. Although poverty and social impact analysis (PSIA) studies initially focused on low-income countries, that focus has since spread to middle-income countries. The integration of the PSIA approach into the World Bank's policy lending operations has provided a critical push to mainstreaming this methodology.

This volume presents a collection of poverty and social impact analyses that assess the impact of a range of policy and institutional reforms. In addition to illustrating the use of different tools and methods, these studies provide lessons that encourage and guide policy makers and practitioners while the PSIA approach is mainstreamed.

Although the analytical work for the studies included in this volume is complete, the ensuing policy dialogue and operations are in different stages. The studies present evidence of their impact on government policy and World Bank operations and reveal the value of evidence-based policy making. In several instances, the PSIA studies have led to a re-evaluation of policy advice or to significant modifications in the design of the policy and institutional reforms.

One final challenge remains: to embed PSIA work within country systems, whereby the analytical work would be solicited, managed, and undertaken by the countries themselves. Thus building country capacity is the main thrust of the next stage of PSIA work.

We are grateful to the German Development Cooperation for supporting the preparation of this volume and for supporting client capacity-building for PSIA into the future.

Steen Lau Jorgensen   Luca Barbone
Director, Social Development   *Director, Poverty Reduction*

January 2006

List of Contributors

Diego Angel-Urdinola is a Young Professional at the World Bank. He obtained his doctorate in economics at Georgetown University, Washington, DC, and conducts applied research in the fields of poverty, inequality, labor markets, international migration, and infrastructure. He has contributed to the development of a series of academic and non-academic publications as well as other operational research for various developing nations, especially in Latin America and Sub-Saharan Africa.

Daniel Artana is chief economist at FIEL, a Buenos Aires–based think-tank. His fields of work are public finance, regulation, and macro-economic analysis. He is currently teaching economics at the National University of La Plata and at the MA in law and economics of the University Torcuato Di Tella, both in Argentina. He has been a consultant to the World Bank, the IDB, AID, the UNDP, and several government and private organizations of Latin American countries. He received his doctorate in economics from UCLA.

Sudeshna Ghosh Banerjee is a Young Professional who has been with the Africa Infrastructure Group since September, 2005. After graduating with a doctorate in public policy from the University of North Carolina in 2001, she has been working as a consultant to the World Bank, primarily in infrastructure and social development groups in the Europe and Central Asia and Africa Regions. Her research focuses on poverty and social impact of infrastructure reforms, privatization, investment climate, and survey methodology.

Elena Bardasi is a consultant in the PREM group of the Africa Region of the World Bank. Her research focuses on income distribution, income inequality, poverty, gender, labor market functioning, and applied econometrics. Before joining the Bank in 2003, she was chief research officer at the Institute for Social and Economic Research (University of Essex, UK) and coordinator of the Luxembourg Employment Study project at the Luxembourg Income Study (LIS).

Sabine Beddies is a social scientist in the Social Development Department of the World Bank. Her research and operational focus is on social inclusion, political economy, and distributional impacts of policy reforms. She contributed to the conceptualization and mainstreaming of the PSIA methodology and the Country Social Analysis framework, and conducted operational work in the water sector, agriculture, local government taxation, and financial resource allocation in the education sector. Her recent focus is on macro social analysis and governance in the Middle East and North Africa, and East Asia.

Florencia T. Castro-Leal is a senior economist and task manager in the Latin America Poverty Group and the Nicaragua and Honduras Country offices of the World Bank. Her current work program focuses on poverty reduction strategy papers (PRSPs), enhanced heavily indebted poor country (E-HIPC) Initiatives, Poverty Reduction Support Credits, Poverty Assessments, and Poverty and Social Impact Analysis. She has regional work experience in countries of Africa, Europe, Latin America, and South East Asia. She joined the World Bank in 1993 as a Young Professional and received her doctorate in economics from the University of Texas at Austin.

Antonio Chambal is financial management adviser to the Ministry of Education and Culture of Mozambique. From 2000 to 2005 he was the national director for Administration and Finance, responsible for managing public and external funds for the education sector. Over the same period, he was also the coordinator for an IDA Credit that supported a sectorwide education investment program. In his capacity as director of finance, he launched a national decentralization program that allocates small block grants directly to primary schools in the country. Prior to this, he was department chief in the National Directorate of Technical Education (1989–91) and a professor of accounting, auditing, and financial planning in various technical training institutions in Mozambique.

David Coady is a technical assistance adviser to the Poverty and Social Impact Analysis (PSIA) Group in the Fiscal Affairs Department of the International Monetary Fund. His research interests include public economics and development economics. Recently his research has focused on the evaluation of the targeting, financing, and impact of conditional cash transfer programs, and he has co-authored a book (with Margaret Grosh and John Hoddinott) reviewing the design and implementation of targeted transfer programs titled *Targeting of Transfers in Developing Countries: Review of Lessons and Experience*. Prior to joining the Fund, he was a research fellow at the International Food Policy Research Institute, 1998–2004 and a lecturer in economics in the University of London, 1992–1998.

Maria Correia is a social development lead specialist in the World Bank's Africa Region. She currently manages a multi-country program to demobilize and reintegrate ex-combatants into civilian life in the greater Great Lakes Region of Africa. Prior to assuming this position, she was responsible for furthering the social development agenda in the Bank's Africa Region, including poverty and social impact analyses. Over the last decade, her research has focused on gender and youth development. She is currently editing a volume on gender issues from a male perspective and another on gender and pension reforms in Latin America.

Malcolm Cosgrove-Davies is a senior energy specialist with over 10 years of experience at the World Bank. He is currently assigned to the Bank's Africa Energy Unit, where he has operational responsibility for ongoing and proposed energy projects in Rwanda, Uganda, and Zambia. These projects focus on rural access, grid rehabilitation and expansion, power generation, renewable energy, transmission, and distribution systems, and also include elements of "cross-sectoral" support in information and communication technologies (ICT), water, health, and education. Prior to joining the Bank's Africa Energy Unit, he had similar responsibilities for projects in East and South Asia, with a particular emphasis on rural and renewable energy.

Aline Coudouel is a senior economist with the Poverty Group in the World Bank. She leads the team working on poverty analysis, monitoring, and impact evaluation and has been coordinating the World Bank Poverty Group's work on poverty and social impact analysis. She has been involved in the Poverty and Social Impact Analysis (PSIA) agenda in the World Bank since its inception, defining the approach and advising teams on its implementation for selected countries and reforms. She is the co-editor, with Stefano Paternostro, of two volumes on guidance for the PSIA of selected sectors (Coudouel and Paternostro, 2005 and 2006).

Anis A. Dani is the social policy adviser in the Sustainable Development Network at the World Bank. His research focuses on the social impacts of infrastructure, agriculture, and institutional reforms and programs. Since 2000, he has coordinated the Social Development Group's work on social analysis and led the production of the *Social Analysis Sourcebook*. He then focused on developing and disseminating analytical tools and methods for PSIA, and the production of the *PSIA User's Guide*, the *Good Practice Note* on PSIA, and the *Tools for Institutional, Political, and Social Analysis for PSIA* in collaboration with other partners. Prior to joining the Bank, he worked on people-centered development in Himalayan countries, based at the International Center for Integrated Mountain Development, Kathmandu (1984–9), and on the nonprofit sector in South Asia (1989–95).

Hermine G. De Soto is a senior social scientist (consultant) in social development and has worked for 15 years in operationally focused social development work. Part of her World Bank work includes social studies/analyses, poverty studies, and social impact analyses in the World Bank's Europe and Central Asia Region as well as in the Sub-Saharan Africa Region. She is a widely published social scientist/anthropologist, both within the Bank and in international academia. Her most recent World Bank publication is *Roma and Egyptians in Albania: From Social Exclusion to Social Inclusion* (2005). Also trained in medical anthropology, she currently assists with operational work in the Sub-Saharan African regional malaria program, control, and management.

B. Essama-Nssah is a senior economist with the Poverty Reduction Group at the World Bank, who works on the development and application of simulation models for the study of the impact of economic shocks and policies on poverty and income distribution. He is the author of a book on analytical and normative underpinnings of poverty, inequality, and social well-being. He was a senior research associate with the Cornell University Food and Nutrition Policy Program from 1990 to 1992. From 1984 to 1989 he was vice dean of the Faculty of Law and Economics, and head of the Economics Department at the University of Yaoundé (Cameroon). He received his doctorate in economics from the University of Michigan.

Leonardo Gasparini is the director of the Center for Distributional, Labor and Social Studies (CEDLAS) at Universidad Nacional de La Plata in Argentina. He works on poverty and inequality issues in Latin America and the Caribbean. His research also includes the analysis of social programs, education, and the distributional impact of fiscal policy. He has been working as a consultant with the World Bank. In particular, he has contributed to several recent World Bank LAC Flagship Reports.

Nils Junge has been a consultant for the World Bank since 2002, and over the past three years he has conducted Poverty and Social Impact Analyses in the Europe and Central Asia and Sub-Saharan Africa Regions. His recent focus has been on labor restructuring. As part of his work, he is currently researching and developing evaluation models for analyzing the welfare impacts of mass layoffs.

Sarah Keener is a senior social development specialist in the Sub-Saharan Africa Region's Environmentally and Socially Sustainable Department of the World Bank. Her current work focuses on policy and institutional analysis in the health, mining, and infrastructure sectors, and in stakeholder participation in the regional Nile Basin Initiative. She has worked in 20 African countries, with a focus on demand-based and participatory design of water, sanitation, and environment projects.

Shashi Kolavalli is a development consultant based in Washington, DC. His research interests are institutions, the public role in private sector–led growth, and strategy development. Some of the issues he is working on are organization of export crop sectors and sanitation. Previously he was a principal economist at the International Crop Research Centre for the Semi-Arid Tropics and professor at the Indian Institute of Management, Ahmedabad, India.

Milton Kutengule has been secretary to the Treasury in the Ministry of Finance in Malawi since August 2004. Between 2002 and 2004, he was permanent secretary of the Ministry of Economic Planning and Development, responsible for monitoring the implementation of various economic and development policies, including the Malawi Poverty Reduction Strategy. Dr. Kutengule received his doctorate from the University of East Anglia (UK) in 2000. His thesis focused on the diversification of sources of income in rural parts of Malawi. He also has considerable experience in the design, management, and review of economic and social development policies and programs in this country. Recently, he has reviewed various decentralization and poverty reduction initiatives in Southern Africa and in Malawi.

Julian Lampietti is a senior economist in the Europe and Central Asia Environmentally and Socially Sustainable Development Group. He is author or co-author of five PSIAs as well as regional studies on the demand for heating and power sector reform. Currently his work program focuses on designing projects and policy in the areas of rural development and agriculture. He is in the process of completing a book about PSIAs and the power sector.

Manuel Francisco Lobo is adviser to the Minister of Education and Culture of Mozambique, and leads the education group that developed the PRSP in the areas of human resource development and decentralization. From 2004 to 2005, he was the national director of Basic Education and led the EFA-FTI team. Prior to this, he worked in the planning unit of the ministry (starting in 1997), in the Pedagogic University, as a provincial director of education (1990–1994), and as a teacher.

Shabih Mohib is an economist in the East Asia and the Pacific Poverty Reduction and Economic Management Unit of the World Bank. His current work focuses on improving public expenditure management and governance, enhancing the efficacy of fiscal policy, and civil administration reform. Before joining the World Bank in 2003, he was a senior economist at the Ministry of Finance in Tanzania where he worked as a fiscal economist and focused on issues pertaining to public expenditure management, the Tanzania Poverty Reduction Strategy, and medium-term macro-fiscal forecasting and reporting.

Miriam Montenegro Lazo is a research analyst working at the Advisory Technical Unit at the Ministry of the Presidency of Honduras. She got her master's degree in economics at the Pontificia Universidad Catolica de Chile. She has experience in PRSP implementation and monitoring as well as in PSIA work. She has been the manager of the Research Unit conducting several studies related to policy and PRSP impact and evaluation since February 2004. She has a lot of training in database management and econometric analysis. She has contributed to the development and publication of research studies in the fields of poverty, inequality, policy incidence, and the labor market.

Ambar Narayan is an economist in the South Asia Poverty Reduction and Economic Management Unit. His work primarily focuses on poverty-related issues—assisting countries to develop methods for monitoring and measuring poverty and design policy interventions, and conducting analysis on microlevel data to support the Bank's operations. He has been involved in a number of reports such as Poverty Assessments and Development Policy Reviews in the South Asia region, as well as in writing the regional Social Protection Strategy. Recently, he has participated in supervising the cash grant component of the Bank's emergency tsunami relief project in Sri Lanka.

David Newhouse is a technical assistance adviser to the Poverty and Social Impact Analysis (PSIA) Group in the Fiscal Affairs Department of the International Monetary Fund. He has assisted with the writing of several PSIA studies, including a number of studies on the distributional impacts of price and tax reforms. His research interests include topics in household income dynamics, health economics, and the economics of education. His work focuses both on developed and developing countries, with special emphasis on Indonesia and the United States. He earned his doctorate from Cornell University in 2002, and subsequently worked as a staff economist at the Federal Trade Commission for two years before joining the Fund.

Antonio Nucifora is an economist in the Poverty Reduction and Economic Management Unit for Southern Africa at the World Bank, where he focuses on Malawi. His current work is being carried out in close collaboration with the government and includes an assessment of the efficiency of public expenditures and a study of the characteristics and determinants of poverty using the data from the 2004/5 nationally representative integrated household survey. He has also been involved extensively in issues of food security and agricultural policy in Malawi. Before joining the World Bank in 2002, he was a visiting professor at the University of Catania, Italy, where he taught courses on agricultural economics and econometrics.

Stefano Paternostro is a lead economist in the World Bank Africa Region Human Development Group. From 2002 to 2005, he coordinated the World Bank Poverty Group's work on poverty and social impact analysis, developing and disseminating methodologies to assess impacts of policy reforms, producing the *PSIA User's Guide* and the *Good Practice*

Note on PSIA, and coordinating with external partners on operational issues. With Aline Coudouel, he is the co-editor of two volumes on guidance for PSIA in selected sectors (Coudouel and Paternostro, 2005 and 2006).

Marc-Olivier Rubin has a background in both economics and political science and has been working with PSIA as a junior professional officer in the Social Development Department of the World Bank. Currently, he is finishing his doctorate on food security and famine while undertaking various consultancies for the World Bank and the Copenhagen Consensus Secretariat.

Issouf Samaké is an economist at the IMF Institute. Before joining the IMF, he worked as a consultant to the World Bank Institute and to the DECVP, as well as the African Region for about three years. He helped to develop the Bank's Poverty Analysis Macroeconomic Simulator (or PAMS) and worked for several governments in Africa on macroeconomic modeling and poverty issues.

Dumitru Sandu is a professor of sociology at the University of Bucharest and also works as a local expert for the World Bank in Romania. His current research focuses on temporary emigration and public action attitudes, with recent articles in *Current Sociology* and *International Journal of Sociology*. His experience in applied sociology is presented in his just-published book, *Community Development: Research, Practice and Ideology*.

Sarosh Sattar is a senior economist in the Europe and Central Asia Region (Poverty and Economic Management Department) of the World Bank. Her current work focuses on macroeconomic and structural issues as well as assessing the extent and main causes of poverty in low- and middle-income countries. Before joining the Europe and Central Asia Region, she worked extensively on these issues and on social sector expenditures analysis in the Middle East and North Africa Region.

Robert Townsend is a senior economist in the East Africa Rural Development Operations Department of the World Bank. He works on analytical support and lending operations to countries in the region. His recent work has focused on supporting improvements in policy and public expenditure alignment to the agricultural growth and poverty reduction objectives of Tanzania and Uganda.

Alexandria Valerio is a senior education specialist in the Latin America and Caribbean Region of the World Bank Group. Her current research focuses on educational policy and decentralization of financial resources and management decisions directly to districts and primary schools, technical vocational education and training, and HIV/AIDS and education. Before joining the Latin America and Caribbean Region, she was responsible for leading the policy dialogue and operational tasks in the education sector in Mozambique and Angola, and she is author of regional research on school-based HIV/AIDS prevention programs for students and teachers.

Tara Vishwanath is a lead economist, PRSP adviser, and poverty coordinator for the South Asia Region's Poverty Reduction and Economic Management Unit of the World Bank. Before joining the World Bank she was a professor in the economics department of Northwestern University. Her work in South Asia provides leadership to the poverty work in the region—which encompasses a wide range of tasks, including survey-based analytical work, the development of monitoring tools, the design of policy interventions and their evaluation, and strategic policy advice. Recent and ongoing work includes managing the cash grant program of the tsunami project, technical support for the welfare reform in Sri Lanka, and select randomized evaluation experiments in the area of education and poverty programs.

Jan Walliser is a senior economist in the Country Economics Unit of the Operations Policy and Country Services Vice Presidency of the World Bank. During 2002–4 he was senior country economist for Burkina Faso, where he coordinated the preparation of several fast-disbursing credits, technical studies on public expenditures, and poverty analysis. Prior to joining the World Bank, Mr. Walliser was an economist at the International Monetary Fund, and a principal analyst at the U.S. Congressional Budget Office. His research has largely focused on macroeconomics of tax reform and pensions, the functioning of annuities markets, and issues in intergenerational redistribution and aging.

Limin Wang is an economist on secondment from DFID to the World Bank. She holds a doctorate in economics from the University of Southampton, United Kingdom. Her research focuses on impact analysis of policy reforms, income inequality, labor market reforms, and determinants of health outcomes in developing countries. She has contributed to a series of academic publications and policy reports for the World Bank.

Before joining the World Bank in 1999, she was a lecturer at the Kings' College, London, and a search officer at STICERD, London School of Economics.

Quentin Wodon is a lead poverty specialist in the PREM Unit of the Sub-Saharan Africa Vice Presidency of the World Bank. After completing business and engineering studies and working in the marketing department of Procter & Gamble, he shifted fields to focus on poverty-related issues and joined, for five years, the ATD Fourth World, an international NGO working with the very poor. Thereafter he completed his doctorate in economics, taught at the University of Namur, and joined the World Bank in 1998. His current focus is on helping African countries prepare and implement their Poverty Reduction Strategies.

Nobuo Yoshida is an economist in the Poverty Reduction and Economic Management Unit of the South Asia Region at the World Bank. He is currently working on poverty, education, health, and social protection issues in India, Pakistan, and Sri Lanka. His research interests are on poverty and inequality measurement at subnational levels, the targeting of social protection programs, and bureaucratic corruption.

Hassan Zaman is a senior economist in the South Asia Poverty Reduction and Economic Management Unit of the World Bank. He was previously in the Africa Region of the Bank working on structural reform and public expenditure issues in Malawi. Prior to joining the World Bank as a Young Professional in 1998, he worked on micro-credit issues in Bangladesh for an NGO and assessed the impact of micro-credit for his doctoral thesis.

Lessons from the Implementation of Poverty and Social Impact Analysis of Reforms

ALINE COUDOUEL, ANIS DANI,
AND STEFANO PATERNOSTRO

I ncreased attention to poverty reduction as the central goal of development has highlighted the need for an improved understanding of how policies affect the poor. With the advent of the Poverty Reduction Strategies (PRS)—vehicles through which countries articulate their strategic choices on policy and institutional reforms—many low-income countries are struggling over the choice of public actions that will have the greatest impact on poverty. This difficulty stems partly from the lack of sound analysis of the distributional consequences of reform. The call for systematic assessment of poverty and social impacts emerged from the recognition that these elements result in differential impact on different social groups. Analysis of winners and losers of reforms helps to inform the design of policies that promote more equitable access to opportunity, particularly for the poor and disadvantaged groups.

THE CHALLENGES OF POVERTY AND SOCIAL IMPACT ANALYSIS

Poverty and social impact analysis (PSIA) is challenging because of the complex nature of reforms and their consequences. The analysis of distributional impacts depends on many elements—the design of the reform itself, of course, but also the political economy of reform and the capacity of implementing and regulatory agencies responsible for the reform program. First, policies affect different groups in very different ways, with some groups losing while others gain. Second, most reforms have distributional impacts that are transmitted to households and individuals through different channels, and these impacts can go in opposite directions for particular groups. Third, impacts may vary over time: some impacts can be expected to occur immediately, while others may take more time to materialize. As the economic impacts and behavioral responses to a policy change evolve, they can lead to alternations of positive and negative impacts over time. Fourth, some impacts derive directly from the reforms, while others take more indirect routes to reach households.

In addition, the interests of stakeholders can have important consequences for the actual implementation of reforms and their success. In particular, stakeholders likely to lose influence, power, or benefits can resist reforms. Resistance from influential stakeholders or elite capture of benefits can undermine reform efforts. Analysis of those interests helps to understand likely reform outcomes.

Finally, the impact of reforms depends on the capacity and willingness of responsible agencies to carry out or oversee reform implementation. Reforms tend to involve a deepening of or change in responsibilities. This change is sometimes linked to the creation of a new organization or the addition of new roles and responsibilities to existing organizations. Internalizing these institutional measures takes time as new staff is hired or existing staff redeployed and retrained, and new systems and procedures introduced. The success of policy reforms thus depends heavily on the related institutional reforms and the political will to support these reform measures unstintingly.

Addressing the Challenge

In January 2001, the Joint Implementation Committee for Poverty Reduction Strategy Papers (PRSP) acknowledged the gaps in the analysis of policy impacts within client countries and asked the Bank to take the technical lead in helping developing countries fill this analytical gap.[1] The analysis of impacts of policy reforms is not entirely new, nor are the analytical instruments for such analysis new inventions. What is new is the application of the tools and techniques of social and economic analysis to analyze impacts of economywide policy reforms before those reforms are carried out (ex ante analysis), and more systematic use of that analysis to inform policy advice and policy design. A quick internal stocktaking in 2001 identified some ongoing analytical work but revealed considerable analytical gaps within Bank- and International Monetary Fund (IMF)-assisted operations. Consequently, the Bank, along with key donor partners, embarked on a program of systematizing PSIA of the policy reforms supported by its lending.[2]

Over the past few years, the World Bank has developed a broad array of guidance materials to stimulate and support PSIA. The first of these was *A User's Guide to Poverty and Social Impact Analysis* (World Bank 2003), which describes the methodological approach recommended for PSIA. The *User's Guide* presents key elements of good practice, highlights the operational principles and existing constraints on PSIA, and summarizes the key tools used by practitioners for PSIA of policy reforms.

The *User's Guide* has been supplemented by additional products focusing on tools and techniques. *The Impact of Economic Policies on Poverty and Income Distribution: Evaluation Techniques and Tools* is a compendium of tools and techniques relevant to PSIA, which range from incidence analysis to tools linking microeconomic distribution to macroeconomic frameworks or models (Bourguignon and da Silva 2003). A second volume (forthcoming), *Evaluating the Impact of Macroeconomic Policies on Poverty and Income Distribution Using Micro-Macro Linkages Models,* will present five approaches through which macro-counterfactual experiments can be modeled and linked to microeconomic data. The World Bank has also released a sourcebook of *Tools for Institutional, Political and Social Analysis (TIPS) in Poverty and Social Impact Analysis,* produced in partnership with the U.K. Department for International Development (DFID), which draws on a range of multidisciplinary tools to complement econometric analysis with what is generically called social analysis (DFID and World Bank 2005).

Two additional volumes—*Analyzing the Distributional Impact of Reforms: A Practitioner's Guide to Trade, Monetary and Exchange Rate Policy, Utility Provision, Agricultural Markets, Land Policy and Education* and its companion volume *Analyzing the Distributional Impact of Reforms: A Practitioner's Guide to Pension, Health, Labor Market, Public Sector Downsizing, Taxation, Decentralization and Macroeconomic Modeling*—present analytical guidance and an overview of the specific issues arising from the analysis of selected categories of policy and institutional reforms.[3] These volumes offer guidance on the selection of economic tools and techniques for economic analysis of distributional impacts most appropriate to the reforms under scrutiny as well as examples of applications of these approaches.

The pilot studies financed between 2002 and 2004 helped to stimulate interest in PSIA.[4] Subsequently, the Bank earmarked funds for scaling up PSIA, resulting in around 40 PSIA studies being conducted annually during the next three years. By 2006, over 150 PSIA studies have been completed or are underway. The majority of these have been conducted in low-income countries, but PSIA has also been extended to middle-income countries. Less than three years after the first studies, the PSIA approach has established a firm foothold within the analytical work undertaken by the World Bank and several other development agencies.

Consolidating PSIA in World Bank Operations

In September 2004, the World Bank provided operational guidance to its staff through the approval of the Operational Policy on Development Policy Lending (OP8.60). The Operational Policy was accompanied by a *Good Practice Note on PSIA,* providing operational guidance for staff and country counterparts on how to integrate PSIA within development policy lending operations. The Bank has also committed itself to place the results of this work in the public information domain through the release of the Program Document for a development policy lending operation after Executive Directors have approved the operation. The Operational Policy describes the obligations of the Bank to undertake due diligence for the policy reforms supported by its operations:

> *Poverty and Social Impacts.* The Bank determines whether specific country policies supported by the operation are likely to have significant poverty and social consequences, especially on poor people and vulnerable groups. For country policies with likely significant effects, the Bank summarizes in the Program Document relevant analytic knowledge of these effects and of the borrower's systems for reducing adverse effects and enhancing positive effects associated with the specific policies being supported. If there are significant gaps in the analysis or shortcomings in the borrower's systems, the Bank describes in the Program Document how such gaps or shortcomings would be addressed before or during program implementation, as appropriate. (OP8.60, *Development Policy Lending:* paragraph 10, World Bank 2004).[5]

The approval of the policy has helped to consolidate PSIA work by making it routine. One noteworthy feature of this policy commitment is that it has extended the application of PSIA beyond low-income countries that prepare a Poverty Reduction Strategy to middle-income countries, since Development Policy Lending is for both groups of countries. PRSP countries are eligible for Poverty Reduction Support Credits (PRSC) on concessional terms, while middle-income countries typically obtain budget support through loans linked to specific policy reforms.

The enactment of the operational policy is an important step toward providing an institutional base for PSIA. In practice, mainstreaming depends on integrating PSIA in strategy and analytical instruments.

Strategy documents—countries' PRSPs and Country Assistance Strategies (CAS)—produced in the past did not systematically identify PSIA priorities, but this is slowly changing. The next generation of PRSPs offers an opportunity to identify priority reforms whose poverty and social impacts would need to be analyzed. On the Bank's side, there is an expectation that this analytical program will be reflected in the forthcoming CASs.

From its inception, PSIA has been identified as an approach, not as a new instrument. To the extent that the PSIA approach within the Bank is well integrated into country analytical work—poverty assessments, public expenditure reviews, country economic memorandum, country social analysis, and Economic and Sector Work—PSIAs do not have to be produced as stand-alone studies. Even when a PSIA is undertaken as a stand-alone piece, operational links and impacts can be achieved by linking it to specific operations. Going forward, PSIAs are being aligned much more closely and integrated within country Economic and Sector Work. This tendency will be strengthened as special funding for PSIA disappears and is replaced by the normal operating budget.

Objective of this Book

Despite the rapid uptake of PSIA, in particular by the World Bank, civil society organizations and bilateral donors point to several areas where they feel PSIA work could be improved.[6] The need for better integration of PSIA into the PRS process, greater stakeholder involvement in the analysis, more systematic disclosure of work carried out by the Bank, and more systematic use of PSIA in informing Bank-supported operations are frequently raised. This collection of case studies provides an opportunity to reflect back on the PSIA work undertaken so far to draw lessons on how the analysis and its operational impact can be improved.

This book contains a selection of examples from the first cohorts of completed PSIAs. The case studies do not cover all the types of reforms analyzed, nor do they provide comprehensive coverage of all the tools and techniques that can be used to analyze policy impacts, but this cross-section of case studies is not atypical. The cases have been selected to illustrate the spectrum of sectors and policy reforms to which PSIA can be applied and to demonstrate the range of analytical tools and techniques that have been used for PSIA. The chapters largely deal with policy reforms in a single sector, such as agriculture (crop marketing boards in Malawi and Tanzania, cotton privatization in Tajikistan), energy (mining sector in Romania, oil subsidies in Ghana), utilities (power sector reform in Ghana, Rwanda and transition economies, water sector reform in Albania), social sectors (education reform in Mozambique, social welfare reform in Sri Lanka), and taxation reform (Nicaragua), but they also include macroeconomic modeling (Burkina Faso).

FIVE ANALYTICAL LESSONS

In the rest of this chapter, we draw on the case studies included in this volume to discuss the analytical and operational lessons. We then present a short synopsis of each of the chapters presented in this volume before concluding with challenges that lie ahead.

Lesson 1: Negative and Positive Impacts

Generically, *distributional analysis* means the analysis of the impact of reforms both on groups that benefit from reforms and on groups that are adversely affected by them. Indeed, although part of the imperative for PSIA emerged from a concern for how reforms affect the poor, the proponents of PSIA recognized that focusing exclusively on the assessment of adverse impacts on the poor would be limiting and counterproductive. Besides the analytical necessity of comparing impacts on different groups to assess the overall impact of a policy, one key concern was that focusing PSIA exclusively on negative impacts would reduce PSIA to an instrument for designing mitigation measures and leave out the possibility of drawing on it to include the poor in the benefit stream of the reforms. For example, the analysis of the tax reform in Nicaragua revealed that some elements of the reform were progressive while others were regressive. Overall, it was important to have a clear understanding of both positive and negative impacts on different groups so that some impacts could be mitigated while building consensus for the reform.

In addition, PSIA recognizes that it is critical to understand the likely impact of reforms on non-poor groups, especially those with significant influence, in order to uncover potential support and opposition for the reform. Taking the political economy of reforms into account when designing them is central to their success or failure. Broadening the analytical scope of PSIA has given it a greater ability to consider alternative designs of policy reforms.

Lesson 2: Impacts on Different Social Groups

The analytical work carried out over the past few years has been quite effective in broadening the scope of distributional analysis. Distributional impacts are often analyzed for different income groups, typically using constructs such as income or consumption quintiles and deciles. For instance, the chapter on Sri Lanka social welfare reform, the two Ghana chapters on electricity tariff reform and oil subsidies, the analysis of Nicaragua's fiscal reform, and the study of Rwanda's electricity reform use deciles or quintiles to analyze impacts and derive policy recommendations. The power sector reform studies in the Europe and Central Asia Region also look at welfare across income groups. These categories are very useful to understand the effectiveness of targeting, compare aggregate impacts of policy alternatives, and determine the optimal level of transfers.

However, quintiles and deciles are artificial constructs that do not necessarily identify meaningful groups. In this sense, such analysis does not lend itself to the examination of preferences and behavioral responses to policy change. Behavioral responses are often conditioned by other individual and household characteristics, including location, social or occupational characteristics, perceptions of benefits and risks, and the extent to which stakeholders feel they can influence outcomes. Hence, the majority of the studies in this volume have also used such characteristics to define groups. For example, the studies of Albania's water sector, Malawi's agricultural markets, Mozambique's education sector, Romania's mining reform, Tanzania's reform of crop boards, and Tajikistan's cotton reform analyze the impacts of those reforms on spatially defined groups. The analysis of education reform in Mozambique and mining reforms in Romania explicitly look at impacts across gender. The model developed in Burkina Faso distinguishes groups according to their place of residence, their labor market situation, and their involvement in the production of tradable versus nontradable goods. In Sri Lanka, the analysis focuses on particular groups defined not only in terms of their demography but also in terms of access to land and housing.

By looking at the impacts on, and influence of, different stakeholder groups that have different interests and degrees of influence on the reforms, PSIA is also able to analyze the political economy of reform. This provides insights into the likelihood of the reform being carried out as intended and into the likely responses of various groups, thereby deepening the understanding of reforms and their impacts.

Lesson 3: Short- and Long-Term Impacts

In order to present a complete picture of the impacts of reform alternatives, it is also essential to consider both short- and long-term impacts. Most reforms have both direct impacts on selected groups, which often occur relatively rapidly, and indirect impacts, which can take longer to materialize. Assessing short-term impacts tends to be easier than assessing longer-term ones, in part because of their more direct nature. A same group of stakeholders can be affected positively in the short term and negatively in the longer term, and vice-versa. Providing a full picture of the net effects over time is critical to inform the debate around the reform options.

For instance, the analysis of the effect of petroleum price changes in Ghana takes into account both the direct effects on households in terms of the energy they consume and the indirect effects they will feel as a result of changes in prices or increased expenditure in other areas. Very often, reforms are expected to have large indirect effects through their effect on the fiscal balance or more generally their broader effects on the economy. Taking these indirect effects into account is complex. In the case of the cotton reform in Burkina Faso, for example, these broad indirect effects are taken into account in the analysis of changes in cotton prices and volumes, and more generally changes in agricultural production.

Lesson 4: Multiple Transmission Channels

Experience has also shown that it is critical for the analysis to consider multiple transmission channels for impacts, including such channels as prices and wages, employment, access to goods and services, assets, transfers and taxes, and authority.[7] Indeed, selected groups of stakeholders might be affected positively through some channels and negatively through others. Neglecting some of these channels could therefore lead to erroneous conclusions in terms of the net impacts.

The case studies included in this volume typically cover 2 or 3 channels. For example, the studies on Malawi and Tanzania were initially approached primarily through the lens of transfers, but the impact analysis suggested that access to marketing services and changes in authority structures were also significant channels through which additional impacts could be transferred. Similarly, the analysis of utilities in Europe and Central Asia, as well as those in Ghana and Rwanda, suggested that in addition to concern for tariffs, access to utilities was an important consideration. The importance of access implies that the traditional concern for affordability and lifeline tariffs may need to be modified to include the possibility of subsidizing connection costs that, in some instances, may be even more helpful to the poor than recurring price subsidies. The analysis of petroleum price changes in Ghana shows how savings made by reducing the subsidy can be better channeled to the poor through interventions in other sectors, including removing school fees and investing in transport and rural electrification.

Lesson 5: Choice of Research Methods and Tools

The choice of research methods and tools tends to be determined by the nature of the research question, the availability of prior data and secondary information, and the resources and time available for the analysis. By and large, multidisciplinary approaches have proved to be invaluable for PSIA. Preliminary findings from one method are often tested and refined through complementary tools to add robustness through triangulation of results. More than half of the studies in this volume used multidisciplinary approaches. For instance, in the Malawi study, the two quantitative analyses came up with somewhat contrary results that were clarified and interpreted by the qualitative study. Similarly, in the Romania mining study, the analysis of household survey data was compared with the results from the community study and the gender study to arrive at more robust understanding of impacts. On the other hand, the studies on Burkina Faso, Ghana (oil subsidies), Rwanda, and Sri Lanka relied mostly on economic analysis; these studies could benefit from complementary analysis to assess different groups' responses to opportunities and risks.

A particular challenge of PSIA is the need to measure likely behavioral responses to policy reforms. To address this difficulty, the studies in this volume rely partly on qualitative techniques, including key informant interviews and focus groups (as in the studies of water reform in Albania and agricultural markets reforms in Malawi), semi-structured questionnaires and purposive surveys (electricity in Ghana or crop boards in Tanzania), and qualitative research at the community level (analysis of mining reforms in Romania). PSIA also relies on quantitative methods to simulate behavioral responses, for instance by embedding dynamic demand or supply functions in models with micro-macro linkages (as in the model developed for Burkina Faso); or by capturing the likely behavioral responses of households to changes in price, quantity, quality or choice—for instance, changes in consumption patterns (utility reforms in Europe and Central Asia) or changes in demand for education (education in Mozambique).

Political economy analysis can help to understand the interests of influential stakeholders. Political economy dimensions can be studied through stakeholder analysis (as for Ghana electricity), institutional analysis (Albania water, Tanzania crop boards), or analysis of secondary data (Romania mining, Tajikistan cotton).

FIVE OPERATIONAL LESSONS

The PSIA process, especially the degree of participation by stakeholders, has generated some degree of debate. During the early years of PSIA, when there was a degree of skepticism about its feasibility, more attention was given to its analytical and operational aspects. Now that the tools and methods have been developed and adopted, some bilateral partners and civil society organizations feel that the PSIA process needs more attention.[8]

Lesson 1: Identification of Priority Reforms for PSIA

The first operational lesson is that the need for PSIA should emerge from the PRS process. The elaboration of the Poverty Reduction Strategy, or similar national development strategies in other countries, has typically been based on extensive participatory processes.[9] That is where the participatory process and policy dialogue rightly belong. The case for establishing yet another participatory process for identification of reform priorities for PSIA is rather weak. Instead, integrating consultations on PSIA priorities more systematically within future discussions of PRSs and country strategies is desirable.

Overall, government agencies and other in-country stakeholders have tended to be the primary source for identifying reforms for PSIA, although some have been proposed by donor agencies. In middle-income countries, the reforms have tended to emerge during consultations regarding country assistance strategies or their medium-term expenditure frameworks. To the extent that countries have an inclusive process of strategic planning, other stakeholders are able to feed into that process. All the chapters in this volume analyze reforms identified by the respective governments and, for at least half of them, by civil society as well.

PSIA is most effective when applied to specific and well-defined reforms. Indeed, it cannot address broad strategies—such as the Poverty Reduction Strategies or broad reform packages—whose distributional outcomes cannot be meaningfully assessed. Since PSIA requires significant time and resources, it is important for low-income countries to focus analyses on key reforms that are likely to have significant distributional impact, and to prioritize the need for PSIA with other analytic gaps. The *PSIA User's Guide* recommends that four criteria be used to select priority reforms:

- the expected size and direction of the poverty and social impacts,
- the prominence of the issue in the government's policy agenda,
- the level of national debate surrounding the reform, and
- the timing and urgency of the underlying policy or reform.

The chapters in this book provide examples of how the PSIA process relates to these criteria. All of the chapters deal with policy reforms that have large impacts both in terms of their fiscal importance and in terms of the number of people likely to be affected. With the exception of Romania, which is not a PRSP country, all the reforms emerged from the interim or final PRSPs of their respective countries. Reforms of public utilities, agricultural markets, and mining are high on the governments' policy agendas, and all of them have generated a good bit of controversy. For instance, the reform of the agricultural markets has been passionately debated for many years in Malawi. In the case of Sri Lanka, PSIA focused on a particular transfer program which was the most critical, both because of its size and because of the political economy surrounding it.

Lesson 2: Design of the PSIA

The choice of tools and methods is driven by the availability and quality of data, the existence of technical capacity, and resource and time constraints. In order to be credible and useful, however, the analytical techniques and research methodologies employed should be both transparent and accessible to all stakeholders. Overall, it is important to address the interest of the public by releasing information on the scope of work early during the analytical process and opening a public discussion of the scope and design of PSIA before the analysis is undertaken.

This, however, is quite different from designing the analytical work in a participatory manner with all stakeholders. Research design is left to professionals who, over time, have established norms and standards for analytical work over several decades as their case load has grown. In fact, in some cases—where the policy reforms can affect influential stakeholders—a participatory research design process runs the risk of being undermined by powerful political economy interests.

The research questions for the PSIA presented in this volume were discussed with the government and key stakeholders before the PSIA was designed for the majority of these studies. The research design was prepared by the PSIA teams, partly in collaboration with in-country researchers, adapting economic and social analysis techniques from other contexts to these reforms.

Lesson 3: Analysis of the Reform

For the PSIA to be credible, the analytical work has to be technically sound and the basis for arriving at conclusions needs to be transparent and able to stand up to public scrutiny by peers. This is the same standard that would apply to any other form of scientific research. Rigorous analysis by specialists does not mean that key stakeholders and those affected by the reform are ignored. Their interests, perceptions, and likely behavioral response are indeed essential data for the PSIA. In practice, however, the analytical process has leaned toward a scientific, technocratic one, rather than a participatory one.

This implies that there is no monopoly on who does the analysis as long as the research methodology is transparent. PSIA can be (and frequently is) undertaken by government agencies, universities, research institutes, nongovernmental organizations, development agencies, or even private companies. There are a few instances (as in Malawi), where nongovernmental organizations have been involved directly in PSIA work, undertaking part of the research and analysis. Their contribution, however, was a scientific and rigorous one, rather than the expression of the views of particular stakeholders.

In order to promote the greater use of the PSIA process, in-country capacity for poverty and social analytical work is essential so that this sort of analysis can be carried out routinely within partner countries. In-country capacity remains a constraint in many borrower countries. In the examples provided in this book—with the exception of the Burkina Faso study, where client capacity building was an explicit objective—client capacity building has tended to occur through on-the-job learning by in-country partners directly involved in the PSIA. In Nicaragua, for instance, the PSIA team comprised a mix of local academics, government analysts, and World Bank staff. In the long run, however, mainstreaming PSIA will require more deliberate, and significantly higher, investments in capacity building for poverty and social impact analysis.

In the examples presented in this volume, stakeholder consultation (rather than involvement) during the analytical phase were common and represented an important source of data. For instance, the Romania mining and Tajikistan cotton studies paid a great deal of attention to stakeholder interests through stakeholder consultations and analysis, but they relied on specialized research teams to ensure analytical rigor and objectivity in the face of political economy interests. As exemplified by the analysis of the oil subsidies in Ghana, even when the analysis is conducted in a quick fashion modeling existing household survey data, it is feasible to enrich the analysis by consulting with key stakeholders who are knowledgeable about the reform.

Another lesson learned from experience in numerous countries is that the agencies responsible for implementing a reform, even though they might not be actually undertaking the analysis themselves, should be kept fully abreast of the analytical process. This permanent involvement is critical to ensure that they understand the analytical findings and are able to both utilize the results and monitor reform impacts effectively. In the case of Nicaragua, the involvement of the tripartite committee (comprised of representatives from the government, civil society, and donors), responsible for the tax reform throughout the PSIA, proved critical to its influence on the policy designs.

Lesson 4: Policy Dialogue

A central lesson that emerges from the chapters in this book is that for the PSIA to be effective, it has to be closely aligned with the ongoing policy dialogue. This means that the research design has to be based on the reforms and public actions effectively under consideration, and that results have to be relayed back into the policy dialogue.

In practice, the PSIA is only one of the inputs into the policy dialogue around the reform. Hence another and related lesson is that establishing a parallel dialogue on the PSIA itself is neither practical nor useful. Rather, the key issue is the dissemination of PSIA results into the broader reform dialogue. This allows for the effective utilization of the PSIA results along with other factors such as the economic and financial returns of the reform, competing expenditure priorities, and the presence of political support for reform when debating policy options.

Policy processes often do not have a clear beginning or an end. More often than not, even a discrete action—such as removing the subsidy from the energy sector—is composed of a series of interrelated fiscal, institutional, and political actions. Consequently, most of the reforms analyzed have been on the table for several years; they may take several more to implement. It is therefore better to think of the PSIA as an integral part of the programmatic process of policy reforms in the relevant sector. For instance, welfare reform in Sri Lanka has a broad agenda covering issues of targeting efficiency, but also exploring alternative options to social protection, such as the move from universal to conditional transfers or self-selection. The PSIA presented in this volume feeds into one of the elements of their broad agenda.

In some of the experiences presented in this volume, such as those of Albania, Burkina Faso, Ghana, and Malawi, governments are effectively drawing on PSIA lessons within their ongoing dialogue with local constituencies and donors.

Long policy processes mean that PSIA can be useful before a reform, during the reform, or later in the process. Although the PSIA has usually been conducted ex ante, it also has relevance during reform implementation and after a certain phase is completed. When reforms are already in the process of implementation, the PSIA can inform policy choice, allowing reform proponents to reconsider choice, design, pace, and sequence of policy and institutional reforms and identify or strengthen mitigation measures. Mozambique education and Sri Lanka social welfare PSIAs were conducted to help those governments reconsider their programs. The studies in Ghana and Rwanda have also helped their governments determine optimal modes of subsidy to facilitate energy access by the poor. In Malawi, the study convinced the Bank to modify its policy advice to continue restructuring the economic functions while protecting the social functions of remote agricultural marketing outlets. Similarly, retrospective analysis of reforms already carried out, such as the utilities studies in Europe and Central Asia, offer lessons for the next phase of reforms.

The key lesson is that the dissemination of results from the analysis is critical to ensure it feeds into the broader policy dialogue. This requires a particular effort to ensure that *all parties* to the reform have access to the same information base. When this was not the case, as in Malawi, even though the final results were made available to the government, other stakeholders were unable to access them and felt left out of the policy process. In practical terms, however, there is a tradeoff between early release of information and ensuring analytical rigor and peer scrutiny prior to dissemination of research results. There is no single solution to this tradeoff. In each case, a judgment needs to be made about the likely impact of disclosing information. Generally, it is good practice to release research results as early as possible to increase their likely impact on the design of reforms.

Many of the studies in this volume have adopted creative solutions to share interim results with stakeholders. For instance, the Burkina Faso PSIA has been carried out directly with the government and local partners, giving them access to information throughout and involving them directly in the analysis. Similarly, the results from the Albania water and the Sri Lanka social welfare PSIAs were shared and discussed with the government while the analytical work was ongoing.

Lesson 5: Monitoring and Evaluating Reforms

One of the innovations of PSIA lies in its focus on ex ante analysis of reform impacts. This ex ante analysis means that the best PSIA includes several assumptions—about the macroeconomy, market trends, global market prices, investor behavior, behavioral responses by affected persons, political support for reform, the pace of parallel reforms, and institutional capacity. Changes in these assumptions are likely to occur, as the context of the reforms changes constantly. These changes affect the expected impacts of reforms, which might in turn call for changes and corrections to the design of some components of the reforms. The need to integrate the critical elements of the PSIA into monitoring and evaluating the reforms is therefore paramount. This is already happening in some of the cases presented in this volume—for instance, in the cases of the Romania mining and Sri Lanka welfare reforms, where governments are using the PSIA findings to refine their monitoring systems.

This integration is best done by integrating the monitoring of elements underlined by the PSIA within existing domestic monitoring systems—either PRS monitoring systems or sectoral monitoring systems. However, the PSIA might lead to a close monitoring of some elements that are not traditionally the focus of national systems. This may necessitate the contribution of other actors to the monitoring efforts, including local civil society organizations.

THE IMPACT OF PSIA ON GOVERNMENT POLICY AND WORLD BANK OPERATIONS: EVIDENCE FROM THE CASE STUDIES

PSIAs are now increasingly being used to inform the design and sequencing of reform policies. For example, the PSIA of utilities (Europe and Central Asia, and Rwanda) has created institutional space for consideration of access to service, and quality of service, besides affordability. Consequently, the standardized solution of lifeline tariffs is being nuanced by reforms that subsidize connection costs to increase access to utility services for the poor, rather than subsidizing recurring charges.

Reforms of agricultural markets (Malawi and Tanzania) tend to be motivated by fiscal imperatives and market failures. However, impact on different groups is conditioned by spatial inequality (primarily access to transportation) and socio-economic characteristics of the households, which determines their ability to manage risks and cope with shocks. Policy recommendations emerging from the studies have led to more location-specific applications of reform alternatives.

Analysis of social sector services (Mozambique and Sri Lanka) revealed that local interpretation of rules prevented achievement of policy objectives. This has resulted in recommendations to eliminate or minimize local discretion for universally provided services in Mozambique, and objectively determined criteria of eligibility for targeted social assistance benefits in Sri Lanka.

We present below an overview of each of the case studies reviewed in this volume with a particular emphasis on the impact that this work has had on the on country policies and World Bank operations.

Fiscal Reform in Nicaragua

Chapter 2 presents the PSIA of fiscal reforms in Nicaragua with particular attention to the development of a new tax system. The PSIA simulates the distributional impact of these reforms, determining the projected revenues from the tax changes included in the Fiscal Equity Law and assessing the distributional impact of projected revenues from value-added tax (VAT), exonerations, excise taxes, and income taxes on household welfare. The analysis finds that using income as the indicator of welfare, the overall tax reform in Nicaragua is slightly regressive. However, when current consumption is used as the indicator, the reform is assessed as slightly progressive. If reform implementation leads to an effective increase in tax revenues, distribution in Nicaragua will become less unequal than it is currently.

The government created a tripartite technical committee comprised of government, civil society, and donors to design the tax reform program and the Fiscal Equity Law. This committee had explicit responsibilities for providing feedback for the Nicaragua PSIA on the tax reform.

The recommendations are (1) to eliminate exonerations and exemptions, thus avoiding loopholes in the reform's regulations; and (2) to strengthen tax administration to diminish tax evasion. The findings presented in the chapter have already been incorporated into a revised PRS, allowing them to be more widely disseminated to decision makers in the public sector and to representatives of other branches of government, such as the National Assembly, as well as to political parties, the private sector, and the media.

Cotton Sector Reform in Burkina Faso

The PSIA in chapter 3 presents the analytical framework of the poverty analysis macro-economic simulator (PAMS) model of cotton sector reform in Burkina Faso. Burkina Faso is a poor landlocked country of about 12 million inhabitants with an extremely narrow natural resource base that is very dependent on cotton fiber exports and therefore vulnerable to external shocks. Analyzing the poverty impact of cotton price fluctuations is therefore a high priority for the country.

The World Bank and the German Technical Cooperation (GTZ) helped the government develop a PAMS model to assess the poverty and distributional impacts of macroeconomic shocks and policies reforms. PAMS modeling provides sets of simulations to inform policy choices. It is now routinely applied to estimate the poverty impact of different macroeconomic scenarios. The fourth and fifth poverty reduction support credits (PRSCs) build on PAMSs work to analyze the poverty impact of cotton price fluctuations and consider development policy choices. PAMS demonstrates the limitations of the cotton sector for quickly reducing poverty across the entire country, so the second PRSP focuses on consolidating achievements in the cotton sector, informing policies that are accompanied by an ongoing effort to raise educational attainment and reduce morbidity and mortality rates.

The Burkina Faso experience has led to the adoption of the PAMS model in other countries of the subregion. The study emphasizes the importance and strong payoffs of building capacity in the government's forecasting team, of close collaboration with other partners, and of the need to make appropriate allowance for collecting and analyzing poverty data when embarking on this sort of modeling.

Education Reform in Mozambique

Chapter 4 presents the results of a PSIA conducted on the effect of school fees and primary school enrollment and retention in Mozambique. The Ministry of Education had been considering policy alternatives for encouraging school attendance and completion. The PSIA was designed to consider demand-side and supply-side constraints as well as contextual factors—school proximity, parental education, and the characteristics of the child. The study finds, perhaps surprisingly, that school fees have little impact on enrollments in primary school but that other expenditures on education are significant.

The PSIA study generated a series of recommendations, the most important of which was to revise the current policy on school fees in order to clarify the type, purpose, frequency, payment mechanisms, and accountabilty of funds. Other recommendations include expanding the resources channeled directly to schools, deploying teachers better, and building schools closer to their communities.

The PSIA has had an impact at three levels: (1) it provided an initial impact assessment of the government decision to abolish all fees beginning in the 2005 academic year; (2) it has informed the second Education Sector Strategic Plan and the ministry's gender strategy; and (3) it has sharpened advice in the context of the PRSC, Joint Partner Initiatives, and Policy Reviews in Mozambique.

Welfare Reform in Sri Lanka

The PSIA summarized in chapter 5 was designed to examine the potential gains to be had by transforming the current subjective method of selecting beneficiaries of the Samurdhi welfare program to a system that applies a set of objective criteria. Poverty in Sri Lanka is concentrated in pockets throughout the country. Rising inequality across households is making it important to target government assistance efficiently.

The PSIA uses a proxy means text formula (PMTF), based on household data, for an ex ante simulation exercise. Recommendations can then be made on the cutoff point and appropriate payment schemes to improve targeting. A pilot targeting survey was conducted to validate the results of the simulations. Three models were simulated; PMTF model III, presented in the chapter, was chosen by comparing models in several criteria, including each model's cutoff point, undercoverage rate, and leakage rate. The PSIA also uses simulations to address issues inherent in the payment scheme for eligible individuals—its feasiblity as well as its welfare implications.

This PSIA has informed the design of the reform and implementation plan, and influenced the basic policy decision to adopt the PMTF approach. A pilot and the linking of the country's statistical systems for monitoring and measuring poverty with the conduct of the proxy means testing exercise proved crucial to its success.

Reforming the Power Sector in Eastern Europe

Success in Eastern Europe in the privatization of the power sector has been mixed. The PSIAs described in chapter 6 are designed to find a way to improve the chances for success and make the transition smoother and less difficult for the poor. The chapter considers energy reform in Armenia, Azerbaijan, Georgia, Kyrgyz Republic, and Moldova—countries that all have cold winters and socialist legacies, and that therefore have common specific requirements for successful power sector reform.

This group of PSIAs has led to a softening on the Bank's position on privatization on the energy sector, affecting overall policy design. It has also influenced the debate over direct income supports versus lifeline tariffs: because the PSIAs found that the existing social protection systems were prone to leakage, there are instances where lifeline tariffs are more useful. Finally, PSIAs have improved the dialogue by bringing policy-based evidence to the table in order to encourage countries (1) to explicitly link tariff increases to service quality improvement, and to raise tariffs more slowly and focus on raising collections before raising tariffs; (2) to consider the role of the public sector in increasing access to gas as a way to offset the impact of tariff increases; and (3) to give priority to metering. The chapter demonstrates the need to adapt the design of the PSIA to the local political economy, to ensure the availability of adequate time and resources, to involve a broad range of stakeholders, to emphasize rigorous analysis, and to recognize the value of both ex ante and ex post analysis.

Energy Sector in Rwanda

In spite of Rwanda's remarkable economic recovery in the decade since the genocide, its energy sector is in crisis. Chapter 7 documents this crisis, explains the need to increase electricity tariffs, and assesses both the impact of such an increase on the poor and the distributive effects of alternative tariff structures.

The energy sector in Rwanda is very small. All electricity in the country comes from hydroelectric power produced domestically, along with imports from two international utilities. Hydropower sources are experiencing unexpectedly low lake levels, exacerbating the problems. The government has approved an increase of electricity tariffs to nearly double the old tariff. The chapter provides simulations of the distributional properties of alternative tariff designs, including the interesting Inverted-U Block Tariff Structure (IUBT) that has been proposed by Eleztrogaz, Rwanda's main energy provider. Their proposal was to provide a reduced price on all consumption below 20 kilowatt hours, along with a price higher than simple cost recovery for all consumption between 20 and 100 kilowatt hours, thus recouping some of the subsidy for the lower bracket.

The analysis attempts to discover which new tariff structure would be appropriate, and whether the new proposals by Electrogaz for an IUBT make sense. The analysis of data shows clearly that connection subsidies can be better targeted than consumption subsidies, although there would still be benefits to providing at least some level of protection, and that volume-differentiated tariff subsidies are better targeted than the others, although the IUBT has some advantages. If such cross-subsidies were to be implemented, it would be relatively straightforward to use the framework presented in the chapter to conduct the necessary assessments with household surveys.

Electricity Tariff Reform in Ghana

The PSIA summarized in chapter 8 was designed as an input into Ghana's poverty reduction strategy. The overall fiscal drain of the electricity sector had, by 2002, become substantial, and deficits of the three electric utility companies approached 11 percent of government spending.

Fieldwork was carried out in the three major urban areas where most electricity in the country is consumed. The study probed two assumptions: (1) that higher prices have a direct impact on the poor, and (2) that those falling in the lifeline band also fall below the poverty line. The Ghana PSIA also made explicit the importance of looking not only at the subsidy, but also at its sustainability over time. To aid those without access to electricity, the PSIA recommended that policy makers review the factors that affect the availability and pricing of kerosene products in rural areas. The PSIA also recommended indicators to monitor the process of energy reform.

This PSIA led to a change in the World Bank's own allocation for new investments to include resources to prepare project components for nontraditional and off-grid sources of energy, thus providing a "voice" for those stakeholders least represented on the stakeholder map—poor rural consumers not yet connected to the grid—and a way to take their needs into account in the design of development projects.

Collaboration among stakeholders resulted in showing that the assumption that the best way to reach the poor was to extend subsidies was false: the majority of the poor are not connected to the grid. This realization allowed the World Bank to shift its lending policy rapidly to target these needs better. Local organizations played a leading role in analyzing data.

Water Sector Reform in Albania

Chapter 9 summarizes the PSIA of water sector privatization in Albania. The Government of Albania has set up two models for decentralized water sector reform: (1) public management of water utilities, led by local governments; and (2) private water utility management, supported by the World Bank's Municipal Water and Wastewater Project (MWWP or the "Project"). The PSIA selected four cities under public utility management and compared them with four Project cities. The study was designed to set baselines in all eight cities. A follow-up study will measure the distributional impacts of the two reform models against these baselines, so that the PSIA compares the reform impacts of two water sector reform models across two points in time. Study findings inform the policy dialogue in-country on decentralization and water sector privatization, and also on Bank operations in the water sector.

Key findings suggest reform adjustments focused mainly on a different sequencing and pacing of the reform. Data from all eight sites suggest that visible improvements in the service quality and in the collection ratio should be made before tariffs are further increased. This sequence is crucial for maintaining consumer satisfaction and to keep consumers paying water charges. Local governments request the Bank to support decentralization reform, as well as to provide technical assistance and capacity building. Study findings illustrate similarities and differences between the two reform models. Reform adjustments could be useful where improvements in service quality and in the collection ratio are made a condition for gradual tariff increases in all eight cities.

The Mining Sector in Romania

The PSIA of the Romania mining sector summarized in chapter 10 was conducted to inform the design of a second Bank loan. Under communism, the mining sector was privileged, with relatively high wages and a politically influential trade union. Sector restructuring was initiated in 1997; however, subsidies and tax exemptions grew to more than US$300 million by 2004, equivalent to 0.5 percent of GDP. In April 2004, the government approved a mining sector strategy to address the fiscal deficit and comply with European Union (EU) requirements to eliminate mining subsidies.

The PSIA examines three sets of distributional impacts of sector reform: impacts on mining and non-mining communities and households; gender impacts; and the distribution of wages and subsidies within the mining sector. The study found (1) considerable diversity among mining towns depending on local infrastructure and economic opportunities, (2) gender bias in impacts and rehabilitation opportunities for women, and (3) inequitable and inefficient use of subsidies caused by political economy interests. Intra-sectoral analysis helped to unpack the cause of the quasi-fiscal deficits.

The study has led to the creation of additional components for community infrastructure, a small grants scheme, especially for women and youth, and the establishment of a subsidy monitoring mechanism to ensure that subsidy management objectives are met. Close collaboration of the PSIA team with the project team enabled the PSIA to have an impact on the reform program even before the report was finalized and led to an agreement that sector reform will require changing institutional arrangements and power relations to manage political economy interests.

The Petroleum Sector in Ghana

The PSIA of the policy and reform of the petroleum sector in Ghana summarized in chapter 11 emphasizes the need to identify the probable impact on the real incomes of the poorest households and alternative approaches to mitigating these effects. The PSIA group collaborated closely with country teams at the IMF and the World Bank before sending a technical assistance mission to Ghana in January 2005.

The PSIA evaluates the distributional implications of petroleum subsidies and first-order income effects of price changes to household real incomes for Ghana and considers a range of alternative approaches to protecting the real incomes of the poor. The analysis simulated different scenarios using the national household survey and assessed the impacts of the different alternatives. The study found that the distribution of the benefits from energy subsidies across households involves substantial leakages of these benefits to higher-income households. The simulations clearly show that targeted subsidies have high returns for protection to the poorest households; maintaining lower kerosene prices is relatively inefficient. Better-targeted programs can help reduce, even eliminate, losses from subsidy leakage.

The results of the PSIA were presented to the government in early February 2005; in mid-February of the same year, the government increased petroleum prices by, on average, 50 percent and emphasized its commitment to continuing sector reforms. It also introduced additional expenditure items in the 2005 budget intended to imitigate the adverse effects of the higher petroleum prices on low-income households. These programs included the elimination of school fees as well as investments in transport and an expansion of the rural electrification scheme.

This study is a very useful example of how household survey data and input-output data together can be used to evaluate the likely impact of higher domestic petroleum prices. The study also helps to highlight the tradeoffs that exist in practice: the desire to be ex ante and timely means that the tradeoffs in this instance were relatively high. However, such tradeoffs are expected to become less sharp as the framework and capacity for PSIA is developed.

Reforming the ADMARC in Malawi

Chapter 12 describes the process and findings of the PSIA on the reform of ADMARC in Malawi. ADMARC is a Malawian parastatal organization mandated to market agricultural produce and inputs; it also plays a food security role in the country's maize market. ADMARC has recently deviated from its core mandate and its importance in agricultural marketing has declined. Many reforms have progressively liberalized agricultural markets over the last 20 years, a strategy that has been supported under various IMF and World Bank programs. This strategy has been less positive than expected, and donors continued to press the government to improve ADMARC's financial position through restructuring and cost cutting.

The PSIA was designed to address the controversy surrounding recommendations to reduce ADMARC's marketing role further and possibly sell off some of its marketing infrastructure. Three background studies were commissioned: two quantitative studies that used econometric techniques to analyze survey data, and one was a qualitative study that used an array of methods to solicit households' and stakeholders' reactions. The PSIA confirmed that ADMARC was wasteful and could be substantially downsized in less remote areas without significant social risks. The PSIA did increase awareness of the emphasis placed by the Bank on maintaining social services and the importance of identifying a more efficient alternative to address market failures in remote areas.

Several NGOs have criticized the limited extent of its consultation during the study's design and the long delay in disseminating its findings. As the process has evolved, the value of wide consultations, inclusiveness, and consensus building has become better understood. The Bank also underestimated the symbolic importance of repealing the ADMARC Act and the politics that became associated with this event.

The findings of this PSIA were incorporated into the new World Bank program. The experience with ADMARC in Malawi shows that policy reforms that have significant social impacts are difficult to implement without an adequate consensus that takes into account the main concerns raised by stakeholders. The combination of quantitative and qualitative methodologies is well worth the trouble. This study has improved the quality of World Bank recommendations by providing a more nuanced stance on ADMARC.

Cotton Farm Land Privatization in Tajikistan

The objective of the PSIA presented in chapter 13 was to analyze the poverty impact of cotton farmland privatization in Tajikistan. The analysis focused primarily on the income implications of cotton farmland privatization, looking at the poverty impact of cotton farmland privatization by different methods deployed in Tajikistan. The two methods were State

Farm Restructuring (SFR) and the World Bank Farm Privatization Support Project (FPSP). The main focus of the study was on access to land, crop choice, and the participation of farmers in the financial affairs of farms.

The study analyzed the cotton production and marketing chains and the distortions that existed within them. A stakeholder analysis was carried out to assess the incentives and relative importance of each stakeholder in the privatization process. The PSIA made an early and important contribution by identifying the main obstacles to improving the welfare of cotton farmers and the main sources of distortion, quantifying the large losses in this sector, estimating their impact on farmers' incomes, and highlighting the opportunity cost to Tajikistan.

The government's options are to (1) privatize all cotton farms on the lines of FPSP, leaving other aspects of the cotton production and marketing chains unaltered, or (2) privatize all cotton farms on the lines of the FPSP while liberalizing the production and marketing chains. The PSIA revealed that Option 2 would be most effective in alleviating the problems with the sector while productivity remains low and farmers' poverty level remains high. The status quo would have significantly negative consequences for the entire economy.

The PSIA helped to understand stakeholder incentives to raising barriers to welfare improvements. Stakeholder analysis structured the multiple factors that led to the observed outcome of high poverty in cotton areas. The analysis was extended to determine the extent of profits (or rents) captured by various groups, which is useful for understanding the degree of resistance to change. The team working on this PSIA benefited from being multidisciplinary and having an in-depth knowledge of the culture, the political players, and the agricultural sector.

Reform of Coffee and Cotton Crop Boards in Tanzania

Chapter 14 contains part of a larger PSIA on Tanzania's coffee, cotton, cashew, and tea industries. The chapter focuses on the first two. Agricultural growth is central to reducing poverty in Tanzania. The institutional structure, which includes the crop boards, for production and marketing affects the competitiveness of export crops. The PSIA was designed to review the sources and use of crop board funds; to assess the existing environment for the cotton and coffee industries; and to analyze the impact of reform options, particularly on smallholder farmers and vulnerable stakeholders. The PSIA used a mixed methods approach with sequenced data collection.

Crop boards perform important public functions but their interventionist stance often handicaps traders. The boards have a mix of public and private activities, including regulation, service provision, and collection of revenue, which can create a conflict of interest. Clearly delineated board functions and accountability structures within the crop industries are crucial. Reform options include (1) boards that are publicly financed and focus on public services; (2) boards that are privately financed; (3) boards that are jointly financed, with associated private services financed by a levy and contracts for public services; and (4) boards that remain as they are. The study team recommends option 1 for the coffee industry, and option 3 for the cotton industry.

The PSIA is expected to inform the future functions of the coffee and cotton boards. The government has already decided to abolish the levy that financed the boards, replacing it with budget financing, and to abolish the crop development funds. The reform affects producers by improving access to market information, increasing competition, and providing greater accountablilty of service providers. Because policy reforms are ultimately political, working on PSIAs from a purely technical angle is often inadequate, and local capacity building along with good analytical work was essential to this PSIA.

LOOKING AHEAD: CHALLENGES TO MAINSTREAMING THE PSIA

As the collection of chapters in this book illustrates, significant progress has been achieved in a relatively short period of time. However, the glass is only half full and much more needs to be done before PSIA can be considered truly mainstreamed. Having tested the feasibility of this approach and moved from pilots toward mainstreaming within donor agencies, the challenge of embedding PSIA within the Poverty Reduction Strategy processes and policy formulation within client countries remains daunting. Mainstreaming will require greater country capacity in three different dimensions.

First, the regular, systematic use of the analysis of distributional impacts can materialize only if there is strong national demand for analysis. Such demand will be more likely if there is growing interest in evidence-based policy making, a much broader agenda to which PSIA can contribute. This will require greater ability and engagement by policy makers to formulate their analytical needs and guide the analysis.

Second, mainstreaming the analysis of the poverty and social impact of reforms requires greater national capacity to effectively analyze and monitor reforms than is presently available. For this, research and analytical capabilities among borrower countries and the information base necessary for the analysis need to be strengthened.

Finally, for decision makers to use information on alternative policy options effectively, there is a need for a greater in-country ability to understand the findings and their implications, alongside a need for greater efforts at disseminating results to all stakeholders in adapted formats.

NOTES

1. The Joint Implementation Committee (JIC) was established in 1999 to facilitate communication and coordination between the World Bank and International Monetary Fund (IMF) on PRSPs.
2. The Department for International Development of the U.K. (DFID) was initially the most active partner of this program; it financed six pilots parallel to the Bank's pilot studies.
3. Coudouel and Paternostro (2005, 2006). These two volumes are available at www.worldbank.org/psia, click on "reform."
4. Financing for the initial PSIA pilots was provided by a Norwegian-Finnish trust fund (TFESSD), which financed six each in 2001–3 (fiscal 2002 and fiscal 2003). Since then, other donors—Belgium, Germany, Italy—have also provided trust funds for PSIA work.
5. The OP 8.60 is available in the World Bank Operational Manual (World Bank 2004).
6. See for example CIDSIE-Caritas Internationalis (2005); EURODAD (2005); Oxfam (2005); GTZ (2005).
7. See the PSIA *User's Guide* (World Bank 2003) and the *TIPS Sourcebook for PSIA* (DFID and World Bank 2005, section 5.1).
8. See, for example, CIDSIE-Caritas Internationalis (2005); EURODAD (2005); Oxfam (2005); GTZ (2005).
9. See the PRSP Sourcebook chapter on participation, available at http://web.worldbank.org/WBSITE/EXTERNAL/TOPICS/EXTPOVERTY/EXTPRS/0,contentMDK:20175742~pagePK:210058~piPK:210062~theSitePK:384201,00.html

REFERENCES

Bourguignon, F., and L. A. Pereira da Silva. 2003. *The Impact of Economic Policies on Poverty and Income Distribution: Evaluation Techniques and Tools.* Washington, DC and New York: World Bank and Oxford University Press. http://www.worldbank.org/psia.

CIDSIE-Caritas Internationalis. 2005. "Submission to World Bank/IMF 2005 PRS Review." Brussels and Vatican City.

Coudouel, A. and S. Paternostro, eds. 2005. *Analyzing the Distributional Impact of Reforms: A Practitioner's Guide to Trade, Monetary and Exchange Rate Policy,*

Utility Provision, Agricultural Markets, Land Policy and Education. Washington, DC: World Bank. http://www.worldbank.org/psia

———. 2006. *Analyzing the Distributional Impact of Reforms: A Practitioner's Guide to Pension, Health, Labor Market, Public Sector Downsizing, Taxation, Decentralization and Macroeconomic Modeling.* Washington, DC: World Bank. http:// www.worldbank.org/psia.

DFID and World Bank. 2005. *Tools for Institutional, Political & Social Analysis (TIPS): Sourcebook for PSIA.* http://www.worldbank.org/tips.

EURODAD. 2005. "EURODAD Submission to the World Bank / IMF 2005 PRS Review." Brussels, Belgium.

GTZ. 2005. "Making Poverty Reduction Strategies Work—Good Practices, Issues, and Stakeholder Views." Eschborn, Germany.

Oxfam. 2005 "Oxfam International Submission to the World Bank/IMF 2005 PRS Review." London, UK.

World Bank. 2003. *A User's Guide to Poverty and Social Impact Analysis.* Washington, DC: World Bank. Available in English, French, Spanish and Russian at www.worldbank.org/psia.

World Bank. 2004. OP 8.60. http://wbln0018.worldbank.org/Institutional/Manuals/OpManual.nsf/BB1704DC5C8434C485256723004B6A53/C22F1032D7DFD30285256E8A00763966?OpenDocument

World Bank. Forthcoming. *Evaluating the Impact of Macroeconomic Policies on Poverty and Income Distribution Using Micro-Macro Linkages Models.*

2

NICARAGUA
The Impact of the Fiscal Equity Law Reform

LEONARDO GASPARINI, DANIEL ARTANA,
FLORENCIA T. CASTRO-LEAL
AND MIRIAM MONTENEGRO

This chapter describes the process and findings of the Poverty and Social Impact Analysis (PSIA) on fiscal reform in Nicaragua.[1] In September 2002, the Nicaraguan government, the World Bank, and the U.K. Department for International Development (DFID) agreed to carry out a PSIA on the impact of the fiscal reform then under design. The Fiscal Equity Law, which was the legal expression of the reform, was approved by the Nicaraguan National Assembly in May 2003, and entered into force in June of that year. This experience illustrates the comprehensiveness of the PSIA approach and provides useful lessons for the future.

The chapter is structured as follows: the next section presents the macroeconomic context, the inequality context, and the reform's main objectives. The following section provides a synthesis of the process used to design the PSIA and its methodology. The next section provides a synthesis of the main findings and policy recommendations of the PSIA, which is followed by a review of stakeholder and risk analysis. The final section presents conclusions and lessons learned.

MACROECONOMICS, INEQUALITY, AND TAX REFORM

To understand the relations between macroeconomics and inequality in a country and its tax reform efforts, we look first at the context in which these three elements operate. In Nicaragua, these three elements show a country in which macroeconomic stability has been hard to attain, there is persistent high inequality, and fiscal balances still need to be strengthened.

The Macroeconomic Context

Fiscal weakness, seen in other Central American countries, has been recurrent in Nicaragua during the last several years. However, following a noticeable deceleration in the rate of economic growth, which dropped to around 1 percent in real terms in 2002, recent macroeconomic indicators in Nicaragua are looking more favorable. In particular, efforts have been made in the framework of an agreement with the International Monetary Fund (IMF) to reduce the fiscal deficit and contain the growing domestic debt by controlling the expansion of public spending and increasing revenues. The tax reform approved by the nation's congress (the National Assembly) is an important instrument for achieving the fiscal goals outlined in the agreement.

The Distributional Context

Nicaragua's ranking for inequality (or the distribution of wealth among the country's population) varies, depending on whether calculations are based on consumption or on income distribution. When measured by consumption, studies rank Nicaragua's inequality more closely to the Latin American average (WIDER 2000; World Bank 2003). But, when measured by income, inequality indicators (such as the Gini coefficient) rank Nicaragua as a nation with a high degree of inequality, both internationally and more specifically within Latin America (see figure 2.1). By either measure, Nicaragua is among those nations with medium to high inequality, higher than neighboring Costa Rica and El Salvador. Nicaragua's distributional evolution over the last decade, however, has been positive. Unlike the Latin American average, unequal income distribution in Nicaragua did not increase in the 1990s and up to 2001, the latest year for which Living Standards Measurement Survey (LSMS) data are available. Moreover, unequal levels of consumption and the poverty rates have dropped significantly; overall poverty declined from 50.3 percent in 1993 to 45.8 percent in 2001, while extreme poverty fell from 19.4 percent to 15.1 percent in the same period.

The most commonly used inequality indicator, the Gini coefficient, showed a drop of inequality in Nicaragua for per capita consumption between 1998 and 2001—from 45.2 to 43.1 nationwide—and for the same period in urban and rural areas, from 43.9 to 41.4 and 37.2 to 34.7, respectively. Poverty rates in Nicaragua have also declined. The poverty

FIGURE 2.1 **Gini Coefficient: Equivalent Household Income Distribution, 1998–2001**

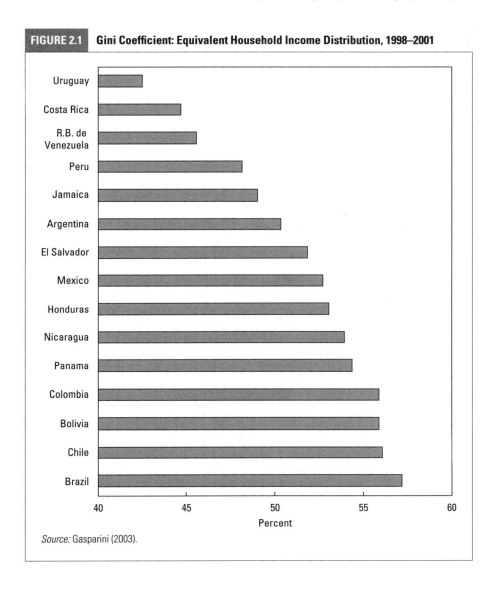

Source: Gasparini (2003).

rate, calculated on the basis of consumption distribution, dropped from 50.3 percent in 1993 to 47.9 percent in 1998, and then to 45.8 percent in 2001 (World Bank 2003). The reduction has occurred in both urban and rural areas. Despite this progress, however, Nicaragua has one of the highest proportions of poor people in the region, as figure 2.2 illustrates.[2]

Because inequality and poverty in Nicaragua were relatively high, albeit declining during the last decade, an additional goal expressed by the

FIGURE 2.2 **Poverty Rate Index: Percent of Population Living on Less than US$2 per Day, late 1990s**

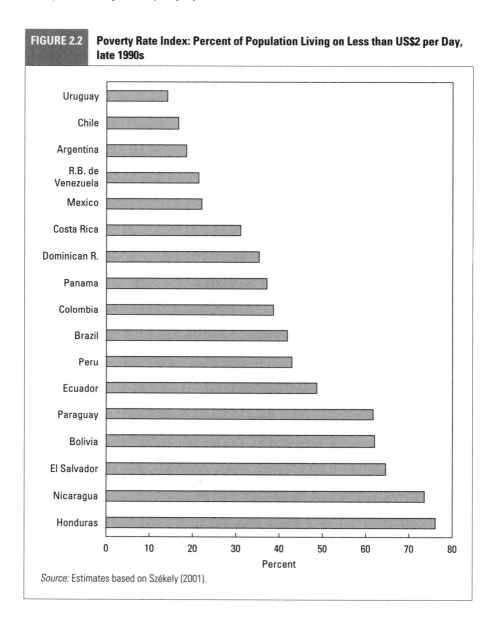

Source: Estimates based on Székely (2001).

Government of Nicaragua (GON) while undertaking this reform was to ensure the distributional equity of the tax reform. Tax reforms worldwide are rigorously evaluated by governments for their fiscal dimension on at least three criteria: impact on revenues, allocative efficiency, and degree of fiscal accountability. Another relevant dimension is their distributional equity. In particular, this PSIA evaluated the effect of the Tax Equity Law on distributing welfare among the population in Nicaragua. Thus, the analysis provided estimates of the degree to which the tax reform modified the distribution of the standard of living in Nicaragua.

The Design of a New Tax System

Public finance development professionals are coming closer to the design of an improved and simplified tax system for market economies to strengthen revenue collection. Such a tax system is based on a value added tax with few exemptions and uniform rates; additional taxes on only some consumer goods to help solve problems related to tax evasion or negative externalities; a progressive individual income tax structure, also with few exemptions and deductions to avoid diluting this progressivity and ensure efficiency; and a uniform corporate income tax aligned to the maximum marginal individual income tax rate—this uniform tax acts as a withholding system for some capital revenues. Together with other economic policy measures, a well-designed and administered tax system generates adequate incentives for investment and growth, and helps—together with targeted social spending policies—to improve income distribution.

Pre-Reform Taxes in Nicaragua

In 2002, Nicaragua's tax system had little transparency or accountability. Exemptions and exonerations for particular economic sectors and activities were widespread, and differentiated treatment was the rule rather than the exception. This tax structure included a multiplicity of special treatment exceptions and exemptions that generated only low revenues. There had traditionally been an enormous range of differentiated rates for sales tax, excise taxes and import duties, and income tax.

The most relevant tax in Nicaragua prior to the reform was the value added tax (VAT), known as the "IGV" (see table 2.1 for the tax structure in 2001). Some 44 percent of total tax revenues were generated by this tax. Excise taxes, particularly those on petroleum derivatives, generated about 26 percent of non-earmarked tax revenues, and taxes on foreign commerce—particularly import duties (DAI)—generated around 8 percent of total revenues. Taxes on individual and corporate income contributed only 19 percent of overall revenues, with corporate income tax generating the larger portion. Other excise taxes, which rounded out the previous Nicaraguan tax structure, are not included in the table.[3]

Table 2.1 Nicaragua's Pre-Reform Tax Revenues (non-earmarked), 2001

Item	C$ millions	Percent
1. Goods and Services	**5,138.1**	**73.1**
Sales Taxes (IGV)	*3,079.5*	*43.8*
Domestic	1,520.6	21.6
Imported	1,558.9	22.2
Excise Taxes (ISC)	*1,857.2*	*26.4*
Oil	1,325.9	18.9
Beer	223.6	3.2
Alcoholic Beverages	103.9	1.5
Tobacco	99.8	1.4
Carbonated Beverages	104.0	1.5
Specific Consumption Taxes (IEC)	*189.6*	*2.7*
Administrative Fees	*11.8*	*0.2*
2. International Commerce	**590.2**	**8.4**
Import Duties (DAI)	450.1	6.4
Temporary Protection Tariff (ATP)	40.7	0.6
35% tax (commerce w/ Honduras/Colombia)	69.6	1.0
Others	29.8	0.4
3. Income and Earnings	**1,302.7**	**18.5**
Declared income	203.8	2.9
Advance corporate income tax payments	415.2	5.9
Other advance income tax payments	10.6	0.2
Wage and Salary Withholding Tax	402.4	5.7
Other Withholding Taxes	270.8	3.9
Total	**7,031.0**	**100.0**

Source: Developed with data from the Treasury Department (MCHP), the Internal Revenue Service (DGI), and the Customs Department (DGA).
Note: C = Nicaraguan córdobas.

There were four VAT rates on consumption in Nicaragua, including customs revenues. A zero-rate tax was applied to various products destined for the domestic market. Many exonerations were based on type of product and specific buyers, along with high levels of tax evasion (around 35 percent, according to IMF estimates). Excise taxes were applied to almost 1,000 products, though such a tax could be justified only for those items generating negative externalities (such as cigarettes, alcoholic beverages, and fuels, the consumption of which is undesirable as it potentially generates costs to the society as a whole—for example, health care expenses of diseases associated with the consumption of cigarettes, or accidents as a result of drunk driving). Both excise taxes and import duties were plagued by exonerations based on the influence of specific buyers. This seriously impeded revenue collection and undermined the economy's equity and efficiency.[4] The income tax structure was geared toward promoting investment by offering an accelerated amortization option and favoring debt-financed investments. Moreover, many exonerations and special treatments promoted investments by specific sectors or organizations.

The 2003 Tax Reform

The Fiscal Equity Law had six main objectives:

- to simplify the tax system,
- to expand the tax base,
- to better manage the nation's public finances,
- to promote equitable distribution of the tax burden,
- to reduce tax evasion, and
- to make the tax system more efficient and progressive.

Thus, Nicaragua's tax reform did not simply attempt to increase taxes but also to modify the tax system. Nicaragua's tax revenues currently account for less than 30 percent of GDP, including social security contributions, so the country's tax pressure—at around 15 percent of GDP—is similar to that of other low-income nations with the same level of development (see figure 2.3).[5]

The Government of Nicaragua decided to modify the tax system by introducing the Fiscal Equity Law. This law was approved by the National Assembly in May 2003 and entered into force in June of that year. The law aimed at increasing government revenues in order to bridge the fiscal gap, reducing distortions, and improving accountability and vertical and horizontal equity.[6] Some of the most important measures, because of their overall fiscal impact, were

- replacing the zero rate (sales tax) with an exemption (which probably increased the price of goods to the consumer),
- eliminating some sales tax exonerations,
- reducing the spread of excise tax rates,
- introducing a tax on assets that acts as a minimum income tax,
- eliminating the accelerated depreciation mechanism for investments, and
- taxing financial profits.

The government expected the application of the Fiscal Equity Law to increase revenues by C$733 million (Nicaraguan córdobas) per year (see

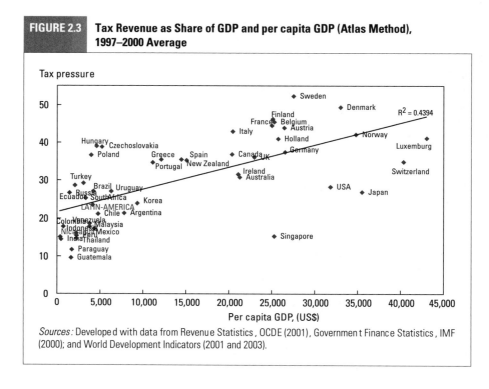

FIGURE 2.3   **Tax Revenue as Share of GDP and per capita GDP (Atlas Method), 1997–2000 Average**

Sources: Developed with data from Revenue Statistics, OCDE (2001), Government Finance Statistics, IMF (2000); and World Development Indicators (2001 and 2003).

table 2.2).[7] Three measures are projected to generate close to two-thirds of the total: elimination of zero-rate VAT exemptions, a change in excise tax rates for imports, and the minimum income tax payment of 1 percent on gross assets.

The reform simplified the tax system by eliminating the zero-rate VAT on the sale of items for the domestic market and lowering excise tax rates;[8] by improving equity by reducing the number of exonerations and exemptions, taxing financial profits, and increasing the income tax rates paid by higher income individuals; and by introducing a minimum tax on corporate earnings. It also strengthened tax administration by implementing various administrative measures and creating related civil service positions. In addition, the government committed to attain sustainable fiscal balances, thereby rationalizing public spending.

The reform's specific measures included modification of the progressive individual income tax rates for those with the highest incomes and instituting a definitive minimum income tax payment by individuals or corporations dedicated to business activities; elimination of the zero-rate for domestic market products and the declaration of products from the

Table 2.2 Nicaragua's Post-Reform Projected Annual Tax Revenue Increase

Item	C$ millions	Percent
VAT tax	**303.9**	**41.5**
Elimination of zero rate sales tax	208.3	28.4
Elimination of sales tax exonerations/ exemptions-domestic	49.9	6.8
Elimination of sales tax exonerations- imported goods	45.6	6.2
ISC	**78.7**	**10.7**
Imported luxury goods	71.7	9.8
Imported vehicles for collective transportation	8.6	1.2
Elimination of excise tax exoneration	0.1	0.0
Refunds to corporations under the "Temporary Import" regime	(1.8)	(0.2)
DAI	**6.9**	**0.9**
IR	**337.6**	**46.1**
30% individual income tax rate, with social security deductions	(26.2)	(3.6)
Minimum 1% payment on gross assets	189.7	25.9
Tax on financial profits	36.8	5.0
Accelerated depreciation	56.2	7.7
20% withholding for nonresident services	22.7	3.1
Withholding: agricultural commodities market transactions	41.6	5.7
Withholding: Imported goods	16.9	2.3
Fishing licenses	**5.8**	**0.8**
Total	**732.9**	**100.0**

Source: Calculations based on data from the Treasury Department (MCHP).

basic basket of consumer goods that had previously been part of the zero-rate regime as exempt. Besides eliminating the zero-rate for many domestic market products, the reform also removed other products from the basic basket of consumer goods that had previously been exempt. Finally, the reform eliminated discretionary exemptions and instituted a legal basis for different taxes and for regulating their application.

The Fiscal Institutions Engaged in Implementing the Reform

The reform professionalized tax and customs administration by strengthening the faculties of the Treasury Department (MHCP), thus aiding its implementation of the new law. It also endowed revenue-collecting agencies such as the Internal Revenue Service (DGI) and the General Customs Department (DGA) with all power needed to fully implement the law's regulation. It authorized the legal and penal systems to exercise their powers in cases of noncompliance. The law also assigned other institutions—such as banks, financial institutions, and NGOs—the ability to collect revenues, giving them normative and supervisory capabilities. Eventually, the reform facilitated the approval of a new tax code and a financial administration law by initiating a broad dialogue on sustainable fiscal balances and the legal and regulatory framework to implement it.

THE DESIGN OF THE PSIA ON FISCAL REFORM

The GON negotiated a Poverty Reduction Growth Facility (PRGF) program, approved by the Board of the IMF in December 2002, which incorporated specific fiscal targets intended to strengthen Nicaragua's fiscal situation and support a path for improving its primary balance.[9] In the context of this new PRGF, the GON started work in 2002 on a fiscal reform package to begin in calendar year 2003. In September 2002, GON, the World Bank, and DFID agreed to carry out a PSIA. The main reasons for selecting a PSIA of the Nicaraguan tax reform (the Fiscal Equity Law) were (1) because the World Bank and DFID were asked by the GON to provide support to analyze the potential distributional impact of this fiscal reform; (2) although attention was given to the quality of the tax reform, the need to generate more revenues was clearly a pressing motivation for the reform, so all stakeholders and donors had expressed concern about its poverty and social impact; and (3) because of the explicit intention expressed by the GON to incorporate these findings into the 2nd Poverty Reduction Strategy Paper (PRSP) progress report.

Establishing a Tripartite Technical Committee

Ownership of GON, participation of civil society, and donor involvement were key objectives for this PSIA. Consequently a tripartite technical committee was established comprising GON, civil society, and donors. This committee—comprised of GON, civil society, and donors—was set up by the Ministry of Finance (Ministerio de Hacienda y Crédito Público or MHCP) to design the tax reform package as well as the Fiscal Equity Law and its operational guidelines. National authorities selected the members for the committee, in consultation with civil society and supported by both multilateral and bilateral donors. The tripartite technical committee had explicit responsibilities for providing feedback for the Nicaragua PSIA on the tax reform package from drafting terms of reference, selecting consultants, and discussing preliminary and final results, to discussing preliminary and final drafts through the completion of the PSIA.

Sources of Data and Welfare Indicators

The PSIA relied on the 2001 Living Standards Measurement Survey (Encuesta de Medición de Niveles de Vida, or EMNV 2001) maintained by the National Institute of Statistics and Census (INEC). The committee, the consultants, and the staff of the MHCP worked together to identify the main changes in the tax parameters and to estimate how these changes were likely to affect people's incomes and the cost of particular products in consumer's baskets analyzed by poverty group (non-poor, poor, and extremely poor, as well as quintiles ranked by per capita consumption).

Information from the EMNV 2001 about household income and consumption in both urban and rural areas was used to analyze the impact of the Fiscal Equity Law on income distribution. This information was organized according to two welfare indicators: income and consumption. The first of these—income—looks at an individual's income situation at the moment of the survey, and therefore is subject to problems related to measurement. In principle, it would be preferable to have information about income patterns over each individual's lifetime. Unfortunately, this information is not available, although it may be approximated on the basis of a person's current consumption. Empirical evidence in Nicaragua reaffirms the permanent income hypothesis establishing that people tend to consume on the basis of estimates of permanent income, smoothing out fluctuations in income through savings. This allows us to use current consumption to approximate an individual's income flow over time.

Methodology

The objective of a tax incidence chapter is to identify who is affected by the tax burden and to evaluate changes in the distribution of welfare in relation to a specific tax or group of taxes. Economic studies about the impact of taxation recognize antecedents as remote as those written by David Ricardo. Interest in studies about such impact—whether for academic or economic policy reasons—has not diminished over time, an interest that is reflected in the large number of recent contributions to academic and professional literature.[10]

Two methodologies are typically used in impact studies. The most sophisticated consists of estimating computable general equilibrium models. To do this, reliable econometric estimates for a series of parameters and elasticities are needed. Unfortunately, these estimates are not available in most developing economies, and Nicaragua is no exception. The second methodology is known as the "shifting assumptions" methodology, and it consists of three stages: (1) selecting different shifting assumptions for each tax, (2) determining the distribution of the tax being analyzed and applying the assumptions from stage 1 and finally (3) adding up the taxes to each group (that is, population quintiles ranked by per capita consumption) to determine overall impact. This less-sophisticated methodology is more commonly applied throughout the world. All government agencies that conduct tax-impact studies in developed nations, for instance, use variations of the shifting assumptions methodology (see Bradford 1995).

In this chapter, the shifting assumptions methodology was selected for the following reasons:

- incomplete information hinders a study using a computable general equilibrium model;
- this methodology offers advantages in terms of comparability with previous studies conducted in Nicaragua and other countries of the region; and
- this methodology provides a greater degree of transparency when communicating results to policymakers.

Two vital steps determine the results of this type of study. The first of these is the selection of the variable to indicate individual welfare; the second is the selection of shifting assumptions for each tax. These two points are explored further in the next section.

The Welfare Variable

The concept of *progressivity* refers to the extent to which the tax burden increases in proportion to the standard of living (Lambert 1993). This definition runs into an operational problem when it is implemented empirically: which variable(s) available in a household study can best approximate an individual's standard of living? The traditional tax literature has used total family income as a proxy for the standard of living. This variable, however, is inadequate in two important respects. First, it does not consider the demographic composition of families. If two households have an equal total income but the first household has ten members while the second only has two, the standard of living of each member of these two families will certainly be different. Therefore, total family income should really be conditioned by the size and composition of the household. The most typical way to do this is to consider per capita income. Another more sophisticated option is to use a scale of "equivalent" adults (in contrast to a per capita scale for which every individual weighs the same, in an equivalent scale adults are given a larger weight because they consume relatively more than children) adjusted to the household's internal economies of scale.

There is a second constraint to using family income that is even more important than the variable for welfare. Household surveys, including those conducted in Nicaragua, tend to report individual and family incomes obtained over a short period of time, usually one month. When a household's income pattern is not stable, current income is a deficient approximation of an individual's standard of living. Even in economies with weak capital markets, families tend to soften consumption over time. A person who works for four months, who receives an advance during the first month and the remainder in the final month, will tend to "equalize" his or her consumption, at least partially, during these four months, saving during the first and using savings and credit during the next two months. If this person is interviewed for the household survey during the second month, his or her income will be zero, but that would not represent his/her true standard of living.[11] This bias creates problems for estimating the progressivity of taxes. An individual whose current income is low only at this moment would erroneously be classified among the poorest percentiles of the population. Since this person's income is only temporarily low, he or she can maintain higher levels of consumption, and therefore indirectly "pay" taxes on the consumption of goods and services. The tax burden on such an individual, computed as the ratio between taxes paid and the reported income level, would be very high (based on a current income of zero, it would in fact be infinite); therefore, the tax would be viewed as regressive.

The artificial bias of classifying taxes on goods and services as "regressive" has concerned analysts, who recommend using "intertemporal" income estimates instead of current income to better approximate an individual's real standard of living (see Caspersen and Metcalf 1994; Fullerton and Rogers 1993; Metcalf 1994; and Poterba 1989). The simplest and most frequently used formula estimates intertemporal income by combining current consumption with an estimate of gifts and inheritance. Our chapter uses the same criteria (ignoring the role of gifts and inheritance because the information in this area is deficient). The results obtained from estimating the standard of living on the basis of current income are also reported.

Shifting Assumptions

We analyze tax impact because the burden of a tax does not necessarily weigh on the person who is legally responsible for its payment. An "agent" (defined as the individual or corporation legally responsible for tax payment) may shift or transfer the tax to other economic "agents" by increasing the price of goods and services that they sell or reducing payments for productive factors or inputs. The possibilities for transferring taxes depend on the market structure and state regulations. The elasticity of the supply and demand of taxable goods and services is a fundamental factor affecting these possibilities.

The analyst should select shifting assumptions, based on the economic structure of the society considered for each tax that is studied. In our analysis, the following assumptions—commonly found in specialized literature about this theme—have been selected. It is assumed, first of all, that the burden of individual income tax is borne entirely by the person who is legally responsible for paying this tax, assuming inelasticity in the supply of labor and savings. This assumption is shared by all authors. However, there are multiple variants of this assumption with respect to corporate income tax. In principle, corporate income tax is assumed by businessmen who derive benefits from their firms and capitalists who obtain financial profit from their investments. However, it is possible that part of this tax may be shifted "forward" to consumption or "backward" in the form of lower salaries, depending on the elasticity of the supply of capital. Our analysis examines these options. The second assumption concerns both VAT and excise taxes (in Spanish these are ISC, which stands for *Impuesto Selectivo al Consumo*), which are taxes on goods and services. In principle, these taxes are transferred to prices, so that consumers bear the burden when purchasing taxable items. Although imported products may easily substitute for certain goods, foreign imports are also generally covered by taxes. Thus, it is assumed that sales tax and excise taxes are charged to the consumer.[12]

Tax Progressivity, Tax Burden, and Tax Pressure

The concentration curve for taxes are calculated for the poorest population ($p\%$) ordered according to the standard of living (variable x). The tax concentration index is computed as the Gini over the tax concentration curve, with t_{ih} representing the tax burden to the individual i who pertains to a given household h and x_{ih} the proxy for standard of living.

This analysis uses the Kakwani progressivity index, which is the index most frequently cited in related literature. The index is computed as the tax concentration index minus the Gini coefficient over the distribution of x. A tax is defined as *progressive* if t_{ih}/x_{ih} increases with x_{ih}. It is defined as *regressive* if it decreases with x_{ih} and as *neutral* if it remains constant.

$$Kakwani\ progressivity\ index = \frac{tax\ concentration\ index}{Gini\ coefficient}$$

Tax pressure is calculated as the share of the tax burden over the share in consumption of each individual in the distribution ranked according to consumption. The tax burden by product for the different quintiles is calculated as the share of each quintile in the tax revenue ordered by consumption.

$$P(C)_{qi} = \frac{tax\ burden(C)_{qi}}{consumption\ share_{qi}}$$

where,

$P(C)_{qi}$ = tax pressure P of the ith quintile (q_i), ordered by consumption

$tax\ burden\ (C)_{qi}$ = tax burden of the ith quintile (q_i), ordered by consumption

$consumption\ share_{qi}$ = participation of the ith quintile (q_i) in the consumption distribution

THE MAIN FINDINGS AND POLICY RECOMMENDATIONS

Tax reform has changed the tax status of various goods and services in Nicaragua from a zero-rate status to a tax-exempt one. This change affects the market prices of products because firms are no longer allowed to get the VAT that they paid on their purchases of inputs back from the government.

The Distributional Impact of the Reform by Tax Type

In this analysis, we simulate the distributional impact of these changes to tax status, determining the projected revenues from each tax change included in the Fiscal Equity Law. We obtain the distributional impact of projected revenues on the basis of the distribution of family consumption and the shifting assumptions explained above for the VAT, exonerations, excise taxes, and income taxes.[13]

Value Added Tax

A detailed analysis of the impact of the VAT is performed on each product for two reasons. This breakdown allows us to make more precise estimates of the overall impact of VAT reform. It also helps to identify areas where actions might be taken to change the tax status of certain goods if a stronger distributional (or re-distributional) impact is desired. Kakwani concentration and progressivity indexes are calculated for a series of products (see table 2.3). The goods are organized in the table according to their decreasing concentration index. An increase in the VAT on salt, for example, has maximum impact on the poor in relation to the most affluent groups, while additional VAT on cooking gas has a minimal distributional impact. According to the numbers found in column 4 of the table, the VAT on all of the goods examined here is considered regressive. However, when consumption is used as the criterion (column 3), the regressivity of taxes on many goods is reduced, even disappearing in some cases.

The analysis of the distributional impact of VAT concludes that the modifications introduced by the Fiscal Equity Law are neutral. In addition, the analysis by product shows that for a few of them—rice, cooking oil, sugar, and beans—the change in VAT status would be clearly regressive. The Kakwani progressivity index does not significantly vary from zero (1.4) when ranked by consumption, confirming neutrality, and is negative (−22.3) when ranked by income.

The tax burden and tax pressure for the aggregate of changes made to the VAT structure was also calculated by quintile. According to a traditional analysis that utilizes per capita income as the indicator of welfare, the VAT reforms in Nicaragua are regressive. However, when current per capita consumption is used as the indicator, the reform is assessed as proportional (see figure 2.4).

Exonerations

Nicaragua's tax system contains an extensive variety of exemptions and exonerations. A wide range of economic sectors receives exceptional tax treatment. The Fiscal Equity Law eliminates various tax exonerations that affect both domestic transactions and imports. With respect to VAT, the government projects revenues of C\$49.9 million from the domestic sector and C\$45.6 million from imports. However, only a fraction of this total revenue corresponds to governmental organizations that will no longer receive exonerations. Most of the remaining increased revenues will result from eliminating exonerations to transportation cooperatives, the mining and manufacturing industries, and, to a lesser extent, to agricultural

Table 2.3 Kakwani Concentration and Progressivity Indexes for Value Added Tax

Item	Concentration index ranked by		Progressivity index ranked by	
	Equivalent consumption	Equivalent income	Equivalent consumption	Equivalent income
Salt	9.0	4.1	−31.3	−49.2
Beans	11.1	2.8	−29.2	−50.6
Rice	12.9	6.2	−27.4	−47.2
Sugar	14.1	9.4	−26.2	−43.9
Coffee	14.6	8.3	−25.7	−45.0
Cooking oil	17.3	11.3	−23.0	−42.0
Household Products	26.0	18.6	−14.3	−34.8
Onion	27.7	16.9	−12.6	−36.5
Tomato	31.3	19.8	−9.0	−33.6
Powdered Milk	31.3	18.5	−9.0	−34.9
Tortilla	33.3	20.8	−7.0	−32.5
White Bread	33.3	22.7	−7.0	−30.6
Pinolilo	33.4	18.0	−6.9	−35.4
Potatoes	35.1	20.4	−5.3	−33.0
Eggs	35.4	22.1	−4.9	−31.3
Plantains	38.1	23.8	−2.2	−29.5
Transportation	38.5	29.6	−1.8	−23.7
Clothes/children	39.4	28.4	−0.9	−25.0
Shoes/adults	42.1	29.7	1.8	−23.7
Pork	43.6	27.9	3.3	−25.5
Cleaning/hygiene prod.	45.1	34.8	4.8	−18.6
Chicken	47.8	34.0	7.5	−19.4
Water Service	48.5	40.1	8.2	−13.2
Fresh milk	49.2	35.2	8.9	−18.2
Shoes/kids	50.2	39.5	9.9	−13.9
Cheese	50.4	33.4	10.0	−20.0
Clothes/adults	53.5	44.1	13.2	−9.3
Cabbage	54.1	29.6	13.8	−23.7
Fish	55.0	43.8	14.7	−9.6
Beef	56.0	40.9	15.7	−12.5
Banana	59.0	39.0	18.7	−14.4
Electricity Service	61.1	51.8	20.8	−1.6
Cooking gas	61.7	49.7	21.3	−3.7
Total	41.7	31.1	1.4	−22.3

Source: Developed with data from the 2001 EMNV.

FIGURE 2.4	Normalized Tax Pressure for Value Added Tax (by quintile)

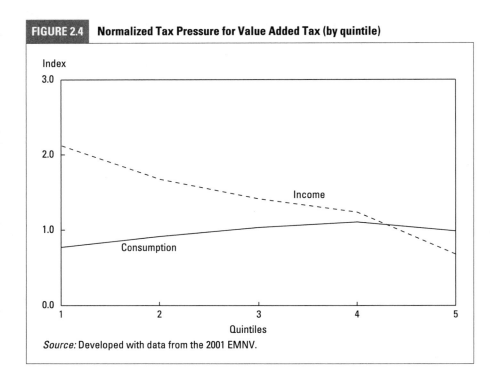

Source: Developed with data from the 2001 EMNV.

cooperatives. For the analysis, it is assumed that the elimination of these exonerations translates into higher prices for the final goods or services sold by these sectors, except for the mining sector. Mining does not generally sell products to end consumers, and because there is no input-product matrix, most of the burden from eliminating these exonerations for mining has been passed on to consumers in general.

The distributional impact of changes to the tax exoneration structure is neutral, with low progressivity indexes. The value of the Kakwani progressivity index (see table 2.4) does not significantly vary from zero (1.7) when consumption is used as the indicator, and it is slightly negative (−20.7) when income is used.

Excise Taxes

The Fiscal Equity Law changes excise tax rates for a long list of products. These tax changes are found to be progressive in an intertemporal framework, and neutral or slightly regressive when ranked by income. The Kakwani progressivity index (see table 2.5) is positive when ranked by consumption. This progressivity is superior for the group of products

Table 2.4 Kakwani Concentration and Progressivity Indexes for the Reduction in Value Added Tax Exonerations

| Item | Concentration index ranked by | | Progressivity index ranked by | |
	Equivalent consumption	Equivalent income	Equivalent consumption	Equivalent income
Foods	34.8	23.0	−5.5	−30.4
Industry	51.5	42.3	11.2	−11.1
Transport	38.5	29.6	−1.8	−23.7
Mining	40.3	30.2	0.0	−23.1
Total	42.1	32.6	1.7	−20.7

Source: Developed with data from the 2001 EMNV.

whose tax rate is uniformly set at 10 percent. The index is 20.2 for the aggregate, 22.2 for the group taxed at 10 percent, and 9.4 for the group of products taxed at a rate of 15 percent.

The tax burden and tax pressure for the aggregate of changes made to the excise tax structure was also calculated by quintile. According to a traditional analysis that utilizes income as the indicator of welfare, the excise tax reforms in Nicaragua are regressive. However, when current consumption is used as the indicator, the reform is assessed as progressive (see figure 2.5).

Income Taxes

The Fiscal Equity Law addressed two types of income tax—corporate and individual. The new legislation, through varied measures, aims to increase equity and reduce evasion.

Table 2.5 Kakwani Concentration and Progressivity Indexes for Excise Taxes

| Category | Concentration index ranked by | | Progressivity index ranked by | |
	Equivalent consumption	Equivalent income	Equivalent consumption	Equivalent income
Total excise	60.5	49.3	20.2	−4.0
10% rate	62.5	51.2	22.2	−2.2
15% rate	49.7	39.3	9.4	−14.1

Source: Developed with data from the 2001 EMNV.

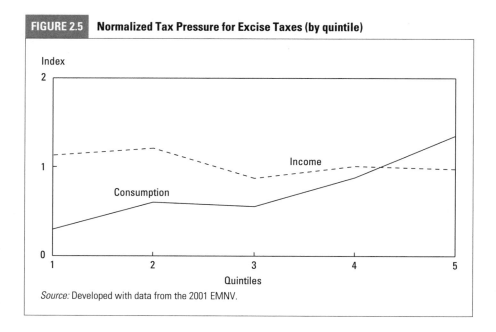

FIGURE 2.5 **Normalized Tax Pressure for Excise Taxes (by quintile)**

Source: Developed with data from the 2001 EMNV.

Corporate Income Tax

The Fiscal Equity Law promotes a series of measures aimed at reducing corporate income tax evasion. The main measure is the minimum payment of 1 percent on the value of gross assets. This measure will contribute C$189.7 million to the national budget. In a similar vein, limits on accelerated depreciation, withholding taxes on agricultural commodity market transactions, taxes on financial profits, and the 2 percent withholding tax on imported goods valued at more than US$2,000 will also help to reduce tax evasion. These measures are expected to generate an additional C$139.2 million in revenues, for a total additional C$328.9 million in revenues overall. This PSIA, therefore, includes estimating the impact of these measures, simulating the distributional impact of increased corporate IR revenues.

The theoretical impact of this tax on corporate earnings has been and remains the subject of intense debate in specialized literature. The competitive general equilibrium model in closed economies predicts that the burden can affect not only capital, but also labor and consumers (Harberger 1962; Kotlikoff and Summers 1987; and Fullerton and Metcalf 2002). Although this is generally a tax that affects the formal sector of the economy, the inter-sector movement of capital implies the tax's transfer to all capital, independent of its destination. Capital may avoid this tax when it has a high level of international mobility. At one extreme, with perfect mobility, the rate of earnings should coincide with independence from the geographic location of the investment. Thus, an increase in the tax on capital should be compensated by an increase in gross earnings. Although mobility is not total in any country, Nicaragua is a relatively open country, with access to international financial markets, particularly in the United States. Hence, capital may certainly elude at least part of the tax burden, transferring this burden as lower salaries or higher prices.

For purposes of this analysis, corporate income tax was evaluated according to three hypotheses. In the first (H1), the total burden weighs solely on capital. As discussed, this is an extreme hypothesis. In the second (H2), the burden is partly transferred to capital and partly to the price of goods; in the third (H3), part of the tax is transferred to capital, the price of goods, and also labor (see Pechman 1984). To develop these alternative hypotheses, the distribution of income from capital and benefits, from salaried labor in the formal sector, and from total consumption were calculated with information from the 2001 EMNV.

Income tax is clearly progressive, even when part of the burden of this tax may be transferred. In Hypotheses 2 and 3, more than 60 percent of the burden weighs on Quintile 5. The concentration and progressivity indexes are clearly higher than those obtained from other taxes (illustrated in table 2.6).

The tax burden and tax pressure for the aggregate of changes made to the corporate income tax was calculated by quintile. According to both the traditional approach, using income as the indicator of welfare, and the most modern approach using current consumption as the indicator, the results of the reform on corporate income taxes are assessed as visibly progressive (see figure 2.6).

Table 2.6 Kakwani Concentration and Progressivity Indexes for Corporate Income Tax

Hypothesis	Concentration index ranked by		Progressivity index ranked by	
	Equivalent consumption	Equivalent income	Equivalent consumption	Equivalent income
H1	82.3	83.4	42.0	30.0
H2	62.5	58.0	22.2	4.7
H3	64.1	62.8	23.7	9.5

Source: Developed with data from the 2001 EMNV.

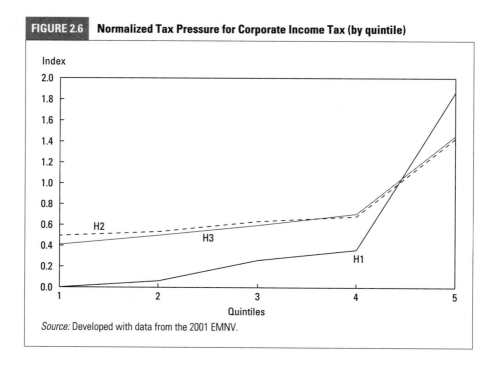

FIGURE 2.6 **Normalized Tax Pressure for Corporate Income Tax (by quintile)**

Source: Developed with data from the 2001 EMNV.

Individual Income Tax

The Fiscal Equity Law also makes some changes to individual income tax. The law's Article 21 sets the marginal income tax rate at 30 percent, unifying it with the corporate rate. Although this measure would imply an increase in revenues, it is complemented by changes allowing deductions for payments to the National Social Security Institute, which will generate a net loss of tax revenues. It is predicted that together both measures will imply a C$26 million reduction in revenues. Individuals will also be affected by the tax on financial profits. Moreover, the reform establishes a 20 percent withholding tax on services provided by nonresidents.

To calculate the impact of these changes, it is assumed (as in almost all relevant literature) that individual income taxes are not transferred, and that the tax burden weighs solely on the individual legally responsible for their payment. The impact of individual income tax was simulated on the basis of income declarations found in the 2001 EMNV, and the rate scales and deductions that were applicable before and after the reform.[14] The tax that in theory should have been paid by each individual surveyed was simulated, based on their income in 2001 and the income tax structure at that time, and alternatively with the current income tax structure.

Two interesting results emerged from this exercise. First, we find that the pre-reform individual income tax structure is already progressive. Prior to the reform, 94.6 percent of the tax burden weighed on individuals from the wealthiest quintile (based on equivalent consumption distribution).[15] The reform increases this to 95.3 percent, making the system yet more progressive (see figure 2.7). Second, the simulation indicates a C$45 million loss in revenues as a result of the reform, which is not significantly different from the C$26 million loss anticipated by the government.

The difference in progressivity between current individual income tax and the individual income tax prior to reform is very minor (see table 2.7). The reform's distributional impact on individual income tax shows two effects that tend to net out. On the one hand, the impact increases given the slightly greater progressivity, but on the other hand it causes a loss in revenues. Thus, there is zero net impact.

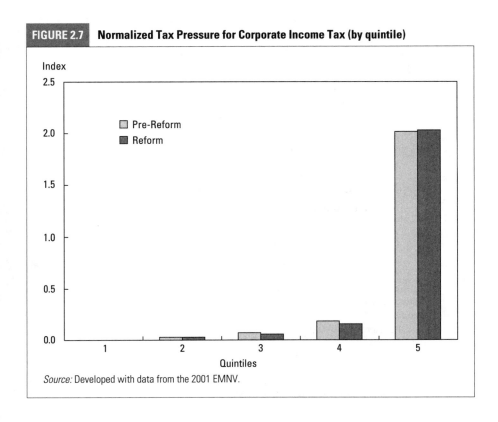

FIGURE 2.7 **Normalized Tax Pressure for Corporate Income Tax (by quintile)**

Source: Developed with data from the 2001 EMNV.

Table 2.7 Kakwani Concentration and Progressivity Indexes for Individual Income Tax

Tax system	Concentration index ranked by		Progressivity index ranked by	
	Equivalent consumption	*Equivalent income*	*Equivalent consumption*	*Equivalent income*
Pre-Reform	91.3	95.5	51.0	42.1
Post-Reform	92.2	96.1	51.9	42.7

Source: Developed with data from the 2001 EMNV.

Impact of the Fiscal Equity Law on Vertical Equity

In considering the overall impact of the Fiscal Equity Law on vertical equity, we find that the reform's aggregate concentration index is 54.6, while the Kakwani progressivity indicator would be 14.3, indicating slight progressivity (see table 2.8). In the case of VAT, the reform is found to be neutral (statistically not significantly different from zero) when we use consumption as the welfare indicator. Eliminating the zero-rate VAT is regressive for some products (for example, rice, salt, beans, sugar, coffee, and cooking oil), although it is progressive for others (cooking gas, electricity, bananas, beef filet, fresh fish, and clothing). The reform's reduction of the spread of excise tax rates is progressive. Reforms to individual and corporate income tax rates, independent of the shifting assumption hypothesis used, have zero net impact and are visibly progressive, respectively.

Table 2.8 Kakwani Concentration and Progressivity Indexes for the Overall Reform

Tax	Concentration index ranked by		Progressivity index ranked by	
	Equivalent consumption	*Equivalent income*	*Equivalent consumption*	*Equivalent income*
Value added tax	41.7	31.1	1.4	−22.3
Eliminating VAT exonerations	42.1	32.6	1.7	−20.7
Excise taxes	60.5	49.3	20.2	−4.0
Income tax	64.1	62.8	23.7	9.5
Total	54.6	47.6	14.3	−5.7

Source: Developed with data from the 2001 EMNV.

The impact of the C$733 million in revenues that are expected from the Fiscal Equity Law is slightly positive (see table 2.9). Although the poorest quintile consumes 6.2 percent of total consumption, it must bear 3.4 percent of the additional tax burden. In contrast, the wealthiest quintile, which consumes 47.1 percent of total national consumption, will pay 59.2 percent of the higher taxes.

Tax pressure increases with the level of consumption, making it progressive. The last column of table 2.9 measures the normalized tax pressure on each quintile (the relationship between the two previously mentioned variables). A frequent indicator of a nation's equitable distribution is the Gini coefficient. This coefficient, calculated on the basis of equivalent consumption distribution, dropped from 42.4 to 40.3 between 1998 and 2001. The Fiscal Equity Law reduces the Gini to 39.2 if additional revenues are spent on a uniform per capita basis, and will drop even more if spending targets the poorest members of Nicaraguan society.

The tax burden and tax pressure for the all reform changes was calculated by quintile. According to a traditional analysis that utilizes income as the indicator of welfare, the overall tax reform in Nicaragua is slightly regressive. However, when current consumption is used as the indicator, the reform is assessed as slightly progressive (see figure 2.8).

Impact of the Fiscal Equity Law on Horizontal Equity

The analysis in the last section considers themes related to vertical equity, estimating progressivity indicators and calculating the reform's distributional impact on personal income distribution. Horizontal equity is

Table 2.9 Consumption Distribution, Reform's Tax Burden and Reform's Normalized Tax Pressure

| | Distribution | | |
Quintile	Pre-reform consumption	Reform tax burden	Normalized tax pressure
1	6.2	3.4	0.5
2	10.6	7.9	0.7
3	14.8	10.9	0.7
4	21.3	18.7	0.9
5	47.0	59.2	1.3
Total	100.0	100.0	

Source: Developed with data from the 2001 EMNV.

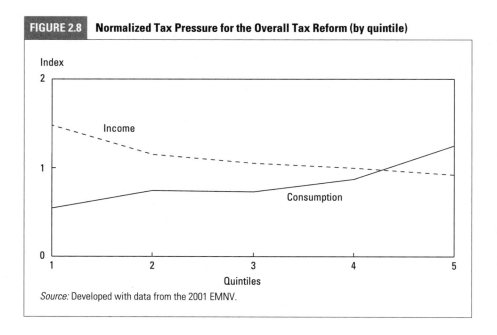

FIGURE 2.8 Normalized Tax Pressure for the Overall Tax Reform (by quintile)

Source: Developed with data from the 2001 EMNV.

another dimension of distributional fairness. It refers to equal treatment of "agents" who are in similar situations. In the realm of taxes, this concept implies similar taxation treatment for individuals in similar economic brackets.

One of the objectives of the Fiscal Equity Law is to reduce the horizontal inequity that results from many types of preferential treatment. The reform significantly reduces a series of exemptions and exonerations received by different sectors of the economy. In addition, the spread of tax rates is also substantially reduced. With respect to VAT, various products are added to the 15 percent tax rate, and most excise tax rates are set at 10 or 15 percent. The marginal tax rate for individuals is raised to the corporate rate. In these ways, the Fiscal Equity Law represents progress toward a more horizontally equitable tax system.

Summary of Main Findings

The recent passage of the Fiscal Equity Law significantly modifies the Nicaraguan tax system. In this chapter, we evaluated the distributional impact of these reforms by applying the shifting assumptions methodology to information about spending and income obtained from the EMNV 2001. We used both consumption and income adjusted to demographic factors as alternative welfare indicators, and applied standard shifting assumptions found in corresponding literature. The distributional impact of each reform measure and the general tax system were evaluated in relation to concentration and progressivity curves and indexes. We found that the tax reform implemented through the Fiscal Equity Law is slightly progressive in distributional terms. If its implementation leads to an effective increase in tax revenues, distribution in Nicaragua will become less unequal than it is currently. In addition, the law's measures promotes horizontal equity.

The results for the tax burden before and after passage of the Fiscal Equity Law are similar, since the reform has only a minor impact on total revenues and its distributional impact does not differ significantly from that of the previous tax system. The poorest individuals are taxed only marginally less after the reform, while the more affluent are only taxed marginally more. These similarities naturally translate into similar tax pressure. The Nicaraguan tax system was slightly progressive prior to the reform, which has only marginally increased its progressivity (see table 2.10).

Table 2.11 provides a summary of the distributional impact of the post-reform Nicaraguan tax system. For purposes of the analysis, the first hypothesis (H1) is where the total burden of the corporate income tax weighs solely on capital; the second hypothesis (H2) is where the burden is partly transferred to the price of goods. If there were equal per capita public spending, changes to the tax system would imply an almost 11-point reduction of the Gini coefficient for the distribution of equivalent family consumption. The reform would be responsible for 1 point of this total. When income is used as the welfare indicator, the distributional impact is less—a 9-point reduction of the Gini.

**Table 2.10 Kakwani Concentration and Progressivity Indexes,
Pre- and Post-Reform**

Tax system	Concentration index ranked by		Progressivity index ranked by	
	Equivalent consumption	Equivalent income	Equivalent consumption	Equivalent income
Pre-Reform	53.1	45.3	12.8	−8.0
Post-Reform	53.2	45.6	12.9	−7.8

Source: Developed with data from the 2001 EMNV.

Table 2.11 Distributional Impact of the Tax System, Pre- and Post-Reform

Impact assessment	Equivalent consumption	Equivalent income
Pre-taxation Gini system	40.3	53.4
Tax progressivity	12.9	−7.8
Spending progressivity (H1)	0.0	0.0
Spending progressivity (H2)	40.3	53.4
Fiscal progressivity (H1)	12.9	−7.8
Fiscal progressivity (H2)	53.2	45.6
Revenues/income	20.1	20.1
Post-taxation Gini (H1)	37.7	54.9
Post-taxation Gini (H2)	29.6	44.2

Source: Developed with data from the 2001 EMNV.

Recommendations for Improving Vertical and Horizontal Equity in Nicaragua

There is a small group of goods with high consumption rates by the poorest stratum of the population. The fiscal equity law currently exempts 53 items, but three-quarters of the food consumption of the extremely poor people in Nicaragua consists of only 11 items (rice, beans, corn, sugar, tortilla, eggs, vegetable oil, coffee, fresh milk, cheese/cream, and chicken), and half of four basic food staples (rice, beans, corn, and sugar) (World Bank 2003). Therefore, for VAT to favor the poorest, only 11 items could be exempted. The budgetary impact of some type of differentiated treatment would be minimal, but the distributional impact would be great since the current loss of revenue comes mainly from the non-poor. The recommendation is to limit tax exemption to the 10 items exclusively.

Generalized exonerations and exemptions, without any clear distributional motive, lead to distortions, horizontal inequity, and little or no distributional gain. This analysis suggests that eliminating sector exonerations is important for making the tax system more transparent and accountable, for increasing its horizontal equity, and for increasing its revenues. The recommendations are (1) to eliminate, in accordance with the law, exonerations and exemptions, thus avoiding loopholes in the reform's package; and (2) to strengthen tax administration to diminish tax evasion.

This analysis illustrates the importance of fully implementing the Fiscal Equity Law to achieve its revenue goals. Because the reform increases the tax structure's progressivity only minimally, most of its distributional impact comes from higher revenues, and therefore the increased social spending it permits. If the reform's objectives are not met and revenues do not grow, it will have little or no impact in fiscal terms and will therefore not constitute any true progress toward fiscal equity.

Improvements in tax administration to enhance tax collection and reduce tax evasion are of fundamental importance for Nicaragua. This administrative measure will also improve the horizontal and vertical equity of Nicaragua's tax system.

STAKEHOLDER AND RISK ANALYSIS

Generally, stakeholders with significant influence over the reform and the possible support or opposition are exporters, consumers, political parties, and civil society and the media. Exporters would wish to maintain their fiscal benefits. Consumers in those population deciles that have a large share of their goods classified within the basic basket could oppose the reform. However, consumers could well be supporters of the reform, given that the impact of the approved package of measures on income distribution is positive. Political parties could generate opposition to this law's implementation because of existing political polarization in Nicaragua. Finally, civil society and the media could exert pressure to take part in the design of the reform's regulations or in defining future legislative reforms.

This PSIA undertook an indirect stakeholder analysis by identifying potentially affected actors, and by analyzing the impact channels and the expected direction and order of magnitude of the impact. This stakeholder analysis was performed by analyzing the published fiscal laws modified by the reform (Law 439, Tax Base Expansion Law; Law 453, Fiscal Equity Law; and other laws). In addition, the Nicaraguan treasury department's method of evaluating the impact of taxation was used, together with revenue estimates from the Internal Revenue Service (DGI) and income estimates provided by the Central Bank of Nicaragua. The chapter evaluates the reform's distributional impact using a shifting assumptions methodology. This PSIA also identified the main risks that could change the expected impact of the reform, their likelihood, and their expected magnitude.

Stakeholders Affected Positively

The export sector is positively affected by maintaining the zero percent VAT rate for exports. The benefit of accelerated depreciation is limited to only those firms participating in the Temporary Import Law, and the minimum annual exports required for participation in the Temporary Import Law is lowered from US$100,000 to US$50,000. The four channels through which stakeholders are affected are prices, access to goods and services, assets, and transfers and taxes. On prices, inputs are less expensive for smaller export firms. On access to goods and services, the acquisition of inputs for small export firms is simplified and therefore made easier. On assets, the accelerated depreciation regime is maintained for most exports. On transfers and taxes, sales tax paid for inputs is refunded, a 1.5 tax credit line is assigned to the FOB value of exports, and a credit of 25 percent of the value of excise taxes paid for fuels toward income tax is permitted. The expected direction and order of magnitude of the impact of the reform is both short and long term. In the short term, the reform facilitates access to imported goods and services for the smallest export firms. In the long term, it maintains the tax regime for the export sector, in a context of important changes to tax norms.

Agriculture, small-scale industry, small-scale fishing, and the coffee sector are also positively affected by the reform, primarily by taxes. The reform allows VAT paid for inputs to be refunded, allows excise taxes paid for fuels to be refunded, and exonerates these sectors from the minimum income tax payment. The expected direction and order of magnitude is short term, realized by permitting these sectors to benefit from temporary fiscal provisions.

Stakeholders Affected Negatively

Individuals with savings accounts of more than US$5,000 or with bonds that mature in less than four years are negatively affected by the new Fiscal Equity Law, primarily because of the 10 percent tax applied to interest. The expected direction and order of magnitude of this effect is both short and long term. In the short term, the tax burden is transferred to individuals with savings accounts, reducing their net revenues. In the long term, it promotes long-term investment, or investment in government bonds (CENIS).

Foreign consultants (either in the form of foreign business partners or as transactions via the Internet) are also negatively affected, primarily because of the 20 percent tax that is applied and withheld by the service contractor (the firm or agency signing the contract with the consultant). The expected direction and order of magnitude of this effect is short term, and although this represents a net loss for foreign consultants, it makes the tax system uniform and increases revenues.

Consumers are also negatively affected by the new Fiscal Equity Law, by both prices and taxes. On prices, the modified tax status of various products from the basic basket of goods (from zero-rate to exempt) could cause price increases to final consumers. On taxes, products not included in the basic basket will continue being taxed. The expected direction and order of magnitude of this effect is both short and long term. In the short term, 53 products from the basic basket will be exempt from VAT. These products, along with electricity service, constitute the basic needs of the lowest-income deciles of the population. Prior to the reform, these products were subjected to a zero-rate VAT. Their exemption eliminates bureaucratic procedures for receiving refunds under the zero-rate system and simplifies the tax system (under the new system, there is a rate of 15 percent VAT for the remaining products). The exemptions, however, will certainly increase prices, since the state will not refund VAT fiscal credits. In the long term, authorities should find a more efficient channel for allocating resources. Possible channels include exempting or zero-rating a reduced number of items consumed by the extreme poor, targeted social assistance, or establishing a voucher system for the poorest members of society.

Sectors that lose exonerations are negatively affected. These sectors are producers of goods and services (transportation and agro-industrial cooperatives, Nicaraguan air transport, forestry, and mining); the social sector (ministries of health and education); the government (state institutions, the executive branch, the electoral branch, National Assembly Deputies, municipal governments, etc.); and other sectors (returning citizens). These stakeholders are affected in four ways: through the labor market, prices, access to goods and services, and transfers and taxes. On the labor market, if sectors lose competitiveness because of the loss of fiscal benefits, there could be income losses and a reduced demand for labor. On prices, sectors that lose benefits and are productive may transfer higher taxes to prices. On access to goods and services, these sectors could experience reduced competitiveness, which would affect the supply of goods and services. On transfers and taxes, the reform eliminates exonerations and exemptions from VAT, excise taxes, income tax, and import duties for sectors that had previously benefited from 57 legal provisions. The expected direction and order of magnitude of this effect is both short and long term. In the short term, the reform permits expansion of the tax base and makes the tax system more neutral, with uniform treatment for all sectors. In the long term, it permits competition on the basis of greater efficiency, not on the basis of special treatment mechanisms that translate into greater tax pressure on other sectors of the economy.

Individuals and corporations dedicated to economic activities are negatively affected by the new Fiscal Equity Law, primarily by transfers and taxes that increase the progressive income tax table for one stratum of the population, and the provision that unifies the maximum individual and corporate income tax rates. The reform also establishes the definitive income tax payment of 1 percent of the total value of gross assets. The expected direction and order of magnitude of this change is both short and long term. In the short term, it eliminates differences in the tax rates paid by individuals and corporations, preventing the erosion of the tax base and increasing vertical equity. It also increases the minimum income tax payment, which increases revenues from this tax by putting a limit on tax evasion. In the long term, it strengthens vertical equity and increases effective tax collection

Small-scale fishing industry is negatively affected by the Fiscal Equity Law, primarily through higher costs, by establishing annual payment for fishing licenses and permits, and by imposing monthly fees to use natural resources. The expected direction and order of magnitude of this change is both short and long term. In the short term, it establishes payments needed to regulate the industry. In the long term, it manages the sustainable use of natural resources.

Potential Risks

Economic policy risks are those related to rent-seeking behavior to maintain fiscal benefits that are not available to other sectors, to civil society and the private sector, and to political opposition groups. Among the first rent-seekers, because some sectors maintain their fiscal benefits, it is possible that they will defend these benefits or want to obtain others by modifying the law's operational guidelines or the law itself. Sectors without access to these fiscal benefits could generate opposition to the reform. Civil society and the private sector could protest because of the law's regulations, or because they have been assigned a greater tax burden. Political opposition groups are manifested by polarization at the National Assembly. Such polarization makes agreement more difficult and weakens good governance.

Exogenous risks come mainly from free trade agreements. If a free trade agreement with the United States is approved in the short term, or if the tariffs of the Central American common market are reduced or unified, revenue goals could be negatively affected because additional measures will be needed to guarantee compliance with the revenue and tax targets.

Institutional risks arise from constitutional provisions that could be applied to some articles of the law because its operational guidelines have not yet been published. Once the operational guidelines of the law are published and implemented, the opportunities for action by sectors opposing the reform will be reduced.

Other country risks include slow economic growth. The government's effort to promote economic growth induces macro and political stability, good governance, the reduction of opposition to the reform, and finally the transition to a more efficient and equitable tax system. The reform contains elements that promote both medium- and long-term growth.

CONCLUSIONS AND LESSONS LEARNED

In September 2002, the GON, the World Bank, and DFID agreed to carry out a PSIA on the impact of the fiscal reform then being designed. The legal expression of the reform, the Fiscal Equity Law, was approved by the National Assembly in May 2003 and entered into force in June of that year. The Nicaraguan PSIA on the Fiscal Equity Law was fully concluded by October 2003. The timing of the PSIA analysis permitted it to have an important impact on the design of the reform, allowing it to influence policy dialogue and policy advice. PSIA major findings were discussed as the PRSC was being prepared, before its presentation to the World Bank Board in February of 2004. This PSIA was reviewed by the IMF, and Fund staff provided useful and favorable comments. Findings were incorporated into the PRSP second Progress Report presented to the Boards of the World Bank and IMF in February 2004.

Discussions of PSIA findings in Nicaragua took place in three workshops, one with the MHCP and donors, another with the fiscal reform committee members, and a third with representatives of civil society members of the National Council for Economic and Social Planning (Consejo Nacional de Planificación Económica y Social or CONPES). At that time, CONPES was the main group for consulting civil society representatives for the PRSP.

At present, multilateral and bilateral donors are working toward a joint financing arrangement (JFA) on general budget support between the GON and the donor group. The Performance Assessment Matrix (PAM) has incorporated a condition that would increase tax collection and that should continue to increase vertical and horizontal tax equity on the basis of the findings of this PSIA. The condition provides for VAT tax exemptions to be limited exclusively to the 11 items identified comprising three-quarters of the food consumption of the extreme poor.

The GON is currently finalizing the preparation of a second-generation PRSP-II. The findings of this chapter have already been incorporated into this revised Poverty Reduction Strategy. This will allow for the chapter to be more widely disseminated to decision makers in the public sector and to representatives of other branches of government, such as the National Assembly, as well as to political parties, the private sector, and the media. Any future components of the reform can also make use of the findings of the chapter.

Stakeholder involvement is absolutely key throughout the process, beginning from the process of drafting Terms of Reference, selection of consultants, discussion of preliminary and final results, discussion of preliminary and final drafts, and through the completion of the PSIA. The relevance and usefulness of the contents and policy recommendations of the PSIA can be ensured only in this way.

Probably the most salient feature of this PSIA was the GON's leadership in creating a tripartite technical committee (GON, civil society, and donors) by the Ministry of Finance (Ministerio de Hacienda y Crédito Público or MHCP) to design of the tax reform, the Fiscal Equity Law and its operational guidelines, and the elaboration of the PSIA. The selection of members for the committee was the responsibility of national authorities, consulted and agreed with civil society, and supported by both multilateral and bilateral donors. The tripartite technical committee had explicit responsibilities for the PSIA

The technical quality of the PSIA was ensured by the full involvement of the staff of the MHCP's Office of Fiscal Affairs, by the GON, by World Bank support in selecting and financing qualified international consultants, and by incorporating qualified national research assistance both to obtain all needed information as well as to ensure knowledge transfer of methodologies.

Finally, close collaboration among multilateral and bilateral donors ensured timely financing and timely review, including the IMF's review of the PSIA, which provided favorable and useful comments.

NOTES

1. The authors wish to thank the valuable collaboration of the Government of Nicaragua: Eduardo Montealegre, Minister of Finance; Luis Rivas, Director Fiscal Affairs Department (OAFE); and Francisco Abea, Research Analyst at OAFE. The authors also want to thank Anis Dani, Aline Coudouel, Carlos Felipe Jaramillo, Ulrich Lachler, and Stefano Paternostro at the World Bank; and Luis Breuer, Oscar Melhado, and Philip Young at the IMF for the many useful comments. The findings, interpretations, and conclusions reported in this document represent solely the authors' views and should not be attributed to the World Bank or to the Government of Nicaragua.

2. Cross-country comparisons should be made with prudence, since a range of other factors vary from country to country, including the value of the basic food basket for the poor, and the variety and quality of basic diets.
3. Contributions to the social security system are noteworthy.
4. For example, there was an extensive list of organizations and sectors receiving exonerations on imports. This list included the print media, radio and TV, manufacturers of medicines for human use, universities and higher education centers, the agriculture and livestock sector, the fishing and aquaculture industries, hotel investments, international organizations and missions, donations and loans from international institutions, exporters, national security agencies, the energy industry, nonprofit associations, transportation cooperatives, mining exploration, hospital investments, and governmental organizations.
5. After the completion of this report, the GON re-estimated the GDP. The new estimate reduced the observed tax pressure to around 22 percent of the GDP.
6. A fiscal policy is equitable in the vertical sense if the wealthiest contribute a greater proportion of their income or consumption than the population with fewer resources. Horizontal equity implies that two individuals with the same capacity to contribute pay the same amount of taxes.
7. The córdoba is Nicaragua's national currency. The exchange rate with the U.S. dollar was 15.364 by mid October 2003.
8. In Nicaragua, various goods were eligible for a zero-rated VAT, which meant that businesses were rebated the taxes paid during previous stages in the production chain. The reform eliminated this mechanism, and various zero-rated products were given tax exemption (these were mostly goods from the basic basket of consumer goods).
9. *Primary balance* describes the fiscal condition where expenditures (excluding interest payment and debt redemption) are covered by revenues excluding bond revenues (deficits). Thus, general expenditures for the year and the tax revenue for the same year are balanced.
10. See the excellent summary by Fullerton and Metcalf (2002).
11. Similarly, if the individual is interviewed in the first or fourth month, estimates of his or her standard of living based on current income will be skewed upward.
12. It is assumed that competition will cause an increase in the market price, independent of the formal or informal nature of a product's sales outlet. This competitive mechanism might not function perfectly in all sectors, making it important to know the differentiated rates of evasion among the stores where different social groups do their buying. The possibility of estimating these rates is beyond the scope of this work. If families with greater purchasing power tend to buy more frequently from "formal" businesses, this analysis' conclusions about sales tax regressivity will have been somewhat overestimated.
13. In each case, those families that consume a specific good produced at home are omitted.

14. For this calculation, the Monthly Wage and Deductions Table was used, based on Categories of the Nicaraguan Social Security Institute.
15. Because of space limitations, the values calculated for the distribution of equivalent income were not presented here. The results are very similar.

REFERENCES

Bradford, D., ed. 1995. *Distributional Analysis of Tax Policy.* Washington, DC: American Enterprise Institute for Public Policy Research.

Caspersen, E., and G. Metcalf. 1994. "Is a Value Added Tax Regressive? Annual versus Lifetime Incidence Measures." *National Tax Journal* XLVII (4), December.

Deaton, A., and S. Zaidi. 2002. "Guidelines for Constructing Consumption Aggregates for Welfare Analysis." Living Standards Measurement Study, Working Paper 135, World Bank, Washington, DC.

Fullerton, D., and D. Rogers. 1993. *Who Bears the Lifetime Tax Burden?* Washington, DC: The Brookings Institution, Chapters 1 and 2.

Fullerton, D., and G. Metcalf. 2002. "Tax Incidence." NBER Working Paper 8829, National Bureau of Economic Research, Cambridge, MA.

Gasparini, L. 2003. "Different Lives: Inequality in Latin America and the Caribbean." *The World Bank 2003 LAC Flagship Report,* Chapter 2. Washington, DC: World Bank.

Gómez Sabaini, J. 2002. "Nicaragua: Desafíos para la modernización del sistema tributario." Mimeo.

Harberger, A. C. 1962. "The Incidence of the Corporation Income Tax." *Journal of Political Economy* 70: 215–40.

Kotlikoff, L., L. and Summers. 1987. "Tax Incidence." In *Handbook of Public Economics,* vol. 2. ed. A. J. Auerbach and M. Feldstein. Handbooks in Economics Series. Amsterdam: Elsevier.

Lambert, P. 1993. *The Distribution and Redistribution of Income.* Manchester: University Press.

Menchik, P., and M. David. 1982. "The Incidence of a Lifetime Consumption Tax." *National Tax Journal* 35: 189–203.

Metcalf, G. 1994. "Life Cycle versus Annual Perspectives on the Incidence of a Value Added Tax." In *Tax Policy and the Economy.* ed. Auerbach. Cambridge, MA: MIT Press.

Pechman, J. 1984. *Who Pays the Taxes?* Washington, DC: Brookings Institution.

Poterba, J. 1989. "Lifetime Incidence and the Distributional Burden of Excise Taxes." *American Economic Review* 79, May.

Stotsky, J., and A. WoldeMariam. 2002. "Central American Tax Reforms: Trends and Possibilities." IMF Working Paper WP/02/227, Washington, DC: International Monetary Fund.

Székely, M. 2001. "The 1990s in Latin America: Another Decade of Persistent Inequality, but with Somewhat Lower Poverty." IADB Working Paper 454, Inter-American Development Bank, Washington, DC.

WIDER. 2000. UNU/WIDER-UNDP World Income Database, Version 1.0.

World Bank. 2003. *Nicaragua Poverty Assessment. Raising Welfare and Reducing Vulnerability.* Washington, DC: World Bank.

3

BURKINA FASO

A Macroeconomic Approach to Analyze Cotton Sector Reform

B. ESSAMA-NSSAH, ISSOUF SAMAKÉ,
AND JAN WALLISER

Burkina Faso is a poor landlocked country of about 12 million inhabitants with a very narrow natural resource base. In 2004, its GDP reached about US$300 per capita. About 20 percent of the population live in urban areas (mainly the capital city Ouagadougou and Bobo-Dioulasso, in the center of the cotton-growing area). Most depend heavily on agricultural activities, which often do not generate significant cash incomes. Macroeconomic performance and progress in reducing widespread poverty therefore remain vulnerable to exogenous shocks such as rainfall fluctuations and changes in world market prices for cotton, Burkina Faso's main export good.

CONTEXT AND DESCRIPTION OF REFORM PROGRAM

Burkina Faso was among the first countries to finalize a full Poverty Reduction Strategy Paper (PRSP) in early 2000. The PRSP is grouped around the following four thematic pillars:

- accelerating growth with equity,
- promoting access to social services,
- increasing employment and income-generating activities for the poor, and
- promoting good governance.

The subsequent translation of the strategy into budgetary priorities was facilitated by the introduction of program budgets and a medium-term expenditure framework (MTEF).

In the context of PRSP monitoring it became increasingly apparent that the government had few analytical tools for establishing targets for poverty rates based on projected growth rates. Moreover, subsequent to the Monterrey summit in 2002, the Burkinabe government and its development partners increasingly focused on the relationship between PRSP objectives and the Millennium Development Goals (MDGs). To tackle this issue, the government expressed interest in formally modeling the links between the macroeconomic framework and aggregate poverty rates in order to more systematically study the poverty impact of different development paths and exogenous shocks.

Burkina Faso depends heavily on cotton fiber exports, which in recent years represented more than 50 percent of the total value of its exports. The cotton sector, in turn, is the major source of cash income for the rural population, with about 20 percent of the population being involved directly in cotton production. Cotton production expanded significantly after the 1994 devaluation, from about 150,000 metric tons in 1994/5 to over 500,000 metric tons in 2004/5—with a fall in production during 1998/9 following the invasion of the white fly pest.

The government followed a two-pronged strategy in managing the cotton sector, which is organized as an integrated filière system.[1] First, increasing responsibility was given to the union representing cotton farmers by a transfer of 30 percent of the shares of the cotton company (SOFITEX) to them, with the government retaining a minority of 40 percent.[2] This process increased the direct interest of producers in the financial stability of the cotton company and resulted in the adoption of a price mechanism that to date has been able to allow SOFITEX to operate without structural losses. Burkina Faso in this respect contrasts favorably with other African cotton producers.

The government decided in 2001 to open the less-developed cotton zones of the center and the east to new investors rather than maintaining a single operator. This process was concluded in 2004, with the sale of ginning plants and exploitation rights in the two zones. Although within each of the zones the filière structure with monopoly exploitation has been maintained, the concessions that allow exploitation of the zones are being limited over time, and thus foster competition for these zones among operators. Moreover, allowing different operators was seen as reducing risks to the sector of financial distress resulting from management problems at a single operator, a factor that had played a role in large deficits of cotton operators in other countries.

With the further expansion of cotton production under the reform efforts and very limited possibilities for diversification, the government was particularly interested in developing a tool to simulate the poverty impact of fluctuations in cotton prices and production. This issue became increasingly important during 2004 with the sharp decline in cotton prices and the appreciation of the local currency, the CFA franc, vis-à-vis the U.S. dollar. The simulations would help to better understand tradeoffs the government faces in making financing decisions for the sector. A second area of focus for the government was the link between poverty rates and different growth paths to gauge whether government policies should be geared particularly toward enabling growth in certain sectors.

In response to the government's request, the World Bank and the German Technical Cooperation (GTZ) offered to help the government customize the poverty analysis macroeconomic simulator (PAMS) for Burkina Faso. PAMS is a modeling tool developed by several World Bank staff in 2002 with the intention of bridging the gap between macroeconomic aggregates and poverty rates by modeling explicitly the links between macroeconomic aggregates and income changes of different socioeconomic groups (Pereira da Silva et al. 2002). PAMS thereby allows a study of the poverty impact of changes in key macroeconomic variables, such as changes in the export price of cotton, as well as the potential impact of government policy responses. The technical support for developing a PAMS model for Burkina Faso was financed with World Bank technical assistance and Poverty and Social Impact Analysis (PSIA) funds, as well as with GTZ resources.

The collaboration on PAMS modeling coincided with the government's work on revising the PRSP that was launched in early 2003. In this context, the government was also conducting a new household survey to study the change in poverty rates between 1998 and 2003. The latter exercise was accompanied by World Bank staff, both through support for technical survey design and through analytical work under a poverty assessment undertaken during 2004. The PAMS modeling was therefore intended to provide additional information on growth-poverty linkages and exogenous shocks to support policy analysis in the revised PRSP, and to help identify key patterns of poverty-growth dynamics during 1998–2003 for the poverty assessment.

The remainder of this chapter is organized as follows: The next section describes the modeling approach of PAMS. The second section discusses simulations undertaken for Burkina Faso. The third section reviews the impact of analytic support, and the final one draws some lessons from the collaboration.

MODELING GROWTH-POVERTY LINKAGES WITH PAMS

The basic idea underlying PAMS is to trace sequentially, in a top-down fashion, the poverty and distributional implications of macroeconomic shocks or policies and of structural policies. The framework can also be used to analyze the poverty incidence of the level and pattern of growth induced by such policies. The framework is composed of three layers: a macro layer, a meso layer, and a micro layer. The top layer is the macroeconomic module that imposes aggregate consistency. The meso layer models the functional distribution of economic welfare represented by income or expenditure. The last module is a poverty and inequality simulator.[3]

The package is conceived as a "shell" that can host data from any country. The minimum requirement is a macro-consistency framework and a household survey. The three layers of PAMS are implemented by four elements:

1. a macroeconomic model to simulate the behavior of the macroeconomy;
2. a labor, earnings, and transfer module to represent the *functional distribution of income* and prevailing redistributive mechanisms;
3. a module to simulate the *size distribution* of income among representative groups, and
4. a module to organize the original household survey data according to the structure of module 3.

Despite PAMS' simplicity, the framework can provide first-order answers to some important macro and (some micro) policy issues that face policymakers in many developing countries in designing poverty reduction strategies. Based on a set of macroeconomic assumptions, the macroeconomic module generates a growth path for gross domestic product (GDP). This level of growth is then translated by the meso-module in a pattern of economic growth consistent with the chosen segmentation of the labor market. The induced changes in disposable income are transmitted to the poverty and inequality simulator to compute the impact on poverty and between-group inequality.

Ensuring Macroeconomic Consistency

The PAMS framework is sufficiently flexible to accommodate various degrees of complexity in modeling the functioning of the economy. All that is needed for PAMS is a model producing macro-consistent output. Macro-consistency frameworks are designed to explain, at an aggregate level, the relationships and changes in key macroeconomic variables such as (1) the production of goods and services, (2) employment, and (3) consumption, savings, and investment. Generically, the building of this module involves three key steps. The first step is to construct an accounting framework that imposes consistency on real and financial transactions of socioeconomic agents. The second is to specify behavioral equations and projection rules for the variables. The last step entails the choice of residual variables used to satisfy underlying budget and system constraints. Such constraints usually take the form of accounting identities.

Five basic sets of macroeconomic accounts are involved in building the PAMS framework. Four of these represent four institutional agents: the public sector, the banking system, the nonfinancial private sector, and the external sector or rest of the world. The final set of accounts, representing the national accounts, traces two different aspects of the production process: factor income from the production of goods and services, and expenditure on the output of the production process.

In the case of Burkina Faso, the macro-consistency model of the authorities to which PAMS was linked had been developed with technical assistance of GTZ over several years. A resident technical advisor to the ministries in charge of finance and economy financed by GTZ had implanted a forecasting tool that became the main instrument for the analysis conducted by authorities themselves. The automated forecasting instrument, known as "IAP" in French, produces the main macroeconomic variables in a detailed spreadsheet and ensures internal consistency of historical data and projections. To ensure close monitoring of macro-micro linkages, PAMS was integrated with IAP; it produces results practically automatically each time the macroeconomic forecasts are adjusted. In addition, the Burkina Faso PAMS model was equipped with a standard World Bank macroeconomic model, called RMSM-X.

Deriving Disposable Incomes

The second or meso layer of PAMS attempts to model distributive mechanisms based on the public budget and factor markets. Indeed, each household in the economy is assumed to get its means of livelihood both from participating in various markets and from the government (as net public transfers).

The main element of the meso level is the labor and wage-income module, which simulates the functioning of a segmented labor market. First, the module divides the economy into two basic components: rural and urban. Then, within each component, we distinguish the formal from the informal sector; within each one of these sectors, we distinguish subsectors that produce tradables from subsectors that produce nontradables.

To derive aggregate incomes by sector, GDP is broken down according to the above sectors. Here again, it is necessary to determine residually the production of certain sectors (for example, the urban informal and the rural subsistence sectors) in order to maintain overall consistency. The simplest way to model the output of the rural economy, which was followed in the case of Burkina Faso, is to make it a constant elasticity function of rural labor supply. Within the urban economy, assuming that all private investment in the economy occurs within the formal sector, the output in that sector can be derived on the basis of an appropriate assumption about the link between output and investment. The production of the public sector, which is part of the urban sector in the model, is exogenously determined by government spending. Once exports in the urban and rural sectors have been computed based on the real exchange rate, the output of the urban informal nontradable sector and rural subsistence agriculture are determined residually.

To link changes in GDP with labor incomes by different population groups, incomes are traced through a simple model of the labor market. Labor supply is assumed to be driven by demographic considerations and migrations of labor and skill categories. In Burkina Faso, PAMS was aligned with the nine socioeconomic groups of the survey:

1. civil service
2. rural nontradable self-employment
3. rural tradable
4. rural family helper
5. rural non-labor force
6. urban formal tradable sector
7. urban formal nontradable sector
8. urban informal sector, and
9. urban unemployed (residual).

Labor demand is broken down by socioeconomic categories, skill levels, and location (rural/urban) and seen as dependent upon sectoral demand induced by output growth as well as on real wages. There is no substitution between types of labor in the production process except migration. The wage rates are derived from supply and demand considerations in the labor market, and the PAMS framework relies on the information of the household survey to proxy the premiums between labor categories.

The module also features a subsection on taxes, transfers, and social expenditures (consistent with the macro model and the government's budget). For each of the country's socioeconomic categories—for example, along the lines of a macro-consistent incidence analysis—it makes average transfers or average taxation of that specific representative agent (RA) with a specific average tax or transfer instrument. These considerations are important in determining disposable income. Disposable income is composed of wage income (or profits) plus social transfers from the budget to a specific labor category, minus taxes paid by that specific category of labor.

Simulating Poverty and Inequality Changes

The third layer of the model deals with household-level information organized in a way that allows easy linkages with the module that derives disposable income. The pattern of income distribution from the base year household survey is assumed to hold throughout the simulation period. Thus, the simulation process projects the mean income of the various RAs in the economy, assuming that there are no changes in the intra-group distribution of income or expenditure.

For each year in the simulation period, the macro module, along with the labor and wage-income module, generates disposable income figures for each of the relevant socioeconomic groups. This income is distributed according to the pattern observed in the household survey. Once internal consistency is assured, the household-level simulator computes common poverty indexes for incidence (the percentage of people below the poverty line) and intensity (the extent to which the living standard of the average poor falls below the poverty line). The simulator also calculates changes in between group inequality using the Gini index of inequality.

There are two caveats for the PAMS approach. First, PAMS inherits the strengths and weaknesses of the models running on top of it. For example, limitations of the macroeconomic forecasting tool inevitably are transmitted via the meso module to poverty projections. The second caveat comes from using the assumption of the RA to determine income (wages, transfers) for each RA. The simulations assume that the mean income growth of each RA affect consistently all households in that particular group (for example, there are no changes in the intra-group distribution of income). Moreover there are no changes in the composition of the population of each RA. For example, there is no endogenous shift between workers from one RA to another for those households that could "migrate" from one to another, given their characteristics and the incentives provided by relative income growth rates. This situation limits the ability of the framework to account for agent heterogeneity in characteristics and behavior.

Implementing the PAMS Model in Burkina Faso

The development of a PAMS model for Burkina Faso was a collaborative effort between the government, the World Bank, and the German Technical Cooperation (GTZ). In Burkina Faso, the Ministry of Economy and Development (MEDEV) is charged with coordinating the PRSP and preparing macroeconomic forecasts. It also supervises the independent National Institute of Statistics and Demography (INSD). Therefore MEDEV was the natural vantage point for developing and installing a PAMS module for Burkina Faso. The macroeconomic analysis and forecasting division of MEDEV, known under its French acronym DPAM, was assigned by the ministry to collaborate with Bank staff on the development of PAMS. DPAM subsequently ensured the close association of INSD with the modeling work. This collaboration was essential for transferring knowledge about PAMS modeling and application to the DPAM.

The advice and support of the GTZ-financed technical advisor unit in improving government access to PAMS was crucial for its success. GTZ-financed experts both assisted the government in verifying the initial calibration and supported the creation of a user-friendly Excel-based interface that allowed them to connect PAMS with macroeconomic scenarios produced by macro modeling tool IAP and RMSM-X. It also permitted them to study changes of poverty against a macroeconomic baseline in numerical and graphical form.

The first step of PAMS modeling was to adapt household data to the income and wage module of the model. To trace incomes, World Bank staff in Washington, DC extracted data from the 1998 household survey, and PAMS was aligned with the nine socioeconomic groups of the survey. In its first calibration, these were each aligned with the level of consumption and income recorded in the 1998 household survey.

The first calibration attempts were discussed with Burkinabe partners in Ouagadougou during the summer of 2003. At the same time, a first training was conducted by Bank staff to introduce the methodology and the data needs of the model to government officials. The training included discussions about the way in which household data can be used, in a fairly simple process, to reproduce poverty rates in PAMS, with subsequent calibration choices for the meso-layer determining long-run dynamics. These first exchanges resulted in an intensive dialogue via electronic mail and videoconferencing on the calibration of the model, both of the poverty simulator and the labor market module. GTZ then financed the visit of a core team of modelers in Washington, DC during the fall of 2003, which resulted in a first calibrated version of PAMS.

During April to July 2003, the government also conducted a new household survey to update the findings of the 1998 survey. Because of urgent data needs for the revision of the full PRSP, INSD presented first results of the survey to the public in August 2003. These results indicated that poverty had remained stagnant during 1998–2003. However, subsequent to the more detailed data analysis by World Bank staff in collaboration with INSD (which was carried out in the context of a poverty assessment in 2004), it was found that the results from the 1998 and 2003 surveys were not comparable because of significant changes in the composition of the consumption basket and poverty line components. On the basis of a comparable consumption indicator, poverty was found to have declined by about 8 percentage points between 1998 and 2003.[4]

One of the difficulties for the collaborative effort was the integration of the 2003 survey into the PAMS framework. With preliminary results already part of the public domain, it proved difficult to base PAMS calibrations on ongoing analytical work that cast doubt on the comparability of the first results. At the same time, it seemed important to base simulations on the 2003 results and to use the information on poverty dynamics between 1998 and 2003 to calibrate the model. It was therefore agreed with the government to calibrate PAMS on the restricted set of comparable consumption items from the 2003 survey. However, the poverty line was adjusted to reproduce the same poverty rate that had already been announced by INSD. Although the calibration takes into consideration comparable poverty levels in 1998, simulations prepared with the government focused on projections from 2003 onward, based on the poverty levels attained in 2003. Table 3.1 summarizes baseline poverty numbers for 2003 by socioeconomic group, which served as baseline for PAMS, and compares those numbers with the poverty numbers for 1998.

A final set of presentations and further training of government officials in the use of Burkina Faso's PAMS model took place during a week-long seminar in June 2004 that brought together participants from MEDEV, the Ministry of Finance and Budget, members of economic

Table 3.1 Socioeconomic Groups and Poverty, 1998 and 2003

percent

Socioeconomic group	Share of population		Share of poor		Poverty headcount	
	1998	2003	1998	2003	1998	2003
Rural area	86.3	79.5	94.1	91.0	62.2	52.7
Urban area	13.7	20.5	5.4	9.0	21.1	20.9
Public sector (urban)	4.1	3.6	0.7	0.3	9.1	3.4
Agricultural tradable (rural)	16.8	18.3	16.4	18.6	53.1	47.1
Other agricultural nontradable (rural)	65.3	59.6	74.6	71.0	61.8	55.3
Family helpers and others (rural)	0.6	0.7	0.3	0.6	30.3	42.0
Non-labor force (rural)	3.6	1.0	3.3	0.8	50.4	38.8
Private formal tradable (urban)	1.0	0.8	0.1	0.1	8.1	7.7
Private formal nontradable (urban)	1.9	2.6	1.2	0.9	33.3	15.7
Informal (urban)	5.6	7.4	2.3	3.4	22.8	21.5
Unemployed (urban)	1.1	6.0	1.0	4.3	47.8	33.1

Source: World Bank (2005, poverty assessment).

planning departments of several line ministries, and donor representatives. Summarizing the collaborative effort and exchanges that had taken over 18 months during 2003–04, the model was presented and training conducted. With these activities, the first phase of the modeling effort was concluded. Further follow-up activities in 2004–05 focused on applying the model to different macroeconomic reform scenarios and included knowledge transfer to other West African countries, in further collaboration with GTZ, based on a Burkina Faso "hub."

USING THE PAMS MODEL IN BURKINA FASO

A first step in using the PAMS model for studying the impact of different macroeconomic scenarios is to choose and analyze a baseline scenario associated with baseline economic policies. For the purpose of this chapter, we have retained a scenario that reflects the lower end of government projections, in assuming an average long-run GDP growth rate of 5 percent driven by secondary and tertiary sector growth of 6 to 7 percent and primary sector growth of 4 percent (table 3.2). Inflation is projected to remain low, at 2 percent per year. Fiscal revenue would increase slowly over time, and government spending as a share of GDP would increase moderately to allow increased spending, notably on education. Export growth would slightly outpace real GDP growth, implying a moderate increase in the export-to-

GDP ratio. Overall, the scenario presented below is somewhat less optimistic about future growth than the revised PRSP that was adopted by the government in 2004 and assumes larger inflows of donor resources.

Baseline Growth and Poverty Scenario

The baseline scenario builds on a certain number of assumptions that, by themselves, would need to be supported by appropriate government policy choices. First, primary sector growth needs to be driven by either a further increase in cultivated land or an increase in agricultural productivity. Second, secondary and tertiary sector growth of 6 to 7 percent will not be possible without growth of private investment, improvements in skill levels, and improvements in infrastructure. Third, the projections

Table 3.2 Baseline Macroeconomic Framework and Poverty Response

Indicator	2003 actual	2004 projected	2005 projected	2006 projected	2007 projected
Selected macro indicator					
Real GDP growth[a]	8.0	4.8	5.3	5.2	5.2
Primary sector[a]	10.8	1.8	4.5	4.5	4.5
Secondary sector[a]	10.4	6.3	6.7	6.6	6.6
Tertiary sector[a]	5.5	6.1	5.3	6.8	6.8
Fiscal revenue[b]	11.3	12.0	12.5	13.0	13.5
Public expenditure[b]	22.0	22.5	22.7	22.9	23.6
Exports of goods[a]	10.7	15.8	16.4	8.5	6.3
CPI (% change)	2.1	2.2	2.2	2.0	2.0
Poverty incidence					
National	46.4	44.1	42.4	40.3	39.2
Rural	53.1	51.4	49.6	47.6	46.6
Urban	20.5	19.7	17.9	16.0	15.4
Demographic structure					
Annual growth rate[c]					
National	5.1	2.4	2.4	2.4	2.4
Rural	4.6	1.9	1.9	1.9	1.9
Urban	7.8	4.3	4.3	4.2	4.2
Share of population					
Rural	79.5	79.1	78.8	78.4	78.0
Urban	20.5	20.9	21.2	21.6	22.0

Source: Authors' projections with PAMS.
a. Real growth rate in percent.
b. In percent of GDP.
c. The growth rate for 2003 reflects 300,000 total displaced people from Côte d'Ivoire.

exclude any shocks to GDP growth from rainfall patterns or terms of trade, thus ignoring the vulnerability of Burkina Faso to these factors. In particular, the baseline scenario also still builds on the assumption of broadly stable cotton prices. Retaining this assumption will later on allow the model to simulate the impact of the steep decline in cotton prices on poverty in Burkina Faso. Finally, the baseline projections build on a very modest shift of population from rural to urban areas.

Based on the macroeconomic assumptions, PAMS produces a set of baseline poverty rates for the whole country, as well as urban and rural areas, and different socioeconomic groups (SEGs). The production of these numbers alongside the macroeconomic scenario can be considered a first major value added of using PAMS. Typically, poverty rate projections build on fairly simple elasticity assumptions and avoid the formalization inherent to the labor income module of PAMS. Modeling the links explicitly exposes the opportunities and risks that arise from a projected macroeconomic environment for poverty reduction. Thereby, it opens opportunities to study alternative policies and macroeconomic environments and their impact on poverty rates.

Under the baseline macroeconomic scenario retained in this chapter, the poverty incidence is expected to decrease substantially—from 46.4 in 2003 to 39.2 percent by 2007 and eventually to 28.7 percent by 2015. The poverty headcount thus declines by about 4 percent per year, with per capita income growing at around 2.5 percent, implying a poverty-growth elasticity of roughly 1.5. With about the same rise in per capita income between 1998 and 2003, poverty declined by about 3 percent per year. The decrease in the rural areas is projected to accelerate slightly, from 3.1 percent between 1998 and 2003 to 3.4 percent during 2004–5, while in the urban areas it is projected to increase sharply, from 0.2 to 5 percent, over the respective two. These projections show that, under the baseline projections, secondary and tertiary sectors are the main engines of growth and thus urban labor demand grows more quickly than rural labor demand, representing an important structural shift from past growth experience.

PAMS permits the tracing of the income developments by SEG for the baseline scenario. The macroeconomic developments affect poverty rates through their effects on the changes in real incomes per capita across SEGs (table 3.3). These aggregate changes are derived from group-specific income growth, which in turn reflects the links that PAMS establishes between the structure of GDP, labor demand, labor supply, and incomes. As can be seen from table 3.3, the baseline structure of GDP growth is projected to benefit the informal sector, the formal tradable sector, and agricultural nontradables, explaining the steady

Table 3.3 Inequality and Household Expenditure Trends

percent

Socioeconomic group	2003 actual[a]	2004 projected	2005 projected	2006 projected	2007 projected
Inequality					
Gini index (inter-group)	44.8	45.7	45.3	47.9	48.2
Per capita income growth by SEG [b]					
Public sector, urban (3.6)	1.7	2.1	0.0	2.9	1.4
Nontradable, rural (59.6)	2.7	1.1	3.3	3.2	1.1
Tradable, rural (18.3)	1.1	3.1	2.8	2.6	2.5
Family helpers, rural (0.7)	0.9	1.0	0.7	1.5	0.8
Formal, tradable, urban (0.8)	3.0	2.4	5.3	10.7	3.2
Formal, nontradable, urban (2.6)	4.1	5.2	2.3	4.5	2.5
Informal, nontradable, urban (7.4)	5.3	2.2	5.7	6.8	5.7
Unemployed (6.0)	0.1	3.6	0.7	2.5	0.5
Non-labor force, rural (1.0)	0.4	0.4	0.2	0.6	0.3

Source: Authors' projections with PAMS.
a. The percentage changes in this column indicate the per annum changes between 1998 and 2003.
b. The numbers in parenthesis indicate the share of each group to the total population in 2003.

decline in poverty in rural areas and the decline in urban poverty that contrasts with past experience. Owing to readjustments of labor supply over time linked to the differential growth rates for rural and urban areas, the income growth fluctuates despite fairly stable GDP growth patterns. For intra-group inequality, the concentration of higher growth in urban sectors in the baseline scenario is projected to exacerbate inequality.

PAMS produces statistics that permit a more formal analysis of the quality of the baseline growth process by way of growth and inequality elasticities. The growth elasticities represent the percentage change of the relevant poverty measure for a 1 percent growth without changes in inequality. The inequality elasticities represent the percentage change for the poverty measure in relation to a 1 percent increase in the Gini index. The inequality-growth trade-off index by Kakwani (2000) shows how much growth (in percent) is needed to keep the respective poverty measures constant if the Gini index rises by 1 percent. PAMS also produces the poverty-equivalent growth rate of Kakwani and Pernia (2000), which denotes the growth rate that would lead to the same level of a poverty measure if growth was not accompanied by any inequality changes, alongside other pro-poor growth statistics.

The baseline scenario implies rising growth and inequality elasticities of the poverty gap and the square poverty gap over time, deepening the growth-inequality tradeoff (table 3.4). The poverty gap reflects the average distance of the poor from the poverty line; the square poverty gap is the average squared distance of the poor from the poverty line. Under the baseline, the pure effect of economic growth on the poverty gap would accelerate from −2.0 in 2003 to −2.2 by 2007—that is, growth becomes more powerful in reducing the distance of the poor from the poverty line. However, along with rising growth elasticity, inequality elasticity rises sharply, from 2.8 to 3.8, implying that the distance of the poor from the poverty line rises more quickly with increases in inequality. Overall, the net changes in elasticities imply a slight increase in the growth-inequality tradeoff. In other words, slightly higher growth is needed to offset the impact of rising inequality. It must be noted, however, that by international standards, the tradeoffs are small and that even under the baseline scenario, Burkina Faso could achieve a fairly broad-based reduction in poverty.

The changes in the growth-inequality tradeoff can be attributed to the rising share of secondary and tertiary sector activities. The urban sector has much higher inequality elasticities, and it benefits to a larger extent from secondary and tertiary sector growth. Thus, as more of national income is channeled to urban areas, inequality rises and the growth-inequality tradeoff becomes more important. Rising inequality also reduces the growth elasticity of the square poverty gap, which places a higher weight on unequal income distributions.

Shocks and Policy Alternatives

The baseline scenario serves as a springboard to study different economic environments and policy responses that could improve the quality of economic growth and potentially accelerate poverty reduction. In general,

Table 3.4 Poverty Elasticity Decomposition

Poverty indicators	2003	2004	2005	2006	2007
Poverty gap					
Growth elasticity	−2.0	−2.1	−2.1	−2.2	−2.2
Inequality elasticity	2.8	3.1	3.3	3.6	3.8
Inequality/growth tradeoff	1.4	1.5	1.6	1.6	1.7
Square poverty gap					
Growth elasticity	−2.5	−2.4	−2.4	−2.4	−2.3
Inequality elasticity	4.7	5.0	5.3	5.6	5.8
Inequality/growth tradeoff	1.9	2.1	2.2	2.3	2.5

Source: Authors' projections with PAMS.

government policies could influence the composition of GDP (for example, through targeted infrastructure investments); change the transmission channels between GDP growth and income (for example, through market regulation or fiscal policies); and enhance the chances of the poorest and most vulnerable of participating in the income creation process. These channels are summarized in figure 3.1.

The government voiced two key concerns about shocks and policy choices in the context of its growth policies. The first concern is about the vulnerability of poverty rates to cotton prices and cotton production because of the exposure of the Burkinabe economy to wide price swings in the international cotton markets. This concern was deepened by the further expansion of cotton-growing areas, limited diversification, and the recent decline of international cotton prices accompanied by an appreciation of the euro and CFA francs vis-à-vis the U.S. dollar. The second concern relates to the relative weight of primary sector growth compared with growth of secondary and tertiary sectors in reducing poverty rates, and the resulting policy recommendations for government investments. Both matters were studied with the PAMS tool to inform policy choices.

Findings of four policy experiments illustrating the contribution of PAMS to poverty analysis are summarized in terms of their impact on poverty and inequality in table 3.5. The first set of experiments concerns the cotton sector, where we simulated a 20 percent decline in export prices

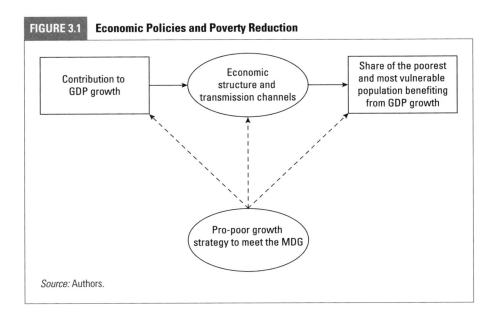

FIGURE 3.1   Economic Policies and Poverty Reduction

Source: Authors.

Table 3.5 Summary of Policy Experiments

Economic variables under different scenarios	2003 actual	2004 projected	2005 projected	2006 projected	2007 projected
Real GDP growth					
Baseline	8.0	4.8	5.3	5.2	5.2
Cotton price: −20%	8.0	4.0	4.3	4.9	5.0
Cotton price and quantities: −20%	8.0	1.2	2.9	3.8	4.3
Other agricultural goods: +20%	8.0	9.3	5.3	4.7	4.9
Change sources of growth	8.0	4.8	5.3	5.2	5.2
Primary sector					
Baseline	10.8	1.8	4.5	4.5	4.5
Cotton price: −20%	10.8	0.9	1.5	3.1	3.9
Cotton price and quantities: −20%	10.8	−8.3	−0.3	2.8	3.7
Other agricultural goods: +20%	10.8	26.3	4.0	4.5	4.5
Change sources of growth	10.8	3.8	3.3	6.6	6.5
Secondary sector					
Baseline	10.4	6.3	6.7	6.6	6.6
Cotton price: −20%	10.4	5.7	5.9	6.0	6.4
Cotton price and quantities: −20%	10.4	3.3	4.3	4.9	5.5
Other agricultural goods: +20 %	10.4	9.1	5.1	5.6	6.6
Change sources of growth	10.4	6.2	6.6	6.5	6.5
Tertiary sector					
Baseline	5.5	6.1	5.3	6.8	6.8
Cotton price: −20%	5.5	4.0	4.8	5.7	6.1
Cotton price and quantities: −20%	5.5	2.2	4.4	4.7	5.5
Other agricultural goods: +20%	5.5	20.0	4.3	5.4	6.8
Change sources of growth	5.5	4.9	4.1	5.6	5.6
Poverty headcount					
Baseline	46.4	44.1	42.4	40.3	39.2
Cotton price: −20%	46.4	45.7	43.4	40.9	39.6
Cotton price and quantities: −20%	46.4	46.6	44.2	41.7	40.2
Other agricultural goods: +20%	46.4	41.2	41.5	40.1	39.2
Change sources of growth	46.4	43.9	42.1	39.4	38.0

Source: Authors'projections with PAMS.

as well as a combined decline in both volumes and prices by 20 percent. The second set of experiments concerns the composition of GDP growth, where we first look at an expansion of agricultural output, including subsistence, by 20 percent, and then study a growth scenario that puts more weight on primary sector growth.

Table 3.5 also retraces each of the experiments in terms of GDP growth and poverty headcount. It displays overall growth rates as well as growth by sector. The impact of the policy experiment can be gauged by comparing the baseline scenario with the policy scenario. For example, the 2005 column shows that the poverty headcount would be one percentage point higher because of lower cotton prices than was simulated under the baseline. The difference in headcounts can thus be attributed to the cotton price decline. What is important to note is that the impact takes into account the price impact on the macroeconomic framework, and its impact is traced though the income module of the model. Below, the mechanics of the experiments and their impact are explained in more detail.

Cotton

In a first set of policy experiments, PAMS was used to study the economic and poverty impact of cotton price fluctuations compared with the baseline projections. For this purpose, two macroeconomic scenarios were developed. Under the first scenario, the cotton price would decline by 20 percent in 2004 and stay lower in the long run, with concomitant effects on growth in future years. Under the second, even more drastic, scenario, both cotton price and volumes were assumed to fall by 20 percent in 2004 and stay at lower levels in the long run.

Compared with the baseline, a sharp decline in cotton prices is estimated to drive up poverty rates by 1.5 percentage points in the first year after the shock (figure 3.2 and table 3.5). This estimate builds on a macroeconomic scenario that recognizes interlinkages between the different sectors and thus reflects the deleterious impact of a decline in cotton prices for the secondary and tertiary sector incomes as well as primary sector incomes. Under the scenario, the fall in the price of cotton induces a decrease of production in the primary sector of about 0.9 percent the first year and 3 percent the second year. In turn, this leads to a fall in output in the secondary and tertiary sectors, where cotton is transformed and marketed and where income from cotton production is consumed. In the first year following the shock, the output of the secondary sector, where cotton transformation takes place, declines by about 0.6 percent. In the second year this output falls sharply, by about 2.1 percent. The tertiary sector shows a similar pattern, but the fall in output is less drastic.

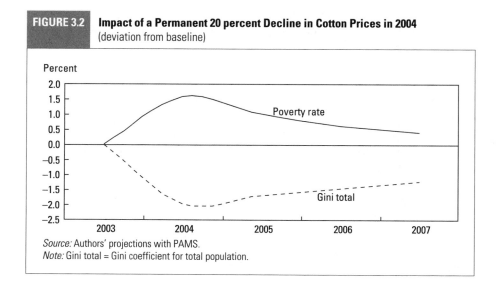

FIGURE 3.2 **Impact of a Permanent 20 percent Decline in Cotton Prices in 2004**
(deviation from baseline)

Source: Authors' projections with PAMS.
Note: Gini total = Gini coefficient for total population.

The poverty impact of the price decline is concentrated on the group of cotton farmers. Cotton farmers comprise about 18 percent of the population, and poverty increases by about 6 percentage points in this group. However, poverty rates also increase slightly for other groups such as unskilled self-employed persons producing nontradable goods and living in rural areas (about 60 percent of the population), who receive part of their revenue in the form of transfers from cotton farmers. At the same time, because cotton farmers enjoy incomes that are higher than those of the average population, the intra-group inequality as measured with the Gini coefficient declines as cotton income declines.

Over the medium run, the impact of the cotton price decline on poverty rates is projected to be mitigated by the recovery in the secondary and tertiary sectors (see table 3.5). The relative performance of the secondary and tertiary sectors combined with the decline in inequality resulting from the decline in cotton production will favor poverty reduction; however, the adverse impact of cotton on poverty will not be completely offset in the medium run.

The poverty impact would be exacerbated if the decline in cotton price was combined with a sharper drop in cotton output. In a second scenario, both cotton prices and quantities are assumed to fall by 20 percent (figure 3.3). Again, the simulations show the direct impact on cotton farmers as well as the impact on output in other sectors. The shock will directly

FIGURE 3.3 **Impact of a Permanent 20 percent Decline in Cotton Prices and Volumes in 2004** (deviation from baseline)

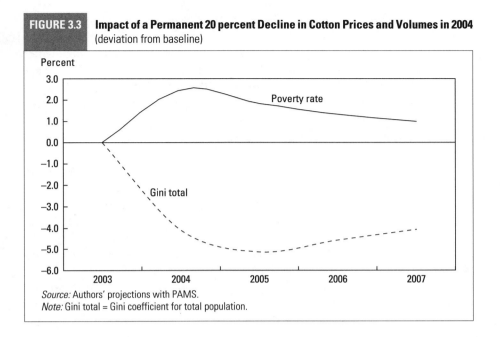

Source: Authors' projections with PAMS.
Note: Gini total = Gini coefficient for total population.

decelerate the primary sector growth from +10.8 percent to −8.3 percent, while the secondary and tertiary sectors growth rates will decrease by 3 points and 3.9 points, respectively. Again, the secondary and tertiary sectors will steadily recover in the medium run (see table 3.5).

The immediate impact of the price and output decline would be an increase in poverty rates of 2.5 percentage points. This impact is composed of an increase of poverty rates by 8.9 percentage points among cotton farmers, alongside increases of 1.3 percentage points for unskilled self-employed persons producing nontradable goods and living in rural areas, and 0.7 percentage points for informal sector workers producing nontradable goods and living in urban areas. As is the case for the price drop, the poverty impact compared with the baseline is mitigated over the medium term by the secondary and tertiary overall steady performance (see table 3.5) that will favor poverty reduction without completely offsetting the adverse initial shock.

The simulations of the interrelationship between cotton prices and quantities and poverty rates underscore the importance of the cotton sector for reducing poverty in Burkina Faso. Sharp fluctuations in prices and quantities have reverberating effects through the economy that can be long-lasting if the shocks are permanent. These findings give strong support to the existing policies of the main stakeholders in the cotton sector aiming at reducing short-term volatility of prices. Currently, the producer price for cotton is set based on a long-run average price floor, which is augmented with a bonus if the sector made a profit in the past year. Loss-making periods are weathered with a cotton support fund financed with cotton sector profits. This mechanism helps to stabilize cotton prices and cotton production by avoiding sharp changes in price signals. Thus far, the price floor has been set low enough to keep the sector profitable.

The PAMS simulations also give some support for government intervention in response to the expected impact of recent cotton price developments. The sharp decline in CFA franc-denominated prices for cotton fiber will lead to a lowering of the producer price, from CFA franc 210/kg (including the bonus of CFA franc 35/kg) to the floor price of CFA franc 175/kg in 2005/6 to keep the cotton sector financially viable. The simulations give some indication that limiting the price decline could diminish its impact by drastically lowering the poverty impact for the directly affected group and limiting the contagion to other economic sectors. However, if prices in CFA francs remain low in the long term, such measures will give only a temporary reprieve and would need to be accompanied by signals allowing a reorientation of agricultural output.

Different Growth Patterns

In a second set of simulations, PAMS was used to study the impact of shocks to agricultural production and different growth paths. The first simulation presents the impact of a 20 percent increase in overall primary sector output, excluding cotton, in 2004 (figure 3.4). These activities include subsistence agriculture (cereals), live animals, leather and hides, meat production, gold mining, and so on, and represent about 50 percent of total exports. The rise in output will increase other exports and will benefit all economic sectors, which provide a livelihood for almost 80 percent of the population. Unskilled self-employed persons engaged in the production of nontradable goods and living in rural areas (which amounted to 60 percent of the population, with a 55 percent poverty headcount in 2003) gain from this development.

Compared with the baseline, given the large number of Burkinabe who work in the primary sector, the 20 percent increase in output would be associated with a 3 percentage point decline in the poverty rate (table 3.5). This large decline reflects not only the direct sectoral impact but also the spreading increase in economic activity resulting from the primary sector growth. In the simulations shown below, the impact is temporary,

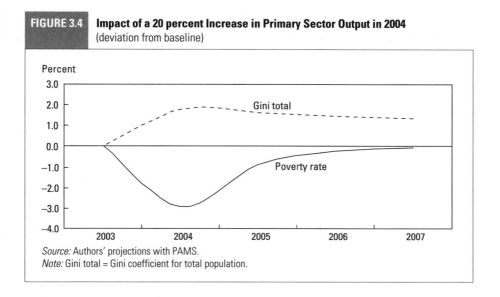

FIGURE 3.4 **Impact of a 20 percent Increase in Primary Sector Output in 2004**
(deviation from baseline)

Source: Authors' projections with PAMS.
Note: Gini total = Gini coefficient for total population.

however, because those activities have a relatively weak connection with other sectors—it is this connection that determines the long-run growth path. In the medium term, the persistence of somewhat higher inequality (signified by the rising Gini coefficient) will also tend to offset the poverty effects. Linking poverty rates to primary sector output also illustrates the large possible swings in poverty rates in response to rainfall conditions—a sharp decline in cereal output (that is, a decrease in primary sector output) would have large impact on living conditions of an important share of the population.

Higher long-term growth in the primary sector could contribute to faster poverty reduction. The growth scenario for the last simulation assumes that overall economic growth remains unchanged, but primary sector growth is about 2 percentage points higher in the long term than under the baseline, compensated by smaller growth of the tertiary sector. Figure 3.5 below, which extends the horizon to 2014, shows that the effects of different sources of growth are cumulative and can be substantial. In this case, higher primary sector growth would lead to faster poverty reduction—about 1 percentage point by 2007 and 4 percentage points by 2015—while reducing inequality.

The simulations reinforce government policy choices supporting primary sector growth. After focusing on food security and promoting small irrigation techniques for food production year-round, the govern-

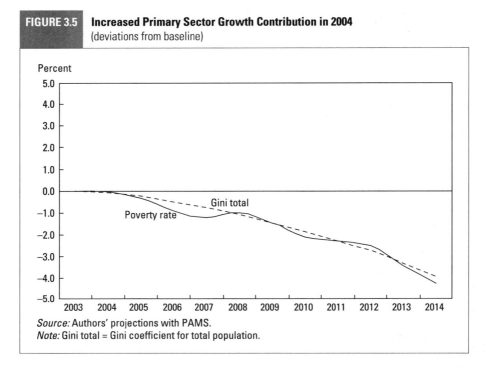

FIGURE 3.5 **Increased Primary Sector Growth Contribution in 2004**
(deviations from baseline)

Source: Authors' projections with PAMS.
Note: Gini total = Gini coefficient for total population.

ment has launched additional initiatives to improve rural infrastructure and market access for producers of alternative crops such as fruits and vegetables. Limited market size for locally produced cereal (corn, millet, sorghum) has proved to be one of the great limitations to the success of the rapid increase in output associated in part with small irrigation. However, as noted earlier, even if farmers are able to increase their ability to market crops, sustained growth in agricultural output projected under this simulation may be very difficult to attain since it hinges on major productivity increases.

The growth simulations also can help to underscore a limitation of the model. The implication of the model to direct government growth policies to the non-cotton primary sector at the margin is largely driven by the presumed stability of the non-cotton farmer group, which in 2003 comprised 60 percent of the Burkinabe population and 71 percent of the poor. To the extent that the population shifts at a higher pace from rural to urban areas than is assumed in the simulations, it may well be that urban sectors at the margin would be most effective in reducing poverty rates.

THE IMPACT OF ANALYTIC SUPPORT

PAMS modeling work has had an impact on the government's policy work and annual PRSP reporting, as well as on the analytical underpinning of Bank lending operations. In the government, the modeling work has strengthened the focus of macroeconomic modelers on poverty issues and the need for coherent poverty data. At the macroeconomic forecasting and analysis department (DPAM), PAMS has clarified some of the multiple layers in which economic activity generates incomes and can change poverty. There is clear understanding of the relevance of the study of these channels, and the model is now routinely applied to estimate the poverty impact of different macroeconomic scenarios produced with the IAP model. There is strong interest by the government in reflecting projected developments in cotton markets and variations in terms of trade.

The 2004 poverty reduction strategy annual progress report, made available in draft form to civil society, stakeholders, and donors in April 2005, draws on PAMS to trace recent poverty developments. Although the report refrains from producing a variety of scenarios, it uses PAMS to obtain a first glimpse of possible poverty headcount changes related to macroeconomic developments in 2003–4. The government is considering expanding the analysis of different macroeconomic scenarios in future reports. On the institutional front, some difficulties arise from staffing limitations of DPAM and its limited involvement in the PRSP process. DPAM is charged with a variety of tasks, including monitoring economic developments, macroeconomic analysis, and macroeconomic forecasting. DPAM has to spend significant time with the statistical institute INSD and other government departments to obtain necessary data. Naturally DPAM also plays a key role in program discussions with the International Monetary Fund. These day-to-day tasks, which receive high priority from the government, limit the time available to DPAM staff to pursue studies on poverty-growth linkages.

In a related area, PAMS implicitly strengthened government focus on poverty statistics and the collection of poverty data. The issue of comparability of the consumption data from the 1998 and 2003 surveys was discussed intensively during the preparation of the World Bank's poverty assessment with technicians at the INSD and DPAM. PAMS also illustrated the incoherence of the macroeconomic variables and the household survey data, which are both produced by INSD. Although the government has maintained its original August 2003 poverty estimates that showed stable poverty rates between 1998 and 2003, the PAMS work has placed additional emphasis on ensuring comparability of survey data. It has also generated interest in conducting smaller poverty surveys between household surveys, and given additional impetus for Burkina Faso's inclusion in the statistical capacity building program (STATCAP) of the World Bank.

PAMS work has enriched the recent World Bank–led poverty assessment for Burkina Faso. In particular, the poverty assessment relied on PAMS simulation to study different growth paths and to consider the impact of external shocks that could enrich future policy discussions. It also built on detailed statistical measures produced in the context of PAMS work about the nature of the linkage between growth and poverty reduction in Burkina Faso during 1998 and 2003. The results of the poverty assessment were presented during a "week of reflection" to government, donor officials, and civil society, and they informed the preparation of the country assistance strategy.

Bank lending, notably the Bank's series of Poverty Reduction Support Credits (PRSC), also draw on PAMS. In particular, early findings showing the potential impact of the Ivorian crisis and justifying additional Bank support of US$10 million were included in the documentation for the third PRSC operation. The policies supported by the fourth and fifth PRSC and other Bank operations build on PAMS work for the analysis of the poverty impact of cotton price fluctuations and the related discussion of development policy choices with the government that took place in 2004–05. In particular, although cotton is an important vehicle for reducing poverty, PAMS also demonstrates its limitations for quickly reducing poverty across the entire country. Cotton remains extremely vulnerable to international price developments, so there is a need for better diversification of income sources. The second PRSP therefore focuses on

- consolidating achievements in the cotton sector, notably be strengthening the government's regulatory role and giving better incentives for soil preservation;
- enhancing off-season farming and increasing food security, especially by spreading adapted irrigation techniques and investment in local infrastructure;
- improving market access for farmers and agricultural infrastructure with projects such as accelerated rural road construction and improvements to export infrastructure;
- improving the business climate and access to credit, electricity, and transport services for small and medium enterprises; and
- enhancing analytical and policy focus on job creation issues in urban areas.

These policies are accompanied by an ongoing effort to raise educational attainment and reduce morbidity and mortality rates.

The Burkina Faso experience has generated interest in the subregion for adopting the model in other countries. To this end, in collaboration with GTZ in Burkina Faso, a regional workshop and technical assistance from the Bank and GTZ have supported the preparation of PAMS in three to four additional countries during 2005.

LESSONS LEARNED

■ The importance and strong payoffs of building a close early collaboration with the government forecasting team figure among the positive lessons learned during the preparation of PAMS. DPAM staff brought a clear set of requirements and questions to the collaboration that helped shape PAMS to their needs, and disseminated it through several training seminars to a variety of government departments. The collaboration allowed DPAM to be strongly vested in the model.

■ A second positive lesson emerges from the close collaboration with local GTZ technical assistance. GTZ-financed colleagues with long-standing modeling experience in Burkina Faso gave frequent ideas for improvements and asked difficult questions on the model calibration. They also contributed actively to linking the existing forecasting tool with PAMS, which was crucial for its quick adoption by DPAM. Without the GTZ-financed assistance, many key features in linking PAMS to the Burkinabe forecasting model and its user-friendly interface could not have been developed.

■ The third lesson from the PAMS development in Burkina Faso relates to the close involvement of World Bank country office staff. Because the work had a champion in the economist located in the country office, the modeling work was undertaken continuously rather than being limited to a few missions. Questions and concerns of DPAM staff as well as feedback from GTZ were relayed without delay to colleagues in Washington, DC, making the modeling work both more interactive and steady.

■ A fourth lesson from the engagement is that there is a need to make greater allowance for collecting and analyzing poverty data when embarking on PAMS modeling. Once official poverty data had been released in August 2003, the World Bank team underestimated the difficulties it would face in introducing data revisions to the poverty analysis that ultimately fed the PAMS model. Despite frequent and frank exchanges on the technical level, the official poverty rates do not yet reflect comparable consumption aggregates, a situation that can hamper further analytical work that underpins poverty analysis and PAMS. In terms of process, it would probably have been beneficial to involve INSD earlier and more closely during the period of poverty data analysis. Stronger engagement would have reinforced earlier the focus on the poverty data collection and analysis in the technical interactions.

NOTES

1. Under the filière system, a single monopoly company with exclusive exploitation rights provides credit and inputs to farmers. When cotton is delivered to the cotton company, the latter subtracts the outstanding credit from the payments made to farmers.
2. The remainder of shares in the company are held by the French company DAGRIS and local banks.
3. For an in-depth description of the PAMS model, see Pereira da Silva et al. (2002).
4. Parallel work financed by GTZ in the context of a pro-poor growth multi-country study piloted by the World Bank came to very similar conclusions about the comparability of 2003 and 1998 data. Using a different poverty line, this analysis arrived at an even larger drop in poverty rates than the poverty assessment prepared by the World Bank.

REFERENCES

Easterly, W., E. C. Hwa, K. Piyabha, and Z. Jan. 1990. "Modeling the Macroeconomic Requirements of Policy Reforms." World Bank Working Paper 417, World Bank, Washington, DC.

Grimm, M., and I. Günther. 2004. *How to Achieve Pro-Poor Growth in a Poor Economy: The Case of Burkina Faso.* Report prepared for the Operationalizing Pro-Poor–Growth Project sponsored by the World Bank, DFID, AFD, GTZ, and KFW.

Pereira da Silva, L., B. Essama-Nssah, and I. Samaké. 2002. "A Poverty Analysis Macroeconomic Simulator (PAMS) Linking Household Surveys with Macro-Models." Policy Research Working Paper 2888. World Bank, Washington, DC.

Kakwani, N. 2000. "On Measuring Growth and Inequality Components of Poverty with Application to Thailand." *Journal of Quantitative Economics* 16: 105–18.

Kakwani, N., and E. Pernia. 2000. "What Is Pro-Poor Growth?" *Asian Development Review* 18 (1): 1–16.

World Bank. 2005. "Burkina Faso: Reducing Poverty through Sustained Equitable Growth." Poverty Assessment Report. 29743-BUR, June.

4

MOZAMBIQUE
School Fees and Primary School Enrollment and Retention

ALEXANDRIA VALERIO, ELENA BARDASI,
ANTONIO CHAMBAL AND MANUEL FRANCISCO LOBO

The Government of Mozambique recognizes the importance of education, including primary education, in advancing economic and social development.[1] Since the Peace Agreement in 1992, significant efforts have been undertaken and substantial progress has been made in increasing access to primary education, particularly lower primary schools (*Ensino Primário do Primeiro Grau* or EP1, grades 1 through 5). From 1992 to 2003, the gross admission rate to grade 1 grew from 59 percent to 123 percent, the gross enrollment rate (GER) in EP1 increased from 60 percent to 112.7 percent, and the number of lower primary schools rose from 2,800 to over 8,000, representing the greatest-ever expansion of access to the system (see tables 4.1 and 4.2 for gender-disaggregated figures).

SELECTION OF THE POLICY REFORM

Although the achievements of the Ministry of Education in increasing enrollment over the last 10 years are laudable, it is widely recognized that the educational system is at a crossroads. Completion, repetition, and dropout rates have not followed the trend of these impressive advances.

Trends in Primary School Enrollment

The proportion of pupils who complete the full lower or upper primary education cycle (through grade 5 or grade 7, respectively) remains well

Table 4.1 GER, NER, and Number of Primary and Secondary Pupils, 1997 and 2003

Indicators	EP1 (grades 1–5)	EP2 (grades 6–7)	ESG1 (grades 8–10)	ESG2 (grades 11–12)
Gross enrollment rate (GER)				
1997	74.8	19.3	6.2	0.3
2003	110.4	35.5	15.3	1.5
Net enrollment rate (NER)				
1997	43.0	2.2	0.6	0.0
2003	67.9	4.3	1.5	0.5
Number of children				
1997	1,744,863	153,102	45,211	2,614
2003	2,826,362	351,575	142,784	18,291
Number of schools				
2003	8,077	950	125	29

Source: EducStat annual school survey (1997, 2003).

below expectations in Mozambique relative to neighboring countries and countries at similar levels of income. Completion rates also vary substantially by gender and across provinces and districts. Girls and children from low-income families in remote rural communities, particularly in the north and central regions of the country, are at a greater disadvantage. Analyses by age indicate that, of 100 pupils who gain access to grade 1, only 37 survive to grade 5. By grade 7, only 15 pupils remain in the system, and by grade 12 only a single pupil remains. For those pupils who stay in the system, it is difficult to ascertain learning achievement, as there is no national assessment mechanism in place to track learning outcomes.

The Ministry of Education is seeking to examine the underlying, multifaceted causes behind the poor primary school completion rates

Table 4.2 GER by Gender, 1997, 2000, and 2003

Indicator	EP1 (grades 1–5)			EP2 (grades 6–7)		
	1997	2000	2003	1997	2000	2003
Total	74.8	91	110.4	19.3	24.2	35.5
Boys	87.6	103	120.6	23.0	29.3	42.9
Girls	61.9	81	100.3	15.6	19.1	28.3
Gender gap	25.7	21	20.3	7.4	10.2	14.6

Source: EducStat annual school survey (1997, 2000, and 2003).

and reevaluate the appropriateness of current policy responses. This is especially important if Mozambique is to achieve the goal of universal completion of primary schooling (through grade 7) by 2015 and, more broadly, a sustained reduction in poverty.

Low Completion Rates: A Supply-Side or Demand-Side Problem?

Many plausible hypotheses might explain the low completion rates (see tables 4.3, 4.4, and 4.5).[2] The most frequently cited ones can be grouped into three categories. First, it has been suggested that *demand-side constraints*—more specifically, the high direct costs and high opportunity costs of schooling because of formal and informal school fees and forgone paid or unpaid work—increase the likelihood that children will drop out of school. Few studies exist that might help determine the extent to which various costs have an impact on school enrollments and pupil retention rates in Mozambique. Anecdotal evidence implies, however, that the costs are significant and may have great influence on schooling decisions, particularly among the poorest households. In a situation in which slightly more than half the population is living below the poverty line, the direct costs and the opportunity costs of education provide a plausible explanation for the low completion rates.

Second, it has been proposed that *supply-side constraints*—such as the poor quality of education, which has been exacerbated by the rapid expansion in access and the poor physical infrastructure of most primary schools—may have an impact on completion rates. The relative increase in the proportion of unqualified teachers, open-air classrooms, and

Table 4.3 Primary and Secondary Repetition, Dropout, and Completion, 1997 and 2003

Rates	EP1 (grades 1–5)	EP2 (grades 6–7)	ESG1 (grades 8–10)	ESG2 (grades 11–12)
Completion rate				
1997	22.0	7.3	2.0	0.6
2003	40.0	17.0	4.6	1.1
Modified completion rate				
2003	60.2	32.1	8.3	1.9

Source: EducStat annual school survey (1997 and 2003).
Note: To estimate the completion rate for lower secondary (grades 8–10) and upper secondary (grades 11–12), the age groups were divided randomly by the number of age years (the 16–17 age group by two, and the 18–24 age group by seven).

Table 4.4 Lower Primary GER, Repetition, and Completion, by Province and Gender, 2003

Province	Boys			Girls			Completion gender gap
	GER	Repetition	Completion	GER	Repetition	Completion	
Cabo Delgado	125.6	17.0	42.1	96.7	17.0	20.0	−22.1
Gaza	136.6	24.9	63.5	131.9	22.9	60.1	−3.4
Inhambane	135.1	27.7	67.0	129.3	26.4	57.6	−9.4
Manica	131.3	23.1	56.4	102.4	22.9	31.0	−25.4
Maputo City	138.2	25.8	94.2	141.7	23.5	96.7	2.5
Maputo Province	152.7	23.0	82.9	152.1	21.1	81.4	−1.5
Nampula	99.9	19.5	38.7	78.1	20.4	18.1	−20.6
Niassa	113.7	18.5	42.9	90.4	18.6	23.3	−19.6
Sofala	117.4	17.9	53.1	88.5	18.2	29.7	−23.4
Tete	111.5	15.9	41.9	92.0	16.1	25.9	−16.0
Zambézia	120.3	25.6	32.1	92.0	26.8	14.6	−17.5
Nationwide	120.6	21.9	48.2	100.3	21.9	31.9	−16.3

Source: EducStat annual school survey (2003).

teacher absenteeism; the deterioration in pupil-teacher ratios; and the scarcity of textbooks and learning materials, particularly in the EP2 grades, lend support to this hypothesis.

Third, *contextual factors,* such as socioeconomic conditions and local traditional practices, can exert harmful effects, especially on the educa-

Table 4.5 Upper Primary GER, Repetition, and Completion, by Province and Gender, 2003

Province	Boys			Girls			Completion Gender Gap
	GER	Repetition	Completion	GER	Repetition	Completion	
Cabo Delgado	31.1	14.2	15.5	14.8	15.6	6.7	−8.8
Gaza	54.2	19.0	27.3	52.3	20.8	23.9	−3.4
Inhambane	61.5	23.3	29.7	51.1	24.9	21.9	−7.8
Manica	50.8	20.8	25.0	25.3	23.4	9.9	−15.1
Maputo City	89.8	20.3	45.8	94.1	23.6	46.2	0.4
Maputo Province	74.7	13.8	37.8	73.5	15.9	31.5	−6.3
Nampula	31.7	18.1	15.9	13.7	17.4	6.0	−9.9
Niassa	42.0	17.5	19.0	20.1	17.1	7.7	−11.3
Sofala	46.0	17.9	24.0	26.8	19.5	11.3	−12.7
Tete	31.5	15.4	15.8	17.5	16.6	8.0	−7.8
Zambézia	31.3	22.6	15.6	13.7	21.9	6.4	−9.2
Nationwide	42.9	18.9	21.5	28.3	20.3	12.6	−8.9

Source: EducStat annual school survey (2003).

tion of girls. Food insecurity and chronic illness in families may also inflate the opportunity costs of children's presence in school.

Recent studies on Mozambique describe the interplay among demand and supply constraints and contextual factors in terms of impact on enrollments and pupil retention rates in primary schools. The findings point to a mix of influences. They highlight the cost of schooling, inadequate household incomes, insufficient human capital development, the distances children must travel to reach school, the quality of education, and the rise in the prevalence of human immunodeficiency virus/acquired immune deficiency syndrome (HIV/AIDS) as key constraints. On the latter point, a study undertaken on behalf of Save the Children U.K. in Mozambique reinforces the evidence for the negative impact of direct costs and, especially, the opportunity costs on the demand for education (Breslin 2003). The study finds that, when a parent or household member is ill, children suffer from emotional problems, uncertainty, and stress. The high level of domestic and caring responsibilities placed on children whose parents or caregivers are chronically sick often translates into children stopping school. The study also finds that illness in the household affects household savings and forces substantial prioritization on expenditures for food, clothing, health, and school materials. The longer the illness, the greater the likelihood that the household will prioritize resources to cover food and health expenditures, thereby affecting children's education, sometimes permanently. On those occasions when parents or caregivers manage to keep children in school despite the illness, the study finds high levels of discrimination among peers and neighbors, resulting in children leaving school prematurely.

Official Policy on School Fees

It is important to note that primary education in Mozambique is neither compulsory nor free.[3] The official policy on school fees was established by ministerial decree no. 6 of 1986 (*Diploma Ministerial no. 6/86*), which outlines the fees payable to the system and the associated rules and regulations governing the use of the fees and the fee exemption procedures (*Regulamento de Propinas e Taxas de Internamento no Sistema Nacional de Educação*). The policy distinguishes among registration fees (registration and attendance), examination fees, boarding fees, contribution quotas, monthly payments, and "other" fees.

Because of the importance of primary education, the policy restricts the number of official fees at the lower levels of the education system. For primary schools, the policy stipulates that pupils must contribute a fixed amount, to be paid in cash, through the Social Action Fund (*Acção Social Escolar,* or ASE) and are to meet boarding costs (the latter, if applicable, only in EP2 grades). Contributions through the ASE are intended solely for the purpose of supporting needy pupils by providing school materials, clothing, and other personal items. There are no fees for teacher education.

For secondary education, literacy programs, and technical and vocational education and training, the policy includes the collection of registration and examination fees and, where applicable, boarding fees. In effect, the ASE contribution acts as a school registration fee. The decree of 1986 makes no mention of whether schools have any freedom to collect additional fees and, if so, for what purpose, nor does it offer guidance on management, decisionmaking, and accountability procedures or on the role of school uniforms.

The ministerial decree of 1986 was revised in 1987 through another decree (no. 152/87) with the objective of adjusting the fees, which had been eroded by inflation. Table 4.6 presents a summary of the types of fees as described in the decree of 1987.

In practice, the majority of primary schools generate revenues locally to cover routine expenses, mainly through school fees (formal and informal) and an array of levies. Direct government budget allocations to cover daily operations in EP1 are extremely rare; only the largest schools located in urban areas receive assistance from the government to pay for water and other utilities. A recent public education expenditure analysis estimated that school fees may account for up to 18 percent of recurrent expenses in EP1 and 23 percent in EP2. The education expenditure analy-

Table 4.6 Annual Fees by Type and Educational Level (MZM)

Level	Registration	Examination (each subject)	Boarding	ASE
Primary education				
EP1, grades 1–5	n.a.	n.a.	n.a.	150
EP2, grades 6–7	n.a.	n.a.	500	250
Secondary education				
ESG1, grades 8–10	2,000	n.a.	1,000	400
ESG2, grades 11–12	3,000	n.a.	1,500	500
Teacher education	n.a.	n.a.	n.a.	400
Adult education				
Level 1	4,000	200	3,000	400
Level 2	6,000	500	5,000	500

Note: n.a. = not applicable. The Mozambican currency is the metical (plural, meticais), or MZM. The approximate exchange rate (January 2005) was US$1 = MZM 18,355.

sis indicated that the bulk of public expenditures are accounted for by teacher and administrative salaries, system administration, textbook procurement, and classroom construction and upgrading.

The Role of School Fees and Schooling Expenses in Household Schooling Decisions

A limitation of previous studies on constraints to enrollment in Mozambique is the lack of specific information on the impact of direct costs and opportunity costs on the financing of primary education or in forcing children out of school. There is little information available on the extent to which various costs (formal and informal school fees) have an impact on school enrollments and pupil retention rates. Several studies, including the Cost and Financing Study (World Bank 2003b), the Sector Expenditure Review (Ministry of Education and Culture 2002), and the Public Expenditure Review (World Bank 2003a), have highlighted the information gap on this issue, particularly in the context of achieving the aims of the World Bank's Education for All program and the Millennium Development Goals. The studies suggested the need for an in-depth study to gain a better understanding on the role of school fees, the relative importance of fees in financing primary education, and the extent to which the fee structure is a barrier for continued enrollment, especially for children in very poor households. The lack of information on the impact of school fees on schooling decisions has also been highlighted at annual consultation meetings between the Ministry of Education and cooperating partners supporting the education sector.

Policy Alternatives

To respond to the problem of low completion rates, the Ministry of Education has been considering intensifying and introducing various policy alternatives as a way forward. Since primary education in Mozambique is neither compulsory nor free, the policy alternative that attracted the public and resonated strongly with the cooperating partners who provide financial and technical assistance in the education sector was the elimination of school fees for primary education. Other policy alternatives under consideration included the expansion of the school network, particularly by constructing schools closer to communities, and the improvement in the quality of education by strengthening and expanding teacher education programs, improving teacher management and deployment practices, supplying basic learning materials, and improving the relevance of the curriculum.

Although it may be worthwhile to implement many, if not all, of these policy alternatives at once, it was important to prioritize them according to the likely costs and potential impacts of each, especially given current financial burdens and the pressing social demand for more expenditure in other areas of the education system. Although the Ministry of Education was already implementing some of these policy alternatives, particularly those related to reducing supply-side constraints, the issue at hand was whether to continue emphasizing supply-side policies or to look for a more appropriate combination of policies to address supply and demand side constraints that would respond more effectively to the challenge of enhancing completion rates and, more broadly, raising the educational attainment, competencies, and skills of the labor force.

Although the relative magnitude of the individual constraints is not known, over the last couple of years there has been a strong and growing sentiment among policy makers in Mozambique that demand-side constraints (direct costs and opportunity costs) pose the greatest challenge to better completion rates. Easing the demand-side constraints by reducing or eliminating school fees is commonly advocated as an important solution at this juncture, one that, ostensibly, should have greater impact on disadvantaged groups.

The Study

In December 2003 the World Bank made available resources to undertake a study and presented the idea to policy makers in the Ministry of Education for their review and consideration. Ministry officials seized the opportunity, assigned a team to work on the study's research design, and launched the study in February 2004. Cooperating Partners working on the education sector in Mozambique supported the undertaking and provided technical and financial support to strengthen the research team.[4]

Against this background, it was agreed that the Poverty and Social Impact Analysis (PSIA) would be undertaken to fill the information gap on the impact of direct costs (formal and informal school fees and related schooling expenses) and opportunity costs on enrollment and pupil retention in primary education, particularly among the poorest who are more likely to be out of school. To the extent possible, it was agreed that the study would be complemented with analyses on the role of supply-side constraints and contextual factors to allow for a more informed comparison among policy reform alternatives. That is, although the study would focus on measuring the impact and magnitude of policy alternatives aimed at lowering all schooling costs, these would be compared with policies for easing supply-side constraints and mitigating contextual factors, for which there is more information and where investment efforts are currently focused. The study could then become an important tool to inform the choice, design, and sequence of policy options and institutional reforms aimed at increasing school enrollment and retention rates, particularly among children from poor and vulnerable households.

The analysis was considered timely and particularly important because, although it is plausible that a fee reduction or elimination might stimulate enrollment and retention, both of which are desirable outcomes for the Ministry of Education, there were concerns that a sudden, sharp expansion in enrollment could also have an unintended, negative effect on the quality of education, ultimately lowering the perceived benefits of education and discouraging parents from sending their children to school. These concerns emanated from experience in Malawi and Uganda where setbacks in educational quality were observed after the elimination of primary school fees in the 1990s. In the case of Mozambique, it was difficult to speculate on the potential impact of a fee reduction policy because, unlike Malawi and Uganda where initial pupil admission rates and gross enrollment rates were low, in Mozambique these indicators were already at nearly universal levels. In Mozambique, therefore, the key question was the extent to which school fees had an impact on pupil retention and completion rather than its impact on initial enrollment.

Relevance of the Proposed Reform

The study was perceived to be relevant for several reasons. First, the Ministry of Education intends to continue moving forward rapidly and aggressively to reach the goals of Education for All and the Millennium Development Goals and was, therefore, examining the option of abolishing school fees as one of the key policy alternatives to stimulate the demand for schooling and to reduce dropout rates.

Second, the study coincided with the final preparatory phase of the government's Education Sector Strategic Program 2005–10. The program envisaged the institutionalization and scaling up of pilot initiatives such as Direct Support for Schools (*Apoio Directo às Escolas*), which channels small grants directly to all primary schools for the purchase of pupil materials and classroom consumables, thereby helping reduce the direct costs of primary schooling.

Third, international experience gathered through fee-reduction schemes in India, Kenya, Lesotho, Malawi, and Uganda indicates that, although such schemes can boost the demand for education, they should not be undertaken without assessing the consequences to post-primary education or without adequate preparation for coping with any sudden, sharp rise in the demand for schooling that may result. One should ensure that there is a pool of potential teachers who can be deployed rapidly, that the infrastructure is in place to serve more pupils without having to cut hours of instruction, and that a supply of basic teaching and learning materials can be guaranteed. Failure to prepare a comprehensive response with a clear strategy for confronting financially and physically any sudden jump in the demand for schooling may be a formula for failure.

DESIGN OF THE PSIA

Figure 4.1 shows the demand-side and supply-side constraints on education considered within the study. On the demand side are factors related to the benefits (returns to education) and the costs, which are divided into direct costs (fees, books, uniforms, other education-related materials, and other costs such as transport) and opportunity costs (forgone work inside and outside the household). On the supply side, the main factors identified are the existence (or absence) and location (distance) of schools, the adequacy and quality of education infrastructure, and the quality of education, including such aspects as the number and the qual-

FIGURE 4.1   Contextual Factors and Demand-Side and Supply-Side Constraints

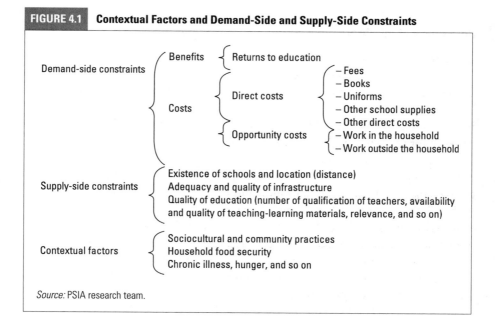

Source: PSIA research team.

ification of teachers, the availability and quality of teaching-learning materials, and curriculum relevance. The contextual factors considered include sociocultural factors, traditional community practices, household food security, and chronic illness in the household.

Conceptual Framework

Since one of the specific objectives of this study was to estimate how government policy on formal or informal school fees affects the demand for primary schooling, the study classifies fees as follows (see figure 4.2): first, the form in which the fees are paid, that is, whether they are paid in cash or in kind (including labor); second, the source of the fees, that is, whether the fees are official (determined by law or regulation) or school based (determined by the school, a practice that contradicts official policy); third, a category labeled "atypical," which incorporates fees that are neither official nor required of all students, including direct payments requested by teachers, special contributions for key events, and so on;

FIGURE 4.2 Typology of Fees

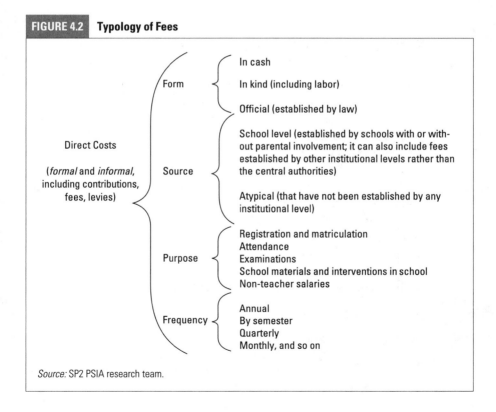

Source: SP2 PSIA research team.

fourth, the purpose of the fee, that is, fees for registration, attendance, examinations, school materials, non-teacher salaries, the maintenance of infrastructure, and so on; finally, the frequency of the payments demanded.

Research Team

The research team was comprised of staff from the Ministry of Education, the National Institute for Educational Development, the World Bank, and the Department for International Development (U.K.). Cooperating Partners working on the education sector lent their technical support by commenting on the research design and methodology prior to beginning field work and by providing feedback and suggestions on various drafts of the study. To broaden participation, preliminary field results were presented during the Ministry of Education's National Basic Education Seminar held in May 2004, which was chaired by the director of basic education and attended by over 100 education staff from the 10 provinces and Maputo City.

Research Design, Study Structure, and Data Sources

It was decided the study would need to include a qualitative research component to incorporate the perceptions of policy makers and technical officials at various levels of the educational system, school-level staff, parents, and community leaders. It would also need a quantitative component to include analysis from a recent national household-level survey. The research team began by establishing a conceptual framework for the proposed analysis (described above) and reviewing the literature on the impact of fee-abolition schemes internationally and trends in education indicators in Mozambique to provide a context to the study.

The main analysis was structured in four parts. A list of questions was prepared for the first three parts of the study to guide the research team in preparing survey instruments, sample selection, interpretation of findings, and report writing (see annex 4.A). A description of each part, including the objective, data sources, and constraints, is presented below.

Part 1: Assessment of the Official Government Policy on School Fees

This first part, an assessment of the official government policy on school fees, had two objectives. The first objective was to provide a thorough description of government policy on school fees, including their type, magnitude, frequency of payment, and exemption mechanisms, as well as the interpretation of these aspects in government strategy documents on education and poverty reduction more generally. The second objective was to provide insights into the way the government policy on fees is interpreted by policy makers, senior officials, and technical officers in selected provinces and districts, including whether the fees are perceived to have an impact on school enrollment and pupil retention.

To achieve the first objective, the assessment relied on a review of legal documents that establish the government's policy for dealing with direct costs in primary education. To achieve the second objective, the assessment relied on the results of in-depth interviews with thirty Ministry of Education officials at various levels and in two provinces to elicit their views and opinions about the impact of school fees on household schooling decisions and, if this perceived impact is negative, how the effects might be mitigated so as to reach the goal of universal completion of primary education. For the interviews in the Ministry of Education, the methodology relied on individual semistructured in-depth interviews. Semistructured focus group discussions and interviews were held at the provincial and district education offices. At the provincial education offices, most heads of departments were not available at the time of the discussions. Their representatives participated instead. At the district education offices, the directors were asked to obtain the participation of the people who were most relevant in terms of the themes under discussion. The themes were communicated to these participants two days before the interviews took place.

Part 2: School- and Community-Level Analysis

The second part of the study, an analysis of school- and community-level perspectives on the role of school fees, was aimed at gauging consistency between the government policy on school fees and the way the policy is interpreted and applied in schools and viewed by parents and community leaders. The analysis gathered qualitative information on school fees, other direct costs, and opportunity costs from a group of stakeholders in schools and their surrounding communities. This allowed for an in-depth, qualitative exploration of the impact of costs on primary schools, enrollment, and pupil retention.

The research method used for the school and community analysis was a case study approach in a select group of schools in districts in four provinces in the northern, central, and southern regions of Mozambique. The criteria for selecting the provinces revolved around enrollment and retention rates in urban and rural areas, the enrollment and retention of girls, poverty indicators, cultural diversity, and logistical considerations.

The 30 schools selected were in the provinces of Niassa (11), Zambézia (10), Gaza (5), and Maputo City (4). Originally, three provinces (Gaza, Niassa, and Zambézia) had been chosen for the survey, but, after consultation with key officials at the Ministry of Education in Maputo, it was decided that Maputo City should be included as an additional province with special characteristics. Maputo City was therefore added to the sample of provinces, and some of the initial schools selected in Gaza were eliminated from the study and replaced by schools in Maputo City. The schools were located in both urban and rural areas, with an emphasis on the latter. More or fewer schools might have been selected, but, given the resources and the time available, the study team decided that 30 schools was an appropriate number. Schools were selected within the districts according to the following criteria: up to three schools in each district, some poor schools with high enrollment rates, some poor schools with low enrollment rates, schools with parent associations, and schools in a range of locations (with an emphasis on rural schools). Because the schools selected were located in 13 districts with different characteristics, the team was able to collect information that lent itself to comparisons across regions and across urban and rural areas and income groups.

The analysis was conducted on the basis of structured and semi-structured interviews and focus group discussions with school directors, teachers, students, parents, and community leaders. In addition, provincial, city, and district directors of education were interviewed. The objective of the interviews was to determine and assess the way the interviewees understood and interpreted the government's official policy on fees, the types and amount of the fees, the mechanisms used in schools to set the fees, the recourse mechanisms typically employed to exempt needy students, the advantages and disadvantages of the fees, the impact of the fees on regular school attendance, and the extent to which the fees and other direct costs deter enrollments. The methods used to finance education, including the extent to which schools rely on fee revenue to cover day-to-day operations, were also examined. Similarly, the analysis sought the opinions of teachers and parents about whether children would be likely to stay in school longer if the fees were reduced or abolished.

The individual interviews were conducted with the aid of semistructured interview manuals containing interview questions and space to record responses. The method was applied chiefly with city, district, and provincial directors of education and school or pedagogical directors. The focus group discussions were conducted with the aid of semistructured discussion manuals, which also contained discussion questions and space to take notes on responses. The focus group method was employed with parents, students, and community leaders. It was decided that the collective interviews or focus groups would involve four to six participants. It was felt that the small number would allow the people in the group more opportunity to speak, unlike the situation in larger groups.

One problem that the team faced during the implementation phase was a lack of communication. When the provincial education offices learned of the team's visits, they had difficulty contacting the district education offices, which subsequently did not notify the rural schools because of the distance, the lack of telephones and vehicles, and so on. This restricted the ability of the team to arrange interviews with parents and community leaders. Nonetheless, the team was able to interview small groups of parents in most schools. The views of community leaders, on the other hand, may be underrepresented in the report because it was difficult to reach them or to arrange meetings.

Another constraint during the implementation phase was the limited time and resources available to cover the 30 schools adequately. At first, the team went as a unit from school to school and split up to conduct the interviews. As the work progressed and came to include larger provinces such as Niassa and Zambézia, the team members understood it would be better to use two vehicles and divide up the work so that the researchers could each cover one school per day and spend more time at the school and in the community. In the provinces of Niassa and Zambézia, an average of four to five hours were spent in each school.

In addition to interviewing teachers, school principals, pupils, parents, and community leaders who are stakeholders in the schools, the team realized after the first week of interviews that they should include the perspectives, if possible, of children of school age who were not attending school and the parents of these children. Although the team attempted to include as many of these people as they could find, relatively few were located. Therefore, the views of such people on the reasons for nonattendance or for dropping out of school are underrepresented in the report. The team filled in some of this gap by substituting the views of parents who could not afford to send all their children of school age to primary school.

Although the sexual harassment of girls and corruption in primary schools may be factors in school nonattendance and dropping out among girls, these issues were not specifically addressed in the manuals for the interviews among teachers, students, and parents. The team touched upon these issues with several provincial and district directors of education. Nonetheless, information on these issues as factors in the problems faced by girls in education, especially in rural areas, is underrepresented in this analysis.

Despite the limitations of the analysis, the team is confident that sufficient quality information was gathered in the 30 schools visited to be able to analyze meaningfully school costs and other factors that may influence attendance, dropout, and completion rates among boys and girls in primary schools and to draw reasonable conclusions and recommendations on the appropriate policy toward school fees.

Part 3: Household Survey Analysis

The third part of the study, a quantitative analysis of the most recent household survey, studied the relationship between demand for education, household expenses for education, and household level of well-being (measured by total consumption) and other characteristics. The analysis was based on the national household budget survey (*Inquérito aos Agregados Familiares sobre Orçamento Familiar,* or the IAF) in 2002–3 that provides detailed information on household income and expenditures in a representative sample of 8,700 households and 44,000 individuals. The survey contains detailed information on the expenditures, transfers, and incomes of Mozambican households, as well as information on the profile of household members and demographic and geographic characteristics. In addition, the survey questionnaire included modules on health, employment, education, housing, poverty indicators, and victimization. Data on daily, monthly, and annual expenditures allowed for the construction of a consumption aggregate that was used as a measure of welfare. Information on annual education expenditures by households was disaggregated by level and type of school (public or private) and by the typology of expenditure (school fees, uniforms, books, and other school supplies).

The household-level analysis consisted of two parts. The first part outlined descriptive statistics on outcomes (attendance, enrollments, dropouts) and on direct and indirect costs of education. The study aimed to investigate whether the outcomes and the costs varied according to the characteristics of individuals, households, and locations. The study relied on the IAF microdata to compute several measures of school attainment. The advantage of using microdata for this type of analysis lies in the availability of a broad range of characteristics of individuals and households that can be linked to school outcomes. No other source of data allows for the analysis of variations in school outcomes when consumption and other household and individual characteristics vary. The second part of the household-level analysis was devoted to an econometric analysis to assess the extent to which the demand for education was sensitive to reductions in school fees, while also taking into account a wide range of factors that may also affect demand.

There were several constraints identified in carrying out the quantitative analysis. The IAF contains information on annual household education expenditures by level and type, as well as expenditures for uniforms, books, and other school supplies.[5] These expenditures are not collected for each child separately, but are recorded by level and type of education as a total household amount.

It was necessary to make a per child calculation for the analysis. The household amount spent on each level of education, public and private combined, was therefore divided by the number of children attending the corresponding level of education. The decision was taken to mix public and private expenditures because, on the one hand, the number of children attending private institutions is negligible (except in the top quintile) and, on the other hand, the expenditures for "church," "community," "nongovernmental," and "other" types of schools that children may attend have been classified rather randomly as public or private by the households.

Perhaps more problematic was the assumption that had to be made in order to calculate the per child expenditure for books, uniforms, and other school materials. This expenditure is given as a cumulative amount for all children going to school, irrespective of the level and type of education. The best that could be done was to divide the total amount by the total number of children going to school, as in the case of the calculation on fees and charges. However, the need for books and uniforms (and their cost) may vary greatly by education level.[6]

Second, it was not obvious which type of fees the household was likely to declare as "household expenditure for education fees."[7] Nonetheless, one may readily speculate about the type of expenditures likely to be included for each education level: any type of school fees paid, in cash, for registration, attendance, examinations, and so on. However, it is not expected that the households report the monetary value of any fee paid in kind (the guidelines given to the interviewers are not very clear on this point), especially fees that are "illegal" or "semi-illegal."

Third, the education expenditures are collected as an annual amount ("in the 12 months before the interview"). Because school attendance is recorded at one point in time, it is possible that the annual expenditure does not exactly refer to the children that are observed to be going to school at a given moment. Nonetheless, it is expected that the discrepancies are small and that the results are valid on average.

Finally, the measurement of opportunity costs also posed some problems. The opportunity cost of going to school is provided by the value of the forgone opportunities open to the child. The exact nature or value of these opportunities is not evident, however. In developing countries, one of the most important alternatives to school is work in the labor market or as an unpaid family member on the farm or in the home. Unfortunately, although questions were included in the IAF on all individuals aged 6 or above in the household who were involved in formal or semiformal work activities in the labor market or as unpaid family members, the survey did not collect information about domestic chores among children or about the children who are employed whether they attend school or not.

Part 4: Assessment of Findings and Recommendations

The fourth part of the study, an assessment of findings, sought to summarize, interpret, and link the findings from the different parts and data sources to present a holistic assessment of the current situation and likely impact of lowering the costs of education. The recommendations listed in the fourth part concern the main question addressed by the study: What is the impact of formal and informal school fees on school enrollments and completion rates? Which are the most relevant, demand-side or supply-side constraints? What is the role of contextual factors? It was hoped that the recommendations would be considered points of departure for discussions on the development of policies toward school fees and related expenditures on primary education. It is important to note that the recommendations emanate not only from the findings of the study, but also from suggestions made during discussions at the National Seminar on Basic Education held in Maputo in May 2004. Given that recommendations have a financial impact, efforts were made to include actions that are financially affordable, relatively straightforward, and effective at meeting the objective.

MAIN FINDINGS

There is a discrepancy between official government policy on fees and what actually happens. Regulations often say one thing, but the reality faced by schools requires them to collect fees beyond those acknowledged in official policy, and the policy on fees no longer reflects the current situation.

Official Policy on School Fees

The official regulations stipulate that, for each primary school pupil, a fixed sum of MZM 150 must be contributed, in cash, to an ASE; another MZM 500 must be paid for boarding costs. The latter fee, if applicable, is supposed to be collected only in upper primary grades. The ASE contributions are intended solely for the purpose of supporting needy pupils in acquiring school supplies, clothing, and other personal items for school. At all levels, students who repeat a class are required to pay an additional 50 percent of the fee except under extraordinary circumstances for which they must present a written document. The policy also stipulates that students who cannot afford the ASE contribution should be provided an exemption and be allowed to register. Unless exempted, students who are not able to pay the required fees within the fixed time limit are not entitled to enroll.

The regulations do not mention whether primary or secondary schools have the freedom to collect additional fees and, if so, for what purpose; nor do they offer guidance on the uses of the funds generated by schools, the role of uniforms, or the financial accountability of schools. Neither the regulations nor the fee amounts have been updated since 1987. The fee policy is considered to be out of step with key developments in the educational system since 1992. Policy documents offer little, if any, guidance.

To cover operational expenses, the majority of lower primary institutions rely on funds they generate. Direct budgetary allocations through the Ministry of Education to meet routine expenses are extremely rare. Only the largest urban EP1 schools receive assistance in paying water and other utility charges. Since primary schools are poorly funded, it is not surprising that the majority are forced to impose fees, including and in addition to the ASE contributions, in order to continue operating.

The fees being required by schools are well above the amounts officially fixed in the government policy documents. Paying fees set by the schools seems to be the norm rather than the exception. Besides the ASE contributions, typical fees include a variety of other, mostly ad-hoc fees. Though the general policy is that no child is to be kept out of school because the fees have not been paid, most schools enforce the payment of fees in all cases.

The application of the government policy on fees varies across provinces and districts. The majority of policy makers, senior officials, and technical officers interviewed during the field study believed that, in the absence of school fees, including ASE contributions, primary schools would operate in a much more negative environment. Over two thirds of all interviewees acknowledged that the funds collected by schools are a key to the expansion of access to education, mainly through the financing they provide for classroom construction and building upgrades using unconventional materials.

Though there is general agreement that the ASE funds should be employed for the benefit of needy pupils, school directors say that the funds, along with other fees generated by the schools, benefit all children by ensuring the normal operation of schools. Few schools visited had safety net strategies in place to cater for vulnerable, disadvantaged pupils.

Direct Costs and Opportunity Costs

Households struggle to pay school fees and expenses. Costs to families include direct expenses and also the cost of the income that is not earned when a child goes to school instead of to work. These costs, when taken together, can make it very difficult for all the children in a family to attend school.

School Fees and School Expenses

ASE contributions are spent by schools for a variety of purposes. Most commonly, the contributions are applied toward the purchase of school consumables, including chalk and blackboards, sports equipment, material for extracurricular activities, notebooks for teachers to use to prepare and plan their activities, pens, writing paper, photocopying, learning materials, and benches, chairs, and tables, as well as to pay for upgrades in infrastructure, including materials for school construction, refurbishment, or maintenance. The funds also sometimes cover the wages of guards, auxiliary staff, and occasional workers; water and telephone bills; food and drink for visitors and teachers during exams; and the organization of sports activities and teacher training.

In addition to the ASE contributions, schools request additional monetary contributions from parents at the beginning, during, or at the end of the school year. These are also considered fees. For example, additional fees are charged for enrollment or registration certificates, passing certificates at the end of a school year, special certificates for the completion of grade 5 and grade 7, examinations (the money is sometimes used to provide lunch for external examination monitors), and test booklets. Some schools charge special fees for the construction or rehabilitation of classrooms, for cleaning materials, school guards, or sports equipment. Although some of these contributions are small, cumulatively they can become significant, especially for parents with several children of school age. For example, in one school in Maputo City, the established registration fee is MZM 50,000 for EP1 and MZM 65,000 for EP2, but, if the extra fees are included, parents pay MZM 90,000 for EP1 and MZM 100,000 for EP2 per child. If the cost of uniforms, school supplies, and books is added, the amount per child rises by an average of MZM 135,659, bringing the total amount per child to MZM 235,659.

In many instances, the cost of uniforms or other clothing for school, routine school supplies, and school snacks was found to pose the greatest barrier to school attendance and to cause dropouts. The cost of uniforms, which are mostly an urban phenomenon, might range from MZM 160,000 to MZM 180,000 per child. Despite this high cost, most parents said that they preferred to buy uniforms rather than to purchase other clothing for their children to wear to school. In rural areas, the cost of regular, everyday clothing for school is a burden, but the special outlays are often necessary, for children may feel ashamed if they must attend school in the same old clothes.

Most parents consider school supplies a significant expense, given that they must make the purchase more than once a year. In the higher grades, teachers require pupils to buy up to 10 blank notebooks and other supplies. The expense is great, especially for the notebooks, which cost an average MZM 5,000 each. Sometimes, because of this expenditure alone, parents may decide not to send all their school-age children to the higher grades in primary school.

Parents also spoke of the food they must provide for their children to take to school or the money they must give them to buy snacks. In rural communities, parents give between MZM 1,000 and MZM 2,000 a day to each child for food. Although this might not seem much, it becomes a considerable sum over the course of a school year.

The main finding relating to orphans and vulnerable children is that the professionals in nearly all schools in urban and rural areas lacked precise knowledge about the number of orphans in their communities and were even unaware of the number of children enrolled in their schools for whom one parent or both parents were deceased. Some school directors and teachers said "yes, we have them," but did not know how many there were. During interviews, parents said that, though they would prefer to send all their children to school, they sometimes had to choose among the children, particularly when they had little money and too many household chores or too much farm work. At the outset of the interviews, most of the parents said they had employed no criteria in selecting the children who would go to school, but, after some discussion, it became evident such criteria had existed. In rural areas and in poor urban settings, if necessary, parents would keep girls back from school to perform tasks at home, while orphans (boys or girls) were used as young house servants. Girls would often also drop out to care for younger brothers or for adults who had fallen ill (see Box 4.1).

BOX 4.1   **Parent Responses in Interviews**

"The orphan cannot study because nobody can come . . . to build the school."

"We have a lot of orphans here, but they stay outside the school. Their uncles and aunts do not care. They cannot afford to have all their children in the school."

—Parents of pupils in Forquia Sede, an EP1 school in Namacurra District, Zambézia Province.

"The school does not accept . . . children who do not pay."

—Parents at Nensenhenge, a full primary school in Sanga District, Niassa Province.

"When the parents cannot pay the fees, the children can continue to study. But a lot of parents do not know about this."

—Parents at Eduardo C. Mondlane, an EP2 school in Lichinga City, Niassa Province.

According to the national household budget survey, annual average expenditure on school fees per child was MZM 21,410 in EP1 and MZM 60,013 in EP2 (see tables 4.7 and 4.8), plus an additional MZM 114,249 for uniforms, books, and other school supplies. Total household and per child expenditures on school fees (the ASE contributions and other school charges) rise as pupils advance from one grade to the next. The total average expenditure for EP2 is almost three times that for EP1; the expenditure on ESG1 is seven to nine times that for EP1, and the expenditure for

Table 4.7 Average Household Expenditure on School Fees
by quintile

	Annual average household expenditure			
Quintile group	EP1 (grades 1–5)	EP2 (grades 6–7)	ESG1 (grades 8–10)	ESG2 (grades 11–12)
1	32,645	64,341	138,285	197,118
2	33,217	60,906	234,210	357,840
3	30,510	65,968	247,692	207,393
4	36,073	102,081	186,175	258,393
5	72,271	203,934	417,263	702,637
All	40,479	105,319	285,871	498,820

Source: Authors' calculation from IAF survey 2002/3.
Note: The averages have been computed on households reporting positive expenditures. The amounts have been spatially adjusted for differences in prices, so that they are comparable across regions.

Table 4.8 Annual Average Expenditure on School Fees per Child
by quintile

Quintile group	Annual average per child expenditure			
	EP1 (grades 1–5)	EP2 (grades 6–7)	ESG1 (grades 8–10)	ESG2 (grades 11–12)
1	15,979	43,124	98,405	146,578
2	16,670	40,303	180,637	328,297
3	16,779	42,623	170,133	98,988
4	19,337	64,720	113,129	220,574
5	41,548	99,173	296,357	490,115
All	21,410	60,013	198,881	357,159

Source: Authors' calculation from IAF survey 2002/3.
Note: The averages have been computed over all children living in households reporting positive expenditures. The amounts have been spatially adjusted for differences in prices, so that they are comparable across regions.

ESG2 is more than one and a half times that for ESG1. These amounts may appear small, especially for lower and upper primary school, for which they barely reach 1 percent of total household consumption and an even smaller share of total household cash income. However, school fees are not only an important source of revenue in schools (in most cases they are the only source of cash revenue)—equivalent to US$2.5 million in EP1 and US$1 million in EP2—but also they are much higher than the official fees stipulated in the ministerial decree of 1987.

The most substantial lower primary school fee occurs in Maputo City (about MZM 70,000 a year), followed by fees in urban areas in Nampula Province (MZM 55,000). The lower primary fees tend to be much less significant in rural areas, although, in some cases, they are not necessarily less than the fees in urban areas (in Sofala, for example). By contrast, the fees for upper primary school are fairly similar in urban and rural areas, the only exceptions being the provinces of Maputo and Nampula. Moreover, everywhere, except in the urban areas of Niassa Province, they are much more substantial than the lower primary fees, sometimes even three times as high (in Nampula, for example). In the case of upper primary fees, Maputo City is not the most expensive area. In urban Nampula and Sofala, households with children in upper primary school pay a higher average per child fee.

In urban areas in almost all provinces, the average per child school fees tend to increase as the level of household consumption rises. Among the three lower quintile groups, the increases are fairly moderate. The most substantial climb is observed between the third and fifth quintiles.

In rural areas, fees are much less responsive to changes in household consumption; only in three provinces (Gaza, Tete, and Zambézia) are larger EP1 fees paid by households in the top quintile. There is also some variation among provinces. However, in general, school fees represent a small part of the total cash expenditures of households in all parts of the country.

The household survey confirms that, for primary school, the average amount spent on books, uniforms, and other school materials is as high, if not higher, than the sum spent on school fees. For example, the average annual amount spent on books is about MZM 43,000 per child, about twice the average fee expenditure for EP1 (MZM 21,410); even more expensive are the uniforms, on average about MZM 73,000 per child, more than the average EP2 fee (MZM 60,013) and more than three times the average EP1 fee.

In summary, cumulative direct costs have a negative impact on enrollments and pupil retention, particularly among low-income parents with large families to support. Although the fees paid to schools, including the ASE contributions, are not a determining factor of enrollment, they are an important factor when added to the cost of uniforms and clothing, school supplies, and food. According to the analysis among schools and communities, the inability to purchase school supplies for children is probably the most important factor in rural areas, whereas the ability of their parents to pay for uniforms and school supplies can be the difference between a child being in or out of school in urban areas.

Management, Accountability, and Fee-Exemption Mechanisms

Fee types and amounts may be determined in consensus with the school council and community or imposed by the school alone. Official policy documents do not offer any guidance. One of the main problems is that school fees are not properly regulated, and the amounts required for official fees and other charges may therefore be substantial for households. Since there is no control or accountability over the use of school fees, including ASE contributions, funds can be easily diverted for nonlearning purposes. The benefits for the schools and pupils are thus limited. In most of the schools visited, parents, community leaders, and even teachers were unable to explain clearly how the ASE funds were used.

Several senior Ministry of Education staff spoke of the problem of the misuse of ASE contributions. The funds had sometimes been spent to build private homes or buy motorcycles. In fact, the significant misuse of the ASE funds prompted the minister of education to issue a declaration in 2004 (*Despacho no. 8/GM/2004*) stating that the funds were to be spent only by the educational institutions to which they belonged and for the purposes fixed according to plans drafted and approved by school councils.

Although the declaration has addressed the issue of school-generated revenue, it does not address other basic issues—such as the amount, type, and frequency of the fees permitted—nor does it offer any guidance on decision-making processes in the establishment of the fees, the management of the funds, or exemption criteria for pupils whose parents cannot afford the fees.

Some school directors and community leaders are aware of school fee exemption mechanisms such as the poverty certificate. However, it is generally agreed that obtaining such a document requires a great deal of stamina, perseverance, and, paradoxically, financial resources. The bureaucratic process involved in obtaining the certificate can be cumbersome and expensive. In some instances, the certificate may cost up to MZM 50,000, excluding the outlays for several trips to the district capital, which, when added to the cost of the certificate, is more than twice the amount of the fees themselves, particularly for lower primary school. Moreover, even when households manage to obtain poverty certificates, they are still required to pay for uniforms or clothing, school supplies, and food. Meeting these costs is problematic in the case of poor and vulnerable children, including orphans.

One area of consensus among school directors, teachers, and parents is that the Direct Support for Schools program is helping to meet the financial needs of primary schools. Stakeholders feel that the program provides clear accountability mechanisms and guidelines on eligible expenditures to ensure that funds are used properly. Schools are employing the funds they receive through the program to purchase educational materials, thereby offsetting some of the direct costs that would otherwise fall to parents. The staff in rural schools believes the program is leading to an increase in enrollments and attendance in lower primary schools.

Opportunity Costs

Opportunity costs are a much more important factor in rural areas than in urban areas. Nonetheless, in cities such as Maputo or Quelimane, children are often compelled to work in order to contribute to the family income. For households in rural areas, children are an important source of labor, especially during the harvest. This affects children's performance in school and contributes to high repetition and dropout rates. Children who have started school late or repeated frequently, a common situation in rural schools, often decide not to complete primary education, and they drop out to seek work in Maputo or in the mines of South Africa.

Parents and teachers at schools in rural districts frequently mentioned that children helped out on small farms (*machamba*). Teachers said that children often disappear for several weeks during the harvest and then either reappear, or drop out of school altogether. There are two harvest times. The first and most important takes place between April and June (corn, beans); the second takes place from November to March. Children who come back after helping their parents with the harvest have usually fallen behind in their school work and tend to fail the examinations at the end of the year.[8] There are high repetition and dropout rates in rural districts, especially in isolated communities and remote schools. The school year does not follow the agricultural cycle, and parents must therefore face a difficult decision if they want to send their children to school, but, at the same time, believe that they need them as helpers during the harvest to ensure the family's subsistence. Often, the latter path wins out.

According to the household budget survey, almost all children who work do not go to school. However, the percentage of children in employment is much lower than the percentage of children not attending school, especially among the 6–10 age group. From the survey, it is not clear what the children who are not attending school are doing. One may speculate that they are employed in some kind of domestic work. A question included in the survey that seeks reasons for children's nonattendance at school might have offered some insight into the alternatives available to children not currently in education. The responses were not particularly enlightening, however. Only a small share of children (0.3 percent of the children in the 6–10 age group and 1.8 percent of the children in the 11–14 age group who are out of school) declared that they were out of school because of work. Even among those who were working, only a small minority (2 percent for both age groups) said that work was the main reason they were not attending school. For the 6–10 age group, the most common response selected in the survey for nonattendance was "other reasons" (44 percent), while, for the 11–14 age group, it was "because of no interest in school" (31 percent).

Supply-Side Constraints

Among the supply-side constraints that play a significant role in low enrollment rates and high dropout rates are insufficient school infrastructure and the poor quality of education, in particular the relevance of the curriculum and the availability of textbooks, learning materials, and qualified teachers. The majority of the primary school facilities visited during the field study, especially in rural areas, were inadequate. Schools often lacked enough class space to accommodate the number of pupils registered. Some teachers were obliged to improvise classrooms under the shade of large trees. A problem in most schools was the lack of school furniture, especially desks for pupils and teachers. Many children had to sit on cement or dirt floors, a situation that is unsustainable for long periods. The lack of school furniture may be a contributing cause in non-attendance and dropping out. In some schools that relied on both regular and makeshift classrooms, children who were in the makeshift classrooms sometimes moved surreptitiously to the better classrooms because they wanted to have desks or, at least, cement floors.

A key factor affecting the quality of the education offered in schools is the availability of good teachers. There were substantial differences in this respect across provinces. Urban areas tended to be better endowed with qualified teachers. For example, the proportion of qualified teachers in EP1 in the provinces of Manica and Niassa was only 58 percent, while, in Maputo City and Sofala Province, it was 94 and 75 percent, respectively.

A related problem is the lack of qualified women teachers. This may have an impact on attendance and dropout rates among girls in primary schools. The lack of qualified women teachers was especially acute in the northern provinces of Cabo Delgado, Nampula, and Niassa and in the central province of Zambézia. In several communities, stakeholders said that the unqualified teachers were recent secondary school graduates, were often young, single men, and, in some instances, lacked maturity and ethical principles. This sometimes led to the harassment of young girls and women students.

Contextual Factors

The two main cultural constraints on pupil retention and completion rates are early marriages among girls and initiation rites among boys and girls. The initiation rites involve ceremonies marking the passage from childhood to adulthood. They constitute a symbolic moment during which substantial elements of traditional education are transmitted. These rites are maintained chiefly in rural areas, but also in cities in the central and northern regions. The rites normally take place after the harvest, when there is an abundance of time and food available for the ceremonies. The initiation rites affect girls more than boys. Girls are normally initiated during their first menstruation, when they are between 12 and 15 years old. When the rites are completed, girls are considered women and may marry. They are thus provided with a clear reason for dropping out of school. The two constraints of early marriage and the initiation rites are therefore interrelated.

Girls usually marry at a young age, especially in rural areas and in the northern and central regions. Marriage may be arranged while the girls are still young. After they menstruate for the first time, they may already begin living with their (older) husbands. Emphasis on early marriage and pregnancy represents a key constraint on the education of girls. Though they are legally allowed to continue their education, pregnant girls often do not remain in school either because they do not feel at ease, or because the community and the school environment fail to encourage them. Role models who can demonstrate how education might allow girls to gain access to a career are lacking in rural areas. Since girls and women have difficulty earning a living or contributing financially to the subsistence of their households, girls and their parents are not encouraged to insist on education as a path to a meaningful future. Table 4.9 summarizes the impact of the various factors, as perceived in the provinces studies, using a ranking that ranged from 1 (highest impact) to 4 (lowest impact).

Impact of Reducing or Abolishing School Fees and Other Direct Costs

The study seeks answers to the question: What would happen to enrollments if school fees were reduced? The multivariate analysis has generated several relevant findings.[9]

The first noteworthy result is that, in general, *school fees have little or no statistically significant impact* on enrollments in lower and upper primary school. This is consistent with the outcome of the school and community analysis and the descriptive analysis of the household survey data. One possible reason for the lack of impact is that only a portion of all school fees—those paid in cash—are accounted for in the household survey. There are, moreover, some geographical exceptions to the conclusion about fees. In urban areas in the central region of the country, higher fees are associated with lower enrollment probabilities. Although in general the impact of fees is not statistically significant, households in urban areas in the central region send fewer children to school when fees are higher, and they send more children to school when fees are lower. For example, if the average fees in EP1 were to reduced to one third, from

Table 4.9 Impact of Demand-Side, Supply-Side, and Other Factors on Primary Enrollment and Completion Rates, Four Provinces

Factors	Niassa EP1	Niassa EP2	Zambézia EP1	Zambézia EP2	Gaza EP1	Gaza EP2	Maputo City EP1	Maputo City EP2
Demand side								
Direct costs								
- School fees (all)	2	2	3	2	2	2	2	1
- Uniforms	3	3	3	3	2	2	1	1
- School supplies	1	1	1	1	1	1	1	1
- School snack	1	2	1	2	1	2	3	3
- Transport	4	3	3	3	4	3	2	2
- New clothing	2	2	2	2	2	2	4	3
Opportunity costs	2	1	2	1	2	1	3	2
Benefits of education	3	2	3	2	2	2	1	1
Supply side								
School access and distance	3	1	3	1	3	1	2	2
Infrastructure adequacy and quality	2	2	1	1	2	2	1	1
Constraints on quality of education	1	1	1	1	1	1	3	3
Availability of financial resources	1	2	1	2	1	2	2	2
Contextual factors								
Socioeconomic	1	2	1	2	1	2	2	1
Cultural	1	1	2	2	1	1	3	3
Family related	2	2	2	2	2	2	2	2
Other*	3	2	2	2	3	2	2	2

Source: The full PSIA Study. This table was developed in the May 2004 seminar with the Ministry of Education staff from national and provincial levels.
Note: Code: 1 = high impact; 2 = moderate impact; 3 = low impact; 4 = no impact. * Sexual harassment and financial corruption were not a special focus of the analysis, but examples of both problems emerged during conversations with parents and pupils. EP1 = grades 1–5; EP2 = grades 6–7.

MZM 21,400—the average per child fee—to slightly more than MZM 7,000, a household that currently sends two in three children to school would be more likely to send the third child to school as well. The impact would be somewhat greater in the case of EP2 fees, but would still be limited to urban areas in the central region.[10]

The impact of fees on dropouts is negligible (see table 4C.3 in annex 4C). An exception is urban areas in the southern region, where an increase in EP2 fees would result in a rise in dropout rates. The cost of uniforms is associated with a *positive* effect on enrollments in EP1 (see table 4C.1 in annex 4C). An explanation for this apparently counterintuitive result has been offered by the minister of education. The uniform has a special egalitarian function in Mozambique. By masking social status, it obscures visual differences among children. For this reason, parents prefer to send their children to school in uniforms. This explanation does not contradict the findings of the analysis.

The second noteworthy result of the study is that *proximity to school seems to be a key variable in explaining enrollments in primary school.* The greater the distance between home and school, the more likely it is that the child will not attend. In rural areas, the probability that a child will enroll in EP1 falls quickly as the distance to the school rises. Relative to a school distance of less than 30 minutes, the probability declines by 11 percent if the school is 30 to 45 minutes away, 19 percent if it is 45 to 60 minutes distant, 27 percent if it is one to two hours distant, and 38 percent beyond two hours away (table 4C.1). If a household is more than two hours from an EP1 school, the probability that a child will enroll more than halves, falling from 68 percent (the general average of the sample) to 30 percent. The probability of dropping out of school is less sensitive to distance. This is understandable since the probability of dropping out was estimated conditional on the child attending school during the previous year. Nonetheless, in a rural area, if the EP1 school is more than two hours distant, the probability that the child will drop out rises by almost 14 percent (table 4C.3).

The third noteworthy result is that the level of *household consumption has an impact on the probability that a child will attend lower primary school.* It also has an impact on the probability that a child will drop out of a lower primary school in a rural area, though the impact is not as great as might have been expected. For example, if the level of consumption of an urban household grew from MZM 14,500 to MZM 39,500 a day, an expansion of more than 170 percent, the number of children in the household who would be attending EP1 would rise from two in four to three in four.[11] Though the coefficient of consumption is highly statistically significant, the variation in levels of consumption must be great in order for substantial changes to be produced in the probability of enrollment. Moreover, according to our estimates, even if the level of consumption increased by more than one and a half times (as in the example above) still not all children in the household would go to school. This may indicate the preference (or need) of the household of selecting which children to send to school and having some of them engaged in household domestic activities. Differences in household consumption do not appear to be associated with substantial changes in the probability of dropping out of or even attending EP2.

The impact of variables such as school proximity, parental education, and the characteristics of the child seem to be greater than the impact of consumption. The lack of a stronger association between household consumption and school enrollment and dropout rates is partly explained by the impact of the educational attainment of the parents on these rates. Parental educational attainment is also associated with household welfare. In other words, the consumption effects appear to be mediated to some extent by parental educational attainment. For example, in urban areas, relative to a child whose father or male guardian has never attended school, the probability that a child will attend EP1 is 5.3 percent higher if the child's father or male guardian has completed EP1, 4.7 percent higher if he has completed EP2, 8 percent higher if he has completed ESG1, and 7 percent higher if he has completed more than ESG1. Even more substantial is the impact of a mother's education; the corresponding probabilities range from 7.6 percent if the mother has completed EP2, to 12.3 percent if she has completed more than ESG1. In rural areas, the impact of parental educational attainment is greater still, and, in this case, the coefficients of the educational dummies of the father are more significant than those of the mother (+13 percent for a father with EP1 and +24 percent for a father with ESG1).

The fourth noteworthy result is that the *personal characteristics of the child, particularly age, gender, and unusual vulnerability, have a large impact* on the probability of enrollment or dropping out. Thus, the probability of attending EP1 rises with age, but at a declining rate. The age impact is greater in rural areas, which is an expected result given that children in rural areas tend to start school later than do children in urban areas. Older girls show less probability of being enrolled relative to boys of the same age, and this effect is also significant in rural areas. Nonetheless, in the case of EP2, age does not seem to have any impact on the probability either of enrollment or of dropping out of school. It needs to be borne in mind, however, that children, particularly girls, attending EP2 are a select sample and that dropouts are estimated conditional upon attendance at school the previous year, which means that the sample of dropouts is also highly select.

Gender is associated with various probabilities of enrollment and dropping out. Very young girls are more likely than boys to be enrolled in EP1. However, this probability decreases very quickly with age. While, for example, a 7-year-old girl in a rural area has 4.5 percent higher probability of being in EP1 than a boy of the same age, a 10-year-old girl has 3.6 percent lower probability than a 10-year-old boy. Moreover, this disadvantage increases with age for girls older than 10. Nonetheless, there is no difference between boys and girls in the probability of enrollment in EP2, nor of dropping out of EP1 or EP2 (though this probability is conditional on having attended school the previous year). Households in which there are more girls enroll a lower share of children; this occurs in both rural and urban areas.

It is not possible to define unambiguously the status of orphans in the dataset, but the variable "not a child of the household head" may include this characteristic and also capture the status of children who are related to, but not offspring of the head of the household and who are therefore potentially also disadvantaged. In fact, the estimated coefficient of this variable is statistically significant and non-negligible in size in the regressions of EP1 and EP2 enrollments and dropouts, especially in urban areas. Not being the child of the household head is associated with a 12 percent reduction in the probability of attending EP1 in urban areas and a 14 percent reduction in the probability of attending EP2. Similarly, dropouts from EP1 increase by almost 3 percent and from EP2 by 5 percent if the child is not the child of the head of household.

The coefficient of the variable that captures the presence of disabled individuals in the household who are potentially in need of care is also negative and significant for EP1 enrollments (−5 percent in both urban and rural areas), but is not significant for the probability of EP2 enrollment, nor for dropping out of EP1 or EP2.

Conclusions

The fees being required by schools are well above the amounts officially fixed in the government policy documents. Paying fees set by the schools seems to be the norm rather than the exception. Typical fees include not only the ASE contributions, but also a variety of other, mostly ad-hoc fees. Though the general policy is that no child is to be kept out of school because the fees have not been paid, most schools enforce the payment of fees in all cases.

The schools and community survey indicates that although the fees paid to schools, including the ASE contributions, are not a determining factor of enrollment or retention, they are an important factor when added to the cost of uniforms and clothing, school supplies, and food. The cumulative direct costs have a negative impact on enrollments and pupil retention, particularly among low-income parents with large families to support. The inability to purchase school supplies for children is probably the most important factor for attendance in rural areas, whereas the ability of their parents to pay for uniforms and school supplies can be the difference between a child being in or out of school in urban areas.

The quantitative analysis assigns to school fees little, if any, impact on enrollments and dropouts. Some caveats apply, however. First, the household budget survey is likely to capture only a part of school fees, namely, the fees that are paid in cash and on which parents have been more likely to agree formally. It is possible that a substantial portion of school fees—perhaps the most controversial of them, such as in-kind fees, extraordinary fees, personal favors to teachers, and so on—has gone completely unrecorded in the survey. It is precisely these types of fee that may result in nonenrollment or dropping out. Second, the amount of school fees reported by households is very small, especially for EP1 and EP2. Such small amounts can have only a limited impact, if any, on the demand for education. Therefore, fee reduction or elimination in primary schools could mitigate the problem, but should not be expected to solve it.

The quantitative analysis highlights, however, the existence of other important constraints on school attendance. One key factor is school proximity (a supply-side constraint). The greater the distance between primary schools and households, the greater the probability that school attendance will fall. This is a crucial factor in rural areas because 35 percent of all rural households are more than 30 minutes distant from a primary school. Improving school access and availability can raise enrollments considerably in EP1 and EP2 and, to some extent, help decrease the number of dropouts, especially in areas where schools are distant.

Some groups of children are especially disadvantaged in terms of school enrollment. Although it appears that, relative to boys, younger girls are less disadvantaged than older girls, there is still a gender gap in enrollments in EP1 and EP2, except for the very young girls (likely a cohort effect). This gap becomes substantial among girls over 14.

Delayed entry and longer stays in EP1 (repetition) are significant problems, especially because older children are much less likely to attend upper primary school and much more likely to drop out of lower or upper primary school. If children were starting school at the proper age and progressing through lower primary school at the appropriate pace, more children would be attending upper primary school, and the probability of dropping out would be substantially reduced.

Poor children are less likely than rich children to be enrolled in EP1. The children of parents with little educational attainment are also less likely to be enrolled. Forming another disadvantaged group are those children who are not the children of the heads of the households in which they live. Many (not all) of these are likely to be orphans.

Finally, it must be stressed that a broad set of variables has a statistically significant impact on EP1 enrollments. Moreover, the estimated coefficients tend to be larger than those in the other regressions, indicating that there is substantial selection taking place from the start. Lower primary school attendance is not equally likely for all. This initial selection continues throughout the educational system. For example, the fact that household consumption is not statistically significant in explaining EP2 enrollments does not mean that poor and rich children are equally likely to attend upper primary school. It means only that, *among those children who have completed lower primary school,* household consumption is not a substantial factor in explaining EP2 enrollments. However, because poor children were already less likely to attend lower primary school and, therefore, because they have not completed that level of schooling, they are also less likely to attend EP2.

Recommendations

The study generated a series of recommendations to ease demand-side, supply-side, and contextual constraints to increase retention in primary schools. To ensure that the recommendations were feasible, actionable, and within the immediate financial scope and implementation capacity of the education system, the research team generated recommendations through a consultative process with policy makers, technical officers, teachers, and key stakeholders from all provinces in Mozambique. A clear message from this process was that recommendations should include a list of actions required to operationalize a given recommendation (see annex 4D). The most important recommendation was to revise the current policy on school fees to clarify the type (if any), purpose, frequency of fee contributions, payment mechanisms, and accountability of funds. Participants also felt that this revision should state clearly that pupils whose parents cannot afford to make contributions should be exempted from paying fees. There was consensus that exemption decisions should be the realm of school councils based on local criteria rather than the possession of a poverty certificate, especially since acquiring the latter requires entering into a bureaucratic process and a cash outlay that is beyond the reach of poor parents and orphaned children.

The second recommendation was to initiate public information campaigns to educate communities on the right of children to attend primary school irrespective of their economic circumstances, the wider benefits of schooling, and the need to start school at the appropriate age. As the study pointed out, delayed entrance into grade 1 often leads to premature dropout, especially in rural areas and for girls.

The third recommendation is related to the need to increase resources that are channeled directly to the schools, mainly through the

Direct Support for Schools program, to ease the burden on households, especially when it comes to purchasing pupils' school materials. The size of the grant could be expanded from the current average of US$1.90 per child per year to about US$4.10 per child per year, while also tying resources to pupil retention (especially girls in rural areas) and overall school performance. The grant, therefore, could be used as a tool to elicit reform from the ground up. If the size of the grant were expanded, the overall outlay from the Ministry of Education would increase from an average of US$5.5 million to US$12 million per year. Compared with the high costs of other inputs in the education system, especially construction, the approach is likely to yield an affordable cost per retained student.

The fourth recommendation is to deploy teachers better to ensure that qualified teachers are distributed more equitably, especially in rural areas where the supply of qualified teachers and female teachers is limited. The schools must be equipped with teachers who have a pedagogically sound foundation and also have access to in-service training that enables them to maneuver contextual factors—including gender and HIV/AIDS prevention—in a manner that is suitable to community practice if the country is to achieve the goal of universal completion or primary education by 2015.

Finally, the fifth recommendation is to build schools closer to the communities they serve to reduce the travel time to school, and to consolidate lower and upper primary schools into one physical plant to increase the likelihood of continuing from one level to the next. The cost implications of this recommendation are higher than the three previously mentioned recommendations; nonetheless it is an important one given the results from the econometric analysis.

THE IMPACT OF THE PSIA

In an effort to promote equitable access to education, as stipulated in the Poverty Reduction Strategy Paper, the Government of Mozambique issued a ministerial decree in 2004 wherein it declared the abolition of the ASE and any other fees and levies in primary education starting in the 2005 academic year, which began in mid-January 2005. The decree of 2004 allows parents, communities, and other interested parties to make contributions in cash or in kind, although only on a strictly voluntary basis.

Although the government's decision to abolish all fees is a bold step to encourage and accelerate enrollment in primary education, the decree of 2004 does not mention whether additional budgetary allocations will be made to cover the shortfall in school-generated revenue (an average of MZM 21,410 per child in EP1 and MZM 60,013 per child in EP2). It also does not mention whether school supplies, textbooks, school uniforms, and other miscellaneous items, which were financed by households (at an average of MZM 114,249 per enrolled child), will be covered by other means. In the event that items previously financed by households are covered by the government and provided directly to schools and students, an additional US$2.5 million for EP1 and US$1 million for EP2 would need to be allocated in 2005 (at current enrollment levels). However, should students who dropped out before completing lower or upper primary school be encouraged to re-enroll, the government's allocation would have to be raised substantially in order to provide for the rise in the number of new or returning students, particularly in upper primary schools. It should be noted that under the current fee abolition scheme and in the absence of additional budget resources, households would still be required to purchase school supplies, uniforms, and, in some grades, textbooks.

It is too early to gauge the initial impact of the government's political decision, but the removal of fees is likely to increase the absolute number of students, especially in upper primary schools, in which only slightly more than 10 percent of the eligible school-age population is currently enrolled and where the social pressure to expand is greatest. It is also possible that students who dropped out before completing EP1 or EP2 will be encouraged to re-enroll. The question of whether returning students will remain in the system until completion will also depend on the household's ability to meet additional expenses to cover school supplies, uniforms, and textbooks or on an extraordinary effort from the government to increase public expenditure to cover school supplies and other miscellaneous schooling expenses for the majority of EP1 and EP2 pupils.

Regarding the PSIA impact at the operational level, the Ministry of Education, the Bank team, and Cooperating Partners have used the study to inform the development of the second Education Sector Strategic Plan (2005–9), where there is a proposal to double the grant size of the Direct Support for Schools program in 2006 and eventually to include an additional, earmarked grant to finance small-scale civil works activities, whether upgrading or adding classrooms. An additional financial incentive mechanism to increase the completion rate of girls and vulnerable children in rural areas is also envisioned under the program. The study is informing the operationalization of the gender strategy in the Ministry of Education at all levels as well. A seminar was held in May 2005, sponsored by Action Aid and Danida, on this topic and for which the study is one of the key documents. The Ministry of Education has requested the Bank and the Cooperating Partners for a similar study to analyze the constraints to enrollment and completion at the secondary education level and for follow-up support to evaluate the impact of the fee elimination reform on key education indicators.

In addition, the Bank team has used the report to inform and sharpen advice in the context of the Poverty Reduction Sector Credit (PRSC), Joint Partner Initiatives, and Policy Reviews taking place in Mozambique.

LESSONS LEARNED

The study verified that the official policy of school fees is not being applied. There is substantial variation in fee levels across schools. Moreover, although some schools rely on active community participation to establish the level of contributions for ASE, others rely on less transparent or arbitrary methods. The variation in fee levels may cause parents to select schools based on the level of fees required rather than on proximity, which results in longer distances to the nearest affordable schools. Finally, the school fees are not fulfilling their intended objective, which was to act as a pool fund to support the needy and vulnerable students.

The elimination of school fees in 2005 was widely supported by parents and stakeholders. In theory, the elimination of school fees will allow parents to select schools based on educational criteria rather than on ability to pay the ASE fee level set forth by the school. Parents cannot any longer use school fees as a justification for not sending all their children to school, irrespective of gender, relation to the household, or poverty status.

However, this measure should be accompanied by various actions to ensure that schools have the necessary funds to function appropriately. Since the ASE funds were covering salaries of auxiliary staff, primarily to maintain and guard the school facilities and grounds, the Ministry of Education must provide resources to ensure that these services take place. This is very important from a school health and hygiene and student security perspective, as the lack of either may result in inconsistent school attendance or dropping out, particularly of girls.

The lessons learned in carrying out the study (see the section on issues related to methodology, team composition, and data constraints) are useful for future follow-up studies or studies of a similar nature. Chief among the positive lessons are that establishing a technically strong, multidisciplinary team is crucial. The team should be composed of technical staff from government, the World Bank, and Cooperating Partners, including NGOs. It should also incorporate continuous consultation sessions with a wide range of stakeholders from provincial and district education offices to include their perspectives and thereby ease potential resistance to the implementation of the study's recommendations. It should be highlighted, however, that consultations require time to ensure genuinely built consensus and financial resources, particularly in a large country such as Mozambique. Similarly, in order to ensure that the insights gained from the analysis were internalized and implemented, great efforts were made to ensure that recommendations would be operationally focused as possible and that they build on existing institutional structures, processes, or programs. As a result, the study has been useful in informing policy makers in the Ministry of Education and Ministry of Finance about a feasible way forward on various aspects impinging on consistent enrollment. This is being done in the context of the revised Poverty Reduction Strategy Paper (PRSP) and Poverty Reduction Sector Credit (PRSC) with the World Bank and Cooperating Partners supporting the Government of Mozambique.

Given the recent change in policy to eliminate school fees without providing additional financing to offset forgone school revenue, it would be useful to undertake a follow-up study to evaluate the impact of the policy change. The study would measure positive and negative effects using quantitative and qualitative methodologies. So far anecdotal evidence suggest that the removal of fees has left schools without operational funds needed to hire school maintenance staff, which has prompted teachers to assign students to do the cleaning, thus cutting back on the already-limited number of hours of instruction. It is not clear whether the collection of other school-based levies continues under a different name and payment structure. Similarly, given that the issue of fees is prominent, perhaps even more so at other levels of the educational system, it would also be advantageous to begin to explore these issues at post-primary levels to inform decision making.

NOTES

1. This chapter is based on the *Poverty and Social Impact Analysis (PSIA) Primary School Enrollment and Retention: The Impact of School Fees.* Report No. 29423, January 2005. www.worldbank.org/psia.
2. The analysis presented in the PSIA study concentrates on the two levels of primary education: lower primary education (*Ensino Primário do Primeiro*

Grau or EP1), which offers grades 1 through 5, and upper primary education (*Ensino Primário do Segundo Grau* or EP2), which offers grades 6 and 7. Most Mozambican schools provide only one level of primary education (EP1 or EP2), but a small share—about 10 percent of all schools enrolling grade 1 pupils—cover all seven grades. Each of these is referred to as a *full primary school* (*Escola Primária Completa* or EPC). The *completion rate* used in this study is defined as the total number of students graduating from the final year of a cycle of education, regardless of age, expressed as a percentage of the segment of the population that is at the age corresponding to the official age for graduation. Since the number of students graduating from the final year of a cycle is likely to be lower than the number of students enrolled in the last year of the cycle, a *modified completion rate* has also been calculated using the enrollment in the final year of the cycle, regardless of age, expressed as a percentage of the segment of the population that is at the age corresponding to the official age for graduation. As anticipated, the latter rate points to higher rates of completion across provinces, ranging from an additional 15 to 30 percentage points for grade 5 completion and to an additional 9 to 35 percentage points for grade 7 completion.

3. The national education system, as currently constituted, was legally established through ministerial decree no. 6, 1992 (*Diploma Ministerial no. 6/92*). The decree does not establish that education, including primary education, should be compulsory or free. Rather, the decree assigns to the Council of Ministers the responsibility for determining the pace at which compulsory education should be introduced, taking into account socioeconomic developments in the country.

4. Cooperating Partners is the consortium of representatives from international agencies and national NGOs that provide financial or technical support to the education sector in Mozambique (also known as "the donors"). There are about 25-plus Cooperating Partners in basic education in Mozambique.

5. The education levels are lower and upper primary school, lower and upper secondary school, elementary technical and vocational, basic technical and vocational, intermediate technical and vocational, higher education, and "other" education. For lower and upper primary school, lower and upper secondary school, and higher education, the survey collected information on fees and charges separately according to institution type (private and public).

6. In the multivariate analysis, the average cost of uniforms was computed by considering only those households with children in lower (or upper) primary school.

7. The exact wording of the questionnaire was "Despensas ensino primário (1°/2°) grau (público/privado) (incl. propinas e matricula)."

8. The school year in Mozambique is divided into trimesters. The first is from January to April, the second is from May to July, and the third is from August to October.

9. See Annex 4B for the details on the econometric techniques and Annex 4C for the results of the multivariate analysis (Tables 4C.1, 4C.2, and 4C.3).
10. Calculations based on the coefficients estimated with the Fractional Logit Model, reported in Table 4C.2.
11. Calculations based on the coefficient estimated with the Fractional Logit Model, reported in table 4C.2.

REFERENCES

Breslin, Lindsey. 2003. *When Someone Is Sick in the House, Poverty Has Already Entered: A Research Study on Home-Based Care, Morrumbala Center, Zambézia Province, Mozambique.* Report prepared for Save the Children U.K. and the Hope for African Children Initiative. Maputo: Estamos-Organização Comunitaria.

Ministry of Education and Culture. 2002. "Sector Expenditure Review." Maputo, Mozambique.

Wooldridge, J. M. 2001. *Econometric Analysis of Cross Section and Panel Data.* Cambridge, MA: MIT Press.

World Bank. 2003a. *Mozambique: Public Expenditure Review, Phase 2: Sectoral Expenditures.* Africa Region. Washington, DC: World Bank.

———. 2003b. "Cost and Financing of Education: Opportunities and Obstacles for Expanding and Improving Education in Mozambique." Africa Region Human Development Working Paper 37. Africa Region, Human Development Sector, World Bank, Washington, DC.

———. 2005. *Poverty and Social Impact Analysis (PSIA) Primary School Enrollment and Retention: The Impact of School Fees.* Report 29423, January. Washington, DC: World Bank. www.worldbank.org/psia.

Research Design: Guiding Questions

PART 1: ASSESSMENT OF GOVERNMENT POLICY: GUIDING QUESTIONS

- What is the official policy on school fees by type of fee and level of education?
- Are there types of fees collected that are not included in the official policy?
- What is the official policy on school fee exemptions by level of education?
- How is the official policy (or any changes to it) disseminated across levels of government, schools and the general public?
- How is the official policy interpreted and applied across levels of government?
- Who decides fee levels and determines whether they are excessive?
- Are the mechanisms in place to regulate excessive fees?
- Are there sanctions against excessive fees?
- What are the recourse mechanisms for parent's whose children are turned away by the lack of income to pay for school fees?
- Are the recourse mechanisms established and is their existence widely shared by Ministry officials across levels of government and localities?
- Do schools receive an annual subvention from the ministry's budget to meet recurrent costs in the school (untied)?

■ If so, what proportion of the school operating expenses is covered by the subvention and what proportion is covered with school generated fees?

PART 2: SCHOOL AND COMMUNITY ANALYSIS: GUIDING QUESTIONS

■ How is the official policy of fees interpreted at school and community level?

■ What are the fees collected at school level? What share of annual expenditures are financed by fees? Are fees used for particular expenditures?

■ Who decides on the level of fees?

■ How is the level of fees determined, on which criteria is it based upon?

■ What are the fees used for? Do they do any good? If so, what sort of good?

■ Is there a relationship between the fees and the perceived quality of services provided?

■ What happens to the student if fees go unpaid?

■ Are the fees mandatory or voluntary?

■ What mechanisms are in place to collect fees?

■ Are there mechanisms to ensure needy children are exempted from school fees?

■ What are those mechanisms, how easily accessible are they and how do they work in practice?

■ In addition to fees, what are other reasons for not attending school?

■ How important are fees relative to other reasons given for not attending school or for dropping out prematurely, particularly before completing EP1?

■ How important are other reasons given for not attending school or for dropping out prematurely relative to school fees, particularly before completing EP1?

■ According to the parents, teachers, and students, how could the impact of fees be best mitigated to ensure students complete at least EP1?

■ Are there household constraints that prevent parents from sending children to school?

■ What are those?

■ How do parents decide who is sent to school? And for how long?

■ What would it take for the schools and the households to ensure that all children complete EP1?

■ Are there shared factors in schools with high enrollment and completion rates? What are those?

- Are there shared factors in households with high enrollment and completion rates? What are those?
- How willing would the household be to continue paying school fees, even if the government ensured a minimum level of expenditure per student?

PART 3: HOUSEHOLD SURVEY ANALYSIS: GUIDING QUESTIONS

- How much do households spend, on average, on education (fees and school-related items) by type of school and level of education?
- How does expenditure vary by household poverty quintile and locality?
- What are the gross and net enrollment patterns for primary school–aged children by poverty quintile, locality, and gender?
- What are the gross and net enrollment patterns for primary school–aged children who have lost a parent by quintile, locality, and gender?
- To what extent can the demand for education be increased by the reduction in school fees, by poverty quintile, locality, and gender?
- What would happen to enrollments if school fees were reduced?
- Which other factors, besides school fees, have an impact on enrollments and dropouts?

Econometric Model

We estimated probit models for the probability of a child being enrolled in EP1 and EP2 separately for urban and rural areas:

$$P(S_i = 1) = P\left(\varepsilon_i \geq -\left(Z_{li}\beta + Z_{hi}\gamma + Z_{si}\delta + \bar{F}_j\lambda + \bar{A}_j\phi\right)\right)$$

where

$P(S_i = 1)$ indicates the probability of the child attending school,

$\quad Z_{li}$ is a vector including child-specific variables (age of the child, the child's sex, and the child's relationship with the household head),

$\quad Z_{hi}$ is a vector including household characteristics (parents' education, female-headed household, presence of disabled in the household, residence, household consumption),

$\quad Z_{si}$ is a vector including school characteristics (distance to school),

$\quad \bar{F}_j$ is a vector including the average level of school fee and the average cost of uniform per child paid in area j (calculated over all children in area j excluding child i),

$\quad \bar{A}_j$ is the average level of other relevant area variables such as level of consumption (calculated in the same way as the average fee level, that is, as a leave-out-mean variable), and

$\quad \varepsilon_i$ is an error term normally distributed.

We decided to include the average area level of school fee (and average cost of uniforms) together with a set of area-level controls (including average consumption $\overline{A_j}$) to alleviate the problem of endogeneity of school fees and uniform expenditures, arising from the fact that the amount of school fees (or uniform cost) paid by each household may depend on how rich parents are and therefore on how rich the area is. Rich parents are more likely to send children to school and at the same time to pay higher fees. For uniforms, we computed the average cost of uniforms using only those households that had only children going to EP1 (or EP2), because the cost of uniforms is collected as a cumulative amount for all children going to school, irrespective of the level. So we had to compute averages over bigger areas to keep the sample sizes meaningful.

The samples are defined, in the case of enrollments in EP1, as the group of children who should be in EP1 (that is, who have completed a level of education lower than EP1) and can be either in EP1 or out of school; in the case of enrollments in EP2, as the group of those who have completed EP1 and can be either in EP2 or out of school. In order to focus on a group of relatively homogeneous individuals we also imposed an age limit—6 to 17 for EP1 and 12 to 19 for EP2.

To assess the robustness of our results, we estimated an alternative model, which used the household as the unit of analysis and where the dependent variable was defined as the fraction of "enrollable" children who are actually enrolled—that is, the ratio of children who go to EP1 (EP2) out of all children living in the household who could potentially go. In other words, all children who are in the age range 8–16 (12–19) and who have not completed EP1 (EP2). In this case, we estimated a fractional logit model.[1]

Finally, we estimated a probit model for dropouts from EP1 and EP2, separately for urban and rural areas. The group "at risk" of dropping out from EP1 includes all those who were going to school last year and have not completed EP1 yet. The group at risk of dropping out from EP2 (or, more precisely, dropping out from primary school before completing EP2) includes all those who were going to school last year and have completed EP1, but not yet EP2.[2] Although ideally it would be interesting to jointly estimate enrollments and dropouts, it is difficult if not impossible to find convincing identifying variables for the two sets of coefficients.

---

1. For an explanation of this model, see Wooldridge (2001).
2. For dropouts we imposed the same age limits as for enrollments.

That is why we have estimated two separate probit regressions. It is therefore important to keep in mind that the probability of dropping out is estimated as a conditional probability (conditional on having been enrolled until last year and on having completed EP1, in the case of dropouts from EP2, for example). Notice that enrollment in EP2 is also estimated conditional on having completed EP1.

4-C

Multivariate Regressions

Table 4C.1 Probit Estimates for the Probability of the Child To Be Enrolled in EP1 and EP2

| | EP1 | | EP2 |
	Urban	Rural	Urban
Age	0.188***	0.283***	0.020
Age squared	−0.009***	−0.012***	−0.003
Female	0.106	0.206**	0.014
Female * age	−0.007*	−0.023***	−0.015
Not a child of the head/spouse	−0.121***	−0.077***	−0.141***
Kid order	0.015***	0.016**	0.022***
Some disabled in the household	−0.050**	−0.056**	−0.035
Female headed household	−0.090	0.011	0.048
No father in the household	0.096**	0.044	0.018
Father some primary education	0.029	0.029	0.043
Father EP1	0.053**	0.132***	0.009
Father EP2	0.047*	0.076	0.063*
Father ES1	0.078***	0.243***	0.058
Father more than ES1	0.071***	0.141	0.105***
No mother in the household	0.047*	0.139**	0.049
Mother some primary education	0.044***	0.071***	0.019
Mother EP1	0.087***	0.075*	0.023
Mother EP2	0.076***	0.118*	0.053*
Mother ES1	0.050	0.025	0.061
Mother over ES1	0.123***	0.213	
North	0.042	−0.155	−0.008
Center	0.190**	−0.066	0.330***
South excluding Maputo City	0.019		0.090
Log (average cons. In the district)	0.016	−0.067**	−0.058
Log (average household cons.)	0.043***	0.056***	0.030*
EP school 30 to 45 minutes distant	0.000	−0.114***	−0.012
EP school 45 to 60 minutes distant	−0.004	−0.191***	−0.520*
EP school 60 to 120 minutes distant	−0.064	−0.270***	
EP school more than 2 hours distant	−0.278**	−0.382***	
Log (average school fee/child in the district)	0.039	−0.015	−0.003
Log (average cost of uniform)	0.025*	0.008***	−0.001
Fees * female	−0.017	−0.016	0.041
Fees * Center	−0.090***	−0.004	−0.115**
Fees * South	0.007	0.021	−0.031
Fees * North	−0.042		0.021
Observations	3994	4817	1446
Pseudo-R^2	0.2346	0.1350	0.2995
Log pseudo-likelihood	−1,444.63	−2661.93	−519.99

Source: Authors' calculations based on the IAF survey 2002/3.

Note: The marginal effect is computed at the mean of repressors. For dummy variables it is given for a discrete change from 0 to 1. * = statistically significant at the 10 percent level. ** = statistically signifi- cant at the 5 percent level. *** = statistically significant at the 1 percent level. The reference categories are: male, child of the household head, father never in education; mother never in education, no disabled in the household, male headed household, living in Maputo City, distance to school < than 30 minutes.

Table 4C.2 Fractional Logit Model (dependent variable: ratio of children going to EP1 and EP2 in each household out of all those who are eligible)

	EP1		EP2
	Urban	*Rural*	*Urban*
No father	2.329*	0.997	
Father some primary education	1.064	1.041	1.212
Father EP1	1.421	1.892***	1.231
Father EP2	1.635*	1.379	1.756
Father ES1	2.203**	4.787***	2.047*
Father over ES1	2.230**	2.537	3.653***
No mother	1.466	2.442**	0.838
Mother some primary education	1.309**	1.466***	1.004
Mother EP1	2.557***	1.447*	0.799
Mother EP2	2.078***	2.279**	1.286
Mother ES1	1.662	1.333	
Some disabled in the household	0.723**	0.815*	0.894
Female headed household	0.580	1.314	
Ratio of enrollable children who are female	0.646***	0.663***	0.780
Ratio of enrollable children who are orphans	0.465***	0.851	0.471***
North	0.849	0.305*	3.731
Center	2.834	0.492	19.023**
South excluding Maputo City	1.056		3.725
Total school fees	1.049	0.910	1.316
Average consumption level in the district	1.036	0.721*	0.735
Average household consumption level	1.522***	1.339***	1.597***
EP school 30 to 45 minutes distant	1.014	0.626***	0.883
EP school 45 to 60 minutes distant	1.171	0.418***	0.000***
EP school 60 to 120 minutes distant	0.871	0.296***	0.000***
EP school more than 2 hours distant	0.303*	0.205***	
Total cost of uniforms	1.075	1.035**	1.008
Fees * Center	0.722**	0.978	0.528**
Fees * South	1.122	0.952	0.737
Fees * North	0.890		0.819
Observations	2205	2616	801
Log pseudo-likelihood	−1,345.52	−2251.61	−495.56

Source: Authors' calculations based on the IAF survey 2002/3.

Note: Odd ratios shown. * = statistically significant at the 10 percent level. ** = statistically significant at the 5 percent level. *** = statistically significant at the 1 percent level. The reference categories are: father never in education; mother never in education, no disabled in the household, male headed household, living in Maputo City, distance to school < than 30 minutes.

Table 4C.3 Probit Estimates for the Probability of the Child to Drop Out of EP1 and EP2

| | EP1 | | EP2 |
	Urban	Rural	Urban
Age	−0.015*	−0.043***	0.019
Age squared	0.001***	0.002***	0.000
Female	−0.030	−0.093*	−0.056
Female * age	0.003	0.008**	0.005
Not a child of the head/spouse	0.027***	0.012	0.048***
Kid order	−0.004**	−0.008**	−0.009***
Some disabled in the household	0.020*	0.013	0.002
Female headed household	0.016	0.042	−0.433***
No father in the household	−0.026*	−0.027	0.983***
Father some primary education	−0.013**	0.007	−0.012
Father EP1	−0.020***	−0.016	−0.011
Father EP2	−0.019***	0.016	−0.019
Father ES1	−0.020***		−0.024**
Father more than ES1	−0.018***	−0.027	−0.031***
No mother in the household	0.005	−0.035	−0.014
Mother some primary education	0.001	0.004	−0.002
Mother EP1	−0.016***	−0.012	−0.009
Mother EP2	−0.007	−0.037	−0.021**
Mother ES1	−0.004		−0.019
Mother over ES1			
North	−0.006	0.027	−0.018
Center	−0.005	−0.001	−0.164*
South excluding Maputo City	0.037		−0.034
Log (average cons. In the district)	−0.002	0.020	0.010
Log (average household cons.)	−0.003	−0.022**	−0.010
EP school 30 to 45 minutes distant	−0.004	0.016	0.035
EP school 45 to 60 minutes distant	−0.004	0.020	0.285
EP school 60 to 120 minutes distant		0.069*	
EP school more than 2 hours distant		0.137**	
Log (average school fee/child in the district)	0.000	−0.001	−0.003
Log (average cost of uniform)	−0.001	0.002	0.000
Fees * female	0.001	0.000	−0.003
Fees * Center	0.004	0.006	−0.007
Fees * South	−0.012	−0.008	0.042**
Fees * North	0.004		0.008
Observations	3242	3095	1243
Pseudo-R^2	0.1946	0.0665	0.2403
Log pseudo-likelihood	−454.55	−788.00	−253.02

Source: Authors' calculations based on the IAF survey 2002/3.

Note: The marginal effect is computed at the mean of repressors. For dummy variables it is given for a discrete change from 0 to 1. * = statistically significant at the 10 percent level. ** = statistically significant at the 5 percent level. *** = statistically significant at the 1 percent level. The reference categories are: male, child of the household head, father never in education; mother never in education, no disabled in the household, male headed household, living in Maputo City, distance to school < than 30 minutes.

PSIA Recommendations

Because recommendations have a financial impact, efforts were made to include actions that are financially affordable, relatively straightforward, and effective at meeting the objective.

DEMAND-SIDE FACTORS

Recommendation 1: Revise official policy (the ministerial decree) on school fees.

- Clarify the type (if any), purpose, and frequency of the fees and contributions that may be charged by schools, the payment mechanisms, and the recordkeeping procedures. Ensure that schools and parents are fully aware of the types of fees and contributions that are not allowed and should not be charged.
- Create strict regulations on the collection of add-on and ad hoc fees in primary schools in order to ensure that mechanisms are in place to encourage financial accountability and discourage unnecessary fees.
- Define the roles, responsibilities, and decision-making authority of school directors, teachers, parents, and community members (outlined in the school council manual) in order to ensure transparency and accountability in the collection and governance of school-generated revenue.

■ Define the exemption criteria for school fees and contributions (that is, the criteria for the exemption of grades 1 and 2 pupils; the exemption of all lower primary school pupils; the exemption of disabled, orphaned, or vulnerable children; and so on) and simplify the steps required to prove exemption eligibility to school administrations.

■ Eliminate or streamline the bureaucratic process involved in obtaining the poverty certificate required for fee exemption. In rural communities, for example, poverty certification should be a simple process based on the oral testimony of local authorities and community members, and the process should be free of charge. For this purpose, develop flexible criteria to be implemented by communities, churches and religious groups, nongovernmental organizations, schools, and community leaders in order to identify children who are out of school, especially orphans, and guarantee that they enroll in school and have access to appropriate school materials and clothing.

■ Increase awareness of the revised official policy through print and radio campaigns and through special brochures to be distributed together with the materials on the Direct Support for Schools program.

Recommendation 2: Design and launch print and community radio campaigns to inform, educate, and disseminate information in the following areas:

■ The rights of children and the benefits of education, especially in rural areas.

■ The importance of ensuring prompt entry into grade 1 at the age of 6 or 7. As the study points out, delay in starting school is one of the most important constraining factors associated with pupil repetition and dropping out.

■ The official policy on school fees and contributions, exemption criteria and mechanisms, the roles and responsibilities of stakeholders, and policies on financial corruption and the misuse of fees. The official policy should recognize that fees in primary education represent a roadblock to improving equity in the access to services.

■ The intergenerational benefits of the education of girls, with an emphasis on ensuring at least completion of the full EP1 cycle, particularly in rural areas. If necessary, provide financial incentives to schools in order to boost the likelihood of the enrollment of girls.

- The ministry policy against sexual harassment in schools, in particular the harassment of girls by teachers.
- The concept that schools should be responsive and adaptive to the socioeconomic, cultural, and political needs and conditions of the community rather than expecting the community to adapt to the needs of the school.
- Schools are active participants in the fight against HIV/AIDS through school-based prevention programs and the dissemination of information regarding the rights and proper care of those who are infected or affected by HIV/AIDS.

Recommendation 3: Expand and institutionalize the Direct Support for Schools program.

- Expand the size of the program's cash grant per school. (Currently the average grant size ranges from US$200 to US$3,000, depending on a school financing formula.) Earmark a portion of the expanded grant to cover operational and educational expenditures. Operational expenditures should be clearly defined and listed in the same way as school consumables are currently presented in the Direct Support for Schools program manual on eligible expenditures.
- Although schools should have the authority to decide the mix of consumables to be purchased using the program cash grants, it should be clear that poor and vulnerable children should receive preferential treatment in the distribution of school materials, since the lack of money to purchase these has been found to represent one of the greatest constraints on sustained school attendance.
- Gradually introduce eligibility criteria for the cash grant in order to ensure that schools continue to receive resources if certain outcomes, mutually agreed, are met. This will mean that the grant will no longer be merely a cash transfer. It will become an incentive mechanism to foster change from the ground up. Eventually, school directors should be required to prepare simple school plans in which they state their objectives for the year.
- Tailor additional interventions for districts in which enrollment and completion rates are extremely low. A one-size-fits-all approach to the problem of inadequate completion rates will not work. For example, programs should be implemented to delay or mitigate the impact of initiation rites among girls in order to ensure that young girls are not permanently excluded from school.

- If the size of the cash grant were to be expanded by, say, 100 percent to cover all essential classroom consumables and school supplies for students, the cost of the program would rise from the current US$5.5 million to about US$12 million per year. This would increase the average benefit per pupil from US$1.90 to US$4.14 per year.

- Consider the possibility of introducing a classroom and infrastructure upgrade allocation to help communities upgrade and equip classrooms with furniture and provide water and sanitation facilities for schools. The resources transferred through the upgrade allocation could be provided on demand through a partnership agreement among the school administration, the school council, and the local community. Most communities in Mozambique are already active in building or upgrading school infrastructure. The shortages are the lack of financial support—mainly for the purchase of conventional construction materials—and technical support to ensure that new school construction is able to withstand the rainy season.

- Consider the possibility of introducing an allocation for orphans and vulnerable children in order to ensure that such children gain access to school and are able to purchase school supplies (exercise books, notebooks, and other consumables). Clear, simple criteria would have to be developed to identify these children and to monitor their sustained enrollment.

Recommendation 4: Simplify school examination procedures and eliminate examination fees.

- Provide guidelines to schools to simplify the procedures for end-of-year and end-of-cycle examinations and, most importantly, eliminate all fees charged for the right to take examinations and receive certification for grades 5 and 7.

SUPPLY-SIDE CONSTRAINTS

Recommendation 5: Build schools closer to communities in order to reduce the average distance to the nearest primary school.

- School proximity is one of the key factors in poor performance for enrollment and dropout indicators. Yet there is little information on appropriate school site selection. It is therefore imperative to accelerate the completion of the school mapping exercise (*Carta Escolar*). The importance of this action should be emphasized.

- Establish and disseminate clear criteria for school site selection in order to ensure that schools are located within easy walking distance in the communities served.

- Gradually consolidate lower primary schools into full primary schools in order to expand access to the upper primary grades in the same school buildings. Information generated through the school mapping exercise is essential for identifying appropriate sites and matching sites with catchment areas.

Recommendation 6: Improve school infrastructure.

- Improve infrastructure so that it complies with the minimum requirements for a pedagogically sustainable teaching-learning process (cement floors, adequate ventilation, durable construction materials, potable water, toilet facilities, and so on).

- Supply the essential furniture (pupil and teacher desks).

Recommendation 7: Improve the quality of education.

- Improve teacher deployment to ensure that qualified teachers are posted in rural areas. A special effort should be made to train more women teachers for rural communities.

- Furnish the essential textbooks and complementary learning materials on time and in sufficient quantities (before or at the beginning of the school year).

- Improve the relevance of education by teaching children with knowledge that counts. This is particularly important in rural areas.

PUBLIC EXPENDITURE ON EDUCATION

Recommendation 8: Improve the effectiveness and efficiency of public expenditure on education, particularly in EP1 and EP2.

- Improve current practices in teacher compensation, deployment, and management in EP1 and EP2. Despite the increase in resources allocated to the sector, the proportion of unqualified teachers continues to rise, particularly in rural areas.

- Although additional resources for primary education are needed to expand the Direct Support for Schools program, upgrade infrastructure, improve quality, and so on, new allocations should be strategically applied so that their impact is likely to be as substantial as possible. Additional resources for hiring teaching staff could be spent so as to send additional qualified teachers to rural schools or to other schools in which there is a shortage of qualified teachers, in particular women teachers. Expenditure on education cannot continue to increase without organized monitoring and evaluation.

5

SRI LANKA
Welfare Reform

AMBAR NARAYAN, TARA VISHWANATH,
AND NOBUO YOSHIDA[1]

The attempt to transform social welfare programs in Sri Lanka represents one of the key reform efforts undertaken by the country during the last five years. The effort has far-reaching repercussions for achieving the stated objective of such programs—namely, to provide consumption support to the poor and to ensure the sustainability of expenditure on such programs in the medium term. The effort to reform the welfare system of the country also offers a lesson on the difficulties in overcoming the systemic inertia that characterizes a long-running program, especially one that has had a history of politicization. Furthermore, it showcases the complex process through which such reforms evolve, and illustrates the way the changing political circumstances of a country govern those processes.

In Sri Lanka, this reform is also a useful test case of the chance of success of reforms that need considerable political will and commitment to implement, in spite of the potential benefits they promise. The critical nature of this particular reform in the country context and the lessons it offers for other countries with similar entrenched programs are the main reasons it was selected for conducting a Poverty and Social Impact Analysis (PSIA).

The engagement of the World Bank in this particular reform has been that of a partner, providing support in developing solutions to the problem of how to select beneficiaries of the program in an objective and transparent manner, and building institutional capacity to implement the decisions that are adopted by the government. The PSIA exercise has evolved organically from the partnership between the Bank team and its government counterparts, driven by their close collaboration in designing technical solutions to achieve better targeting and in operationalizing those solutions on the ground. Much of the exercise described below has emerged from the work conducted to support the government in designing the reform. This work included consultations with the government and other stakeholders, empirical exercises using household data to develop a targeting method, a pilot to corroborate the ex ante analysis of impact, and workshops with stakeholders.

While the reform is still ongoing, it is instructive to document this PSIA case study for two reasons: first, to illustrate how ex ante impact analysis can be used to motivate and provide impetus to the reform process itself; and second, to underscore the importance of building institutional capacity to enable implementation—a key factor in realizing the benefits of the diagnostic insights in a PSIA.

WELFARE PROGRAMS IN SRI LANKA: THE CURRENT STATE

To put the role of welfare programs in Sri Lanka into context, it is useful to briefly refer to the status and pattern of poverty in the country. Over the last two decades, decline in poverty has been modest and marked by rising inequality. Between 1990/1 and 2002, the national poverty head-count ratio fell by around 3 percentage points (from 26.1 percent to 22.7 percent), and was at the same time accompanied by rising inequality (see table 5.1). Poverty incidence in urban areas was almost halved, but it fell by only 5 percentage points in the rural sector and increased by

Table 5.1 Poverty Headcounts for Sri Lanka

Classification	1990–1	1995–6	2002
National	26.1	28.8	22.7
Urban[a]	16.3	14.0	7.9
Rural[a]	29.4	30.9	24.7
Estate	20.5	38.4[b]	30.0

Source: HIES data for relevant years, using official poverty lines (DCS).
Note: a. The classification of urban and rural areas is different between HIES 1990–1 and HIES 1995–6 onward: all town councils were classified as rural areas after 1995–6. The changes do not alter the arguments on the poverty trend, although the levels of headcount ratios (urban and rural) need to be cautiously interpreted.
  b. Comparability of estate headcount for 1995–6 with that for other years may be affected by the fact that HIES in 1995–6 was sampled differently for the estate sector.

10 percentage points in the estate or plantation sector; differences in inequality across provinces have also been pronounced, with a headcount rate (in 2002) of around 11 percent in Western Province contrasting sharply with one of around 35 percent in Sabaragamuwa and Uva (see figure 5.1). Rising inequality is reflected by the fact that, although mean per capita consumption for the country increased by about 29 percent in real terms between 1990/1 and 2002, the increase was around 50 percent for the top quintile (of per capita consumption expenditure) and only 2 percent for the bottom quintile.

Poverty in Sri Lanka is thus concentrated geographically, not only in the poorer provinces but also in pockets of deprivation even in the better-off provinces. The heterogeneity across areas and the rising inequality across households make it all the more important for social welfare programs to target government assistance effectively to those in need, ensuring a minimum level of consumption while remaining consistent with the equity objective of redistributing some of the benefits of growth. Typical clientele for such assistance would consist of the poor, and especially the vulnerable among them—the disabled, the aged, children, and households headed by single women.

When measured against these broad objectives, the social welfare sector in Sri Lanka presents a decidedly mixed picture. On the one hand, a long history of countrywide programs for the poor and vulnerable have created an enabling environment and a consensus around such

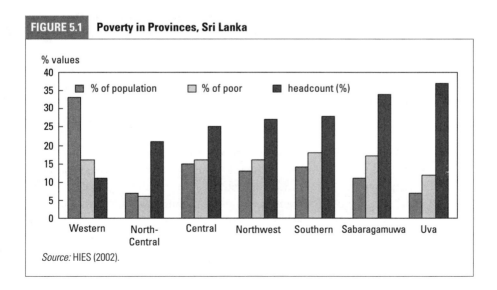

FIGURE 5.1 **Poverty in Provinces, Sri Lanka**

Source: HIES (2002).

programs; on the other hand, the effectiveness of these programs has been far below their potential because of inefficient targeting and inadequate coordination across programs.

A multitude of overlapping programs administered by a number of ministries constitutes the social welfare sector in Sri Lanka. Total expenditure for welfare programs is sizeable, amounting to an estimated 3.2 percent of GDP and 12.2 percent of total government expenditure in 2003. This expenditure is distributed among programs such as Samurdhi consumption grants to poor households, pensions to retired government personnel, fertilizer subsidy, expenditures on school uniforms and textbooks, payments to disabled soldiers, and dry rations to refugees.[2] A large share of social welfare programs is administered by the Ministry of Social Welfare, which targets the disadvantaged sections of society, and the Ministry of Samurdhi, which also subscribes to development objectives that go beyond that of a welfare/income support program.[3] The Samurdhi transfers program is the most significant of targeted welfare programs; expenditure on this program constitutes the second highest budget item in welfare spending (after pension payments to retired public servants). At its peak in 2002, expenditures of the Ministry of Samurdhi consumed close to 1 percent of GDP and 4 percent of the government budget.[4]

A review of expenditures of the Ministries of Samurdhi and Social Welfare reveals that more than two-thirds of the budgets of the two ministries are spent on direct transfers to households, although the stated objective of Samurdhi would suggest otherwise (see annex 5A). Together, the two ministries cover as much as half of the population of the country as beneficiaries. In the case of the Ministry of Samurdhi, the transfer goes into the payment of the Samurdhi consumption grant to poor households. In the case of the Ministry of Social Welfare, a large part of the transfer payments goes to disabled soldiers and families of soldiers killed in action (92 percent of transfers in 2003), leaving only a small share for other beneficiaries such as vulnerable children or those affected by natural disasters, disability, or old age.

There is little coordination between the ministries, with the result that there appears to be considerable overlap between the beneficiaries of their programs. Along with expenditures on transfers, the other significant category of recurrent spending is administrative costs, including payments on personal emoluments—especially for the Ministry of Samurdhi, which relies on a large cadre of staff to administer the program. The large salary bill of the Samurdhi program in particular constitutes a drain on the ministry and reduces the welfare impact of spending.[5]

Efficiency of welfare expenditure in terms of its impact can thus be enhanced by better rationalization between the programs of different ministries in terms of their stated objectives, target groups, and coverage of beneficiaries. Effectiveness of spending, it also appears, is adversely affected by large-scale errors in targeting beneficiaries. This is particularly the case for the Samurdhi program, which dominates the other transfer programs in terms of budget and coverage. A number of evaluations in the past have indicated serious flaws with the Samurdhi program that have led to significant mis-targeting, which has in turn led to a much-reduced impact. As described in the section on this program this is largely the result of employing highly subjective criteria for identifying house-holds eligible for Samurdhi benefits.

THE IMPETUS FOR WELFARE REFORM

The need for reforming the welfare system to achieve a better outcome for the considerable expenditure in this sector was identified as a high priority in its reform agenda by the government of Sri Lanka in its PRSP of 2003. This view has subsequently been shared by the World Bank's Country Assistance Strategy of 2003. Responding to this need, the new Welfare Benefit Act was enacted by the Sri Lankan Parliament on July 12, 2002. The purpose of the Act was to rationalize the legal and institutional framework of all social welfare programs, reduce politicization in the selection of beneficiaries of the program, and improve the targeting performance of the Samurdhi foodstamp program in particular. The passage of the Welfare Benefits Act was also one of the policy actions undertaken by the government as a part of its commitment to the reform program supported by the World Bank's budgetary support Poverty Reduction Support Credit-I (PRSC-I).

In order to implement the reform along the lines envisaged by the Welfare Benefits Act, in 2003 the government of Sri Lanka requested technical advice and assistance from the World Bank. Responding to this request, a Bank team has worked over the last two years in close collaboration with a team comprised of local officials and international consultant; a steering committee, comprised of senior officials from key ministries and statistical organizations, provided overall direction during the early stages of the process. The Welfare Benefits Board (WBB), set up according to the guidelines provided by the Act, has been the implementing agency for coordinating the exercise, including both the completed pilots and the actual implementation process that is currently underway in some parts of the country. Although the rationalization of the targeting and beneficiary selection across all welfare programs is the ultimate objective of this exercise, reforming the Samurdhi transfers program was identified as the first priority because it accounts for the bulk of spending on transfers (excluding payments to disabled soldiers and families of armed forces). Therefore the most substantive analysis of targeting has been conducted for this program.

In accordance with this priority, the PSIA examines the potential gains to be had in terms of impact on poverty and coverage of specially vulnerable groups—including households headed by widows and those with children, disabled people or the aged—by transforming the process of selection of beneficiaries from the current system that relies on subjective judgments by Samurdhi development officers to a system that applies a set of objective criteria to identify beneficiaries. The results of this exercise have been instrumental in designing the actual implementation of the reforms on the ground. Moreover, as described below, the results of ex ante analyses have been corroborated with the help of a pilot program that involved simulating the targeting exercise that is central to the reform and comparing those results with results from the ex ante simulations using household survey data.

THE SAMURDHI PROGRAM AND KEY PRINCIPLES OF THE REFORM

A recent evaluation conducted by the World Bank (2002) suggested that Samurdhi's targeted foodstamp and cash transfer program, which constitutes 80 percent of the total program budget, misses about 40 percent of households ranked in the poorest consumption quintile, while almost 44 percent of the total budget is spent on households from the top three quintiles Qualitative results suggest that political factors, including party affiliation or voting preferences, influence the allocation of Samurdhi grants. Large-scale leakage of benefits has led to the program covering as much as half of the population. The result is that the benefits are spread too thinly and the small size of transfers has little impact on poverty.[6] The high incidence of errors in targeting is also evident in the large discrepancies between the distribution of Samurdhi beneficiaries across districts (or provinces) with that of poor population across districts (or provinces) available from independent household surveys.[7] Thus it appears quite obvious that an improvement in targeting, by reducing leakage and exclusion, can potentially have a sizeable impact on poverty.

It is widely agreed that the errors of the current targeting of the Samurdhi program are related to a number of factors. Perhaps foremost among them is the way the program is administered. The criteria for selecting beneficiaries are stated as a combination of the income of a family and the number of family members; how these criteria are applied is left completely in the hands of the program officers. Since income is generally unobservable and almost impossible to corroborate, this results in a process of selection that depends entirely on the subjective judgment of the program officers. Identifying beneficiaries is left to the program officers (more than 22,000 in number), without any process of community validation or any community-based mechanism for redressing grievances or monitoring entry into and exit from the program. This results in a process that is inherently nontransparent to beneficiaries and nonbeneficiaries alike. It is also a process that is vulnerable to political capture and patronage.

There are a number of other factors that further distort the outcomes of this program. The fact that it targets by "families," rather than the more easily identifiable and objective concept of a "household," provides incentives for households to split themselves into families to obtain multiple payments. There is little or no monitoring of the status of beneficiaries, with the result that once a family enters into the program, there is no transparent or easily enforceable way of "graduating" the family out of the program. Exit from the program, therefore, when it occurs, is imposed rather arbitrarily on families—usually as a result of budget cuts that compel the Ministry of Samurdhi and Poverty Alleviation to eliminate a certain number of beneficiaries from the program without a clear set of criteria for doing so (this occurred in 2003 when the Samurdhi budget was reduced). There are no formal mechanisms for lodging appeals or redressing grievances, which adds to the nontransparent nature of the selection process.

The problems with the current Samurdhi system extend to the processes governing the payments of benefits. A large number of beneficiary families actually end up getting little or no transfers in effect, primarily because a "forced saving" component (and smaller compulsory contributions for social insurance and a housing lottery) is held back and deposited in Samurdhi banking societies in the beneficiaries' names. Assessments have shown that the beneficiaries have restricted access to these "savings," and in many cases even lack the knowledge of how much savings have accumulated in their accounts. Because the Samurdhi transfers are intended to provide support to augment the consumption of poor families, there seems to be little justification for the forced deductions for savings and other purposes; there is even less when the savings are not readily available when needed, as appears often to be the case.

The Welfare Benefits Act that set the parameters of the reform seeks to address the key structural deficiencies of the Samurdhi program summarized above. Specifically, the Act mandates an independent WBB and lower-level committees to set eligibility criteria, validate entry and exit into the program, and redress appeals. The Act also envisages setting objective criteria for selecting beneficiaries to minimize the level of subjectivity in the selection process and lend the process greater transparency. The institutional separation between the selection of beneficiaries and the payment of benefits—with the WBB undertaking the former task and the Ministry of Samurdhi having the responsibility for the latter—is intended to reduce the incentives for distortion of the selection process. The role of the WBB also includes monitoring entry into and exit out of the program through periodic collection of data, and setting the rules for redressing grievances through an appeals process. The actual operation of the appeals process will be managed by village or Grama Niladhari (GN) division level committees.

Although the Act sets the broad institutional parameters of the reform, it is in the process of operationalizing these broad principles that many of the other problems of the Samurdhi program can be addressed. In the course of describing the PSIA exercise below, some of the most important features of the operational design of the reform will be highlighted. This will help understand how the reforms address the multiple shortcomings of the current program—which are indeed critical for realizing its potential benefits—and also point to potential areas of risks in implementation on the ground.

REFORMS AND THE ROLE OF THE PSIA: THE CURRENT STATUS

After the national elections and the subsequent change in government in March 2004, the momentum for reform has slowed, largely because of the inherent political difficulties in reforming a program that provides handouts to a large number of people. At the same time, an effort is currently underway, led by the WBB in collaboration with the Ministry of Samurdhi, to extend the Samurdhi program to the conflict-affected areas of the North and East. This represents the first-ever attempt to integrate the North and East into a national safety net program. Encouragingly, the government has decided to adopt the formula-based targeting system that constitutes the crux of the proposed Samurdhi reform in these areas. Although implementation of this system has begun in the North and East, it is still unclear when a similar effort will be extended to the South, where additional political difficulty arises from the need to transform an entrenched system.

Successful realization of the program in the North and East will demonstrate the benefits from such a program when implemented properly, which may in turn provide a fillip to the prospects of a similar system to be adopted in the rest of the country. Furthermore, because the government is still in the process of deciding whether to extend the reform to the South, the PSIA exercise takes on an added role. By clearly identifying the impact on poverty and the distributional implications of the reform, results from the PSIA could play inform the government's decision-making process as well as the World Bank's policy dialogue with the government on this key reform agenda.

The role of the PSIA in moving the reform agenda forward has assumed added importance because of the challenges facing the welfare system of Sri Lanka in the aftermath of the tsunami of 2005. As a part of its post-tsunami recovery program, the government introduced a cash grant program in the affected areas. This program is supported by the Bank's emergency assistance project, and the Tsunami Emergency Reconstruction Project is intended to be a short-term livelihood support to the worst-affected households. But as the program winds down, as it is expected to by June 2005, there will be a need to integrate the most vulnerable among the affected, who will need continuing support, into the existing welfare system. The potential entry of this vulnerable population will represent an additional challenge to the current Samurdhi system in terms of budgetary needs as well as the institutional capacity to identify and target such households. Addressing this challenge will become much easier if the Samurdhi reform is implemented: the reform would increase the efficiency of spending or targeting, and it would put into place a targeting mechanism that is able to objectively identify beneficiaries and track and monitor entry and exit into the program.

DESIGN OF THE PSIA

As mentioned above, the PSIA for Welfare Reforms in Sri Lanka has evolved out of the technical support to the government by the Bank team over the past two years; it is therefore, in large part, the product of joint work undertaken by the Bank team and their counterparts on the government side. The PSIA exercise incorporates the following components, all of which were also central to the process of designing the reform and building institutional capacity necessary for implementation.

Technical Analysis Based on Household Data

The objective of this exercise is threefold. First, it is intended to develop an objective set of criteria to identify beneficiaries of the Samurdhi program through an econometric exercise for deriving a viable proxy means test formula (PMTF). In principle, conducting a direct "means test" that correctly measures the earnings of a household is the best way to determine eligibility when the poor are the target group, as is the case with Samurdhi. In practice, however, such straightforward means tests suffer from several problems, the most important being that verifying incomes of households is very difficult in developing countries where reliable income records do not exist. Thus the idea of using a PMTF that avoids the problems involved in relying on reported income is appealing.

A PMTF involves using information about household or individual characteristics correlated with welfare levels in a formal algorithm to proxy household income or welfare. These instruments are selected based on their ability to predict welfare as measured by, for example, consumption expenditure of households. The obvious advantage of proxy means testing is that good predictors of welfare—such as demographic data, characteristics of dwelling units, and ownership of durable assets—are likely to be easier to collect and verify than are direct measures such as consumption or income.[8] For these reasons, which have led to PMTFs being widely used around the world for targeting safety net programs, the steering committee set up by the government of Sri Lanka to guide the technical aspects of the reform process decided to adopt a PMTF to identify the target group for Samurdhi benefits.

Specifically, a PMTF is derived using a regression of the measure of welfare (in this case per capita household consumption) on a set of welfare predictors to identify the set of predictors that are (1) best able to "predict" the actual welfare of households, and (2) easy to observe among households, and conversely difficult for households to distort. Once a PMTF is derived, in order for it to be applied, information on the welfare predictors must be collected from all applicant households using a simple application form. For every applicant household, the collected information is used to compute a PMTF "score," which is then used to accept or reject the household from the program based on a pre-decided selection "cutoff" score.

Second, once the PMTF is derived from a regression exercise using suitable household survey data, recommendations can be made (1) on the cutoff point in terms of the score computed by the PMTF that defines the target group, which in turn determines what proportion of the population is targeted; and (2) on appropriate payment schemes that optimize impact on welfare and take into account distributional concerns *within* the target group, for a given budget constraint. These in turn make it possible to ex ante simulate the impact of targeting by the PMTF (with the selected cutoff and payment scheme) on targeting accuracy, the distribution of beneficiaries across income/consumption groups and the consequent impact on selected poverty measures, and coverage of vulnerable groups of interest, relative to the existing system employed by the Samurdhi program.[9]

Third, the above ex ante simulation exercise using household data can also be used to identify the implications of different budgetary allocations for the program, by clearly measuring the outcomes or impacts corresponding to different levels of allocation.[10]

Corroboration from a Pilot

In order to validate the results of the simulations using household sample survey data, the Welfare Benefit Board conducted a pilot targeting survey covering 48,000 households in 114 GN divisions. The pilot's primary objective was to test the proxy means–tested application process for selection of beneficiaries of the Samurdhi program, using an application form that collects information on all household characteristics that constitute the welfare predictors of the PMTF. The results from applying the PMTF to the pilot data were compared with the results predicted by simulations using household data. Final results from this analysis were used to fine-tune the selection cutoff and to adjust the criteria for selection, to correct for shortcomings of the PMTF in certain cases. Finally, for a subsample of pilot GN divisions, a field validation exercise was conducted. In this exercise, the list of households selected as eligible by applying the PMTF was validated through visits to households and consultations with community elders and GN-level officials. The objective of this exercise was to gauge how far the identification of eligible households using the formula resonates with the perceptions of poverty held by local inhabitants.

The results and insights from the pilot—on technical aspects of using the PMTF as well as on the application process and design of application forms—constituted a key input into the PSIA of the reform, which in turn influenced the design of the reform. By allowing corroboration of the ex ante simulations with results from an actual application process along key dimensions—such as coverage rates among the population, among specific vulnerable groups, and in areas with special characteristics such as those affected by conflict—the pilot greatly enhances the reliability of the analysis to identify the poverty and distributional impact of welfare reform.

Consultations with Stakeholders

Another key element of the PSIA exercise—and more broadly, the entire process of supporting the reform—was the consultations with stakeholders.

Formal forums for consultation consisted of two workshops with wide participation that were conducted at different phases of the pilot exercise. These workshops were supplemented with many consultations and field visits with local Samurdhi officers and program beneficiaries, as well as with regular meetings and brainstorming sessions with the steering committee and the WBB. Consultations with stakeholders were thus not limited to the formal setting of organized workshops, but instead they took the form of an evolving partnership with the drivers of the reform, the ministries involved in implementing the program, and technical experts from the central bank and the Department of Census & Statistics (DCS).

To understand the process of consultations, it is useful to start with the institutional setup to support and implement the reform. At the onset of the process, a steering committee was set up to provide direction to the process. This committee included representation from relevant line ministries (Samurdhi, Social Welfare) and senior officials from the Treasury Department, the Central Bank of Sri Lanka, and the DCS. The committee was assisted by a small group of technical staff, working in partnership with the World Bank team and two international consultants—one with extensive experience in the implementation of safety net programs, and the other with experience in management information systems (MIS), required to administer and monitor such programs.

The steering committee's role was to coordinate across all stakeholder departments and facilitate (with policy decisions as necessary) the work needed to develop the PMTF and to design and implement the pilot. The committee also coordinated the process of wider consultation with insights from the pilot and developed an MIS for program management and monitoring. Much of the work that forms the core of the PSIA described here—the econometric work used to derive the PMTF, the subsequent analysis of impact using household data along the dimensions described above, and the analysis of the pilot data—was conducted jointly by the World Bank team with local statisticians and other technical staff appointed by the steering committee. With time, as the WBB was constituted as a formal body in accordance with the guidelines of the Act, it gradually adopted the role of overseeing and facilitating the work and coordinating across different line ministries, while the steering committee adopted the role of providing guidance on technical issues.

Consultations with the results and insights from the pilot were held in two workshops organized jointly by the WBB and the Ministry of Samurdhi. The first workshop was held just after the fieldwork for the pilot was completed. This workshop focused on learning from the experiences of field staff who invited applications from households and suggested solutions for logistical problems.

The second workshop was held after the pilot analysis was complete, and enjoyed wide participation from all relevant line ministries and departments as well as administration officials of some districts and field-based program staff. The objective for this workshop was to discuss the implications of the pilot results and identify ways forward. A number of issues surrounding key policy recommendations were considered, among them:

- the eligibility cutoffs and size of the target group,
- the schedule of benefits (how benefits are determined, and whether they should depend on household characteristics),
- the kind of benefits (for example, whether benefits should be in the form of cash, checks, or foodstamps),
- the modalities of payment (whether payment should by through commercial banks, Samurdhi banking societies, or post offices), and
- the critical question of whether forced savings and the provision of microcredit should be linked to the cash transfers program as they are currently.

The workshop participants also focused on the question of how the targeting method and application form should be modified for conflict-affected areas of the country. This discussion benefited greatly from the active participation of experienced government officials from those parts of the country.

As the next section will elaborate, the discussions and feedback from the workshop were instrumental in formulating the final targeting criteria and schedule of benefits, particularly in the context of certain special cases where the PSIA showed that applying the PMTF directly may lead to higher rates of error. These adjustments were made in specific cases such as small households, households with certain categories of vulnerable members, and conflict-affected areas.

In the section that follows, the main results of the PSIA, drawing from the different components described above, are elaborated.

RESULTS FROM THE POVERTY AND SOCIAL IMPACT ANALYSIS

As apparent from the description above, the technical analyses of the poverty and social impact of welfare reform are built around the econometric exercise for deriving the PMTF for targeting Samurdhi. A discussion of the main findings of the analyses must therefore be preceded by a description of the PMTF exercise, which will then lead to the results from the simulation exercises using household survey data and the results from the pilot data.

Developing a PMTF for Sri Lanka

The PMTF exercise involves defining an indicator for welfare of a household—which in this case was chosen to be monthly per capita household consumption expenditure—and then identifying a set of easily observable variables or predictors that together serve as the best proxy for the welfare indicator.[11] To derive the PMTF, the consumption variable is regressed using the ordinary least squares (OLS) method on different sets of explanatory variables. The case for using OLS to predict welfare is driven primarily by convenience and ease of interpretation. The OLS method is especially convenient when a large numbers of predictor variables (including continuous variables) are available; and it is amenable to intuitive interpretation of the coefficients of the welfare predictors, making it easily understandable to a policymaker (see annex 5C for further discussion).

The primary source of data for the PMTF exercise was the Sri Lanka Integrated Survey (SLIS), conducted by the World Bank in collaboration with local institutions in 1999–2000 and designed to be representative of all of Sri Lanka at the national and provincial levels. However, because of the conflict in the North and East at the time, the sample from those areas did not turn out to be reliable. Thus, for the purpose of this exercise, the North and East sample was excluded, leaving a sample of around 5,600 households, which by design is representative for the country excluding the North and East (using sample weights). By all accounts, the SLIS appears to be well suited to the developing the PMTF. Being a multitopic household survey in the style of a Living Standard Measurement Survey, it has rich and detailed information on most correlates of poverty, along with information on the benefits received from the existing Samurdhi program. At the time of the exercise, the SLIS was also the most recent source of representative household data available for Sri Lanka. Exclusion of the North and East, while unfortunate, should be seen in the context that no survey has managed to cover the region during the past decade of conflict.

Identifying potential variables to predict welfare considered two separate criteria:

1. correlation between the measure of welfare and the predictor, which will determine accuracy of the prediction, and

2. verifiability of the predictor, which will determine the accuracy of information used to impute welfare.

There is often a tradeoff between these two criteria, so a certain amount of subjective judgment is required in the final choice of the model. The types of predictors used for this exercise fall into the following broad categories:

- location variables,
- community characteristics,
- housing quality,
- household characteristics,
- ownership of durable goods or farm equipment, and
- ownership of productive assets (including land).[12]

Very briefly, the steps for arriving at the PMTF run as follows. After identifying the original set of potential variables belonging to the six broad categories, the set of selected predictors are introduced in a weighted OLS regression of (log of) per capita monthly consumption expenditure. Different subsets of variables are checked for possible multicollinearity, and adjustments made accordingly. A stepwise regression is then used with the remaining set of variables to eliminate variables that are not statistically significant and do not increase the model's overall explanatory power. Through this process, different models evolve based on the subset of variables entering into the regression, which are evaluated against each other to decide on the final model for the PMTF.

Determining Eligibility by Using PMTF

Each model predicts a certain level of welfare, as measured by (log of) per capita monthly consumption expenditure. These predicted welfare levels are used to assign individuals to eligible or ineligible groups, based on an eligibility cutoff point. The eligibility cutoff point is determined by the welfare level of a certain percentile of the individual welfare distribution, using "true" welfare as measured by actual per capita consumption. For the purpose of analysis, a range of cutoff points were considered, defined by specific percentiles of actual or true per capita consumption expenditures (e.g., 25th, 30th, 40th). The eligible group identified by the PMTF constitutes all households whose predicted consumption (or PMTF score) falls below the cutoff point.

It is important to note that the selection of the cutoff point is a policy decision, not a technical one—a decision that depends on the proportion of the population that the government would like to target with the program. The role of the analysis was to inform this decision by simulating a wide range of scenarios that correspond to different cutoff points for the selected model. In this context, the analysis had two objectives: first, to show the sensitivity of the model and its attendant errors in targeting to changes in cutoff points; and second, to help the government decide what the cutoff point should be, taking into account the tradeoffs inherent in choosing a relatively higher cutoff vis-à-vis a low one.[13]

Evaluating a Targeting Formula

As with all regression analyses, different specifications of the model and different samples of the population yield different results; it is not always easy to determine which specification is superior. However, a variety of tests can be conducted that, taken together, can be used to select one model over another, as well as to compare the selected model with the current targeting of Samurdhi. The first criterion, used to evaluate alternate options for the PMTF, is the regression's R^2, which is the proportion of the variation in consumption that is explained by the regression model. The higher the R^2, the better a particular set of variables is in predicting welfare.

The second criterion involves looking at measures that indicate the ability of various models, and the existing Samurdhi system, to identify the poor properly. Following standard practice with PMTFs, targeting accuracy is evaluated using Type I and II errors from which rates of undercoverage and leakage are derived, and incidence of benefits across consumption groups.[14] To apply this criterion, it is important to clarify certain concepts. The target population is defined as a group of individuals whose actual per capita consumption expenditure is below a selected threshold (*a poverty line*), while the eligible population comprises individuals whose PMTF score is below the selected *cutoff point for eligibility*. A Type I error, or error of exclusion, refers to an individual incorrectly excluded by the formula (i.e., an individual who belongs to the target group but not the eligible group). A Type II error, or error of inclusion, refers to a person incorrectly identified as being eligible (i.e., an indivdual who belongs to the eligible group and not the target group). The *undercoverage rate* is calculated by dividing the number of Type I errors by the size of the target group. The *leakage rate* is calculated by dividing the number of Type II errors by the size of the eligible group. Undercoverage reduces the impact of the program on the welfare level of the intended beneficiaries, but carries no budgetary cost. Leakage increases program costs and can also be welfare reducing in the presence of a budget constraint: the higher the leakage of benefits to the nondeserving, the lower the amount available for transfers to those who truly deserve.

It is worth noting that undercoverage and leakage rates are useful in evaluating targeting accuracy *only* if the targeted population and the eligible population are defined consistently. It is easy to see that for a given target group, as the eligible group expands (i.e., as the eligibility cutoff is raised), undercoverage falls while leakage increases; conversely, as the eligible group shrinks, undercoverage increases and leakage falls.[15] This represents the tradeoff between undercoverage and leakage for a given target group, as the eligibility cutoff is shifted.

For the sake of simplicity and to ensure consistency for comparison, the analyses presented here are for cases where eligibility cutoff is held to be *identical* to the threshold that defines the target population. These cases turn out to be enough to highlight the main results. Note that when these two lines move together, raising the eligibility cutoff (and thus also the "poverty line" or threshold that defines the target group) would lead to lower undercoverage and leakage, simply because the "burden" on the formula to accurately predict welfare is reduced. Given the program's budget constraint, these adjustments come at the cost of reducing the amount available for each beneficiary, which has important welfare implications, particularly for the poorest. This illustrates the key tradeoff that policymakers need to consider before deciding on the eligibility cutoff.

The last criterion to evaluate targeting efficiency is involves looking at how a specific PMTF allocates potential beneficiaries across the expenditure distribution. It is preferred that a model has good incidence—that is, most of the identified beneficiaries should belong to the bottom of the consumption distribution and relatively few, if any, to the top of the distribution.

Selecting a PMTF Model

A large number of specifications were tried out and evaluated according to the criteria described above. All specifications involve OLS regressions of (log of) per capita monthly consumption measured in Sri Lankan rupees on a set of predictors, with only those variables retained whose statistical significance is 80 percent or above. It was found that a model that includes province and rural/urban location dummies, along with a list of variables belonging to other categories as described above, yields the highest R^2 and the lowest rate of undercoverage and leakage for cutoffs

Table 5.2 Results from Different Models

Model	Undercoverage rate for different cutoff percentiles			Leakage rate for different cutoff percentiles			R^2
	25th	30th	40th	25th	30th	40th	
I. Full model	0.51	0.42	0.30	0.39	0.35	0.29	0.58
II. Restricted and excluding province dummies	0.52	0.43	0.28	0.39	0.36	0.31	0.56
III. Restricted and excluding province and rural/urban dummies	0.53	0.43	0.28	0.39	0.35	0.31	0.56

Source: Staff estimation based on SLIS (1999–2000).
Note: The 25th, 30th, 35th, and 40th percentiles of actual consumption amount to SR Rs 1129, 1201, 1270, and 1347 monthly per capita (at 2000 prices) respectively. The target group in every case is defined by the cutoff point for the eligible group—that is, when the cutoff is the 30th percentile of consumption, the target group is the bottom 30 percent of the population by consumption.

set at 25th, 30th, and 40th percentiles of actual per capita consumption (model I in table 5.2).[16] However, for a number of reasons, it would have been difficult to incorporate province-specific and rural/urban location variables into the final PMTF: not only would this test the limits of what is politically acceptable, but the census definitions for rural/urban sectors are out of date and do not conform to people's perceptions. Moreover, it made sense to restrict the set of predictors further—to reduce the information burden in applying the PMTF—as long as this restriction did not lead to significant increases in targeting errors.

Dropping the province and rural/urban location dummies and retaining only the set of highly significant variables (those with a significance level of 99 percent or higher) did not lead to an appreciable change in the results. This is seen from comparing models I and III in table 5.2. More disaggregated analysis also showed that, although model I yields aggregate results that are slightly superior, the undercoverage rate varies widely across provinces. This is problematic. Eliminating province weights from the PMTF, as in models II and III, reduces such variations considerably. Similarly, a comparison between models II and III in table 5.2 shows that excluding the rural/urban location variable leads to little or no change in targeting errors and R^2. Analysis disaggregated by sectors also showed that III has lower undercoverage for urban areas than II, which results in a much smaller gap in undercoverage rates between rural and urban areas—a feature that is appealing to policymakers.[17]

Model III was thus the final choice for the PMTF (for a concise description of pros and cons of each model, see annex 5C). The set of predictors with appropriate weights comprised:

- community characteristics (presence of a bank or divisional headquarters in the community);
- household assets (consumer nondurables, farm equipment);
- household's ownership of land and livestock;
- characteristics of household head (age, education, main activity, marital status);
- household demographics (household size, whether all children attend school); and
- housing characteristics (owned housing or not, type of wall and latrine, ratio of rooms to number of household members).

The results of model III compare well with those from similar exercises conducted for other countries. For an eligibility cutoff equal to the 30th percentile of actual per capita consumption, model III yields an undercoverage rate of 43 percent and a leakage rate of 35 percent. For the same cutoff in percentile terms, a similar exercise using Jamaica data for 1989 yields undercoverage and leakage rates of around 41 and 34 percent respectively; and using data for 2000, the rates are 69 and 44 percent. The corresponding rates are 39 percent and 24 percent for urban Bolivia, and 54 and 35 percent for urban Peru (1990 data for both cases).

Model III, the selected PMTF, is presented in detail in annex 5A, (along with the closest alternative, model II). Both models are based on the regression results listed in table 5A.2. The formula is more likely to assign benefits to larger households; households where all children do not go to school; households with few durable goods and amenities, little land and livestock, and poor housing; households with older heads; and where the head is a female widow, has lower levels of education, and does not work as a salaried employee. The weights thus seem to be appropriate in terms of increasing the chance of households that are more likely to be poor or with vulnerable members to be selected.

To check whether the methodology used for the estimation can be improved in terms of impact on targeting efficiency, two alternative methods of estimating the PMTF were explored. Both involve using a subset of the sample for estimation (see details in annex 5C). These exercises did not yield results that were significantly better in terms of targeting outcomes, nor did they yield insights that would introduce doubt about the robustness of the selected model and its predictions.

As an additional cross-check, in parallel with the estimation exercise using SLIS, a similar exercise was conducted using the Consumer Finance and Socio-Economic Survey (CFSES) (1996–7) dataset of the Central Bank of Sri Lanka. This exercise yielded a PMTF that confirmed the main characteristics of the model developed using SLIS, confirming the suitability of the selected model. At the same time, the SLIS-based model was found to outperform the CFSES-based one on the pilot data, primarily because the CFSES had less information on poverty predictors and was an older survey. This is a particularly important reason why the CFSES of 1996–97 was not the ideal data source for this exercise: consumption patterns had changed over the years that have elapsed, a change that in turn reduced the reliability of many of the welfare predictors, especially those related to the ownership of household durable goods.

Implementing the PMTF on Targeting Efficiency: Ex Ante Results

One of the important questions to address is how the new selection criteria based on the PMTF compare with the current Samurdhi program in identifying the poor. Tables 5.3 and 5.4 illustrate how undercoverage and leakage rates of the selected PMTF and the current Samurdhi program vary as the cutoff line (equal to the threshold to define the target group) increases from 25th percentile to 40th percentile of actual per capita consumption expenditure distribution.[18]

A fair comparison between the PMTF and the current Samurdhi program can be conducted only for a cutoff set at the 40th percentile of the actual per capita consumption expenditure, which implies that the targeted population is the bottom 40 percent of consumption distribution and that program coverage is around 40 percent.[19] The choice of the 40th percentile for the threshold is justifiable for two reasons. First, coverage of the current Samurdhi program is around

Table 5.3 Undercoverage Rates

	Total			Rural			Urban		
Cutoff[a] →	25	30	40	25	30	40	25	30	40
PMTF	0.53	0.43	0.28	0.51	0.42	0.27	0.67	0.53	0.35
Samurdhi	n.a.	n.a.	0.42	n.a.	n.a.	0.40	n.a.	n.a.	0.62

Source: Staff estimation based on SLIS (1999–2000).

Note: n.a. denotes not applicable, since the current Samurdhi covers 40 percent of the population. All point estimates have a standard error; for confidence intervals and standard errors of undercoverage and leakage using PMTF, see annex table 5A.3.

a. *Cutoff* indicates a percentile of the actual per capita consumption expenditure distribution.

Table 5.4 Leakage Rates

Cutoff[a] →	Total			Rural			Urban		
	25	30	40	25	30	40	25	30	40
PMTF	0.39	0.35	0.31	0.39	0.35	0.30	0.47	0.38	0.36
Samurdhi	n.a.	n.a.	0.43	n.a.	n.a.	0.42	n.a.	n.a.	0.57

Source: SLIS (1999–2000).
Note: n.a. denotes not applicable, since the current Samurdhi covers 40 percent of the population. All point estimates have a standard error; for confidence intervals and standard errors of undercoverage and leakage using PMTF, see annex table 5A.3.
a. *Cutoff* indicates a percentile of the actual per capita consumption expenditure distribution.

40 percent of entire population. Second, given Samurdhi's coverage of 40 percent and its clear intention to cover the poorest section of the population, the assumption that the targeted population is the poorest 40 percent of the consumption expenditure distribution is perfectly reasonable.

When the 40th percentile is chosen as the threshold, both undercoverage and leakage rates of the PMTF are found to be *substantially lower* than those of the current Samurdhi program—both nationally and separately for urban and rural sectors. The difference in undercoverage rate is 14 percentage points nationally and in leakage is 12 percentage points; the gaps are much higher for urban areas. These results indicate that replacing the current Samurdhi selection criteria with the PMTF would significantly improve targeting accuracy.

However, given the existing budget constraints, having a safety net program intended to target the poor cover 40 percent of the population seems excessive. A cutoff equal to the 30th percentile of actual per capita consumption expenditure appears to be more reasonable in terms of program coverage (program coverage of around 27 percent of the population is predicted), while ensuring tolerable levels of undercoverage and leakage. This was the recommendation for eligibility cutoff presented by the technical team at the workshop, and it was accepted by the policymakers and other workshop participants.

Interestingly, the targeting errors from using the PMTF for a cutoff at the 30th percentile is superior to those of the current Samurdhi *even* when the cutoff is set at the 40th percentile (see tables 5.3 and 5.4). Undercoverage rates are very close for the two cases, and leakage rates are higher by 8 percentage points for Samurdhi. Even when the target and eligible groups for the Samurdhi program are allowed to be larger than that of the PMTF, which should naturally lead to lower targeting errors for the former, the PMTF comes out as clearly superior. Moreover, this gain is *just* on the dimension of targeting efficiency. It does not account for the welfare gains arising from the larger benefits received by the beneficiaries under the PMTF regime.

The last measure for evaluating the targeting efficiency of the PMTF is the incidence of coverage across the distribution of actual per capita consumption expenditure (table 5.5). Again, a fair comparison with the current Samurdhi would be for the 40th percentile as the cutoff line and the threshold for defining the target group. If the PMTF is used to select beneficiaries with the cutoff at the 40th percentile, more than 20 percent of population in the poorest decile and 15 percent of the 2nd decile will be added as beneficiaries, while the proportion of coverage of the top 3 deciles will be reduced by between 5 and 13 percent. Even when the cutoff point is set at the recommended 30th percentile level for the PMTF, the coverage of the bottom decile is significantly higher than that for Samurdhi, and leakage to the richest 30 percent of population is dramatically reduced in comparison with the current Samurdhi program.[20]

Table 5.5 also shows that targeting using the PMTF, regardless of which eligibility cutoff is used, is highly progressive. This is consistent with the distributional objectives of an income transfer program. Moreover, as shown in figure 5.2, the degree of progressiveness in coverage is much higher for the PMTF, for either eligibility cutoff, than that for the current Samurdhi.

Table 5.5 Incidence of Benefits by per Capita Consumption Deciles

Cutoff line[a] decile	40th percentile		30th percentile PMTF
	PMTF	Samurdhi	
1	0.91	0.69	0.76
2	0.75	0.60	0.55
3	0.69	0.54	0.45
4	0.55	0.49	0.30
5	0.47	0.47	0.27
6	0.34	0.43	0.19
7	0.24	0.36	0.13
8	0.16	0.25	0.07
9	0.05	0.18	0.02
10	0.01	0.06	0.00
Total coverage	0.42	0.41	0.27

Source: SLIS (1999–2000).
a. Numbers in the cutoff line denote a percentile of the *actual* per capita consumption expenditure distribution.

FIGURE 5.2 **Incidence of Benefits by Consumption Deciles**

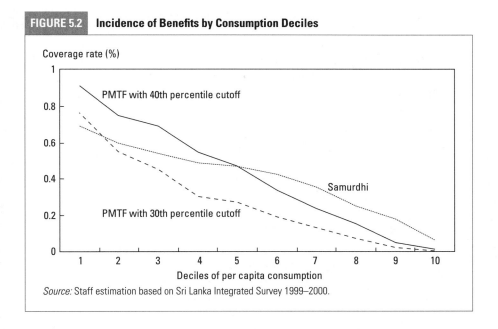

Source: Staff estimation based on Sri Lanka Integrated Survey 1999–2000.

These results also indicate which segments of the population (distributed by consumption) will gain from the PMTF regime, and, conversely, which will lose—just in terms of the proportion of individuals receiving benefits. The biggest winners will obviously be the poorest group—the bottom decile—whose coverage will increase by 7 percentage points after reform. Clearly the richest groups will lose the most, with the proportion of individuals in the top 4 deciles who receive benefits expected to fall from 21 percent pre-reform to less than 6 percent post-reform. The reduction in coverage will be less for the middle group (4th to 6th deciles), from 46 percent pre-reform to 25 percent post-reform; and it will be almost negligible for the bottom 3 deciles, from 61 percent covered pre-reform to 59 percent covered post-reform.

These statistics, however, do not reflect the full extent of gains and losses for each group, since they *do not* take into account the changes in amounts received. One of the important benefits from the reform is expected to be the significant increase in transfers for those selected by the PMTF, since the same budget is now being distributed among 27 percent of the population (and not 41 percent as under the current Samurdhi). The next section attempts to quantify the net welfare gains from the reform, using an appropriate distribution-sensitive welfare measure.

Selecting a Payment Scheme for Eligible Individuals

So far we have examined the PMTF exclusively from the point of view of targeting efficiency. A related and equally important question is how to set the amounts for benefits to eligible beneficiaries for the selected eligibility cutoff (equal to 30th percentile of actual per capita consumption). The challenge is to identify a payment scheme that maximizes the welfare objectives of the program.

It is necessary first to define appropriate welfare measure(s) that represent the program's main objectives. Although Samurdhi's objective is to reduce consumption poverty of the beneficiaries, the simplest measures of poverty—such as headcount poverty or the poverty gap—do not take into account the *distribution* of transfers among the poor. Therefore, to evaluate the welfare impact of different payment schemes, we consider Sen's poverty index and squared poverty gap. Both these measures reward progressiveness in distribution of benefits—that is, they both register an increase in welfare when the marginal rupee goes to the neediest.

For operational purposes, the feasibility of a payment scheme is as important as its welfare implication. The most ideal payment scheme from the point of view of distributional impact also turns out to be almost impossible to implement.[21] Moreover, analysis also shows that the welfare levels attained by the "ideal" redistributive scheme are achievable to a large extent by employing simpler schemes—for example, one that provides each eligible household a sum comprised of two components: a *fixed* component that is to the same for all eligible households, and a *variable* component that has a fixed amount per member or appropriately defined subsets of members so that it varies by the number of members in the household. Within this class of payment schemes, the most appealing to policymakers and stakeholders was the scheme where the variable amount was defined *per vulnerable member* of the household, where the vulnerable are defined as children aged between 0 and 15, elderly aged 66 and above, and those who are disabled or permanently ill.

Such a payment scheme is easy to justify since such individuals cannot, or should not, earn income for the household, and they are also the ones most affected by shocks to the livelihood of the household. Such a scheme turns out to be progressive because of the high correlation between the ranking of households by consumption and the number of such vulnerable individuals in the household. Moreover, such a scheme is not difficult to implement with a well-designed MIS. Creating such a database has been an important part of building institutional capacity for implementing the reform.

Optimal Payment Scheme: Impact on Welfare and Benefit Incidence

The next step is to find the optimum value of parameters a and b for a monthly payment level of $(a + bX_k)$ to household k, where a is the fixed component, b is the payment per vulnerable member, and X is the number of vulnerable members in household k, subject to a budget constraint (equal to the recent annual budget for Samurdhi transfers). This payment scheme also allows for a high degree of flexibility in choice, since varying degrees of progressiveness can be induced by selecting different levels for a and b.[22]

The search for an optimal combination of (a, b) was conducted using simulations from SLIS (1999–2000) data, taking Sen's index and squared poverty gap as the relevant aggregate welfare measures. Two other features of the analysis are important:

■ First, the simulations attempt to measure the impact of *replacing* the existing system of payments with a new one.
■ Second, the budget for the program was taken as SL Rs 9 billion at 2004 prices (the budgetary allocation for 2004), adjusted to 1999–2000 figures by appropriate inflation rates.

The simulations reveal $(a, b) = (80, 197)$ in 1999 Sri Lankan rupees, or (115, 284) in 2004 Sri Lankan rupees, to be the most desirable payment scheme—that is, one for which both Sen's index and squared poverty gap are minimized. Furthermore, for this payment scheme, around 15 and 17 percent reduction is achieved in Sen's index and squared poverty gap respectively compared with the existing Samurdhi scheme. The existing scheme represents the aggregate welfare impact of the reform, when the optimum level of payments are implemented.[23]

Using the above optimum payment scheme, simulations on SLIS show the incidence of benefits to be far more progressive than they are under the existing Samurdhi scheme. This is reflected by the amount of benefits per capita per month for every decile (annex table 5A.5), as well as the share of every decile in the total amount of benefits (table 5.6). As table 5.6 shows, the share of benefits for the bottom 3 deciles under PMTF is much higher—and conversely the share of top 3 deciles is much lower—than it is under the existing Samurdhi. Although there is little progressiveness in the distribution of benefits under the current scheme (share of benefits is almost the same for the lower 8 deciles), the PMTF optimal payment scheme implies that the share of benefits declines progressively for higher deciles of per capita consumption. These results show clearly that, in terms of benefits received, the winners from this reform will be poorest 40 percent of the population, at the cost of losses

Table 5.6 Incidence of Payments
percent

Decile	PMTF[a] (optimal payments)	Samurdhi[b]
1	25.4	10.9
2	20.3	11.8
3	17.2	12.0
4	12.2	11.6
5	11.5	13.0
6	6.4	11.8
7	4.1	10.9
8	2.0	9.0
9	0.8	6.5
10	0.2	2.6
Total	100	100

Source: Staff estimation based on SLIS (1999–2000).
a. The share of budget for each decile if beneficiaries are chosen by the PMTF and each household receives an amount given by the optimal payment scheme.
b. The share of Samurdhi budgets received by each decile.

suffered by the top 60 percent of the population, with the losses being especially large (100 percent or more) for the top 4 deciles.

As an *operational recommendation* for the program's payment scheme, the following ranges are prescribed: $a =$ (SL Rs 100–110) and $b =$ (SL Rs 270–280) at 2004 prices. Both the fixed and the variable components recommended are slightly lower than the optimal amounts to keep some budgetary margin. This is important because these simulations are rough calculations using a number of simplifying assumptions, and there may be hidden implementation costs.

It is also useful to reflect on the implications of changes in program budget for welfare. A reduction of budget from the current level of SL Rs 9 billion (at 2004 prices) would necessarily imply a decrease in either the number of beneficiaries or payment amounts. The analysis showed that current payment amounts are the minimum necessary to yield meaningful benefits. Any budget reduction would have to be accommodated by a reduction in the number of beneficiaries (lowering of cutoff point *below* the current level). This would lead to an increase in the error of exclusion and therefore a reduction in overall welfare. On the other hand, if there were an *increase* in the budget, significant welfare gains would be obtained by increasing the payment amounts while keeping the number of beneficiaries unchanged (maintaining the recommended cutoff point). Higher payment amounts to eligible households would ensure that beneficiaries are able to reach consumption levels closer to that of the poverty line.

Evaluating PMTF Using Data from the Targeting Pilot

The analysis so far has been limited to simulating impact on welfare by targeting efficiency and distribution using household survey data, a limitation like those for similar exercises in many countries. However, there are at least three important limitations on this type of analysis in the Sri Lankan context.

- First, since SLIS was conducted more than five years ago, it is important to ascertain whether the analysis applies to current patterns of household consumption.
- Second, it is an important policy question as to whether the information necessary for the PMTF will be reported accurately by households during an application process that is inherently different from the data collection for a household survey like SLIS.
- Third, SLIS is not appropriate for analyzing the targeting impacts of the PMTF at a more disaggregated level due to its limited sample size.

The pilot targeting exercise was conducted over 12 districts and 114 GN divisions, where each GN division was covered in its entirety, to simulate as far as possible the application process for the actual reform when it is implemented.[24] Enumerators distributed application forms to all households in selected GN divisions, explaining that the information collected could be used for selecting future welfare beneficiaries. The forms included variables for the PMTF. The household was left to decide whether or not to return the application form to the enumerator. In many cases, the enumerators helped the households to fill the forms; in most cases, the information was checked before the forms were accepted and signed by the Samurdhi Development Officer of the area.

The sample GN divisions were drawn by the DCS, based on criteria for selection of pilot areas developed jointly with the steering committee. The sample was not specifically designed to be statistically representative for the country, but since it was very large and distributed across different districts (see table 5A.5), it was expected that the results would largely reflect the country as a whole.

The pilot data address many of the limitations of SLIS data discussed above: they were recent, they simulated the expected real application process, and around 27,000 households filled out and sent back their application forms. Nevertheless, these data also have important limitations. First, they do not include per capita household consumption expenditures, making it impossible to compare actual consumption with consumption predicted by the PMTF (i.e., the PMTF score), and therefore it is impossible to measure undercoverage and leakage. Second, and most important, households in the pilot sample were self-selected, and around 45 percent of households did not return the application form. However, because of the way the pilot was conducted, it is reasonable to assume that nonrespondents are largely those who are well-off and not interested in receiving benefits from the welfare program. A comparison of the distribution of PMTF scores from the pilot with those from SLIS confirms that the universe of pilot respondents are poorer on the average than the survey sample (see annex figure 5A.2); it does not, however, rule out the possibility of some households who did not or could not fill the application even if they had wanted to participate in the program.

Among the numerous questions that can be addressed by the pilot data in conjunction with SLIS, three are considered most important from the perspective of a PSIA:

1. How does the coverage (percentage of population identified as beneficiaries) of the selected PMTF for different measure up to what was simulated from SLIS?
2. Does the PMTF discriminate against groups that are likely to be especially vulnerable?
3. What additional insights are available for the North and East, which was not included in the SLIS sample?

Aggregate Coverage of the PMTF

Addressing question 1 above serves as a basic check of the validity of the prediction of the simulations using household data. To compute coverage rates from the entire population of pilot GN divisions, it is assumed that not all nonrespondents would be eligible for the program even if they had turned in their application forms. This is reasonable in theory since the pilot sample is a self-selected sample of poorer households.

Coverage rates predicted from SLIS turn out to be reasonably close to the coverage rates from the pilot, especially if the cutoff scores are low. Table 5.7 shows that when the cutoff score is set at the 20th or the 25th percentile of actual consumption distribution, the coverage rate for pilot areas are within 1 to 2 percentage points of those predicted by SLIS. Although this gap expands for higher cutoff points, for the cutoff of 30th percentile the gap is still less than 3 percentage points, indicating that the SLIS predictions of coverage are not off the mark. For obvious reasons, the coverage rate is much higher among pilot households who *had* turned in their application forms.

Table 5.7 Applying the Selected PMTF to the Pilot Sample:
Program Coverage

Percentile of actual per capita consumption (SLIS)	Cutoff scores for PMTF	Coverage (%) predicted from SLIS	Coverage (%) from pilot GN divisions	
			NE	All pilot areas
20th	695	13.1	13.8	11.6
25th	703	21.0	22.1	18.5
30th	709	27.5	28.9	24.6
40th	721	43.5	43.0	37.0

Source: SLIS (1999–2000) and data set from the pilot (2003).
Note: Number of population in non-Northeast is census population in 2001. When calculating coverage, it is assumed that all nonrespondents would not have been eligible even if they had applied.

It is useful to explore why the difference between coverage rates predicted from SLIS and from the pilot increase as the cutoff rises. One plausible reason has to do with the assumption about the eligibility of the pilot nonrespondents described above. This assumption is less likely to be valid as the cutoff is raised, because most of the nonrespondents would be ineligible at the cutoff of 25th percentile even if they applied, whereas some of them may have been eligible when the cutoff is raised to the 40th percentile. If this is indeed the case, as the cutoff rises, there is likely to be an *underestimation* of true program coverage because of false exclusion of some nonrespondents. As a result, the difference between the two coverage rates should be expected to widen. This would imply that the pilot coverage rates should be referred to as the lower bound of expected program coverage.[25]

Thus the pilot results appear to be consistent with the expected coverage of the PMTF, which indirectly enhances credibility of other analyses (such as undercoverage and leakage rates) based on SLIS data.

Coverage of Vulnerable Groups

Whether the PMTF discriminates against certain vulnerable categories of people (question 2 above) is an important policy question, even in the face of satisfactory overall targeting. To examine this question, coverage rates of certain categories of households that are likely to be vulnerable— those with (a) disabled household heads, (b) those with single female household heads; (c) those with less than 1 acre of cultivable land, (d) those with the head of the household aged 70 or above, and (e) those with a very large number of members (7 or more)—are looked at.

Table 5.8 Coverage Rate for Likely Vulnerable Groups

Households	SLIS actual	SLIS PMTF	Pilot PMTF
a. Disabled head	0.37	0.34	0.43
b. Single female head	0.35	0.31	0.39
c. Land owned <1 acre	0.31	0.29	0.41
d. Age 70+ head	0.34	0.32	0.42
e. Household size 7+	0.49	0.58	0.75
General population	0.30	0.28	0.39

Source: SLIS (1999–2000) and data set from the pilot (2003).
Note: Eligibility cutoff is 30th percentile of actual per capita consumption.

Table 5.8 presents the results for these categories, but only for the recommended cutoff of 30th percentile. Deciding whether a vulnerable group of households is inadequately covered by the PMTF is easily answered by comparing coverage rates for each category with that of the general population (the shaded cells). The pilot coverage rates here refer to calculated coverage from the pilot data with no adjustment for nonrespondents, so that (as expected) coverage rates of the pilot sample are higher than those of the SLIS data for all categories of vulnerable households.

The results of table 5.8 do not indicate any bias in the PMTF against these likely vulnerable groups. Interestingly, the coverage from PMTF predictions in SLIS data is quite close to the target group defined by actual SLIS consumption data for all vulnerable categories except large households. For example, actual SLIS consumption data identifies 34 percent of individuals in households with disabled heads to be in the poorest 30 percent of the population, and the PMTF selects 32 percent of such individuals as eligible. The PMTF, however, covers a significantly larger proportion of large households than the proportion reflected by actual consumption figures, indicating that the formula tends to favor large households.

Finally, table 5.9 also shows that the undercoverage rate among these potentially vulnerable categories of households is in fact lower than the undercoverage rate among the general population for different cutoffs between 25th and 40th percentile of consumption (the target group is taken to be equal to the cutoff percentile). Undercoverage is particularly low among large households and those with an elderly head of household. This is further evidence that the PMTF covers the poor among these

Table 5.9 Undercoverage Rates among Vulnerable Groups

Cutoff (percentile)	Disabled head of household	Single female head of household	Land owned <1 acre	Age 70+ head of household	Household size 7+	General population
25th	0.51	0.50	0.52	0.42	0.28	0.52
30th	0.40	0.41	0.41	0.33	0.20	0.43
35th	0.32	0.35	0.34	0.32	0.17	0.37
40th	0.26	0.27	0.26	0.25	0.12	0.28

Source: SLIS (1999–2000).

vulnerable groups as well as, or even a little better, than it does the poor among the rest of the population.

Pilot Insights for the North and East

Addressing question 3 from above is critical in view of the impact of long-standing conflict in the North and East and the lack of information on this region provided by other surveys, including the SLIS. Table 5.7 indicates that there are systematic differences in coverage rates between the pilot areas in the North and East and in the rest of the country, with the coverage in the North and East being consistently higher for different cut-off points. This is completely explained by the much higher response rate to the application process in the North and East—66 percent of households (69 percent of the population) applied in the North and East, compared with 52 percent of households (55 percent of the population) in the South. Among those who applied, coverage was in fact lower in the North and East than in the rest of the country. For example, for the 30th percentile cutoff, coverage rate among those who applied was 41 percent for the North and East GN divisions and 43 percent for other GN divisions (see annex table 5A.6).

There are a number of potential explanations for the higher response rate in the North and East. One, offered by people and agencies working in the area, is that the people of this region have been receiving assistance from a number of relief agencies because of the war conditions that have prevailed for some time, and are more used to the idea of receiving benefits by filling forms. Another possible explanation is that the application process in the South was not able to extend opportunities to all those who would have liked to apply, and because some poor people have received nothing in the past and therefore see no point in filling an application form. A third explanation is simply that the people of North and East are worse off because of the conflict, and therefore they apply in greater numbers for such programs.

Although there is no way to pick one of these explanations as more plausible than the others, they raise important issues that the actual program must take into account. The most important is the need to ensure, with strong outreach efforts and information campaign if necessary, that *all* who would like to receive welfare payments are able to actually apply. This may be a particular challenge in areas where the existing program is visibly present—in those areas, people who are currently excluded may not be hopeful enough about receiving benefits to take time to fill in the application form.

The pilot data also revealed that most household characteristics in North and East pilot districts do not differ significantly from those in the other pilot districts. One difference that does emerge, however, is the presence of a higher incidence of single female headed households in the North and East: 14 percent of all households there are headed by a single woman, compared with 12.6 percent in the other pilot areas.

On the whole, the pilot did not suggest any major systematic difference between household characteristics in the North and East and the rest of the pilot districts that would question the usefulness of the same PMTF for the North and East. The only large difference in the data—the response rates—clearly has no bearing on the applicability of the PMTF-based selection criteria. These conclusions must remain tentative at this stage, however, partly because the pilot was conducted in just two districts from this region, and partly because—in the absence of consumption data from these areas—there is no proper benchmark against which the predictions from the PMTF model can be compared. Implementation of the program in the North and East must therefore be tempered with caution.

PMTF Beneficiaries and Existing Welfare Recipients from the Pilot Sample

The distribution of Samurdhi beneficiaries was found to be somewhat correlated with PMTF scores in the pilot areas of North and East where Samurdhi was operating; there was, however, little correlation between the two in non-North and East districts (see annex figure 5A.3). If the PMTF is applied with the cutoff set at the 30th percentile (which covers about 25 percent of the pilot population), then 63 percent of beneficiaries are current Samurdhi recipients, 6 percent benefit from other welfare programs (but not Samurdhi), and 31 percent currently receive no benefits. Moreover, in these 114 GN divisions from 12 districts, 53 percent of current Samurdhi beneficiaries will not receive benefits under the

PMTF regime with the selected cutoff. On the other hand, 35 percent of those who receive no benefits now will do so, and so will 45 percent of those who currently receive benefits (likely to be much smaller) only from other programs. Clearly, these represent the potential winners and losers of the reform in the pilot areas.

Addressing Special Cases: Small Households, Homeless Households, and Conflict-Affected Areas

The scrutiny that the PMTF and the pilot were subjected to in various forums, including the workshops and other consultations, raised many questions and led to important adjustments in the selection criteria and the way the PMTF would be applied. Some of the questions raised were resolved by clarifying the idea behind the PMTF without significant changes in the selection criteria.[26] The interactions engendered in the course of the scrutiny played a valuable part in improving the analysis and building consensus around the notion of introducing objectivity into selecting beneficiaries through a targeting formula—a novel idea in most countries that have not tried it before.

Small Households

The interactive process also helped first to identify, and then to resolve, a particular concern under the selected eligibility rule: a high rate of exclusion of small households (defined as a household size that is less than or equal to three), which is critical from an equity point of view. It turns out that for this special group, almost 80 percent of the target group (the bottom 30 percent of the consumption distribution from SLIS data) are not identified as eligible by the PMTF. The pilot sample also confirmed the PMTF's apparent "bias" against such families: most households with three or fewer people had higher scores than the cutoff, *including* those households for whom all other poverty predictors suggested they are very likely to be poor.

This results from a structural problem of the PMTF approach. Since poor households on the average are more likely to be larger, the PMTF puts a large negative weight on a large household size to improve the prediction of consumption expenditure for the whole sample. In other words, what works well for the population as a whole, strongly biases it against a small subgroup, because households that are poor *and* small are much less likely to be selected.

The only practical way of addressing this problem is to devise additional criteria for the special case of small households of three or fewer.

Based on careful simulations, where a large number of possible criteria were considered, adjustments to the eligibility criteria were made to

- maximize the coverage of the poor small households;
- minimize leakage to non-poor small households; and
- involve simple, transparent and easily implementable criteria.

The adjusted criteria involved two cutoff scores for eligibility: the original one (corresponding to the 30th percentile) and a higher one (the 75th percentile).[27] All households above the higher cutoff are eliminated, and all below the lower cutoff are selected. Those between the two cutoffs are selected if the following are fulfilled:

- household size is less than or equal to three;
- number of rooms (excluding kitchen, bathroom, garage, verandah) is equal to one;[28] and
- at least one "vulnerable" household member (that is, single female, age 15 years or less, disabled or permanently ill, age more than 60).

Using the revised selection criteria, substantial improvements in results were found among small households (see annex table 5A.7). This is the case nationally, as well as for urban and rural/estate regions separately. *Without* using the criteria described above, the coverage rate among households of size three and less was about 7 percent in SLIS data, compared with a target group of 17 percent. In contrast, with the revised criteria the coverage of this group increases to 18 percent. Substantial reductions in under-coverage rates among small households are achieved by using the new criteria. Furthermore, the new revised criteria induced little change in the aggregate results for the population—including coverage, undercoverage and leakage rates, and incidence of benefits. This is expected since the proportion of small households in the total population is quite low, and the eligible group is only a small proportion of such households.

Homeless Households

The homeless posed some issues, since the SLIS data on which the PMTF was estimated, like most household surveys, did not include homeless households. The paucity of data makes it difficult to even estimate the proportion of homeless households in the total target population. A consensus was reached during the workshop that *all* homeless households should be included in the program automatically, without applying the PMTF, which would be difficult to calculate in any case. This does not lead to any significant change in the coverage and other estimates, as homeless households are only about 1.3 percent of all applicant households in pilot areas, and the average household size is much lower for homeless households, which translates to relatively low amounts per household using the payment scheme described previously.[29]

Applying PMTF in Conflict Areas

The pilot results did not uncover any evidence to suggest that the PMTF should not be applied in the conflict areas. However, a number of issues were raised by workshop participants about the need to change the way certain variables were defined and interpreted for the North and East, which would in turn imply a change in the instructions for the application form for North and East. A number of these changes were incorporated in the questionnaire manual for the North and East when implementation started in that region. Changes included, for instance, the definition of cultivable land, which is a variable in the PMTF. In the North and East, the definition of *cultivable land* will exclude land that cannot be cultivated next season because it may now have landmines, even though this land may have been cultivable in the past. Similar adjustments may also have to be made to the definitions of other variables such as ownership and quality of dwelling. These adjustments are expected to improve the welfare impact of the PMTF in the North and East by taking into account special conflict-related circumstances.

Field Validation of the Eligibility of Pilot Households

A field validation exercise, conducted in four GN divisions of the 114 pilot GN divisions, showed encouraging results. The primary objective of the exercise was to validate the list of selected households in each GN division with local officials and elders to test the way the formula's predictions resonate with the local subjective perceptions about poverty. A second objective was to visit households that GN-level officials believe to be cases of targeting error—that is, households that had been selected by the PMTF but did not deserve it, or that had not been selected by the PMTF even though they are actually poor—to ensure that their information was recorded correctly, and if so, to discover the precise reasons for the PMTF score.

This exercise helps correct errors in information and disseminate knowledge about the way the PMTF works, and it also provides valuable clues about why perceptions may depart from statistics, which in turn is critical for anticipating future problems and devising strategies to address them.

The exercise also helped design the rules and mechanisms for the appeals process, which is the only way to ensure that (1) targeting errors arising out of incorrect or distorted information are corrected; and (2) there are some clear mechanisms to make allowances for special circumstances. Special circumstances, however, need to be appropriately defined—if they are overly broad and applied too often, the process would be arbitrary and subjective, taking away the entire point of applying the PMTF.

Institutional Reform to Support Implementation

In order to implement the PMTF-based selection mechanism as described above, the Act and the WBB already provide the broad institutional framework. The stipulations in the Act imply that the responsibilities for selecting beneficiaries according to the eligibility criteria set by the formula, monitoring entry and exit into the program, and setting the rules of the appeals process will reside with the Board. The existing program officers of Samurdhi will continue to administer the application process under the supervision of the WBB and district and divisional administrators, and to facilitate the necessary information campaigns and the community validation process. The separation of roles between the program officers and WBB is fundamental to implementing an objective selection mechanism. Furthermore, community validation will also build in a mechanism to enforce accountability of the program officers and to minimize the likelihood of political influence in the selection process.

Because the reform will result in paring down the list of current beneficiaries, an appeals process with clear and transparent guidelines will be necessary. Appeals will be handled by community-level committees with representation from a broad range of community representatives, subject to guidelines that ensure consistency in redressing grievances across communities and minimizing arbitrary judgments. A detailed operational manual that specifies the roles, responsibilities, and guidelines has been prepared and submitted to the government for approval.

A number of changes in the methods of payments have also been recommended by the policy workshop participants. The two most important among them are

- first, to distribute the cash transfers through accounts created in post offices (instead of Samurdhi banking societies as is the current practice), preferably in the name of the female member of the household; and

■ second, to eliminate the current practice of compulsory withholding of savings and insurance premiums from the benefits.

The de-linking of transfers from savings and insurance and using post offices for distributing benefits will ensure that access to insurance, savings, and credit services from the Samurdhi banks are not contingent upon selection for Samurdhi payments. This is desirable because the cash transfers serve objectives that are completely different from those that are served by microfinance/insurance programs.

THE IMPACT OF PSIA

At various stages along its path, the PSIA informed the design and preparation for implementation of the reform because it was closely integrated with the Bank's support and policy dialogue for the reform. The PSIA-type of analysis, initiated with the exercise intended to derive a PMTF for Sri Lanka, was supplemented by other, equally important activities. Together they added up to the full range of support necessary to bring about the institutional capacity to undertake the reform of a program as large as Samurdhi. The previous sections have described in some detail the analytical part of the support and the specific elements of the exercise that influenced key changes in the design of the reform or led to introduction of compensatory measures to mitigate negative impacts. Some of these are summarized below.

To start with, the basic policy decision to go forward with a PMTF approach—which was the precursor to all the other decisions that followed on eligibility, payments, and so on—was greatly influenced by the analysis that used SLIS and CFSES data to explore its feasibility and the gains that can be expected from adopting it. At a later stage, the results from the analysis of ex ante impact and the subsequent analysis with the pilot data were the moving force behind the discussions and agreements reached at the policy workshop in December 2003. The discussions at the workshop led to decisions on a number of key elements of the reform, including the choice of the PMTF, the eligibility cutoff for selection, and the schedule of payments for beneficiaries. In addition, a number of recommendations emerged from the workshop on the composition of the appeals committee, the enrollment of beneficiaries into the program, and the steps necessary to build a functioning MIS database.

A number of examples of the analysis informed adjustments to the design of reforms to mitigate potential adverse impacts or induce additional benefits. One example is the exercise undertaken to mitigate the potentially high likelihood of exclusion of small, poor households (with three or fewer members) by the PMTF-based selection criteria. Since this group represents a small share of the population, this exclusion has only negligible impact on aggregate targeting errors; however, the adjustment was necessary to minimize adverse impact on a potentially vulnerable section of the population who are likely to rely on social assistance (e.g., aged people or couples living by themselves, or with a grandchild).

As mentioned in the section on the current status of the reform, the most recent policy impact of the work on designing and preparing for the reform—which includes the technical analysis that is the subject of this paper, as well as institutional capacity building, policy dialogue, and MIS development—has been the decision to introduce the Samurdhi program targeted by the PMTF in the North and East. The enduring analytical work will be critical in implementing the scheme in the North and East. The PSIA thus remains an ongoing exercise, and it must remain so if it is to continue providing solutions to potential problems.

The current status—the program being introduced in the North and East, but an uncertain future for reform in the South—puts the onus on the potential role of the PSIA to prove its worth. It must inform policy debates with a view of generating consensus around the need to undertake such reform for the South also. The section on the current status of reforms refers to the additional strain expected for the country's welfare system with the imminent phasing out of the cash grant program for tsunami-affected families. Accommodating the additional demand for benefits this will generate will require exploring options to make Samurdhi much more efficient in targeting the poor. The proposed Samurdhi reform has identified a way to achieve precisely that objective, and more importantly one that appears to work—in pilots, and now, it is hoped, with similar success in actual operation in the North and East. The PSIA is in the unique position to bring these facts and their implications out clearly, and to inform and influence the policy dialogue that can revive the impetus for this reform.

LESSONS LEARNED

As the discussion above has shown, the PSIA for welfare reform in Sri Lanka has played an integral part in both motivating the reform process and influencing its design. The lessons gained from such an exercise are numerous; they range from the technical issues relevant for similar PMTF exercises and the design of safety nets to broader lessons about the process of PSIAs and the role they can play in facilitating reform.

Lesson One: The Importance of a Pilot

On the technical side, the PSIA exercise has generated a number of lessons that are highly relevant for designing safety net interventions, and especially for deriving a PMTF. Two of these lessons are considered the most important. The first key lesson is that a pilot is extremely important, primarily because household surveys—which are inherently different in nature from the exercise of actually collecting data from applicants to the program—cannot replicate the local incentives and logistical difficulties that may affect the quality of data. A pilot carefully designed to replicate the actual exercise is therefore critical to test the validity of the targeting formula as well as to indicate whether the process is adequate in terms of (1) collecting the relevant information accurately, and (2) including all potential applicants for the program, especially those in vulnerable groups and remote areas. Moreover, as was the case in Sri Lanka, the pilot is also valuable for checking whether certain specific groups are being excluded by the PMTF, and how consistent the selected list of beneficiaries are with local perceptions. Even when the pilot cannot involve the best option of actual payment of benefits, as was the case in Sri Lanka, it can still be of enormous value along the above dimensions, if designed appropriately.

Lesson Two: Linking Measurement and Proxy Means Testing

The second lesson relates to the strong link between a country's statistical systems for monitoring poverty and social indicators and measuring poverty on the one hand, and the feasibility of conducting a proxy means testing exercise on the other. In Sri Lanka's case, although the one-off exercise of SLIS turned out to be a boon, using this survey to derive the PMTF raises the question of how the PMTF will be updated in future, since the SLIS in its current form will never be repeated. The future plans of Sri Lanka's official survey agencies offer viable options: DCS's plan involves expanding their current Household Income and Expenditure Survey (HIES), which currently has little information on welfare predictors, into one that is closer to the form of an LSMS.[30] As such a survey becomes available, there is now the requisite capacity among the technical staff within the WBB to update the PMTF, based on their experience with developing and piloting the current PMTF.

The recent resolution of the poverty line and measurement issue, by ensuring a consensus about poverty incidence in the country, has also helped provide a clear benchmark for the size of the target group for the PMTF. The Bank's efforts in supporting these activities have been able to exploit synergies with the progress on welfare reform. The externalities flow both ways: resolution of poverty measurement and survey plans are essential to make the estimation and the future updating of the PMTF feasible; and the adoption of the PMTF has in turn generated the impetus for appropriate surveys.

Lesson Three: Linking Analysis, Capacity Building, and Legal Framework

On the broader issue of the role of the PSIA in facilitating the reform process, an important lesson pertains to the links between the analytical work on the one hand, and institutional capacity building and legal framework on the other. In the case of Sri Lanka, the passage of the Welfare Act by the country's parliament provided the critical legal framework for the reform. Equally critical was the work done to build institutional capacity, which helped in internalizing the insights from analytical work into the design of the reform and enabling an institution such as the WBB to be in a position to actually implement the design.

Lesson Four: The Importance of Ongoing Engagement

Related to above is a lesson for international agencies such as the World Bank on the role of PSIAs: an effective PSIA must be a continuing engagement rather than a one-off exercise. This is all the more crucial in the case of reforms such as the one discussed here, which involves changing the institutional mindset of a well-entrenched program where there are strong political incentives to maintain status quo. Such fundamental reforms are also intrinsically different, in terms of design and implementation challenges, from stroke-of-the-pen policy reforms such as removing certain distortions in trade policy or reducing fuel subsidies. In the case of Sri Lanka's welfare reform, even when the enabling legal and institutional framework was in place (as with the Act and the WBB), there was a need for continuing technical assistance to integrate the PSIA-type analysis into its broader objectives. Furthermore, in such cases it is also important to recognize that PSIAs may need multi-year engagement to not only provide analytical solutions but also help create the enabling environment for implementing these solutions locally.

Lesson Five: Embed Reform within a Broader Policy Framework

Another lesson is the importance of embedding reform in the context of the broader policy framework of the country. In the case of Sri Lanka, the broader policy dialogue on the evolution of safety net programs in the country must also take into account the potential for moving from an exclusive reliance on unconditional transfers to a role for conditional transfers. In Sri Lanka, this potential includes public works programs to address the long-standing problems of mistargeting by inducing an element of self-selection into the program. The future of this policy dialogue will be critical for implementing the welfare reform countrywide, easing the transition into a more selective Samurdhi program by clarifying the role and clientele of such programs, and providing alternative opportunities for those who do not qualify for unconditional transfers such as Samurdhi. The country is currently poised to consider this issue seriously. The additional challenges to the welfare system created in the aftermath of the tsunami, and the PRSP progress report's endorsement of the role of programs such as public works, have both had an impact on this consideration. The work for this PSIA and other related exercises—including the Bank's support for tsunami-related safety net programs—can play an important role in informing this important debate.

NOTES

1. This chapter draws from work done under the technical assistance for Welfare Reform which included, in addition to the main authors of this paper, Francisco Ayala, Yoko Kijima, Hernando Quintero, S. Sivakumaran, and Princess Ventura. Comments and suggestions from Anis Dani and Kapil Kapoor are gratefully acknowledged. We also acknowledge support from Peter Harrold and Sadiq Ahmed. All remaining errors are the sole responsibility of the authors.
2. Other than programs run by different federal agencies, the provincial ministries also implement social welfare programs—notably the disbursement of the "Poor Relief"—that are financed by the decentralized budgets.
3. An average of 13.2 billion Sri Lankan rupees was allocated to Samurdhi between 2000 and 2003, which amounts to 1 percent of annual GDP, or over 10 percent of social service expenditures and a third of welfare expenditures. The Ministry of Social Welfare and its two associated departments consume only 0.2 percent of GDP, which is 3 percent of the social services expenditure and 7.5 percent of the spending on welfare.
4. The transfer component of the Samurdhi program had an allocation of 9 billion Sri Lankan rupees (around US$90 million) in FY 2003, which amounted to 0.75 percent of GDP and about 3 percent of total government spending.

5. For instance, in 2003, recurrent spending for the Samurdhi Ministry accounted for Rs. 12.2 billion Sri Lankan rupees out of a total of 12.5 billion rupees, of which 9.2 billion was spent on consumption grants or transfers and 2.8 billion on the salary bill of the Samurdhi Authority (about 22 percent of the total expenditure of the program).

6. See Glinskaya (2000) for a detailed evaluation of the Samurdhi program.

7. See the annex (figure 5A.1) for a comparison of the share of the poor population (using the official survey—HIES 2002) with the share of the Samurdhi transfer budget received by each province. Uva and Sabaragamuwa provinces account for 29 percent of the poor population, but receive only 22 percent of Samurdhi transfers. Western, North-Central, and Northwest provinces together account for 38 percent of the poor, but receive 47 percent of the transfers.

8. The efficacy of proxy means testing is indicated by a recent comparative study of targeting in Latin America (Grosh 1994), which has found that, among all targeting mechanisms, proxy means tests tend to produce the best incidence outcomes in developing countries. For more on the theory and academic evidence on proxy means tests, see Annex 5B.

9. This is possible since the household survey data used to derive the PMTF for Sri Lanka also contains information about who receives Samurdhi benefits.

10. For some of these projections, data from the Census of Population (2001) is used.

11. In development literature, consumption expenditure is generally considered a more accurate measure of welfare than income for several reasons. First, consumption expenditures are more likely to indicate the household's "true" economic status, as a result of households with sporadic incomes smoothing their consumption patterns over time. Second, consumption is generally measured with far greater accuracy than income in a household survey, primarily because households' sources of income may include home-based production and own farms; calculating the flow of *net* incomes from households' sources of income is thus problematic.

12. See annex 5A for a more detailed discussion on each category of variable vis-à-vis the two main criteria.

13. A useful reference point here is that the headcount poverty rate for Sri Lanka was estimated at 25 and 22 percent, using HIES data from 1995–96 and 2002, respectively. One must, however, keep in mind that there is no way to compare the *n*th percentile from SLIS data with the poverty line computed from HIES; the former can, at best, serve as an indicative poverty threshold for the SLIS.

14. See Grosh and Baker (1995) and related literature for other countries.

15. Two extreme examples help illustrate this point clearly. If a program selects the entire population as eligible, undercoverage rate is zero regardless of how the target population is defined. Conversely, if the targeted population is the entire population, the leakage rate is zero, no matter what the selection criteria that determines the eligible population.

16. As mentioned previously, all calculations are made for the case where the eligibility cutoff is *equal* to the threshold to define the target group.

17. For example, for the 30th percentile cutoff point, undercoverage rates of model II were 41 and 71 percent for rural and urban areas respectively, while those of model III were 42 and 53 percent respectively.

18. Note that this means that if the threshold is the 25th percentile, the target population is the bottom 25 percent of the actual consumption distribution, and the eligible/beneficiary population is a group of individuals whose per capita consumption expenditure is below the 25th percentile.

19. Setting the cutoff line at 40th percentile of actual per capita household consumption expenditure does not guarantee the program coverage also becomes 40 percent. This is a coincidence. If the cutoff is set at 30th percentile, the program coverage becomes 27 percent (see table 5.5).

20. Note that the total coverage, if the 30th percentile is used for the cutoff line, is less than 30 percent. This is related to the fact that predicted per capita consumption expenditures tend to be larger than actual consumption for poor households, and eligible households are defined if their predicted consumption is lower than the 30th percentile of actual consumption.

21. For example, one of the most customized payment schedules is to determine the level of payment to eligible households sequentially: the poorest household receives enough to achieve the consumption of the next poorest; next, the two poorest households receive enough to attain the consumption of the next poorest, and so on, till the budget is exhausted. This type of payment scheme has the most egalitarian or redistributive impact, but it is almost impossible to implement.

22. There can be tradeoffs: by increasing b, progressiveness is increased on the average; however, for a limited budget, this implies a lower a, which affects eligible households that are poor but have few or no vulnerable members. At the margin—that is, when b is high enough that a has to be set to zero, it turns out that as many as 5.5 percent of households belonging to the poorest decile of *actual* per capita consumption fall below the PMTF eligibility cutoff but do not receive any benefits.

23. These gains are somewhat overstated, since the simulations use a budget constraint of SL RS 9 billion for the optimum payment scheme under PMTF, which is higher than the total budget implied by the existing Samurdhi benefits received by households in SLIS. However, separate simulations with the budget held constant yield comparable results: for example, squared poverty gap shows a reduction of at least 10 percent from the existing Samurdhi payments when the PMTF is used to distribute payments.

24. The pilot covered each GN division in its entirety. Total population of pilot areas (from the Population Census) is 199,151 (48,501 households), out of which around 26,703 households (with a total population of 115,580) applied. Out of a total of 114 GN divisions, 23 were from the North and East,

with an estimated population of 42,568 (10,367 households), from which 6,876 households (with population 29,271) applied.

25. Experiences from pilots in other countries also show a similar pattern, where the coverage rate of pilot areas are lower than predicted by household data, giving credence to the argument made here.

26. For example, a typical concern was that the positive weight of owning a radio might penalize the poor since a radio is so cheap that everyone including the poor can own it. This perception was, however, not supported by either SLIS or pilot data—both showed that a significant number of poor households do not own a radio, which explained why radio ownership turns out to be a good predictor of poverty in combination with other predictors.

27. These cutoffs translate to PMTF scores of 709 and 767 respectively.

28. As an alternative for the number of rooms criterion, it is possible to use a floor condition—type of floor unprepared earth or prepared clay. However, the number of rooms criterion is slightly superior to the floor type criterion, especially for urban areas.

29. Twenty-four percent of homeless households comprise a single member, compared to 1 percent of those living in homes. Five percent of homeless households comprise 6 or more members, compared to 37 percent of those living in homes.

30. The Central Bank of Sri Lanka has also recently completed its own Consumer Finance and Socio-Economic Survey (CFSES) of 2003–4, which contains information on many of the welfare predictors. The future surveys by DCS and the Central Bank will both afford opportunities to evaluate or even update the PMTF using more recent data when they become available.

31. Simple means tests are performed as part of the food stamp programs in Jamaica (prior to 2002), Honduras, Sri Lanka, and Zambia. In Jamaica and Sri Lanka, this evaluation has been largely subjective and does not contain any systematic examination or weighting of certain factors. Evaluations reveal that the two programs delivered only 56 and 57 percent of its benefits respectively to those in the poorest 40 percent of the population.

32. Glewwe (1990) took the same basic approach of predicting welfare. Instead of using regressions, he solved a poverty minimization problem to derive weights for each household variable. While theoretically more appropriate, the poverty minimization technique is much more difficult to compute, and produces results not dissimilar from those based on regression analysis.

33. See Grosh and Baker (1995), Annex I for a fuller discussion.

34. Grosh and Baker (1995) present a case where they use only the poorest half of the population as the basis for building the targeting models, and show that such an approach leads to significantly lower undercoverage.

35. See Grosh and Glinskaya (1997) and Hentschel et al. (1998) for applications of this method.

REFERENCES

Census of Population. 2001. Sri Lanka Department of Census and Statistics, Census of Population and Housing (2001).

Coady, D., M. Grosh, and J. Hoddinott. 2004. *Targeting of Transfers in Developing Countries: Review of Lessons and Experience.* Regional and Sectoral Studies. Washington, DC: World Bank.

Glewwe, P. 1990. "Efficient Allocation of Transfers to the Poor." Living Standards Measurement Study Working Paper 70, World Bank, Washington, DC.

Glewwe, P., and O. Kanaan. 1989. "Targeting Assistance to the Poor: A Multivariate Approach Using Household Survey Data." Policy, Planning and Research Working Paper 225, Washington, DC: World Bank.

Glinskaya, E. 2000. "An Empirical Evaluation of Samurdhi Program." Background paper to Sri Lanka Poverty Assessment. SASPR, World Bank, Washington, DC.

Government of Sri Lanka. 2002. *Regaining Sri Lanka: Vision and Strategy for Accelerated Development.*

———. 2005. *Sri Lanka New Development Strategy: A Framework for Economic Growth and Poverty Reduction.*

Grosh, M. 1994. *Administering Targeted Social Programs in Latin America: from Platitudes to Practice.* Washington, DC: World Bank.

Grosh, M., and J. Baker. 1995. "Proxy Means Tests for Targeting Social Programs: Simulations and Speculation." LSMS Working Paper 118, World Bank, Washington, DC.

Grosh, M., and E. Glinskaya. 1997. "Proxy Means Testing and Social Assistance in Armenia." Draft. Development Economics Research Group, World Bank, Washington, DC.

Haddad, L.J., Sullivan, J., and Kennedy, E. 1991. "Identification and evaluation of alternative indicators of food and nutrition security: some conceptual issues and an analysis of extant data." Informal. Washington, DC, USA, IFPRI.

Hentschel, J., J. Lanjouw, P. Lanjouw, and J. Poggi. 1998. "Combining Census and Survey Data to Study Spatial Dimensions of Poverty: A Case Study of Ecuador." Policy Research Working Paper 1928, World Bank, Washington, DC.

HIES. 2002. Sri Lanka Department of Census and Statistics, Household Income and Expenditure Survey 2002.

Narayan, A., and N. Yoshida. 2004. "Proxy Means Test for Targeting Welfare Benefits in Sri Lanka." Informal. Forthcoming South Asia Policy Working Paper Series. World Bank, Washington, DC.

Ravallion, M., and K. Chao. 1989. "Targeted Policies for Poverty Alleviation under Imperfect Information: Algorithms and Applications." *The Journal of Policy Modeling* 11 (2): 213–24.

World Bank. 2002. *Sri Lanka—Poverty Assessment, Volume 1.* World Bank: Washington, DC.

————. 2003. *Sri Lanka Country Assistance Strategy.* Report No. 25413-CE. World Bank, Washington, DC.

————. 2005. "A Poverty Map for Sri Lanka—Findings and Lessons." Policy Note (draft). South Asia Region.

Expenditure Composition of Ministries of Samurdhi and Social Welfare

An average of SL Rs 13.2 billion was allocated to Samurdhi between 2000 and 2003, which amounts to 1 percent of annual GDP, over 10 percent of social service expenditures and a third of welfare expenditures. Total Samurdhi expenditures (nominal) increased from around SL Rs 10 billion in 2000 to SL Rs 15.2 billion in 2002, and then declined to around SL Rs 12.2 billion in 2003—largely due to changes in the size of the transfer component. Recurrent spending typically accounts for about 98 percent of total expenditure, and about 97 percent of that consists of consumption grant to households and salaries paid by the Samurdhi Authority to a 26,000+ cadre of staff that administer the program. For instance in 2003, recurrent spending accounted for SL Rs 12.2 billion out of a total of SL Rs 12.5 billion, of which SL Rs 9.2 billion was spent on consumption grants or transfers, and SL Rs 2.8 billion on the salary bill of the Samurdhi Authority (about 22 percent of the total expenditure of the program).

In contrast to the Ministry of Samurdhi, the Ministry of Social Welfare and its two associated departments consume only 0.2 percent of GDP, 3 percent of the social services expenditure and 7.5 percent of the spending on welfare. The breakdown of expenditures of the three institutions shows that recurrent expenditure accounts for about 98 percent of the total. Mirroring the pattern seen for Samurdhi, there was a steady increase in total expenditures from 2000 to 2002, from around SL Rs 2.5 billion to SL Rs 4.4 billion, followed by a decline to around SL Rs 4 billion in 2003. The increase is primarily explained by an increase in the size of the transfer component; the share of this component in the total budget has also significantly increased over time, from 79 percent in 2000 to 94 percent in 2003. As much as 92 percent of transfers in 2003 went for social security for disabled soldiers (including families of soldiers who have lost their lives), leaving only 8 percent for beneficiaries within other vulnerable groups.

Table 5A.1 PMTF (Weight on Each Variable for the Selected Models)

Variables	Dummy	Model II	Model III selected as PMTF
Location			
Rural/Estate	*	−10	0
Community characteristics			
Public/private bank in community	*	7	8
Divisional secretariat in community	*	8	9
Household assets			
Car/van	*	40	40
Cooker (kerosene/gas/electric)	*	15	17
Bicycle/tricycle	*	4	4
Fan	*	11	11
Refrigerator	*	11	12
Motorcycle/scooter	*	9	8
Radio/CD/cassette player	*	4	4
Sewing machine	*	7	7
Tractor	*	15	15
TV/video player	*	7	8
Land and livestock			
Cultivable land owned by household :			
1 < Acres < = 2	*	8	7
2 < Acres < = 4	*	8	8
Acres > 4	*	17	16
Livestock (any)	*	8	8
Household head			
Not a female who is widowed/ separated/divorced	*	6	5
Age: 70–79	*	−6	−5
80 and above	*	−13	−13
Education: Passed OL or grade 11	*	7	7
Passed AL/GAQ/GSQ	*	10	10
Has degree/PG/diploma	*	17	16
Work: Salaried employment or in business	*	5	5

Table 5A.1 PMTF (Weight on Each Variable for the Selected Models)
     (*Continued*)

Variables	Dummy	Model II	Model III selected as PMTF
Household demographics			
Household size: 3–4 members	*	−22	−23
5–6 members	*	−39	−39
7–8 members	*	−51	−52
> 8 members	*	−59	−59
All children age 5–16 attend school	*	7	6
Housing characteristics			
Dwelling owned by hhold	*	4	4
Fuel for cooking: gas/electricity	*	12	13
Toilet: private and flush type	*	16	16
No. of rooms (excl. kitchen/bath) *per* hhold member		17	16
Walls: *Not* cabook/mud/plank/cadjan	*	6	6
Constant		715	707

Source: Staff estimation based on SLIS (1999–2000).

Note: All scores are derived from regressions of (log of) per capita consumption expenditure on a set of variables. The score for each variable is its coefficient in the regression, *multiplied* by 100, and *rounded* to the nearest integer. The aggregate score for each household is calculated as *constant +/− the weight on each variable:* for each dummy variable (indicated by *), multiply the score by 1 *if true* for household, by 0 *if not true;* for each continuous variable, multiply the score by the value of the variable for the household. Regressions include only variables with significance level of 99 percent and above.

Table 5A.2 Regression Results from OLS Estimations

(dependent variable: log of actual per capita monthly
consumption expenditure of household)

Variable	Description of variable	Model II	Model III
non_urban	1 = lives in rural/estate	−0.098	
	0 = lives in urban area	(6.11)**	
car_van	1 = hhold has car/van	0.402	0.403
	0 = otherwise	(16.33)**	(16.32)**
cooker	1 = hhold has cooker (kerosene/	0.147	0.166
	gas/electric); 0 = otherwise	(7.58)**	(8.68)**
cycle	1 = hhold has bicycle/tricycle	0.040	0.036
	0 = otherwise	(3.68)**	(3.27)**
fan	1 = hhold has fan	0.108	0.114
	0 = otherwise	(6.77)**	(7.15)**
fridge	1 = hhold has refrigerator	0.112	0.118
	0 = otherwise	(5.92)**	(6.20)**
m_cycle	1 = hhold has motorcycle/scooter	0.089	0.083
	0 = otherwise	(5.39)**	(5.01)**
radio	1 = hhold has radio/CD player/	0.044	0.043
	cassette player; 0 = otherwise	(3.21)**	(3.12)**
sew_mach	1 = hhold has sewing machine	0.073	0.073
	0 = otherwise	(5.93)**	(5.95)**
tractor	1 = hhold has tractor	0.149	0.149
	0 = otherwise	(3.87)**	(3.88)**
tv_vcr	1 = hhold has TV/VCR	0.072	0.075
	0 = otherwise	(5.68)**	(5.87)**
bank_com	1 = public/private bank in community	0.073	0.083
	0 = otherwise	(5.59)**	(6.46)**
ds_com	1 = divisional secretariat in	0.083	0.091
	community; 0 = otherwise	(3.88)**	(4.24)**
wid_f	0 = Head is female and widowed/	0.056	0.053
	separated/divorced; 1 = otherwise	(3.49)**	(3.25)**
ageHcat4	1 = hhold head age: 70–79	−0.055	−0.054
	0 = otherwise	(2.69)**	(2.61)**
ageHcat5	1 = hhold head Age: 80 +	−0.134	−0.133
	0 = otherwise	(3.95)**	(3.89)**
edulevH4	1 = hhold head passed OL or grade 11	0.065	0.065
	0 = otherwise	(4.16)**	(4.16)**
edulevH5	1 = hhold head passed AL/GAQ/GSQ	0.103	0.103
	0 = otherwise	(4.32)**	(4.33)**
edulevH6	1 = hhold head has degree/PG/	0.169	0.163
	diploma; 0 = otherwise	(3.86)**	(3.71)**
activH34	1 = hhold head in salaried employment	0.049	0.050
	or business; 0 = otherwise	(3.80)**	(3.89)**
landown2	1 = cultivable land owned by household:	0.075	0.069
	1<Acres< = 2; 0 = otherwise	(3.48)**	(3.19)**

Table 5A.2 Regression Results from OLS Estimations (*Continued*)
(dependent variable: log of actual per capita monthly
consumption expenditure of household)

Variable	Description of variable	Model II	Model III
landown3	1 = 2 < acres < = 4	0.084	0.079
	0 = otherwise	(3.31)**	(3.09)**
landown4	1 = acres > 4	0.166	0.159
	0 = otherwise	(3.74)**	(3.58)**
lstk	1 = hhold has livestock (any)	0.084	0.082
	0 = no livestock	(4.39)**	(4.24)**
dhsize2	1 = hhold size: 3–4 members	−0.220	−0.227
	0 = otherwise	(7.49)**	(7.71)**
dhsize3	1 = hhold size 5–6 members	−0.387	−0.393
	0 = otherwise	(12.67)**	(12.84)**
dhsize4	1 = hhold size 7–8 members	−0.512	−0.516
	0 = otherwise	(15.30)**	(15.36)**
dhsize5	1 = hhold size 8 + members	−0.587	−0.586
	0 = otherwise	(15.02)**	(14.94)**
rsch5_16	1 = all children in hhold of age 5–16	0.065	0.062
	attend school; 0 = otherwise	(3.67)**	(3.45)**
dwellten1	1 = dwelling owned by hhold	0.038	0.035
	0 = not owned by hhold	(3.09)**	(2.82)**
fuel1	1 = fuel for cooking: gas/electricity	0.122	0.126
	0 = other	(5.37)**	(5.53)**
latrtyp1	1 = toilet: private and flush type	0.163	0.162
	0 = other	(9.93)**	(9.80)**
rmsmem	No. of rooms (excl. kitchen/bath)	0.165	0.159
	per hhold member	(11.50)**	(11.05)**
walltyp137	0 = walls: cabook/mud/plank/cadjan	0.062	0.063
	1 = other	(4.77)**	(4.80)**
Constant		7.145	7.071
		(175.16)**	(181.02)**
# Observations		5257	5257
R^2		0.56	0.56

Source: Staff estimation based on the Sri Lanka Integrated Survey 1999–2000.
Note: **denotes significant at the 99 percent level.

Table 5A.3 95 Percent Confidence Intervals for Undercoverage and Leakage Rates with PMTF (Model III)

Cutoff percentile	Undercoverage	Leakage
25	[0.48, 0.57]	[0.34, 0.44]
	(0.021)	(0.027)
30	[0.39, 0.46]	[0.31, 0.39]
	(0.019)	(0.022)
35	[0.33, 0.40]	[0.30, 0.38]
	(0.018)	(0.020)
40	[0.25, 0.31]	[0.27, 0.34]
	(0.017)	(0.018)

Source: Staff estimation based on SLIS (1999–2000).
Note: All calculations take the threshold for the target group to be same as the eligibility cutoff; confidence intervals are in square brackets; standard errors are in parentheses.

Table 5A.4 Per Capita Benefits (1999 SL Rs/Month)

Decile	PMTF with optimal payment scheme	Current samurdhi
1	93.8	55.2
2	64.6	48.8
3	51.8	44.4
4	36.1	42.1
5	34.4	44.0
6	18.6	38.6
7	12.5	35.4
8	5.9	25.0
9	2.3	16.4
10	0.7	5.9
Total	30.6	35.1

Source: Staff estimation based on SLIS (1999–2000).
Note: Calculations are made taking all households for a decile as the denominator, not just the households receiving (or designated to receive) benefits.

Table 5A.5 Composition of Pilot Applicants by District

District name	No. of GN division	No. of households
Colombo	3	1,739
Kalutara	5	845
Kandy	4	862
Nuwara-Eliya	14	4,104
Galle	23	2,652
Matara	6	1,680
Hambantota	21	2,973
Vavuniya	6	1,813
Trincomalee	17	5,063
Badulla	4	695
Monaragala	5	2,282
Ratnapura	6	1,995
Total	114	26,703

Source: Data from the Targeting Pilot Exercise (2003).

Table 5A.6 Coverage Rate of Pilot Areas in the North and East Compared with Rest of the Country

Percentile of actual per capita consumption (SLIS)	Cutoff score from SLIS model	Coverage (%) predicted from SLIS	Coverage (%) in pilot sample		Coverage (%) in population in pilot districts	
			North & East	Rest of the country	North & East	Rest of the country
20th	695	12.0	19.9	20.4	13.8	11.2
25th	703	19.6	31.2	33.0	22.1	18.1
30th	709	26.3	40.9	42.9	28.9	23.6
35th	715	33.7	51.3	53.0	36.4	29.1
40th	721	41.9	61.1	62.8	43.0	34.5

Source: Data from the Targeting Pilot Exercise (2003).

Table 5A.7 Results with Revised Eligibility Criteria for Small Households

Sample with household size <=3

Facility criterion	Coverage	Proportion of poor	Undercoverage	Leakage
No. of rooms <= 1	0.18	0.17	0.53	0.56
Original	0.07	0.17	0.77	0.47

Sample with household size <=3 (Rural/Estate)

Facility criterion	Coverage	Proportion of poor	Undercoverage	Leakage
No. of rooms <= 1	0.18	0.18	0.56	0.57
Original	0.08	0.18	0.79	0.51

Sample with household size <=3 (Urban)

Facility criterion	Coverage	Proportion of poor	Undercoverage	Leakage
No. of rooms <= 1	0.15	0.08	0.10	0.49
Original	0.05	0.08	0.46	0.13

Source: Staff estimation based on SLIS 1999–2000 data.
Note: Original refers to the original PMTF being used to identify eligible households. *Coverage* refers to the percentage of population in households of size <=3 selected by the criteria. *Proportion of poor* refers to the true percentage of poor in households of size <=3 (using SLIS data).

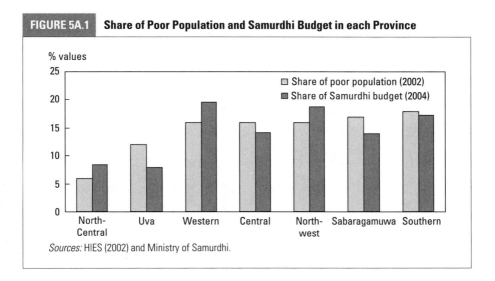

FIGURE 5A.1 **Share of Poor Population and Samurdhi Budget in each Province**

Sources: HIES (2002) and Ministry of Samurdhi.

FIGURE 5A.2 **Comparison of Score Distribution**

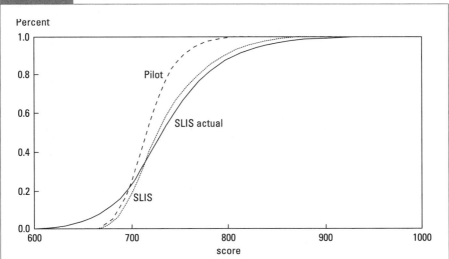

Source: Staff calculations based on SLIS 1999–2000 and data from the targeting pilot exercise (2003).
Note: Scores are log points times 100. SLIS actual is log per capita expenditure times 100; SLIS refers to predicted score from SLIS data, and Pilot score is calculated by the PMTF using the entire sample including the North and East provinces.

FIGURE 5A.3 **Coverage of Samurdhi and PMTF in Pilot Areas**

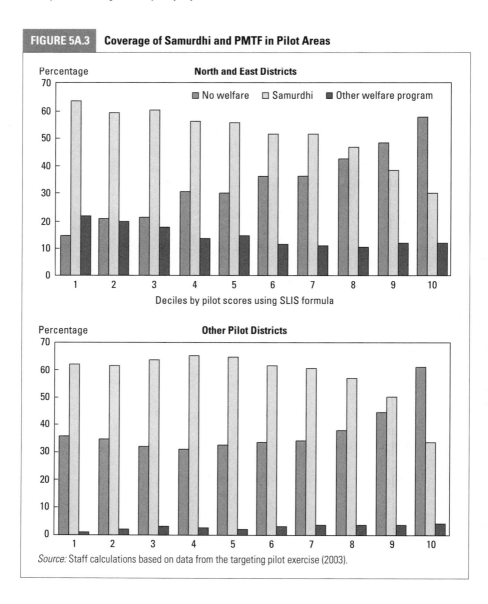

Source: Staff calculations based on data from the targeting pilot exercise (2003).

PMTF : Rationale and Evidence

Targeting benefits to the poor first requires a precise definition of the target group. Once the target group is established, a methodology must be found to identify individuals or households who are in that group and to exclude those who are not.

RATIONALE FOR THE PMTF TO IDENTIFY BENEFICIARIES OF A TRANSFER PROGRAM

In principle, conducting a *means test* that correctly measures the earnings of a household is the best way to determine eligibility when the poor are the target group, as is the case with Samurdhi. In practice, however, such straightforward means tests suffer from several problems. First, applicants have an incentive to understate their welfare level, and verifying that information is difficult in developing countries where reliable records typically do not exist. Second, income is considered an imperfect measure of welfare in developing countries, since it is unlikely to measure accurately imputed value of own-produced goods, gifts and transfers, or owner-occupied housing. Incomes of the poor in developing countries are also often subject to high volatility because of factors ranging from seasonality of agriculture to the sporadic nature of employment in the informal sector. Since adjustments for such volatility are hard to make in practice, actual welfare from income measures are likely to be highly distorted. In the light of these difficulties, rigorous means tests are largely reserved for industrialized economies where a well-educated labor force is concentrated in jobs in which cash is paid regularly and payments are reported to tax or welfare authorities. Where means-testing is used in developing countries, it is greatly simplified, at a considerable cost to accuracy.[31]

Because of administrative difficulties associated with sophisticated means tests and the inaccuracy of simple means tests, the idea of using proxy means tests that avoid the problems involved in relying on reported income is appealing. Proxy means testing involves using information on household or individual characteristics correlated with welfare levels in a formal algorithm to proxy household income or welfare. These characteristics are selected based on their ability to predict welfare as measured by, for example, consumption expenditure of households. The obvious advantage of proxy means testing is that good predictors of welfare— such as demographic data, characteristics of dwelling units, and ownership of durable assets—are likely to be easier to collect and verify than direct measures such as consumption or income. The efficacy of proxy means testing is indicated by a recent comparative study of targeting in Latin America (Grosh, 1994), which has found that, among all targeting mechanisms, proxy means tests tend to produce the best incidence outcomes in developing countries.

ACADEMIC EVIDENCE AND PRACTICAL EXPERIENCE WITH PROXY MEANS TESTS

A number of simulations in academic papers by various authors show how proxy means test could work, and the welfare gains likely produced by implementing such a targeting system. Haddad, Sullivan, and Kennedy (1991) used household survey data from Ghana, the Philippines, Mexico, and Brazil to show that some variables that would be very simple to collect could serve as good proxies for the measures of caloric adequacy that are usually used as the standard measures of food and nutrition security. These standard measures are harder to collect as they rely on the memory of individuals and on the anthropometric indicators of preschool children. Glewwe and Kanaan (1989) have used regression analysis on a data from Côte d'Ivoire to predict welfare levels based on several combinations of variables that are fairly easy to measure. Their paper demonstrated that simple regression predictions could improve targeting markedly over untargeted transfers.[32] In a recent study, Grosh and Glinskaya (1997) used regression analysis with data from Armenia to show how the targeting outcomes of a current cash transfer program can be improved by using a suitable proxy means test formula.

Grosh and Baker (1995) carried out simulations on Living Standards Measurement Survey data sets from Jamaica, Bolivia, and Peru to explore what kind of information can best be used in a proxy means test and how accurate such tests might be expected to be. Their results show that more information is generally better than less for a targeting formula, though there are diminishing returns. The proxy systems all have significant undercoverage, but they cut down leakage so much that the impact on poverty is better with imperfect targeting than with none.

Although academic exercises have been useful in developing such a proxy means test system, more insights on the implementation of such programs can be gained by looking at actual experiences on the ground— in Chile where it has existed since 1980, and more recent programs in Costa Rica, Colombia, and Jamaica. The Ficha CAS in Chile uses a form filled out by a social worker that collects information on household characteristics such as location, housing quality, household composition, and education and work of household members. Scores are assigned using a complicated algorithm and then used to determine eligibility for two large cash transfer programs and for water and housing subsidies. If the household is determined to be eligible, the same scores are used to determine the level of subsidy.

Issues in Deriving PMTF for Sri Lanka Using SLIS Data

PREDICTING WELFARE: THE CHOICE OF ORDINARY LEAST SQUARES (OLS)

The first problem with using an OLS model is that many of the explanatory variables are likely to be endogenous to (and thus not independent explanators of) household welfare. This problem is however is of less concern to us, since our objective is solely to *identify* the poor and not to explain the *reasons* for their poverty. Second, as Grosh and Baker (1995) point out, strictly speaking OLS is inappropriate for predicting poverty since the technique minimizes the squared errors between the "true" and the predicted levels of welfare, which is a different theoretical problem from that of minimization of poverty.

That said, OLS is considered convenient and useful by Grosh and Baker when a large numbers of predictor variables, including continuous variables, are available. An algorithm that does solve the problem of minimizing poverty is found in Ravallion and Chao (1989), and this could be a better tool for designing a transfer scheme than the OLS model. However, this algorithm is very difficult to use when a large number of predictive variables are available, and is difficult for policymakers to interpret.[33]

VARIABLES TO CONSIDER FOR THE PMTF

Selecting variables to predict welfare as measured by per capita consumption should take into account two separate criteria: correlation between the welfare measure and the predictor, which will determine accuracy of the prediction, and verifiability of the predictor, which will determine the accuracy of information used to impute welfare. The types of predictors used for this exercise, discussed below, were arrived at after judging all possible predictors on the basis of these two criteria (including the trade-offs that at times exist between them).

- *Location variables* are obviously the most easily verifiable, and the same is true for characteristics of the community when it is defined in simple terms such as the presence of a bank or administrative offices.
- *Housing quality* may also be easily verified by a social worker visiting the home.
- *Household characteristics,* such as the number of members and dependents, and age, education, and occupation of the house-hold head, are less easy to verify. However, it is generally felt that these data are not overly difficult to verify, and also that households are less likely to misrepresent such information. Using program officers who live in the same community as the applicant households to collect the information—as is envisaged for Sri Lanka—makes it more likely that such information will be reported correctly.
- *Ownership of durable goods or farm equipment* is verifiable by inspection, although this can be misrepresented by the household removing the goods from the home during an expected visit by the social worker, which is easier to do with small or mobile items than for items such as stoves or refrigerators. The general presumption in the literature is also that people are more willing to lie about ownership of such durable goods than they are about household characteristics. However, these variables tend to have high predictive power for welfare, and therefore including them can reduce mistargeting substantially.
- *Ownership of productive assets* is again not easy to verify. The presence of livestock is verifiable to some extent. Although land ownership may not be measured perfectly, one can reasonably expect that program officers who belong to the community will have local knowledge about whether a household owns a large amount of land or not, which will deter misrepresentation. The fact that these variables are likely to have high correlations with poverty in rural areas makes a strong case for including them as predictors of welfare.

FORMULA RECOMMENDATIONS FOR PMTF: COMPARING MODELS I, II, AND III

Although the final choice for the PMTF was model III, it is useful to summarize the pros and cons of each model.

- Model I is the most comprehensive model, incorporating province dummies and variables from all categories mentioned above.
  - It yields the best fit and the lowest error rates on the aggregate.
  - Its province weights may be hard politically to incorporate in a formula; and some weights are not intuitive, which reduces their acceptability.
  - Because of the weights, rates of undercoverage vary widely. Some provinces are covered far better than others.
- Model II omits province location variables and restricts the set to variables that are highly significant (99 percent level and above).
  - Its fit and error rates are close, but not identical, to those for model I.
  - It avoids the problems in model I by using province weights.
  - Undercoverage rates are more uniform across provinces in model II than in model I, which is desirable.
  - Its use of fewer variables reduces the information required to apply the model.
- Model III is identical to model II, with urban location variables omitted. Therefore all the pros and cons of model II vis-à-vis model I apply.
  - Model III yields overall error rates very similar to those for model II.
  - It reduces urban undercoverage compared with model II, at the cost of a slight increase in rural undercoverage (this is possible since the number of urban poor is very low compared to that of rural poor).
  - It should be selected over model II since the gap in undercoverage rates between rural and urban areas is much smaller.

COMPARING SELECTED MODELS WITH THOSE USING ALTERNATIVE METHODS OF ESTIMATION

To check whether the methodology used for the estimation can be improved upon in terms of impact on targeting efficiency, two alternative methods of estimating the PMTF were implemented. The first method consisted of using the poorer segment of the population to derive a PMTF, which may lead to better results since it puts more emphasis on accurately predicting the welfare of those near the bottom of the distribution, where the improvements are most relevant to the goal of poverty reduction.[34]

Applying this approach, a model estimated on the bottom 80 percent of the population performs marginally, but not significantly, better than model III above. This improvement is not large enough to justify its choice over model III for a number of reasons.

- First, the improvement is not unambiguous, since less undercoverage from using the new model vis-à-vis model III has to be weighed against the lower leakage rates from the latter.
- Second, even the improvement in undercoverage is not very high (between 2 and 5 percentage points) for the cutoff points likely to be the most relevant (25th and 30th percentiles).
- Third, the method of estimating the poverty predictors using only a certain part of the sample, depending on the poverty ranking of households, appears to be rather arbitrary.

For these reasons, model III is easier to understand and explain. Because the advantages of the alternate model are marginal, model III still appears to be the best choice.

The second alternative method consists of using *half the sample* to run the regressions to predict welfare, and testing the predictions from this model by calculating undercoverage and leakage rates on the *other half of the sample*. The utility of this lies in reducing the likelihood of "overfitting" the sample.[35] By separating the estimation and the testing of the model between two non-overlapping parts of the sample, the model is likely to be subjected to a harder test—minimizing the bias in favor of the model that may occur when its predictions are used on the same observations used to derive the coefficients. This is important to consider, so as to mimic as far as possible the real-world situation where our models will be applied to impute the welfare of households who will not be the same set of households for whom the formula is estimated. This exercise is conducted as a test for the sensitivity of the existing models in two ways: first, to see whether the coefficients of the model using this method are significantly different from those derived using the whole sample; second, to see how the targeting errors are when the new method, involving a "harder test" of accuracy in targeting, is used.

This exercise is conducted for the two sets of variables used in model II and III, and the two new models are called IIa and IIIa respectively.

■ First, the coefficients from model IIa turn out to reasonably close to those from the original model II, and similarly those from model IIIa to the original model III. This suggests that the original models are quite robust to adjustments for overfitting.

■ Second, the error rates using the new method are close to those of the original models for various cutoff points and poverty lines, with the former being usually higher by 2 to 3 percentage points.

Thus subjecting the methodology to a harder test does not lead to significant increases in targeting errors. Moreover, the coefficients or weights of the variables, after adjusting for overfitting, are similar to those of the original models. These results essentially validate the OLS models and the methodology underlying them, as well as the results from the simulations of targeting errors with these models.

6

EUROPE AND CENTRAL ASIA
Power Sector Reform

JULIAN A. LAMPIETTI AND NILS JUNGE[1]

A reliable supply of electricity is essential for a modern economy, but pushing through the necessary reform process to its conclusion often involves difficult choices. Political will, sound design, and proper sequencing are essential to helping consumers make the painful transition from inexpensive and irregular service to a self-financing and reliable service. Privatization of the power network has been embraced as the key component of most countries' reform programs, but success in Eastern Europe has been mixed. For both the Bank and the governments, two main questions stand out. First, can a way be found of improving the chances for success? Second, can the transition process be made smoother and less onerous for the poor?

In the fall of 1999 the Europe and Central Asia Socially Sustainable Development Department of the World Bank launched a study on the social dimensions of utility price increases in Armenia. The objective of the study was to assess the impact of public service tariff increases on household welfare, with particular attention to the accessibility and affordability of these services for the poor. When it was completed, "Utility Pricing and the Poor: Lessons from Armenia" triggered intense debate, at times acrimonious, within the country team about the possible consequences of the ongoing power sector reform program.

The timing of this study was fortuitous. The financial crises of the late 1990s contributed to a private sector that was reluctant to take on new commitments and pulling out of many of its previous commitments. Client countries were increasingly unhappy with the conditionalities in Bank sector operations. And pressure from outside stakeholders had translated into an institutional movement to better understand why some badly needed reforms were not being taken up as expected.

In the following years, similar power sector reform studies, now called Poverty and Social Impact Analysis studies (PSIAs), were commissioned for Azerbaijan, Georgia, Kyrgyz Republic, and Moldova. At the same time regional studies were commissioned on heating (World Bank 2002) and on power sector reform (World Bank 2004a).

This chapter is about the early group of power sector PSIAs, the impact that they have had, and the lessons that have been learned about power sector reform and the PSIA process in general.

THE CHOICE OF REFORM

In Europe and Central Asia many governments are barely able to keep the power sector on life support through a complicated web of explicit and implicit subsidies. The system is plagued by inefficient use of resources and weak governance. Continuing along this path is unsustainable for governments that face severe resource constraints. Power sector reform is therefore a critically important issue for many governments in the region.

In addition to being essential for a modern economy, the performance of the power sector is a potentially volatile issue. When governments cannot afford to maintain their electricity infrastructure, service quality deteriorates and people complain. Businesses and industry also suffer, and there are ripple effects on economic growth and employment. In the worst case, the residential sector is supplied with electricity for only a few hours per day. Although reform promises to improve service, tariff increases and disconnections of nonpayers are particularly unpopular, and the public often views the sale of state assets to the private sector with skepticism. Problems are compounded by a sense of entitlement associated with the legacy of the socialist social compact. The compact resulted in publicly owned, vertically integrated, and highly centralized energy infrastructure, with almost 100 percent of households having access to a reliable supply of inexpensive electricity.

Since the early 1990s the World Bank has been advising governments in Europe and Central Asia on how to undertake power sector reform. This advice, which is detailed in the Bank's 1998 Europe and Central Asia energy sector strategy, includes raising prices to cost recovery levels, improving metering and cutting off nonpaying customers, establishing predictable and transparent regulations, introducing competition in generation and supply, and selling industrial assets to private strategic investors (World Bank 1998: 29–30). Where appropriate, the Bank advocated that price increases be coupled with direct income transfers to help offset welfare losses of higher prices, particularly for poor households. The intended outcomes are reduced fiscal deficits, efficient resource use, increased production efficiency, and ultimately improved consumer service.

Despite these attractive outcomes, governments have been slow to adopt the reform package. Although many countries have introduced some parts of the package, very few have actually transferred management control to strategic investors. More common are partial reforms. For example, after taking the initial steps, the Moldovan government has privatized only part of the network and has repeatedly failed to attract financially attractive bids for the remainder.

The combination of low household incomes, high international prices for fuel, the need for utilities to rely on internally generated funds for capital investment, and the political ramifications of removing subsidies at a time of general economic decline have led to a "worst of all worlds" situation. In light of these problems, several countries concluded that investment capital may be better used and efficiency improvements may be better achieved by increasing competition and private sector participation. The downside to this conclusion is that it might, at least in the short term, lead to higher utility prices, leading in turn to rising popular concern about the social and environmental impacts of energy reform.

Although broadly similar across countries, the context of reform for each country in Europe and Central Asia was slightly different.

- *Armenia:* In Armenia, increasing costs recovery for utilities was a cornerstone of the government of Armenia's economic reform program. In the beginning of 1999 the Armenian authorities made decisive moves in several politically sensitive areas, increasing electricity tariffs and reshaping the family benefits system. Since 1995 the electricity supply has become more reliable, tariffs have been raised, cross-subsidization has been reduced, and payment discipline has improved. An energy law was adopted and an independent Energy Commission established to regulate prices.
- *Azerbaijan:* One of the most vexing problems in Azerbaijan is the domestic power supply. Despite being a net energy exporter, power supply outside the city of Baku is limited. This is because of a combination of problems, including badly maintained infrastructure, high

commercial losses, high nonpayment rates, and low tariffs. These problems worsened as strong economic growth increased demand for electricity. The opportunity cost of supplying the sector with low-cost domestic oil and gas also rose as international oil prices increased, contributing to a significant expansion in state subsidies to the sector.

■ *Georgia:* The Georgian government—with the support of the donor community—undertook a program of utility sector reform in the expectation that gains in efficiency and service quality would, over time, offset both welfare losses from higher prices and potential negative externalities from restricted access. With living standards falling throughout the 1990s, the government began to partially privatize the power sector and established a legal and regulatory framework to govern it. Households continued to have high levels of access to network services, but the numbers masked supply shortages and poor service, particularly outside Tbilisi. Despite rapid increases in the price of electricity and non-network fuels, the share of spending on energy remained constant.

■ *Kyrgyz Republic:* Reforming the energy sector was one of the key challenges on Kyrgyz Republic's policy agenda. The technical and commercial losses of the sector were estimated to be 5 percent of GDP, causing a significant drain on the fiscal and quasi-fiscal deficits. Subsidization of residential electricity consumption alone amounted to 2.7 percent of GDP in 2002. Moreover, there were frequent disruptions of electricity service, requiring costly repairs on a regular basis. Restructuring the energy sector was therefore considered necessary for improving the efficiency of electric power companies.

■ *Moldova:* Moldova launched its reform program in 1997, strongly supported by donors, to address urgent problems in the energy sector. Regular blackouts, especially in urban areas, and a steep drop in household electricity consumption—to an average of 50 kilowatt hours per month—underlined the seriousness of not just the problems of the energy sector but of Moldova's poor economic health in general. Reforms resulted in substantial improvements in supply to consumers, but the dialogue in more recent years has been accompanied by acrimonious debate among stakeholders. Much of the disagreement centered on the private operator, Union Fenosa, a Spanish-based company, which purchased almost two-thirds of the electricity distribution network in 2000. Since privatization began, accusations, counteraccusations, and lawsuits have led to a climate of uncertainty for continued reform. One of the central complaints, which the study sought to examine, was that privatization had adversely, and disproportionately, affected the poor.

Europe and Central Asia is unique in that people at the same income level as those in other regions are worse off because of the additional and necessary heating costs during the cold winters.

Over the last decade electricity prices have increased substantially so that it threatens to become one of the most expensive components of household consumption. Unless incomes keep pace with price increases, this in turn raises the specter of negative environmental externalities because people may turn to wood and coal for their power needs, as these remain among the less expensive fuels.

Although the social implications of reform are receiving increasing attention, the environmental implications of reform remain largely uncharted. On one hand, the reform process may induce cleaner and more efficient electricity production and reduced consumption. On the other hand, there may be unanticipated social costs associated with the rising price of electricity. The combination of a cold climate and the collapse of clean, safe heating alternatives (such as district heating) may be pushing households, especially poor households, to substitute less expensive dirty energy (such as wood, coal, and kerosene) for electricity in heating. Burning dirty fuels lowers indoor and outdoor air quality, leading to negative health outcomes. Burning wood can also contribute to deforestation and the loss of valuable forest functions. The social costs associated with substitution are not addressed by direct income transfers, and these costs must be taken into account in the design of reform programs.

Difficulties in implementing reforms are exacerbated by the cold climate, the legacy of high levels of service, and the public's sense of entitlement. Rising electricity prices can have substantial welfare consequences when access to less expensive substitutes is constrained because people must have energy to survive during the cold winters characteristic of the region. Difficulties are compounded by a stock of housing and heating infrastructure designed under conditions when energy was virtually free. In Europe and Central Asia, gaining access to electricity is less of an issue than maintaining access. Virtually 100 percent of urban households had access to reliable electricity supply before the transition. Higher prices and the threat of disconnections combined with public sector wage arrears—especially when juxtaposed against the socialist legacy—contribute to a sense of entitlement where nonpayment is a widely accepted practice.

In this context, the PSIA appears to have been the right instrument at the right time, bringing a new perspective to power sector reform in

Europe and Central Asia. First, it provided an opportunity to conduct a more robust empirical analysis of the social consequences associated with elements of the sector reform program, particularly for the poor. Specific analytic innovations associated with this type of empirical analysis are discussed further below. Second, it provided a starting point for bringing a greater number of stakeholders into the design of the reform.[2] Third, by being multidisciplinary, it contributed to new operational ideas on how to mitigate the negative impact of reform.

THE DESIGN OF THE PSIA

The theoretical framework for the PSIAs has its origins in the social cost-benefit literature. Costs and benefits accrue to key stakeholders in the reform process—these are generally identified as households, government, and the power utility.[3] The PSIAs are designed to try to identify the direction and magnitude of the impact of reform on these groups so that this information can be used in project or program design; they are also designed to encourage public discourse on the reform. For example, some of the most hotly debated issues that the PSIAs started addressing were how different quintiles of the population would respond to electricity tariff increases and who pays and who does not.

Electricity is an important input into the production of many goods and services. Reform of this sector therefore can profoundly influence the cost of the basic consumption basket, yet the direction and magnitude of this effect is unclear. It may be negative if higher costs are passed on to consumers, or it may be positive if service quality improvements lead to increased competition between producers and efficiency gains. Ideally the reforms should be analyzed in a general equilibrium framework that takes into account these linkages. However, general equilibrium modeling is data intensive and very sensitive to a large number of assumptions, which are often rather arbitrary. Thus, there are strengths and weaknesses to both approaches. The partial equilibrium analysis presented in these PSIAs should be thought of as one of many inputs to the decision-making process. A key advantage of the partial equilibrium approach is that it is relatively transparent and easy to explain to stakeholders.

The household analysis generally consists of two major components. The first is a qualitative analysis intended to improve our understanding of the relationship between utility availability, price changes, and household behavior, with an emphasis on the behavior of the poor. The second is a quantitative analysis intended to assess the impact of tariff changes on the welfare distribution.

Qualitative Analysis

The qualitative research typically includes focus group discussions and in-depth key informant interviews. It is designed to generate testable hypotheses about behavior in response to higher tariffs and thus informs the design of the quantitative survey. Key informants include representatives from the different utilities, government, private sector, regulator, and households. The information gathered this way is used to inform the design of the quantitative analysis.

Qualitative Research in Moldova

In the case of Moldova, for example, qualitative research was designed to test the validity of the findings on household consumption behavior gleaned from the quantitative analysis. Focus groups with participants from different socioeconomic strata in urban and rural locations were held across the country to obtain the perspective of a range of consumers. We were interested whether perceptions between poor and non-poor, and between households supplied by the private company and by the state-owned company, differed, and if they did, how these perceptions differed. These findings guided our interpretation of the quantitative results.

Although the hard data painted a generally positive picture of changing consumption behavior among the poor, exemplified by rising electricity consumption, rising incomes, and a decreasing share of electricity in the household budget—all in the face of rising electricity tariffs—the qualitative findings caused us to temper our enthusiasm. For example, the very poorest, although glad to again have 24-hour electricity availability, were still experiencing serious deprivations, and were coping by unplugging appliances and using low-wattage bulbs. Qualitative research also allowed the study to explore the service quality aspects of reform, which received less than positive reviews. Finally, qualitative findings were important in maintaining a perspective on real world experience—although the study found that average consumption increased from 50 to 55 kilowatt hours over a three-year period, few consumers perceived this improvement, which was understandable given the very low consumption levels at issue.

Qualitative Research in Georgia

In Georgia, qualitative research was used to help understand changes in expenditures among different fuel types. Relatively stable energy expenditure shares and consumption levels suggested that households in Tbilisi were replacing electricity with less expensive fuels. Breaking down total expenditure into its components revealed this to be the case. Households had increased the share of electricity in total energy from 45 to 51 percent from 1996 to 2002 (from 3 to 7 percent of income.) The share of kerosene dropped. And shares of LPG (liquid petroleum gas) and fuel wood (purchased) stayed constant. More significant, the share of gas increased from 2 to 20 percent, with the greatest increases occurring in 1999.

Focus group sessions examined the factors underlying the changing expenditures shares in greater detail, addressing the impact of access to gas on the energy mix of households. Most participants expressed a desire to have gas, preferring it to other fuels for both cooking and heating, and to some extent for heating water. Participants noted that gas was cheaper than electricity and cleaner and more comfortable than kerosene or wood. Almost all participants with no gas connections said that they used kerosene or wood for heating and cooking. After getting access to gas, they gave up these fuels. In fact, many said that they dislike both kerosene and wood so much that they used them only when no other option is available or affordable. Gas access gives them a desirable substitute.

Quantitative Analysis

The second component of the PSIA is usually a household survey used to collect data on energy consumption and expenditures. The possibility of using an existing data set such as a living standards measurement study survey (LSMS) or a household budget survey (HBS) is explored first. If appropriate data are not available, then a new primary data collection exercise is initiated, paying careful attention to making sure that the sampling frame and parts of the questionnaire are consistent with the most recent poverty assessment. The latter is important because it enables the PSIA work to be linked to the broader poverty dialogue. A typical household survey will contain the following sections:

- household roster,
- income and expenditure,
- electricity,
- electricity substitutes,
- contingent valuation, and
- attitudes and perceptions toward sector reform and tariff increases.

One of the key analytical innovations in this group of PSIAs has been collecting billing and payment records from the utility and then merging them with either an existing data set or a new data set. Although this step requires complicated database manipulation and can be extremely time consuming, it has clear advantages. Self-reported electricity data (as well as energy expenditure data in general) collected in the traditional poverty monitoring surveys such as an LSMS or an HBS may be confounded by recall error, under- and overreporting, and the presence of arrears. This makes it almost impossible to identify current and historical consumption. Matching household-level income and expenditure data with household-level data from the utility on electricity billing consumption and payment allows a much more sophisticated analysis of the residential demand and the distributional consequences of price changes. For example, it allows the analyst to determine whether price changes in the past have contributed to theft of electricity or to changes in consumption, or both. Good data on consumption also allow a thorough evaluation of the potential social and fiscal impact of alternative social protection measures such direct income transfers versus lifelines.[4]

Quantitative Analysis in Georgia

In Georgia data from the private utility AES Telasi allow careful examination of household electricity consumption patterns over the last three years. Although prices have increased, mean household consumption has remained constant at around 125 kilowatt hours per month (figure 6.1). This consumption level has two important implications for policy. First, current consumption levels are low. Basic minimum needs are likely to

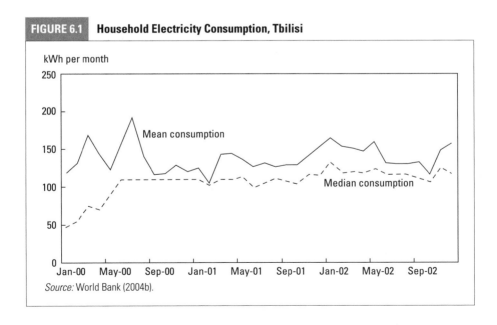

FIGURE 6.1 **Household Electricity Consumption, Tbilisi**

kWh per month

Source: World Bank (2004b).

be approximately 125 kilowatt hours per month.[5] Second, demand in Tbilisi, where service has been quite reliable for the last few years, remains constant despite price increases, suggesting inelastic demand and large welfare losses from future price increases.

In addition to allowing more sophisticated analysis of household behavior, household-level utility data provide the analyst with a unique opportunity to model the impact of different reform measures on the revenues of the utility. It also allows a careful evaluation of the quality of record keeping by the utility and identification of technical versus non-payment losses.

Quantitative Analysis in Armenia

In Armenia, total household electricity consumption dropped 17 percent—from 2.2 million kilowatt hours in March–November 1998 to 1.8 million kilowatt hours during the same months of 1999 (table 6.1). Despite this drop in consumption, the new tariff resulted in a 16 percent increase in total billings. But utility revenues from the households increased only 6 percent, as household payments failed to keep pace with billings. Calculated collection rates—the ratio of total payments to total billings—fell 9 percentage points, from 97 percent in 1998 to 88 percent in 1999.

Quantitative Analysis in Moldova

The combination of billing and payment records from the utility and household income data allowed detailed comparison of the impact of public and private sector utilities on consumer behavior in Moldova, thus answering a key stakeholder question about the difference in the impact of privately and publicly managed utilities on consumers. The multivariate demand model below (table 6.2) shows that once other factors (tariff rates, income, household size, apartment size) are taken into account, a dummy

Table 6.1 Aggregate Impact of Electricity Tariff Change*

Household	1998	1999	Change between 1998 and 1999	
			Units	Percent
Consumption (million kWh) (a)	2.22	1.83	−0.38	−17%
Billings (million Armenian drams) (b)	39.57	45.79	6.22	16%
Payments (million Armenian drams) (c)	38.22	40.33	2.11	6%
Collection rate (percent) (c/b)	97%	88%		−9 pp.**

Source: World Bank (2001).
Note: *For sample households only; **percentage points.

Table 6.2 Factors that Explain Differences in Consumption

Dependent variable = log household kWh	Coefficient	Standard error	Z	P > z	95% confidence interval	
Elec_Net	0.1129609	0.1593886	0.71	0.479	−0.1994349	0.4253568
LNtariff_ Elec_Net[a]	0.391911	0.1516937	2.58	0.010	0.0945967	0.6892253
Lntariff	−0.8179857	0.1078821	−7.58	0.000	−1.029431	−0.6065406
LNexp_ Elec_Net[a]	−0.0257354	0.0157094	−1.64	0.101	−0.0565253	0.0050545
LNexp	0.4073425	0.0101895	39.98	0.000	0.3873715	0.4273135
hhsize_ Elec_Net[a]	0.037604	0.0089831	4.19	0.000	0.0199975	0.0552105
hhsize	0.0774905	0.0052413	14.78	0.000	0.0672178	0.0877632
Centralgas	−0.0315774	0.0172559	−1.83	0.067	−0.0653983	0.0022436
Central heating	0.2400001	0.0218951	10.96	0.000	0.1970865	0.2829138
Large cities	0.3621006	0.0266468	13.59	0.000	0.3098739	0.4143272
Small towns	0.352343	0.0182673	19.29	0.000	0.3165397	0.3881463
LNapart_area_ Elec_Net[a]	0.0523831	0.0275835	1.9	0.058	−0.0016796	0.1064458
LNapart_area	0.1292712	0.0167569	7.71	0.000	0.0964282	0.1621142
quarter2	−0.1061795	0.0138249	−7.68	0.000	−0.1332758	−0.0790832
quarter3	−0.0973005	0.0142535	−6.83	0.000	−0.1252369	−0.0693641
quarter4	−0.0338091	0.0137512	−2.46	0.014	−0.060761	−0.0068573
_cons	−0.2031077	0.1033946	−1.96	0.049	−0.4057573	−0.000458
sigma_u	0.38643982					
sigma_e	0.48026545					
Rho	0.39299847	(fraction of variance due to u_i)				

Source: World Bank (2005).

Note: The dependent variable is the log of household kWh consumption. The independent variables are electricity network, log tariff × electricity network, log tariff, log income × electricity network, log income, household size × electricity network, household size, central gas, central heating, large cities, small towns, log apartment area × electricity network, log apartment area, quarter 2 (April–June), quarter 3 (July–September), quarter 4 (October–December), constant.

Random-effects GLS regression	Number of observations = 17,510
Group variable (i): hhid	Number of groups = 10,726
R^2 within = 0.0486	Observations per group: Minimum = 1
R^2 between = 0.4391	Average = 1.6
R^2 overall = 0.3875	Maximum = 3
Random effects u_i ~ Gaussian	Wald chi^2 (16) = 8,634.93
corr (u_i, X) = 0 (assumed)	Probability > chi^2 = 0.0000

a. Interaction variables (variable of interest multiplied by "poor" dummy). These are: Dummy "poor": 0 if not poor, 1 if poor. Dummy "CentralHeating": 0 if central heating not available, 1 if available. Dummy "CentralGas": 0 if central gas not available, 1 if available. Dummy "LargeCities": 0 if household not located in large city, 1 if in large city. Rural: excluded category. Dummy "SmallTowns": 0 if household not located in small town, 1 if in small town. Dummy "Elec_Net": 0 if Union Fenosa, 1 if NRED.

variable for the service provider is not statistically significant. This enabled the team to determine that household electricity consumption patterns were not different for the private and public distribution networks.

Engagement with Stakeholders

Another important element in the design of these PSIAs is engagement with stakeholders. Traditionally the sector specialists working on the reform program in both the government and the Bank have few incentives to engage in public discourse on the design of the reform before it is complete. This is understandable because public discourse can slow down or delay the process, and can sometimes contribute to a less-than-optimal program design. For all these PSIAs, however, a working group of government, civil society, and nongovernment stakeholders are brought in at the concept stage to participate in the analysis and discuss the findings. This kind of open process of information gathering and discussion with the various stakeholders fosters local ownership of the policy process and provides input to the team working on the analysis.

Take, for example, the Azerbaijan PSIA stakeholder analysis. A series of in-depth interviews was conducted with representatives from the presidential administration, the cabinet of ministers, the Ministry of Economic Development, the Ministry of Fuel and Energy, the Ministry of Labor, the Ministry of Environment and Natural Resources, parliament, energy sector enterprises, the media, and NGOs. The objective of these interviews was to identify key elements of the reform package that are not supported by the stakeholders and why.

The interviews found that there is general consensus among stakeholders from various backgrounds on the key elements of reform. These elements include

- that there is a need for tariff reform;
- that mitigation policies must be place to cushion adverse social effects of reforms;
- that metering and collection rates must be improved first, before implementing the reform;
- that higher tariffs and collection rates should be accompanied by improved service; and
- that private sector participation is necessary.

Consensus on the broad reform measures suggests that the risks of controversy when engaging in a more transparent dialogue are low.

The conclusion from this analysis was that a more transparent forum for dialogue on reform measures was necessary because only a limited number of key players in the Ministry of Economic Development and the Ministry of Finance are fully aware of the actions being considered as part of the reform program. Other stakeholders are less well informed, and they often feel excluded from the process or have different views. For example, some of the stakeholders do not think the Tariff Council, with its limited mandate of tariff setting, is the appropriate institution to facilitate the dialogue.

Another conclusion from the stakeholder analysis was that senior government staff need and want more information on the full set of reform options. They are particularly keen to learn from the experience of other countries that have undergone similar reform programs. Some of the most pressing questions relate to mitigating social impacts, tariff design, and attracting private sector investors. Although a fair amount of technical assistance is already being provided in this area, it may be possible to enhance this assistance through a series of study tours to countries where the reform program has been very innovative.

MAIN FINDINGS

The countries of Europe and Central Asia, with their cold winter climates and socialist backgrounds, have specific requirements for a beneficial reform in the power sector. There are eight main findings from this analysis of the early group of power sector PSIAs that apply to these countries.

- As noted earlier, the starting point for reforms is different in Europe and Central Asia. The socialist system gave almost all households access to reliable, inexpensive electricity. Thus welfare gains from increased access—often one of the most immediate and tangible benefits of power sector reforms—is not a consideration in most of these countries. This leads to our first finding, which is that the welfare gains come from improvements in service quality, not increases in access. This finding reinforces the need for reform that will emphasize outcome-based indicators of service quality.
- Without ex-ante disaggregated baseline data on service quality, reform appears to be closely linked to a fall in welfare. This leads to the second finding, which is that electricity spending as a share of income has often increased, especially for the poor, while consumption stayed the same or fell. Where actual household data on consumption has been collected (directly from the utilities), consumption is very low, sufficient only to satisfy basic subsistence needs. In countries with very low consumption, demand for electricity is relatively inelastic, suggesting that there may be large welfare losses associated with future tariff increases.

■ The third finding is that households consistently spend somewhere from 2 to 10 percent of their income on electricity, and the bottom quintile consistently spends a larger share than the top. That the bottom quintiles, or poor, devote a higher share of income to electricity indicates that electricity is a necessary good. Although the top quintile may be capturing a larger share of sector subsidies in absolute terms, it is a larger share of income for the poor. This suggests a greater proportionate welfare loss for the poor, who undertake a more active search for substitutes when tariffs are increased to cost recovery levels.

■ The fourth finding is that rural households spend a lower share of income on electricity than urban households. This may be because they have greater access to inexpensive substitutes such as wood and coal. If true, then under certain circumstances a move to raise tariffs to cost recovery could lead to negative externalities such as indoor air pollution, outdoor air pollution, and deforestation. All of these negative externalities have social costs that the public sector may not want to ignore.

■ The fifth finding is that the poor are much more likely than the rich to report zero electricity payment. Nonpayment is one of the most vexing problems in Europe and Central Asia; a key power sector reform objective has been to resolve this problem. In addition to the poor being more likely to report zero payment, nonpayments are positively correlated with expenditure ratios. This suggests that policies designed to both raise collections and tariffs at the same time will disproportionately affect the poor.

■ The sixth finding is related to the design of measures to mitigate the impact of tariff increases. Existing social protection systems are typically not very well correlated with poverty. Leakage and coverage in these systems is generally positively correlated. By comparison, the performance of lifeline tariffs on both these measures is a function of the percentage of the population below the poverty line. The greater the number of poor people, the higher the coverage and the lower the leakage. Coverage is also generally negatively correlated with inequality, suggesting that—compared with income transfers—lifelines will produce the biggest gains in coverage in countries with high inequality.

■ The seventh finding is that proper sequencing is key to making reform acceptable. For example, although a poverty-targeted income transfer is more efficient, it may take years to become operational. This is because the existing social protection systems (and energy-specific safety nets) in Europe and Central Asia are usually based on categorical privileges. Reformulation of categories can be politically difficult, time consuming, and ultimately quite expensive. Another problem is that the amount of compensation is often subject to political lobbying. Thus, in the near term, the only feasible solution may be to channel compensation through the existing social protection system.

■ The eighth finding is that reliable longitudinal data on deforestation and fuel switching behavior were not available, making it impossible to separate the potential health consequences of power sector reform from other factors. Although anecdotal evidence suggests that in many places there has been an increase in the use of dirty fuel, this cannot be unambiguously attributed to power sector reform. It may, for example, be a result of a concomitant collapse in district heating. There is, however, evidence that poor households burn more dirty fuel than non-poor households, especially for heating. Survey data indicate that fewer households would use wood and coal if they had access to gas. Of course, in many countries the gas sector is also in need of reform before it can operate on a sustainable basis. More data are needed to evaluate the impact of reforms on fuel switching, energy use, substitution effects, and health and social effects.

THE IMPACT OF THE PSIA

This group of PSIAs has had an impact on both overall policy design and operational design. Some of these are explored in more detail below.

Impact on Policy Design

In terms of overall policy design, the main impact of these PSIAs has been to contribute to softening the Bank's position on privatization. This point was largely driven home by the Armenia PSIA, which found that reform-induced electricity prices increased and consumption fell significantly more than expected when the national power company was put on commercial terms in preparation for eventual sale. Ultimately, the government of Armenia did not collect nearly as much new revenue as it had hoped, and the arrears for the poor increased. As noted in the *Wall Street Journal:* "The Armenia study landed with a thud at the World Bank; it implied that free-market ideology had trumped clear thinking when the World Bank had prodded the Armenian government to commercialize the power company" (Phillips 2003).

The second major area where the PSIAs have had an influence is on the debate over direct income supports versus lifeline tariffs. In the late 1990s there was a very strong emphasis on direct income transfers as the best way to mitigate the impact of tariff increases on the poor. However, the PSIAs found that the existing social protection systems were prone to leakage and it would take years to establish new systems. The question of whether lifeline tariffs or targeted subsidies are more appropriate in a transition context depends on the timeline for reform, the leakage of the existing social protection system, and the available budget. Lifeline tariffs can be effective, as long as the size of the blocks of consumption levels at which different tariffs come into effect is set to minimize capture by the non-poor (this can also become a political issue) and the government explicitly compensates utilities for any social transfers they are asked to provide. Ultimately the tradeoffs between lifelines and income transfers through social protection system depend on country-specific circumstances.

In terms of influence on the public policy debate within the country, the PSIAs have generally improved the dialogue by bringing policy-based evidence to the table. For example, in Moldova reform opponents were claiming that electricity is a merit good and therefore should be provided by the public sector. They were also claiming that consumers were getting a bad deal (from the private sector) because the regulatory system is weak and prone to pressure from the private company. Proponents of reform were arguing that privatization made the electricity sector more efficient and financially stable. In this context the PSIA set out to answer two questions about reform. First, did reform affect the poor differently from the non-poor? Second, were household consumption patterns different for private and public distribution networks? To get at these issues the study analyzed a range of household welfare indicators after the implementation of privatization, including access, consumption, and expenditures on electricity. It also analyzed coping mechanisms, the roles played by the social assistance compensation system, and consumer perceptions.

Although it is early to determine the impact of the Moldova PSIA on policy—it is still being disseminated and requests for copies from various agencies are received regularly by the resident mission—it has changed the terms of the debate on energy privatization. By concluding that there was no statistically significant difference between the impact on poor and non-poor, this issue in the dialogue with the Bank and the government has been clarified. The latter has, in effect, dropped its past arguments against privatization—that the poor were hurt by its consequences. (The report found that differences in consumption are more closely linked to location than to the electricity provider.)

Impact on Operational Design

There are several areas where the PSIAs are expected to have an impact on operational design. The first expected impact is that countries' reform programs will encourage an explicit linking of tariff increases to improvements in service quality. As noted earlier, there might be a mismatch between the timing of the costs (higher tariffs) and benefits (improved service quality) of tariff reform. In this case, the welfare loss from raising tariffs can be minimized by explicitly linking tariff increases to improved service quality. This can be particularly important for poor people because they often suffer from the lowest-quality service. It is also likely to generate more political will to support the reform.

The second expected impact is that countries will consider raising tariffs more slowly. The shock therapy programs of the 1990s included sudden radical increases in tariffs. Although this approach has its proponents and opponents, there is little doubt that sudden changes in tariffs require changes in behavior that cannot be as rapid as the shocks that initiate them. Raising tariffs slowly minimizes welfare losses by allowing consumers to adjust their consumption patterns, take advantage of income growth, and increase their use of substitutes. However, it also is likely to have significant fiscal costs, especially if tariffs are well below cost recovery. If sudden large tariff increases are absolutely necessary, they should be accompanied by programs that provide households with the resources necessary adjust to the new tariff structure.

The third impact is that countries' reform programs will try to focus on raising collections before raising tariffs. Given higher nonpayment among the poor and assuming uniform enforcement of collections, the poor will likely face bigger effective tariff increases than the non-poor. Although this was not the case in every country (an exception being Moldova), it implies that the poor will require slightly more compensation than the non-poor if both tariffs and collections are increasing at the same time. The timing of collection efforts is crucial and should be closely linked to improvements in service quality. Alternatively, efforts could be made to raise collections first, because otherwise the tariff increase is likely to translate into a nonpayment problem.

The fourth impact is that countries' reform programs will carefully consider the role the public sector should play in increasing access to gas as part of the reform program. Because the poor have less access to the LPG infrastructure, increasing access to allow use of clean and inexpensive substitutes might be one of the best ways to offset the impact of electricity tariff increases, particularly where a large number of people heat with electricity. Increasing access to gas can be done through a variety of instruments, as long as the government explicitly compensates the utility for any social transfers it provides. An example would be bidding out competitive subsidies to encourage the extension of natural gas networks to poor neighborhoods. Particularly promising, especially in areas where large increases in clean fuel prices are expected, are investments in efficiency and insulation that can produce substantial reductions in consumption. These investments must be coupled with innovative financial instruments that enable consumers, particularly the poor, to distribute capital costs over a longer period.

Finally, metering is and should continue to be a priority, especially for the poor. In an environment of tariff reform, meters offer consumers information about and control over their energy use, leading to savings and possibly to more efficient consumption. Recent advances in smart metering technology are particularly promising. The simplest form of smart metering is a display meter that allows consumers to monitor consumption in money terms rather than kilowatt hours. Such a meter can be combined with a keypad or smartcard reader that could link to prepayment systems, thereby potentially reducing costs and allowing consumers to take advantage of lower tariffs generally offered to prepayment customers. Internet-linked systems offer other services, including welfare benefits payments. Realizing the full potential for smart metering requires piloting the technology to establish the real value to customers. It is unrealistic to expect low-income households to meet the cost of installing expensive new systems.

LESSONS LEARNED

Several lessons that apply across countries with difficult climate conditions and complex historical backgrounds can be learned from the groups of PSIAs addressed in this chapter. Common to all these lessons is the understanding that each country has a unique set of circumstances, and the implication that therefore each reform must be tailored to those particular circumstances.

■ **Adapt the design of the PSIA by taking into account the local political economy.** Every one of the PSIAs described here is slightly different and was carefully tailored to address issues and problems raised by the primary stakeholders. For example, the Moldova PSIA addressed the question of differential impacts of privately and publicly managed utilities on the poor. By contrast, the Azerbaijan PSIA focused more on the potential future welfare effect of raising tariffs and how people would need to be compensated to mitigate this effect.

- **Make sure adequate time and resources are made available.** It is worth stressing the importance of adequate time and budget resources when assessing sensitive issues such as utility privatization and tariff increases. Rigorous, high-quality analysis cannot be undertaken under unrealistic time constraints. Sufficient time is also required for the stakeholders, including those within the Bank, to understand the implications of the study, participate in a meaningful way in consultations, and respond to the findings. All the energy PSIAs under discussion were given a relatively long timeframe and significant resources with which to proceed. The average time period was one year, and the cost of the work for each PSIA was about US$100,000. By contrast, more recent PSIAs have been hurried through the pipeline and consequently have not become part of the policy dialogue. Also, without enough time to collect high-quality data, the robustness of the analysis has been questioned. The result is a study with correspondingly less influence.

- **Involve a broad range of stakeholders.** The PSIA was found to be a good instrument for initiating a broad-based dialogue on energy reform. Through discussions with all the stakeholders, including potentially affected population groups, and doing so openly, the PSIA became a forum for the discussion. The attitude of the PSIA team sought to make all stakeholders welcome and encouraged them to speak their minds. Their views and contributions, to the extent possible, were then reflected in the final result. Previously, discussion and debate was usually dominated by one or more powerful stakeholders. Introducing a broad spectrum of actors can "democratize" the debate and bring into the open hitherto neglected information and opinions. Ultimately this helps galvanize support for the findings. When all the antagonists are asked to contribute to a study and its findings, they are naturally more inclined to support its findings. Having contributed to some degree to the planning and design of the study, they are more likely to have a stake in its outcome. It is therefore important to acknowledge their contribution during the process. Instead of back-and-forth accusations in the media and a partial and biased understanding of the issue, the PSIA analysis can and should ground the discussion in sound evidence.

- **Emphasize rigorous analysis.** The more controversial the issue and the more unexpected the findings, the more important it is to base the study on sound evidence. A clear advantage of conducting PSIAs on energy reform was the availability of extensive and rich data to draw upon, as mentioned earlier. Aside from the opportunities for a nuanced analysis of many issues related to consumption behavior, rigorous data analysis can serve as a backstop should the findings be questioned. Having data that are recognized to be of good quality, such as HBS or utility billing data, can give the PSIA instrument the strength it needs. Often, of course, such data are unavailable or not applicable. In this case, the amount of care that should be given to the research design, data collection, and analysis cannot be emphasized enough. In addition to analytic rigor, clarity is crucial. Using a sound methodology, comprehensible to the layperson, and laying out the findings in a lucid manner accessible to those without the theoretic or analytic background (who make up the majority of the stakeholders) can move the discussion away from speculation, theorizing, and finger-pointing via the media or other channels to a constructive dialogue on the purpose and implementation of the reform.

- **Ex ante and ex post analysis can both be valuable tools.** Although the PSIA instrument was originally conceived as an ex ante analytical instrument, it has great value when conducted ex post as well. Armenia, Georgia, and Moldova PSIAs were ex post studies; Azerbaijan and Kyrgyz Republic PSIAs were ex ante. Ex post analysis has the advantage of using actual data and not relying on projections, and it helps set the tone for future actions. It can also help slow a reform program that is going off track or keep a reform program on track when it is going off. An example of the latter is Moldova: when the communist party came to power on an anti-reform platform, after-the-fact analysis helped keep the program on track.

- **Reframe controversial issues.** By reframing a problem, a PSIA can sometimes foster a more constructive dialogue by moving it in a direction more conducive to resolution. In the case of Moldova, the government contended that rising tariff prices were hurting the poor and increasing overall poverty. Because of the difficulties of establishing causal relationships, the study reframed this issue by asking whether the poor were consuming more or less electricity after privatization. It held as its hypothesis that, if post-privatization consumption of electricity was decreasing along with decreasing overall consumption, then raising electricity prices would cause the poor to cut back on electricity consumption. Data analysis, however, showed that the poor's consumption of electricity was increasing. Poverty indicators were found to be decreasing as well. Thus the study did not address causal movements, but instead showed that increasing prices, and much greater electricity availability, occurred simultaneously with increases in consumption, and let the audience draw its own conclusions. Another way of framing the debate would have been to argue that rising prices were preventing the poor from reaching previous, much higher, levels. This could easily have fueled another debate.

The use of the PSIAs shows that the analysis process can indeed increase the chances for a successful power sector reform program, and can also smooth the transition for the poor. Reform of the sector is both essential and sensitive for each of the countries of Central Europe and Asia addressed in this chapter, and it is enhanced substantially by the PSIA studies.

NOTES

1. This chapter builds on the work of many people, including Anthony Kolb, Sumila Gulyani, Varham Avenessian, Hernan Gonzalez, Margaret Wilson, Ellen Hamilton, Sergo Vashakmadze, Taras Pushak, Nora Dudwick, Katelijn Van Den Berg, Grant Milne, Maria Shkaratan, Xun Wu, Karin Fock, and Irina Klytchnikova.
2. There has been considerable debate about the costs and benefits of the different elements of reform. In the majority of cases, the decisions about the best course of action are made behind closed doors and revealed to the full range of stakeholders only when the program is a fait accompli. This group of PSIAs is contributing to a more open, participatory process that offers the possibility of bringing more stakeholders on board at an earlier stage.
3. Although business is clearly a key stakeholder, there is little doubt about the direction and magnitude of the impact of reform on this group and therefore there is relatively little emphasis on this group in the literature.
4. A *lifeline* consists of a lower price for a given level of essential consumption.
5. A refrigerator (manual defrost 5–15 years old) consumes about 95 kWh/month; three incandescent light bulbs consume another 30 kWh per month.

REFERENCES

Phillips, Michael. 2003. "World Bank Wonders about Utility Privatizations." *Wall Street Journal* July 21: A2.

World Bank. 1998. "Energy in Europe and Central Asia: A Sector Strategy for the World Bank Group." Discussion Paper 393, World Bank, Washington, DC.

World Bank. 2001. "Utility Pricing and the Poor: Lessons from Armenia." Technical Paper 497, World Bank, Washington, DC.

World Bank. 2002. "Coping with the Cold: Heating Strategies for ECA's Urban Poor." Technical Paper 529, World Bank, Washington DC.

World Bank. 2004a. "Power's Promise: Electricity Reforms in Eastern Europe and Central Asia." Working Paper 40, World Bank, Washington, DC.

World Bank. 2004b. "Revisiting Reform in the Energy Sector: Lessons from Georgia." Working Paper 21, World Bank, Washington, DC

World Bank. 2005. *Moldova. Sharing Power: Lessons Learned from the Reform and Privatization of Moldova's Electricity Sector.* Report No. 30376-MD, World Bank, Washington, DC.

7

RWANDA
Electricity Tariff Reform

DIEGO ANGEL-URDINOLA,
MALCOLM COSGROVE-DAVIES,
AND QUENTIN WODON

I nternal political stability, policy reforms, and foreign aid have helped Rwanda stage a remarkable economic recovery over the decade since the genocide. Real GDP growth averaged more than 7 percent per annum over the period 1998–2002, slowed to 3 percent in 2003, and is estimated to be around 4 percent in 2004 and 6 percent over 2005–7. Despite the growth in GDP, however, poverty remains widespread (Government of Rwanda 2002; World Bank 2003), and infrastructure bottlenecks have emerged as a significant constraint to continuing economic growth and human capital development. This is the case for the energy sector, especially the provision of electricity, which is currently in a state of crisis. The objective of this chapter is to document this crisis, explain the need to increase electricity tariffs, and—most importantly—assess the impact of such an increase on the poor and also analyze the distributive properties of alternative tariff structures.

ELECTRICITY IN RWANDA: CURRENT CONTEXT

The modern energy sector in Rwanda is very small. Wood and charcoal remain the most significant—and often the only—fuels available to households and the productive sectors of the economy. Most of Rwanda's electricity has traditionally come from hydroelectric power produced domestically, along with imports from Sinelac (which is a utility owned jointly by Rwanda, Burundi, and the Democratic Republic of Congo) and SNEL (a utility company from the Democratic Republic of Congo). Electrogaz, Rwanda's main energy provider, provides service to fewer than 70,000 customers or about 7 percent of the households (nearly two-thirds of them in Kigali alone). Peak electricity demand—which is currently not being met—is about 50 to 55 megawatts. Grid extension beyond the urban areas has been extremely limited. At about 20 to 25 kilowatts per year, per capita consumption of electricity in Rwanda is among the lowest in the world. Electrogaz is in a difficult situation because strong demand growth is combined with unexpectedly low lake levels in both domestic and shared hydropower sources. The financial situation of Electrogaz is also problematic, and supply shortages and unreliability (there have been extensive and lengthy power cuts beginning in early 2004) have raised the cost of doing business for firms in Rwanda and weakened the prospects of attracting new investments.

Rwanda is facing a severe electricity crisis because of increased demand and production costs coupled with reduced revenues over time in real terms per kilowatt-hour distributed. The government's strategy has been to respond to the twin objectives of extracting the sector from its crisis situation and establishing a sound basis for future growth and development. Over the medium term, the government intends to establish policies and institutional frameworks that would create incentives for developing indigenous energy resources, ensuring the sustainable and efficient performance of sector entities, and increasing access to electricity and enhancing the flow of investments, both from development partners and from the private sector. In the near term, the government intends to use a transition strategy to address the power shortage by investing in thermal generation and by reviving the performance of Electrogaz. Finally, immediately, the government's focus has been on raising electricity tariffs to increase revenues for Electrogaz and avoid large deficits in the sector.

Objectives and Findings of this Analysis

A doubling of electricity tariffs was recently approved, from a flat rate of 42 Rwanda francs (RF) per kilowatt hour to a flat rate of RF 81.25 per kilowatt hour. The new tariff became effective in January of 2005. However, the new flat rate may not be appropriate for protecting some of the poorer residential customers of Electrogaz from the increase in the level of electricity tariffs. This chapter provides simulations for the distributional properties of alternative tariff designs, including an interesting Inverted-U Block Tariff Structure (IUBT) proposed by Electrogaz. In the next section of this chapter, which is based on material prepared for the Urgent Electricity Rehabilitation credit recently granted to Rwanda (World Bank 2004), we document the current state of crisis of the electricity sector and its origins, and explain the need for the upward revision of electricity tariffs. In the subsequent section, which closely follows a framework for the analysis of utility tariffs proposed by Angel-Urdinola and Wodon (2005), we assess the distributional characteristics of alternative potential tariff structures using recent household survey data.

It is important to note that this chapter was prepared as part of broader work at the World Bank on Rwanda's energy sector. This work includes the Urgent Electricity Rehabilitation credit, which has a detailed discussion of the difficulties encountered in the electricity sector (World Bank 2004), and a second Poverty Reduction Strategy Grant or PRSG II (World Bank 2005), which was approved by the Bank's board in November 2005 and includes further measures related to this sector. Specifically, one of the triggers for the PRSG III (that is, one of the measures that should be implemented by the authorities to benefit from a third PRSG) is the passage of electricity and gas legislation that includes tariff reform in order to improve energy sector performance.

Our findings in this chapter can be summarized as follows. Because few people have access to the electricity network, the share of the implicit subsidies that prevailed before the increase in tariff and that benefited the poor was very low. Today, consumption subsidies are still likely to be badly targeted to the poor, and the IUBT proposal would improve targeting performance slightly. Nevertheless, the IUBT tariff structure is less pro-poor than a volume-differentiated tariff (VDT) would be. Furthermore, if substantial subsidies (or cross-subsidies) were to be implemented in the future, it would probably be more effective from a poverty reduction point of view to give priority to subsidies for new connections to the network for the poor rather than providing subsidies for consumption for those households already connected. Yet there may still be some benefit to also providing some level of protection for households that are already connected and that consume small amounts of electricity, especially if such protection is not too expensive and if a careful analysis of the distributional properties of the proposal is carried out.

Rwanda's Electricity Sector: A Brief Review

In 2003 and in 2004, Rwanda's demand for energy was about 50 to 55 megawatts per year. However, domestic power generation facilities consist of only four hydroelectric plants that together can produce about

28.6 megawatts per year. The largest two of these plants (with a combined capacity of about 24 megawatts) are based on interconnected lakes, the levels of which have declined precipitously in recent years. As a result, energy demand is not being met and the country is critically dependent on imports of modern energy sources. Petroleum products are transported from Mombasa in Kenya via pipelines to Eldoret in Uganda, then by road to Kigali and elsewhere in the country (which introduces very high transportation costs and several duties and taxes).

In 2004, on average, about 20 percent of the peak demand and energy requirements were not met. The lack of energy was more severe during the dry period of August/September 2004, when as much as 50 percent of the energy requirements during peak hours were not met. The extent of hydroelectricity supply shortfall in the face of growing demand is expected to continue for several years.

Apart from weaknesses in production, the national transmission and distribution network is small and dilapidated. Some of the network was damaged during the civil war period (in 1994), but all of it suffers from inadequate maintenance, compounding the bulk supply problems. Technical and nontechnical physical losses—the difference between energy sent out and energy billed—were about 25 percent in 2003. These losses are attributable mainly to poor network conditions and metering equipment, though there may also be a small amount of illegal use. Although investment requirements in network rehabilitation are high, only a small amount of urgent patchwork repair and replacement has been done. Over the next three years, it will be urgent not only that sufficient resources be made available for expanding overall capacity to meet demand growth, but also that Electrogaz revenues be adequate for financing the sharp increases in variable (fuel and other operating) costs of using new capacity.

Electrogaz is Rwanda's largest company. It is a 100 percent publicly owned utility for grid electricity and urban water supplies. Although national in scope, most of its distribution network and sales are concentrated in Kigali. Although the government abolished its legal monopoly on power distribution in 2000, it remains the only operator in the sector. A five-year management contract to Lahmeyer International has been in place since November 1, 2003. The government of Rwanda has postponed a decision on privatization of Electrogaz until the end of this management contract. Transforming Electrogaz into a well-run, commercially oriented utility is a major challenge. The success of the management contract with Lahmeyer depends on the availability of funding for system rehabilitation and expansion, and there have been delays in mobilizing the necessary resources. In addition, considerable effort has had to be devoted to addressing the ongoing power shortages on a crisis basis, which has hindered the longer-term task of system planning and improving Electrogaz's commercial performance.

Electrogaz is in a difficult financial situation. Revenue collection has been poor until recently, but this has apparently improved since new management took over in late 2003. More than half of all Electrogaz's customers—these are customers in both residential and commercial or government sectors, most of them in Kigali—are on pre-paid meters, contributing to advance payment on some 25 percent of the company's total sales. As with the supply infrastructure, there has been little new investment on the customer service end: meters, billing, and accounting systems are old and their reliability low. Still, the number of low-voltage customers has grown about 60 percent since 1997, at an average of 4,000 new connections per year.

Electrogaz's electricity and water tariffs were last revised in 1997. Since then there has been nearly 50 percent real decline in electricity tariffs in U.S. dollar terms—from about US$0.150 per kilowatt hour in 1997 to about US$0.072 per kilowatt hour in 2004. During this period, imports from the jointly owned company Sinelac increased rapidly. Largely because of its high lending terms and capitalization of debt service, Sinelac tariffs have reached levels that cannot reasonably be passed through to the customers. Electrogaz had a flat tariff of RF 42 per kilowatt hour (before 18 percent value added tax [VAT]) charged to all customers, irrespective of type of activity, individual supply voltage or consumption volumes from mid- to late 1997 to end-2004, when it was revised to a flat tariff of RF 81.25 per kilowatt hour. The flat tariff structure limits the ability to target effective cross-subsidies to existing and prospective low-volume/poor household customers.

Background and Objective of this Analysis

In recent negotiations between the World Bank and the Government of Rwanda on a credit to the country for urgent electricity rehabilitation, financial cost recovery objectives were agreed upon. The terms of the agreement specify that during fiscal 2005 and 2006, cash revenues from sales should be sufficient to cover cash operating expenses. Thereafter, during fiscal 2007, cash revenues from sales should be sufficient to cover cash operating expenses and debt service. Finally, effective in fiscal 2008, Electrogaz should set tariffs such that cash revenues from sales should be sufficient to cover cash operating expense, debt service, and 25 percent of the investment program during that year.

In setting these targets, it was assumed that Electrogaz would be exempted from all taxes on generation fuels. Thus, the tariff adjustments have been designed to enable Electrogaz to meet its financial objectives in the respective years. In practice, as a temporary measure, a doubling of electricity tariffs was recently approved, as mentioned earlier. The rate rose from a flat rate of RF 42 per kilowatt hour to RF 81.25 per kilowatt hour.

More recently, the Bank and the authorities of Rwanda agreed that a trigger for the next Poverty Reduction Support Grant (PRSG III) would be the adoption by the authorities of electricity and gas legislation that would include tariff reform to improve energy sector performance. The question now is which new tariff structure would be appropriate, and whether the new proposals for an IUBT (discussed below) by Electrogaz make sense. In the next section of this chapter, we try to answer these questions by looking at the impact of the tariff structure on the poor using recent household survey data, and we also simulate the distributional characteristics of alternative tariff structures.

Before presenting our framework for analysis and key results, it is worth noting the limits of the exercise. Our objective was not to conduct a full Poverty and Social Impact Analysis (PSIA) as this analysis is traditionally understood. We did not have a request from the government to do such a full analysis, nor did we have funding for a large scale study. We aimed to provide a rapid appraisal of the main distributional features of alternative tariff structures, since this was the main issue to be acted upon by the authorities in order to complete the trigger for the PRSG III. We focused on a rapid benefit incidence analysis and, by extension, on a poverty impact analysis, without carrying out a social analysis of the potential impact of the reforms. For example, we did not conduct any stakeholder analysis, nor did we conduct qualitative work on the perceptions of key stakeholders, especially the poor, of the tariff reform. We also did not carry out institutional work on the capacity constraints for implementing specific policy proposals.

Most of the results provided here were presented at a workshop in Kigali in March 2005. The workshop was organized jointly by the World Bank and the Rwandese government unit in charge of the preparation, implementation, and revision of Rwanda's Poverty Reduction Strategy. One of the sessions of the full-day seminar was devoted to electricity tariffs, with representation from the management of Electrogaz. The work that had been prepared by the Bank team for that session focused on comparing the flat tariff structure existing in Rwanda at the time with traditional inverted block tariffs (IBTs) and volume-differentiated tariffs (VDTs). As discussed in Komives et al. (2005), IBTs are typically based on the assumption that poorer consumers have lower levels of consumption, so that reduced tariffs at low levels of consumption provide a higher degree of affordability for the poor, while supposedly targeting only the poor in so doing. Thus it is often believed that subsidies are not provided to other classes of customers who consume higher levels of electricity and presumably have the means to pay the full cost for it. But the problem with IBTs is that all customers benefit from the lower price for the first bracket(s) of consumption, and this leads to high leakage of the implicit or explicit subsidies to the non-poor.

VDTs, the alternative to the IBTs, provide the lower price at low levels of consumption to only those households that consume less than a given threshold. This threshold is often referred to as the *lifeline* level of consumption that should be affordable to all. In many countries, IBTs and/or VDTs have more than two levels of pricing for different blocks of consumers. It can then be shown that VDTs tend to be better targeted than IBTs, both of which have better distributional characteristics than flat tariff rates such as the flat fee that had prevailed in Rwanda for many years. This was also the case in Rwanda, and these were the results that were presented by the Bank team. Unfortunately, as pointed out by the seminar participants, VDTs have one weakness: they imply a discontinuity in the amount of the bill for the customer. For example, assume that the lifeline is set at 40 kilowatt hours per month per household, that a lower price per kilowatt hour applies to households with consumption levels below that lifeline, and a higher price applies to all households where the consumption level is above the lifeline. This means that a household consuming 40.5 kilowatt hours per month will have a much higher bill than the household consuming only 39.5 kilowatt hours, although both households may be equally poor. In addition, some households might move from one price to another depending on their monthly consumption and the billing system.

The idea of the IUBT came from the staff of Electrogaz. Their proposal was to provide a reduced price on all consumption below 20 kilowatt hours, along with a price that is higher than the cost-recovery level for all consumption between 20 and 100 kilowatt hours. The price for units consumed above 100 kilowatt hours were to be set at cost-recovery level. This was an interesting idea because it aimed to recoup some of the subsidy provided in the lower bracket by requesting above-cost contribution in the middle bracket. Under some circumstances, this type of tariff structure can achieve a better targeting performance than a simple IBT, while also avoiding the discontinuity in price under VDTs. After the seminar, the Bank team estimated the extent of the difference engendered by the IUBT idea. These results are provided below, and then compared among other tariff structures with the targeting performance of a VDT.

THE DISTRIBUTIONAL PROPERTIES OF ALTERNATIVE TARIFF STRUCTURES

Our aim in this section is to provide a rapid appraisal of the distributional characteristics of alternative tariff structures. For this we use data from a household survey and a basic analytical framework proposed by Angel-Urdinola and Wodon (2005).

Data and Basic Statistics

The analysis in this section is based on data from the Integrated Household Living Conditions Survey (*Enquête Intégrale sur les Conditions de Vie des Ménages au Rwanda*) conducted by the National Statistical Office between October 1999 and July 2001. Data were collected between October 1999 and December 2000 in urban areas, and from July 2000 to July 2001 in rural areas. The estimates of poverty presented in Rwanda's Poverty Reduction Strategy suggest that 62 percent of the population is poor (Government of Rwanda 2002), with the poverty line set at 64,000 Rwanda francs per adult equivalent per year (the use of the equivalence scale implies that not all household members are considered to have the same needs). Only 10 percent of the population is considered to be living in urban areas, which is where access to the electricity network is concentrated.

Table 7.1 provides data on access to electricity in Rwanda's population (at the national level and in urban areas), as well as average consumption and expenditure for electricity. At the national level, access to electricity is virtually nonexistent in the bottom seven deciles of the distribution of consumption per equivalent adult essentially because access is not available in rural areas, where close to 90 percent of the population lives. This means that almost no one among the poorest 70 percent of the population at the national level has access to electricity. The distribution is different in urban areas, where access rates start to pick up in the third decile. However, according to the official poverty estimates in the country, because only 14 percent of the urban population is considered poor, access among the poor remains very low (as shown by the data for the bottom two deciles of the distribution of consumption per equivalent adult in urban areas). Note that the share of households paying for electricity is close to the share of households declaring in the survey that they use electricity. This suggests that the amount of fraud or illicit

Table 7.1 Electricity Access, Consumption, and Expenditure in Rwanda, 1999/2001

Decile expenditure per equivalent adult	Total expenditure equivalent adult per month[a]	Household size per equivalent adult	Expenditure in electricity per equivalent adult per month[a]	Average kWh consumed per month per household	Access to electricity (%)	Share paying for electricity (%)	Access to electricity at the PSU level (%)	Take up rate (%)
National level								
1	1,333.38	5.78	0.00	0.00	0.00	0.00	4.08	0.00
2	2,172.59	5.88	0.00	0.00	0.00	0.00	5.08	0.00
3	2,751.59	5.78	0.00	0.00	0.16	0.00	4.42	3.63
4	3,321.85	5.57	0.00	0.00	0.00	0.00	4.58	0.00
5	4,007.26	5.54	1.16	0.33	0.54	0.47	4.53	12.01
6	4,829.01	5.22	0.10	0.01	0.20	0.08	8.86	2.23
7	5,811.95	5.23	1.16	0.20	0.54	0.39	7.99	6.73
8	7,270.61	5.42	11.72	2.30	3.29	3.29	13.70	24.01
9	9,861.02	5.18	30.75	5.30	7.85	7.12	21.79	36.00
10	23,798.89	5.41	248.45	34.00	39.94	33.49	63.04	63.35
Urban areas only								
1	3,431.03	6.44	10.81	3.10	5.07	4.36	71.16	7.12
2	5,486.05	5.97	12.02	2.00	7.01	4.53	82.78	8.47
3	7,714.26	6.81	59.45	13.00	22.16	21.92	88.51	25.04
4	9,778.16	6.46	188.28	33.00	42.25	37.78	89.24	47.34
5	12,349.32	6.25	139.25	22.00	44.20	36.77	94.19	46.92
6	15,094.02	6.08	130.24	21.00	40.41	29.00	92.31	43.78
7	18,788.44	5.87	266.60	46.00	56.70	49.83	93.98	60.33
8	23,440.77	5.49	334.94	48.00	54.77	45.28	94.53	57.94
9	30,665.18	6.22	427.62	68.00	70.29	64.99	98.73	71.19
10	57,860.51	5.06	1,030.07	115.00	92.90	79.32	99.34	93.51

Source: Authors' calculations, based on Rwanda's EICV 1999/2001.
a. In local currency (Rwanda francs).

connections in Rwanda is relatively low (higher levels of fraud have been observed in other countries).[1]

Table 7.1 also shows that consumption levels are very low. In urban areas, in the first six deciles of the population, the average consumption is below 40 kilowatt hours per month, which is often considered as a possible lifeline level. Consumption is above 60 kilowatt hours per month only in the top two deciles. Total expenditure for electricity is also very low both in absolute terms and as a percentage of the total expenditure per equivalent adult of the households. This implies that an increase in tariffs would have only a very minor impact on poverty among households connected to the network. Therefore, instead of looking at the impact of tariff hikes on the poor (this impact would be negligible, especially at the national level, because most of the poor simply do not consume any electricity), we will look at the distributional properties of the implicit subsidies that existed until recently in Rwanda for electricity consumption. These subsidies are implicit because, although no cash is distributed directly to the consumers of the electricity, the cost of its production is higher than the price charged. We will then assess how different tariff structures would affect these distributional properties.

A Framework for Assessing the Targeting Performance of Consumption Subsidies

In order to analyze the distributional characteristics of electricity subsidies, we use the very simple analytical framework proposed by Angel-Urdinola and Wodon (2005; see also Komives et al., 2005, for an application of this framework to a large set of countries).[2] Our key parameter of interest is Ω, which is the share of the subsidies, implicit in the tariff structure, received by poor households and divided by the share of the poor in the population. In mathematical terms, this is

$$\Omega = \frac{S_P}{S_H} \times \frac{H}{P}, \tag{7.1}$$

where S denotes the nominal implicit subsidies, subscript P denotes the population of poor people, and subscript H denotes the population as a whole, P denotes the number of poor households or individuals, and H represents the total number of households or individuals.

If Ω takes a value of 1, this implies that the subsidy is roughly neutral from a distribution and poverty point of view, so that the share of benefits going to the poor is equal to their population share. A value above (below) 1 implies that the program is somewhat pro-poor (not pro-poor), since the poor benefit from a larger (smaller) share of the total benefits than their population share.

In practice, many poor households in the population do not receive subsidies, and thus the value of Ω is usually less than 1. There are several reasons for this. First, access to networks may not reach poorer areas. If we denote access to networks by A, this means that in many cases $A_P < A_H$. Also, poor households, although they may have access to the networks, may be less likely than the population on average to use the services because they cannot afford to. If we denote the share of all households that have access to the service in their neighborhood and actually use the service as $U_{H|A}$, this would mean that $U_{H|A} < U_{P|A}$ in most cases. While $U_{H|A}$ represents the take-up rate of connections among those with potential access, $A_H \times U_{H|A}$ represents the actual household connection rate, with the same relationships for the poor (denoted by the subscript P).

Now denote the share of eligible utility service users who are beneficiaries of a subsidy by $T_{H|U}$. In Rwanda, since the consumption of all households was subsidized under the flat rate (before this rate was increased), all users received the subsidy and therefore $T_{H|P} = T_{H|U} = 1$. The share of households receiving the subsidy was equal to the share of all connected household times the share of households eligible for subsidy (that is, $A_H \times U_{H|A} \times T_{H|U}$). Similarly, the share of poor households receiving the subsidy is $A_P \times U_{P|A} \times T_{P|U}$. We will use below the variable B to capture this beneficiary incidence, so that:

$$B_H = A_H \times U_{H|A} \times T_{H|U} \tag{7.2}$$

$$B_P = A_P \times U_{P|A} \times T_{P|U} \tag{7.3}$$

A second important variable for assessing the targeting performance of subsidies is the rate of subsidization or the difference between what households pay per kilowatt hour of electricity and what it actually costs to produce, transmit, and distribute that kilowatt hour. Denote the average unit cost of producing, transmitting, and distributing the good by C. Then the average rate of subsidization is $R_{H|T} = 1 - E_{H|T} / (Q_{H|T} \times C)$, with $Q_{H|T}$ being the average quantity consumed by *subsidy recipients* and $E_{H|T}$ being their average expenditure on electricity. Again, these parameters can be estimated for the poor as a group (by using the subscript P instead of H). The average subsidy benefit per household receiving (and per poor household) in the population as a whole (and among the poor) can then be written as

$$\frac{S_H}{H} = B_H \times R_{H|T} \times Q_{H|T} \times C \tag{7.4}$$

$$\frac{S_P}{P} = B_P \times R_{P|T} \times Q_{P|T} \times C \tag{7.5}$$

The benefit targeting performance indicator Ω, which again represents the share of the benefits of the subsidy obtained by the poor and divided by the share of the poor in the population is equal to

$$\Omega = \frac{A_P}{A_H} \times \frac{U_{P|A}}{U_{H|A}} \times \frac{T_{P|U}}{T_{H|U}} \times \frac{R_{P|T}}{R_{H|T}} \times \frac{Q_{P|T}}{Q_{H|T}} \tag{7.6}$$

Thus five ratios determine the value of the overall performance parameter Ω: access, uptake, targeting, rate of subsidization, and quantity consumed. The ratio of access rates (A) will in most cases be lower than 1 simply because the poor tend to live in areas without access to electricity. The usage or take-up ratio (U) will also be less than 1 if the cost of connecting to the network is high for the poor, or if they live farther away from the grid even when there is access in their neighborhood. This means that the product of the R and Q ratios must be greater than 1 for the subsidy to be progressive. As we will see, in Rwanda (and as has been observed elsewhere), this is rarely the case.

Analyzing Empirical Results for Consumption Subsidies in Rwanda

We analyze the targeting performance of three different types of subsidies or tariff structures: inverted block tariffs, volume-differentiated tariffs, and U-shape tariffs. Table 7.2 provides estimates of Ω at the national level and for urban areas using the official poverty line to define the poor. The benchmark case is the situation that existed before the doubling of tariffs at the end of 2004. At the national level for the benchmark case, Ω takes a value of 0.007, which is extremely low, suggesting that less than 1 percent of the subsidy (or lack of cost recovery) that existed before the increase in tariffs benefited the poor, even though the poor accounted for 62 percent of the population. When estimations are performed for urban areas only, the value of Ω increases to 0.035 but this is still very low, in part because of low official rates of poverty in urban areas (14 percent of the urban population).

The low values of Ω are driven by the comparatively low electricity connection rates among the poor compared with the connection rates of the population as a whole. There are lower access rates (A_P) in the neighborhoods where the poor live than the overall access rate (A_N), and lower take-up rates where there is potential access among the poor U_P than the overall take-up rate (U_N). Because all households that were connected to

Table 7.2 Distributional Characteristics of Alternative Tariff Structures

Parameter	Benchmark flat tariff (price = 42 Rwanda francs/kWh)	Inverted block tariff			Volume-differentiated tariff			Perfect Targeting
		L = 20 kWh	L = 40 kWh	L = 50 kWh	L = 20 kWh	L = 40 kWh	L = 50 kWh	
		National: Absolute poverty definition						
A_H	0.12	0.12	0.12	0.12	0.12	0.12	0.12	0.12
A_P	0.04	0.04	0.04	0.04	0.04	0.04	0.04	0.04
$U_{H|A}$	0.30	0.30	0.30	0.30	0.30	0.30	0.30	0.30
$U_{P|A}$	0.01	0.01	0.01	0.01	0.01	0.01	0.01	0.01
$T_{H|U}$	1.00	1.00	1.00	1.00	0.06	0.30	0.45	0.01
$T_{P|U}$	1.00	1.00	1.00	1.00	0.63	0.72	0.72	1.00
$R_{H|T}$	0.48	0.11	0.20	0.23	0.48	0.48	0.48	0.48
$R_{P|T}$	0.48	0.17	0.25	0.28	0.48	0.48	0.48	0.48
$Q_{H|T}$	88.26	88.26	88.26	88.26	13.15	25.43	32.74	38.46
$Q_{P|T}$	38.46	38.46	38.46	38.46	10.11	11.83	11.83	38.46
A	0.38	0.38	0.38	0.38	0.38	0.38	0.38	0.38
U	0.05	0.05	0.05	0.05	0.05	0.05	0.05	0.05
T	1.00	1.00	1.00	1.00	10.58	2.41	1.58	101.52
R	1.00	1.62	1.27	1.23	1.00	1.00	1.00	1.00
Q	0.44	0.44	0.44	0.44	0.77	0.47	0.36	1.00
Ω	0.007	0.012	0.009	0.009	0.138	0.019	0.010	1.726
		Urban areas: Absolute poverty definition						
A_H	0.86	0.86	0.86	0.86	0.86	0.86	0.86	0.86
A_P	0.70	0.70	0.70	0.70	0.70	0.70	0.70	0.70
$U_{H|A}$	0.37	0.37	0.37	0.37	0.37	0.37	0.37	0.37
$U_{P|A}$	0.04	0.04	0.04	0.04	0.04	0.04	0.04	0.04
$T_{H|U}$	1.00	1.00	1.00	1.00	0.05	0.28	0.42	0.01
$T_{P|U}$	1.00	1.00	1.00	1.00	0.63	0.72	0.72	1.00
$R_{H|T}$	0.48	0.10	0.19	0.22	0.48	0.48	0.48	0.48
$R_{P|T}$	0.48	0.17	0.25	0.28	0.48	0.48	0.48	0.48
$Q_{H|T}$	92.49	92.49	92.49	92.49	12.73	25.11	32.54	38.46
$Q_{P|T}$	38.46	38.46	38.46	38.46	10.11	11.83	11.83	38.46
A	0.81	0.81	0.81	0.81	0.81	0.81	0.81	0.81
U	0.10	0.10	0.10	0.10	0.10	0.10	0.10	0.10
T	1.00	1.00	1.00	1.00	11.78	2.60	1.72	90.78
R	1.00	1.69	1.33	1.27	1.00	1.00	1.00	1.00
Q	0.42	0.42	0.42	0.42	0.79	0.47	0.36	1.00
Ω	0.035	0.060	0.047	0.045	0.794	0.104	0.053	7.699

Source: Authors' calculations, based on Rwanda's EICV 1999/2001.
Note: Simulation uses standard definition of the poor using the consumption aggregate and the official absolute poverty line. Absolute poverty line = 65,145 Rwanda francs per equivalent adult per year. Unit cost is 81.25 Rwanda francs per kilowatt hour. L = lifeline.

the network benefited from the low tariff rate before the increase in tariff, the targeting parameters T_P and T_N were both equal to 1. Finally, the low value of Ω was also a result of higher consumption levels among the connected population as a whole (who therefore benefited more from the below-cost flat rate) than the consumption levels among the poor.

Table 7.2 also provides results from various simulations. We first consider inverted block tariff structures with two brackets, so that consumption below and above the lifeline—the threshold for the lower consumption bracket, denoted by L in the table—have different costs per kilowatt hour. Lifelines of 20, 40, and 50 kilowatt hours are considered. In addition, we also simulate the value of Ω under volume-differentiated tariffs for small customers. With this structure, only those who consume less than the lifeline reap the benefit from the lower cost per kilowatt hour. When simulations are conducted at the national level, none of the scenarios generates a high value for Ω. In urban areas, Ω takes a significantly higher value only for the volume-differentiated tariff and a lifeline of 20 kilowatt hour. In this case, the value of Ω is 0.79, which is better, but implies that the poor still benefit less than the population as a whole from the implicit subsidy.

Additionally, table 7.2 provides simulations under which there is perfect targeting of the subsidy or special tariff to the poor. In practice, however, such perfect targeting cannot be achieved. These values should simply be considered as the best that could be achieved under perfect information and implementation given the current structure of connection rates. In fact, it is unclear whether a good proxy means-testing mechanism could and should be implemented in Rwanda's urban areas at this time, especially considering that poverty is much higher in rural areas.

In table 7.3, the simulations for the urban sample are reworked by considering that 40 percent of the urban population is poor. This is an arbitrary threshold, with poverty defined in relative terms and a much higher poverty headcount than occurs under the official measures of poverty. In a political economy setting, considering such alternative definitions of poverty in urban areas may be warranted by a desire to protect part of the connected population (which is located, for the most part, in urban areas) from the increase in tariffs. With this alternative definition of the poor, the value of Ω is 0.30 in the benchmark case. The value of Ω reaches 1.35 with the volume discount applied to the consumption below 20 kilowatt hours. Note that, with perfect targeting, increasing the population considered to be poor reduces the value of Ω.

Finally, we analyze results for the IUBT structure proposed by Electrogaz. This tariff structure assumes, as before, a cost of RF 81.25 per

Table 7.3 Distributional Characteristics of Alternative Tariff Structures in Urban Areas

Parameter	Benchmark flat tariff (price = 42 Rwanda francs/kWh)	Inverted block tariff			Volume-differentiated tariff			Perfect Targeting
		L = 20 kWh	L = 40 kWh	L = 50 kWh	L = 20 kWh	L = 40 kWh	L = 50 kWh	
				Urban areas: Relative poverty definition				
A_H	0.86	0.86	0.86	0.86	0.86	0.86	0.86	0.86
A_P	0.78	0.78	0.78	0.78	0.78	0.78	0.78	0.78
$U_{H|A}$	0.37	0.37	0.37	0.37	0.37	0.37	0.37	0.37
$U_{P|A}$	0.18	0.18	0.18	0.18	0.18	0.18	0.18	0.18
$T_{H|U}$	1.00	1.00	1.00	1.00	0.05	0.28	0.42	0.18
$T_{P|U}$	1.00	1.00	1.00	1.00	0.15	0.45	0.57	1.00
$R_{H|T}$	0.48	0.10	0.19	0.22	0.48	0.48	0.48	0.48
$R_{P|T}$	0.48	0.15	0.24	0.28	0.48	0.48	0.48	0.48
$Q_{H|T}$	92.49	92.49	92.49	92.49	12.73	25.11	32.54	63.01
$Q_{P|T}$	63.01	63.01	63.01	63.01	13.55	21.99	27.45	63.01
A	0.91	0.91	0.91	0.91	0.91	0.91	0.91	0.91
U	0.49	0.49	0.49	0.49	0.49	0.49	0.49	0.49
T	1.00	1.00	1.00	1.00	2.87	1.62	1.38	5.65
R	1.00	1.42	1.31	1.27	1.00	1.00	1.00	1.00
Q	0.68	0.68	0.68	0.68	1.06	0.88	0.84	1.00
Ω	0.30	0.43	0.39	0.38	1.35	0.63	0.51	2.50

Source: Authors' calculations, based on Rwanda's EICV 1999/2001.
Note: Simulation uses a relative poverty line that identifies 40 percent of the urban population as poor. Relative poverty line = 40 percent of households. Unit cost per kWh = RF 81.25/kWh. L = lifeline.

kilowatt hour. It also considers two thresholds: the lower price for fewer than 20 kilowatt hours and the baseline price for more than 100 kilowatt hours, with the middle consumption bracket priced at above-cost levels in order to recoup the subsidies provided in the lower bracket. As presented in table 7.4, this alternative structure increases the value of Ω over the value of the IBTs in table 7.3, but not by a lot (from 0.43 to 0.52, assuming a lifeline of 20 kilowatt hours). Additional results are provided in table 7.4 for alternative thresholds with the IUBT.

Apart from considering alternative tariff structures, there is another way to provide benefits to the poor: by providing connection subsidies instead of consumption subsidies. As seen above, consumption subsidies are often difficult to target well because of the role played by access and usage factors in attempting to channel subsidies to non-poor households. With connection subsidies, access and usage factors

Table 7.4 Distributional Characteristics of the Proposed IUBT

Parameter	Proposed block tariff structure	Simulation 1	Simulation 2	Simulation 3	Simulation 4
	1.00	1.00	1.00	1.00	1.00
T_{PIU}	1.00	1.00	1.00	1.00	1.00
R_{HIT}	0.04	0.02	0.09	0.12	0.16
R_{PIT}	0.07	0.04	0.12	0.17	0.21
Q_{HIT}	92.49	92.49	92.49	92.49	92.49
Q_{PIT}	63.01	63.01	63.01	63.01	63.01
T	1.00	1.00	1.00	1.00	1.00
R	1.72	2.22	1.46	1.35	1.30
Q	0.68	0.68	0.68	0.68	0.68
Ω	0.52	0.67	0.44	0.41	0.39

Source: Authors' calculations, based on Rwanda's EICV 1999/2001.

Note: Simulation uses the urban areas sample and the relative poverty measure. A and U parameters are equal to those in table 7.3. Relative poverty line = 40 percent of households. Unit cost per kWh = 81.25 RF/kWh.

Proposed block tariff structure: 0–20 kWh : P1 = 42; 20–100 kWh: P2 = 88; >100 kWh : P3 = 81. Simulation 1: 0–15 kWh : P1 = 42; 15–100 kWh: P2 = 88; >100 kWh : P3 = 81. Simulation 2: 0–30 kWh : P1 = 42; 30–100 kWh: P2 = 88; >100 kWh : P3 = 81. Simulation 3: 0–40 kWh : P1 = 42; 40–100 kWh: P2 = 88; >100 kWh : P3 = 81. Simulation 4: 0–50 kWh : P1 = 42; 50–100 kWh: P2 = 88; 100 kWh : P3 = 81.

can play in the other direction. Since the poor tend to not have access, they may benefit the most from connection subsidies. This is, however, not necessarily the case, because it depends on who exactly will receive the connection subsidy (this depends on how the extension of the network takes place).

The methodological details for considering different scenarios are explained in Angel-Urdinola and Wodon (2005). We present here the results from three scenarios:

■ First, the households that receive connection subsidies are selected randomly from those households in population without a connection today, which—from a measurement point of view—would be the same as giving a connection subsidy to all the population not connected today (scenario 1 in figure 7.1).

■ Second, the beneficiaries of the connection subsidy are selected from the population with access but without usage or take-up (scenario 2 in figure 7.1). This means that to benefit from access, households must not currently use the service but must live in an area where the service exists.

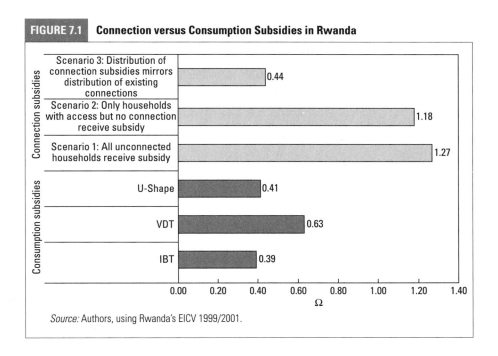

FIGURE 7.1 Connection versus Consumption Subsidies in Rwanda

Source: Authors, using Rwanda's EICV 1999/2001.

■ Third, the beneficiaries of the connection subsidy have the same distributional characteristics as the households connected today because, for example, of a complete lack of targeting in the connection subsidy design and a low access rate. This lack or targeting and low access would essentially prevent the poor from participating in the benefits of the increase in connection rates that are made feasible by the connection subsidy.

The key results for the value of Ω in all three scenarios are presented in figure 7.1. They are compared with the values of Ω for consumption subsidies in the case where the lifeline is set at 40 kilowatt hours (the latest proposal of Electrogaz was to set the lifeline at 20 kilowatt hours, but the results are similar for alternative lifelines and can be found in tables 7.3 and 7.4). In all scenarios presented in figure 7.1, we have used the urban sample and the relative poverty line for the estimations.

Clearly, connection subsidies have the potential to be better targeted than consumption subsidies. This conclusion is similar to the one drawn by Estache, Foster, and Wodon (2002) in their review of the evidence for Latin America. But this may not be necessarily the case, however—it could depend on how the mechanism for providing eligibility for connection subsidies would be implemented in practice.

Indeed, although connection subsidies have promise, they need to be implemented well to ensure good targeting and limit costs. For example, in their study on social or subsidized water connections in Abidjan and Dakar, Lauria and Hopkins (2004) explain how social connections were financed through a water development fund paid for with a surcharge on water tariffs. Unfortunately, poor targeting resulted in 90 percent of residential connections in Abidjan being eligible for the subsidy. In fact, some of the connected households paying the surcharge were found to be poorer than many of the households receiving the new social connections. The program suffered from distorted incentives because the flat fees paid for each social connection to private operators were an incentive for those operators to maximize the number of subsidized connections while at the same time seeking for these social connections richer households that were likely to consume more water and were located closer to the pipes. In this way the utilities would reap higher revenues and minimize the cost of connecting in the first place. According to the authors, these distortions may in fact have led to reductions in connection rates or at least to an increase in the time needed to get connected among the poorest households located in informal settlements. The fact that the social connections required households to own the land on which their dwelling was located also probably undermined the targeting performance of the program. This example makes it clear that for connection subsidies as well as for consumption subsidies, a good design of the eligibility mechanism is required for the subsidy to actually reach the poor.

CONCLUSION

The electricity sector in Rwanda is currently in a state of crisis. The country is simultaneously experiencing a growing demand for electricity, rising costs resulting from the need to rely increasingly on thermal power generation in the near term, and, until recently, very low tariffs that had remained unchanged for seven years and did not permit the national operator Electrogaz to break even. The government has recently approved a near doubling of tariff rates; its present consideration of alternative tariff designs is part of an effort to protect the poor from this increase in tariffs.

The objective of this chapter has been to document the extent to which the poor did benefit from past subsidies (in the form of tariffs that were well below cost recovery rates), and to discover whether they would benefit from alternative implicit or explicit cross-subsidies. Because access rates to the network are very low among the poor, the share of the implicit subsidies that prevailed before the increase in tariff and that benefited the poor was also very low. In other words, previous subsidies were badly targeted. Today, because tariffs have been increased to cost-recovery level, there are no more implicit subsidies in Rwanda's tariff structure.

Still, the government is considering amending the tariff structure to protect poorer consumers, and Electrogaz has proposed an interesting IUBT structure to achieve this objective without compromising the objective of cost recovery. We have shown that, in Rwanda, the subsidies or cross-subsidies under the IUBT would be better targeted to the poor than those existing under the previous flat tariff structure. The IUBT performed only slightly better than a more traditional IBT, but less well than a VDT. It remains to be seen—by looking at other case studies for other countries—if, under other circumstances, the IUBT idea could be proven to have a stronger positive impact on the overall targeting performance of subsidies. Although the IUBT in Rwanda would have the advantage over the VDT of avoiding the discontinuities that exist in VDT systems between customers just below and just above the lifeline level, the targeting performance of the VDT was superior. Therefore the VDT is the structure that could probably be recommended for poverty reduction in Rwanda.

Another important result of our analysis was the finding that it would probably be better for poverty reduction to give priority to a subsidy mechanism for new connections to the network rather than a subsidy for consumption for those households that are already connected. Such a new-connection subsidy would enable more households to benefit from electricity (this has been proven to generate positive externalities for outcomes related to education and health, for example). It would target a population currently without access, which tends to be poorer than the population with access. In fact, recent trends in new connections show a strong demand from households and small commercial as well as institutional customers. Although in the near term Electrogaz bulk supplies and network and metering capacities are extremely constrained, once the Electrogaz capacities have been rehabilitated, there is a considerable potential for expanding the electricity market in the immediate proximity of its current distribution network.

Even if subsidies for higher rates of connection appear to be better targeted for poverty reduction (and perhaps for achieving other development objectives related to the Millenium Development Goals) than subsidies for consumption among users currently connected, it must be recognized that there would be benefits in providing at least some level of protection from higher tariffs for those households consuming small amounts of electricity. This level of protection would be important also for new and potentially poorer households that are newly connected to the network. If such consumption cross-subsidies were to be implemented, they could take place either in the form of VDTs or IUBTs as well as IBTs. A detailed evaluation of the different pricing alternatives would need to be considered, following the preliminary assessment provided here. It is relatively straightforward to use our framework to conduct such assessments with household surveys.

NOTES

1. Casual observations and discussions suggest that there is a considerable degree of "subsidiary connections," however, so that some agents (external to Electrogaz) extend lines to other households. These external agents extract higher unit prices for electricity than the prices they pay to Electrogaz.
2. For simplicity of exposition, we will assume throughout the rest of this chapter that households have a zero elasticity of demand to changes in prices. Given the very low levels of consumption recorded in the survey, and given the fact that households are unlikely to adjust their consumption downward significantly with an increase in prices, the elasticity is indeed likely to be low, so that the assumption is not likely to result in severe bias in the empirical results.

REFERENCES

Angel-Urdinola, D., and Q. Wodon. 2005. "Do Utility Subsidies Reach the Poor? Framework and Evidence for Cape Verde." Mimeo, World Bank, Washington, DC.

Electrogaz. 2005. Presentation of Utility Tariff Adjustment 2005 made at the March 2005 World Bank workshop on poverty reduction in Kigali, Rwanda.

Estache, A., V. Foster, and Q. Wodon. 2002. *Accounting for Poverty in Infrastructure Reform: Learning from Latin America's Experience.* WBI Studies in Economic Development. Washington, DC: World Bank.

Government of Rwanda. 2002. *A Profile of Poverty in Rwanda.* Kigali: Ministry of Finance.

Komives, K., V. Foster, J. Halpern, and Q. Wodon, with support from R. Abdullah. 2005. *Water, Electricity, and the Poor: Who Benefits from Utility Subsidies?* Washington, DC: World Bank.

Lauria, D., and O. Hopkins. 2004. *Pro-Poor Subsidies for Water Connections: Cases from West Africa.* Consultant's Report, University of North Carolina, Chapel Hill, N.C.

World Bank. 2003. *Rwanda: Poverty and Human Development.* Washington, DC: World Bank.

————. 2004. Project Appraisal Document on a Proposed Credit in the Amount of SDR 16.7 million (US$25 million equivalent) to the Republic of Rwanda for an Urgent Electricity Rehabilitation project (December 27, 2004), Washington, DC.

————. 2005. International Development Association Program Document for a Proposed Grant in the Amount of SDR 37.6 million (US$55 million equivalent) to the Republic of Rwanda for a Second Poverty Reduction Support Grant (October 13, 2005), Washington, DC.

8

GHANA
Electricity Tariff Reform

SARAH KEENER AND
SUDESHNA GHOSH BANERJEE

I n May 2003 the Government of Ghana was in the process of preparing its first Poverty Reduction Support Credit (PRSC) in support of its poverty reduction strategy (GPRS). As part of the stakeholder consultations on the preparation of the PRSC, a number of areas were identified where poverty and social impact analysis (PSIA) would strengthen the process of design, monitoring, and evaluation of key policies. The World Bank agreed to support one of the topics selected by stakeholders—an analysis in the energy sector—after assessing (1) the breadth of potential impact from the reform, (2) the level of sensitivity of the public to the reform, and (3) the level of public consensus and need for dialogue.[1]

The main objectives of electricity sector reform in Ghana—an area of reform that has been under discussion since 1994—are

- to meet the demand for expanding capacity for electricity generation by opening the market to private investment and deregulating part of the market;
- to improve the efficiency of the sector through performance contracts, competition among power producers, and tariffs that reflect the cost structure; and

This work is based on a report and field work completed with Kumasi Institute of Technology (KITE) under the leadership of Ishmael Edjekumhene. Ramboll Consultants also provided support to the PSIA implementation.

- to reduce the fiscal drain of the sector on the government budget by gradually moving tariffs toward full cost recovery.[2]

The topic of the PSIA was chosen in collaboration with stakeholders (see the next section). The PSIA did not focus on the entire spectrum of sector reform because a broader Economic and Sector Work on the Energy Sector was already underway at the World Bank, and because of the limited time available to incorporate the findings into the GPRS and PRSC.

CONTEXT OF THE ENERGY SECTOR REFORM IN GHANA

The PSIA for electricity sector reform in Ghana was included in the initial list of areas needing research because of public concern over a combined increase of 72 percent in the end-user electricity tariffs in August 2002 and March 2003, and the subsequent enactment in 2003 of an automatically adjusting tariff formula for electricity. After further stakeholder consultation in Ghana, this research was narrowed to focus on (1) whether the lifeline tariff (households consuming less than 50 kilowatt hours per month receive a government subsidy) was an effective tool in protecting the poor from tariff increases and, on an indicative basis, and (2) assessing how consumers were coping with the higher tariffs. This analysis was deemed important because of concern over the automatic tariff adjustment mechanism, which at the time was expected to lead to further tariff increases. In spite of the heated debate on electricity tariffs, little analytical work had been completed on issues of affordability and the relationship between expanding electricity services and having an economically viable sector. Both these objectives are contained in the GPRS.

The overall fiscal drain of the electricity sector had, by 2002, become substantial: in 2002, deficits of the three electricity utility companies—the Volta River Authority (VRA), the generator; the Electricity Company of Ghana (ECG), the southern distributor; and the Northern Electricity Department (NED), which is part of the VRA and distributes electricity in northern Ghana—approached 11 percent of government spending, or 4 percent of GDP.[3] Of this US$204 million deficit, US$124 million alone stemmed from interest and exchange rate losses. Projected losses for 2003 were expected to rise to the equivalent of 17 percent of total government spending for the previous year, or 6 percent of GDP. This financial situation affected the utility's ability to maintain, upgrade, and extend its current infrastructure and resulted in inadequate generation reserve, transmission network constraints, overloaded transformers, and degraded distribution networks. All of these factors reduced the quality of service to customers, particularly in the more populated areas outside northern Ghana. Aging equipment increased system losses and indirectly added to the cost of producing and distributing electricity. If full cost recovery as well as full debt service were to be included, total costs in 2003 would be near US$0.08–0.10 per kilowatt hour. New financial needs for restructuring and revitalizing the sector were, at the time, calculated to add additional debt service of at least US$0.01 to this average price per kilowatt hour.[4]

The attempt to reform electricity tariffs in Ghana is not a recent phenomenon—in fact, it predates other major reform initiatives in the power sector. As table 8.1 illustrates, there is a long history of attempting to reconcile the desire to have tariffs that reflect economic costs with the desire to keep electricity affordable to consumers. Tariffs that adjust regularly to reflect fluctuations in costs (such as fluctuations in exchange rate or inflation) were implemented between 1994 and 1997. In pursuance of the agreement to ensure that tariffs approximate the long-run marginal cost (LRMC), the government of Ghana (GOG) continued to increase electricity tariffs without any opposition until an increase of over 300 percent in May 1997. This substantial increase provoked intense nationwide objection, with the Association of Ghana Industries (AGI), the Trades Union Congress (TUC), and the Civil Servants Association (CSA) at the forefront of the protest.[5] Following this increase, draft legislation was enacted to establish an independent regulatory agency. The Public Utility Regulatory Commission (PURC) bill became law shortly thereafter, in October 1997, and an eight-member PURC board was sworn in on November 10, 1997.

Ghana's residential tariff structure has moved from five subgroups, based on levels of consumption, to four and then three during the 2003 tariff review process (table 8.2).[6] The lowest group, the lifeline, offers a flat rate to customers consuming 50 kilowatt hours per month or less, and was originally created to minimize the cost to the utility of billing small accounts. Starting in August of 2002, the government of Ghana introduced a subsidy for those consuming within the lifeline amount; this subsidy came to be used as a tool for ensuring that lower-income users were protected from tariff increases. When the automatic adjustment formula for tariffs was planned to start in 2002, the GOG increased the subsidy on the lifeline to protect this block from the automatic adjustment; the adjustment with the formula did not actually take effect until October, 2003.

At the start of the PSIA, tariff increases had brought the average end-user tariffs to the point where they covered the PURC-defined economic costs. However, these do not include an allowance for current inefficiencies (estimated to be about US$0.02 per kilowatt hour; PURC 2002).[7] More recent financial analysis of the sector pointed to the fact that consumers in

Table 8.1 The History of Tariff Reform in Ghana

Year	Event
1976–86	No changes in tariff.
1986	Coopers & Lybrand perform the first major tariff study, which recommends tariffs based on LRMC, classifying consumers by groups of those who impose similar costs on the systems, and classifying residential consumers by level of consumption. This tariff is progressive, with a lifeline consumption level of 50 kWh applying to all consumers. The government also adopts a uniform national tariff structure.
1988	The level of tariffs recommended by Coopers & Lybrand is substantially adopted; it approximates 75 percent of LRMC.
1989	Tariff increases, ranging from 6 percent for low-income consumers to 20 percent for nonresidential consumers, are implemented to enable the VRA to continue to earn an 8 percent and ECG a 6 percent ROR. However, in fixing the tariff, the GOG expressed concern at the prospect of further adjustments to domestic tariffs that reflected recent devaluation and inflationary pressures at a time when the service remained unreliable. The GOG expressed the wish to reexamine certain aspects of the 1986 tariff study, which led to their commissioning next major tariff study (ACRES).
1990–2	The ACRES study: • points out that the inverted block rate structure recommended by Coopers & Lybrand was cumbersome to administer and a source of customer discontent, • recommends adopting "adjusted LRMC"—an LRMC adjusted to reflect the financial requirements of the utilities, and • recommends merging all residential tariff structure into a single energy rate with the exception of the lifeline tariffs. New electricity tariffs, based on the recommendation of ACRES International (which was actively supported by the World Bank), were introduced in January 1992.[a]
January 1993	The GOG agrees to adopt a formula-based approach to tariff adjustment and to provide regular and systematic adjustment of the tariff thereafter on the basis of the agreed-upon formula. This formula essentially provided for phasing-in prevailing tariffs to LRMC, adjusting for inflation and exchange-rate fluctuation. Tariff increases were implemented in January 1993, and an agreement was reached for further increases to take place in 1994 and 1995 within the framework.
1994–7	Tariffs continue to increase per the agreed-upon formula, although the focus is on a set ROR for the utilities rather than LRMC.
1997	Tariff increases of over 300 percent prompt nationwide protest. President Rawlings suspends any increase until a regulatory commission is formed. The regulatory commission PURC was formed and placed in charge of tariff setting.

Table 8.1 The History of Tariff Reform in Ghana (*Continued*)

Year	Event
February 1998 September 1998 May 2001 July 2002	PURC tariff adjustments
2001	PURC outlines a transitional plan for tariffs to cover 2001–4, including regulations for consumer consultation on tariffs.
January, 2003	Tariff formula allowing for automatic adjustment to reflect exchange rate and inflation is enacted and supposed to take effect July 2003.
October, 2003	First automatic adjustment of the tariff per the formula.
2005	PURC scheduled to carry out major tariff review.

Source: Authors elaboration.
Note: HV = high voltage; LRMC = long-run marginal cost; LV = low voltage; ROR = rate of return; VRA = Volta River Authority. a. The main features of the 1992 tariff increase were: tariffs for residential consumers increased from 20 to 30 percent of LRMC; nonresidential tariff mirrored LMRC; and LV and HV industrial tariffs moved from 26 percent and 33 percent of LRMC to about 42 percent and 54 percent respectively in the case of ECG, and to about 70 percent in the case of VRA.

the middle tariff band (51–300 kilowatt hours) were paying below actual average cost, and they were therefore being subsidized along with those in the lifeline band.

THE PSIA PROCESS: STAKEHOLDER INVOLVEMENT AND METHODS

Because tariff policy had such a high profile in Ghana, the PSIA placed as much emphasis on informing policy discussion and involving national

Table 8.2 Residential Tariff Structure
Ghanaian cedis per kilowatt hour

Kilowatt hours/ month	February 1998	September 1998	May 2001	August 2002**	March 2003	October 2003***
0–50 kWh/ month	2,000 (cedis/kWh)	4,000 (cedis/kWh)	7,800 (cedis/kWh)	9,000 (cedis/kWh)	13,000 (cedis/kWh)	13,000 (cedis/kWh)
0–50*	87	174	339	391	565	565
51–300	50	120–150	242–304	400	550	610
Over 300	75–180	220–350	570	960	960	1,065

Source: PURC (2003).
Note: *Flat rate, assuming average consumption levels of 23 kilowatt hours /month; **Government subsidy of ¢5,000 starts; ***Government subsidy increased to ¢6,080 to keep lifeline constant.

stakeholders in the research process as it did on the technical research issues. The research was led by national consultants and guided by a multi-stakeholder steering committee to increase the chances that the analysis would lead to enhanced policy debate and operational changes. National involvement therefore had several elements:

- The multistakeholder group was involved from the beginning in the elaboration of terms of reference, and in vetting interim field reports and drafts. Some members also participated in a two-day training session and portions of the fieldwork.[8]
- Consultants collecting information were required to share all background reports and analysis, as well as information on methodology, with the steering and technical committees (compiling and sharing available background studies and methodology guidance on CD-Roms) to increase local knowledge of the tradeoffs in the policy being considered.
- National capacity and experience with evidence-based policy analysis was developed by contracting local research partners not only to implement field work but to lead the analysis and report writing as well. The PSIA was guided by the Kumasi Institute of Technology and Environment (KITE), a Ghanaian nongovernmental organization (NGO) active in energy policy issues.[9]

The steering committee for the PSIA research comprised the minister of energy (chairman); the minister of state and economic planning, and chief executives of the National Development Planning Commission (NDPC)—the body tasked with monitoring the GPRS, the PURC, and the VRA. The chairman was well disposed to report on the PSIA to the cabinet. To facilitate ongoing collaboration, a technical committee was also formed, and comprised representatives of stakeholder institutions: the ministry of energy, the ministry of finance and economic planning, the NDPC, the Ghana Statistical Service, the VRA, the electricity distributor companies for both the north and the south of the country (ECG and NED), PURC, the World Bank, and two NGOs representing consumer interests.

The Ghana PSIA presented special challenges to the steering committee. It had a limited time frame in which to inform the electricity tariff policy because this policy was included in the PRSC and GPRS, and primary data specific to the issue at hand were lacking. In particular, although tariffs had increased substantially, the most recent household income data were from 1998–9, prior to tariff increases. Further, these data did not identify "lifeline" customers as such. Based on discussion with the Department of Statistics, it was clear that one could not impute quantities consumed because of the common error of taking the arrears section of the bill to be the current bill. As the PSIA research later revealed, arrears for urban slum households tended to be many multiples of arrears for other groups; thus using these data to impute the impact of higher tariffs on household budgets would not have been accurate. Finally, as noted above, updated household surveys and a thorough tariff review were planned in 2005; the PSIA was not meant to replace these, but rather to inform policy in the interim period.

The PSIA research approached these constraints in two ways: (1) it focused on testing assumptions behind the policy reform using existing data, and (2) it used utility data on all customers to assess the behavioral response to tariff increases and to identify any major reactions. PSIA research also used a small sample of more in-depth primary research to provide insight into why consumers were reacting as they were and to identify specific groups that could not be identified through utility data. The PSIA recommended that future nationally representative household surveys on ability and willingness to pay be undertaken to inform the thorough tariff review planned for 2005. The small-scale survey for the PSIA covered 318 households, both compound and individual, and was complemented by focus group discussions and interviews with key inform-ants. In addition, the PSIA analyzed how different stakeholders influenced the implementation of previous tariff reforms. Finally, although the PSIA focused on the specific lifeline tariff policy being debated, it also recognized that access to and costs of biomass, fuelwood, and kerosene have a much larger impact on the majority of the poor who tend to be concentrated in rural areas dependent on these sources of fuel.

The fieldwork was carried out in Tamale, Accra, and Kumasi, the three major urban areas where the majority of electricity consumers are concen-trated. These areas represent the country's three main ecological zones: coastal, forest, and savannah. For the in-depth quantitative surveys, and for some of the key informant interviews, 90 customers from customer data-bases in ECG (which services Accra and Kumasi) and NED (which services Tamale) were randomly selected within the following categories:

- urban areas with low- to middle-income residents (URBAN),
- rural areas (those that were included in the self-help electrification program, or SHEP),[10] and
- urban slums (SLUM).[11]

All three categories are said to have a significant share of lifeline customers.

Customer data related to consumption, current bill, and arrears from ECG, the largest distribution utility, were collected on as many of those households interviewed as possible. The customer identification number was used as the common key, allowing the research team to pair this information with households' responses, and, most importantly, to show trends in electricity consumption over time for these same households. In addition, for some of the specialized surveys, specific neighborhoods and consumer groups—such as neighborhoods with problems with disconnection or illegal connections—were targeted. Finally, housing in Ghana includes shared compound houses; policy makers were concerned that these households were not able to benefit from lifeline tariffs although they were assumed to be among the most vulnerable. In summary, the following methods were used:

- New analysis of nationally representative existing data (the Ghana Living Standards Survey 4 [GLSS4] of 1998 to 1999, preliminary results from the Core Welfare Indicators Questionnaire 2003, and utility records to assess the recent behavioral response to tariff increases).
- In-depth focus group discussions with a sample of compound house dwellers as well as rural and peri-urban customers.
- Limited quantitative surveys of SHEP, URBAN, SLUM, and compound house dwellers and landlords.
- Key informant interviews with specific stakeholder groups. These groups comprised disconnected consumers, commercial consumers, bonded cashiers of ECG, district technical officers of ECG, ECG loss control units, NED officials, and urban and rural non-connected alternative energy consumers—for example, those who used solar, LPG, fuelwood, kerosene, and candles—and high-consumption customers and commercial illegal consumers.
- Financial modeling of both the cost of the lifeline and of its sustainability over time by a financial analyst, using the utility's base financial model.

STAKEHOLDER PERSPECTIVES AND INCENTIVES

Stakeholder analysis revealed the incentives and diverse perspectives of the different institutions within the electricity sector as well as those outside it. The analysis also revealed the likely degree of influence of each stakeholder group over tariff reform. In general, one can posit that three basic mechanisms exist for funding the investments needed to improve utility company performance and reduce losses. These mechanisms are:

- government investment, which may not materialize because of financial shortfalls and because it could jeopardize macroeconomic stability;
- recovery of costs and establishing an investment margin through tariffs, which must be sensitive to the willingness and ability of consumers to pay; and
- private investment, which requires a financially strong sector and some form of government guarantee.

Much of the debate over tariffs in Ghana revolved around which of these methods is most appropriate. A particularly contentious issue concerned whether electricity tariffs in Ghana were already too high or too low. Those who saw it as too low generally believe that consumers should pay the cost of service provision, and those who saw it as too high generally believed that the government, through overall taxes or other sources, should bear a greater share of the cost of service provision.

The VRA, the ECG, the ministry of finance, and some development partners were the main proponents of tariff reform. These groups all asserted that tariffs were too low, largely because they themselves face mounting costs from increased reliance on more expensive thermal generation. These costs are directly affected by changes in international oil prices, which are denominated in U.S. dollar terms. International energy experts also tended to view tariffs in per kilowatt hour terms and to compare them with the tariffs of neighboring countries, which were higher.

The PSIA found that although Ghana's tariffs were lower than those of other countries in the region, these comparisons did not take into account Ghana's higher rates of access. These rates of access affect both the political economy and willingness to pay. In Ghana the newest consumer is poorer than current consumers who have had access for some time and also poorer than consumers in these other countries where only the highest-income consumers have access to electricity. As table 8.3 illustrates, although Ghana had lower tariffs than neighboring countries such as Benin or Togo, it also had substantially higher rates of access and thus was reaching beyond the the highest-income consumers who are likely to be connected to the grid first.

Further, protection of the middle tariff band in Ghana—which at the time of research was subsidized—largely reflects middle-class customers who are concentrated in high-voting urban areas, areas that wield considerable political power in a democracy such as Ghana. As figure 8.1 shows, tariffs increased most sharply for the top tariff band that was covering costs; further, up until 2003 lifeline customers were, on average, paying slightly more or the same per unit as the next two tariff bands comprising those consuming between 51 and 300 kilowatt hours per month.

Table 8.3 Cross-Country Comparison of Electricity Tariffs

Country	Connection rate 2000 (%)	Inhabitants with electricity (millions)	Average household tariff (US cents/kWh)	**Social tariff (US cents/kWh)	GDP per capita (PPP) (2002)
Côte d'Ivoire	50	8.0	8.5	5.0	1,500
Ghana	43	8.0	7.2ᵃ	6.3ᵇ	2,130
Benin	22	1.4	12.4	10.4	1,031
Burkina Faso	13	1.6	14.9	13.2	1,012
Togo	9	0.4	10.7	10.5	1,458

Sources: Connection rate and number of inhabitants: IEA World Energy Outlook (2002); average household tariff: Layec (2004); GDP per capita: World Bank (2004).

Note: a. Updated from ECG and NED data February 2003. b. The range of unit costs here depends on the individual level of consumption of the consumer because this is a flat tariff for all consuming 50 kWh or less. The cost per kWh ranges between US$0.029 cents and US$1.49 if one consumes 50 or 1 kilowatt hours per month respectively. The rate for the average consumption level (23 kWh hours per month) is presented here and reflects the price to the consumer.

FIGURE 8.1 Evolution of Tariffs by Residential Bands (in Ghanaian cedis)

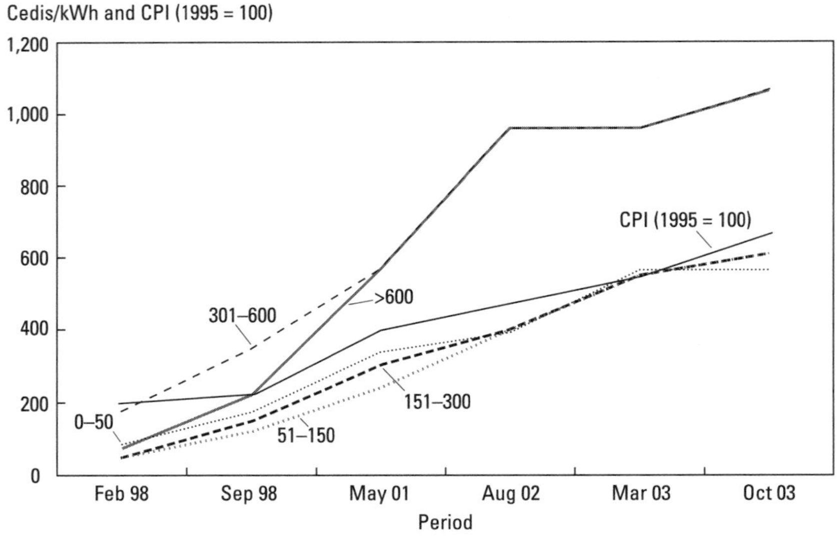

Source: PURC (2003).
Note: Average lifeline consumption is assumed to be 23 kilowatt hours.

Consumers and the press, in contrast to the other stakeholders, saw tariff increases in cedi terms. These increases generally followed the Consumer Price Index (CPI), except for those of the highest consumption category (600 kilowatt hours per month).

Figures 8.2 and 8.3 illustrate the influence various stakeholders have on tariff reform, as well as their degree of support or opposition to tariff increases. It should be noted that the symbols are based on a qualitative ranking emerging from a review of documents and stakeholder interviews. Some groups of consumers have more direct influence over reform because they have power and are well organized. High-consumption industrial customers, for example, have more direct influence because they generate a significant share of the utilities' revenue and can, on occasion, bargain directly with the utilities for more favorable payment terms. The VRA has historically been perhaps the most influential stakeholder in tariff reform because it proposes the initial tariffs that form the basis for subsequent negotiations. It was able to bypass the ministry of energy and report directly to the president, and it generated substantial foreign exchange from sales to the major international aluminum company, VALCO. VALCO had been consuming about one-third of the electricity available from a main power source, the Akosombo Dam. VALCO enjoyed low rates because of a long-term contract, which was under dispute at the time of the PSIA. Because of this dispute, VALCO operations ceased during this period. As the percentage of VRA's revenues from VALCO—and thus foreign exchange—have decreased, the personal emoluments accorded to VRA staff have also decreased. VALCO has thus pushed harder to recover costs from other areas such as consumer tariffs.

More dispersed customers, such as residential customers mapped to the bottom right quadrant of figure 8.3, have less direct influence than other stakeholders over tariff reform in between electoral periods, but are very likely to be harmed by tariff increases. Their primary avenue of influence stems from their votes around electoral periods. As a result, the central government (number 1 in figure 8.3) tends to move away from tariff increases close to electoral periods, or may try to influence the regulator, PURC, to delay such increases. The perceptions of these less-organized consumers are heavily influenced by the media—in particular, through the large number of FM radio stations (there are over 70 FM stations). Among the residential consumers, it is important to note that the majority fall within the middle tariff band (50–300 kilowatt hours), which were paying tariffs below average cost though they were consuming one-third of residential electricity. These consumers are also likely to represent the bulk of

FIGURE 8.2 **Stakeholders in the Tariff-Setting Process**

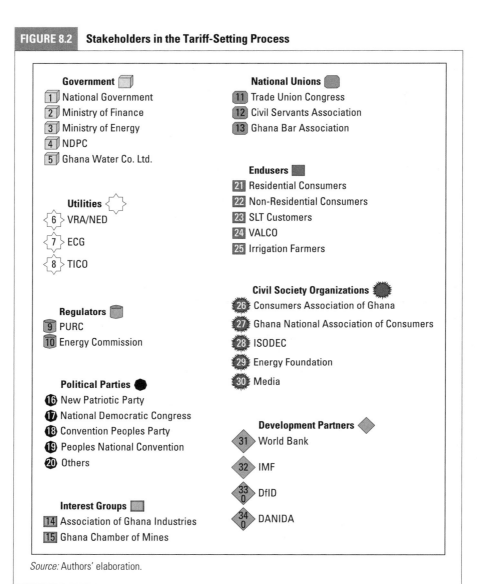

Source: Authors' elaboration.

voters in densely populated urban areas, so they may therefore have a fair degree of influence leading up to electoral periods. Alternative avenues of influence consist of only two consumer associations with a small staff and low level of funding. These associations therefore have only limited power, though they do represent consumers at PURC public hearings.

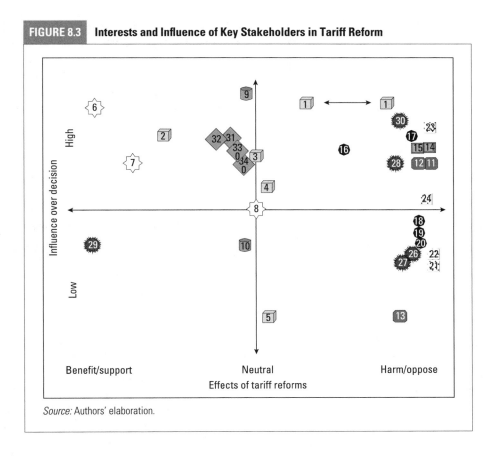

FIGURE 8.3 **Interests and Influence of Key Stakeholders in Tariff Reform**

Source: Authors' elaboration.

PURC has a mandate to oversee the tariff-setting process to ensure that the interests of the consumer are represented. Final decisions, in principle, are not subject to any executive or legislative consent and/or concurrence. In practice PURC remains dependent on the government for the majority of its operating budget, a fact that has caused some to question whether it is put under pressure by the GOG during pre-electoral periods. Although both PURC and the government acknowledge that tariffs must be rationalized to economic and cost-reflective levels, concerns about the likely impact of tariff reforms on end-users have led to some resistance from these two major stakeholders against the steep increases in tariffs proposed by the utilities.

Opposition political parties, unions, and associations have often vehemently opposed tariff increases in the public press. Three groups that have had some influence over the public discourse on tariffs, and are therefore found in the upper right-hand quadrant of figure 8.3, are the Civil Servants

Association, which has branches in all regional capitals; the Association of Ghana Industries, which has the clout of the large industrial consumers behind it; and the Trades Union Congress, which has a membership of 600,000. This contrasts with both the consumer organizations, which are comparatively small in size and budget, and the group for which there is no formal representation—rural consumers both on and off the grid.

RESULTS

Based on discussions with staff of the southern electricity distributor, ECG, the research team found that two factors may influence the degree to which local staff implement the move toward greater cost recovery. First, some staff felt that they were working for the VRA (the distributor) because they viewed VRA's tariffs as increasing faster than ECG's and therefore felt their company received less benefit from higher tariffs. Second, with the exception of rural collectors, frontline staff feel only the brunt of tariff increases—they deal with more angry customers, more illegal connections, and higher arrears but none of the benefits, as their remuneration is not directly tied to collection rates. This may represent one factor in the arrears growth that accompanied tariff increases.

Finally, tension exists between political imperatives and the incentives of a commercially oriented utility for the following reason. The way to ensure the greatest returns from substantial capital expansion costs is to maximize the density of connections rather than spreading connections over broader physical or regional areas. A high density also reduces costs of providing and maintaining service for the distribution utility. However, through the self-help electrification program (SHEP, described in the next section), the political goal and the goal of poverty alleviation targets is to extend electricity to as many communities as possible rather than to concentrate density in currently connected communities. Therefore, although access is increasing, it is increasing largely to low-consumption dispersed customers. This in turn leads to a higher number of new consumers who have lower (lifeline) consumption, are more rural, and are potentially more dispersed than existing customers. This creates upward pressure on tariffs for other categories of consumers and increases in cross-subsidies.

The Context of Poverty

Beginning the decade with half of its population below the poverty line, Ghana managed to reduce its poverty incidence to 42 percent by 1998/9, a decrease driven in part by robust growth rates of around 5 percent at the end of the 1990s. But poverty reduction and human development have been uneven, and most of the improvement has occurred in the more urbanized Accra and the forest zone. In the rural Savannah (primarily northern, upper east, and upper west regions), poverty remained unchanged throughout the 1990s. These three regions also have the lowest access to health care facilities, water, and electricity (Demery 2003). Poverty remains a largely rural phenomenon, with 80 percent of the poor living in rural areas (table 8.4).

The Lifeline Tariff

In 2002 the GOG introduced a 5,000 cedi subsidy per consumer in the lifeline band (those who consume 50 kilowatt hours month or less), to be paid by the ministry of finance to the ECG and NED, the electricity distributors. In October 2003 the lifeline subsidy was raised from ¢5,000 per lifeline customer to ¢6,080 in order to keep the lifeline tariff at a constant ¢13,000, while tariffs for other customers increased according to the newly implemented automatic formula.

Broader Issues of Targeting

The first key assumption that the PSIA probed was whether the poor had access to electricity—a precondition for higher prices having a direct impact.[12] A review of existing national household survey data clearly demonstrated that in broad terms, those that fall under the poverty line do not tend to have access to electricity in rural areas, where the majority of the poor are concentrated; only 7 percent of rural poor people use electricity for lighting, while 93 percent use paraffin or kerosene.[13] Among the

Table 8.4 Ghana Regional Poverty Incidence, 1988/9

Region	Poverty incidence (%)
Greater Accra	7
Western	25
Ashanti	36
Volta	37
Brong Ahafo	39
Eastern	48
Central	50
Northern	69
Upper West	88
Upper East	89
Ghana	42

Source: Demery (2003).

smaller number of urban poor, roughly 54 percent use electricity for lighting.[14] These figures reflect trends in other developing countries, where households move up the "energy ladder" using cleaner fuels such as gas for cooking and electricity for lighting as their incomes rise (figure 8.4). Overall, the poor are not likely to rely on electricity. They are much more affected by price and access to paraffin, kerosene, or wood.

The PSIA found that the gap in access to electricity was largest in the poorer northern regions (in the NED distribution area) in spite of the existence of SHEP, which provided very low connection fees to rural communities (5,000 cedis or less than US$3) within 20 kilometers of the network. As shown in figure 8.5, only 10 percent of the communities earmarked for electrification in the fourth phase of the SHEP program (SHEP 4) were in the three poorer savannah regions (upper east, upper west, and northern regions) where less than 30 percent of the population has electricity access. SHEP has focused on more populated areas with less endemic poverty such as the Ashanti region, in part because it is supposed to assess the ability of customers to pay, and wants to maximize connections, which is easier to

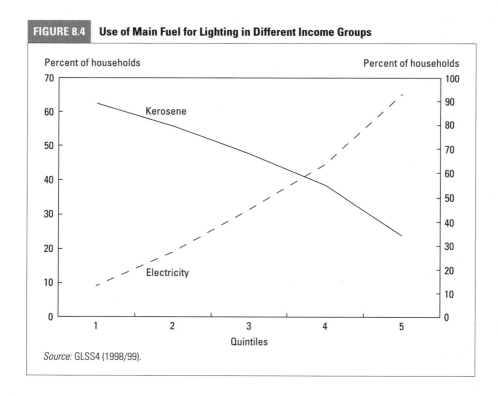

FIGURE 8.4 Use of Main Fuel for Lighting in Different Income Groups

Source: GLSS4 (1998/99).

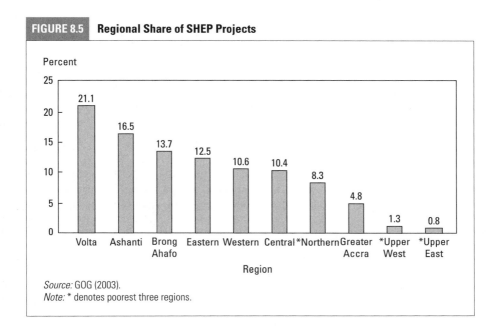

FIGURE 8.5   **Regional Share of SHEP Projects**

Source: GOG (2003).
Note: * denotes poorest three regions.

do in more densely populated areas. Thus, new investments in rural electrification are not adequately reaching the very poorest northern regions, which saw a decreased share in new rural electrification funding.

Targeting Poor Electricity Users

A second issue that the PSIA probed was the assumption that those falling in the lifeline band also fell below the poverty line. Although national-level household surveys did not identify which consumers fell in the lifeline tariff band, and because imputing consumption patterns from reported expenditures could have introduced a heavy bias because of the intermingling of arrears with current charges, the research team focused on using indicators not related to electricity consumption (income, poverty) from the 1998/9 household survey data. The team subjected this to a sensitivity analysis, projected forward. Even if the lifeline were to reach all poor electricity consumers, roughly half the lifeline subsidy would still "leak" to households that do not fall below the upper poverty line.[15]

On the other hand, if one assumes that new customers are poorer than existing customers (assuming 20 percent of all new customers fell below the poverty line) then the leakage could drop to 46 percent, but would still be substantial. Further, KITE survey data showed that lifeline customers are no more vulnerable (using the criteria of missing meals and selling assets) than other customers. The minority of customers who exhibited signs of vulnerability (such as taking children from school because of an inability to pay school fees or selling assets) were as likely to be consuming above the lifeline as below it; no statistically significant difference could be found between the lifeline and nonlifeline customers on most proxy indicators for vulnerability.[16] Clearly, at present the lifeline tariff represents an imperfect mechanism for reaching poor electricity users.

If one were to try to target the lifeline better, where would the poorer electricity users be found and how would one target them? In 1998/99 poorer electricity users were more likely to be found in rural areas, and in specific regions (figure 8.6). Although very few poor rural households have electricity, among the rural residents that do have electricity, about 20 percent fell below the poverty line in 1998/9, compared with less than 1 percent in Greater Accra and only 12 percent in other urban areas. In other words, in poorer regions, even low rates of access can reach a proportionally larger number of poor people. For example, in the central, Volta, and upper east regions, 27 percent of people with electricity access fell below the poverty line, compared with only 3 percent in Greater Accra.[17] But, as noted above, overall access rates remain low in the poorer northern regions, and those regions' share of investments for new connections is also disproportionately low.

The rationale for narrowing the lifeline to reduce leakage would make sense only if it were more likely to reach poor households and/or if the administrative and transaction costs of such refined targeting was outweighed by the direct savings incurred. During discussions with stake-

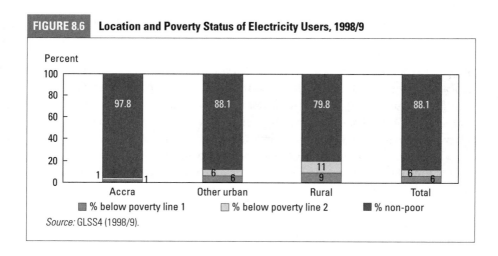

FIGURE 8.6 **Location and Poverty Status of Electricity Users, 1998/9**

Percent

Accra	Other urban	Rural	Total
97.8	88.1	79.8	88.1
1 / 1	6 / 6	11 / 9	6 / 6

■ % below poverty line 1   □ % below poverty line 2   ■ % non-poor

Source: GLSS4 (1998/9).

holders on these preliminary findings, and through the financial analysis carried out as part of this PSIA, the following became clear.

- The financial cost of the lifeline is minimal, as, at present, lifeline customers use only 2 percent of residential consumption.
- To the utilities, the lifeline was not originally a poverty tool, but rather it was a tool to minimize the administrative costs of small accounts. An initial discussion of options among technical committee members revealed that they were not interested in lowering the lifeline for this reason.
- The much larger issue is that the households in the lifeline exhibited no statistical differences in terms of poverty (or few) compared with nonlifeline customers. This was true even of those at the lower end of the lifeline consumption bracket.

Thus, although it is true that, on a per unit basis, those at the lower end of the lifeline pay less, the larger poverty issues are that many who could do not actually take advantage of the lifeline, instead ending up in arrears or disconnected. Also the majority of the poor do not have access to electricity.

Indicative Indicators of Social and Poverty Impact of Higher Tariffs

On the consumer side, in the absence of household survey data before and after tariff increases, the research team looked at positive or negative impacts from tariffs using a continuum of behavioral responses as rough indicators of whether these tariffs were having major impacts. This analysis was not meant to replace the analysis of national household survey data but to indicate any urgent problems that could not wait for the completion of the latest Ghana Living Standards Survey (GLSS) and that should be taken into consideration in the PRSC II and the GPRS. The objective was to ascertain whether the impact of higher electricity prices was so widespread that they could not be addressed through a lifeline or other targeted scheme. Thus, the approach was to select a small random sample within strata, using the utility database as the sample frame, and then to triangulate this with information on consumption for all consumers and for subsets of consumers from the utilities. Although such a small sample is not statistically significant, combined with evidence on consumption patterns from all consumer accounts (from the utilities) it nonetheless provided useful insights into people's coping mechanisms and into how better to design a targeting program.

The continuum below posits that if consumers responsible for bills are not aware of the price increase, it is less likely that the increase had a significant direct impact. Consumers may respond to higher tariffs by conserving energy, such as turning out lights when not in use or using more energy-efficient appliances or bulbs. Further along the continuum of behavioral response lie responses that may have negative impacts, such as reducing use of lights when such use is not excessive, or reducing productive uses of electricity. A common response—accumulating arrears—might have a negative impact on the consumer only if fines or disconnection are actually imposed by utility workers. Finally, substituting with dirty fuels such as wood or coal would have significant negative externalities (figure 8.7).

Although the researchers expected there to be extensive knowledge of price increases among consumers because of a high level of media coverage, they found that just over half of connected respondents ($n = 90$) interviewed in a subset of areas (urban, slum, and rural electrification areas)

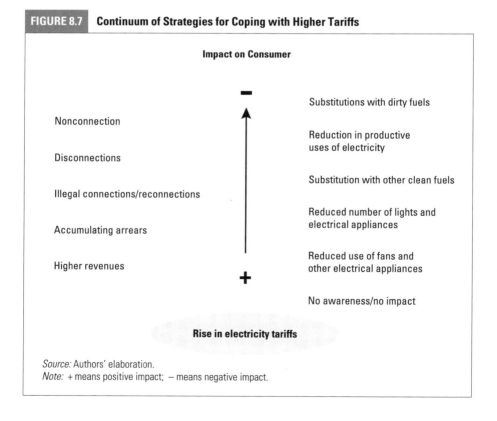

FIGURE 8.7   Continuum of Strategies for Coping with Higher Tariffs

Impact on Consumer

Nonconnection

Disconnections

Illegal connections/reconnections

Accumulating arrears

Higher revenues

Substitutions with dirty fuels

Reduction in productive uses of electricity

Substitution with other clean fuels

Reduced number of lights and electrical appliances

Reduced use of fans and other electrical appliances

No awareness/no impact

Rise in electricity tariffs

Source: Authors' elaboration.
Note: + means positive impact; − means negative impact.

recalled that tariffs had risen. These same households were asked follow-up questions about problems with bill payment and coping strategies. Of those aware of the price increase, almost half did nothing in response. The observations from the survey reinforce the results found by examining trends in utility data; some people are having trouble paying bills, but it does not reflect the situation of the majority of consumers. Fourteen percent of the medium- to low-income consumers interviewed cited rising electricity prices as the main reason for difficulty in paying bills, followed by changes in financial situation (9 percent) and seasonality of income (9 percent) (table 8.5).

The most significant finding is the difference between urban and rural respondents in terms of their awareness of the link between consumption and lower bills, with a clear gap among rural residents, probably because of lower literacy rates. Although the research team expected widespread

Table 8.5 Coping Responses to Price Increase

Response	Urban n = 30 (%)	Slum n = 30 (%)	SHEP n = 30 (%)	Total n = 90 Effective n = 49 (%)
Did not make changes	19	40	78	47 (n = 23)
Flat rate	33	17	7	13
Bill is affordable	33	17	29	26
Unaware of the link between price and conservation measures	33	67	64	61
Already conserving before increases	0	0	0	0
No other alternative than to pay	0	0	0	0
Made changes	81	60	22	53 (n = 26)
Borrowed money	0	0	25	4
Sold assets	0	0	0	4
Disconnected	0	12	0	4
Reduced number of electrical appliances	15	25	0	15
Used energy-saving bulbs	23	12	25	19
Reduced use of lighting	38	37	50	38
Reduced use of fan and other electrical appliances	0	12	0	4
Switched or used alternative sources of energy.	8	0	0	4
Combination of measures	16	0	0	8

Source: KITE Survey (2003).

knowledge of tariff increases, only about half of residential consumers were aware of such increases, and of these only half made changes in their consumption in response. In many cases consumers made no changes in their behavior in response to tariff increases because of a lack of knowledge in rural areas about how the lifeline works. Among those who did make changes (a group more predominant in urban areas), the most common response was to reduce the use of electricity for lighting.

Qualitative research on particular customer groups pointed to one group that felt that it was being acutely affected by higher tariffs, but that would not have been captured in the broader analysis or by looking at utility data. This was the group of small commercial enterprises such as corn millers, whose customers were not high income and who had competition from other firms that used diesel or other energy sources. Interviews with utility staff further confirmed that problems with illegal connections were particularly persistent among this group of customers.

During the field research, it became clear that consumer attitudes toward arrears were generally lax; it was very common for consumers to pay only some portion of the current bill, assuming that as long as arrears do not become too large, they are not likely to get disconnected. As the existence of arrears often does not imply disconnection, households often did not attach a high priority to paying the electricity bill, giving priority instead to other expenditures for which the penalties are much clearer and predictable, such as school fees or water bills. Questioned on the frequency with which a household defaults on payment, 31 percent of respondents indicate bill default every month. A smaller percent—17 percent of all consumers interviewed—attested that defaulting on their bill was because of financial constraints. According to consumers, such difficulty in payment can occur every month (21 percent), at least every 3 months (21 percent), once every 6 months or less (27 percent), or rarely (24 percent).

One coping mechanism of particular concern both for the consumer and for the utility is disconnection. The survey data revealed that the practice of cycling in and out of connection is widespread; almost half of all the households interviewed reported that they had been disconnected at one point in time, with disconnection more frequent in slum areas and less frequent in rural electrification areas (table 8.6). In urban slum areas the phenomenon is even more common, and is reflected in the larger debt accumulation among consumers in these areas, and thus the higher reconnection costs (table 8.6). A little over half of these households were disconnected for two weeks or less. This points to a problem with monthly bill payments and the regularity of income from informal enterprises.

Table 8.6 Disconnection and Reconnection Cost

Household connection status	Urban (n = 30)	Slum (n = 30)	SHEP (n = 30)	Total (n = 90)
Households disconnected before	50%	57%	37%	48%
Households reconnected	100%	88%	100%	95%
Reconnection cost (cedis)	37,672	235,810	116,545	131,323

Source: KITE Survey (2003).

A more drastic reaction to tariff increase is to seek illegal connection or to tamper with the meter. During focus group discussions, people openly admitted that this occurs, often after someone has been disconnected for nonpayment. It is difficult to assess the growth in these "nontechnical" losses, since estimates of these losses are not made on an annual basis. The most recent estimate in 2001 of technical and nontechnical losses (billing error, illegal connection, meter problems) showed that 11 percent of the electricity produced was lost in this manner.[18]

In Ghana, the potential for substituting alternative fuels lies primarily for the fuel used for lighting, as most of the respondents already were at the "bottom of the energy ladder" for cooking, using mainly charcoal or firewood because of the high relative cost of electricity for this purpose (figure 8.8). Outside of Ghana and large urban centers, the use of LPG

FIGURE 8.8 Cooking Fuel Cost

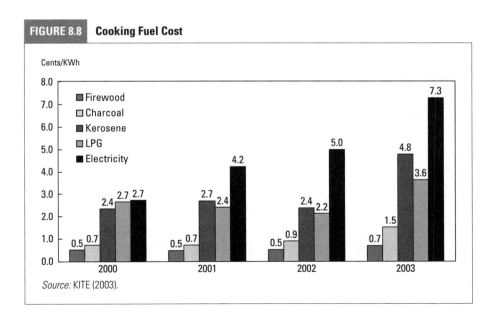

Source: KITE (2003).

(gas) is unlikely because of the higher cost of equipment required and limited availability.[19] Of potential concern for the future of Ghana's wood resources is the low cost of wood when compared with electricity. However, as indicated in table 8.5, only a small proportion of those aware of tariff increases actually switched to alternative fuels (4 percent overall). Further research is needed about the dependence of poorer households on kerosene and wood because of the increased price and limited availability of kerosene.

In order to test the validity of some of the indicative data above, the research team analyzed utility data on consumption overall and by tariff band over time for all customers in ECG areas. The analysis confirmed that the total amount of electricity used by residential consumers shows little or no permanent overall reaction to the tariff increases (figure 8.9). Although consumption levels may drop just after a tariff increase, they have tended to move back to an equilibrium that is not significantly lower than previous consumption levels. Variations in the total demand are mainly the result of variations in the demand in the highest band; these variations are related to seasonal changes in outdoor temperatures and holiday periods (the use of air-conditioning). Although some households are negatively

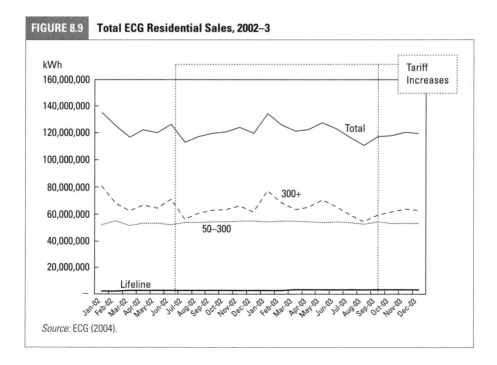

FIGURE 8.9 Total ECG Residential Sales, 2002–3

Source: ECG (2004).

affected by tariffs and are accumulating arrears or cycling into disconnection and reconnection consumption data on all customers confirms the results from the qualitative and small scale-research: that this is neither a generalized phenomenon nor is it significant in scale. Nonetheless, indicators for certain subgroups merits attention in future sector research.

The Ghana PSIA made explicit the importance of looking not only at the subsidy, but also at its sustainability over time. If the overall cost of the subsidy were too high, it might lead to indirect effects that could ultimately harm the poor. These harmful effects include contributing to fiscal deficits that could feed inflation. They could also lead to declines in service quality or to informally implemented limitations on electricity access of poorer groups by the utilities.

Incorporating a financial analysis of the utility into the PSIA allowed for this holistic approach.[20] Although the nominal cost of a lifeline tariff may be affordable to the utility at present, if the number of customers needing such a lifeline grows, and if the central government does not pay its subsidy on time (this was the case at the time of the PSIA) or does not cover the full cost of service provision, then the utility will tend to rely on informal cross-subsidies among consumers as long as there are enough consumers paying at cost to cover the others. As noted in the stakeholder analysis, the middle band of consumers represents a politically important block of urban voters. This has tended to limit the utilities' willingness to charge full cost to this group, resulting in higher increases for the upper tariff bracket consumers than for others. Moreover, such an implicit cross-subsidy would be threatened by one of the proposals for sector reform that was being considered, which was to allow larger industrial customers to purchase electricity directly from the generator (VRA) at bilaterally agreed prices, rather than going through the distributor (ECG or NED) and paying formally regulated prices.

There was, indeed, an increase of consumers in the lower tariff bands in ECG areas over the period of tariff increases. The number of lifeline consumers in ECG increased, from 19 percent of residential customers to 21 percent of residential customers from February 2002 to February 2003 (table 8.7). This increase may be the result of the combined effect of many new connections falling in the lifeline and a decrease in consumption by those above the lifeline. The annual increase in the total number of residential ECG customers is around 5 percent. A general decrease in average consumption is observed for all consumer categories, but again, as illustrated in figure 8.9, these are small changes. In NED service areas, there has been more growth in higher-end consumers (table 8.8) than in ECG areas.

Table 8.7 ECG Consumption and Customer Trends during Tariff Increases

Tariff band	Number of residential consumers			Share of residential consumers			Average consumption			Share of residential consumption		
	February 2002	February 2003	Change (%)	February 2002 (%)	February 2003 (%)	Change (%)	February 2002 (kWh)	February 2003 (kWh)	Change (%)	February 2002 (%)	February 2003 (%)	Change (%)
Lifeline	106,360	124,707	17	19	21	11	25	23	–8	2.1	2.3	10
50–300 kWh	336,510	344,341	2	60	58	–3	162	159	–2	44	43	–2
300 +	122,365	123,312	1	22	21	–5	555	555	0	54	54	0
Total residential	565,235	592,360	5	100	100		221	213	–4	100	100	

Source: ECG (2004).

Table 8.8 NED Consumption and Customer Trends during Tariff Increases[a]

Tariff band	Number of residential consumers			Share of residential consumers			Average consumption			Share of residential consumption		
	July 2002	February 2003	Change	July 2002 (%)	February 2003 (%)	Change (%)	July 2002 (kWh)	February 2003 (kWh)	Change (%)	July 2002 (%)	February 2003 (%)	Change (%)
Lifeline	—	46,400	n.a.	24	23	−4	27	28	−4	14	13	−7
50–300 kWh	—	67,556	n.a.	52	57	10	134	134	0	65	67	3
300+	—	10,496	n.a.	7	8	14	784	851	−8	16	18	13
Total residential		124,492										

Source: NED (2004).

Note: "0" consumers are not included.—not available; n.a. not applicable.

a. Based on a sample of 71,000 NED customers.

Because consumption has not responded in significant terms to tariff increases, one question the research team asked was whether the increases simply translated into greater arrears. The team used utility data to analyze the growth in arrears (1) overall and (2) within a random sample of specific consumer groups to assess whether these arrears were associated with specific consumer groups.[21] Overall, the value of arrears in cedis for residential customers increased by 34 percent between 2002 and 2003. However, arrears expressed as number of corresponding months of billing had not gone up, and in fact had decreased from a ratio of 6.3 to 6.0 (table 8.9).[22]

In addition to analyzing arrears for all customers, the research team sought to discover which groups were having the most difficulty with arrears. The team analyzed a random sample of customers from the ECG supply areas Accra East, Accra West, and Ashanti from each of the tariff bands over the past two years. They concluded that the trend at the aggregate level is similar to the trend of the overall utility data. Although arrears have increased considerably within the past two years, revenues have also increased. Within this random sample, the overall trends in arrears mask significant variations. In Kumasi, for example, the average arrears among lifeline customers has increased from ¢12,000 in July 2002 to ¢80,000 in February 2004. In Accra East arrears for lifeline customers have almost doubled, but at a much higher level, from ¢200,000 at ¢400,000 (corresponding to about 2.5 year's payment) during the same period. This means that lifeline customers in Accra East have paid a very small fraction of their bills since July 2002. Further, absolute levels of arrears in Accra are quite high. This level may reflect the number of slum areas where arrears have tended to be high, in contrast to the more general trend outlined in tables 8.7 and 8.8. Nonetheless, this tendency in arrears points to the need for more

Table 8.9 EGC Trends in Arrears

Tariff band	Average monthly bill			Ratio arrears over charges		
	February 2002 (cedis)	February 2003 (cedis)	Change (%)	February 2002 (cedis)	February 2003 (cedis)	Change (%)
Lifeline	7,824	14,002	79	7.4	5.6	−24
50–300 kWh	37,289	63,414	70	3.3	3.0	−9
300 + kWh	217,978	355,908	63	7.8	7.5	−3
Total residential	70,861	113,900	61	6.3	6.0	−6

Source: ECG (2004).

detailed and disaggregated analysis of affordability by tariff band once more recent GLSS data become available.

Finally, the survey team secured the ECG utility records of the inter-viewed households. It is evident from the arrears-to-current bill ratio that the households in compound and slums in Accra and Kumasi are more likely to react by accumulating arrears, particularly in 2003. Further, the ratio of arrears to current bill for slum households shows more fluctuations than for rural electrification and urban households. The households that have answered "Yes" to any of the four vulnerability indicators (sent away family members, took children out of school, had one meal yesterday, sold assets) are more likely to accumulate higher arrears than nonvulnerable households. Although the mean arrears of nonvulnerable households are ¢190,719, the arrears are more than twice this for households exhibiting any one of these vulnerability indicators. The rural electrification house-holds in the Accra region appear to be paying their bills on time: the ratio of arrears to current bill is less than 1 for the entire sample period. Over the period of tariff increases, arrears have increased substantially, particularly for some customer groups, including those in the lifeline (in spite of a flat tariff). However, the increase in arrears has not yet affected either the util-ity's overall revenues, which have increased, or the ratio of arrears to cur-rent billing.

CONCLUSIONS, POLICY RECOMMENDATIONS, AND IMPACT

In order to provide better energy services to the poor, future research in the energy sector needs to compare costs—including the implied ongoing operational and capital costs—of achieving energy access through contin-ued central-grid electricity expansion with the costs of other achieving such access through other alternatives. These alternatives include increasing access, price, and efficiency of biomass fuels such as fuelwood, kerosene, diesel, renewable energy sources, and other off-grid alternatives.

The lifeline tariff represents an imperfect mechanism of targeting the 5 to 20 percent of consumers who show signs of vulnerability. In fact, the lifeline tariff tariff was not originally designed to target the poor, but to ease the administrative burden on the utility and to provide a "basic needs" level of service. Nonetheless, the tariff has the potential to provide vital protec-tion to the minority of electricity consumers who have exhibited indicators of vulnerability and who have stated that they are having trouble paying their bills. At present, many of those who are having trouble paying bills are not using the lifeline, which points clearly to what was witnessed during fieldwork: many people do not know how to manage electricity resources and do not understand the protection the lifeline tariff offers. This lack of information appears particularly acute among those it is most likely to protect—poorer rural and less literate customers.

The current nominal cost of the lifeline subsidy is less than 1 percent of ECG revenues (about US$1.5 million per annum), and there is no impetus to refocus it in the short-term. The administrative cost of more detailed targeting schemes is unlikely to outweigh the savings generated, particularly since there were no more signs of vulnerability among those in the bottom half of the lifeline band than in the top half. A more efficient use of resources would be to educate vulnerable groups—especially those in rural areas—about how to take advantage of the lifeline tariff. Consumer education about billing and energy savings is needed, particularly in rural areas and among those who do not see the bill, in a way that is accessible to customers with less education.

Utilities should promote public information about why electricity tariffs are increasing, and about how people can save energy to safeguard themselves. If sector reforms that consolidate NED and the ECG move forward it may be necessary to review the tariff structure again, because electricity losses are considerably higher in NED areas (up to 40 percent higher in poorer northern regions).

Policy makers should carefully consider the indirect impacts on residential consumers of allowing large customers to negotiate agreements with the VRA (a type of partial deregulation). At the time of the PSIA, these customers provided an informal cross-subsidy for the lifeline and for those in the middle tariff brackets. Losing these large customers, which contribute a significant proportion of current charges, risks a further deterioration of the utilities' financial position. If this happens, the utilities may limit access to the poor or may reduce quality indirectly. The alternative would be for the ministry of finance to cover the cost of providing such a lifeline in a timely manner.

To aid those without access, the PSIA recommended that policy makers review the factors that affect the availability and pricing of kerosene products in rural areas in the interim, possibly through the related PSIA on petroleum products. In future research, it will be important to assess the best methods of facilitating clean and efficient access to energy in low-density poorer rural areas (such as more fuel efficient stoves, alternative energy sources, and so on) for those who may not be able to afford electricity services. Policy makers should consider whether the indirect subsidies currently provided to non-lifeline electricity consumers could be better used for expanding clean energy access and energy efficiency in these rural areas.

In addition, the PSIA recommended indicators to monitor the process of energy reform. These indicators include information about the average processing time needed for new connections, the number of new connections, the ratio of arrears to current payment by tariff band, changes in the prices of electricity dependent products or services, and the level of awareness of the lifeline among different groups of consumers compared to a baseline. For future reforms, the PSIA recommended providing incentives for improved quality of service as part of any future management contract for electricity, with specific input from consumers on those indicators of most value to them.

Following the completion of this PSIA (in late June 2004), the World Bank changed its own allocation for new investments to include resources to prepare project components for nontraditional and off-grid sources of energy (in the context of the Ghana Energy Development and Access Project of over US$70 million). These investments would better target areas where the poor are concentrated in the north of the country, where the share of new investment for electricity was declining. In effect, the PSIA provided a "voice" for those stakeholders least represented in the stakeholder map—poor rural consumers not yet connected to the grid—and a way to take their needs into account in the design of development projects.

After the PSIA was completed a new energy minister took office following the elections in November 2004. The government continued its use of the lifeline tariff, and its findings were integrated directly into the PRSC II. The policy recommendations that require more complex responses by others—such as the recommendation to increase education for rural consumers—may require more follow-up. The government, particularly the ministry of energy, expressed its interest in managing the dissemination process, which is still in a nascent stage. The National Development Planning Commission (NDPC) that is coordinating these activities aims to involve the media during the planned dissemination in 2006. The PSIA has nonetheless received attention from the NGO community, including Eurodad and ISODEC, which recently concluded an assessment of five Ghana PSIAs conducted in 2003–4 to understand the PSIA selection mechanism, country ownership, client dialogue, local capacity building, and impact on policy.

LESSONS LEARNED

The first lesson is one of the importance of collaboration. Collaboration among stakeholders throughout the PSIA process was crucial for ensuring that there was sufficient internal discussion of the PSIA findings. This collaboration required additional time commitment of both Bank staff and consultants as well as government personnel within a finite policy-planning timeline. The PSIA was therefore divided into what could be done within the time available (so that it would be able to feed into the PRSC and GPRS). Although this means that there is still more analysis to be done, the analysis that was completed was nonetheless able to inform some of the broad assumptions behind different policy options and to take concrete steps to ensure that evidence informed approaches. One example was the initial assumption that the best way to reach the poor was through electricity subsidies. The majority of the poor, however, were not connected to the grid, at least in the poorest northern regions. These regions saw a declining share of new electricity investments because of competing incentives for stakeholders, which took the form of the electricitiy company choosing between financial sustainability or extending access. Addressing this assumption about subsidies as the best way to reach the poor with existing data allowed for a relatively rapid shift in World Bank lending to target the needs of the poor in the poorest regions of Ghana better.

A second lesson is that local organizations have a leading role to play not only in collecting data but also in its analysis, and this requires a substantial investment in capacity building and training. One of the accomplishments of the PSIA was to engage a local energy-sector NGO—KITE—to lead the PSIA with support from the World Bank. Such an association not only raised the feeling of ownership among the Ghanaian stakeholders but also raised Ghanaian capacity to undertake evidence-based policy analysis. However, additional time is needed to train teams on evidence-based policy analysis specific to the sector at hand.

The third lesson learned in the course of this project is that, for policy measures involving new resources or a diverse set of stakeholders, the process of policy analysis and formulation starts once the PSIA has been completed. Ensuring that the findings continue to be integrated requires two elements: a local-level "champion" for the PSIA who is central to the policy discussion, and continued resources for follow-up.

And the fourth lesson is that the dissemination process cannot be hurried. The level of ownership of the PSIA by the lead agency, the Ministry of Energy in this case, is evident in its desire to drive the dissemination process. However, the existence of many competing demands mean that this process may take longer than anticipated. This was the case for all of the five donor-funded PSIAs undertaken in Ghana in 2003–04 (Eurodad 2005). It is crucial to have a well-defined dissemination strategy built into the work program of PSIA.

NOTES

1. This PSIA on the energy sector was made possible by the support of the Energy Sector Management Technical Assistance Program (ESMAP) of the Danish trust fund, and of the Trust Fund for Environmentally and Socially Sustainable Development (TFESSD).
2. In June 1994, the government, through a policy paper, outlined the strategic framework for power sector reform and established a power sector reform committee (PSRC) to oversee the reform of the sector.
3. This result is based on government spending as reported in PRSC II, less amortization, foreign assistance, and arrears.
4. This figure is from a draft financial model for ECG constructed as part of this PSIA.
5. The only opposition to tariff increase between 1994 and 1997 arose when the Ministry of Energy approved tariffs that were to take retrospective effect. This decision was challenged in court by a group of consumers seeking clarification about the legality of the retroactive billing. The court ruled against the retroactive billing and instructed the utilities to obtain parliamentary approval before enforcing the 1994 and 1995 tariffs.
6. There are five main tariff categories, including residential. The residential, non-residential, and Special Load Tariff–Low Voltage (SLT-LV) customers are supplied electricity at nominal voltage levels of 415/230V and are together classified as low-voltage customers for the purposed of cost allocation; Special Load Tariff–Medium Voltage (SLT-MV) and Special Load Tariff–High Voltage (SLT-HV) customers. PURC approved an average increase of 72 percent, which was implemented in two steps. The first round of increases, totaling 60 percent, came into effect in August; the second round was introduced in March 2003. So the March 2003 increase can be considered an extension of the July 2002 tariff increase rather than a major tariff review.
7. PURC sets benchmarks for efficiency and bases its tariffs on the assumption that these efficiency targets are being met, and that the end-user should not pay for inefficiencies in the utility.
8. The training covered (1) PSIA concepts and methodology, (2) the application of these concepts to research on tariffs, (3) an analysis to date of existing information, (4) focus group techniques, and (5) the use of the field instruments. The field survey was preceded with testing of the draft questionnaires for validity, accuracy, clarity, and timing.
9. World Bank staff and consultants provided support and training throughout the process. An international consulting firm, Ramboll, provided some assistance as well, but was not involved in writing up the final report. SHEP was introduced to assist communities that are within 20 kilometers of all existing 33kV or 10kVnetwork, that have procured low-voltage poles, and where 30 percent of houses are wired to get power ahead of their respective scheduled dates of connection under the National Electrification Scheme. At the time of

community connection, households pay ¢5,000 to get connected. Within these communities, houses that are more than 25 kilometers away from the low-voltage network pay an additional fee to have the distribution wires extended to their houses.

11. These 90 are out of the total sample of 318 households. The rest include compound households, commercial customers, high-income residential customers, and disconnected customers. For the purpose of this paper, only results from individual households are presented.

12. Access is one of the key transmission channels in PSIA; people with electricity access will be most directly affected by changes in price or quality. Indirect or second-order effects would include price increases by those using electricity as an input cost. Such indirect effects were not analyzed in the Phase I PSIA.

13. These are preliminary results, taken from Ghana Statistical Service CWIQ 2003.

14. It is important to keep in mind that there are far fewer poor people in urban than in rural areas; for example, in 1999 only 20 percent of those in other urban areas and less than 5 percent of those in greater Accra fell below the upper poverty line.

15. The lifeline is currently extended to approximately 24 percent of residential consumers; yet in 1999, 12 percent of those with electricity fell below the poverty line (GLSS4). The leakage calculation assumes that the composition of new customers is similar to the composition of old customers, and that all of those who are poor consume in the lifeline bracket (which is unlikely). Different assumptions could move this leakage up or down; overall poverty has declined since 1999, so there may be fewer poor electricity consumers. On the other hand, new electricity consumers are likely to be rural and lower-income than existing customers. If one assumes that new customers are poorer than existing customers (assuming 20 percent of all new customers fell below the poverty line) then the leakage could drop to 46 percent.

16. The KITE data focused on consumers in middle- to low-income areas and were not meant to be representative of the entire customer base. Among this specific group, it found that about 20 percent exhibited at least one sign of vulnerability (selling assets).

17. Ghana Statistical Service 2000.

18. In spite of additional efforts since 2001 to reduce these losses, the overall electricity losses (technical and nontechnical) to the sector are stagnant, remaining around 25 to 26 percent of the electricity produced.

19. Only about half of urban areas in Ghana have an LPG-filling facility in the area. The coverage in the rural areas is negligible. LPG is exempted from taxes and levies as part of a policy to promote the substitution away from charcoal for cooking purposes.

20. For further information on this integrated methodology, see Keener and Banerjee (2005).

21. NED data on arrears were not available.

22. It is important to understand the billing cycle. The cycle is two months long from the time the meter is read to the point where the bill is delivered to the customer. Further, the customer gets a period of close to 40 days to settle the bill, meaning that the billing and collections cycle is approximately three months long. Finally, old arrears—which are unlikely ever to be paid—remain on the books and are not written off.

REFERENCES

Demery, L. 2003. "Poverty Reduction without Much Growth: Ghana during the 1990s." Mimeo, World Bank, Washington, DC.

Edjekumhene, I., and N. Dubash. 2002. "Achieving Public Benefits by Default." In *Power Politics: Equity and Environment in Electricity Reform,* 117–37. Washington, DC: World Resources Institute.

ECG (Electricity Company of Ghana Limited). 2002. *Compound House Survey Report.* Customer Services Directorate, ECG, Accra, Ghana.

Energy Commission. 2003. "The Electricity Sector: Current Situation and the Critical Issue." March 14, Accra, Ghana.

Eurodad. 2005. Experimenting with Poverty and Social Impact Assessments: Ghana.

Ghana Statistical Service, 2000.

Ghana Statistical Service. 2003. "Core Welfare Indicators Questionnaire." Accra, Ghana.

IEA (International Energy Agency). 2002. *World Energy Outlook 2002: Energy and Poverty.* IEA.

Keener, S., and S. G. Banerjee. Forthcoming. *Measuring Consumer Benefits from Utility Reform: An Exploration of Consumer Assessment Methodology in Sub-Saharan Africa.* Washington, DC: World Bank.

KITE (Kumasi Institute of Technology and Environment). Survey, 2003. Kumasi, Ghana.

Layec, M. Presentation on West African Power Pool, January 2004, Energy Sector Management Assistance Program, World Bank.

Opam, M., and J. K. Turkson. 2000. "Power Sector Restructuring in Ghana." In *Power Sector Reform in Sub-Saharan Africa,* ed. J. K. Turkson, 50–82. London: Macmillan Press.

PURC. 1999. *Annual Report.* Accra, Ghana.

———. 2000. *Annual Report.* Accra, Ghana.

———. 2002. *Transitional Plan.* Accra, Ghana.

World Bank. 1993. *Republic of Ghana, National Electrification Project.* Staff Appraisal Report. Washington, DC.

———. *World Development Indicators 2004.* Washington, DC: World Bank.

9

ALBANIA
Decentralization and Water Sector Privatization

SABINE BEDDIES AND HERMINE DE SOTO[1]

The Government of Albania (GOA) aims to provide equitable access to safe water and affordable tariffs through a water sector reform that experiments with decentralization under two parallel water utility management models, one private and the other public.[2]

REFORM CHOICE AND RATIONALE

Although Albania has abundant water resources, its drinking water and sewerage infrastructure is considerably aged, damaged, and inefficient in both urban and rural areas. The GOA included water sector reform in its National Strategy for Socio-Economic Development (NSSED, the country's Poverty Reduction Strategy Paper [PRSP]) to improve service provision efficiency and effectiveness, ensure access to basic infrastructure services, and improve the targeting of the poor. The Bank assists the GOA's decentralization and water sector reform through the Municipal Water and Wastewater Project (the "project" or MWWP). The project introduced the first private sector management contract in four Albanian cities. In line with the "Strategy for Decentralization and Local Government" in the NSSED and the Country Assistance Strategy (CAS), the privatization of the water sector is expected to improve the management of water and wastewater services by establishing transparent and inclusive mechanisms at the local government level for decision making and implementation and the management of natural resources and public services. The GOA and the Bank agreed to examine the distributional impacts of the reform through a poverty and social impact analysis (PSIA).

Reform Context and Choice for the PSIA

The study aimed to assess the impacts of this reform by comparing the two models across eight cities and over a period. Four cities with private water utility management, supported by the Bank's MWWP sites, were compared with a control group of four cities with public water utility management. The study will also compare the two models across two time periods—before and after private sector participation. It was therefore first conducted when the private operator started its engagement (MWWP 2002). A follow-up study will measure the visible reform impacts in about two years' time. The study examined the changes in institutional rules that the decentralization reform entailed, and it assessed the impacts that the changes in authority had on price (tariffs), access, and transfers (DFID et al. 2005; North 1990; Kessides 2000; Birdsall et al. 2003).

Rationale for the Reform Choice

The dilapidated water supply and sanitation networks called for urgent rehabilitation. In almost all urban areas, water supply through the network was intermittent and unreliable. The quality of drinking water was often compromised by the lack of adequate treatment and disinfection facilities and by the unreliable supply of chemicals. The dilapidation of the water supply and sanitation facilities is believed to have triggered several waterborne diseases and epidemics over the last decade, and is seen as a major cause of the rise in infant mortality in Albania (Republic of Albania 2001).

    Inefficient operation systems and lack of financial viability caused water utilities to operate below cost recovery and to drain public sector funds. Most customers had only two to four hours of water a day; some had water only a few times a week without prior notice of actual supply; and a few had no water supply at all. To make things worse, inadequate network maintenance and repair and a lack of metering and operational control of supply have resulted in excessive water losses. These losses were estimated to be greater than 50 percent of water production in all cities. The poorest population groups were hit hardest by the dire water conditions, suffering from lower access and higher costs in both relative and absolute terms. Government subsidies became an increasingly insufficient and unsustainable means for funding the provision of water and wastewater services.

The GOA called for urgent reform to improve water supply and sanitation service delivery and efficiency. The government considered the implementation of the decentralization process to be one mechanism for improving the public delivery of water and wastewater services. Following consultations with the Bank, another mechanism was considered. This mechanism involved elaborating the participation of the private sector through a management contract that includes provisions to ensure benefits to the poor and other vulnerable groups. The GOA saw this as a rapid way to improve public sector service quality and efficiency of operations, and agreed to World Bank assistance through a private management contract of the four utilities in Durrës, Fier, Lezha, and Saranda (Republic of Albania 2001; MWWP 2002; World Bank 2004).

Impacts of the decentralization reform and water sector privatization were expected to be high. The water sector privatization affects all 12 regions in Albania and about 35–38 percent of the urban population—1.294 million people (MWWP 2002).

The severity of the water problems, inefficient utility operation, unsatisfactory service provision, and tariff increase sparked intense public debate. According to the 1999 Decentralization Law, which became effective in January 2002, the water utilities, together with local governments, have the right to make all decisions on operations, investment, and tariff setting to reach eventual cost recovery (Republic of Albania 1999). Civil society responded with demonstrations in April 2003 against tariff increases without service improvement. The policy debate on water tariff increases and lack of service improvements gained further momentum during the run-up to the local government elections in October 2003.

The decentralization reform has advanced at two speeds. Progress has been made toward a reasonably strong legal framework for fiscal decentralization. Implementation, however, has fallen behind. Factual decentralization remains constrained by several issues. These include the lack of local absorptive capacity as well as political and bureaucratic obstacles that hamper reform efforts. For instance, local governments lack capacity in capital and project planning and in water resource management—all of which are essential for a tariff policy with cost recovery for utilities and affordability for customers, as well as for water conservation, quality service provision, and customer service measures. Weak governance and limited institutional capacity continue to remain major challenges that need to be addressed to implement the NSSED fully (UNDP 2002; Kessides 2000).

Gradually, local governments have been gaining representation in the supervisory councils of the water companies, particularly in the cities with privately managed utilities under the Bank water projects. However, these councils remain under the control of the central government. Furthermore, all local governments have increased water utility tariffs. In an attempt to move the water utilities toward cost recovery under the reform, local governments in cities with privately managed utilities have increased tariffs substantially. Local governments with public utility management, however, are likely to pursue a more conservative approach to tariff increases because of perceived public pressure (World Bank 2003).

This finding was reflected in the PSIA pilot study where—at the beginning of the reform—the publicly managed utilities initially maintained the preliberalization water tariffs of 15 leks[3] per cubic meter in Vlora and in Gjirokastra, while the privately managed utilities had increased their tariffs to about 48 percent in Durrës (to 31 leks per cubic meter) and 100 percent in Saranda (to 26 leks per cubic meter). After these selective tariff increases, water tariffs represented 1 to 2 percent of the monthly household budget in the pilots in these four cities compared with monthly household expenditures for electricity of about 7 to 9 percent of the budget. After the universal tariff increase in all cities that is part of the reform implementation, tariffs in all eight study sites comprise 1.3 percent of household expenditure. Nevertheless, consumers remain unwilling to pay higher tariffs without visible service improvements (World Bank 2003).

Table 9.1 presents pertinent details for the eight cities covered by this study.

METHODOLOGY

The hypothesis that the two reform models have different distributional impacts on similar socioeconomic groups guided the choice of analytical methodology. A multidisciplinary team of local researchers and World Bank staff chose tools and methods that would allow a comparison of distributional impacts on social groups in the eight cities studied. Furthermore, the study methodology chose a comparative case study approach for detailed insights into consumer perceptions and coping strategies (Strauss and Corbin 1990; Krueger et al., 2001; Yin 1994). The team selected the four cities under the Bank's MWWP with private utility management (Durrës, Fier, Lezha, and Saranda) and four cities under public utility management (Vlora, Korça, Lushnja, and Gjirokastra) as a control group. The selection criteria for the control group counterfactual cities were similarities with Project cities in terms of size, socioeconomic conditions, and water sector issues. The study assessed consumer/beneficiaries' perceptions of, and satisfaction with

- tariff increases,
- access to water and wastewater services through public and private provision, and
- transfers or subsidies for the poor (a lifeline tariff of 20 liters per capita per day, and service connection and meter installation offered free or included in regular charges over time).

The focus was on analyzing stakeholders, institutions, and social impacts. The study was designed to illustrate the current constraints, opportunities, and risks attached to private and public water utility management. Government and Bank consultations identified the need for concrete insights into the structure, functioning, and impacts of the two reform models. Therefore, the study was designed to illustrate constraints, opportunities, and risks of the process of decentralization per se, the water sector, and its future development for different social, ethnic, and income groups. The research methodology was chosen to allow a degree of comparability of results and also to allow isolation of reform impacts that are intrinsic to each model. The team highlighted the similarities and difference within and across the two reform models by comparing the eight cities at the beginning of the water sector reform in late 2003. Additionally, the team chose to include a longitudinal component by using the analysis as a baseline in all eight cities for a comparative analysis in the future. This way, the analysis will provide insights into distributional impacts at two points in time—at the beginning of the reform and during its implementation.

Multidisciplinary expertise and skills were strategically combined for a comprehensive sector overview. A multidisciplinary team with a strategic skill mix collaborated closely throughout the study's design and implementation. Local and international team members were selected to complement one another's expertise and experiences in decentralization, impact analysis, and water sector reform in Albania. The local team consisted of 15 researchers with expertise in the Albanian water sector, urban governance, and multidisciplinary field research. The Bank team consisted of 4 staff members with applied expertise in the water sector, distributional impact analysis, social and political science, and country knowledge.

Table 9.1 Condition and Access to Water and Sewerage Infrastructure in Eight Target Cities

	Cities under private management contract				Counterfactual cities (public management)			
	Durrës	Fier	Lezha	Saranda	Korça	Gjirokastra	Vlora	Lushnja
Area (km sq)	433	720	437	149	1,530	1,137	1,609	712
Population (2001 census)	113,465	76,166	16,592	14,553	58,911	22,866	85,180	38,336
Population (municipality data)	173,542	109,925	33,000	32,000	84,000	34,250	115,396	61,000
Population growth rate (%, 1989–2003)[a]	210	255	340	203	132	142	160	204
Unemployment rate (%, 2001)	27.05	20.07	12.88	19.58	21.76	23.12	27.23	27.05
Families under economic assistance	1,010 (2.27%)	1,330 (5.2%)	792 (13%)	153 (1.9%)	1,944 (8.3%)	320 (3.5%)	2,007 (7%)	1,500 (10%)
Main economic activities (water-related)	Tourism and services	Food processing services	Fishery, tourism, services	Tourism, fishery, services	Brewery, food processing	Food processing	Tourism, fishery, services	Food processing
Main economic activities (non-water related)	Trade, apparel, construction, transportation, agriculture	Construction, trade, apparel manufacturing, agriculture	Construction	Construction	Apparel manufacturing, trade, construction	Construction, apparel manufacturing.	Construction, apparel manufacturing, trade	Apparel manufacturing, construction, industry
Water utility coverage	Regional	Municipal	Municipal	Municipal	Municipal	Municipal	Municipal	Municipal

Billing system	Dominant flat rate combined with metered consumption	Dominant flat rate combined with metered consumption	Dominant flat rate combined with metered consumption	Dominant flat rate combined with metered consumption	Metered consumption	Flat rate	Dominant flat rate combined with metered consumption	Flat rate
Tariffs: domestic consumers (2003–04, flat rates = 4-person households)	840 Lek flat rate; 31 Lek/cubic meter	30 Lek/cubic meter	28 Lek/cubic meter; about 840 Lek flat rate	30 Lek/cubic meter; about 620 Lek flat rate	32 Lek/cubic meter	240 Lek flat rate	About 550 Lek flat rate	18 Lek/cubic meter; about 600 Lek
Collection ratio (%)	60	40	67	60	98.83	60	50	60
Water loss (%)	68	55	55	60	10	55–60	60	60
Condition of sewerage system	Dire, some investments through MWWP	Dire	Some investments through MWWP	Dire	Dire, funds provided, project not implemented	Dire, lacking investments	Dire, system upgrade in 2003 by PHARE	Dire, lacking investments
Hours of supply	1.5	4.5	13	4	24	2.4	7.5	1.3
Monthly household income (Lek)	39,139	60,292	46,644	74,127	50,023	58,716	66,555	29,964
Population (%) with access to water service	88	85	62	92.4	100	100	100	96.3
Population (%) with access to sewerage	69	86.3	36.7	64.6	95	76.5	87.8	76.8

Source: Household Questionnaire, key-informant interviews, and focus group discussions for the PSIA, December 2003–January 2004.

Note: a. Based on population data obtained from municipal sources. b. Hours of supply presented here are an average of summer and winter supply.

Data Collection Tools and Methods

The team chose a mixed-method approach. Qualitative and quantitative data collection methods and tools provided comprehensive insights into the reform structure and processes of the two models. The study was preceded by a pilot during April and June 2003 to test and refine the research methodology. The team conducted a Stakeholder Analysis, an Institutional Analysis, and a Social Impact Analysis (North 1990; Bianchi and Kossoudji 2001; Brinkerhoff and Crosby 2002). The study compiled secondary data through a desk review of existing material; it collected primary data through 110 key-informant interviews, 32 focus group discussions, 664 socioeconomic household surveys with domestic utility customers, and 8 city profiles to provide context on socioeconomic conditions, the decentralization process, and water sector issues. A local team conducted the fieldwork, using tape recordings for the key-informant interviews and focus groups. Quantitative data were processed and analyzed with Statistical Package for the Social Sciences (SPSS). The tape-recorded, qualitative data were transcribed and analyzed. The local team drafted a report outline, and both teams elaborated the organization, structure, and presentation of the data in the draft report. The Bank team provided substantial guidance and quality control throughout the analysis, as well as the write-up of the study report.

Systematic fieldwork preparation and data collection with secondary research bolstered primary data collection. The secondary literature and data review helped to shape the study approach and methodology (De Soto et al. 2001). It covered key documents and laws on the organization and functioning of local government decentralization, as well as specific water and wastewater sector issues By building on the existing knowledge, the team was able to save time and financial resources. The primary data were collected based on research instruments that the team had elaborated for each data collection method (North 1990; Strauss and Corbin 1990; Bianchi and Kossoudji 2001; Brinkerhoff and Crosby 2002; Foster, Tiongson, and Ruggeri Laderchi 2005) (box 9.1).

Rationale for Choice of Methodology and Process with Regard to Constraints Faced

The study design was chosen to illustrate the constraints, opportunities, and risks associated with the two reform models. The team used stakeholder, institutional, and impact analysis to gain insights into stakeholder

BOX 9.1 Primary Data Collection Methodology

Key-informant interviews gave insights into organizational structures, formal and informal institutions, stakeholder perceptions, and sector dynamics. The team elaborated a thematic topic guide that allowed the necessary free conversation yet covered the themes of interest, such as progress of political and financial decentralization, water access, tariffs, subsidies and transfers. The sampling was purposive to cover all organizational stakeholders directly involved in decentralization and water sector issues from the public and private sectors and civil society. At the central government level, data were collected through eight expert interviews conducted with representatives of the line ministries—the Ministry of Territorial Adjustment and Tourism (MOTAT), the Ministry of Local Government and Decentralization (MOLGD), and the Ministry of the Economy (MOE) and officials of the water regulatory entity (WRE) and the national water council. At each site, a minimum of 12 interviews were completed with representatives of local government, all eight water utilities, some businesses, civil society organizations, and interest groups.

Focus group discussions yielded feedback on consumer satisfaction and coping strategies. The team explored community perceptions on municipal governance and water sector institutions, water access, tariffs, willingness and ability to pay, subsidies and transfers, and employment. Four focus groups were conducted at each site. Sampling was purposive to obtain a balanced site representation regarding demographic and socioeconomic characteristics such as gender, ethnic background, and income group, which the Qualitative Poverty Assessment identified as very poor, poor, non-poor, and relatively well off (see annex 9B). Sampling was also guided by the water and wastewater service quality, such as different water pressure zones based on where respondents lived within the supply network; network coverage for respondents living inside and the service area; and previous participation in the Bank's metering program through its 2000 Water Supply Urgent Rehabilitation Project.

Socioeconomic household surveys revealed basic data on domestic consumers, main water and wastewater problems, and willingness to pay at the household level. The household survey drew on the Social Assessment for the Bank project. It covered issues such as consumer satisfaction with municipal governance, tariffs and willingness and ability to pay, pressure and reliability, and water safety. The respondents were domestic consumers from different socioeconomic, ethnic, and geographical backgrounds. The team drew a representative sample and interviewed a minimum of 80 households at the purely urban sites, and 100 households in the urban-rural region of Durrës to account for this city's larger service area. Sampling was first stratified to cover specific categories of households, such as coverage or lack of coverage by the network, different pressure zones, presence or lack of meters, income group, and participation in the metering program of the Bank's Urgent Rehabilitation Project. Within each category, sampling was random to obtain a balanced representation of households.

Community profiles provided a disaggregated spatial context for socioeconomic conditions and water sector issues. The local researchers produced a profile for each site. These profiles provided a contextual and disaggregated account of water and wastewater conditions, private and public service provision, decentralization progress, and the socioeconomic status of the population.

Source: Authors' compilation.

perceptions—the "black box of decision making"—and the effects the reform on different socioeconomic groups (North 1990; Strauss and Corbin 1990; Bianchi and Kossoudji 2001, Brinkerhoff and Crosby 2002). As part of the institutional analysis, the team produced two organizational maps of the new institutional setting for water sector management under the two regimes (see annex 9A).

The availability and reliability of in-country data and collaboration with local, national, and international partners were limited. As decentralization and water sector privatization are very recent processes in Albania, data on these are scarce (UNDP 2002; MWWP 2002). Owing to methodological and analytic irregularities of the statistics available from the National Statistical Institute (INSTAT 2002, 2003), the team decided to focus on primary data collection and drew heavily on the expertise and resources of local, national, and international partners (ESMAP 2003; UNDP 1997) (box 9.2).

Operational relevance and direct links to a Bank operation provided benefits. The study was designed to feed directly into MWWP, which helps the government to implement its water sector reform within the PRSP context.

The study needed to adapt its timeframe and methodology to local conditions and study deadlines. The study team decided to postpone the fieldwork until after the local elections to avoid having to repeat the fieldwork with the newly elected mayors, and to be able to build the intended basis for future policy dialogue with the local government representatives. This created time and resource constraints for the data collection, analysis, and write-up within the given fiscal year deadline, however. Hence, the team adapted the methodology to schedule a parallel collection of qualitative and quantitative data.

The reform's operationalization was monitored from the beginning through a baseline. The team timed the study to coincide with the start-up of the private operator's engagement in the operation and management of the four water companies under the MWWP. This enabled the team to gather data before reform impacts were visible. Hence the team set a baseline of pre-reform water sector conditions against which future reform impacts can be measured through a follow-up study.

MAIN FINDINGS

This section starts with an overview of key findings, followed by a detailed presentation of reform impacts through decentralization, tariffs, access, transfers, and second-order effects.

BOX 9.2   **Gaining Access to Data and Information Sources through In-Country Collaboration**

- **The team benefited from the country knowledge of local researchers, built capacity, and invested upstream for quality results downstream.** The multi-disciplinary team conducted the study with a local research team that had expertise and a proven track record on conducting a mixed-method study of urban governance and water sector reform. The team conducted a two-day training on the approach of poverty and social impact analysis, with concepts and tools tailored to the water and wastewater sector in Albania. The classroom experience was further grounded through a two-day application of classroom knowledge in the field. Local researchers and Bank staff completed a rapid appraisal to deepen mutual knowledge of water sector reform and PSIA tools and methods. This process was chosen to build the local capacity of the research team to conduct the study and analyze distributional reform impacts.
- **Cooperation with central and local government, civil society, and private sector enabled data collection and an ongoing policy dialogue.** The local team conducted the study in collaboration with the central government's line ministry and worked closely with the eight municipalities, representatives of the private sector, and civil society. Thus, apart from gathering crucial information on water sector decentralization and privatization, the team set the stage for an ongoing policy dialogue, ownership of study findings, and collaboration for the second round of impact assessment against the set baselines.
- **Collaboration with international partners supported the analysis and implementation of proposed reform changes.** As the reform is new and the study methodology was considered innovative, there was considerable interest for the study findings from the relevant central and local-level line ministries, donor agencies, civil society organizations, and domestic and private sector consumers. The United Nations Development Programme (UNDP) joined forces with the study team under its democratic governance program and provided substantial financial resources for the study.

Source: Authors' compilation.

Key Findings

Key findings suggest reform adjustments that are focused mainly on a different sequencing and pacing of the reform. Data from all eight sites suggest that visible improvements in the service quality and in the collection ratio should be made before tariffs are further increased. This sequence is crucial for maintaining consumer satisfaction and to keep consumers paying water charges. The surveyed utilities cannot afford service improvements without first increasing the tariff. Customers in all eight cities are either unable or unwilling to afford the proposed tariff increases without visible service improvements. Whereas nonpayment can be attributed to poverty or the inability to pay for the "very poor" and "poor" groups, service dissatisfaction is usually the cause of nonpayment among the better off.

Local governments request the Bank to support decentralization reform, especially in regard to the transfer of assets and the tariff-setting authority, as well as to provide technical assistance and capacity building. Study findings illustrate similarities and differences between the two reform models (box 9.3).

Reform adjustments could be useful where improvements in service quality and in the collection ratio are made a condition for gradual tariff increases in all eight cities (box 9.4).

The decentralization and water sector privatization reform is accompanied by changes in authority. Two examples of specific impacts emerged as a consequence of changes in power, structures, and processes that govern the function of the institutions involved:

- Tariff increases are higher in the cities with privately managed utilities. The private operator works on a commercial basis with performance-based indicators. The operator has developed a clear strategy for covering operation and maintenance costs. The increase in tariffs is a means to recover costs.

- The urban poor in cities with privately managed utilities have specific support. The private operator mitigates the negative impacts of tariff increases on the urban poor by introducing a lifeline tariff (20 liters/day/capita) and by installing water meters to measure and bill for actual household water consumption.

Key Stakeholders

The council of ministers is responsible for the legal components of the reform; it drafts and presents laws to parliament and issues bylaws. Data collected, however, showed that the institutional basis supporting the reform is still incomplete, and revisions on the current laws and bylaws on decentralization and water sector reform are necessary. MOTAT is responsible for the design of the water sector strategy and policy, including asset transfer to local government, the planning and distribution of investment funds, and the design of subsidy policy. The ministry represents central government on the supervisory council of the water companies and on the executive committee. The directorate of decentralization within MOLGD is the main actor responsible for pushing the reform forward, and it also represents central government on the executive committee of the four water utilities with the private management contracts.

BOX 9.3   **Summary of Key Findings for Utilities under Public and Private Management**

Findings across All Sites Irrespective of the Type of Utility Management

- Decentralization reform has progressed more slowly than expected owing to a lack of coordination and transparency, a lack of capacity for new roles and responsibilities, and socialist norms and practices.
- Changes in authority that determine the success and pace of the reform concern asset transfer, financial viability, and the legal framework.
- New institutional structures (that is, supervisory councils) in the water companies were established with the utilities' transformation into shareholder companies, but a two-thirds majority representation by central government still prevails.
- The tariff-setting authority has been transferred to local government from central government (that is, the water regulatory entity [WRE]), which is reluctant to relinquish authority.
- Owing to incomplete asset transfer and lack of ownership, local governments do not push utilities to increase tariffs for cost recovery.
- Utilities do not operate on a commercial basis; they still receive central government subsidies.
- High commercial losses and entrenched consumer mentality present challenges to cost recovery for utilities.
- Tariffs need to be increased to recover costs, but already-low consumer satisfaction and a high number of illegal connections are obstacles.
- Many consumers perceive water to be a free public good.
- Dominant flat-rate billing without measuring actual water consumption means there are no incentives for water conservation, leading to water misuse.
- Access to the water supply is greater than access to wastewater service.
- Civil society has limited influence in the water sector, and there is a lack of consumer voices in decision making.

Specific Findings for Privately Managed Utilities

- Privately managed utilities have two additional institutional structures: the technical contract monitoring unit, which improves the managerial capacity of water utilities and provides technical and physical support; and the political executive committee, which manages the Bank credit and revises and approves actions undertaken by the private operator.
- Higher tariffs are needed to reach cost recovery, but consumer satisfaction is already low.
- Service coverage is poorer than it is for publicly managed utilities as a result of substantial in-migration, which leads to population growth and the emergence of new and often illegal settlements in the urban peripheries outside network areas.
- Increased demand owing to higher rates of illegal connections and septic tanks strain the system.
- Reliability, duration of supply, and pressure are enhanced owing to the Bank's previous Water Supply Urgent Rehabilitation Project (WSURP).
- A meter installation program measures and bills for actual consumption for all households.
- There is explicit support for poor groups through a free 20 liter/capita/day lifeline tariff.
- Performance measurement indicators are used.

(*continued*)

| BOX 9.3 | Summary of Key Findings for Utilities (*Continued*) |

- The utilities have a clear strategy for covering operation and maintenance costs.
- There are explicit strategies to build sector stakeholders' capacity for management of water and wastewater services, to establish consumer panels, and to raise consumer awareness about water services and the need to pay for consumption.

Specific Findings for Publicly Managed Utilities

- Tariffs are lower than in the Project cities.
- Billing is based on a flat rate and is unrelated to consumption because of the lack of individual meters.
- Consumer satisfaction is higher in counterfactual cities in terms of the level of piped water services received and tariffs charged.
- Access to water supply and wastewater is higher than in Project cities.
- There is no clear strategy for covering utilities' operation and maintenance costs and for defining measurable performance indicators.
- For very poor and poor consumers there is still no proposed subsidy scheme.
- The institutional structures are still not separated, a fact that affects accountability, decision making, transparency, and action plan development.
- There is a need for a capacity building strategy for stakeholders in the sector.

| BOX 9.4 | Recommendations for Reform Adjustments |

Adjustments in Cities with Private Utility Management (Project cities)

Consumers in Project cities consider tariffs high and often unjustified, since service improvements are not yet visible. Hence, reform adjustments in these cities should focus on accelerated efforts to complete the meter installation program before tariffs are raised. In these cities, many non-poor consumers are willing to pay higher tariffs for better services and a meter-controlled consumption. Furthermore, poor and vulnerable groups could then benefit from the introduction of the lifeline tariff.

Adjustments in Cities with Public Utility Management (counterfactual cities)

Cities with publicly managed utilities face challenges about the delayed implementation of the sewage tariff law and the merging of the water and sewerage enterprises. Reform adjustments should concentrate on the implementation of the tariff law, and should be accompanied by public awareness campaigns and the collection of user fees. Reforms should also focus on accelerating the enterprise merger with further enforcement measures to facilitate this aspect of reform.

The MOE is responsible for transforming water utilities into shareholder companies. The Ministry of Finance (MOF) provides subsidies to the water utilities, most of which have inherited central government debts that slowed down the asset transfer. Given the current financial situation of water utilities, the role of the MOF is crucial in accelerating the pace of the reform. Finally, the WRE, formerly the central government's tariff-setting entity and independent since 1996, did initially oppose the decentralization of this function to local government. One major institutional issue that emerges is the attitude of the WRE in light of its changing role and responsibility.

At the local government level, key stakeholders include the mayor, water utility directors, and the supervisory councils as the boards of the water utilities, where central government is represented. In Project cities, there is also an executive committee, the contract monitoring unit, and the private operator. Qualitative data confirmed that the local government is in a better position to set the tariff and is more accountable toward both consumers and water utilities. The greatest challenge for local government was perceived to be in setting tariffs when the assets of the water company belong to more than one local government unit, as is the case of Durrës. At the community level, there are domestic and business customers, as well as registered and unregistered consumers.

Institutional Dynamics within the Reform

Some aspects of decentralization are moving faster than others. There is a political reform commitment at the central government level, and progress has been made regarding the issuance of laws and bylaws, such as the two key documents that guide the water sector reform—"Organization and Functioning of Local Governments" (Law No. 8652), issued in June 2000; and the Albania Water Supply and Sanitation Sector Strategy, issued in June 2003 (Republic of Albania 2000a, 2003). The implementation and enforcement of these changes in the legal framework, however, are still a challenge.

Asset transfer from central to local government is a key implementation challenge. MOTAT conducts the asset inventory of the water utilities, and together with MOLGD, monitors the asset transfer of water utilities from central to local government. As the owner of the assets, MOE is responsible for transforming water utilities into shareholder companies. The asset inventory has been completed for all 53 water utilities except for Korça, where the inventory has to be calculated considering the

Kreditanstalt für Wiederaufbau (KfW) investment. This will be followed by the classification of water utilities according to their service area, starting with the less complex utilities (basically those serving only one municipality or commune) and ending with more complex ones (regional companies). Asset inventory has proven difficult for the regional water systems, especially in Durrës, which affects the pace of the reform. Asset transfer is also slowed down by the utilities' inherited debts to the Albanian electricity body, KESH (Albanian National Power Company) and respective write-offs by the MOF.

Local government supports the reform, sets conditions, and faces challenges. In general, local governments have limited technical resources and capacity to take over the water systems, and thus prefer assistance from the water utilities. The Water Utility Association of Albania is very supportive of the decentralization, as it anticipates closer links and effective institutional support from the municipalities. Local governments have set reform conditions, however, including the rehabilitation of water networks, the writing-off of central government debts prior to decentralized service provision, and asset transfer. The demands have created a stop-and-go decentralization progress pattern, and local authorities are faced with three major challenges:

- Lack of utility management and administration expertise. Durrës municipality, for instance, illustrates the difficulties and ambiguities stemming not only from the complexity of the urban-rural system, but also the lack of capacity to address problems.
- Vulnerability of water utilities to the political process. The reform is subject to politicization because some of the new administrators are political appointees rather than technical experts. This could be of particular concern for Korça, where the utility company is operating efficiently.
- Loss of institutional memory. Local authorities are faced with this problem in the aftermath of the necessary downsizing of civil servants.

Because of a delay in the decentralization process, municipalities have not been able to exercise all of their rights as established by law. The lack of ownership of the water utilities impedes local governments' ability to realize decentralization's full potential. At present, none of the municipalities really uses the power given to it by the law. Local government is now operating in a new institutional environment, which includes a new status for the water utilities, a draft service agreement signed between the municipalities and the water utilities, a new water code, and the executive council where the four local governments have representation. Local governments in the four Project cities are expected to play a more active role through their participation in the executive council. Local governments request the Bank to support the decentralization reform, especially in regard to the transfer of assets and the tariff-setting authority, as well as provide technical assistance and capacity building.

Central and local government views vary on private sector participation. The central government's support for private sector participation in the water sector is reflected in its decisions in Project cities. Local government in Durrës and Saranda supports the private operator based on the government's involvement in the project preparation and high expectations for quick service improvements. In Gjirokastra, the private sector's participation was made conditional on prior network improvements by the water utility, and it remains limited to a management contract. In the counterfactual city of Vlora, municipal officials support public management, but the water company management supports private sector management.

Reform beneficiaries include local government, water utilities, and consumers. The reform will bring all local governments' greater autonomy, and those in Project cities will have additional roles attuned to the approved action plan of the private operator. The utilities in Project cities, which will be transformed into shareholder companies, are expected to benefit from the increase in company revenue and better qualified staff. Public, private, and domestic customers within the network boundaries and with legal or illegal access to the water supply network have benefited from increased access to piped drinking water, higher pressure, and greater water availability (more hours per day and more days per week). In Project cities, very poor households that cannot afford their water bills benefit from the lifeline tariff as long as they have meters installed. Stakeholders negatively affected include poor households located outside the network; they pay higher prices to private vendors for drinking water.

Reform Impacts through Decentralization and Changes in Authority

The decentralization reform changed power, structures, and processes that govern the function of public institutions in the water sector. These changes in authority altered the institutional environment, which in turn shaped the impacts on tariffs, access, and transfers.

New institutional structures differ between the two reform models. As the role of the central government is changing from one of service provider to that of regulator and facilitator, new institutional relationships are emerging among various stakeholders (for a graphical overview, see annex 9A). With decentralization, all Albanian water utilities were transformed into shareholder companies, and supervisory councils replaced the former boards of the utilities after October 2003. The decentralization process, however, is still incomplete. About two-thirds of the supervisory councils still belong to central government (MOTAT and MOE), and only one local government member, usually the deputy mayor, is represented. A bylaw, pending approval by the council of ministers, will fully implement decentralization, and change the majority of the supervisory councils in favor of local government.

Project cities have two additional bodies—the executive committee and the contract monitoring unit. As the technical entity, the contract monitoring unit builds on the experience of the 2002 WSURP and aims to improve the managerial capacity of water utilities, while supporting them with technical and physical interventions. The executive committee was established by the council of ministers for the management of the Bank credit, and is a political entity. As the main decision-making body, it oversees the contractual relationship with the private operator on behalf of the water utilities, and can revise and approve actions undertaken by the operator. The committee consists of seven members appointed by the council of ministers—one from each of the central government line ministries (MOTAT, MOLGD, and MOE) and four local government representatives.

Changes in authority that determine the success and pace of the decentralization in the water sector include asset transfer, financial viability, and the legal framework. The asset inventory and transfer of powers to the local government has slowed down the reform progress. Specifically, the asset inventory of regional water systems has proven to be difficult. Furthermore, the assessment of the financial situation and current type of management for each water utility contributes to asset transfer delay. Issues involved include writing off water utility arrears to the Albanian electricity body KESH (discussed earlier), and local governments' capacity to generate investment funds apart from the limited central government grants. Finally, the completion of the legal framework is crucial for the reform's success, and currently the lack of efficient enforcement mechanisms to implement laws has hampered progress.[4]

The reform has had slow progress, owing partly to incomplete information about new roles and responsibilities, diverging interests, and central government resistance. In the current reform process, stakeholders often do not have the necessary information about their respective roles and responsibilities. Lack of transparency and information disclosure underlies the tension between central and local government stakeholders. Reform progress is slower than expected also because of the still incomplete asset transfer. Some central government bodies resist a full reform implementation, citing the lack of local government capacity. The MOLGD and MOE have the political will for reform, but the loss of power and decision-making authority seems particularly challenging to the self-image of MOTAT and WRE. Reluctant parties either refuse to accept the new roles and responsibilities assigned to local governments through decentralization, or they perceive themselves as being left out of the process. For instance MOTAT, the line ministry for the reform, does not advance the decentralized asset transfer as scheduled because it does not want to reduce its authority. WRE, although not opposed to decentralization, resists the loss of tariff-setting authority to local government and the limited responsibilities for setting policies and enforcing standards. And although MOLGD has been able to get a council of ministers' approval for the Water Decentralization Policy Paper, the implementation of the paper's recommendations does not receive the proper attention by MOTAT, MOE, or WRE.

Reform Impacts on Tariffs, Access, and Transfers

Apart from changes in institutional structures and dynamics, the reform has impacts on tariffs, access, and transfers.

Tariffs

Tariff increases have been applied to reach cost recovery. The water sector reform was accompanied with tariff increases to move water utilities toward cost recovery and operation on a commercial basis. Tariff increases were higher in Project cities, where the private operator aims to make utilities attractive to investors and encourages training water utility staff in the commercial business approach, which has proven very successful in Korça. Local government officials of Lezha support a gradual tariff increase to match consumers' ability to pay. Diverging views exist in Vlora, where the water utility director aims to reach cost recovery not through tariff increases but through an increased collection ratio, since an optimal collection ratio at the current tariff would allow the company to cover operation and maintenance costs. Municipal authorities in Vlora, however, plan to increase the water tariff once the asset transfer entitles them to set tariffs.

Cost recovery can be increased through improved collection and billing rates. Increasing the collection ratio is a high priority of water companies. In seven assessed cities, the ratio was 72–75 percent; for Korça it was 99 percent. The main reasons for low collection ratios are twofold: customer reluctance to pay and the lack of proper enforcement measures. Another factor is gaps in the billing itself, as only about half of the consumed water is actually billed by the utilities in seven cities; the exception is Korça. Inappropriate billing is mainly caused by leakages, water abuse, and overconsumption of water.

It is necessary for water companies to update their database to reflect the real number of consumers, and to contract consumers in the new residential areas who obtain water though illegal network connections. It is in the interest of most water utilities to contract illegal consumers, but no measures have been taken in this regard. The current legal base regarding the value added tax (VAT) might be the reason for this. At present, the water utilities calculate the VAT over the billing rate so that the more consumers they bill, the more VAT they charge. For this reason, it is recommended that the utilities base VAT rates on the collection ratio. However, there is a caveat: contracting additional consumers would not necessarily mean collecting more revenue, especially in the new settlements where the social and economic problems are more prevalent, and where most households do not have an address to which the bill can be sent. Increased collaboration between the water utilities and local governments would be useful in addressing this problem.

The piped water bill is not the only monthly household expense for drinking water. In both reform models, the monthly piped water bill accounts for about 1.3 percent of household expenditure. Hence, it would appear that affordability would not be a problem for most families, were piped water the only drinking-water expense. Qualitative data collected, however, showed that the piped water bill is only one of several household expenditures for drinking water. Many households perceive piped water as unsafe and unreliable. Hence, they often have to buy water from vendors, travel to obtain water, incur additional electricity expenses to operate the necessary water pumps, buy water tanks for storage, and are required to cover costs for repairs in their houses caused by the humidity that is a side effect of the use of water tanks.

Poverty hampers affordability to pay and access in urban peripheries. For the most vulnerable population groups (see figure 9.1), such as the urban poor, tariff increases have had negative effects. Very poor households constitute the largest proportion of nonpayers. The figures for irregular payments drop as the poverty level decreases. The lack of

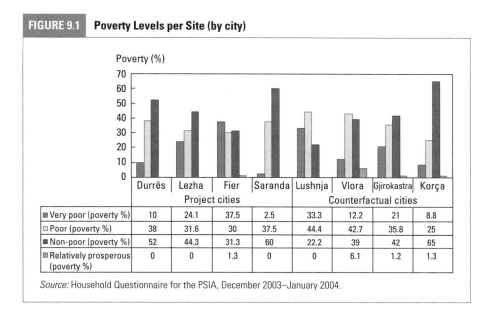

FIGURE 9.1 **Poverty Levels per Site (by city)**

	Durrës	Lezha	Fier	Saranda	Lushnja	Vlora	Gjirokastra	Korça
		Project cities				Counterfactual cities		
■ Very poor (poverty %)	10	24.1	37.5	2.5	33.3	12.2	21	8.8
▢ Poor (poverty %)	38	31.6	30	37.5	44.4	42.7	35.8	25
■ Non-poor (poverty %)	52	44.3	31.3	60	22.2	39	42	65
▨ Relatively prosperous (poverty %)	0	0	1.3	0	0	6.1	1.2	1.3

Source: Household Questionnaire for the PSIA, December 2003–January 2004.

financial means was the most frequently cited reason for not paying by those groups classified as "very poor" or "poor." These include households of retirees, households in the new settlements, and small businesses, although lack of piped water supply and unwillingness to pay also contribute to nonpayment by poor and non-poor households.

Poor groups on the outskirts of Durrës, for instance, reported that they were able to afford the water bills at current tariff levels, but would be unable to pay if tariff rates were to be increased. Further tariff increases would also negatively affect business consumers, especially those operating in the service sector, and small and medium enterprises with smaller profit margins. The very poor and the poor are more disadvantaged in terms of network coverage and service quality (about 28 percent of the very poor and about 17 percent of the poor do not have water access at all). Assuming a 150 liter per capita per day consumption level of drinking water and an average residential tariff of 27.4 leks per cubic meter (2004), a medium-income household would pay around 1 percent of household income. If these tariffs were raised to full cost recovery levels, this would increase to 3 percent. With the same tariff and level of consumption as above, a low-income household (US$2.25 per person per day) currently would pay 2 percent of its income on water and sanitation; this would rise to almost 6 percent if full cost recovery tariffs were charged (and no lifeline tariffs were in place). The generally accepted affordability level for water and sanitation expenses is up to 5 percent of household income.

Willingness to pay is low because of consumer dissatisfaction with tariff increases in the absence of service improvements. For non-poor households, dissatisfaction with the service was the main reason for non-payment of water bills. Other reasons for nonpayment included non-connection and lack of service of piped water. In Project cities, 73.9 percent of consumers were dissatisfied with the water tariff they paid for their current level of service, compared with 39.3 percent in counterfactual cities (figure 9.2 and table 9.2).

Consumer satisfaction with improved services outweighs the negative impacts of tariff increases. Although the water tariffs increased substantially in all cities, the impact of the increase on the majority of household budgets remains low because the water bill remains a small portion of overall monthly household expenditure. Most public, private, and domestic customers consider tariff increases to be a multidimensional issue, whereby the benefits of improved water quality and service and increased access outweigh the tariff increases and negative impacts on household budgets.

FIGURE 9.2 **Consumer Satisfaction with Tariff for the Type of Service Received (by city)**

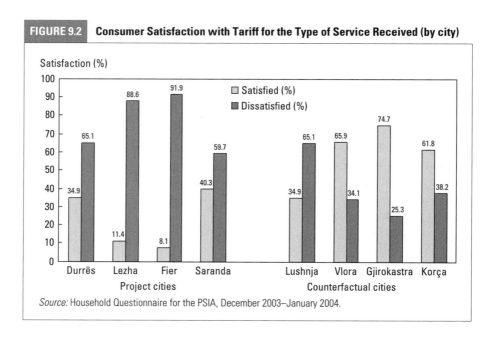

Source: Household Questionnaire for the PSIA, December 2003–January 2004.

Table 9.2 Reason for Nonpayment of Water Bill (by poverty group)

		Poverty group		
	Reasons for nonpayment of bill	*Very poor (%)*	*Poor (%)*	*Non-poor (%)*
Project cities	Perception that water should be free	25.0	30.0	0.0
	Lack of financial means	45.8	25.0	0.0
	Dissatisfaction with the service	16.7	10.0	43.8
	Did not receive a bill	0.0	5.0	12.5
	Long wait to pay at utility office	0.0	0.0	6.3
	Inconvenient office opening hours	0.0	0.0	6.1
	No enforcement	4.2	10.0	18.8
	Other	8.3	20.0	12.5
Counterfactual cities	Perception that water should be free	4.2	0.0	0.0
	Lack of financial means	66.7	8.0	8.3
	Dissatisfaction with the service	4.1	20.0	41.7
	Did not receive a bill	0.0	32.0	0.0
	Long wait to pay at utility office	0.0	0.0	8.3
	Other	25.0	40.0	41.7

Source: Household Questionnaire for the PSIA, December 2003–January 2004.

Flat-rate billing undermines the effort to keep consumption levels low. In all cities except Korça, flat-rate billing is most common. (Owing to substantial donor investment and technical assistance, Korça has moved to metered billing.) According to respondents in the water utilities, the current lack of consumption-based billing encourages major water abuses and consequently prevents them from covering actual production costs. Data collected show that because of flat-rate billing, tariff increases did not affect consumers' water consumption. The perception of water as a free public good was higher in Project cities, and particularly among very poor and poor groups. Project cities witnessed a larger influx of migrants from North Albania, where water is mainly obtained for free from natural sources such as springs or reservoirs. This issue requires particular attention by the private operator, water utility staff, and local governments to raise awareness among customers and consumers that water is a commodity, and to encourage consumption-based payment. As in other countries, civil society involvement in awareness campaigns could help improve collection ratios and water conservation.

Meter installation is key to a fair tariff system based on actual consumption. One major component of reform is the application of universal metering to address issues of water misuse and sustainable water management. Data collected showed that the installation of meters and consumption-based billing have improved household overconsumption and curbed the misuse of drinking water for unintended purposes, such as watering gardens. Unauthorized consumers and businesses, such as car washes or construction companies that use drinking water for their businesses, will be negatively affected by the installation of meters that allow consumption-based billing, as their water bills will increase. Poor groups and retirees reported the positive effects of universal metering, which enabled them to monitor and control their consumption and water expenses. In addition, poor households in Project cities will benefit from metering through the lifeline tariff. The cost of meter installation, however, poses a major problem for most households, including relatively well-off groups. Although poor households are simply unable to pay for the meter installation, non-poor households consider the unexpected charges excessive, unfair, and fraudulent. Specific provisions for poor households coupled with extended information campaigns could be useful.

Greater efforts for enforcement on nonpayment and illegal connections are needed. In Project cities, regular nonpayment is more prevalent than in counterfactual cities because of the higher numbers of illegal settlements and lack of enforcement. The water utilities reported that they are unable to improve enforcement without the active participation of local authorities. Enforcement should be targeted at the group with the highest consumption and least bill payments, which 70 percent of respondents identified as the private sector, followed by public institutions. In both city groups, 24 percent consider financial penalties to be the best way to improve enforcement, followed by cutoff of nonpayers and mailed reminders. Fifteen percent of Project city respondents felt awareness campaigns would be effective, compared with only 8 percent of counterfactual city residents.

Access to Water and Wastewater Services

Access to water supply and wastewater is higher in counterfactual cities than in project cities. About 82 percent of respondents in Project cities and about 99 percent in counterfactual cities have a (legal or illegal) water supply connection; 64.5 percent and 84.3 percent, in respective city groups, have a wastewater connection. Differences in access are to the result of larger numbers of people living outside the water and sewerage coverage area in Project cities, which is in turn the result of the significantly larger inflow of migrants in those cities (who tend to settle at the urban periphery). The partial investment in the water network in Project cities is unable to meet the increased demand for services. Counterfactual cities witnessed less in-migration, and sufficient investment in the network enables Korça to cover all customers. The very poor and poor are more disadvantaged in terms of network coverage and service quality—28 percent and 17 percent of these groups, respectively, have no access to piped water. Network coverage needs to be extended (figure 9.3).

Spatial and ethnic dimensions affect access to piped water. Service quality, measured in "hours of supply" and "water pressure," depends on the geographical distance of the household to the urban center—the closer the household, the better the quality of the water supply. Households in the urban peripheries experienced lower service quality. In Project cities, service quality was slightly better owing to past efforts through the WSURP in 1999. Unconnected poor households outside the water and wastewater network cannot benefit from the reform's investments and service improvements, which are focused on rehabilitating the existing network area. These households continue to pay higher prices to private vendors for drinking water. Thus these negative impacts are not linked to lack of affordability, but simply to these households' location. There is also an ethnic dimension to the impact of the reform. Roma households, which mostly settle on urban peripheries, may not benefit from the reform if they remain excluded from service access as the networks are not expanded to reach their settlements (Gore, Figueiredo, and Rodgers 1995; De Soto, Beddies, and Gedeshi 2005). Finally, links to

FIGURE 9.3 **Household Access to Water Supply Networks and Sewage Networks (by city)**

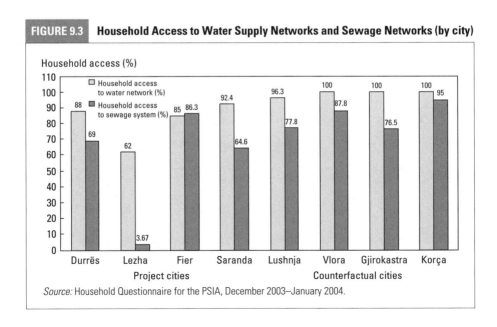

Source: Household Questionnaire for the PSIA, December 2003–January 2004.

property rights introduce a legal reform dimension. The water sector reform might have indirect impacts on the legalization of illegal settlers on the urban peripheries through their connection to the network as legal customers—a step that is supported by water utilities and municipalities.

Access for network customers and very poor households is higher in the Project cities than in counterfactual cities. Public and private sector customers and domestic customers located within the network area, with legal or illegal access to the network, have benefited from increased access to piped drinking water, higher pressure, and availability for more hours per day and more days per week.

Termination of unauthorized access will have a negative impact on illegal domestic and private sector consumers. One of the provisions of the national water sector strategy includes terminating unauthorized access to piped water (Republic of Albania 2003). Illegal domestic consumers will be negatively affected, as they will have to purchase water from providers, such as a vendor, with a direct charge of user fees. The likelihood that the government will be successful in cutting off all illegal connections is slim. Past attempts by the water utilities proved unsuccessful, and currently the government lacks a comprehensive approach toward illegal settlers. Unauthorized business users, such as car washes and construction companies that use drinking water for their businesses, will be negatively affected by the discontinuation of water supply, leading to dissatisfaction with reform.

Inadequate system coverage has direct and indirect consequences. The most common way to cope with inadequate water coverage is to tap the network illegally (table 9.3 and figure 9.4). Poorer households are more likely to have an illegal connection than those that are relatively bet-

Table 9.3 Presence of Illegal Connections (by poverty group)

	Poverty group	No illegal connection	One illegal connection	Two illegal connections
Project cities	Very poor	44.20	53.50	2.30
	Poor	84.40	5.60	0.00
	Non-poor	88.90	10.40	0.70
	Relatively prosperous	100.00	0.00	0.00
Counterfactual cities	Very poor	85.20	14.80	0.00
	Poor	90.50	8.60	0.90
	Non-poor	93.20	6.10	0.80
	Relatively prosperous	100.00	0.00	0.00

Source: Household Questionnaire for the PSIA, December 2003–January 2004.

| FIGURE 9.4 | Presence of Illegal Connections (by city) |

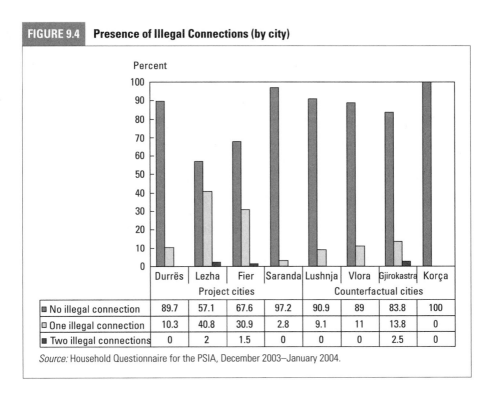

	Durrës	Lezha	Fier	Saranda	Lushnja	Vlora	Gjirokastra	Korça
	Project cities				Counterfactual cities			
■ No illegal connection	89.7	57.1	67.6	97.2	90.9	89	83.8	100
▢ One illegal connection	10.3	40.8	30.9	2.8	9.1	11	13.8	0
■ Two illegal connections	0	2	1.5	0	0	0	2.5	0

Source: Household Questionnaire for the PSIA, December 2003–January 2004.

ter off. The incidence of illegal connections was higher in Project cities because these cities have more settlements outside the coverage area and higher poverty rates. Other strategies to cope with inadequate coverage include digging wells by households or, as seen in Durrës, by hotels. Households also purchase tanks to store water because the system cannot provide 24-hour coverage. Water tank prevalence is 79 percent in Project cities and 57 percent in counterfactual cities, except for Korça, where excellent piped water supply renders tanks necessary. Purchasing water pumps is very common to counteract the lack of water pressure, which poses access problems for households on upper floors. Electricity shortages also affect piped water access.

Poorer households report having limited ability to afford water pumps and tanks; they store water in buckets or basins. Buying water from vendors is especially prevalent in Lushnja, where water access has been unacceptable for years and drinking water needs of entire neighborhoods (80 percent of the respondents) are met with water trucks. Seasonal demand for water from these trucks was reported in Saranda and

Durrës, which complement drinking water needs in the summer, when access to piped water is poorer.

Another coping mechanism is the establishing of additional, mostly illegal connections. The incidence of illegal connection is especially high among the group of very poor, and this percentage drastically goes down as the poverty group moves toward the relatively well off. Inadequate wastewater network coverage is coped with by purchasing septic tanks by 31.6 percent of households in the Project cities, and 15.5 percent in the counterfactual cities. Reliance on septic tanks is particularly high in Gjirokastra where the network is extremely dilapidated.

Coping strategies have negative financial and environmental effects. Money spent buying water tanks and water pumps, higher electricity bills, noise brought on by water pumps, and the cost of house repairs that result from humidity are some of the side effects of coping mechanisms summarized above. Water tanks also favor water abuse. Security valves are usually broken and it is not uncommon to see water overflowing from the tanks during supply hours. Uncontrolled illegal connections and wells lead to excessive groundwater pumping, with negative consequences, such as erosion and aquifer overuse, for sustainable water management and the environment. The widespread use of septic tanks contributes to the contamination of aquifers through infiltration, with irregular cleaning constituting an additional health risk. Hence, sustainable water management is one of the priorities of water sector reform.

Network connection does not imply reliability of water supply and a high quality of access. Both days and hours of supply vary depending on the season. Poorer access during the summer can be explained mainly by the misuse of drinking water for irrigation, which reduces water availability for urban areas. Current water supply in seven out of the eight cities is inadequate. Korça is an outlier in this respect, with its 24 hours of high-pressure water supply. The situation seems worst in Durrës, Lushnje, and Gjirokastra (table 9.4). Out of all the households that reported having access to water service, daily supply was available to only 45.4 percent of Project city respondents and 60.3 percent of counterfactual city respondents. For households without daily access, average days of supply for the summer were 17 and 14 days a month, for the respective city groups; winter supply was about 25 and about 20 days a month, respectively. Thirty-two percent of connected households in Project cities have water less than two hours a day during the summer; this percentage drops to 25.7 percent during the winter.

Poverty and social exclusion has some effect on the number of days and the hours per day of piped water. In Project cities, supply levels seem

Table 9.4 Network Connection and Water Supply

	City	Household access to water network (%)	Households with daily water supply access (average summer & winter) (%)	Hours of water supply per day		Days of water supply per month for households without daily access (aggregated)		Population growth ratio (%) (1989–2003)
				Summer	Winter	Summer	Winter	
Project cities	Durrës	62.00	42.00	1.4	1.7	17	25	210
	Lezha	85.00	31.10	11.7	14.4			340
	Fier	92.40	4.30	3.5	5.6			255
	Saranda	96.30	60.30	3.3	4.6			203
Counterfactual cities	Lushnja	100.00	35.90	1.3	1.4	14	20	204
	Vlora	100.00	46.90	6.7	8.7			160
	Gjirokastra	100.00	60.00	1.9	2.9			142
	Korça	100.00	100.00	24	24			132

Source: Household Questionnaire for the PSIA, December 2003–January 2004.

321

slightly related to poverty and social exclusion. Piped water provision increases by about two hours a week as the poverty level dips and households move up the strata from "very poor" to the "relatively prosperous." In counterfactual cities, the hours of daily supply appear to be slightly related to the poverty level—the very poor tend to get about two fewer hours of supply than do the poor, who in turn receive about two fewer hours than do the non-poor.

Support for the Poor via a Lifeline to Services

Lifelines for poor households in Project cities draw varying responses. As noted above, cities under private management have a lifeline tariff of 20 liters per capita per day free of charge. Although the water bill is only a small part of monthly household spending, very poor families cannot afford to pay for this service. Expert and consumer opinions differ with respect to the lifeline tariff. Some believe that it is a suitable form of subsidy. Others suggest alternative forms of subsidy, such as increasing the amount of state economic assistance to families in need or providing direct subsidies to water utilities to recover the cost of unpaid water bills. In the Project cities, stakeholders affected positively are very poor households, who will benefit from the lifeline tariff once the meter installation program has been implemented.

Equity and efficiency are key to providing water and wastewater service. Families in need must be identified accurately to balance the responsibility of local governments for public water provision with the need of water utilities for cost recovery and financial viability. The study compared data on beneficiaries of state economic assistance with unemployment rates and other proxies. Discrepancies in these data might be explained by the fact that a number of very poor households are not included in the social assistance plan, owing to flaws in the selection process or because they do not meet the eligibility criteria. Another explanation could be that people tend to report being poor even though they are not. Data showed diverging views on the subsidy format and on beneficiaries. Some water utilities consider lifelines to be a viable subsidy for poor groups because there is no room for the kind of abuse inherent in cash subsidies. Local governments, and especially representatives of the municipal social assistance unit, however, consider direct household subsidies through an increase in state economic assistance to be more adequate. In Fier and Korça, water utility representatives state that any increase of subsidies should go directly to the utilities that have to operate on commercial principles with cost recovery.

Meter installation is a prerequisite for the application of lifeline tariffs. In Project cities, the proposed lifeline tariff benefits poor households that have a meter and are billed according to their actual water consumption. For poor households without meters, billing is based on flat-rate consumption and the lifeline tariff cannot mitigate the negative effects of a tariff increase. Hence, meters should be installed before tariffs are increased, so that poor groups can benefit from the lifeline tariff. Until meters are installed, a lower flat rate could be applied to this group.

Second-Order Impacts of Reform on the Local Economy, Employment, and Gender

Albania, because of the transitional nature of its political economy, is still characterized by chronic unemployment. Local household economy is still based on migration and remittances. The overall reform in water and infrastructure will enable the development of local small and medium businesses, which in turn will have a positive impact on gender and employment. These impacts will need to be studied further in the second round of the research.

Businesses in the services sector, mainly bars and restaurants, expect their businesses to grow after the water supply situation improves. Coastal cities such as Durrës, Saranda, Vlora, and Lezha expect improved water and wastewater services to translate into higher attractiveness and increased tourism. This, in turn, will have positive implications for the businesses themselves—such as the food processing industry, which is the main economic activity for the cities of Lushnja, Fier, and Gjirokastra, and the largest brewery and soft drink plants in Korça. Development of the local economy also contributes to the improved financial viability of local governments through increases in own-raised revenues. An indirect impact is thus seen in the potential strengthening of local government finances. In the same vein, inadequate sewerage services and lack of treatment plants hamper local economic development, especially tourism in coastal cities.

Some negative impacts are expected to result from the restructuring of the privately managed water utilities in Project cities, where some utility employees could be made redundant, which may generate opposition and dissatisfaction.

Data from Durrës and Gjirokastra show that women have to wait at home for piped water supply in order to carry out household chores. An improved water supply should render women's responsibilities less bound to the household and thus allow them to seek employment outside the home.

CURRENT AND EXPECTED IMPACTS

The current and expected impacts of reform consider both the in-country dialogue and Bank operations.

Impact of Reform on In-Country Policy Dialogue

Because MOTAT representatives are highly interested in the progress of the reform, they welcomed the study's objective of measuring reform impacts across the two models and across time. In particular, the study is expected to help the newly founded water utility association, the municipal authorities, and the central government to understand better the perception and expectations of the population toward the reform as it is implemented. The study offers recommendations on policy dialogue and reform adjustments. Key issues appear below.

Tariffs

In both Project and counterfactual cities there is a lack of reliable data on consumer affordability and willingness to pay. The policy dialogue with local authorities—especially the social assistance unit and labor office, with inclusion of civil society—has to focus on continuous monitoring of consumers' ability and willingness to pay. Because of decentralization, local municipalities and local civil society groups, including local research groups, still lack technical knowledge in survey techniques and methods. These stakeholders need continued Bank technical assistance for capacity building. Assistance is also needed to mount awareness campaigns.

In both Project and counterfactual cities most customers are excluded from discussions on tariff setting. The policy dialogue needs to focus on the establishment, with Bank assistance, of consumer panels that will represent the customers' interests. To avoid potential opposition, the dialogue should make clear that consumer panels will cooperate with local law enforcement.

Access to Water and Wastewater Services

The policy dialogue needs to focus on completing the coverage of the water and sanitation networks in Project cities as well as counterfactual cities. Infrastructural help from both the Bank and the donor community is needed to improve access and increase quality in the framework of the poverty reduction strategy. Policy dialogue will have to focus on unsatisfactory water quality, lack of wastewater treatment plans, and improper consumer attitudes toward water consumption. Donor and Bank operational assistance must focus on the rehabilitation of the water and sewerage networks as well as the construction of treatment plans. The Bank, the GOA, businesses, and nongovernmental organizations (NGOs) also need to launch an awareness campaign.

Support for the Poor

The policy dialogue will have to focus on the inadequate criteria for support standards and qualifications that are used for both Project and counterfactual cities. The dialogue will have to focus on alternative methods for covering the poorest households. To avoid abuse and corruption, the government, together with civil society, needs to measure systematically which households would need the support. Since completing meter installation depends on tariff increases, other forms of subsidies—such as an increase in state economic assistance—need to be discussed in the policy dialogue. This money would need to go to the water utilities, in order to enhance cooperation between them and municipalities.

Institutional Constraints

The policy dialogue needs to address alleviation or removal of institutional constraints. Institutional constraints in Project cities include inadequate asset transfer (especially in regional systems), inadequate management presence by the local water utility, and inadequate restructuring of water utilities accompanied by ineffective mitigating (that is, compensation) measures. Policy recommendations for these constraints include transfers of shares instead of assets, intensification of information exchange to increase transparency, development of labor market strategies that promote market and job opportunities for the losers of restructuring, and maximum cooperation among water utilities, local governments, and local business.

Institutional constraints in Project and counterfactual cities include the sluggish transfer of assets or shares to local sectors, the perceived inadequacy of supervisory councils, the lack of local government capacity, the lack of updated water and sanitation network maps that will guide the rehabilitation process, corruption and/or weak motivation and commitment at the water utility level, the perception by consumers that the reform progress is being slowed down by the political events in the country, and failure to establish trust relationships with customers. Policy recommendations for these constraints include alternative ways to transfer assets, enhanced information exchange, technical assistance by the Bank and donor community to train local governments, dissemination of study findings and information, Bank technical assistance in cooperation with local government experts to help local water utilities update existing maps, and institutional capacity building that focuses on new incentive systems (such as salary increases and other benefits).

In counterfactual cities, the policy dialogue needs to focus on the failure to complete the merger between water and sewerage enterprises. Policy options include accelerating the merging and facilitating the reform progress by strengthening implementation and enforcement mechanisms.

Legal Constraints

The legal framework necessary to support the implementation of the reform is still incomplete, in both Project and counterfactual cities. The policy dialogue needs urgently to proceed with the remaining by-laws and government decisions that are still pending. Technical assistance with the support of the donor community—especially the European Union, because of its comparative advantage in this field—needs to strengthen enforcement structures and establish new ones at the municipal level, especially for paying bills.

Private Sector Participation

Both Project and counterfactual cities experience difficulties with full privatization. It is not easy for private operators to enter the subsidized sector. The policy dialogue needs to address partial privatization (which can start with the privatization of sales units) and the need for water companies to phase out subsidies. This would enable private operators to enter the cities. Most consumers believe that private operators perform more efficiently than the public operator.

Impact of Reform on Bank Operations

This study has a specific impact on the Bank's Municipal Water and Wastewater Project (MWWP 2002) and the Integrated Water and Ecosystems Management Project (IWEMP 2004). For the Municipal Water and Wastewater Project, the study provides additional information and insights into the ongoing reform process. It identifies the perceptions and expectations of authorities and population groups in terms of the scope, objectives, and implementation of the Project. Specifically it measured public perception and understanding of the government process and the major concerns and priorities of the general public, as well as the poor, about the involvement of the private sector in providing water services in Albania. For instance, an extension of the water network is planned specifically for Durrës, Fier, and Lezha; however, the legalization of the current illegal settlements and the incomplete land valuation need to be addressed before the water and wastewater network can be expanded. Furthermore, the study complements the Project's public communication program and the benchmarking of water utility activities.

The next steps are to measure reform impacts against the set baseline in the same cities during the implementation of the Project. The comprehensive picture emerging from those steps will certainly have an impact on the options for future private sector participation that are to be discussed after the termination of the management contract in the Project. For the Integrated Water and Ecosystems Management Project, the study provides insights into the Project's ongoing monitoring and evaluation.

LESSONS LEARNED

- **The study helped address the analytical gap on data for reform and policy.** The counterfactual and comparative analysis of this study offers new reform data and policy data as well as recommendations for the central and municipal water sector policy makers. In addition, the sociological data obtained from the baseline study will anchor the follow-up study and the participatory monitoring and evaluation component of the sector reform. This comparative aspect proved essential to the Project and the study, and to their respective policy recommendations and policy dialogue. These insights will help policy makers assess the two municipal water reform models.

- **The mixed-method approach was effective.** The mixing of qualitative and quantitative methods and their research tools for fieldwork and data collection was effective in capturing the current challenges of the water sector reform. In order to enhance the impact of study findings, important next steps need to include dissemination through national and regional stakeholder workshops and participatory monitoring and evaluation.

- **The multisectoral team's skill mix contributed substantially to the analysis.** The team designed the study proposal, developed the terms of reference, conducted the rapid appraisal, assisted in selecting and training the local research team, provided feedback for the completion of the final report, and designed the dissemination strategy. Previous training of the local research team in qualitative and quantitative social science methods and tools contributed to the efficacy of the study, and provided the basis of the local teams' rapid understanding of the study framework. The Bank team benefited from established rapport and working relationships with the donor community, which helped to raise interest in the study, leading to buy in and UNDP partnership.

■ **Sufficient planning for time and resources were essential to setting the baseline and measuring against it to capture fully the impact of the reform.** Upstream capacity building of the local team was essential for understanding the PSIA framework and methods, including the context of the specific sector reform. Capacity building and training require careful planning and organization. Resources should also be sufficient to create an effective policy dialogue that is based on study findings and to disseminate the findings to beneficiaries and stakeholders. This study was able to draw on resources for its first part—the setting of the baseline. More resources are now required for the dissemination of and policy dialogue on the baseline study, which will include stakeholder workshops and a participatory monitoring and evaluation of impacts, and for the follow-up study.

■ **In-depth country knowledge contributed significantly to the scope and quality of the study.** For the last six years, the Bank had conducted qualitative and quantitative analytical economic and sector work that was available for the desk review and for designing the questionnaires and the final analysis. Additionally, Bank team members had long-standing operational experience in Albania, including knowledge of the decentralization process, the organization and structure of formal and informal institutions, and the socioeconomic status of consumer groups.

■ **More capacity building is needed.** Poverty and social impact analysis is still a new concept in Albania. Although some local NGOs have previously received training in tools and methods for Social Assessments, Poverty Studies, Needs Assessments, Beneficiary Impact Assessments, and Rapid Appraisals, most NGOs and local research centers are not yet familiar with the methodology of distributional impact analysis. As noted above, at the beginning of this study, a local NGO was trained by two Bank social scientists and two Bank water sector experts. Time and resource restrictions limited the two-day training, but the Bank social scientists substantially assisted and supervised the local team throughout the study, including the analysis and the report writing. Both Bank teams assisted the design of the quantitative and qualitative questionnaires. Local teams need more assistance and time with the questionnaire design and with asking the "right" questions to elicit answers needed for a distributional impact analysis of reforms. The capacity of local teams is still limited to collecting field data and preliminary analysis, but those that have received adequate training complete this task very well. The most difficult part for local teams is applying the conceptual framework to analyze data, and to reflect disaggregated poverty and social impacts. For future capacity building, a five-day training course would be more realistic, and would need to include the successful transfer of analytical skills and instruction on how to apply these skills to analysis and final report writing.

NOTES

1. This chapter presents the PSIA, which was conducted from July 2003 to June 2004, and completed in December 2004. The analysis team consisted of Co-Plan–Institute for Habitat Development, Tirana (Dritan Shutina, Sotir Dhamo, and Jorida Cila) and a World Bank team (Andreas Rohde, Sabine Beddies, Hermine De Soto, Arben Bakllamja, and Xavier Chauvot de Beauchene). The special contribution by Arben Bakllamaja is highly appreciated. Financial support from the World Bank and the United Nations Development Programme (UNDP) in Tirana is gratefully acknowledged.
2. Due to the 2005 general elections, the following changes in government occurred that are relevant to the reforms: Ministry of Economy (MOE) changed to Ministry of Economy, Trade and Energy (MOTE), Ministry of Local Government and Decentralization (MOLGD) changed to Ministry of Interior (MOI), and Ministry of Territory Adjustment and Tourism (MOTAT) changed to Ministry of Public Works, Transport and Telecommunications (MOPWTT); the Ministry of Agriculture, Food and Protection of Consumers (MOAFPC), and Ministry of Environment, Forestry and Water Administration (MOEFWA) have been newly created. For consistency with the PSIA report and research, the chapter retains the previous names and function of the institutional offices. During dissemination, government counterparts in MOI and MOPWTT fully supported the findings, and pledged to continue the reforms.
3. The lek is the Albanian currency unit. Exchange rate US$1.00 = 97.5 leks (November 22, 2004).
4. Although the Law No. 8975 (November 21, 2002) "On Giving the Drinking Water Tariffs the Executive Title" exists, existing enforcement structures for law implementation need to be strengthened or newly established at the local level, especially in relation to the payment of bills.

REFERENCES

Bianchi, R. R., and S. A. Kossoudji. 2001. "Interest Groups and Organizations as Stakeholders." Social Development Paper 36, World Bank, Washington, DC.

Birdsall, N., and J. Nellis. 2003. "Winners and Losers: Assessing the Distributional Impact of Privatization." *World Development* 31 (10): 1617–33.

Brinkerhoff, D., and B. L. Crosby. 2002. *Managing Policy Reform: Concepts and Tools for Decision-Makers in Developing and Transition Countries.* Bloomfield, CT: Kumarian Press.

Colin, J., and H. Lockwood. 2002. "Research and Survey Series: Making Innovation Work Through Partnerships in Water and Sanitation Projects." BDP Water and Sanitation Cluster. London.

DFID (Department for International Development) and World Bank. 2005. *Tools for Institutional, Political and Social Analysis in PSIA: A Sourcebook.* Washington, DC: World Bank and DFID. http://web.worldbank.org/WBSITE/EXTERNAL/TOPICS/EXTSOCIALDEVELOPMENT/EXTTOPPSISOU/0,menuPK:1424015~pagePK:64168427~piPK:64168435~theSitePK:1424003,00.html

De Soto, H., S. Beddies, and I. Gedeshi. 2005. "Roma and Egyptians in Albania: From Social Exclusion to Social Inclusion." Working Paper 53, World Bank, Washington, DC.

De Soto, H., N. Egamberdi, and the Center for Economic and Social Studies (CESS). 2001. *Albania Municipal Water and Sanitation Project: A Social Assessment. ECSSD.* Washington, DC: World Bank.

De Soto, H., P. Gordon, I. Gedeshi, and Z. Simoimeri. 2002. "Poverty in Albania: A Qualitative Assessment in Ten Regions." World Bank Technical Paper 520, World Bank, Washington, DC.

ESMAP (Energy Sector Management Assistance Programme). 2003. *Stakeholder Involvement in Options Assessment: Promoting Dialogue in Meeting Water and Energy Needs—A Sourcebook.* Joint UNDP/World Bank Energy Sector Management Assistance Programme and Bank Netherlands Water Partnership Program (BNWPP).

Foster, V., E. Tiongson, and C. Ruggeri Laderchi. 2005. "Utility Reforms." In *Analyzing the Distributional Impact of Reforms: A Practitioner's Guide to Trade, Monetary and Exchange Rate Policy, Utility Provision, Agricultural Markets, Land Policy, and Education,* ed. A. Coudouel and S. Paternostro. Washington, DC: World Bank.

Gore, C., J. Figueiredo, and G. Rodgers. 1995. "Introduction: Markets, Citizenship, and Social Exclusion." In *Social Exclusion: Rhetoric, Reality, Response,* ed. G. Rogers, C. Gore, and J. Figueiredo. Geneva/ New York: IILS/UNDP.

INSTAT (Albanian Institute for Statistics). 2002. *The Population of Albania in 2001.* Tirana.

———. 2003. *Statistical Yearbook of Albania, 1993–2001.* Tirana.

IWEMP (Integrated Water and Ecosystems Management Project). World Bank, Infrastructure Sector Unit, Europe and Central Asia Region, 2004.

Kessides, C. 2000. *Cities in Transition: World Bank Urban and Local Government Strategy, Infrastructure Group Urban Development.* Washington, DC: World Bank.

KPMG. 2000. *Private Sector Participation in the Durres, Saranda, Fier and Lezha Water Supply and Sewerage Enterprises—Phase 1 Report.*

Krueger, R. A, M. A. Casey, J. Donner, S. Kirsch, and J. N. Maack. 2001. "Social Analysis: Selected Tools and Techniques." Social Development Paper 36, World Bank, Washington, DC.

MWWP (Municipal Water and Wastewater Project). 2002. Infrastructure and Energy Sector Unit, Southeast Europe Country Unit, Europe and Central Asia Region. Washington, DC.

North, D. 1990. *Institutions, Institutional Change and Economic Performance.* New York: Cambridge University Press.

Republic of Albania. 1999. *National Strategy for Decentralization and Local Autonomy.* Tirana.

———. 2000a. Council of Ministers. *Law on the Organization and Functioning of Local Governments.* No. 8652. Tirana.

———. 2000b. Council of Ministers. *Document of Policies on Decentralization of Water Supply and Sanitation Sector.* Law 550. Tirana.

———. 2001. Council of Ministers. *National Strategy for Social and Economic Development (NSSED).* Tirana.

———. 2002. Council of Ministers. *Giving the Drinking Water Tariffs the Executive Title,* Law 8975. Tirana.

———. 2003. Ministry of Territorial Adjustment and Tourism, General Directorate of Water Supply and Sewerage Enterprise. *Albania Water Supply and Wastewater Sector Strategy.* Tirana.

Strauss, A., and J. Corbin.1990. *Basics of Qualitative Research: Grounded Theory Procedures and Techniques.* Newbury Park, CA: Sage Publications.

World Bank. 2003. *Albania Water Sector Decentralization and Privatization—PSIA Pilot.* Washington, DC: World Bank.

———. 2004. *The World Bank Group's Program for Water Supply and Sanitation.* Washington, DC: Water Supply & Sanitation Sector Board, World Bank.

UNDP (United Nations Development Programme). 1997. "Governance for Sustainable Growth and Equity." Report of International Conference, United Nations, New York, July 28–30, 1997.

———. 2002. *Human Development Report Albania 2002: Challenges of Local Governance and Regional Development.* http://www.undp.org.al.hdr.undp.org/docs/reports/national/ALB_Albania/Alabania_2002_en.pdf

WSURP (Water Supply Urgent Rehabilitation Project). 2000. World Bank, Infrastructure Sector Unit, Europe and Central Asia Region, Washington, DC.

Yin, R. K. 1994. *Case Study Research, Design and Methods.* Thousand Oaks, CA: Sage Publications.

Organizational Maps of Albanian Water Sector Reform

FIGURE 9-A.1 Institutional Organization of the Water Sector in Albania

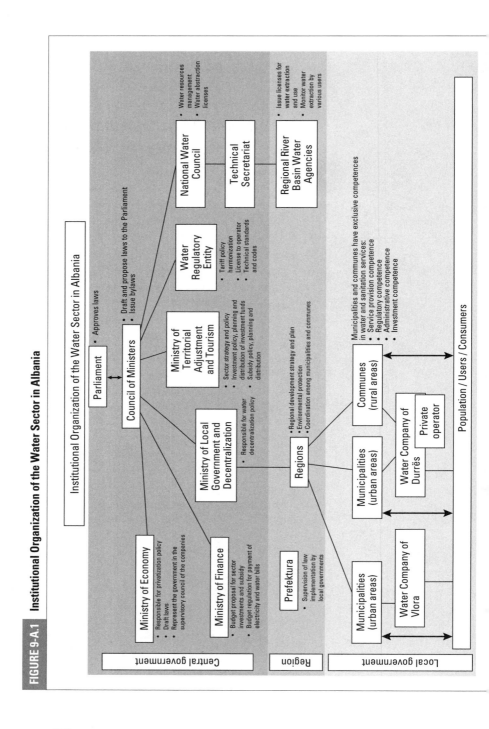

Institutional Organization of the Water Sector in Albania

Parliament
- Approves laws

Council of Ministers
- Draft and propose laws to the Parliament
- Issue bylaws

Central government

Ministry of Economy
- Responsible for privatization policy
- Draft laws
- Represent the government in the supervisory council of the companies

Ministry of Finance
- Budget proposal for sector investments and subsidy
- Budget regulation for payment of electricity and water bills

Ministry of Local Government and Decentralization
- Responsible for water decentralization policy

Ministry of Territorial Adjustment and Tourism
- Sector strategy and policy
- Investment policy, planning and distribution of investment funds
- Subsidy policy, planning and distribution

Water Regulatory Entity
- Tariff policy harmonization
- License to operator
- Technical standards and codes

National Water Council
- Water resources management
- Water abstraction licenses

Technical Secretariat

Regional River Basin Water Agencies
- Issue licenses for water extraction and use
- Monitor water extraction by various users

Region

Prefektura
- Supervision of law implementation by local governments

Regions
- Regional development strategy and plan
- Environmental protection
- Coordination among municipalities and communes

Local government

Municipalities (urban areas)

Water Company of Vlora

Municipalities (urban areas)

Water Company of Durrës

Private operator

Communes (rural areas)

Municipalities and communes have exclusive competences in water and sanitation services:
- Service provision competence
- Regulatory competence
- Administrative competence
- Investment competence

Population / Users / Consumers

FIGURE 9-A.2 Municipal Water and Wastewater Project—Institutional Organization

Municipal Water and Wastewater Project: Institutional Organization

Government

- Water Regulatory Entity
- Ministry of Territorial Adjustment and Tourism
- Ministry of Economy
- Ministry of Local Government and Decentralization

Local Government

- Durrës Region
- Fier Municipality
- Lehze Municipality
- Saranda Municipality

Contract Monitoring Unit

Executive Committee

Water companies

- Supervisory Council — Water Company of Durrës — Private operator
- Supervisory Council — Water Company of Fier — Private operator
- Supervisory Council — Water Company of Lezhe — Private operator
- Supervisory Council — Water Company of Saranda — Private operator

Population / Users / Consumers

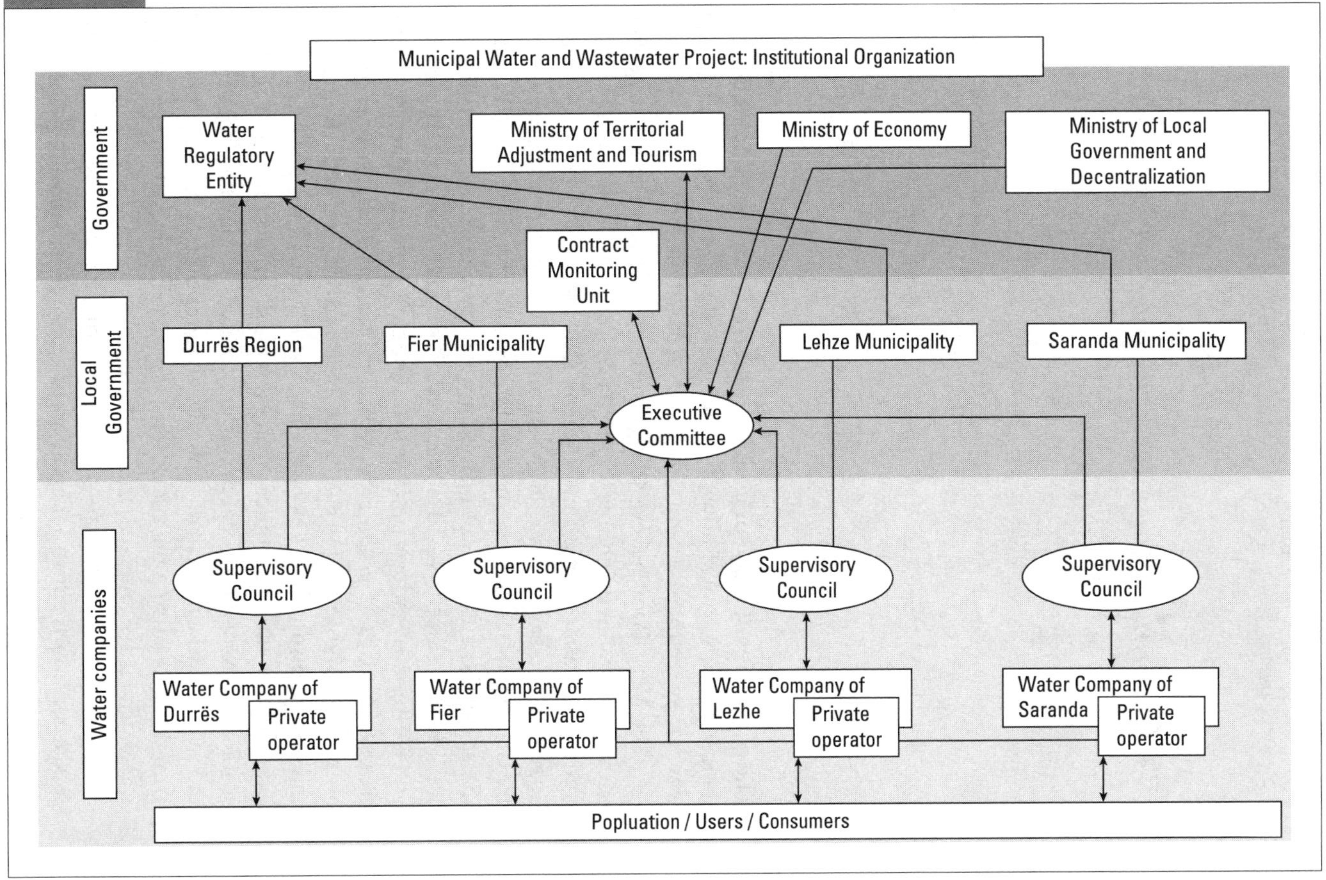

Definitions of Qualitative Poverty Categories

The definitions of the poor groups are based on how households defined themselves in terms of how they understand poverty and the degree to which they see themselves as impoverished.

The Very Poor believe that poverty primarily means not getting enough to eat, not being able to purchase clothes, an inability to continue traditions that are important to them, and a feeling of defenselessness, hopelessness, fear, ignorance, and humiliation. Their principal problems are lack of food, lack of clothing and shoes, and poor water quality. Their sparse diet is causing health problems, which many feel have worsened considerably since 1990. In some places, the incidence of child malnutrition is estimated by local officials to be about 50 percent. Other problems are psychological stress and the poor condition of their home. A smaller proportion of the group feels that an ability to obtain healthcare services and sewage disposal are key problems. Two-thirds of the group says that lack of employment and income are the most important causes of these problems. About 87 percent of this group owns a small two-room home and a third own a median of about five dynyms of land (usually inherited from the state during the transition). Approximately half receive remittances, which are crucial to their welfare.

The Poor believe that poverty is primarily hopelessness, defenselessness, exclusion from social and commercial life, low ability to provide basic necessities for the household, and an inability to continue traditions. In contrast to the Very Poor, Poor households say they eat more, and fewer say they have health problems and psychological stress. Their principal problems are infrastructure related—little or no transportation and electricity shortages—as well as lack of clothing. Secondary problems are the poor condition of their homes and water shortages. The main causes of their problems are unemployment, low or no income, and lack of security. Due to their greater concern about infrastructure-related problems, about half the group says unresponsive or inadequate government is an important cause of their problems. About 86 percent own a small two-room home with basic household items, and about 40 percent own a median of five dynyms of land (usually received from the state during the transition). Approximately half of the Poor receive remittances, but they earn more income from remittances than the Very Poor because the remittance rates of their migrants are higher.

The Non-Poor define poverty primarily as difficulty getting accurate information, and secondarily as exclusion from social and commercial life, an inability to continue some of their traditions, and hopelessness and defenselessness. They have greater material wealth than the Poor and Very Poor, including more income from remittances due to the higher remittance rates of their migrants. Because of their greater material wealth, they are less concerned about food and clothing, and more concerned about infrastructure and public security. Their main problems are heat (short and expensive supplies) and security (crime, lack of trust, and psychological stress). Secondary problems are water (low quantity and quality), sanitation/sewage, and the inability to access health care. Ninety-five percent of them own a small two-room home and 56 percent own a small amount of land (usually received from the state during the transition).

The Relatively Prosperous see themselves as poor only in that they experience difficulty obtaining information. They have little psychological stress from lack of food, clothing, and health care. Members of this group say their health is good, except for the problems of getting old, and many own cars and major household goods such as refrigerators and televisions. Some have second homes. Few in this group receive remittances or use other informal coping mechanisms. But like the other three groups, they feel that key problems are infrastructure and security. Their infrastructure priorities focus more on sewage and water, but also include heat (too expensive) and electricity. Matters of crime, trust, and resulting stress are also considered significant by this group.

Source: De Soto et al. (2002: xii–xiii)

10

ROMANIA
Mining Sector Reform

ANIS DANI, MARC-OLIVIER RUBIN,
DIMITRU SANDU, AND LIMIN WANG

In addition to the sector specificities of the mining sector, in the Europe and Central Asia region, mining sector reform has been a high priority because it involves two challenges: restructuring and downsizing of loss-making state-owned enterprises, and managing the expectations of a politically powerful sector. The Romania study illustrates the typical challenges faced by mining sector restructuring in this region, where the development of domestic mineral sources used to be an integral part of the development strategy in former communist countries, with relatively closed economies. Mine workers were the elite of the proletariat, working under dangerous conditions on tasks of national importance. As such they were relatively well paid, well organized, and influential prior to 1990, even when the productivity of mines declined and mineral extraction became uneconomical. When much cheaper alternatives became available in the 1990s and subsidies mounted, mining sector restructuring became inevitable.

MINING IN ROMANIA: THE COUNTRY CONTEXT

In the early 1990s, Romania had an estimated 464 mines for coal and other minerals. By 2004, production has ceased in 344 of the most uneconomic mines; 82 have been completely closed and the physical closure of 191 mines contracted out. The remaining 71 are currently under care and maintenance, awaiting ultimate closure. At the beginning of 2004, an estimated 120 mines were still operating, but many remained un-economical and dependent on budget subsidies and debt write-offs, generating quasi-fiscal deficits estimated to be 0.5 percent of GDP.

The closure of uneconomic mines has triggered large-scale redundancies in the mining sector in Romania since 1997. The workforce dropped from 171,000 in 1997 to 50,000 in 2004; significant downsizing occurred in 1997 through a process of voluntary redundancies induced by a generous severance package of 12–20 months' wages.[1] Layoffs have continued since then, with 5,000–10,000 workers leaving the industry annually. Implementing the mining sector strategy will require additional mine closures in some regions. Although social protection obligations in terms of payment of wages, severance pay, and unemployment benefits have been met, the mining towns affected by sector restructuring have faced severe hardships in the form of high unemployment and a decline in quality of life, local infrastructure, and social services.

The mining sector in Romania falls under the jurisdiction of the Ministry of Economy and Commerce (MEC). It is subdivided geographically into 12 mining companies, each with a specialization for different minerals. The largest companies are the National Hard Coal Company (CNH Petrosani) and National Lignite Company Oltenia (CNLO); these are geographically concentrated, while the others are more dispersed. The smallest two—for uranium and salt—employ around 1 percent of the mining sector workforce each.

Under communist rule, the mining sector was a privileged sector, with relatively high wages and a politically influential trade union. As was the case for many other state-owned industries, the relationship between the trade unions, the mine managers, and government in Romania has historically been quite close. This legacy continues to influence current relationships, making reform more challenging.

Despite the first phase of mine closures and mass layoffs, direct budget subsidies to the sector doubled in nominal terms, from US$99 million in 1999 to US$188 million 2004. Production subsidies (capital allocations), arrears on national and local government taxes, and social taxes (for unemployment and health care) also increased, forcing the government to write off some of these tax arrears. The combined fiscal impact—of direct subsidies, capital allocations, and tax arrears or write-offs—is estimated to be US$300 million in 2004, or 0.5 percent of GDP (see the section on distributional impacts in the mining sector and table 10.6 for a fuller discussion of subsidy).

In April 2004, the government of Romania approved a mining sector strategy that lays out plans for restructuring the sector to address its fiscal deficit and the mounting debts of unsustainable mines. The new strategy is also intended to meet the requirement of European Union (EU) accession: to eliminate all subsidies to minerals other than coal by 2007 and to coal mines by 2010.

The Poverty and Social Impact Analysis (PSIA) of the mining sector in Romania was conceived as an analytical input to help the government of Romania implement its mining strategy and inform the design of the second Bank loan—the Mine Closure, Environmental, and Socio-Economic Regeneration project (MCESER). The PSIA was designed through a consultative process with MEC, other relevant public agencies, and Romanian resource persons knowledgeable about the mining regions. Stakeholder workshops, organized in October 2004 and May 2005, provided important inputs into the design and analysis. Continued dialogue with mining sector colleagues within the government and the Bank ensured relevance of the PSIA to sectoral issues and enhanced ownership of the PSIA process.

The Socioeconomic Environment

To put this study in perspective, it is necessary to recognize that the period under review is one of considerable hardship, typical of the early years of transition from a centralized to a market economy. GDP growth was negative until 2000, the economy taking its time recovering from the downturn. Inflation remained over 30 percent through 2001, falling to 15 percent in 2003. This obviously had an adverse effect on poverty.

The World Bank's 1997 Poverty Assessment estimated 21.5 percent of the Romanian population to live below the poverty line. By 2002, poverty rose to 29 percent, with even higher levels of dissatisfaction even for the non-poor: 42 percent consider their income insufficient to cover their food needs, and 59 percent assess that their current incomes are not enough to cover current expenditures (World Bank 2003).

Mining activities are dispersed over six of the eight regions in Romania but are concentrated in the west and northwest (see figure 10.1), where historically mining was the dominant economic activity. Prior to 1989, mining employed some 350,000 people directly and generated another 700,000 jobs indirectly. As in other centralized economies, the remit of mining enterprises extended beyond economic production to provisioning infrastructure and social services in mining towns. Services were gradually devolved to municipalities, while employment opportunities contracted. Because most mining towns were mono-industrial, the

FIGURE 10.1   **Mining Regions in Romania**

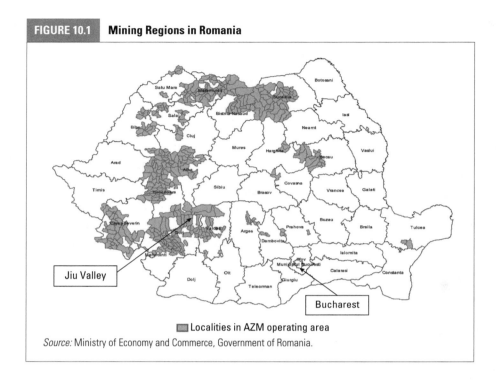

Jiu Valley

Bucharest

▨ Localities in AZM operating area

Source: Ministry of Economy and Commerce, Government of Romania.

impact was particularly severe when these boom towns went bust. Mine closure led to adverse impacts on mining localities both through loss of jobs in secondary enterprises as well as through deterioration of local infrastructure and social services.

The Operational Context

The World Bank has assisted the government of Romania through a US$44.5 million Mine Closure and Social Mitigation Project (MCSMP). The social mitigation component of this project was originally designed to support job creation among unemployed individuals laid off from the mining sector. Measures to induce former miners to accept alternative lower-paying jobs were not very successful, and the target group was broadened to include families of laid-off mine workers, and subsequently all unemployed within the mining localities. Recently, the MCSMP was restructured and a social development subcomponent added to encourage community action for local development.

The National Agency for Programs Development and Implementation for the Reconstruction for the Mining Regions (AZM) was created in 1997 as a consequence of an agreement between the government and the mining trade unions, which wield considerable influence in Romania. AZM is the designated implementing agency for the social mitigation component of the MCSMP. AZM functioned as an autonomous agency until 2001, when it was subordinated to the MEC. This led to a closer relationship between the MEC and mining professionals, but it was disadvantageous because it reduced effective collaboration with other agencies—such as the National Agency for Employment and Training (NAET), which is overseen by the Ministry of Labor, Social Solidarity and Family (MLSSF), as well as with the agency for small and medium enterprises (SMEs), the Romanian Social Development Fund (RSDF), and local governments.

The second Bank loan, MCESER, provides US$120 million in Bank financing, increasing the support for socioeconomic regeneration of the mining regions to three times that of the first loan. MCESER is scaling up job-creation measures for individuals and strengthening the ability of local governments and local communities to improve local infrastructure and services. This will necessitate greater involvement of other agencies including the MLSSF, NAET, the RSDF and local governments, than was required for the first Bank-financed project.

DESIGN AND METHODOLOGY OF THE STUDY

The PSIA consists of a series of product and process tasks undertaken in fiscal 2005, four of which are discussed in this chapter:

1. a comparative study of six towns in mining regions;
2. an analysis of the gender impacts of mining sector restructuring;
3. an ex-post quantitative analysis of program impacts of mining sector restructuring;
4. comparative analysis of the budget of mining companies the mining sector.

The objective of the PSIA was to examine three sets of distributional impacts to inform the policy choices facing the government:

- the differences in impact between mining and non-mining communities and households;
- the impact of reform across the gender divide; and
- the distribution of wages and subsidies within the mining sector.

Community-Level Analysis

The comparison of mining and non-mining communities was intended to compare former mining towns with other similar towns to assess the impact of sector reform at the community level, and to assess the ability of municipalities in those towns to maintain local infrastructure and social services to their constituency. The study involved qualitative field-work in three matched pairs of towns, selected to control for cultural differences (Comanesti with Moinesti in the east, Baia de Aries with Sebis in the west, and Borsa with Negresti-Oas in the north), representing three different subcultural regions of Romania (figure 10.2).

The working hypothesis for the community study was that mining communities affected by mine closure would be affected even further if communities lack the resilience, and local municipalities lack the resources, to maintain local infrastructure and services. This in turn would constrain socioeconomic regeneration of these mining communities. The methodology involved an examination of:

■ the state of physical and social infrastructure and the availability of resources for infrastructure development;

FIGURE 10.2   Regional Location of the Six Selected Towns

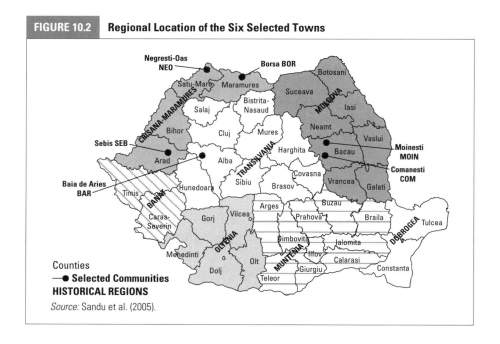

Counties
—● Selected Communities
HISTORICAL REGIONS

Source: Sandu et al. (2005).

- key social characteristics, livelihood strategies, and power relations;
- external communication links;
- effects of antipoverty and development programs;
- the impact of main economic stakeholders; and
- social stakeholders and associational life.

Key socioeconomic, cultural, infrastructure, and institutional information were collected through focus groups discussions, key informant interviews, and official regional statistics. Official data sets provided by AZM and the National Institute of Statistics (census) were also used to supplement the comparative analysis.

Welfare Impact on Different Stakeholders

The welfare impact was assessed by comparing effects between mining and non-mining households captured in annual household surveys commissioned by AZM. The three analytical components of this assessment were

- analysis of the welfare impact of mining sector restructuring on various stakeholder groups defined at the household level;
- examination of the gender impacts of mining sector reform (discussed later); and
- impact assessment of programs designed to mitigate the adverse effects of mining sector downsizing.

This section will focus primarily on the first analytical component, with some discussion of the second to bring out the methodological lessons. The data for the econometric analysis were obtained from four rounds of annual Social Impact Monitoring (SIM) data collected for annual SIM reports (2001 to 2004), commissioned by AZM as part of project monitoring. SIM surveys are purposely designed household surveys of slightly more than 1,200 households annually, conducted across 34 mining settlements, which are representative of the population in the mining regions.[2] The 34 mining localities are randomly selected from a sampling base of 139 localities. These surveys were administered using a standardized questionnaire to collect information for monitoring and impact evaluation of the programs administered by AZM. The household surveys are accompanied by focus groups and secondary analysis of data collected from sector departments within the mining regions.

The welfare impact on different households as a result of mine closure is measured by four outcome indicators (driven mainly by data availability):

1. change in living standards (purchasing power)[3]
2. per capita household income,
3. per capita food consumption, and
4. change in access to basic medical services since 1997.[4]

The study also assessed the overall performance of the program in terms of targeting (gender and locality) and output (AZM program awareness and interests in AZM programs). In the analysis, the change of living standard is expressed as the probability of a household being worse off than it was before the mining sector reform. The econometric models and estimation methods are presented in annex 10A.1

The outcome of any social program depends crucially on the process through which the program is placed and implemented across localities. AZM's programs are distributed across mining localities by inviting enterprises and individuals to apply for individual components of the program.[5] This procedure suggests that the program placement is likely to be in favor of "better-off" localities, because localities with stronger local government capacity (for example, with active and supportive mayors), a better social network, and more active business activities may cause more enterprises to apply for Employment and Training Incentives Scheme (ETIS) and/or more individuals for microcredit than they do in disadvantaged localities.

To address the potential bias caused by endogenous program placement, the PSIA used the difference-in-difference method. The challenge in evaluating program impact lies in separating the impact of programs from that of other factors that affect both program placement and outcomes in the non-randomization experiment setting. However, many regional factors—such as the local economic structure, investment conditions, infrastructure development—as well as the capacity of local organizations to implement social and economic regenerating policies, which in turn affect the probability of program placement and outcomes under consideration, are not observable. Without controlling for these unobservable regional factors, it is not possible to attribute the changes in outcome indicators to the program impact.

The difference-in-difference method, to some extent, can correct the evaluation bias caused by the unobservable factors if they remain relatively stable over time. This method disentangles the program impact by comparing the differences in key outcome indicators, before and after program implementation, between program and nonprogram localities. Qualitative data were collected through semi-structured interviews and focus group in four mining regions (Petrosani, Deva-Brad, Balan, and Gura Humorli) to assess the general perception of AZM program implementation.

Gender Analysis

The gender analysis was designed to assess whether women were disproportionately affected by mining sector reform, and if targeted measures are needed to reach them. This was done by secondary analysis of four rounds of SIM data, supplemented by field research on gender impacts of mine closure in two mining towns (Uricani and Brad) by a research team with prior experience in the mining regions. The data were collected through focus groups' interviews with women from different types of households and local authorities in the two communities. Data on gender were also obtained from the community studies in the six towns, described above.

Understanding the Political Economy of the Mining Sector

An analysis of mining companies' budgets was conducted to understand the dynamics and political economy issues within the mining sector and to help the government decide how to manage subsidies and sector downsizing among the mining companies in order to achieve the objectives of the mining sector strategy. Anecdotal evidence of political economy interests abound; these are often manifested through trade union pressure on the government for higher than average severance and early retirement entitlements, as well as for significant non-wage benefits. The PSIA attempted to quantify these entitlements and to examine who was benefiting from them by analyzing secondary data on employment, wages, and budgets in different mining companies. These data included projections based on the mining sector strategy. Data on employment and wages were readily available. However, data on subsidies and hidden transfers or exemptions had to be compiled for individual companies and then aggregated to understand the political economy dynamics within the mining sector.

The need for the PSIA originally emerged during the dialogue with MEC on the mining sector strategy with the realization that a number of vital questions lacked empirical evidence and sound analysis. From the beginning, the project implementation team in Romania was directly involved in the PSIA design and PSIA process. MEC provided substantive inputs into the design and methodology, identified research locations for community studies, and provided access to household survey and budget data. MLSSF and NAET also provided data and advice on active labor market measures. Two workshops were organized—one on gender impacts (October 2004), and one on broader impacts—to discuss the results with in-country stakeholders and validate analytical findings, which have been disseminated as a Policy Note (World Bank 2005). Key interlocutors at MPF and MEC engaged with the team throughout the project preparation cycle, drawing on interim results for project design, providing feedback on results, and sharpening the task team's focus on the operational implications of this study.

ANALYTICAL RESULTS

Space constraints do not permit presentation of the data in much detail. This section therefore focuses primarily on the main results of the community studies.[6]

Comparison of Mining and Non-Mining Localities

Infrastructure and social indicators reveal lower quality of life in mining than non-mining towns. The comparison of census data for the three mining towns—Baia de Aries, Comanesti, and Borsa—with their matching pairs indicates that the economic dominance of the mining industry, which determined the quality of life of mining sector workers, has come to an end. Physical capital (measured by the percentage of dwellings with piped water, and living floor space per dwelling) in the three mining towns is visibly lower than it is in their respective comparator towns. Field reports also indicate that housing quality is poorer in the mining towns. Infant mortality is significantly higher in two of the three mining towns but not in Comanesti, and the average age is slightly lower in the three mining towns. In two of the three mining towns this seems to be driven by higher fertility rates. Mining towns no longer attract workers—non-mining towns reflect higher numbers of in-migrants.

There is considerable diversity in economic performance and resilience of the mining towns. The main determinants of performance of these communities are (1) mono-industrial or dual economies, (2) age of restructuring process, and (3) prior history of market integration beyond the mining regions. Not surprisingly, towns that are mono-industrial have a harder time adjusting to mine closure, not least because of the immediate effect of job losses. Borsa is the hardest hit both because it is mono-industrial and because the restructuring process started early, in 1997, so its negative effects are fully visible while the socioeconomic regeneration is at an early stage. The impact of restructuring on Baia de Aries has been less severe so far, partly because mine closure is a relatively recent phenomenon, but also because its dual economy includes textiles with mining. This has proved to be a boon to women, but men have a hard time finding alternate employment when they lose their mining jobs. In contrast, Comanesti, the third mining town, has a diverse and resilient economy. One immediate implication is that a socioeconomic regeneration strategy should have the flexibility to adapt to these local variations. The local response to sector reform and relations between local public administration and mining companies is also conditioned by the nature of the particular mining town. A centrally planned, one-size-fits-all approach for all mining towns will not work.

Dependence on mining companies and other state-owned enterprises continues but is being reduced. Mining and non-mining state enterprises used to contribute to local communities through in-kind services or donations for social services and cultural activities. Mining companies have drastically reduced such involvement in community life because their finances were constrained and they started accumulating debts. This is gradually changing the relationship between the mining company and the local community, which no longer perceives the company as the dominant local patron.

The impact of mining companies on local infrastructure and social services goes beyond their inability to maintain those services adequately. All three mining towns studied have accumulated moderate to large debts to local municipalities, which two of them—Borsa and Baia de Aries—are unable to repay (table 10.1). These negative effects are greater in mono-industrial than in economically diverse towns. Romania has a long tradition of heavy involvement by frontier industries, such as mining, in the creation and management of housing and public infrastructure facilities at the local level. The case of Borsa is typical, with the mining company functioning like the de facto mayor for Baia-Borsa, the mining settlement in Borsa. The company finds it easier to manage local infrastructure around Baia-Borsa than to clear their tax arrears, but this also perpetuates local dependency on the mining company. The transfer of utilities to the mayor's office after mine restructuring is complicated by the fact that the municipality does not have the funds to maintain the facilities that are to be transferred from the mining company.

The existing data and indicators do not allow for a thorough assessment of the impact of taxes owed on the performance of local authori-

Table 10.1 Mining and Local Public Administration: Qualitative Profiles

Indicator	Baia de Aries	Sebis	Comanesti	Moinesti	Borsa	Negresti Oas
Demographic / economic features	Very small town; mining/textile dual economy	Very small town of high economic diversity	Medium multi-industrial city	Medium size oil city	Medium size, mono-industrial mining city	Small town of high economic diversity
Employment dynamics after 1989	Advanced mine closure with high unemployment for men	*	Mine closure advanced, economy diversified, temporary emigration high	*	*	None of the former SOEs were closed; private sector proliferating
Attraction for foreign investment	Medium	High	High	Medium	Low	High
Tax payments by companies to local budget	Not so large debts (about 20 million ROL)	Good payers	Large debts of mining company to local budget (0.5 billion ROL); they pay utilities	*	Large debts of mine company and forest company to local admin	Good payers (except small bankrupt firms)
Local firms as sponsors for the community activities	*	*	Coal & wood processing companies—active sponsors of community	*	Mine company provided housing and utilities; now declined	*
Mayor's house as client to local companies	Unable to pay bills due to arrears from mine company	*	*	*	Unable to pay bills due to arrears from mine company	*

Source: Sandu et al. (2005).
Note: * Close to average values with less significance from the social point of view (field assessment).

ties, but it is visible. The community studies were carried out at the microlevel, which, in most cases, was below the unit where administrative budgets are managed. Taxes are collected centrally and then recycled back to local municipalities, so local authorities have no mechanism to enforce tax collection. The financial autonomy accorded to the towns and the capacity to plan and manage finances efficiently varies from town to town. The city hall in Borsa declared their inability to manage records of debts owed by different entities. All three mining companies have tax arrears, but in varying degrees. Moinesti, for example, is a better performer, with 90 percent of taxes collected, compared with 80 percent in Comanesti, but Comanesti has greater financial autonomy than Moinesti. The mayors of Borsa and Baia de Aries claim they are unable to meet their bills to service providers because of the arrears owed by mining companies.

Financial needs for rehabilitating local infrastructure in the mining towns are larger than the resources currently available. Local authorities do not expect tax arrears to be cleared in the near future and are concerned about the deterioration of local infrastructure, which makes these towns even less attractive to potential investors. Mitigating adverse impacts of mining sector restructuring would need to go beyond active labor market measures to include investments in local infrastructure that would encourage enterprise development.

Field evidence suggests that investment in community capacity building can help mobilize local communities to engage more proactively in development processes. The early years of mining restructuring were characterized by general apathy and despondency in mining towns. Among the mining towns studied, two patterns are visible. The smaller, more isolated towns (Sebis, Negresti Oas) display more church-based initiatives. Larger towns with a more diversified economy, such as Comanesti, are more conducive to the growth of civil society organizations. In mono-industrial towns such as Borsa, dependency on the mining industry continues even in civic life, but AZM has played an effective role in facilitating community-based activities. This facilitating role played by AZM is also reported positively from other towns, such as Comanesti.

Policy Implications of Community Studies

The findings of the community studies suggest that a social mitigation program focused exclusively on social protection and active labor market measures will, by itself, not lead to socioeconomic regeneration. Measures will also have to be directed toward local communities to induce more proactivity in development processes. And the range of institutional actors needed for socioeconomic regeneration needs to be diversified.

These findings are consistent with the lessons from restructuring of state-owned enterprises in other transition countries of the region. Fretwell argues that "labor redeployment programs, in and of themselves, do not create jobs" (2004: 24). Well-designed, targeted schemes need to be complemented with a more holistic approach to employment creation (Fretwell and Wilson 1999). To meet short-run demand it is important to have well-targeted and designed labor market policies, but for longer-term employment and economic regeneration, policies that target whole communities are essential.

Haney and Shkaratan (2003) further highlight the importance of a community-based approach to sector restructuring. Their analysis of the coal mining industry in Russia and Ukraine found that a community focus is needed since mining activities in these countries not only provided employment, but also used to supply housing as well as social services to the wider public. During the period of 1993–2001, approximately 354,000 non-miners formerly employed in auxiliary services lost their jobs, a number larger than the number of miners retrenched from the coal industry. In response, Russia extended entitlements of severance and social protection payments from laid-off miners in closed mines to include other groups affected indirectly by mine restructuring, such as underemployed coal miners from operational mines, and finally to staff from other related industries. The related Coal Pilot Project in Russia was also a community-based initiative. That program was designed specifically to combat the effects of coal mine closures on the broader community and deal with adverse impacts of restructuring on housing, social assets, and social infrastructure that affected the mining community.

When it comes to specific active labor market measures, Fretwell stresses the need to implement country specific policies adapted to the country context. Although some successful generic principles can be identified, no single universal design has been successful across countries. Fretwell's study found that

- training programs in general have a positive impact on employment and earnings;
- the net impact of wage subsidy programs is mixed;
- public service employment has no impact, or even a negative impact, on employment and earnings in a post-program setting;

- there is evidence of synergies—for instance, employment services improve the impact of retraining policy; and
- women and youth benefit disproportionately from active labor market programs.

Based on the cross-country experience, Fretwell also emphasizes the fact that successful programs often included direct dialogue between key stakeholders—both before and during the restructuring program. This finding is reinforced by the Haney and Shkaratan (2003) study of Russia and Ukraine.

The second lesson from regional experience is that the range of institutional actors needed for effective socioeconomic regeneration needs to be diverse. In the case of Russia, the program evolved from heavy reliance on the Ministry of Fuel and Energy (equivalent of MEC) in the first phase, into a partnership with the Ministry of Labor and local government bodies, with funds being channeled directly by the Treasury to those entities to avoid leakage to the mining companies. The investments in local infrastructure and small and medium enterprises helped accelerate the process of socioeconomic regeneration, while enabling flexibility needed to design investments according to local priorities. This was made possible by the separation of funding for different activities that were then channeled directly to each organization.

These lessons are consistent with the findings in mining communities in Romania. The key messages are

1. since restructuring generates both direct and indirect adverse impacts, the target group should be broadened beyond mining sector workers to the mining community;
2. active labor market measures need to be complemented by investments in local communities;
3. diverse measures require diverse institutional actors (local governments and other agencies) with earmarked funds for local development that are protected from leakage to the companies being restructured;
4. local governments should not be deprived of much-needed revenue to finance local infrastructure and social services; and
5. smaller, more isolated towns would benefit from more active investment in community capacity building to facilitate a more direct relationship between the community and local authorities. In part, this will depend on the ability of mining companies to retreat from their patronage stance to allow other actors at the local level to come into their own.

Mining Has a Gender Bias

Women have been proportionately more affected in terms of direct job loss than men. When mining sector restructuring began in 1997, women were 16 percent of the workforce; by 2004, their proportion had declined to 7 percent (see figure 10.3). Women constituted 20 percent of the cumulative layoffs from 1997 to 2004.

Mine restructuring affects women more than other sectors do. Employment trends from the mining sector were compared with national unemployment data. The results show greater disparity in the mining sector. National unemployment rates for men and women in Romania were 5.7 percent and 6.4 percent respectively in 1997. By 2002, male unemployment jumped by to 8.9 percent, more than 50 percent over its 1997 level, while female unemployment rose more slowly to 7.7 percent. In the mining sector, however, the pattern of employment is the reverse, with the female labor force in 2005 declining to 87 percent of its 1997 level, while the male labor force declined by much less, to 67 percent. Figure 10.4 illustrates these two opposing trends in national and mining sector unemployment. The two upper lines depict the national unemployment rate, while the lower lines reflect gender-disaggregated downsizing from the mining sector. Although the employment situation has worsened overall, both nationally and in the mining sector, the relative deterioration between the genders is very different. Within the mining sector the gender gap has continued to worsen over time.

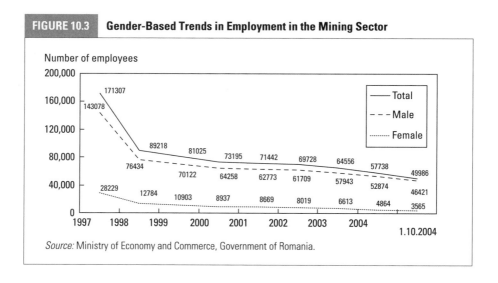

FIGURE 10.3 **Gender-Based Trends in Employment in the Mining Sector**

Source: Ministry of Economy and Commerce, Government of Romania.

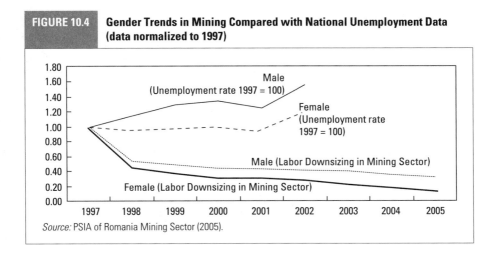

FIGURE 10.4   **Gender Trends in Mining Compared with National Unemployment Data (data normalized to 1997)**

Source: PSIA of Romania Mining Sector (2005).

A second finding that emerges from this graph is that the gender divergence increases after 1997–8, when the layoffs were voluntary. This is consistent with the finding from the qualitative gender study that 41 percent of women (compared with 24 percent of men) reported being pressured by management to take voluntary redundancy (Pislaru and Rughiniș 2004: 3). Empirical evidence thus points to a gender bias in layoffs from the mining industry.

Mining sector restructuring has affected the welfare of women in multiple ways—through employment, increased burden of domestic responsibility, intra-household tensions, and the impact of migration induced by mine closure. The welfare impact on women was analyzed using multiple data sources, including case studies, focus group interview, and analysis of SIM household surveys.

Table 10.2 compares gender-based results for three outcome indicators based on SIM surveys. The results provide clear evidence that women are disadvantaged in the labor market. There is evidence that women are active job seekers in the mining regions. On average, in the mining areas in the period 2001–4, around 30 percent of women and men under the age of 40 declared that they were searching for a job (SIM 2001–4). Within the subsample of redundant persons, 46.4 percent of women aged less than 50 declared at the time of the interview that they were looking for a job, compared with 50.3 percent of men of the same age. But, everything else being equal,[7] female laid-off workers have far fewer chances of being reemployed than males. Women's reemployment probability was

Table 10.2 Impact of Mine Closure on Women

Indicator	2001		2002		2003		2004	
	Male	*Female*	*Male*	*Female*	*Male*	*Female*	*Male*	*Female*
Reemployment probability (percent)	39	12	46	21	43	27	Na	na
A drop in living standards (compared with 1997) percent now vs. before 1997)	40	41	47	47	45	46	41	43
Access to medical care (worse than before 1997) percent	49	49	42	39	45	48	32	33

Source: 2001–4 SIM surveys.
Note: The three indicators—reemployment probability, a drop in living standards (compared with 1997), and access to medical care (worse than before 1997)—are predicted probabilities using a probit model (see annex 10A for explanations).

12 percent, compared with 39 percent for men in 2001. The gap diminishes over time but still remains large.

Survey data do not show significant differences in welfare impact caused by the reform between male- and female-headed households, except for health care. The 2003 data show a very significant drop in access to medical care by female-headed households, compared to 1997, which is likely to have multiplier effects on the family.

Women are entrepreneurial but concerned about risks associated with informal work. There are significant differences between men and women regarding informal sector work (Rughiniş 2001; Pislaru and Rughiniş 2004). This appears to be because of adverse conditions (such as uncertain hours and delays in payments) that prevail in "black market" jobs, where employees depend on the goodwill of their employer. In the subsample of redundant persons from the SIM surveys (2001–4), fewer women (22 percent) said they would be willing to take a job in the "black market" than men (36 percent). But women do not lack entrepreneurial spirit. The microcredit scheme under the MCSMP reports that 36 percent of borrowers are women.

Women are just as likely to express an interest in migration as men. Work in the European Union, legal or clandestine, has offered an exit strategy for a significant number of households, especially where alternative employment is missing. Young or middle-aged, women or men— all consider migration to be a very profitable option. On the other hand, the cost for legal migration (estimated at 600 euros, a cost that needs to be paid on departure) is relatively high and represents an impediment for impoverished families. Illegal migration is frequent from mining localities. However, in many cases attempts to migrate to native localities in the countryside of Moldova region have failed after conflicts with the older generation (given the background of rural poverty in Moldova).

Women suffer more from second-order impacts. The study reveals that women are more vulnerable to domestic violence and other forms of exploitation than men, making them more wary of the informal sector. At the same time, women bear the brunt of the burden of providing for the household. As a result of mine closure, the traditional system of family organization is under pressure. The SIM Annual Reports (Hart Group 2002, 2003a, 2004) and other qualitative research in mining regions (Rughiniș 2001) report visible consequences of restructuring on family relations. These can take the form of inducing increased stress and tensions—either because of shortages and unemployment, as in the Jiu Valley, or because of economic role reversal, as in Brad. Typically women became the main bread earner when husbands were laid off, but in most cases, the reform has forced women to assume a double burden of the adverse economic shocks— taking responsibilities for earning income or being forced to seek jobs outside households while taking full responsibility within the household.

Impoverishment has had visible costs on family life. These costs are seen within the couple and also in the extended family. Qualitative research findings reported in the SIM Annual Reports by Hart Group et al. in the mining areas provide evidence of a notable increase in conflict and domestic violence caused by financial difficulties. Domestic violence is highly visible in the Jiu Valley, with more than half of the respondents having encountered cases of battered women among their acquaintances, and around one quarter also encountering cases of battered men. Divorce rates are also reportedly much higher among redundant workers, sometimes triggered by emigration (Pislaru and Rughiniș 2004).

Gender-blind programs do not reach women equitably. There is considerable evidence that, despite disproportionate adverse impact, the program has not reached out to women effectively. On average, women are far less informed about existing programs. Table 10.3 clearly reveals that women in program localities have significantly higher probability of stating they never heard of AZM programs than their male counterparts, holding all other factors constant. This indicates that, even in AZM program localities, their outreach to women leaves much to be desired.

Program Impacts of Sector Reform

Program impacts were assessed by looking at the overall welfare impact of sector restructuring on households in the mining regions as well as by

Table 10.3 Program Targeting: Gender Focus

Predicted probability (percent)	All individuals			Women	
	All localities	Program localities	Nonprogram localities	Program localities	Nonprogram localities
(1) Never heard of the following:					
Microcredit	66.7	69.0	63.5	80.5	76.2
ETIS	65.7	65.9	65.5	81.1	73.2
Information/counseling	63.7	64.0	63.2	79.4	67.6
Incubation center	69.8	70.5	68.9	84.2	76.4
Support/consultancy	71.6	73.0	69.7	82.6	74.7
Other activities	75.3	77.2	72.5	84.7	75.1
(2) Not interested in AZM program	25.0	25.5	24.2	27.6	28.2

Source: 2001–4 SIM surveys.
Note: Figures in the above table are average predicted probability, which indicates the differences in program awareness or interests between women and an average person in the sample after controlling for all observable covariates.

looking at the impacts of mitigation programs piloted under the first mining project.

The impact of mine closure on household welfare is transmitted through several channels, including employment, access to basic services and government transfers.[8] In the short run, when the process of economic diversification and reemployment generation is limited, the laid-off workers in the mining regions are expected to experience a sharp drop in welfare as a result of income losses, although well-targeted social protection measures can reduce the extent of the negative effect. The welfare impact of the reform is also transmitted through households' access to basic services. Evidence shows that regions with major mining sector downsizing are likely to observe a deterioration of basic services (health, education, electricity, and water). A case study shows that in Anina, a small mining town, only three doctors remain at the hospital that struggles to maintain medical equipment. Human capital losses have also affected the quality and availability of local basic services, with many qualified teachers and medical staff leaving mining towns as a result of mine closure.

At the household level, to a large extent the welfare impact of mining sector downsizing depends on the ability of households to cope with the adverse economic shocks caused by mine closure. Household capacity, however, differs substantially because of differences in their financial assets, human capital (education and health), and social capital (connections to various organizations) across different household groups.

The local social and institution conditions can also affect a household's ability to cope with mining sector downsizing. For example, in regions where the local government has stronger fiscal capacity or is effective and committed to implementing social and economic regeneration programs it may provide more support for disadvantaged groups or better target the neediest population than in a region where local government has weaker fiscal control or is less pro-poor.

Table 10.4 summarizes the welfare impact using four indicators (predicted probability of experiencing a reduction in purchasing power, per capita income and food consumption, and probability of deterioration in access to medical services). The table also includes data on selected human capital indicators and land ownership across the nine different groups or stakeholders (defined by the head of household's labor market status).

Three interesting observations emerge from this table. First, households headed by laid-off miners evidently experienced the largest negative welfare impact of the reform, with the estimated probability of experiencing a reduction of living standards being about 73 percent, compared with the average of 40 percent. Households headed by unemployed persons from other sectors have a 58 percent probability of a drop in living standards (the second highest, although the sample size is small for this group). These two groups are also the poorest measured by income and food consumption per capita.

However, these two groups, in particular laid-off miners, are probably not the most disadvantaged or vulnerable group. There are two pieces of evidence supporting this finding. First, laid-off miners are relatively well educated and generally younger and in better health, so their unemployment is likely to be transitory and they are less immediately affected by worsening basic health services. Secondly, the miners laid off in 1997–9 received a generous severance package, consisting of 12 to 20 months' wages. An in-depth study of laid-off miners in Petrosani reveals that most laid-off miners declined the jobs created in the water-distribution system under the public works schemes financed by the labor redeployment program (Larionescu et al. 1999) because the minimum wages offered by the public work schemes were unattractive compared with the generous compensation packages provided by the government.

Currently employed miners are clearly better off: their probability of experiencing a drop in living conditions is the lowest among the different stakeholder groups, while their income and food consumption per capita are the highest. In addition, miner households, on average, receive higher wages and substantial in-kind income.[9] The Jiu Valley study shows that miners and retired miners' households continue to receive subsidies

Table 10.4 Welfare Impact of Mining Sector Downsizing across Stakeholders

Stakeholder	Probability of experiencing a drop in purchasing power (1997–2001) (percent)	Monthly income per capita (1,000 ROL)	Monthly food expenditure per capita (1,000 ROL)	Deterioration in access to medical services (1997–2001) (percent)	Head of household with little education (percent)	Incidence of illness (percent)	Self assessed poor health status (percent)	Own land (percent)	No. households
Miners	20	1,469	584	49	14	9	9	28	229
Non-miners in state-owned enterprises	25	951	454	42	19	14	13	39	77
Private sector	42	981	462	44	22	7	10	29	103
Retired miners	43	1,053	542	53	48	40	39	38	148
Retired other	39	1,040	565	49	49	49	45	53	105
Laid-off miners	73	482	302	55	34	15	18	27	144
Other unemployed	58	591	318	38	29	20	26	31	34
Housewives	49	680	373	54	61	21	32	27	148
Other	37	985	465	49	26	16	17	33	243
Total	40	979	469	49	33	20	22	33	1231

Source: 2001 SIM survey.

Note: The probability of experiencing a drop in purchasing power and deterioration in access to medical services are for the period between 1997 and 2001 is estimated based on a probit model (see annex 10A). Estimation results are presented in annex table 10A.1. Heads of household with less than the first cycle of high school are defined as *little education.* ROL is the Romanian currency leu (US$1 = 35,000 leu in 2001).

for heating and electricity. This reflects the traditionally strong political power of mining companies and trade unions, compared with workers from other sectors, particularly those in the newly emerging private sector or informal sector in the mining regions.[10] It is also worth noticing that households with retired persons (pensioners) tend to have a better living standard in terms of household income and food consumption.

The estimated probability of experiencing a reduction in living standards is also high for households headed by unemployed persons from outside the mining sector, housewives, and those who are currently working in the private sector. The estimated probability for these three groups is 58 percent, 49 percent, and 42 percent, respectively. This finding indicates that household income among those groups also depends largely on the existence of mining companies, and that they are highly vulnerable to economic shocks caused by mine closure. Laid-off miners are the obvious targets of social protection programs and are recipients of various subsidies financed through central budget as part of the government's mining restructuring package. Those who are employed outside the mining sector (for example, in the private sector or informal sector) are unlikely to receive any compensation despite the fact that their living standards are also vulnerable to second-order effects of mining sector downsizing. On the other hand, older people (retirees from mining sector) who are vulnerable to the worsening of social services because of poor health do benefit from pensions and other entitlements such as coal subsidies for winter heating. Unlike some other transition countries, in Romania these benefits are paid on time.

The above findings suggest that the design of social protection policies in the mining regions should ideally be based on in-depth analysis of the differential welfare impact of mining sector restructuring across different stakeholders. A better understanding of the entitlements and influence of the stakeholders through a PSIA is particularly important to inform both the design and the implementation of social mitigation programs. Households employed in the private sector are often heterogeneous and less organized than those employed in state-owned enterprises, particularly those in the mining sector. As a result, they are inadequately represented by trade unions or other civil society organizations and are less likely to be involved or consulted in the reform process. Their interests may not be taken into account when decisions on mining sector restructuring are reached.

The lessons for future program implementation derived from the above findings are twofold. First, social mitigation and protection programs can be effective only if the design of these programs explicitly takes account of the influence and power relations among different socio-economic groups in the context of mining sector reform. Second, the issue of targeting social assistance to the most deserving households in mining regions is particularly critical for effectively mitigating adverse social and economic impacts during mining sector contraction.

Having reviewed the welfare impact as a whole, we now turn more specifically to the ex-post assessment of the social mitigation programs implemented under the first mining loan. Table 10.5 presents trends in four outcome indicators based on 2001–4 SIM surveys. The results show that for all localities, reemployment prospects increased from 32 percent in the base year 2001 to about 38 percent in 2002–3, matched with an

Table 10.5 Impact Analysis of Social Mitigation Programs

	2001 *(percent)*	2002 *(percent)*	2003 *(percent)*	2004 *(percent)*	*Difference between* 2004 *and* 2001
Program localities					
Reemployment probability	38	43	47	n.a.	9
Experience a drop in living standards (compared with 1997)	42	46	47	44	5
Life not worth living (often think so)	16	11	10	10	−6
Access to medical care (worse than 1997)	57	44	49	36	−22
Nonprogram localities					
Reemployment probability	23	32	30	n.a.	7
Experience a drop in living standards (compared with 1997)	38	49	43	39	1
Life not worth living (often think so)	15	11	9	11	−4
Access to medical care (worse than 1997)	37	35	43	29	−8
All regions					
Reemployment probability	32	38	38	n.a.	6
Experience a drop in living standards (compared with 1997)	41	47	45	42	1
Experience a drop in living standards (compared with previous year)	45	47	45	36	−9
Life not worth living (often think so)	16	11	9	10	−6
Access to medical care (worse than 1997)	49	40	46	32	−17

Source: 2001–4 SIM surveys.
Note: n.a. denotes not applicable. Full estimation results for reemployment probability are presented in annex table 10A.2.

improvement in pessimism about welfare prospects. Based on subjective living standard measures, no major improvement in the mining regions is observed during the survey period 2001–4, although by 2004, the SIM survey shows that access to medical care slightly improved compared with that before the mining sector reform.

The impact evaluation of AZM-led programs is presented in the first and second panels of table 10.5. The program impact is assessed by comparing changes in the four outcome indicators before (SIM 2001 is used as the baseline) and after program implementation, using data from the SIM 2001 survey as the baseline and from the SIM 2004 survey as the post-program data. For example, to examine the impact of programs on reemployment probability, we compare 9 with 7 in the last column of table 10.5. The results show that the program regions seem to be more successful in reemploying unemployed than the nonprogram regions (see figure 10.5), despite the fact that both regions show an upward trend in reemployment probabilities over time. The comparison for other outcome indicators between the program and nonprogram localities does not show any systematic pattern. It should be noted that the sample size in SIM surveys are relatively small and there are several deficiencies in the survey design.[11] In particular, the program participation rates are very low, ranging from 2 to 4 percent of the sample during the years 2001–4. The low participation rates can result from several factors, including the delayed start of program activities and narrow eligibility criteria—which were broadened in 2003 to increase coverage—and loan restructuring in the later years of the first project. The participation rate reduces our

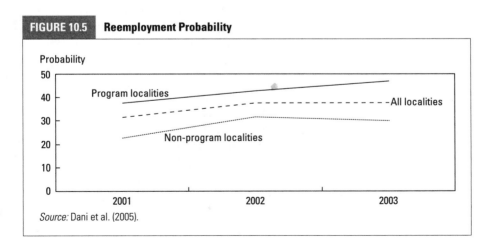

FIGURE 10.5   Reemployment Probability

Source: Dani et al. (2005).

confidence in the results of program impact evaluation, which should be interpreted with some caution.

The program was also evaluated using qualitative data collected through semi-structured interviews and focus groups across four mining regions that had undergone restructuring.[12] The interviews were conducted with representatives of distinct categories of entrepreneurs, including formal and informal entrepreneurs, with or without employees. Focus groups were organized with laid-off workers, workers still employed in the mining industry, and women from those mining towns.

Qualitative data provide some evidence that general opinions about the implementation and outcome of the social mitigation programs are not entirely positive. The survey reveals a large variation in the residents' awareness of the AZM program across the four mining regions. There is also a perception of lack of transparency about entrepreneurs' access to AZM programs and a lack of trust in the selection procedures for social mitigation schemes. These observations need to be tempered by the fact that residents in the mining regions tend to display an attitude of dependency or despondency, sharing the negative perceptions about welfare trends in the country as a whole.

Overall, at the output level, programs supported by AZM are effective in generating jobs for laid-off miners. Compared with an initial target of 10,000 jobs under the MCSMP, AZM has created well over 13,000 jobs, with another 6,448 jobs created or sustained by the microcredit program. In terms of outcomes, socioeconomic conditions in program localities are not significantly better than in nonprogram localities. Because the decline in welfare in mining towns was more severe than in non-mining towns, this result is not surprising. To some extent, however, it may also reflect the reality that the measures undertaken so far were insufficient to deal with the magnitude of the problem both in terms of target size and in terms of depth of the measures undertaken.

The comparison of mining communities with non-mining communities discussed earlier suggests that there is a need to broaden the objectives of future social mitigation programs and to emphasize support for developing local infrastructure and social services to complement active labor market measures. This will have implications about how to manage the transfer of the management and financing of local services, and how to manage the institutional transition and capacity building of local government, which should be the key policy questions for the design of the next stage of the social program.

Distributional Impacts within the Mining Sector

In the 1970s and 1980s, the mining sector in Romania was a growing industry that provided jobs and spurred economic activity in many regions of Romania. By the early 1990s, however, it was a loss-making industry urgently in need of restructuring. The influence of the mining trade unions and their relatively close relationship with the political leadership posed considerable challenges to sector restructuring. The trade unions have been able to negotiate higher rates of severance for mining sector workers on the grounds that they worked under difficult conditions and that reintegration into the labor market would be more difficult for mine workers.[13] After the first wave of layoffs in 1997, when an estimated 90,000 out of 171,000 left the industry, 5,000 to 10,000 layoffs occur annually. In 1997, most of the redundancies took place on a voluntary basis, making it possible to start closing uneconomic mines. By 2004, the number of mines in operation was down to an estimated 120. However, the fiscal benefits of downsizing have not yet materialized, and the hard coal sector (CNH Petrosani) has been granted an extension until 2010. The PSIA assessed the impact of this extension.

There is considerable confusion on the exact status of transfers to the mining industry. Part of this confusion arises out of continuously evolving terminology and ambiguity in the use of terms. The data in table 10.6 classify operating subsidies (that is, ongoing operations of the mining companies) and severance payments as direct subsidies. During the period 2002 to 2004, severance costs increased dramatically, from 3 percent to 20 percent of what MEC classifies as direct subsidies, the increase in operating subsidies exceeding severance payments by a factor of 2 to 1.

Table 10.6 Budget Subsidies to the Mining Industry
US$ millions

Category	Year					
	1999	*2000*	*2001*	*2002*	*2003*	*2004*
Direct subsidies	99.00	91.10	90.50	97.50	169.60	188.00
Operating subsidies	99.00	91.10	90.50	94.40	151.80	156.20
Severance payments	0.00	0.00	0.00	3.10	17.80	31.80
Social allocations	17.70	20.40	20.30	22.70	23.80	19.20
Investment	27.40	25.90	17.70	14.80	16.60	14.30
Total	**144.10**	**137.40**	**128.50**	**135.00**	**210.00**	**221.50**

Source: Ministry of Economy and Commerce, Government of Romania (figures not adjusted for inflation).

The scale and timing of the increase in severance is interesting. The increase in severance is not consistent with the time path of inflation, nor can it be explained by an increase in the number of layoffs. The most significant increase in severance costs, in 2003, coincides with the period when MEC was negotiating with the mining trade unions over the mining sector strategy to get ownership of the strategy and acceptance of the principle of phasing out mining subsidies in accordance with EU accession requirements. The government appears to have made significant concessions to the mining unions to obtain political support for the mining strategy. Despite the increase in severance rates, these payments account for a small part of the subsidies to the mining sector, which implies that downsizing alone does not explain industry losses.

The capital allocations (investments) and social allocations (which include safety equipment, uniforms, transportation, and meals for workers), which typically would be considered production costs, are not classified as such in Romania; nor are they included in the category of subsidies. However, they do involve a budget transfer to keep the mining companies functional.

A third budgetary cost that is even harder to disentangle is the revenue needed to cover current debts to the state budget—social insurance, health insurance fund, and the unemployment fund, from which the mining companies are exempted under Article 33 of the budget regulations for the mining sector (GO 87/2003). This cost consists of current exemptions and does not represent historical debts. These debts have been approved by the Competition Council according to the agreement with the EU and are classified as exemptions, not subsidies. However, from a fiscal point of view, these transfers need to be accounted for.

Aggregate figures for exemptions under Article 33 could not be obtained. However, data from the budgets of mining companies allow us to estimate the total value of these exemptions. Although direct subsidies (including severance payment and operating costs) account for almost two-third of the transfers, the value of capital allocations and exemptions under Article 33 are nontrivial, and the operating costs are also production costs. Taken together, these subsidies and exemptions—which we shall define as ***real transfers***—amounted to more than US$300 million in 2004 (see figure 10.6). In effect, despite the major wave of downsizing in 1997 and the continuing layoffs from the sector, the mining industry generated a quasi-fiscal deficit of 0.5 percent of GDP. The budget analysis in the rest of this section attempts to analyze some of the underlying causes of this deficit.

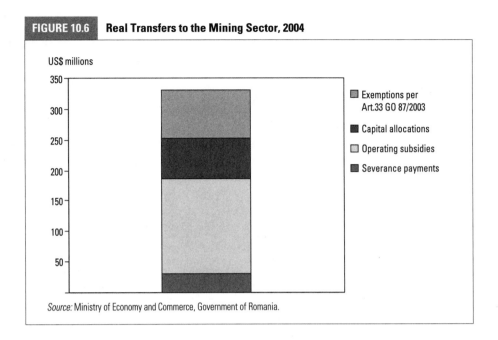

FIGURE 10.6   Real Transfers to the Mining Sector, 2004

US$ millions

Legend:
- Exemptions per Art.33 GO 87/2003
- Capital allocations
- Operating subsidies
- Severance payments

Source: Ministry of Economy and Commerce, Government of Romania.

The nine companies included in the analysis cover a significant part of the mining sector. The total number of employed at the beginning of 2004 was 40,065, which is about 70 percent of the total number of employed in the sector in 1997.[14] The results obtained from these nine companies thus contain a substantial degree of generalizable power. As figure 10.7 illustrates, the nine companies differ considerably in size (measured by both employees and revenue) with CNH Petrosani standing out as the largest company, followed by three medium-sized companies and five smaller companies.

Figure 10.8 compares wages in 2003 as well as the salaries projected for 2004–10 across the nine mining companies, while figure 10.9 shows the projected salaries adjusted for inflation and PPP. All mining companies pay salaries in excess of the Romanian average of 204 US dollars (unadjusted);[15] the wage bill at CNH Petrosani is an outlier.

CNH Petrosani pays considerably higher wages than the other eight companies affecting the industry average. The explanation for this difference was sought in differences in productivity. Table 10.7 illustrates the 2003 output per worker across the nine mining companies. The table reveals that CNH Petrosani indeed produces more output per worker compared with most of the other mining companies, but this is offset by

FIGURE 10.7 **Revenues and Workers in Nine Mining Companies, 2003**

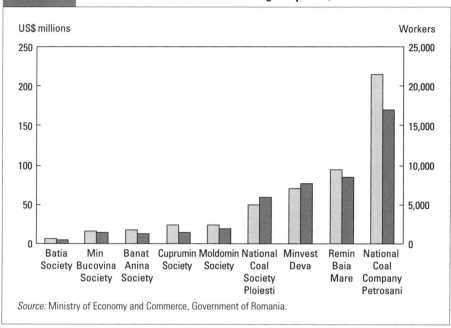

US$ millions   Workers

Source: Ministry of Economy and Commerce, Government of Romania.

FIGURE 10.8 **Gross Salaries: Actual (2003) and Projected (2004–10)**

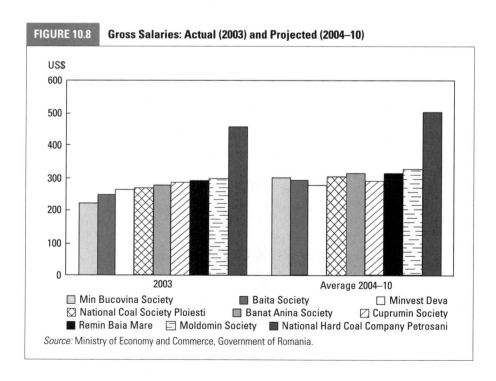

US$

Legend:
- Min Bucovina Society
- Baita Society
- Minvest Deva
- National Coal Society Ploiesti
- Banat Anina Society
- Cuprumin Society
- Remin Baia Mare
- Moldomin Society
- National Hard Coal Company Petrosani

Source: Ministry of Economy and Commerce, Government of Romania.

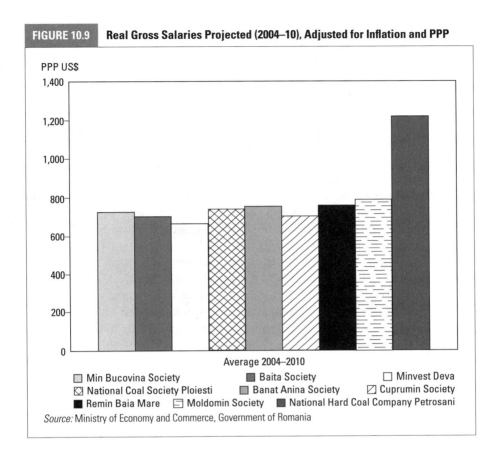

FIGURE 10.9 Real Gross Salaries Projected (2004–10), Adjusted for Inflation and PPP

Source: Ministry of Economy and Commerce, Government of Romania

Table 10.7 Output, Wages, and Output-to-Salary Ratio, 2003

Company	Output (US$ millions)	Wages (US$ millions)	Output-to-Salary Ratio
Minvest Deva	13.2	20.7	0.64
Moldomin Society	4.6	6.4	0.72
Remin Baia Mare	22.1	27.7	0.80
Min Bucovina Society	4.0	4.0	0.99
National Hard Coal Company Petrosani	91.2	91.2	1.00
Cuprumin Society	5.8	4.7	1.22
Baita Society	1.9	1.5	1.24
National Coal Society Ploiesti	24.6	16.3	1.51
Banat Anina Society	8.8	4.1	2.12

Source: Ministry of Economy and Commerce, Government of Romania.

the higher wage bill. If an output-to-salary ratio is applied, CNH Petrosani's value of 1 falls in the middle of the nine companies. This implies that the value of the output generated per worker is about the same as the salary of the worker. The worst-performing company with respect to this ratio is Minvest Deva, with a value of 0.64; the best performer is Banat Anina, with an output value of 2.1 times the salary.

Figure 10.10 separates the nine mining companies' production structure into capital (including raw materials and electricity) and labor (including personnel expenses). The figure reveals very different production structures across the companies, ranging from the labor-intensive CNH Petrosani, where 73 percent of the expenses are for personnel costs, to Bucovinas' share of only 27 percent. The higher wage bill at CNH Petrosani indicates that reduction of the workforce there would lead to faster reduction of transfers to the sector.

The mining sector relies on state support in the form of direct subsidies, capital allocations, and transfers based on Article 33, GO 87/2003. These state transfers to the mining sector must be eliminated by 2010 for Romania to comply with EU accession requirements. In 2003, state transfers to the mining sector amounted to US$275 million, to be reduced by US$110 million by January 1, 2006. In percentage terms this is 40 percent of the 2003 level—approximately the same rate as the reduction in

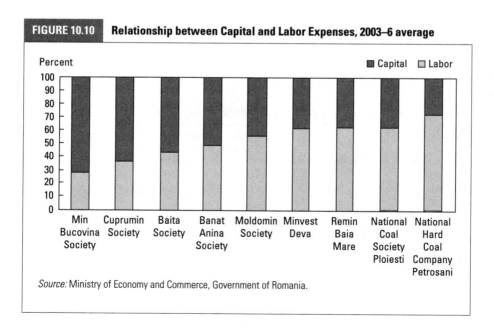

FIGURE 10.10 Relationship between Capital and Labor Expenses, 2003–6 average

Source: Ministry of Economy and Commerce, Government of Romania.

employment. Mining companies are also expected to pay revenue to the state in the form of different kinds of taxes. However, these were found to be negligible: they came to US$10,500 in 2003 and were projected to be US$8,000 in 2004, US$7,800 in 2005, and US$7,200 in 2006.

An interesting question is which company benefits the most from the subsidies and whether the subsidies are allocated on the basis of the companies' running deficits. With regards to the latter, figure 10.11 seems to support the conclusion that, in general, companies with larger budget deficits receive more state transfers. Furthermore, for one company—Bucovina—the transfer is larger than the actual deficit, which could help explain why the company is the only one reported to generate actual profits in 2003. CNH Petrosani has the largest absolute budget deficit and has also been allocated the most state transfers.

Table 10.8 presents the ratios between state transfer and the deficit (value of the output subtracted from company costs) for 2003. Again there

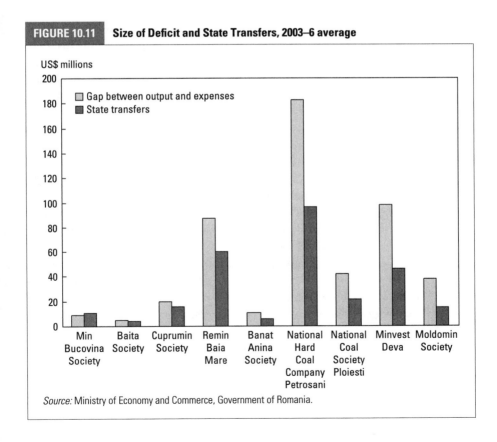

FIGURE 10.11 **Size of Deficit and State Transfers, 2003–6 average**

Source: Ministry of Economy and Commerce, Government of Romania.

371

Table 10.8 State Transfers in Relation to Budget Deficit and Total Revenue, 2003

Company	State transfer/deficit	State transfer/total revenue
Min Bucovina Society	1.25	0.71
Baita Society	0.92	0.66
Cuprumin Society	0.77	0.66
Remin Baia Mare	0.69	0.64
Banat Anina Society	0.54	0.34
National Hard Coal Company Petrosani	0.53	0.45
National Coal Society Ploiesti	0.51	0.44
Minvest Deva	0.47	0.65
Moldomin Society	0.39	0.64

Source: Ministry of Economy and Commerce, Government of Romania.

seem to be large divergences between the companies, with Bucovina's ratio of 1.25 at one end at the spectrum and Moldomin's 0.39 at the other. Calculating the ratio of state transfers in relation to total revenue reveals much less divergence. In part this is because state transfers are part of the total revenue (unlike the state transfer-to-deficit ratio) and because the revenue measure does not consider differences in expenses. The pattern of the two ratios across companies is largely the same, though, with a few exceptions (most notably Banat Anina's low state-transfer-to-revenue ratio): Bucovina is enjoying most state transfers as a percentage of both revenue and deficit.

For state transfers per worker, the above result does not hold. Instead, as figure 10.12 shows, Cuprumin is receiving the highest state transfers per worker (US$277 per worker) followed by Remin (US$239 per worker) and Moldomin (US$222 per worker). A high state-transfer value in these mines is caused by a relatively aggressive downsizing strategy (driving up the per worker ratio) rather than by an increase in overall state transfers. The reason that state transfers are not reduced at the same pace is not only because of institutional rigidity but is rather a result of the fact that downsizing is costly. Downsizing is especially expensive the first few years because of the lump sum severance payment for workers being laid off.

Figures 10.13 and 10.14 show the projected development of state transfers (2003 = 100) in terms of overall transfers and transfers per worker. In the first figure, CNH Petrosani clearly stands out as a company with a comparatively modest reduction in subsidies during the period. When taken per worker, Minvest Deva surpasses CNH Petrosani, but only because the labor force in Minvest Deva has been more than halved,

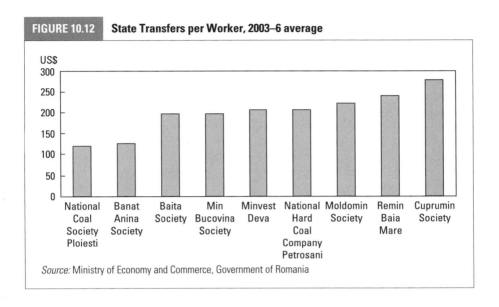

FIGURE 10.12 **State Transfers per Worker, 2003–6 average**

Source: Ministry of Economy and Commerce, Government of Romania

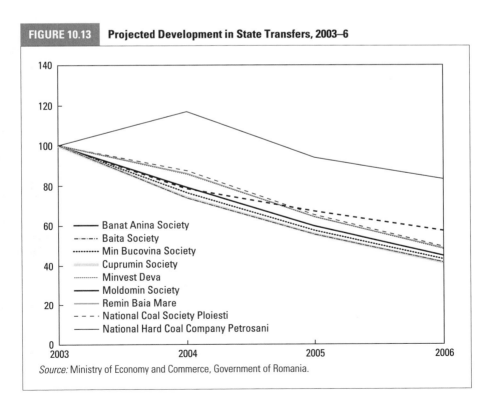

FIGURE 10.13 **Projected Development in State Transfers, 2003–6**

Source: Ministry of Economy and Commerce, Government of Romania.

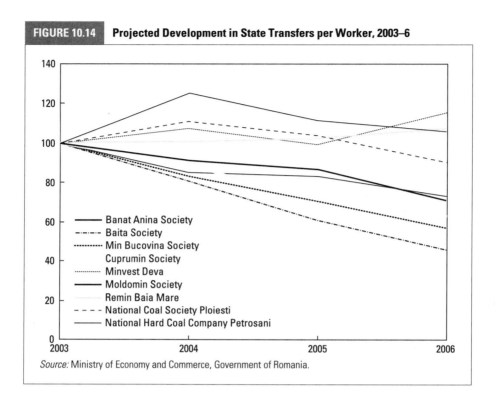

FIGURE 10.14 | Projected Development in State Transfers per Worker, 2003–6

Legend:
- Banat Anina Society
- Baita Society
- Min Bucovina Society
- Cuprumin Society
- Minvest Deva
- Moldomin Society
- Remin Baia Mare
- National Coal Society Ploiesti
- National Hard Coal Company Petrosani

Source: Ministry of Economy and Commerce, Government of Romania.

and the transfers therefore reflect higher proportion of one-off severance payments. If state transfers to CNH Petrosani were to be reduced by the same percentage as the remaining eight companies (53.1 percent), about US$35 million could be saved in state transfers in 2003–6. Note, however, that the US$35 million reduction in state transfers will result in budgetary savings only if a hard budget constraint is imposed on CNH Petrosani.

The strategic choices made for sector reform are not always justified by the budget figures. The economic rationale for further downsizing in CNH Petrosani was convincing, but a political decision has been made to spread this until 2010. With regard to state transfers, with the exception of Bucovina, transfers seem to be largely correlated with the running deficit to cover a large chunk of the companies' shortfall. The apparently slower planned reduction of state transfers for CNH Petrosani can be attributed only to their success in claiming a higher share of subsidies as rent for political capital. As the largest loss-making company, the cost of modestly reducing state transfers to CNH Petrosani relative to the other companies is estimated at US$35 million. To this must be added the cost of its slower restructuring. What is evident is that political economy factors have generated distributional issues within the mining sector, so that some companies and regions—especially CNH Petrosani—are more privileged than others.

LESSONS LEARNED

The PSIA of the mining sector in Romania has provided an opportunity for analyzing the complex problems inherent in reforming a privileged state-owned enterprise sector, which has had a history of close alliances among politicians, company managers, and the trade unions. Several methodological and sectoral lessons emerge from the analysis:

1. The most important lesson is that close alignment of the study team with the team working on sector reform provides access to data and insights that allow the analytical work to go hand in hand with the policy dialogue. In the case of Romania, this enabled the PSIA to have an impact on the reform program even before the results were finalized.
2. The second lesson is that although macrolevel analysis helps to identify aggregate fiscal costs, intrasectoral analysis is essential to unpack different elements that contribute to quasi-fiscal deficits.
3. The third lesson is that social mitigation programs should also address the needs of those indirectly affected by industrial downsizing, basing program design on rigorous analysis of the welfare impact of sector reform. The results illustrate that, although laid-off miners experienced the largest drop in welfare, they were not the most vulnerable group in the mining regions.
4. The fourth lesson is that even when intentions are benign and policies appear to be gender neutral, being blind to gender can disadvantage women. Analyzing actual gender impacts can reveal structural or behavioral constraints that need to be countered if gender equity is to be maintained.
5. The fifth lesson is that many insights can be gleaned by questioning assumptions by re-analyzing existing data. In the Romania mining study, the bulk of the analysis was conducted through analysis of existing household survey data and company budget data. However, this needed to be complemented by community-level case studies.
6. The sixth lesson is that even for qualitative research samples, communities need to be selected carefully to establish meaningful comparisons. The Romania study had the benefit of client involvement to ensure careful selection of study sites.

7. The seventh lesson is that it is very difficult to eliminate subsidies from sectors that have grown dependent on them. Analysis of the nature of transfers and public disclosure of these data help to build broader support for reform, even when there are political economy interests among sectoral stakeholders.

8. The final lesson is that sector reform requires changing institutional arrangements and power relations to avoid conflict of interest. It is inevitable that the interests likely to be weakened by the reform will resist change. The challenge is to show those interests the cost of maintaining the status quo, and to mobilize other partners to avoid backsliding on reform.

NOTES

1. This severance package was considerably more generous than it was in Russia and Ukraine, where severance pay was equivalent to three months' wages; it was, however, comparable to that of Poland.

2. The SIM surveys included 1249, 1247, 1226, and 1226 households in 2001, 2002, 2003, and 2004, respectively.

3. In the SIM surveys, respondents are asked to rank their purchasing power for the survey period, and before 1987. Five levels of purchasing power are specified: (1) can have money to pay utilities only (2) have money only for utilities and food; (3) have money for utilities, food and clothing; (4) can afford basic things (utility, food and clothing) and have some savings; (5) can afford luxury goods. In the analysis, we regroup the above into three groups by combining 3, 4, and 5 because of the small sample size for these levels.

4. Outcome indicators (1) and (4) are measured as an average predicted probability of a representative household to experience a drop in living standards and a worsening in access to medical services respectively. A probit model is used both to predict the average probability and to estimate the impact of the AZM-implemented social mitigation programs (using a program dummy variable to capture the program effect), controlling observable individual, household, and regional level covariates. The estimation results are presented in annex table 10A.2.

5. There are five key subcomponents in the overall social mitigation program implemented by the AZM agency: ETIS, microcredit, workspace center, enterprise support and workspace management (ESWM), and public information and social dialogue. Enterprises are invited to apply for relevant components (for example, ETIS, ESWM) and individuals for microcredit. The applicants are reviewed, verified and approved through well defined procedures involving both regional and central AZM offices.

6. For a profile of the six communities studies, see Table 5.1 in the Policy Note (World Bank 2005: 20). The six community-level background studies are available on file.

7. The reemployment probability is predicted based on a probit model that controls all individual, household, and region covariates, with the gender effect being captured by the gender dummy variable.

8. Some of the data supporting the findings are presented in the tables in annex 10A but the detailed arguments are in the reports for SIM data analysis (Dani et al. 2005).

9. It should be noted that higher wages in the mining sector might be a reflection of higher risks and poorer working conditions associated with mining activities.

10. The classification of stakeholders based on household labor market status is likely to be correlated with household socioeconomic characteristics, such as education and age, which are also the key determinants of household earning capacity. To check the robustness of estimated probability, the probit model is re-estimated controlling for these covariates. We find the estimated probabilities of experiencing a drop in living standards across all groups are robust to the different model specifications.

11. Among many issues associated with the survey design, which was undertaken by AZM's external consultants, the two most obvious deficiencies are (1) the questionnaire design for the annual surveys, in particular on employment status and AZM program awareness, are not consistent between the years 2001–2004; and (2) key outcome indicators (for example, reemployment status) used in the analysis were derived ex-post, and not well constructed when the questionnaire was designed.

12. SIM Annual SIM Reports (Hart Group 2001–4).

13. Mining sector workers accepting voluntary redundancy under Ordinance 22 (1997) were entitled to 12–20 months' wages, depending on length of service—much more than the national average of 6 months severance. Although severance was reduced in 2002, it is accompanied by 20–24 months additional wages as an incentive for early retirement.

14. The data from CNLO Targu Jiu have not been included in the analysis.

15. Romania, National Institute of Statistics, http://www.insse.ro/Indicatori/San_2004/eng/socindic_year2004.htm.

REFERENCES

AZM (National Agency for Development and Implementation of Reconstruction Programs in Mining Regions). June 2001–April 2005. *Quarterly Progress Reports.*

Dani, A., M. Rubin, D. Sandu, and L. Wang. 2005. "Evaluation of Social Programs in Mining Regions in Romania: Findings from SIM Survey 2001–2004." Bucharest: World Bank, January.

Fretwell, D. H. 2004. "Mitigating the Social Impact of Privatization and Enterprise Restructuring." Social Protection Discussion Paper 0405, Human Development Network, World Bank, Washington, DC.

Fretwell, D. H., and S. Wilson. 1999. "Public Service Employment: A Review of Programs in Selected OECD Countries and Transition Economies." Social Protection Discussion Paper 9913, World Bank, Washington, DC.

Government of Romania. 2002. *National Anti-Poverty and Social Inclusion Plan Concept*. Bucharest: Anti-Poverty and Social Inclusion Commission (CASPIS).

Haney, M., and M. Shkaratan. 2003. "Mine Closure and Its Impact on the Community: Five Years After Mine Closure in Romania, Russia and Ukraine." Social Development Discussion Paper 42, Social Development Department & Infrastructure and Energy Department for Europe and Central Asia, World Bank, Washington DC.

Hart Group, with Vienna Survey Centre and CURS SA. 2001. *Fourth Annual Social Impact Monitoring Report, for year 2000*. Bucharest, Ministry of Economy and Commerce, Government of Romania.

————. 2002. *Fourth Annual Social Impact Monitoring Report, for year 2001*. Bucharest, Ministry of Economy and Commerce, Government of Romania.

————. 2003a. *Fourth Annual Social Impact Monitoring Report, for year 2002*. Bucharest, Ministry of Economy and Commerce, Government of Romania.

————. 2003b. *Evaluation of the Employment and Training Incentives Scheme*. Bucharest, Ministry of Economy and Commerce, Government of Romania.

————. 2004. *Fourth Annual Social Impact Monitoring Report, for year 2003*. Bucharest, Ministry of Economy and Commerce, Government of Romania.

Kideckel, D. A. 2004. Miners and Wives in Romania's Jiu Valley: Perspectives on Postsocialist Class, Gender, and Social Change. *Identities* 1 (11) 39–63.

Koletsis, G. 2004. *Strengthening Cohesion and Lessons Learning within the Social Mitigation Project*. Bucharest. Report produced for Department for International Development (DfID) and National Agency for Development and Implementation of Reconstruction Programs in Mining Regions (AZM).

Larionescu, M., S. Rădulescu, and C. Rughiniș. 1999. *Cu ochii minerului*. Bucureşti: Gnosis. Translated from Social Assessment of Mining Sector Restructuring in Romania. Bucharest, LAMARASO Group, 1998.

Ministry of Economy and Commerce. 2004. *The National Strategy of the Mining Industry, 2004–2010*. Bucharest, Romania.

Pislaru, E., and C. Rughiniș. 2004. Gender Impact of Mining Sector Restructuring. Bucharest, Ministry of Economy and Commerce, Government of Romania, background paper.

Pop, S., B. Popa, and V. Goldberg. 2004. *Communities Regeneration Report*. Produced for Department for International Development (DfID) and National Agency for Development and Implementation of Reconstruction Programs in Mining Regions (AZM).

Rughiniș, C. 2001. "Mine Closure and its Impact on the Community: Five Years After Mine Closure in Romania, Russia and Ukraine." Background paper on Romania, Energy and Infrastructure Department, Europe and Central Asia Region, World Bank, Washington, DC.

Sandu, D., M. Constantinescu, A. Dusa, D. Nitulescu and M. Stanculescu. 2005. "Poverty and Social Impact Analysis of Mining Sector Reforms at Community Level in Romania: Synthesis Report." Background Paper for *Poverty and Social Impact Analysis of Mining Sector Reform in Romania,* World Bank, Washington, DC, May.

World Bank. 2003. *Romania Poverty Assessment* (in two volumes). Report No. 26169-RO. World Bank: Washington, DC.

————. 2004. *Mine Closure, Environmental and Socio-Economic Regeneration Project, Project Appraisal Document.* Report No. 30517-RO. World Bank: Washington, DC.

————. 2005. *Poverty and Social Impact Analysis of Mining Sector Reform in Romania.* Social Development Department, Policy Note. Report No. 32772-RO. World Bank: Washington, DC.

Econometric Models and Estimated Results

We present here the econometric models used for estimating the welfare impact of the mining sector reform, focusing mainly on change in purchasing power.

The welfare impact, measured by changes in purchasing power between 2001 and before 1997, is defined as a relative change in purchasing power. The three respective levels of purchasing power as defined in the questionnaire can be presented by A_t (can only afford utility), B_t (can afford utility and food), and C_t (can afford utility, food, and additional commodities), where t represents the two periods of 2001 and before 1997. The possibilities of changes in purchasing power can be summarized in the following matrix:

Period	A (only utility)	B (utility + food)	C (utility + food + other)
Before 1997	Z_{11}	Z_{12}	Z_{13}
2001	Z_{21}	Z_{22}	Z_{23}

The three outcomes for purchasing power for a household—(1) it increases, (2) it remains constant, and (3) it decreases—can be captured by combining the cells in the above matrix. If a household's responses for the two periods correspond to one of the combinations of (Z_{11}, Z_{22}), (Z_{11}, Z_{23}), or (Z_{12}, Z_{23}), then the household is defined as experiencing an improvement in living standards (that is, it has an increase in purchasing power between 2001 and 1997). No change in living standards corresponds to (Z_{11}, Z_{21}), (Z_{12}, Z_{22}), or (Z_{13}, Z_{23}); a reduction in living standards corresponds to (Z_{12}, Z_{21}), (Z_{13}, Z_{21}), or (Z_{13}, Z_{22}).

The ordered probit model is used to estimate the probability of the three outcomes, with the ordinal variable being defined as *decrease, no change,* and *increase.* The probability of observing outcome i is as follows:

$$\Pr(\text{outcome } i) = \Pr(k_{i-1} < \beta_1 x_{1j} + \beta_2 x_{2j} + \cdots + \beta_k x_{kj} + u_j < k_i), \quad (10.1)$$

where u_j is assumed to be normally distributed,
x is a vector of covariates, including individual, household, and regional level independent variables, and
$k_1 \, k_2, \ldots k_{I-1}$ are the cutoff points, with I being the number of possible outcomes.

The complete estimation results are presented in the annex tables 10A.1 and 10A.2.

The above model is applied to estimation of access to medical services, and assessment of life worthiness. The reemployment probability is estimated based the probit model.

The gender impact with regard to reemployment probability, change in living standards and access to medical services are derived from the coefficient of the female dummy variable included in the above models. It should be interpreted as the net impact on women controlling for all other covariates.

KEY ESTIMATION RESULTS

Table 10A.1 Estimation Results: 2001 SIM Data

Outcome variable Estimation method	A reduction in purchasing power (2001 vs. 1997) probit		A worsening in access to medical care (2001 vs. 1997) ordered probit		Often think life is not worth living ordered probit	
	Coef.	z	Coef.	z	Coef.	z
household head education						
1st cycle high school	0.11	0.66	−0.04	−0.15	0.42	1.59
vocational school	0.09	0.72	0.10	0.49	0.45	2.25
above high school	−0.23	−1.69	0.01	0.06	0.36	1.63
Ref: below 5–8 class						
spouse education						
5–8 class	−0.14	−0.77	−0.10	−0.36	0.33	1.28
1st cycle high school	−0.01	−0.05	−0.25	−0.79	0.09	0.31
vocational school	−0.21	−1.10	0.01	0.02	0.38	1.36
high school	−0.45	−2.35	0.12	0.40	0.86	3.02
College	−0.39	−1.41	−0.05	−0.11	0.68	1.53
higher education	−0.65	−2.55	0.29	0.81	1.56	3.40
age of household head	0.00	0.83	−0.01	−1.76	−0.01	−1.40
female (=1)	0.03	0.30	0.22	1.47	−0.26	−1.47
own land	−0.12	−1.27	0.32	2.46	0.03	0.20
region dummy						
Ploiesti	−0.29	−1.14	1.59	4.19	−2.19	−2.75
Comanesti	−0.24	−0.88	−1.68	−2.89	−4.09	−5.22
Voievozi	−1.12	−4.35	0.25	0.73	−2.96	−3.82
Rodna	−0.55	−1.99	0.37	1.01	−2.45	−3.08
Anina	−0.23	−0.88	0.32	0.76	−2.54	−3.16
Moldova Noua	−0.28	−1.00	−0.21	−0.49	−3.15	−4.05
Tg Jlu	−0.41	−1.97	0.63	2.18	−2.67	−3.56
Balan	−0.44	−1.65	0.76	2.36	−1.33	−1.60
Petrosani	−0.63	−3.01	0.08	0.26	−2.32	−3.08
Deva-Brad	−0.41	−1.80	1.24	3.57	−1.49	−1.87
Baia Mare	−0.44	−1.83	0.39	1.15	−2.66	−3.39
Baia Borsa	−0.11	−0.41	0.40	1.01	−3.04	−3.70
Gura Humorului	−0.19	−0.75	0.56	1.68	−1.16	−1.42
Reference: Alba						

Table 10A.1 Estimation Results: 2001 SIM Data (*Continued*)

Outcome variable Estimation method	A reduction in purchasing power (2001 vs. 1997) probit		A worsening in access to medical care (2001 vs. 1997) ordered probit		Often think life is not worth living ordered probit	
	Coef.	z	Coef.	z	Coef.	z
Occupation dummy						
mining sector	−0.03	−0.17	0.22	0.89	0.44	1.25
private sector	0.55	2.57	0.39	1.30	−0.29	−0.80
retired in mining	0.33	1.49	0.07	0.25	0.53	1.34
retired other sector	0.31	1.29	−0.13	−0.38	−0.25	−0.58
unemployed in mining	1.20	5.78	−0.22	−0.78	−1.02	−2.92
unemployed in other sector	1.21	4.14	0.23	0.55	−0.56	−0.99
house wife	0.58	2.76	−0.56	−1.85	−0.34	−0.97
Others	0.39	2.06	−0.05	−0.20	−0.31	−0.93
reference: SOE non–mining						
_cons	−0.06	−0.16				
_cut1 |			0.08		−4.26	
_cut2 |			2.19		−2.99	
Obs	1151		1151		1151	
Pseudo R^2	0.14		0.06		0.13	

Source: 2001 SIM survey.

Note: Due to sample size issue for purchasing power estimation, in the analysis we regrouped households into two groups: reduction versus no change in purchasing power and use the probit model. The three outcomes for medical service access are "worse than 1997," "no change," and "better than 1997." The outcomes for "often think life is not worth living" include "often think so," "sometimes think so," and "do not think so."

Table 10A.2 Reemployment Probability: Probit Model Estimation

Explanatory variables	2001		2002		2003	
	Coef.	*z*	*Coef.*	*z*	*Coef.*	*z*
household head						
Age	−0.03	−0.27	0.13	0.84	−0.08	−0.71
age sq	0.00	−0.25	0.00	−1.16	0.00	0.42
female (=1)	−1.01	−3.79	−0.72	−2.66	−0.49	−1.89
own land	0.24	1.13	−0.06	−0.24	−0.55	−2.28
household head education						
1st cycle high school	−0.25	−0.67	0.06	0.12	0.54	1.13
vocational school	−0.04	−0.13	0.65	1.40	0.31	0.78
above high school	0.40	1.31	0.83	1.69	0.21	0.54
Ref: below 5–8 class						
locality with AZM program (=1)	−0.08	−1.97	0.04	0.16	0.34	1.19
region dummy						
Ploiesti	0.09	0.16	1.14	1.38	−0.10	−0.13
Comanesti	0.86	0.76	−0.17	−0.19	0.38	0.46
Voievozi	0.82	1.27	0.22	0.20	−0.46	−0.55
Rodna	0.67	0.90	0.33	0.40	−0.51	−0.68
Anina	0.52	0.47	0.03	0.04	−0.34	−0.49
Moldova Noua	0.79	0.99	−0.53	−0.49	−0.76	−0.75
Tg Jlu	1.00	0.97	−0.07	−0.10	−0.11	−0.16
Balan	3.35	3.11	0.68	0.90	0.33	0.45
Petrosani	2.13	1.81	0.05	0.06	0.07	0.09
Deva-Brad	2.05	1.63	−0.19	−0.20	0.14	0.18
Baia Mare	2.57	1.80	0.74	0.95		
_cons	1.33	0.66	−2.20	−0.75	2.09	0.84
Obs	266		166		176	
Pseudo R^2	0.23		0.20		0.15	

Source: 2001–3 SIM surveys.

11

GHANA
Evaluating the Fiscal and Social Costs of Increases in Domestic Fuel Prices

DAVID COADY AND DAVID NEWHOUSE

R ecent increases in international oil prices have resulted in substantial fuel subsidies in many developing and emerging market economies. After a long period of stability over the last two decades, international oil prices increased substantially from 2002. Prices increased from around US$25 per barrel in January 2003 to over US$65 per barrel by August 2005, an increase of about 260 percent. Rising fuel subsidies reflect the fact that many countries regulate domestic prices and, especially in the face of sharp price increases, do not pass on higher world prices to domestic consumers.[1]

These subsidies have adverse consequences both for government finances and the efficient use of energy. Large subsidies redirect public expenditures away from other valuable social expenditures or contribute to unsustainable budget deficits. Low energy prices fail to provide the appropriate incentive to households to be more efficient in their use of energy, which would help to mitigate the adverse effect of higher international prices on households and the economy. In fact, given the relatively low price elasticity of energy demand and the negative consumption externalities associated with its use, taxing energy consumption is generally regarded as an efficient way of raising government revenue.

A key motivation behind such price subsidies is to protect the real incomes of households, especially poor households. However, it is also the case that energy subsidies may not be a very cost-effective approach to protecting the real incomes of poor households and that large cost savings can be provided through the use of better-targeted subsidies, transfers, or other social expenditures. Therefore a comprehensive evaluation of energy price reforms must explicitly incorporate both the range of alternative social protection mechanisms that could be used and other public expenditures that could be financed from the budgetary savings resulting from the reduction or elimination of fuel subsidies.

Over the course of 2004–5, for a number of countries, the Poverty and Social Impact Analysis (PSIA) Group at the International Monetary Fund (IMF) evaluated the fiscal and social implications of domestic fuel price increases. In this chapter we present the analysis undertaken for Ghana, which was the first of the evaluations undertaken by the group.[2] The format of the chapter is as follows. In order to provide some general insights into the PSIA process and to motivate our approach to PSIA in the present context, in the second section we briefly describe the policy background and timeline of the analysis and how the IMF engaged with the government and other stakeholders during its execution. In the following section we describe the methodology used to evaluate the likely real income effects of price increases and present the model used to calculate these effects. The methodology employed reflects the tradeoff between modeling complexity and resource requirements and the need for a timely policy analysis that informed policy decisions that were to be taken in the very short term. In the fourth section we briefly set out the structure of the petroleum sector and the background to the proposed price reforms. In the fifth section we present the results of our application of the model to evaluate the effect of higher domestic petroleum prices in Ghana. Special emphasis is given to the identification of alternative approaches to mitigating the adverse effects on the real incomes of low-income households as well as identifying alternative public expenditures that could be financed by the budgetary savings resulting from the elimination of fuel subsidies. In the next section we conclude by summarizing the general policy lessons from the evaluations, emphasizing the limitations of using fuel subsidies to protect the real incomes of low-income households. We also discuss the policy responses of the government subsequent to the analysis. Finally, we highlight some lessons for the PSIA process and the importance of recognizing the tradeoffs that need to be incorporated in practice when determining the nature and role of PSIA.

BACKGROUND

Reform of the petroleum sector has been an important component of the IMF-supported Poverty Reduction and Growth Facility (PRGF) program in Ghana (IMF 2004). A combination of low government-controlled petroleum prices and operational inefficiencies has continually resulted in large quasi-fiscal deficits and sector debt in this country. The cost of petroleum subsidies reached 2 percent of GDP in 2002, and in January 2003 the government introduced a pricing formula linking domestic prices to world prices, resulting in an average increase in domestic prices of approximately 90 percent.[3] However, the formula had been effectively abandoned and further increases in world prices were not passed onto consumers: the total subsidy bill in 2004 reached 2.2 percent of GDP. Faced with rising budgetary costs, in early 2005 the government announced that it intended to introduce a new pricing formula. Concerns about the adverse effect of higher domestic prices on the real incomes of poor households led the government to request the IMF to provide technical assistance to evaluate the likely magnitude of these effects and to identify measures to help mitigate them.

In early January 2005, the PSIA Group at the IMF began working on an ex-ante evaluation of the likely impact of higher domestic petroleum prices on household real incomes and how these would be distributed across the population. Particular emphasis was placed on the need to identify this probable impact on the real incomes of the poorest households as well as on identifying alternative approaches to mitigating these effects. Existing PSIA reports on the petroleum sector had focused on the sources and uses of energy and broader structural reforms of the sector (Armah and Associates 2004; Mercados et al. 2004), but little detail had been provided on the magnitude of the likely real income effects from price increases or on the alternative approaches that could be used to mitigate the adverse effects on poor households. For this reason, the government felt unable to proceed with price reforms until such information was available.

Prior to visiting Ghana, the PSIA Group worked very closely with the country teams both at the IMF (including its resident representative in Ghana) and at the World Bank. Through a number of meetings over a period of three weeks the group was able to clarify the policy background and issues, to identify existing reports related to proposed government reforms in the petroleum sector, and to identify and gain access to the data necessary to undertake the analysis.[4] The group also contacted various academic economists who had previously worked on economic analyses in Ghana and also had information on important stakeholders.[5] The U.K. Department for International Development, which has a very active engagement with the government and other policy actors and stakeholders, also provided valuable information and was kept informed of progress with the report. By being able to secure quick access to many of the data prior to visiting Ghana, the group was in a position to undertake a preliminary analysis that would help to identify key gaps in terms of their knowledge of the policy background and further data requirements. This facilitated the scheduling of important meetings with government and other stakeholders during the first few days of trip to Ghana.

In late January 2005 the PSIA Group sent a technical assistance mission to Ghana, made up of the two authors of this chapter. The first few days of the trip were allocated to prescheduled meetings with various government departments and other stakeholders. Meetings with government officials from the Ministry of Finance and the Central Bank helped to clarify the policy context for the analysis and issues they saw as crucial to address in the report. Meetings with the Ministries of Education and Health helped to identify alternative uses of some of the budgetary savings from eliminating energy subsidies and their likely effectiveness at mitigating the adverse impacts of price increases on poor households. Meetings with the Ministry of Energy provided a clearer picture of energy requirements and sources in Ghana as well as broader energy-related policies. A meeting with the Ghana Statistics Service helped to identify data that could be used for the analysis. With all of these government departments we highlighted and discussed the importance of having access to reliable, up-to-date data for credible and relevant policy analysis more generally. A common emphasis by each of the ministries, as well as by stakeholders outside of government, was the importance of identifying in the report measures to mitigate the adverse impact of price rises on the poor.

Extensive discussions were also held with various policy actors, including the Institute of Statistical Social and Economic Research (ISSER) and the Centre for Economic Policy Analysis (CEPA).[6] We also met the authors of an existing study of petroleum use by households (Armah and Associates 2004) as well as the authors of a study on structural reforms in the petroleum sector in Ghana (Mercados et al. 2004). With each of these stakeholders we discussed the purpose of our report and the details of the methodological approach we would use.

Before leaving the country, the results of a preliminary analysis were presented at a meeting organized by the Ministry of Finance at which a number of the above stakeholders were present. We discussed a range of issues that arose during the discussion and how we would try to address these in a future revised version of the report. Based on comments received at this presentation, the report was revised and reviewed at the IMF headquarters. The revised report was completed by mid-March 2005 and sent to the government in May 2005. Permission to circulate the report widely was received from the government in early July 2005. Since then the PSIA

Group has continually monitored the progress in price reforms and the implementation of mitigating measures to ensure that the findings of the report are integrated into the PRGF program.

APPROACH AND UNDERLYING MODEL

This section sets out the details of the approach used to evaluate the likely impact of increases in petroleum prices on the real incomes of households as well as the approach to identifying alternative measures that help mitigate the associated adverse effects on household real incomes. The approach adopted reflects the necessity to trade off modeling sophistication against data and time resources (see Coady 2005 for more detailed discussion on methodologies). However, we believe that the approach taken provides extremely valuable quantitative information for the policy debate, especially when nuanced through a more qualitative discussion of broader policy implications.

Typically the bulk of total petroleum products is not consumed directly by households but indirectly through their consumption of other goods and services that use petroleum products as inputs. Therefore, the welfare effect of higher petroleum prices on household real incomes will depend both on the *direct effect* of higher prices for petroleum products consumed by households and on the *indirect effect* arising from higher prices for other goods and services consumed by households to the extent that higher petroleum costs are passed on to consumer prices.

Modeling the direct effect, and how it is distributed across income groups, essentially requires information on the level of direct consumption of various petroleum products (for example, gasoline, kerosene, diesel, LPG) by households in different parts of the national income distribution. Modeling the indirect effect requires a model of price-shifting behavior. We start by describing the model underlying our calculation of the price effects resulting from the increase in the price of petroleum products, which are intermediate as well as final goods. This is followed by a discussion of how the resulting price changes can be translated into changes in real income and used as the basis for an analysis of the distributional impact of price changes.

A Price-Shifting Model

To analyze the distributional consequences of price changes for commodities that are intermediate goods one needs to specify a price-shifting model that allows one to identify how higher petroleum costs are shifted on to prices in other sectors of the economy. The implications of higher costs for output or factor prices will, of course, depend on the structure of the economy—for example, whether commodities are traded internationally or nontraded, the nature of commodity taxes, and whether prices are controlled by the government. We therefore start by grouping commodities into three broad classifications reflecting the assumed relationships between higher production costs and output prices:

- **Cost-Push Sectors.** These are sectors where higher input costs are pushed fully on to output prices. We can therefore (loosely) think of these as nontraded commodities (for example, government services, public utilities, construction, trade and transportation, and retail and wholesale trade).
- **Traded Sectors.** These are sectors that compete with internationally traded goods and that have output prices determined by world prices and the import or export tax regime. Therefore, higher input costs are not pushed forward onto output prices, so the brunt of these higher costs is borne by lower factor prices or lower profits.
- **Controlled Sectors.** These are sectors where output prices are controlled by the government. The relationship between output prices and production costs depends on if and how the government adjusts controlled prices. If controlled prices are not adjusted, then the burden of higher costs will be borne by factor prices, profits, or government revenue.

When modeling *price changes* it is useful to think of "aggregate" commodity categories (for example, the aggregate categories available from an input-output table) as made up of a certain proportion of cost-push, traded, and controlled commodities, with these proportions given by α, β, and γ respectively. These proportions should obviously sum to unity and never be negative, that is, $0 \leq (\alpha, \beta, \gamma) \leq 1$ and $\alpha + \beta + \delta = 1$. The technology of domestic firms is captured by a standard input-output coefficient matrix, A, with typical a_{ij} denoting the cost of input i in producing one unit of output j—think of units of output defined such that they have a user price of unity so that price changes below can be interpreted as percentage changes. Consistent with the interpretation of A as capturing an underlying Leontief (that is, fixed coefficient) production technology, we can interpret a_{ij}s as the change in the cost of producing a unit of j due to a unit change in the price of input i.

For *traded* sectors, user prices, q^*, are determined by world prices, p^w, and by trade taxes (including tariffs and sales taxes), t^*:

$$q^* = p^w + t^* \tag{11.1}$$

In this sense, foreign goods are deemed to be perfectly competitive with domestically produced traded goods. Changes in the user prices for traded sectors are then given by

$$\Delta q^* = \Delta p^w + \Delta t^* \qquad (11.2)$$

and both terms on the right-hand side will be specified exogenously by the reform package under consideration.

For *controlled* sectors, producer prices are determined by pricing controls (say, $\tilde{p}$) and we can think of domestic taxes as zero for convenience, so that

$$\tilde{q} = \tilde{p} \qquad (11.3)$$

Alternatively, one could think of the difference between user prices and average unit production costs as an implicit tax. The formula for price changes is then given simply as

$$\Delta \tilde{q} = \Delta \tilde{p} \qquad (11.4)$$

where the right-hand side is specified exogenously in the reform package.

For *cost-push* sectors, the relationship between user and producer prices is given by

$$q^c = p^c + t^c \qquad (11.5)$$

where q^c is the price paid by users of a commodity and p^c is the price received by producers, the difference between these being any sales or excise taxes, t^c, imposed by the government. Producer prices are, in turn, determined as follows:

$$p^c = p^c(q,w) \qquad (11.6)$$

where q are the user costs of intermediate inputs and w are factor prices. For these sectors, cost increases are assumed to be fully pushed forward onto user prices so that factor payments are fixed. From (11.5) one gets

$$\Delta q^c = \Delta p^c + \Delta t^c \qquad (11.7)$$

Using (11.6), the input-output coefficient matrix and assuming factor prices are fixed, and the change in producer prices is derived as

$$\Delta p^c = \Delta q^c.\alpha.A + \Delta q^*.\beta.A + \Delta \tilde{p}.\gamma.A \qquad (11.8)$$

where Δ signifies a price change, all price changes are interpreted as $n \times 1$ row vectors where n is the number of commodity groups, (α, β, γ) are now $n \times 1$ diagonal matrices, and A is an $n \times n$ input-output coefficient matrix. Substituting in from (11.7) and (11.2) one gets

$$\Delta p^c = \Delta p^c . \alpha . A + \Delta t^c . \alpha . A + \Delta p^w \beta . A + \Delta t^* . \beta . A + \Delta \tilde{p} . \gamma . A$$

so that

$$\Delta p^c = \Delta t^c . \alpha . A . V + \Delta p^w . \beta . A . V + \Delta t^* . \beta . A . V + \Delta \tilde{p} . \gamma . A . V \qquad (11.9)$$

where $V = (I - \alpha . A)^{-1}$ with I being an $n \times n$ identity matrix. The typical element of the inverse matrix V, v_{ij}, captures the combined direct and indirect use of cost-push sector i used to produce one unit of cost-push sector j. Notice that if the only price changes are changes in controlled prices, then we have $\Delta t^c = \Delta p^w = \Delta t^* = 0$ so that the final term of (11.9) gives the effect on cost-push sectors of a change in these controlled prices and also $\Delta q^c = \Delta p^c$. The change in sector aggregate prices is then given by

$$\Delta q = \alpha . \Delta q^c + \beta . \Delta q^* + \gamma . \Delta \tilde{q}. \qquad (11.10)$$

In our applications below we assume that all petroleum products are within the controlled sector and all other products are cost-push sectors. Given that the nontraded domestic trade and transport sectors are the main consumers of petroleum products and the effect on traded good prices would come through this component, this assumption is likely to be a good approximation of reality.

Applying the Model

Applying the model to an evaluation of the likely real income effect of petroleum price increases and its distribution across different income groups requires two sets of data. First, one requires information on consumption patterns across households, including direct household consumption of petroleum products (for example, consumption of gasoline, diesel, liquid petroleum gas and kerosene). Typically one finds very different consumption patterns for petroleum products across households with, for example, low-income households allocating a relatively high proportion of total consumption to the consumption of kerosene and a relatively low share to gasoline. Note that one should validate how adequately consumption of petroleum products is captured by the household survey used, for example, by dividing total consumption expenditures for each product by the price pertaining at the survey date to get physical quantities and by comparing total physical consumption to secondary data on aggregate national consumption.

Second, one needs information on the production structure of various sectors of the economy—that is, an input-output matrix showing the use of various sectoral inputs in the production of sectoral outputs, in particular information on the use of petroleum products as inputs by various sectors. Often one has information only for an aggregate amount of petroleum product inputs, that is, the data are not broken down into different petroleum products. In this case one can try to use secondary information to disaggregate these sectors, which involves disaggregating the petroleum product inputs for each sector in the economy as well as disaggregating the petroleum product technology by product type. Alternatively, one can undertake the analysis of indirect price effects using an aggregate petroleum price change while using the disaggregated information available in the household data to evaluate the direct effect for each petroleum product separately.

Using information on the likely increases in petroleum product prices one can use (11.10) to evaluate the impact on consumer prices for the range of sectors available in the input-output table. One then maps the detailed consumption information available in the household data into the input-output sectors to get the budget shares for each commodity category and for each household. Multiplying the budget shares for each commodity category by the corresponding price increase for that commodity gives the percentage change in household real income that is the result of that specific price increase. One can then calculate separately the direct effect by aggregating these real income changes across petroleum products and the indirect effect by aggregating these real income changes across all other commodities. To analyze the distribution of these real income effects one can categorize households by income groups—typically this is based on some household consumption measure such as per capita consumption or consumption per adult equivalent—and, for each income group, look at the average of the real income effect as a percentage of total household income. The direct and indirect effects are added to get the total effect. Where the percentage loss in real income increases (decreases) with household income, the distribution of the total burden is said to be progressive (regressive).

Alternative Mitigating Measures

Since a key motivation for energy subsidies is to protect the real incomes of poor households, it is important to identify alternative approaches to achieving these ends and to compare these to the situation under energy subsidies. Below we consider the following range of alternatives:

■ maintaining kerosene subsidies,
■ using some of the budgetary savings from eliminating subsidies to finance the introduction or expansion of a cash or in-kind transfer program, and
■ using these savings to finance other increases in social expenditures.

The first of these options essentially involves analyzing alternative reforms of energy prices. The last two options can typically be evaluated using information available in household surveys on access to existing transfer programs or existing utilization patterns of other social services such as education and health services. Alternatively one can simulate hypothetical targeted transfer programs in order to highlight the potential returns from introducing such programs or reforming badly targeted existing programs. Note that even if the distribution of existing subsidy benefits is progressive, in the sense that the benefit as a percentage of household incomes is higher for lower income groups (that is, lower income groups receive more than their income share), the subsidies can be badly targeted because the lower income groups receive less than their population share. The policy objective then is to identify alternative and better-targeted programs to protect the real incomes of poor households.

How a government goes about choosing from among these alternatives will, of course, depend as much on political economy issues as on pure economic considerations. Successful packaging of the subsidy removals with one of the above approaches can play a crucial role in generating acceptance of the reforms by the public and avoiding social conflict. A successful reform strategy is likely to generate substantial efficiency gains by providing appropriate price incentives for more efficient use of petroleum products as well as by providing the funds necessary to increase other development and social expenditures.

In this chapter, we are primarily (although not exclusively) concerned with evaluating the distributional implications of petroleum subsidies. Our evaluation focuses on the first-order income effects of price changes—that is, it implicitly assumes that demand and budget shares are fixed. Where households can avoid taxation by switching between commodities, these first-order effects will tend to overestimate the adverse income losses from price increases (Banks, Blundell, and Lewbel 1996). Therefore, our estimates below should be interpreted as upper bounds on the magnitude of income effects. Note, however, that to the extent that responses are similar across income groups, our evaluation of the distributional implications of price changes is likely to be more robust. Our focus on first-order effects reflects the combination of data and time constraints that typically face policy analysts.

THE PETROLEUM SECTOR AND PRICE REFORMS

In this section we apply the approach described above to evaluate the impact of increases in petroleum products on household real incomes for Ghana. We start with a brief discussion of the structure of the petroleum sector and the structure and magnitude of the proposed price reforms. We then present the results in terms of the direct, indirect, and total real income effects and how these are distributed across households in different parts of the national income distribution. This presentation is followed by a discussion of alternative approaches to protecting the real incomes of poor households, which can be used to mitigate the adverse poverty effects of price increases. We conclude with a discussion on policy implications of the analysis.

The Petroleum Sector and Price Reforms

Petroleum products constitute around 30 percent of total energy demand in Ghana (ISSER 2004). The total supply of petroleum products in Ghana was 1.64 million metric tons in 2003, of which diesel accounted for 50 percent, gasoline 32 percent, and kerosene 10 percent. The transport sector is the main consumer of petroleum products, accounting for over 80 percent of total consumption in 2003. Households accounted for 6.2 percent, industry 6.7 percent, and agriculture 4.2 percent. In general, household use of petroleum products is generally restricted to the use of LPG and kerosene for cooking and lighting, respectively.

Ghana has little domestic supply of crude oil; most of its crude oil demand is met by imports from Nigeria. In September 1996, the state-owned Tema Oil Refinery (TOR) acquired sole responsibility for importing crude oil and refined petroleum products into Ghana. TOR is able to meet only around 70 percent of Ghana's demand for petroleum products. The domestic supply of petroleum products is supplemented with imports from Europe. Both imported and domestically produced petroleum products are stored at TOR's refining facilities for further domestic distribution. In 2004, imports of refined products stood at 153,000 metric tons of diesel and 85,000 metric tons of premium gasoline.

Liberalization of the petroleum sector is currently underway to allow private sector participation in the procurement of crude oil as well as the private import of refined products through tenders. Since the beginning of 2004, TOR ceased to have a monopoly on the importation of petroleum products, and from July 2004 it has been prohibited from importing petroleum products. In March 2004, private oil marketing companies (OMCs) participated in the first competitive tender for gasoline with financing provided by a syndicate of banks. The National Petroleum Tender Board (NPTB) arranges for procurement of crude oil for TOR through international competitive bidding. Eventually, it is intended that only the OMCs will be allowed to import both crude oil and petroleum products; TOR will be converted to a tolling refinery that operates and maintains the refining facility and processes crude oil for a fee. There are currently 26 OMCs, but four of them (Shell, Mobil, Total, and GOIL) control over 80 percent of the market. GOIL, which has an obligation to supply products in all outlying and remote areas, is the only state-owned company distributing oil products and has a market share of around 23 percent.

According to the new formula being discussed by the government, domestic ex-pump prices were to be linked to world prices adjusted for international and domestic distribution costs but also including various taxes and levies. The cost, insurance, and freight (CIF) world price is taken as the sum of the free on board (FOB) Mediterranean price (averaged for the previous three Platt's Oligram Price Report calendar months), the suppliers commission, and insurance costs. Import margins are set to cover the costs of getting imports from the port to TOR facilities and set at 13.8 percent of the import CIF price. Taxes and levies include a 15 percent ad valorem excise tax levied on the CIF price, specific excises, a road fund levy, an energy fund levy, an exploration levy, a stock fund levy, and a debt-recovery levy. The domestic distribution margin includes the cost of bulk storage and transportation services, a primary distribution margin, a margin that equalizes domestic prices across the country, a dealers margin, and a marketing margin.[7]

Current ex-pump prices are substantially below those required by the above formula. Table 11.1 compares actual (A) to formula (F) prices for the various petroleum products, and indicates the required increase in prices under the formula. Although all products are currently heavily subsidized *relative to the formula price,* which includes taxes, the extent of the subsidy varies substantially across products. The required increases are highest for LPG and diesel (at 108 percent and 67 percent, respectively) and lowest for premium gasoline and kerosene (at 17 percent and 49 percent, respectively).

Table 11.1 Actual and Formula Petroleum Product Prices and Subsidies
Ghanaian cedis

Components of formula	Petrol per liter	Kerosene per liter	Diesel per liter	Fuel Oil per liter	LPG per kilogram
World CIF price (F)	2,890	3,761	3,884	1,750	5,355
Total taxes (F)	1,711	1,342	1,811	1,141	1,543
Domestic margins	577	677	577	0	990
Ex-pump price (F)	5,179	5,780	5,940	2,891	7,888
Ex-pump price (A)	4,444	3,889	3,556	1,927	3,800
Required increase in current prices	17 percent	49 percent	67 percent	50 percent	108 percent

Source: Ministry of Finance, Ghana.
Note: A and F denote that prices are based on actual and formula levels, respectively. Ex-refinery price F is based on an average of Platt prices for October–December 2004, an exchange rate of 9,133.33 cedis per U.S. dollar and import margins at 13.8 percent of import CIF price. Included in taxes is an ad valorem excise set at 15 percent of the ex-refinery price.

The Welfare Impact of Price Increases

Determining the total impact of price increases on the welfare of poor households requires one to identify both the direct impact from the higher fuel prices paid by households as well as the indirect impact from higher prices for other goods and services when higher fuel costs are passed through to these prices. We discuss each in turn.

Direct Impact

The top panel of table 11.2 presents the budget shares of households by welfare quintile for petrol, kerosene, and LPG. The highest budget share is for kerosene—on average, households allocate 3.5 percent of total consumption to kerosene consumption; this is higher for lower-income households. Petroleum consumption is also an important consumption item for households in the top quintile, where it accounts for just over 2 percent of total consumption.

The second panel of table 11.2 presents the direct effect on households of the planned price increases if the pricing formula were applied. For each household, the budget share of each petroleum product is multiplied by the percentage price increase to get the equivalent percentage change in household real income. These are then aggregated across products and divided by total household consumption to get the total percentage decrease in household real income. On average, households experience a 1.9 percent decline in real income. The incidence of this

Table 11.2 Real Income Effects and Share of the Burden of Price Changes

Budget shares, income effect, and burden shares	Bottom	2nd Quintile	3rd Quintile	4th Quintile	Top	All
Household budget share (item expenditure/total expenditure)						
Petrol	0.001	0.001	0.002	0.002	0.021	0.006
Kerosene	0.059	0.041	0.034	0.024	0.016	0.035
LPGas	0	0	0	0.001	0.002	0.001
Real income effect (percentage change in consumption)						
Direct effect	0.029	0.020	0.017	0.013	0.014	0.019
Indirect effect	0.062	0.066	0.067	0.069	0.068	0.067
Total effect	0.091	0.087	0.085	0.082	0.082	0.085
Indirect as percent of total	68 percent	77 percent	80 percent	84 percent	83 percent	80 percent
Share of the aggregate loss (household loss/total loss)						
Direct effect	0.135	0.160	0.180	0.193	0.332	1.000
Indirect effect	0.077	0.137	0.184	0.256	0.346	1.000
Total effect	0.088	0.142	0.184	0.244	0.343	1.000
Mean consumption (Ratio to bottom quintile)	1.00	1.76	2.55	3.80	7.48	3.31

Source: Authors' estimates.
Note: Quintiles are based on the national per equivalent adult consumption distribution. Budget shares are calculated using data from the Ghana Living Standards Survey (GLSS) 1999. Expenditures on petroleum products have been increased to reflect the substantial increase in their real prices between 1999 and 2004, and total consumption has also been adjusted accordingly. Percentage real income effects are calculated by multiplying household budget shares by the price increases presented in table 11.1, aggregating across petroleum products and dividing by household total consumption. Mean consumption is based on per adult equivalent consumption.

decrease is regressive in the sense that the poorest households are worst hit, experiencing a 2.9 percent decrease in real income, compared with a 1.4 percent decrease for households in the top consumption quintile.

The bottom panel of table 11.2 translates these percentage changes into the share of the aggregate direct real income loss borne by each quintile. We find that the top two quintiles account for around 53 percent of the total loss while the bottom two quintiles account for less than 30 percent of the aggregate loss.

Indirect Impact

Table 11.3 presents the impact of higher petroleum prices on the prices in other sectors. Multiplying these price increases by the corresponding household budget shares and aggregating across goods and services gives

Table 11.3 Indirect Price and Real Income Effects by Sector

Sector	(Budget share (item expenditure/ total expenditure) BS	Price effect (proportionate (increase in prices) dP	Impact = BS*dP
Agriculture	0.452	0.066	0.030
Utilities and mining	0.021	0.116	0.002
Manufacturing	0.253	0.052	0.013
Construction	0.000	0.107	0.000
Trade	0.070	0.107	0.007
Transport	0.032	0.267	0.008
Business	0.025	0.025	0.001
Community	0.097	0.048	0.005
Electricity	0.008	0.000	0.000

Source: Authors' estimates.

Note: Budget shares are derived from GLSS 1999 based on commodity groupings that match the more aggregated input-output table sectoral breakdown available in the 1993 Social Accounting Matrix for Ghana constructed by Powell and Round (1998). Petroleum products are separated from the Manufacturing sector, creating separate entries for five different petroleum product categories: Diesel, Petrol, Liquid Petroleum Gas, Residual Fuel Oil, and Kerosene. The relevant coefficients on individual fuel types were based on information on fuel usage in different sectors available in ISSER (2004). The single Electricity and Mining sector was separated into "Utilities and Mining" and "Electricity" components to allow for the fact that the price of electricity is controlled by the government.

the percentage decrease in consumption due to the indirect price increases. The total indirect real income effect is also presented in table 11.2. On average, indirect price increases decrease household real income by 6.7 percent. These losses are moderately progressive, with the bottom quintile experiencing a 6.2 percent decrease in consumption compared with 6.8 percent for the top quintile. The bottom panel of table 11.2 translates these percentage changes into the share of the aggregate real income loss borne by each quintile. Reflecting their share of total petroleum product consumption, the top two quintiles account for over 60 percent of the total loss whereas the bottom two quintiles account for just over 20 percent of the loss.

Direct and Indirect Impacts

In the second panel of table 11.2, the direct and indirect effects are combined into the total effect. Overall, the average effect is substantial, with the removal of petroleum subsidies resulting in an 8.5 percent decrease in real income. The incidence of this burden is slightly regressive, with the bottom quintile experiencing a decrease of 9.1 percent compared with an 8.2 percent decrease for the top quintile. On average, the indirect effect accounts for 80 percent of the total effect. It is also noticeable that the share of the indirect effect is lowest for the poorest households, accounting for 68 percent of the total effect for the lowest quintile compared with 83 percent for the top quintile.

The bottom panel of table 11.2 translates these percentage effects into the share of the real income loss borne by each quintile. The relatively high share borne by the top two quintiles reflects the same patterns observed for both indirect and direct effects earlier. The top two quintiles account for just below 60 percent of the total loss, compared with 23 percent for the bottom two quintiles. Of course, this also highlights the fact that the benefits from the existing subsidies are very badly targeted, with enormous leakage to higher income households.

Alternative Mitigating Approaches

The above results show that although the direct effect of the removal of petroleum price subsidies looks regressive, with the percentage decrease in income being highest for the poorest quintiles, this effect is dominated by the indirect effect, which is slightly progressive. The total loss from the removal of price subsidies is, thus, only slightly regressive. However, more important from the perspective of poverty reduction is the magnitude of the impact on the poorest households. Our results indicate that the effect for the poorest households is substantial, with the poorest quintile experiencing a 9.1 percent decrease in real income.

Although price subsidies are often justified as a way of protecting the real incomes of poor households, the results above clearly indicate that a very small share of either the total direct or indirect benefits inherent in the price subsidies reach the poorest households, with substantial leakage to higher-income households. It is important therefore to consider alternative approaches to protecting the incomes of the poor, which can be used to mitigate the adverse impacts of petroleum subsidy removal on the poorest households. One can think of a range of approaches, including:

■ *Differential petroleum taxes.* Instead of increasing all petroleum prices to world prices and applying the present system of taxes, one could adjust the taxes so that those products that are more important for the poorest households are taxed at a lower rate or even subsidized. In the present context, this would involve lower price increases for kerosene, which is by far the most important petroleum product directly consumed by the poor.

■ *Increase expenditures on social services.* Some of the public funds generated through subsidy savings can be used to increase social expenditures on such things as public education, health, and nutrition services. The relative impact of these expenditures on the poor will depend on such things as the existing level of access of the poor to these services, and whether these expenditures can be targeted to the poor through, for example, expansion of services into the poorest areas.

■ *Increase "related" expenditures.* A key policy issue concerns the issue of access to clean and affordable energy by the poor. Often the poor have to rely on unclean fuels with adverse consequences for their health and environmental degradation. Similarly, the poor often lack access to efficient public transport or quality roads. Higher fuel prices may thus further exacerbate the situation. To address this, some of the budgetary savings generated by subsidy removal could be used to finance expenditures aimed at improving mass transport systems in urban areas, or the rural roads system, or an intensification of the rural electrification scheme. The transport sector is the most energy-intensive sector, so improving access to efficient transport services can help to mitigate the effects of increases in the prices of petroleum products. Similarly, electricity is typically a cheaper and cleaner source of energy than petroleum-based fuels for households.

■ *Targeted social protection programs.* The budgetary savings of removing or reducing subsidies could be used to increase financing for an existing social protection program or to create a new targeted program.

In order to evaluate the above alternatives we use information in the national household survey for 1999 (GLSS 1999). For education expenditures, we identify households that have children aged 5–11 years enrolled in school and give a uniform transfer to each of these households. Using existing access as the basis for determining transfers can be interpreted as an expansion of existing education expenditures, and thus it captures the "average benefit incidence" of education expenditures. However, there apparently have been some attempts to target additional expenditures better toward the poorest areas of the country so that the incidence of expenditures allocated to expanding these schemes may be substantially more progressive that the average benefit incidence of all existing expenditures—that is, the "marginal benefit incidence" of public expenditures may be substantially better than the average benefit incidence. In education, the concept of capitation grants has been introduced since September 2004 in 40 of the most deprived districts in the country (out of a total of 138 districts).[8] To evaluate the likely distributional impact of this program we use information on the districts currently participating in the scheme and identify beneficiary households as those with children in primary school.[9]

A similar procedure was followed to determine which households would receive health subsidies based on existing access patterns in all districts as well as the same targeted districts. The Community Health Compound scheme targets areas without basic health facilities, constructs health compounds in these areas, and provides a community nurse, basic infrastructure, training, and basic transport. This scheme also targets communities in the poorest 40 districts.

We also simulate the likely incidence of expenditures on rural electrification and urban transport programs. For rural electrification, we identify villages in the sample in which no household reported using electricity as their main source of lighting and evaluated the incidence of giving a uniform transfer to all households residing in these villages. This simulation can be interpreted as capturing the marginal benefit incidence of expenditures on rural electrification. To simulate the average benefit incidence of a transportation subsidy, the analysis gives a transfer to urban households in proportion to their expenditure on intra-city bus transport.

Finally, we simulate the benefit incidence from a program that identifies beneficiaries through a proxy-means algorithm based on a consumption model, with 30 percent of households with the lowest predicted consumption receiving a uniform transfer. Since the transfer could be either in cash or consist of health, education, energy, or other subsidies, this program can be interpreted as an alternative approach which could be used to improve expenditure targeting.[10] It may be that one can achieve better incidence outcomes using a more sophisticated statistical approach than the one used here, or by combining proxy-means targeting with other targeting methods. However, one should also recognize that the proxy-means outcomes evaluated implicitly assume perfect implementation, when in practice we know that implementation effectiveness is as important as design in determining the actual performance of programs.[11]

Table 11.4 presents the distribution of transfers across income quintiles for each of the transfers programs. In the case of kerosene subsidies, only 39 percent (that is, 17.8 percent plus 21.1 percent) of transfers go to the poorest 40 percent of households. This targeting performance is dominated by all of the other transfer programs considered with the exception of health subsidies. Below we focus solely on the targeted education transfer (where 48 percent of transfers accrue to the poorest 40 percent of households) and the hypothetical proxy-means targeting approach (where 65 percent of transfers accrue to these households). We analyze the

Table 11.4 Share of Benefits from Alternative Transfer Programs

household benefits/total benefits

	Bottom	2nd Quintile	3rd Quintile	4th Quintile	Top
Benefit share					
Education					
Untargeted	0.215	0.225	0.219	0.187	0.154
Targeted	0.204	0.279	0.249	0.17	0.098
Health					
Untargeted	0.149	0.193	0.208	0.207	0.244
Targeted	0.148	0.229	0.208	0.226	0.189
Rural electrification	0.329	0.251	0.212	0.135	0.074
Urban transport	0.299	0.128	0.185	0.28	0.376
Proxy-means targeting	0.373	0.277	0.205	0.111	0.347
Kerosene subsidy	0.178	0.211	0.227	0.209	0.174

Source: Authors' estimates.
Note: Quintiles are based on the national distribution of household consumption per adult equivalent.

net real income effects when petroleum prices are increased in line with the formula, but where a fixed amount of revenue is returned to households through these three programs.

Table 11.5 presents the revenue implications of removing all petroleum subsidies and shows clearly that the bulk of the revenue will come from diesel (54 percent) and petrol (38 percent). In all cases, the net

Table 11.5 Revenue Effects from Subsidy Removal and Zero Kerosene Tax

Supply characteristic	Diesel	Petrol	Kerosene	LPG	Fuel oil
Total supply (million liters)	968	726	87	58	53
Ex-refinery price (F)	3,552	2,890	3,761	5,355	1,750
Tax rates (percentage of ex-ref. F)	0.51	0.59	0.36	0.29	0.65
Revenue (billion Ghanaian cedis)	1753	1243	117	90	60
Revenue share (product revenue/total revenue)	0.54	0.38	0.04	0.03	0.02

Source: Authors' estimates.
Note: Supplies are for 2003. A billion is 1,000 million. Nominal GDP in 2004 was 79,865 billion Ghanaian cedis. Total revenue from the above petroleum is ¢3,263 billion, which is approximately 4.0 percent of GDP. Total tax revenue in 2004 was estimated by the IMF (2004) at ¢16,761 billion, which was around 21.3 percent of GDP. In addition to tax revenue, under the assumption that the production activities of the Tema refinery break even at the current world prices, increases in the ex-refinery prices result in a lower quasi-fiscal deficit equivalent to 3.2 percent of GDP.

revenue raised (or funds allocated to the transfer programs) is kept constant across programs. The transfer budget is determined by the revenue lost by keeping the kerosene tax at zero compared with the price formula level of 36 percent, which leads to a decrease in revenue of 3.6 percent compared with the full price adjustment. We then ask how net benefits would be distributed if we allocated this same revenue using alternative transfer programs—that is, if we used a targeted education program and a hypothetical transfer program based on a household proxy-means approach.

Table 11.6 (top panel) presents the magnitude and distribution of the real income effect when 3.6 percent of revenue is returned to households under three transfer programs: a zero kerosene tax, a targeted education subsidy, and a proxy-means targeted transfer program. Focusing first on the case of zero kerosene taxes, the lower increase in kerosene prices results in a smaller aggregate real income decrease (from 8.5 to 7.3 percent) as well as a smaller decrease for the poorest quintile (from 9.1 percent to 7 percent). The share of the poorest quintile in the aggregate real income loss falls from 8.8 percent to 7.8 percent. Although the aggregate real income loss is even lower for the two other transfer programs, this simply reflects the different distribution of the same absolute aggregate loss. Under the targeted education subsidy the share of the poorest quintile decreases to 7.1 percent. Under the proxy-means targeted program this share decreases even further, to 4.4 percent.

Of course, the net loss for the poorest quintile could be reduced further if a greater proportion of revenue was transferred back to households under the programs. Table 11.6 (bottom panel) presents the same simulations as above, but now the revenue that is returned to households is increased by 50 percent—that is, 5.4 percent of the revenue is returned to households. The aggregate net loss to households is now lower in all cases. Under this scenario, the net loss to the poorest quintile under the proxy-means targeted program is near zero. These simulations clearly show that, in terms of providing protection to the poorest households, the two targeted transfer programs dominate low kerosene taxes and also avoid the efficiency costs associated with this tax profile. There are also clearly high returns to developing a well-targeted transfer program.

CONCLUDING REMARKS

With the substantial increase in world oil prices since 2003, the issue of petroleum product pricing, and energy pricing more generally, has become increasingly important in developing countries. Reflecting a reluctance of governments to pass these price increases onto energy users, energy price

Table 11.6 Benefit Incidence for Alternative Expenditure Programs

household income impact divided by household total income

Alternative expenditure scenarios	Bottom	2nd Quintile	3rd Quintile	4th Quintile	Top	All
Returning 3.6 percent of revenue						
Net real income loss						
Price formula alone	0.091	0.087	0.085	0.082	0.082	0.085
With zero kerosene tax	0.070	0.072	0.073	0.074	0.077	0.073
With targeted education subsidy	0.057	0.064	0.070	0.075	0.079	0.069
With proxy-means targeting	0.031	0.063	0.073	0.078	0.081	0.065
Share of aggregate loss						
Price formula alone	0.088	0.142	0.183	0.243	0.343	n.a.
With zero kerosene tax	0.078	0.134	0.178	0.248	0.363	n.a.
With targeted education subsidy	0.071	0.122	0.174	0.254	0.378	n.a.
With proxy-means targeting	0.044	0.121	0.180	0.264	0.391	n.a.
Returning 5.4 percent of revenue						
Net real income loss						
Price formula alone	0.091	0.087	0.085	0.082	0.082	0.085
With zero kerosene tax	0.061	0.066	0.068	0.070	0.074	0.068
With targeted education subsidy	0.042	0.054	0.063	0.072	0.078	0.062
With proxy-means targeting	0.003	0.053	0.067	0.075	0.081	0.056
Share of aggregate loss						
Price formula alone	0.088	0.142	0.183	0.243	0.343	n.a.
With zero kerosene tax	0.071	0.129	0.176	0.250	0.373	n.a.
With targeted education subsidy	0.062	0.111	0.169	0.260	0.398	n.a.
With proxy-means targeting	0.019	0.109	0.178	0.276	0.418	n.a.

Source: Authors' estimates.

Note: n.a.: not applicable. Quintiles are based on the national distribution of consumption per adult equivalent.

subsidies are absorbing an increasing amount of scarce public resources, thus exacerbating the constraints to increasing government expenditures in areas such as social and infrastructure expenditures. Governments are often especially concerned about the adverse impact of such price increases on the poorest households. In this chapter, we identify the fiscal implications of these subsidies for Ghana. Our analysis is concerned primarily with evaluating the likely magnitude of the impact of price increases on household real incomes and how these increases are distributed across households at different parts of the income distribution. We also identify alternative approaches to mitigating the adverse effects of price increases on poor households and actual government policy responses.

It is clear that the distribution of the benefits implicit in energy subsidies across households involves substantial leakages of these to higher income households. This finding is extremely robust across a range of countries for which we have recently undertaken similar analyses. It even holds true for kerosene, subsidies on which are often promoted as a way of improving the targeting of energy subsidies. Reflecting this, the real income burden resulting from a withdrawal of energy subsidies is borne disproportionately by higher income households. That said, lower income households do suffer sizeable real income decreases from subsidy removal. Any credible policy strategy therefore needs to address the mitigation of these adverse effects.

In the context of Ghana, our analysis estimates that the poorest households experience a 9.1 percent decline in real incomes. Maintaining lower kerosene prices is a relatively inefficient approach to protecting these households from such losses because of the extent of the leakage of subsidy benefits to high-income households. Better-targeted programs can help to substantially reduce or even eliminate these losses. Of course, to the extent that it takes time to develop well-designed and well-implemented targeted transfer programs, one may wish to gradually introduce price increases, especially for products such as kerosene that are relatively more important for the poorest households. However, there may be substantial efficiency as well as revenue costs associated with such a strategy, related to the substitution of kerosene for other sources of energy. For example, kerosene is often substituted for diesel and even gasoline when substantial price differentials exist between kerosene and these products. Therefore, it is important to see such an approach as a very short term strategy. In addition, since higher prices may exacerbate the lack of access by poor households to clean fuels (with associated negative health and environmental implications), some of the budgetary savings from eliminating fuel subsidies could be allocated to improving access to electricity (typically a cleaner and cheaper source of energy) as well as to rural roads and urban mass transport.

The results of this analysis were presented to the government in early February 2005. In mid-February 2005 the government increased petroleum prices by, on average, 50 percent and announced its intention of introducing a new pricing formula in order to remove the government from pricing decisions. It also emphasized its commitment to continuing sectoral reforms that would further increase private sector participation in the import and distribution of petroleum products. In May 2005, the government established the National Petroleum Authority to monitor the implementation of the pricing mechanism and facilitate the withdrawal of government from the politically sensitive issue of petroleum pricing. The composition of the authority includes representatives from government, oil-marketing companies, trade unions, nongovernmental organizations such as the association of Ghana Industries, and various experts. This system seems to be working since prices were increased again in June 2005 in response to a continued increase in world petroleum prices.

Of equal importance was the introduction of additional expenditure items in the 2005 budget that were intended to mitigate the adverse effects of higher domestic petroleum prices on low-income households. These included the removal of fees charged to primary and junior secondary schools as well as investments in transport and an expansion of the rural electrification scheme. These budgetary expenditures, equivalent to approximately 0.35 percent of GDP, are to be financed by a special "mitigation levy" that was included in the pricing formula.

Our analysis gives a very useful example of how household survey data and input-output data can be used to evaluate the likely welfare implications of higher domestic petroleum prices. The approach presented can be implemented at relatively low resource cost, yet can provide very valuable information for the policy debate surrounding the issue of petroleum price reform. We have emphasized the importance of identifying the trade-offs inherent in alternative measures that can be used to mitigate the welfare losses for low-income households. In the context of Ghana, the government found this information especially important when designing the policy reform package in a way that was politically acceptable. More generally, it is clear that access to an effective formal social protection system provides a useful mechanism for introducing much-needed structural reforms because it enables the associated efficiency gains to be achieved while simultaneously providing some protection to the poorest households against any adverse effects in the short term.

Finally, the background and timing to this PSIA study helps to high-light the tradeoffs that exist in practice when attempting to undertake "quality PSIA" in order to inform the policy debate. The request for PSIA support came very close to the government budget discussions in parliament during which the policy on price reform was to be announced and debated. This presented a very tight deadline, which strongly influenced the approach adopted in executing the PSIA. Hayes (2005) summarizes the key characteristics or objectives of a "quality PSIA," highlighting that such analyses should be:

- *rigorous* in order to be credible and useful;
- *ex ante* and *timely* in order to influence policy;
- *broad* (that is, include a focus on social, political and institutional as well as economic issues) in order to improve understanding of policy environment in a country and enhance probability that good policies get adopted; and
- *participatory* in order to promote domestic ownership of analysis and its implications, to enhance the chances that the insights will influence policy design, and to help to build domestic capacity for such analyses over time.

In the context of the present Ghana PSIA, the desire to be ex ante and timely meant that the tradeoffs with the other objectives were relatively high, especially the tradeoff with the participatory nature of the process and the breadth of the analysis. For example, in carrying out the PSIA we were able to consult only a relatively narrow group of stakeholders and, reflecting the need for a review and clearance process, the report did not have very wide circulation prior to the policy debate in parliament.[12] However, it should also be recognized that a substantial amount of policy analysis and discussion on the issue already existed and, in fact, were the basis for the government's request for further analysis. The main contribution of the current PSIA was to address in more detail the magnitude and distribution of the likely real income effects resulting from price increases as well as to identify alternative mitigating measures and uses of budgetary savings from elimination of fuel subsidies.

Such tradeoffs across objectives will always exist in practice when undertaking a PSIA. However, one expects that these tradeoffs will become less sharp as the framework and capacity for PSIA is developed over time. In a sense, this is a key contribution of the PRSP process, which is intended to identify a set of policies to be implemented by the government over the period of a few years. This should provide a longer timeline for a higher-quality PSIA process to occur. But even a thorough PRSP process will not be able to incorporate unanticipated economic shocks, such as a sudden leap in world oil prices, and the need for immediate policy responses. In such situations, having access to lessons from countries that faced similar shocks can be a very valuable input to the policy process. It is hoped that the present analysis, and similar ones being carried out at the IMF, have added value from this perspective.

NOTES

1. See IMF (2004: 20, Box 3), Federico, Daniel, and Bingham (2001), Gupta and Mahler (1995), and Gupta et al. (2002) for more details on fuel pricing in developing and developed countries.
2. The results presented here are based on Coady and Newhouse (2005), which can be consulted for greater detail.
3. Historically, relatively large increases in petroleum prices have not been uncommon. For example, kerosene, diesel, and gasoline prices rose in real terms by 161, 214, and 156 percent, respectively, from 1983 through 1987 (Addison and Osei 2001; Gupta et al. 2002).
4. The following people from the World Bank provided invaluable assistance regarding information on the policy context and reform process in Ghana as well as providing access to household-level and input-output data: Marcelo Andrade, Maurizio Bussolo, Carlos Cavalcanti, Vijay Iyer, and Hans Lofgren.
5. In particular, Ravi Kanbur (Cornell University), Jeff Round (University of Warwick), and Stephen Younger (Cornell University) provided important information on data sources and identified various policy stakeholders and analysts that should be contacted.
6. We benefitted greatly from detailed discussions with Felix Asante and D. Twerefou (both at ISSER) and Nii Sowa and Abena Odouro (both at CEPA).
7. The revised formula also allowed for the adjustment of domestic ex-refinery prices to reflect changes in world prices and/or the exchange rate. Prices would be adjusted according to the formula if there were: (1) a monthly average change in the FOB price of +/−US$5/metric ton (2) a monthly average change in the exchange rate of +/−50 cedis/U.S. dollar, or (3) when the combined effect of the above changes registers an absolute change of 10 cedis/litre compared with prevailing ex-refinery prices.
8. The participating districts were chosen based on an index constructed from annually collected school-level data using information that included the furniture in the school, students' performance in matriculation exams, the number of trained teachers, enrollment rates, participation by girls, and the availability of core textbooks. The objective of the program was to increase the amount of public resources going to these schools to replace the levies typically being charged to households by district assemblies. It is hoped that this

program will also increase participation by girls and children from the poorest households.

9. Note that this simulation may underestimate the marginal benefit incidence of expenditures, since the extra expenditures may act to increase enrollments of children from the poorest families.

10. Recently, such statistical approaches have been used extensively in "conditional transfer programs," which have become increasingly popular in developing countries, especially in Latin America. These programs give cash to identified poor households, but condition receipt of the benefit on regular attendance by children at school and regular attendance of pregnant/lactating women or women with young children at health clinics for basic health and nutrition information and services. These programs have also been found to have a substantial impact on improving the human capital of children from very poor families and help to break the intergenerational transmission of poverty and destitution. For a summary of the design, implementation, and impacts of the most well known of these programs see Morley and Coady (2003) and Rawlings and Rubio (2003).

11. See Coady, Grosh, and Hodinnott (2004) for a more detailed discussion of alternative targeting methods and their targeting performance.

12. For an interesting discussion on the interaction of the PRSP and PSIA processes more generally in Ghana, with a particular focus on the quality of the PSIA process, see Azeem (2005).

REFERENCES

Addison, T., and R. Osei. 2001. "Taxation and Fiscal Reform in Ghana." Discussion Paper 97, WIDER, Helsinki, Finland.

Armah and Associates. 2004. "Distributional Impact and Effects of Ghana's Petroleum Pricing Policy." Draft Report submitted to NDPC/UNDP (November).

Azeem, V. with C. Ayamdoo. 2005. "Experimenting with Poverty and Social Impact Assessments: Ghana." Background Report commissioned by Eurodad. http://www.eurodad.org/psia.

Banks, J., R. Blundell, and A. Lewbel. 1996. "Tax Reform and Welfare Measurement: Do We Need Demand System Estimates?" *Economic Journal* 106 (438): 1227–41.

Coady, D. 2003. "Alleviating Structural Poverty in Developing Countries: The Approach of PROGRESA in Mexico." Background Working Paper, World Development Report 2004, February, Washington DC: World Bank. http://www-wds.worldbank.org/servlet/WDS_IBank_Servlet?pcont=details&eid=000160016_20031015131911.

Coady, D. 2005. "The Distributional Impacts of Indirect Tax and Public Pricing Reforms." In *Analyzing the Distributional Impact of Reforms: A Practitioner's Guide to Pension, Health, Labor Market, Public Sector Downsizing, Taxation, Decentralization and Macroeconomic Modeling.* Vol. 2, 2006, ed. A. Coudouel and S. Paternostro. Washington, DC: World Bank.

Coady, D., M. Grosh, and J. Hoddinott. 2004. *Targeting of Transfers in Developing Countries: Review of Lessons and Experiences.* Regional and Sector Studies Series. IFPRI and World Bank: Washington, DC.

Coady, D., and D. Newhouse. 2005. "Ghana: Evaluation of the Distributional Impacts of Petroleum Price Reforms." Technical Assistance Report, Fiscal Affairs Department, International Monetary Fund, Washington DC.

Federico, G., J. Daniel, and B. Bingham. 2001. "Domestic Petroleum Price Smoothing in Developing and Transition Countries." IMF Working Paper 75, International Monetary Fund, Washington, DC.

Ghana Living Standards Survey. 1999. Accra, Republic of Ghana: Ghana Statistical Source.

Gupta, S., and W. Mahler. 1995. "Taxation of Petroleum Products: Theory and Evidence." *Energy Economics* 17 (2): 101–16.

Gupta, S., B. Clements, K. Fletcher, and G. Inchauste. 2002. "Issues in Domestic Petroleum Pricing in Oil-Producing Countries." IMF Working Paper. 03/140, International Monetary Fund, Washington, DC.

Hayes, L. 2005. "Open on Impact: Slow Progress in World Bank and IMF Poverty Analysis." Eurodad, Christian Aid, Save the Children UK, and Trocaire. http://www.eurodad.org/uploadstore/cms/docs/OpenonImpact.pdf.

ISSER (Institute of Statistical, Social, and Economic Research). 2004. "Socio-Economic Impact of Petroleum Deregulation Policy." Final Report, submitted to Ministry of Energy by Resource Center for Energy Economics and Regulation, ISSER. Legon, Ghana: University of Ghana (December).

IMF (International Monetary Fund). 2004. "Ghana: Second Review Under the Poverty Reduction and Growth Facility." IMF Country Report 04/210. http://www.imf.org/external/pubs/ft/scr/2004/cr04210.pdf.

Mercados, A. P., and J. Kofi Bucknor and Associates. 2004. "Determination of Deregulation Policy." Draft Policy Paper prepared for Ministry of Energy of Ghana (December).

Morley, S., and D. Coady. 2003. *From Social Assistance to Social Development: Targeted Education Subsidies in Developing Countries.* Washington, DC: Center for Global Development and the International Food Policy Research Institute.

Powell, M., and J. I. Round. 1998. *A Social Accounting Matrix for Ghana: 1993.* Accra, Republic of Ghana: Ghana Statistical Service.

Rawlings, L., and G. Rubio. 2003. "Evaluating the Impact of Conditional Cash Transfer Programs: Lessons from Latin America." Policy Research Working Paper 3119, World Bank, Washington, DC.

Skoufias, E. 2001. "PROGRESA and Its Impact on the Human Capital and Welfare of Households in Rural Mexico: A Synthesis of the Results of an Evaluation." Research Report, International Food Policy Research Institute, Washington, DC.

12

MALAWI
Agricultural Development and Marketing Corporation Reform

MILTON KUTENGULE, ANTONIO NUCIFORA,
AND HASSAN ZAMAN

his chapter describes the process and findings of the Poverty and Social Impact Analysis (PSIA) on the reform of the Agricultural Development and Marketing Corporation (ADMARC) in Malawi.[1] The reform of ADMARC has been a bone of contention between donors and the Malawi government because of disagreements over the role of parastatal organizations in food security in Malawi. In late 2001, the government and the World Bank agreed to carry out a PSIA on the impact of restructuring ADMARC. The experience with the reform of ADMARC illustrates the usefulness of the PSIA approach and also provides some useful lessons for future reforms.

The chapter is structured as follows: the next section presents the structure and purpose of ADMARC and its role in agricultural produce, input marketing, and food security, and briefly reviews Malawi's experience with ADMARC reforms since the 1980s. The following section provides a synthesis of the methodology, findings, and recommendations of each of the three background studies conducted as part of the ADMARC PSIA. The next section provides a synthesis of the overall findings and policy recommendations of the PSIA, and the following one reviews the process of the PSIA and its main shortcomings, as well as recent progress in the implementation of the findings. The final section presents some tentative lessons and conclusions.

BACKGROUND TO THE AGRICULTURAL DEVELOPMENT AND MARKETING CORPORATION (ADMARC)

ADMARC is a Malawian parastatal organization created in 1971 with the mandate to market agricultural produce and inputs, and to facilitate the development of the smallholder agricultural subsector through marketing activities and investments in agro-industry enterprises. In addition, ADMARC was given a food security role in maize markets by acting as a buyer and seller in remote areas, providing grain storage across seasons, and supporting a large marketing structure with distribution or market centers located in most urban and rural areas. This role reflects the strategic importance of maize in Malawi, where the population's diet is so dependent on the single staple crop that the word *maize* is often equated with the word *food*. Hence the ADMARC role in food security was especially critical at times of maize scarcity.

This social role—the buying and selling of maize at reasonable prices in remote areas—was reflected in the pan-territorial and pan-seasonal pricing system for smallholder farmers, particularly maize farmers, and the establishment of markets in nonprofitable areas. Until 1987 ADMARC enjoyed a monopoly in the importation, marketing, and storage of grain.

The Structure and Purpose of ADMARC

To fulfill its mandates, ADMARC operated a maize price band system that remained in effect until the mid-1990s. Further, it rapidly developed an extensive network and infrastructure of markets across the country comprising regional offices, divisional offices, area offices, storage depots, parent markets, unit markets, and seasonal markets (figure 12.1).[2] These markets were used to conduct sales of farm inputs, purchase commodities from smallholders, and sell food crops to net consumers.

Apart from its agricultural marketing activities, ADMARC also invested heavily in equities and loans in various enterprises and is directly involved in estate agriculture. In fact, by the mid-1980s, ADMARC had equity investments in 34 commercial enterprises and owned numerous agricultural estates.[3] Until 2002, ADMARC also ran various subsidiaries (for example, a cotton ginning company, a bus company, and a cold storage company), many of which were loss making. In 2002, the ministry of finance assumed control over its four largest loss-making subsidiaries in preparation for public sale. Three of these companies have since been privatized. ADMARC also runs many support departments, including printing services, building services, carpentry services, tailoring services, a

FIGURE 12.1　ADMARC Market Locations and Main Road Network, 2002

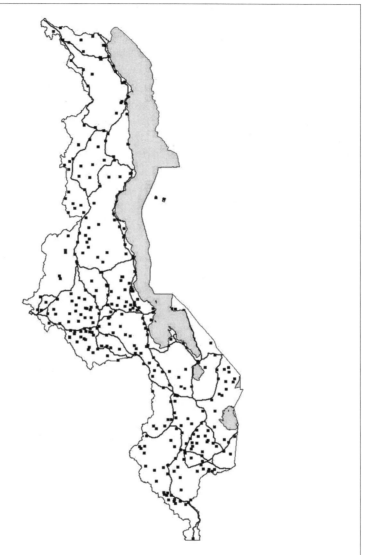

Source: This map has been provided by Todd Benson, based on information collected in Benson et al. (2002).
Note: ADMARC provided a list of 363 markets. Locations were found for 344.

hospital, football clubs, a rice mill, a groundnut grading factory, guest houses and cottages, and urban housing. ADMARC currently employs about 3,250 permanent employees, with an annual cost structure of around 500 million Malawi kwacha (MK).

Over the years ADMARC has deviated from its core mandate of agricultural development and food security to engage in other business activities. Harrigan (1991) argues that ADMARC used the surplus reaped in its trading activities to invest in industrial activities in various sectors of the economy. Kydd and Christiansen (1982) note that between 1971 and 1979 ADMARC extracted about MK182 million from the smallholder sector, of which 14 percent was used to cross-subsidize smallholder food production and consumption while the remainder was used for equity investments and loans to subsidiaries; only 4.3 percent of such investments were related to the development of the smallholder agriculture subsector.

ADMARC's Role in Agricultural Marketing and Food Security

The importance of ADMARC in the marketing of agricultural commodities and inputs has declined steadily since the late 1980s. ADMARC's role in maize trading increased rapidly between 1975 and the late 1980s, but after a few years of significant variations in traded volumes, ADMARC maize trading activities started to decline in the early 1990s (figure 12.2).

The role of ADMARC in trading maize has declined partly because of competition from new entrants. At the time when ADMARC held a monopoly up to the mid-1980s, it purchased some 18 percent of the national maize crop. By the late 1990s, this figure had fallen to between 1 and 8 percent of annual national maize production (table 12.1).[4] In fact, ADMARC's decline in market share applies across all commodities: the share of tobacco purchased dropped from 100 percent to 10 percent, the share of cotton dropped from 100 percent to 50 percent, and the share of groundnuts dropped from 20 percent to an insignificant share (O&M Associates 1999). Similarly, ADMARC's supply of inputs has been reduced to 10 percent of the country's total input supply, although it still accounts for a much larger share of smallholders fertilizer and seed use (see O&M Associates 1999; Kherallah et al. 2001).

In parallel, there has been a sharp reduction in ADMARC's marketing infrastructure during the 1990s. In 1990, ADMARC operated about 1,300 seasonal markets, 217 unit markets, 80 area offices, 12 district headquarters, 3 regional offices, and 18 storage depots (ADMARC 1990). However, as of late 2004, ADMARC had been reduced to 300 seasonal

FIGURE 12.2 **ADMARC Maize Sales and Purchases, 1970–2001**

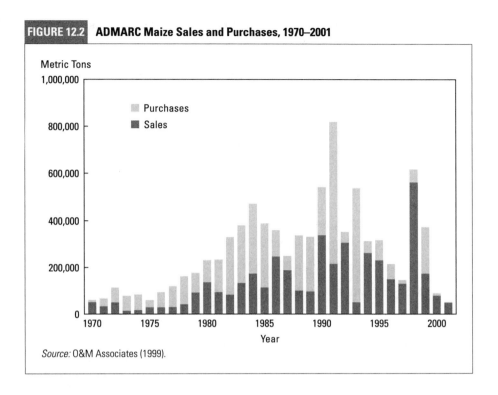

Source: O&M Associates (1999).

Table 12.1 ADMARC Participation in the Maize Markets, 1995–2001

Key elements of maize markets	1995	1996	1997	1998	1999	2000	2001
Smallholder production (millions of metric tons)	1.33	1.79	1.22	1.53	2.48	2.50	1.71
Imports (millions of metric tons)	0.23	0.08	0.05	0.32	0.03	0.00	0.04
ADMARC purchases as a percentage of smallholder production	4.60	4.90	7.90	0.80	2.30	7.90	0.10
ADMARC purchases as a percentage of marketable surplus	18.40	19.60	31.60	3.20	9.20	31.60	0.40

Source: World Bank (2004).
Note: ADMARC purchases are lowest in marketing year 1997/8, as a result of the poor harvest of 1996/7 (and also 1997/8), and again in marketing year 2000/1 when ADMARC storage facilities were full of the grain purchased in 1999/2000. ADMARC eventually sold the entire grain reserves at very low prices just before the poor harvest of 2001/2 (and was left with no stocks to mitigate the impact of the 2001/2 draught). ADMARC's maize purchases have remained very low since 2001/2 (not shown), because of moderate harvests and its precarious financial situation.

markets, 400 unit markets, 15 district headquarters, 3 regional offices, and 9 storage depots (World Bank 2003).

Until December 2000, ADMARC also managed Malawi's strategic grain reserves. In 2001 the government mandated the National Food Reserve Agency (NFRA) to manage the strategic grain reserve. A few years later it established the Department of Poverty and Disaster Management (DoPODMA) in the Office of the President and Cabinet to act solely as a disaster and emergency relief agency, thus taking over the core of ADMARC's social functions. In line with these changes, in 2002 ADMARC's storage capacity—which in the 1990s used to reach approximately 468,000 metric tonnes, or 20 to 25 percent of an annual harvest—was reduced to about 200,000 metric tonnes with the transfer of storage infrastructures to the NFRA.

The Impact of Previous Rounds of ADMARC Restructuring

Many reforms over the course of the past 20 years have progressively liberalized agricultural markets and facilitated growing private sector participation and, therefore, eroded the role of ADMARC. First, the government changed its maize pricing policies and reduced ADMARC's gross maize trading margin from 57 percent in the 1967–79 period to 25 percent in the 1980–6 period. As a result of this reduction in trading margin, ADMARC began experiencing financial difficulties in the early 1980s. These problems were compounded by the deterioration in terms of trade arising from the 1980/1 economic crisis. In addition, in 1987, partly as a result of pressure from the World Bank and the International Monetary Fund (IMF), the government removed ADMARC's monopoly on maize (and other agricultural produce) trading and allowed the liberalization of agricultural marketing to private traders (Chirwa 1998; Scarborough 1990).

This strategy of progressive liberalization has been supported under various IMF and World Bank programs during the late 1980s and the 1990s. The aim was to end government intervention in the maize market and allow private traders to take over the functions performed by ADMARC, which was to be commercialized and privatized, while at the same time providing targeted food subsidies to the poor.

Research conducted by the International Food Policy Research Institute (IFPRI) and Malawi's Bunda College of Agriculture on the impact of market reforms on smallholder farmers (a sample of approximately 800 households and local traders in aggregate) suggests that liberalization has led to an increase in private sector activity (Fafchamps and Gabre-Madhin 2001). Between 1995 and 1998, the number of commodity wholesalers increased in 59 percent of the locations where the survey research was conducted; similarly, the number of commodity retailers increased in 81 percent of the locations. The number of input wholesalers and retailers increased in 46 percent and 70 percent of the areas, respectively, between 1995 and 1998. These data are validated by a survey of small-holders, with 43 percent of households surveyed reporting an increase in the number of input sellers and 60 percent reporting an increase in the number of crop buyers (Kherallah et al. 2001; see also Evans 1990).

Nevertheless, the experience with adopting the liberalization agenda from 1987 with respect to produce marketing in Malawi has been less positive than was expected. Inefficiencies in factor input markets, market information, and credit delivery, along with inadequate infrastructure have constrained sectoral growth. Private traders have not uniformly stepped in where ADMARC's state market presence was removed.[5] The relatively weak response of private sector traders in filling the gap left by the withdrawal of ADMARC reflects the real constraints faced by traders. These constrainst include high transport costs, limited external finance, a lack of brand names and trademarks, a lack of quality certification, a lack of organized commodity exchange, extremely decentralized production and consumption, limited availability of information about input and output prices, and limited contract enforcement (Fafchamps and Gabre-Madhin 2001). These difficulties are exacerbated by the volatile policy environment, since the extent and modalities of government intervention in the agricultural produce market continue to be pervasive, substantially increasing the uncertainty facing traders (World Bank 2004; Rubey 2004).

In spite of the various reforms and the reduced role of ADMARC in agricultural markets, by the late 1990s the financial performance of ADMARC had become increasingly poor, and ADMARC was a major source of concern for the government and the international financial institutions. ADMARC's market interventions continued to be expensive for the budget because the government bore the costs of these operations by repeatedly bailing it out (table 12.2).[6] These bail-outs continued to derail the macroeconomic framework (claiming 1.6 percent of GDP in 1997/8 and 1.9 percent of GDP in 2000/1).

In addition to the negative fiscal impact of government bail-outs, several analysts argued that ADMARC's interventions continued to distort prices and other market signals. Others argued that the presence of ADMARC markets and warehouses continued to discourage private sector participation in maize trade, marketing, and storage, thus impeding the development of the market and leading to a longer-term inefficiency

Table 12.2 ADMARC's Financial Performance 1998/9 to 2002/3

MK Thousands

	1998/9	1999/2000	2000/1	2001/2	2002/3[a]
Net profit after taxation	*376,545*	*−350,943*	*−615,611*	*−898,719*	*−389,358*
GDP at current market prices (million MK)	445,552	916,389	1,090,597	1,445,149	1,984,181
ADMARC profits / (losses) as a percentage of GDP	0.6	−0.4	−0.6[b]	−0.6	−0.2

Source: ADMARC Annual Financial Statements
Note: a. Data are for actual performance to 10/31/2002 (first half of financial year 2002/3).
  b. This amount does not include the losses incurred by NFRA in 2000/1 resulting from ADMARC's sale of NFRA's stocks.

in marketing operations (see, among others, Abbott and Polin 1996 and Rubey 2003). Furthermore, ADMARC's operations continued to be surrounded by a lack of transparency, and they often raised governance issues. Notably, the recent reports of mismanagement of grain reserves at the onset of the 2001/2 food crisis renewed the doubts surrounding ADMARC's role in food security.

As a result, donors continued to press the government to improve the financial position of ADMARC through in-depth restructuring and the adopting cost-cutting measures. Several proposals were considered during the period 2000–2, including the possibility of privatizing or liquidating ADMARC's largest loss-making subsidiaries, auctioning part of ADMARC's marketing and storage infrastructure (ADMARC's management proposed the closure of about 200 markets) and, once again, repealing the ADMARC Act and incorporating ADMARC as a limited liability company to be eventually privatized.

Significant controversy surrounded these recommendations to reduce ADMARC's marketing role further, and possibly to sell off a considerable portion of its marketing infrastructure. First, the government and civil society expressed concern, again, about the existence of market failures in remote areas, noting that if these remote markets were closed because they were inefficient, it would be unlikely that they would be replaced by private traders because transportation costs are high relative to the return on maize sales. This was likely to be true especially in the rainy season when the condition of rural roads worsens significantly.

Second, there was concern that ADMARC fulfilled an important service by maintaining adequate food storage for preventing shortages during the lean seasons, and acting as a last-resort source of supply in times of scarcity. By maintaining warehousing facilities across the country, ADMARC could store purchased maize in secure markets in the food-deficit areas or in a proximate central location for transportation during the rainy season.[7]

Third, the government had significant concerns about the political implications of closing down ADMARC's markets, because the public perception of ADMARC's importance in agricultural marketing and food security is much higher than its actual importance, supported by the available data. There was concern that closing the markets rapidly would give rise to considerable public resentment and political difficulties. As a result, some members of government suggested that the decision to close the markets was politically untenable.

THE PSIA ON RESTRUCTURING ADMARC

Given the sensitivity of the issue and the potentially large social and economic consequences for the poorest groups of the population, in late 2001 the World Bank and the government decided to carry out a PSIA. Specifically, an agreement was reached between the World Bank and the National Economic Council (now the Ministry of Economic Planning and Development) to carry out an in-depth study on the likely poverty and social impacts of the privatization of ADMARC marketing activities. The idea was that the preparation of a joint study between the World Bank and the government, in consultation with other stakeholders, would go a long way to ease the gap in perceptions and understanding of the issues involved, and could contribute to the identification and adoption of a shared reform agenda.[8]

The government and the donors agreed it was critical to prevent ADMARC from causing further fiscal shocks to the economy. They were aware, however, of the importance of proceeding cautiously because of concerns about the disruption of the social function provided by ADMARC's markets in remote areas. The PSIA would study the poverty and social impacts of the proposed closure of some of ADMARC's agricultural markets and, more generally, it would examine the role of proximity to ADMARCs facilities (and services) for household welfare. The goal was to minimize the impact on the budget while allowing the operation of social activities to be financed in a transparent manner.

The study was launched in early 2002 and was one of the pioneer studies using the PSIA approach.[9] Food policy reforms, by definition, have very large social and poverty impacts, so the PSIA approach is well suited to these reforms (Lundberg 2004).

Three background studies were commissioned, each using a different methodology. The first study was a quantitative study that used econometric techniques to analyze data from the 1997/8 Integrated Household Survey (IHS-1) to investigate the relationship between access to ADMARC's services and household welfare. This study was prepared by a World Bank consultant.

A second quantitative study used econometric techniques to analyze data from the IHS-1 and the 2002 Complementary Panel Survey (this is the fourth round of follow-up panels on the IHS-1) to investigate the relationship between access to ADMARC's services and *changes* in household welfare that occurred between 1997/8 and 2002. This study was prepared by a team from the Centre for Social Research (University of Malawi) and the IFPRI.

The third study used a qualitative methodology to carry out field research in 20 rural communities on the combined effect of the closing of markets and the sharp decline of ADMARC's marketing activities in recent years. The study used an array of qualitative research methods to solicit households' and other stakeholders' reactions during field interviews in 2002. This study was carried out by a local research consulting company (Wadonda Consulting), using local researchers from the University of Malawi.

The individual pieces of the analysis were prepared during 2002 and, after several delays, completed in early 2003. A brief description of the methodology used and the main findings of each study are provided in the following sections.

Quantitative Analysis of Data from the 1997/8 Integrated Household Survey

The importance of ADMARC services has been quantified using household data from the nationally representative 1997/8 Malawi IHS-1. The IHS-1 questionnaire was administered over a 12-month period to 12,960 households, divided into 29 primary sampling strata. Out of this total, only 6,586 households were judged to have reliable expenditure and consumption information for use in deriving the consumption and expenditure-based indicator of household welfare. This sample of 6,586 households was used in this analysis.[10]

Methodology: An Econometric Model of Household Expenditures in 1997/8

The impact of ADMARC on household welfare has been assessed by testing for the existence of statistically significant differences in per capita household expenditures depending on proximity to ADMARC facilities.[11] The general model used to assess the importance of ADMARC is

$$Log\ y_i = \beta_0 + X_{1i}\beta_1 + X_{2i}\beta_2 + \delta_1 D_{ADMARC\ 1} + \delta_2 D_{ADMARC\ 2}$$

$$+ \delta_3 D_{ADMARC\ 3} + \mu_1 + e_i \qquad (12.1)$$

where y_i is the log of per capita expenditures, X_{1i} is a vector of nonlabor assets (in logs, including variables such as land), X_{2i} is a vector describing characteristics of household labor (including the level of education, gender, skills and occupation of the household head), $D_{ADMARC1}$ is a dummy variable that takes a value of 1 when time to nearest ADMARC is less than half an hour, $D_{ADMARC2}$ is a dummy variable that takes a value of 1 when time to nearest ADMARC is half to one hour, and $D_{ADMARC3}$ is a dummy variable that takes a value of 1 when the time to nearest ADMARC is one to two hours (table 12.3 and figure 12.3). The base scenario when distance to ADMARC is more than two hours is embedded in β_0. Finally, μ_i is a fixed-effect term specified at the survey enumeration area (EA) level that controls for unobserved location characteristics, and e_i is a stochastic error term.

The δ_s thus provide an estimate of the impact of ADMARC. Distance to the nearest ADMARC facility may affect household consumption through several channels. Rural households may use ADMARC facilities for buying inputs, selling their outputs and purchasing maize for consumption. All of these functions can be expected to have a positive impact on per capita household consumption because they are assumed to grant the household access to input and crop markets at relatively lower transaction costs than would otherwise be the case. Thus, our null hypothesis is that the ADMARC variables are jointly significant, indicating that access to ADMARC facilities is important. Consistency would also require that

Table 12.3 Household Distance to Nearest ADMARC Market (in IHS-1 sample)

Time taken to reach nearest ADMARC	Percent
Half hour or less	21
Over half hour to 1 hour	25
Over 1 hour to 2 hours	29
Over 2 hours	25
No response	1
Total	100

Source: Authors' calculations using data from IHS-1.

FIGURE 12.3 **ADMARC Market Locations and Mean Distance to Primary and Secondary Roads**

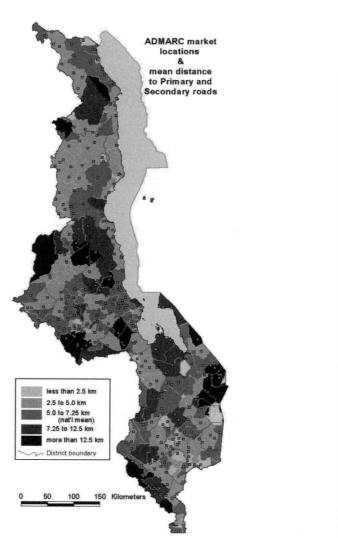

Source: This map has been provided by Todd Benson, based on information collected in Benson et al. (2002).
Note: ADMARC provided a list of 363 markets. Locations were found for 344.

$\delta_1 \geq \delta_2 \geq \delta_3$, indicating that, all else being equal, the impact is greater for households nearer to ADMARC.

Estimating equation (12.1) using ordinary least squares technique cannot guarantee unbiased estimates of the parameters because the placement of ADMARC facilities across different locations cannot be assumed to be random. Similarly, road-building decisions may be based on the existence of other complementary infrastructure or on a region's agro-climatic potential (see, for instance, Binswanger et al. 1993). It is reasonable to expect that placement decisions are related to local socioeconomic-political conditions. The use of fixed effects at the enumeration area level have been specified to sweep out unobserved factors that are likely to be correlated with factors influencing placement (as well as other unobservable factors such as area-specific price levels, for inputs as well as outputs, and components of area-specific transactions costs).

It is reasonable to expect that ADMARC's impact on consumption levels will also depend on the availability of alternative marketing channels. The degree of commercialization surrounding the household determines both the opportunities for engaging in trade and the efficiency of those transactions.[12] To test the hypothesis that the impact of ADMARC services is proportional to the degree of remoteness, we have split the sample of households on the basis of proximity to the nearest primary or secondary road (to proxy for market accessibility conditions),[13] and have estimated two regressions separately for the two subsamples.

Basic Findings from the Quantitative Analysis of the 1997/8 Integrated Household Survey Data

The results of the estimation are presented in table 12.4. The results underline the importance of household education and access to land as major determinants of household welfare. This finding is in line with previous studies on the determinants of poverty in Malawi (National Statistical Office 2000). Household consumption is higher by about 5 percent for households whose head has primary education (when compared to households where the head has received no formal education), 17 percent for households whose head has received secondary education, and 50 percent for households whose head has received higher education. The strong importance of household education is also confirmed by the strong statistical significance of the joint F-test on the three education regressors. Another major determinant of household income is access to land, with per capita household consumption increasing by 2 to 3 percent for every additional 1 percent of land available.

Table 12.4 Results of Regressions to Assess the Impact of ADMARC on Household Welfare Using Data from the IHS-1

Dependent variable: log (per capita expenditure)

	Near to main road		Far from main road	
	Coefficient	t-statistic	Coefficient	t-statistic
Independent Variables				
Household demographic variables from IHS				
Female-headed household	−0.078	(3.01)**	−0.093	(3.47)**
Share of children < 5	−0.481	(6.91)**	−0.466	(6.78)**
Household size	−0.089	(16.81)**	−0.092	(17.34)**
Land	0.029	(1.600)	0.018	(1.030)
Age	−0.005	(1.420)	−0.000	(0.120)
Age^2	0.000	(0.790)	0.000	(0.160)
Occupational Categories				
Administrative	−0.011	(0.150)	0.032	(0.410)
Clerical	0.018	(0.280)	0.002	(0.040)
Sales	0.037	(0.800)	0.044	(1.010)
Services	0.042	(0.840)	−0.047	(0.920)
Agriculture	−0.000	(0.010)	0.051	(1.440)
Other	0.006	(0.100)	0.090	(1.400)
School Categories				
Primary	0.026	(0.880)	0.071	(2.410)*
Secondary	0.169	(5.510)**	0.171	(5.740)**
Higher	0.509	(11.860)**	0.459	(10.140)**
Time to ADMARC				
Half hour or less	0.111	(2.040)*	0.199	(3.650)**
Over half hour to 1 hour	0.041	(0.830)	0.063	(1.430)
Over 1 hour to 2 hours	0.003	(0.060)	0.003	(0.090)
Constant	2.797	(28.560)**	2.580	(26.690)**
Observations	2703		2655	
R^2		0.430		0.450
F-tests				
ADMARC (3)	2.16^		5.70**	
Education (3)	52.94*		36.97**	
Age (2)	4.87**		0.03	
Enumeration area dummies	4.67**		6.50**	

Source: Authors' calculations.
Note: Absolute value of *t*-statistics in parentheses; ^ significant at 10 percent; * significant at 5 percent; ** significant at 1 percent.

Other important factors include the gender of the household head, total household size, and the number of dependents. Per capita household consumption is 8 to 9 percent lower for female-headed households. Household size also has a negative impact on per capita consumption, with per capita consumption lower by about 9 percent for each additional household member. Finally, the dependency ratio of children to adults reduces per capita consumption by almost 5 percent for every 10 percent increase in the share of young children in the composition of the household.

Distance from ADMARC markets also appears to be statistically significant. Although, only the ADMARC variable for distance less than 30 minutes are individually significant, the F-test of joint significance confirms that proximity to ADMARC has a significant positive impact on household consumption. Specifically, per capita consumption is estimated to be between 11 to 20 percent higher for households that reported living within 30 minutes to the nearest ADMARC facility (compared with households living over 2 hours away), and 4 to 6 percent higher for those living 30 to 60 minutes from the nearest ADMARC facility. Further, the relative magnitude of the three ADMARC variables is logically consistent. It is worth highlighting that ADMARC proximity appears to have a smaller impact in less remote areas, where households live close to major access roads. In areas where private market infrastructure is developed and market services function, the impact of ADMARC facilities on farm households is not very significant.

These results are in line with the finding discussed above that ADMARC's impact depends on the availability of alternative marketing channels. The benefits can be attributed to the fact that presently agricultural market institutions and infrastructure are not developed in poor, remote areas. Households that are located in areas where infrastructure is the most readily accessible are less dependent on ADMARC. The degree of commercialization surrounding the household determines both the opportunities for engaging in trade and the efficiency of those transactions. In less remote areas, higher competition can be expected to lower marketing margins, hence reducing the benefit of access to ADMARC's pan-territorial prices. More remote areas have less developed private markets, and alternatives to ADMARC services are less likely to exist there.

Obviously, the finding that ADMARC's marketing services are highly valued in remote areas does not in itself indicate that the services are cost efficient. The additional consumer surplus generated by the pan-territorial pricing would have to be compared with the transfers of resources ADMARC receives from taxpayers.[14] However it supports the thesis that public marketing services provide a significant boost to incomes in remote rural areas and confirms the case for a public role in support of markets in remote areas.

Quantitative Analysis of Data from the 1997/8 Integrated Household Survey and the Complementary Panel Survey

The importance of ADMARC for household welfare has also been assessed by combining data from the 1997/8 IHS-1 with those of the fourth round of the Complementary Panel Survey (CPS). The CPS was implemented by the Center for Social Research whereby data was repeatedly collected from a subset of the households that participated in the 1997/8 IHS-1. Four rounds of the CPS were conducted between January 2000 and September 2002.

The fourth round of the CPS (CPS-4) collected data from 291 households. This round was implemented primarily to collect information that would allow household welfare comparisons to be made between the 1997/8 IHS-1 and the 2002 CPS-4. Consequently the CPS-4 questionnaire was designed to include questions on all of the components of the welfare indicator used in the IHS-1 poverty analysis. The CPS-4 also collected information on a number of household transactions with ADMARC, including travel time to the nearest ADMARC facility, the role of ADMARC in supplying fertilizers and improved maize seed, and the role of ADMARC in providing staple goods for consumption. A detailed description of data is provided in Sharma et al. (2002).

Methodology: An Econometric Model of Changes in Household Expenditures between 1997/8 and 2002

The analysis seeks to explain changes in household welfare between 1997/8 and 2002 by access to ADMARC services, controlling for other major determinants of household welfare. The general model used to assess the importance of ADMARC is

$$\left(LNEXP02\right)_i - \left(LNEXP97\right)_i = \log A + \alpha\left(ADMARC\right)_i + X^i\beta + \upsilon_i \quad (12.2)$$

where *LNEXP02* is the (log of) per capita total household expenditure of household in year 2002 and *LNEXP97* is the initial (log of) welfare position of the household in base year 1997.[15] The changes in household welfare are a function of a constant term, *a*, access to *ADMARC*, a vector of household characteristics X^i,[16] and stochastic error term, e_i.[17] The parameters α and β describe the importance of ADMARC access, and a vector of household characteristics, respectively.

It is noted that a positive impact of ADMARC on improvements in expenditure levels implies that $\alpha < 0$ since ADMARC is measured as distance to the nearest facility. It is also reasonable to expect the impact of ADMARC on household welfare to be conditional on factors such as access to other types of marketing channels,[18] reliability of the household's own food supply,[19] and access to various types of safety net services or social assistance policies.[20] Several interactive dummy variables have been included to test these hypotheses.

The use of panel data is better suited to account for the endogeneity of unobserved factors that are likely to be correlated with factors influencing placement. Nevertheless, estimating equation (12.2) using the ordinary least squares technique cannot guarantee an unbiased estimate of α because placement of ADMARC across different locations cannot be assumed to be random (see, for instance, Binswanger et al. 1993). It is reasonable to expect that placement decisions are primarily a function of local socioeconomic-political conditions. For this reason, fixed effects at the traditional authority (TA) level have been specified to sweep out unobserved factors that are likely to be correlated with factors influencing placement.

In addition, it is worth noting that the model in equation (12.2) allows us to control for the possible underlying but unobserved factors that may affect both LNEXP02 and LNEXP97. If a simple version of equation (12.2) had been estimated, where the term LNEXP97 were moved to the right side, the presence of any common unobserved factors would result in biased estimates of the regression parameters (see, among others, Deaton 1998).

Basic Findings from the Quantitative Analysis of Data from the IHS-1 and CPS-4

The results of the regressions indicate that improvement in household welfare between 1997 and 2002 is strongly related to changes in the size of the household and changes in cultivated land area (table 12.5). In a predominantly low-technology agricultural economy such as Malawi's, increase in access to cultivatable land is the principal determinant of increases in household welfare; increases in household size chip away at per capita resources since land, not labor, is the binding constraint on increased production.

The results of the estimation suggest that proximity to an ADMARC facility has no impact on household income. The ADMARC coefficient is not significant (and carries an unexpected positive sign, suggesting that the farther away from ADMARC facilities, the better).[21] The estimated

Table 12.5 Results of Regressions to Assess Impact of ADMARC on Household Welfare Using Data from the IHS-1 and CPS-4

		Regression on LOGDIFF: difference between logged CPS4 and logged IHS welfare indicators (In MK)	
		Coefficient	t-statistic
admarc	distance to nearest ADMARC (km)	0.019	(0.75)
Household demographic variables from IHS			
agehhh	age of head of household	−0.003	(−0.92)
dpndrat	dependency ratio: dependents/hh	0.422	(−2.17)*
hhhlit	literate head of household (0/1)	−0.147	(−1.13)
farmer	household member with agricultural occupation	0.215	(1.48)
manufact	household engaged in manufacturing	−0.208	(−1.18)
prof	household member with professional or administrative job	−0.356	(2.12)*
maxyrsed	maximum years of education in household	0.020	(1.24)
Access to key consumption smoothing assets or institutions			
stock	variable that equals one if household owned stocks of staples at time of interview in all of the four CPS survey rounds (0/1)	0.131	(0.72)
pclvsval	per capita livestock value (MK)	−0.00006	(−0.93)
soccap	household reported in IHS giving or receiving income transfer (0/1)	−0.202	(1.95)+
snpartic	household participated in at least one safety net or social assistance program as reported in CPS1 (0/1)	0.297	(1.34)
Change in access to key human and physical assets			
hhchange	change in household size betweeen IHS and CPS4	−0.145	(6.21)**
change_cult	change in cultivated land area of household betweeen IHS and CPS4 (acres)	0.050	(2.30)*
Interacted variables			
admarc_disturb	interaction of distance to ADMARC with distance to nearest urban center	0.0002	(1.11)
admarc_stock	interaction of distance to ADMARC with whether household usually possesses staple food stocks	0.025	(1.41)
admarc_snpartic	interaction of distance to ADMARC with whether household participated in safety net programs	−0.037	(1.75)+
disturb	distance to nearest urban center (km)	−0.005	(−0.69)
	constant	0.257	(0.47)
	R^2	0.2103	
	Observations	261	
	Number of TA fixed-effect variables	19	

Source: Authors' calculations.
Note: t-statistics in parentheses: + significant at 10 percent; * significant at 5 percent; ** significant at 1 percent

value of the joint effect of proximity to ADMARC and distance from urban centers suggests that the impact of ADMARC decreases with distance from urban centers. This is contrary to our expectations (and also contrasts with the results presented in the previous section, as it suggests that proximity to ADMARC is less important in remote areas. The estimated impact is not statistically different from zero, however. The other interactive variables also suggest that ADMARC is less important for those households that are able to carry stocks of the basic staples and is higher for those households that are in a position to participate in social welfare programs. None of these estimated impacts is statistically different from zero, however. The results, therefore, do not provide any evidence of ADMARC's impact on household welfare.[22]

However, it must be noted that CPS-4 survey consists of a fairly small sample size and that it suffered from a high level of drop outs in remote rural areas, as the interviewers had no resources for a second visit if they could not meet with the respondent during a first trip. Further, data collection coincided with an emerging income and food crisis in Malawi. In fact, the timing of the study appears to explain the counterintuitive results. Since ADMARC did not have much to offer during the study season (because of its financial problems), it is not surprising that the impact of ADMARC decreases with distance. More generally, it could well be that the impact of ADMARC was simply drowned out by the far more overwhelming effects of the recent deep decline in agricultural production.

In sum, the results of the analysis presented in this section (of the IHS-1 and CPS-4 data) do not appear to support a statistically significant impact of differential access to ADMARC facilities (and services) on changes in household welfare. However, put against the weaknesses of the CPS dataset and the timing of the study, it is not surprising that strong evidence for or against the continued operation of ADMARC cannot be found in the analyses of the CPS data presented here. In light of these considerations, the results presented in this section should not be interpreted to indicate that there is no significant impact of ADMARC on household welfare, but rather simply that the dataset was unable to provide useful information on the role of ADMARC.

Qualitative Study on the Impact of ADMARC and the Role of the Private Sector in Agricultural Marketing

The qualitative study was designed to carry out an ex post assessment on the various social groups of the impact of closing selected ADMARC markets in recent years. Participatory learning methods were used to explore well-being categories, poverty dynamics, and the relation of households to ADMARC's marketing services. The results also provide valuable insights into the operation of the private sector in maize markets. The results of the study, however, cannot distinguish between the combined impact of the closure of seasonal markets and the sharp decline in ADMARC's business activities during the preceding years (see figure 12.2).

Methodology: A Qualitative Study of the Impact of ADMARC Closure in 20 Villages

The study was conducted within the catchment areas of 10 ADMARC unit markets (table 12.6). A range of qualitative research methods were used to solicit reactions of households and other stakeholders. Focus group discussions using variants of participatory learning methods were the main method for collecting data.[23] Interviews with key informants in the selected sites were also conducted.[24] Finally, semistructured interviews with policy and decision makers in stakeholder institutions were also carried out.[25]

In each of the 10 ADMARC unit markets, participatory rural appraisal methodologies, focus group discussions, and key informant interviews were conducted in two villages. A total of 20 villages were included in this study, resulting in a total of 40 focus group discussions (half with women groups), 54 semistructured interviews, and 44 key informant interviews (of which 9 were interviews with ADMARC officials, 3 were interviews with private traders, and 32 were interviews with other key informants). The fieldwork was carried out between April and June 2002.

The 10 ADMARC unit markets include six unit markets that had been proposed for closure and four unit markets that should continue to operate. In the six unit markets earmarked for closure, interviews were conducted in villages in the catchment area of closed seasonal markets, as it turned out that there were no unit markets that had been closed in the past five years.

The location of the ADMARC markets was selected through purposive sampling on the basis of their remoteness and their dominant livelihood characteristics in order to cover the existing diversity in terms of regional and geographical criteria, farming, and livelihood systems as well as other social and cultural criteria.[26] The rationale for choosing remote markets underlies the assumption that ADMARC's marketing services would make the biggest difference in areas where infrastructure is poor because private traders would be less likely to operate in those areas. Thus all 10 sites are in remote rural areas and characterized by very poor road infrastructure, and therefore are difficult to access particularly in the rainy season (except

Table 12.6 Location and Basic Infrastructure of Sites Selected for Qualitative Study

Site	District	Region	Status	Roads	School	ADMARC market	Health facility	Post office	Police post
Nthalire unit market (Kamphyongo seasonal)	Chitipa	North	Closed	Difficult to access	In village	3 km	15 km	14 km	15 km
Mpata unit market	Karonga	North	Open	Fairly accessible	2 km	15 km	15 km	15 km	15 km
Eswazini unit market (Emoneni seasonal)	Mzimba	North	Closed	Accessible In village	11 km	11 km	11 km	62 km	
Chikho unit market (Mzandu seasonal)	Ntchisi	Center	Closed	Difficult to access	In village	In village	1 km	34 km	34 km
Lipiri unit market (Kamtepa seasonal)	Dowa	Center	Closed	Difficult to access	In village	10 km	15 km	15 km	15 km
Mikundi unit market	Mchinji	Center	Open	Fairly accessible	1 km	1 km	1 km	1 km	22 km
Chiondo unit market	Nkhotakota	Center	Open	Fairly accessible	In village	5 km	5 km	5 km	5 km
Kasongo unit market	Phalombe	South	Open	Difficult to access	In village	5 km	27 km	27 km	27 km
Lundu unit market (Mkumba seasonal)	Blantyre	South	Closed	Difficult to access	In village	7 km	7 km	7 km	7 km
Kakoma (Tombondera seasonal market)	Chikwawa	South	Closed	Fairly accessible	2 km	2 km	10 km	10 km	10 km

Source: Authors' survey.

the Eswazini site). All except three sites had a primary school located within the community. However, other essential infrastructure such as a market place, health facilities, police posts, and post offices were often located far from the communities, generally between 5 and 15 kilometers away. All 10 sites present a fairly diversified agricultural sector in terms of both crops and livestock types. There are also a significant number of nonfarm activities. Staple food production did not differ dramatically across the 10 sites, as they all produced maize as well as other food crops such as groundnuts, cassava, and sweet potatoes. However, there are considerable differences in cash crops, with three sites producing cotton and the rest being more involved in tobacco production, but with some households also producing other cash crops such as soybeans and paprika.

Basic Findings of the Qualitative Study

The results of the interviews and focus group discussions indicate that private traders—both large-scale traders and small vendors—are progressively replacing ADMARC as buyers/sellers of crops, especially in markets with well-developed infrastructure. Large-scale traders are not many, and they specialize mainly in the purchase of crops, particularly cash crops. Small-scale unlicensed traders (or small vendors), on the other hand, are very common and provide an accessible marketing channel for buying and selling maize in the rural areas.

It is these small vendors that to some extent have bridged the gap left by ADMARC's inability to provide reliable and efficient marketing services. Small vendors tend to have more regular supplies of maize than ADMARC markets, and they appear to be active in all villages and now constitute the preferred marketing channel for selling of produce. During the recent food crisis in 2002, vendors operated in all villages and had maize to sell throughout the famine, albeit at unaffordable high prices. Even after the government made available—through ADMARC—maize at subsidized prices, small vendors were able to undercut the subsidized price and continued to be the main provider of maize in rural areas (apart from humanitarian assistance).

ADMARC often does not have adequate cash to buy produce from farmers. However, since most small traders work at the local level and almost exclusively engage in short-term arbitrage, they may be unable to guarantee food security in times of shortage (as reflected in the persisting wide price variations between pre-harvest and post-harvest periods). Thus the function of interregional and interseasonal arbitrage performed by ADMARC has not been taken over by these smaller agents.

Compared with the crop produce market, private sector involvement in the agricultural input market remains highly underdeveloped, with only a few private traders selling inputs in rural areas. Small vendors do not sell inputs to farmers, since most are mobile vendors who do not meet the capital and storage requirements of the input business. The agricultural input market in the rural areas is still dominated by ADMARC with a few large-scale wholesalers or limited companies in selected sample sites. Since most of the private traders who deal in inputs are located in urban and peri-urban centers, closure of markets has led to an increase in transport and transaction costs of input procurement for a large proportion of the rural population.

Further, the withdrawal of ADMARC does not appear to be compensated by an equivalent increase in private sector activity, resulting in overall lower competition (and efficiency) in marketing institutions. On the contrary, the immediate effect of closure of a seasonal market or decline in ADMARC business is the reduction in marketing institutions and hence a more concentrated market structure. Since farmers are not organized in marketing cooperatives or associations, the few private traders that access remote rural markets experience an increase in their monopsony power in buying produce from smallholder farmers, and an increase in their monopoly power in the sale of maize and inputs.

This finding is similar to the results of the Oxfam-financed study by Nthara (2002), which indicates that the number of private traders in particular markets is not positively correlated with the absence of ADMARC markets. This finding is also confirmed by the observation that in many closed seasonal markets (and in the many nonfunctional unit markets), rural households now use the services of ADMARC in alternative active markets, and the distance traveled is longer than before seasonal markets were closed. This implies that immediate effect of the closure of markets is to reduce the profitability of smallholder agriculture, as reflected both in the increase in transaction costs for farmers and higher margins for the traders. This is reflected in the negative views expressed in the focus group discussions, which suggest that a range of negative effects has been experienced by communities (and particularly smallholder farmers) as a result of marketing liberalization (as experienced both through the closure of ADMARC seasonal markets and the decline in ADMARC's business at unit markets).

The price competitiveness of private traders is also an important indicator of the effect of the closure of ADMARC markets. In contrast to ADMARC's stable prices, small vendors' maize prices tend to be very volatile from one community to the next, or even within the same community. The high volatility of prices reflects the fact that most private traders face little local competition and are able to operate as monopsonists/

monopolists in the local maize markets. This supports the findings of Fafchamps and Gabre-Madhin (2001), who find relatively high profit margins for Malawian traders, suggesting that there is little competition among traders, and therefore the low efficiency of the private marketing system in Malawi.[27] Where active, therefore, ADMARC also plays an important role in benchmark prices through open access to information to smallholder farmers.

Finally, another issue of concern is the lack of regulation and enforcement of fair trading practices of private traders in rural areas. The poor quality of business practices negatively affects the efficiency of private marketing channels. It also leads to widespread claims of cheating on measurement and weights on the part of small vendors. Similarly, the lack of a clear standard for quality grading gives rise to many commercial disputes.

In sum, ADMARC markets in rural areas appear to play an important role as distribution networks for affordable maize in the lean season and in times of famine, in providing benchmark prices, in providing a reliable source of inputs, and in purchasing crop produce from farmers. Even in markets where private traders are particularly active, notably border markets, the withdrawal of ADMARC markets may have negative consequences for food security and regular access to input.

However, given the qualitative nature of the study, caution must be exercised in generalizing the results of the study. First, it is important to note that the perceptions on closure of markets cannot be filtered out from the effects of other factors that are affecting ADMARC's performance. Moreover, the study was conducted against the background of the famine that engulfed Malawi and southern Africa in the 2001/2 season, and some of the views from the smallholder farmers could be influenced by the famine situation.[28] Further, the study focuses on 10 sites of the many markets ADMARC has throughout the country and, therefore, the results allow only some general insights in the operations of agricultural marketing systems in Malawi.[29] In addition, there were no closed-unit markets in the sample, and the impact of closure of unit markets is inferred from closed seasonal markets and the general situation of declining ADMARC business activities in most of its markets. Also, very few interviews were conducted with private traders.

THE MAIN FINDINGS AND POLICY RECOMMENDATIONS OF THE PSIA STUDY

Three studies have been carried out as part of the PSIA to investigate the impact of access to ADMARC on household welfare. Two studies use econometric techniques on data from the IHS-1 and the CPS-4, while the third study uses an array of qualitative research methods to solicit households' and other stakeholders' reactions during field interviews in 2002.

The results of the analysis indicate that access to ADMARC has a positive impact on household welfare. Specifically, the results indicate that per capita consumption can be up to 20 percent higher for households living closer to ADMARC facilities. This can be taken as evidence that ADMARC facilities provide rural households with valuable access to a marketing channel for buying inputs, selling their outputs, and purchasing maize for self-consumption.

This conclusion is supported by an analysis of price behavior. In contrast to ADMARC's stable prices, small vendors' maize prices tend to be very volatile across communities, or even within the same community. The high volatility of prices probably reflects the fact that most private traders in remote areas face little local competition and are able to operate as monopsonists/monopolists in the local maize markets. This is also supported by the findings of Fafchamps and Gabre-Madhin (2001) who find relatively high profit margins for Malawian traders, suggesting little competition among traders, and therefore low efficiency of the private marketing system in Malawi. Where active, ADMARC appears to improve the operation of markets by increasing competition and providing information on benchmark prices.

The second major finding follows directly from the first one: the beneficial impact of proximity to ADMARC markets is more important in remote rural areas, far from major roads. More remote areas have less-developed private markets, and alternatives to ADMARC services are less likely to exist there. In other words, ADMARC's impact depends on the availability of alternative marketing channels. In less remote areas, higher competition can be expected to lower marketing margins, hence reducing the benefit of access to ADMARC's pan-territorial prices. Indeed, this is confirmed by the finding that in areas where private market infrastructure is developed and market services function, ADMARC facilities do not have a significant impact on farm households.

The third and final finding is that the role of ADMARC is important in maize sales during the hungry season, but much less important during the harvesting season. This reflects the fact that small traders engage mainly in buying maize from farmers after harvest, and less on selling maize to consumers during the lean season. They transport maize out of remote areas and do not generally engage store it. Similarly, small traders are not generally involved in agricultural input supply in remote areas.

A number of policy recommendations follow from the findings of the PSIA study:

■ First, completely eliminating ADMARC facilities may ignore the fact that well-functioning market institutions and infrastructure do not exist uniformly throughout the country. In the short run, providing ADMARC facilities may be beneficial in some areas that are underserved. The question then becomes whether ADMARC can play this useful function in a cost-effective manner, or this social function could be executed more effectively through other market-based mechanisms. In broad terms, two main options for providing the social services have been identified. However, neither their operational feasibility nor their advantages and disadvantages have been assessed as part of the PSIA, and need to be explored by expert consultants:

➢ Option A: The establishment of a specific (public) enterprise responsible for undertaking "social activities" on behalf of government. This organization would (1) take over and manage ADMARC's physical infrastructure located in clearly identified "remote/social markets"; (2) have a lean work force; (3) be managed transparently on the basis of clear policies and procedures; and (4) be funded through a subsidy specifically identified in the government budget. Ideally, although the infrastructure may remain government property, the management of the "social ADMARC" should be subcontracted to a credible and independent third party. An analysis of ADMARC's financial operations will provide some information on the extent of overheads and administration infrastructure (and personnel) needed to operate the "remote/social" market facilities and the amount of public subsidy required.

➢ Option B: The tendering by government of specifically identified "social marketing programs," on a least-cost basis, to any eligible enterprise (including ADMARC). This option would in theory be more transparent and efficient and would not require any implementation capacity on the government side. However, it may be more difficult to implement, essentially because of the difficulty for government to make sure that commercial operators carry out the agreed activities. Hence, it would require a heavy dose of monitoring by a credible neutral party.

■ Second, maintaining ADMARC in its current form is wasteful. Its services are not required in less remote areas of the country, where the activity of the private sector is already well established. ADMARC's facilities in developed parts of the country should be auctioned off to the private sector. All of ADMARC's other nonmarketing activities should also be sold to private operators. These activities are not needed for the operation of the remote markets, and hence should be operated as a private company.

■ Third, in the medium term, as the private sector expands its marketing activities in remote parts of the country, the role for the government to facilitate food marketing in remote areas will diminish. The government can accelerate this process by investing in market infrastructure in remote areas and facilitating the development of institutions that bring greater transparency and competition in market transactions. These measures will enhance private sector participation in the agricultural sector and eventually eliminate the need for such government support.

In sum, the findings of the study partly address the objections to the privatization that had been raised by the government and Civil Society Organizations (CSOs). They also confirm the donors' position that ADMARC was wasteful, and that it could be substantially downsized in less remote areas without significant social risks. Hence, though the study did not substantially alter the policy advice provided by World Bank to the government, it has increased the awareness and emphasis that the Bank places on maintaining social services, and the importance of identifying a more efficient alternative to address market failures in remote areas.

SHORTCOMINGS IN THE PROCESS OF THE ADMARC PSIA AND PROGRESS IN DISSEMINATING ITS FINDINGS

The process followed in the ADMARC PSIA has not been without its flaws and misunderstandings. In fact, several NGOs have criticized the ADMARC PSIA for the limited extent of its consultation at the design stage, and the long delay in disseminating the findings of the study.

Consultations for the PSIA and the Parallel Oxfam Study

Various stakeholders were consulted in the early stages in the design and execution of the ADMARC study, but the consultative process was not as widespread as it could have been. In large part, this is because the study was one of the initial pilot studies carried out using the PSIA approach. It is only as the PSIA process evolved that the value of wide consultations, inclusiveness, and consensus building became better understood. In hindsight, it is clear that wider consultations at the beginning would have contributed to reduce controversy and foster greater local ownership of the PSIA and the proposed reforms.

A few months prior to the Bank starting the PSIA, Oxfam Malawi commissioned a paper on ADMARC. The study was prepared by the Department of Economics of the University of Malawi and involved a survey of rural poor (via a household questionnaire and focus groups) and a literature review of other countries' experiences with marketing boards (Nthara 2002). The survey targeted areas in all the three regions of the country where ADMARC is still operational and where ADMARC has closed its markets.

The findings of the Oxfam study are similar to those of the PSIA report, highlighting the important role ADMARC plays in food security, particularly with respect to maize sales and input markets. The study finds that ADMARC's role in purchasing agricultural produce from small-holder farmers is limited, even in markets where it is still operational, because of its price uncompetitiveness, its late opening of markets in the season, and its lack of cash for most of the buying season. However, with respect to selling food commodities to food-deficient households and selling inputs to smallholder farmers, Nthara (2002) finds that ADMARC still plays a critical role. This is confirmed by the findings of our PSIA qualitative study.

The Oxfam study acknowledges that maintaining the status quo would not be the best way forward. It recognizes that, although ADMARC has played an important social role, this has cost the government, and hence Malawians, more than necessary, mainly because of political inter-ference in the operation of ADMARC's social activities. At the same time, the study contends that total privatization is not a panacea either. In fact, it is likely that a privatized ADMARC may decide to pull out of those areas where it not making a profit. The Oxfam study's proposed solution takes the form of a joint venture between the government and the private sec-tor. The private sector would have a majority shareholding in ADMARC, with the government having some direct influence through its board of trustees to safeguard the interests of the Malawian people. Although this arrangement amounts to privatization of ADMARC, the form the priva-tization takes is a qualified one.

In hindsight, the fact that the findings of the Oxfam study are remarkably similar to those of the PSIA report, and that the study was independently commissioned by civil society, has strengthened the PSIA process. In fact, the Oxfam report has effectively become a fourth study of the PSIA process, and one that is fully "owned" by the civil society organizations.

Disseminating the PSIA Findings and the Repeal of the ADMARC Act

The findings of the various studies were widely debated at a seminar in early January 2004. Although the dissemination workshop benefited from broad participation by civil society and donors, it was nevertheless surrounded by controversy. In order not to postpone negotiations for a new World Bank credit, the government decided to repeal the ADMARC Act prior to wide dissemination of the findings of the PSIA. The president called the parliament for an emergency session between Christmas and New Year's to discuss and approve conversion of ADMARC into a limited company, in spite of strong opposition within parliament and across the country, and prior to the dissemination workshop in January 2004.

The World Bank did not interfere with the procedure chosen by the president to repeal the ADMARC Act. The Bank's view was that the repeal of the Act was merely a political decision, and no real restructuring was going to take place by repealing the Act (and indeed none has taken place as yet). The repeal of the Act was merely a gesture on the part of government to show commitment to the restructuring process, which would be undertaken as part of the credit agreement. The decision regarding the type of restructuring to be undertaken was to be defined at a later stage—only after consultations with stakeholders had taken place, and with the assistance of technical experts/consultants who would prepare detailed restructuring plans. The understanding with government was that the restructuring, notably in the area of social markets, would be consistent with the findings/recommendations of the PSIA (which had already been shared with government several months earlier).

Although the repeal of the Act did not, in itself, introduce any changes to the operation of ADMARC, in the absence of a clearly articulated government plan for ADMARC reforms it raised concerns across civil society. In fact, some in civil society organizations went so far as to suggest that the dissemination of the findings of the PSIA had been purposefully delayed because the World Bank wanted to suppress its findings. However, the background studies had been placed on the World Bank PSIA Web site in mid-2003, several months before the dissemination workshop, and were publicly available. Also the draft PSIA synthesis report was shared with the government in September 2003, and its main findings were informally discussed with civil society leaders (from the Malawi Economic Justice Network, MEJN) also in September 2003.[30]

In hindsight, therefore, it seems clear that the Bank may have underestimated the symbolic importance of repealing the ADMARC Act and the politics that became associated with this event. It would have been wiser to ensure that the dissemination seminar had occurred well before the debate in parliament on the Act's repeal. The World Bank could have used its leverage better by requesting that a short public awareness campaign be carried out before the government went ahead to repeal the ADMARC Act, in line with the general principles and guidance of the PSIA approach (which encourages transparency and involvement of all stakeholders at each step).

In spite of the controversy, the dissemination workshop was very well attended by government officials, CSO representatives, donors, and a few members of parliament. Oxfam Malawi was invited to present the findings of their study, which were presented by Dr. Nthara. The similarity of the findings from the two studies helped to bring together the different parties to focus on the next steps. Civil society organizations issued a statement at the workshop confirming their agreement with the findings of the PSIA, though criticizing the manner in which the process of preparation of the study was handled and the timing of its dissemination.

In this context, it is important to emphasize that probably the major achievement of the ADMARC PSIA is that its findings and recommendations have been accepted by all stakeholders. Moreover, the initiative showed that the Bank was prepared to review its longstanding demand that ADMARC be privatized entirely. The recommendations of the PSIA are more nuanced than earlier proposals and constitute a much better basis for restructuring ADMARC and improving the operation of agricultural markets in Malawi.

Follow-up to the PSIA Report and Progress in Implementing the Reforms

Shortly after the January 2004 workshop, the findings of the PSIA were incorporated into the new World Bank Structural Adjustment Program, which was approved in April 2004. In a nutshell, the restructuring will separate ADMARC's social and commercial functions so that they are managed by separate institutional entities with lean organizational structures. Commercial functions involve undertaking profitable marketing and production operations. Social functions involve running those rural markets for produce as well as farm inputs that are not commercially viable because the volumes of trade are low and the costs of transportation are high. Since the envisaged commercial and social institutions are to have lean organizational structures, the restructuring process will also inevitably require that a substantial number of staff be retrenched.

In line with this agreement, the government has recently set in motion the process to restructure ADMARC. In early 2005, the government advertised internationally to hire a team of technical advisers on a consultancy basis to work collaboratively in operationalizing the restructuring of ADMARC: a business reengineering adviser, a human resources adviser, a financial services adviser, and a social functions adviser. The consultants are expected to

- develop a detailed and clear business structure and action plan for the new commercial company, with a leaner corporate structure (for example, as a single commercial holding conglomerate controlling individual strategic business groups as independent companies), as well as implement the action plan;
- design a system and action plan to provide social marketing services (currently being carried out on behalf of the government by ADMARC Ltd) in a transparent and cost-efficient manner under a separate organizational structure, as well as implement the action plan;
- develop a retrenchment strategy complete with an action plan, as well as implement the action plan;
- design organizational structures for the proposed commercial company and the proposed institution for the management of social functions, develop human resource plans for the two institutions, and then implement the plans; and
- undertake a valuation of assets and property, and produce business and financial plans (with full costings) relating to the proposed commercial company and the proposed system of delivering social functions.

For the restructuring to be operationalized, a detailed business restructuring plan, a financial plan, a human resources plan, and a plan for the operations of the social functions will need to be prepared by ADMARC's management with technical assistance from these experts. Once the government has approved it, the plan will form the basis for the restructuring of ADMARC's operations along separate commercial and social lines. The expectation is that this process would be complete by late 2006.

CONCLUSIONS AND LESSON LEARNED

The experience with the restructuring of ADMARC in Malawi shows that policy reforms that have significant social impacts are difficult to implement and require adequate consensus, which takes into account the main concerns raised by the stakeholders, is built about the way forward.

In the case of ADMARC, the PSIA approach has allowed the World Bank to review the evidence jointly with the government and stakeholders, and to adjust its policy advice to account for some the objections raised by stakeholders. It is hoped that this process has created more understanding and may lead to ownership of the reforms, and increase the likelihood of achieving successful reform outcomes. As the reform process has not yet been completed, it would be precipitous to declare this approach successful. Nevertheless, a few lessons can be drawn from the experience thus far.

- First, on a technical level, the combination of quantitative and qualitative methodologies promoted by the PSIA approach provides a rich understanding of issues and facilitates understanding by all stakeholders. In turn, this greater understanding facilitates ownership of the findings and consensus on the subsequent reforms.
- Second, the consultative process advocated in the PSIA approach raises the profile of the debate and provides a basis for policy decisions "owned" by the government and CSOs. It is crucial to ensure that the consultations are as wide as possible from the beginning of the process, and that transparency and information exchange are maintained throughout the process. This was not done adequately in the ADMARC PSIA, a lack that has been a cause of significant misunderstandings.
- Finally, the joint PSIA study has improved the quality of the World Bank recommendations by providing a more nuanced stance on ADMARC. In fact, the recommendations adopted after the PSIA take into account some of the earlier objections raised by stakeholders about the unconditional privatization of the entire ADMARC structure, and the inefficiencies associated with the limited private sector capacity to fill in the gap left by ADMARC's withdrawal in remote areas.

The World Bank has started a new PSIA study in Malawi, in collaboration with the Ministry of Agriculture and all the stakeholders, to investigate the distributional impacts of liberalizing various aspects of tobacco marketing and sales in Malawi. The lessons learned in the process of the ADMARC PSIA have been applied well so far. The consultative process has been more inclusive and the findings are expected to result in significant policy improvements during 2005–6.

NOTES

1. The authors wish to thank the Norwegian Trust Fund (administered by the World Bank) and GTZ for funding this study. GTZ provided support in terms of the analytics as well as funding for the dissemination seminar. Reiner Forster (GTZ and World Bank) supervised the qualitative study and Renate Kirsch (GTZ) provided substantial comments and advice. The authors also wish to thank Philippe Le Houerou, Anis Dani, Stefano Paternostro, Sudhir Chitale, Maxwell Mkwezalamba, Louise Fox, Jean Paul Chausse, Stanley Hiwa, Francis M'Buka and Tijan Sallah for the many useful comments. The findings, interpretations and conclusions reported in this document represent solely the authors' views and should not be attributed to the World Bank or to the Government of Malawi.

2. *Seasonal markets* are mobile selling points that are opened on demand with a temporary sales force. They operate mainly during the harvesting seasons and are used to purchase and sell produce from farmers. *Unit markets* have permanent structures such as small storage facilities and offices with staff. They generally operate throughout the year and buy and sell produce and farm inputs. *Parent markets* combine permanent storage facilities with administrative offices that oversee unit and seasonal markets.

3. ADMARC investments as of September 2003 included Mitco (100 percent owned), Tobacco Marketing Ltd (100 percent), Malawi Finance Company (100 percent), Manica Malawi Ltd (50 percent), Alexander Forbes (49 percent), Auction Holdings Ltd (47 percent), Indebank (27 percent), the National Bank of Malawi (17 percent), Nedbank (2.7 percent), Illovo sugar (7 percent), Clark Cotton (49 percent), and National Investment Trusts Ltd (15 percent).

4. It should be pointed out, however, that this corresponds to as much as 20 to 30 percent of domestic *marketed* production.

5. In addition, the impact of market liberalization reforms on different categories of smallholder farmers and laborers is not clear. For example, some studies suggest that agricultural laborers who earn less than the legislated minimum wage are the most food insecure. In 1993, the importation and distribution of fertilizer were opened up to the private sector, and in 1994/5 subsidies were reduced to 5 percent. The reduction in subsidies, combined with the devaluation of the Malawi kwacha, led to a doubling of the real cost of fertilizer and had a negative impact on fertilizer usage.

6. ADMARC's accounts are not regularly audited and, hence, reliable data on the financial performance of ADMARC is not readily available.

7. In fact, as government support has dwindled, in recent years ADMARC and has had to introduce restrictions on the quantity it is able to purchase, and it has had difficulties in meeting demand in times of low production.

8. It was agreed that the study would serve to guide the formulation of a detailed proposal to restructure and/or privatize ADMARC. It was also agreed that some of the heavily loss-making subsidiaries of ADMARC, which were not related to ADMARC agricultural marketing functions, could be earmarked

for privatization (notably David Whitehead & Sons, Cold Storage, Shire Bus Lines, and Cotton Ginning).

9. Funding was provided by GTZ and the Norwegian Trust Fund administered by the World Bank.

10. For a full report on the IHS-1 methodology and findings, see National Statistical Office (2000) and Benson et al. (2002).

11. Household expenditure is a widely accepted proxy for overall household welfare.

12. More remote areas have less-developed private markets, and alternatives to ADMARC services are less likely to exist there. Higher competition can be expected to lower marketing margins, hence reducing the benefit of access to ADMARC's pan-territorial prices.

13. In this chapter, road access is measured as the straight-line distance in kilometers of the household's enumeration area to the nearest primary or secondary road (primary roads are generally tarmac roads, while secondary roads are mostly dirt). In the first sample, on average households are located about 1.3 kilometers from the nearest primary road. In the second sample, on average households are located about 6.5 kilometers from the nearest primary road.

14. As discussed, however, it is virtually impossible to disentangle the cost of the ADMARC's marketing activities from its other operations.

15. The dependent variable is thus defined as $LOGDIFF = LNEXP02 - LNEXP97$.

16. Specifically, three sets of control variables (elements of $X\beta$) are included in the regressions: (1) demographic characteristics that have an important bearing on households' ability to manage economic change, including sector and type of employment; (2) variables that control for access to resources and institutions that assist households to uphold or smooth consumption in face of changing incomes; and (3) changes in key asset variables that are likely to affect income earnings in the household.

17. As mentioned in Sharma et al. (2002), it is likely that reported 2002 expenditure levels are higher simply because of improvements in survey administration. The systematic part of this conflation factor is also embedded in A.

18. As private sector market-related institutions are more concentrated around urban centers, the impact of ADMARC is expected to increase with distance from the urban center.

19. All else being the same, households that consistently carry stocks of staples are less likely to go to ADMARC to procure them.

20. The dummy variable for "participation in safety net or other social assistance programs" provides an important control for the availability of such programs in the area and also for the household's access to them. Households that benefit from social safety nets are less dependent on marketing their agricultural product (compared with households without access to such programs). Hence, ADMARC services are likely to be less useful for such households, and its impact, therefore, is correspondingly lower.

21. For the same reason, even though the *F*-test on the joint significance of all ADMARC coefficients rejects the null hypothesis that ADMARC proximity has no impact (at 10 percent probability level), interpretation remains problematic.

22. It should be noted that proximity to ADMARC appears to be weakly significant in the results of the regression in levels (equation 12.2). The *F*-test of the joint impact of all ADMARC coefficients rejects the hypothesis of zero impact with a 10 percent probability. In terms of the individual impacts, the impact of proximity to ADMARC is not statistically different from zero but has the expected negative sign, implying that the impact of ADMARC decreases as distance to ADMARC increases. The interactive impact of proximity to ADMARC and distance from urban centers is statistically different from zero, and suggests that the impact of ADMARC decreases with distance from urban centers (reducing to zero as distance approaches about 26 kilometers). As discussed, this is contrary to our expectations. The results on the other interactive dummies are similar to those for the preferred model presented above.

23. The selection of interviewees and discussion partners accounted for differences with respect to social and economic stratification, ethnic and livelihood diversity, and gender; this was done in consultation with local leaders and local extension staff. The discussions focused on perceptions of well-being and trends in the last five years, livelihood strategies and cropping patterns, the problem analysis, cause-effects diagrams, trend analysis, institutional analysis and analysis of opportunities, and coping and survival strategies.

24. Different stakeholders existing or operating in the areas were interviewed, such as traditional leaders, private traders, shopkeepers, extension agents, food security organizations, and nongovernmental organizations. In each location at least 12 key informants' interviews, including key informants in the surroundings of the sites were conducted, with at least one informant for each well-being group identified by the community in focus group discussions.

25. The institutions and stakeholders visited included ADMARC management, the National Association of Smallholder Farmers, the National Economic Council, Grain and Milling Limited, the Smallholder Farmer Fertilizer Revolving Fund, the World Food Programme (WFP), Bharat Trading Limited, and the Ministry of Agriculture and Livestock Development. The purpose of the institutional interviews was to assess the objectives, motivations, interests, concerns, and resistance of different stakeholders and institutions to the closure of ADMARC markets.

26. Note however that the sample was limited to remote rural areas; no urban, semi-urban, or locations close to a main road were included.

27. Fafchamps and Gabre-Madhin (2001) show evidence that the private marketing system is dominated by petty traders with substantial financial and capacity constraints, and that interseasonal and interregional arbitrage does not form part of the activities of this class of traders. They note that the aver-

age private trader in Malawi operates within a radius of 53 kilometers. They also find evidence that the efficiency of private traders is constrained by the high transaction costs in the form of search and transport costs.

28. As drought and crop failures are becoming increasingly regular in Malawi, however, the timing of the study may also be regarded as an advantage.

29. Purposeful sampling of a few villages was used to provide "ideal type" situations and to explore typical situations in remote rural areas; therefore, the sample was not drawn to be statistically representative at the national level.

30. The government postponed the dissemination workshop, originally planned for November 2003, because the counterpart official in the ministry traveled abroad to participate in workshops in the Netherlands and the United States during October 2003. The final printed version of the report was shared with the government in mid December 2003, with a request to disseminate it to stakeholders in preparation for the dissemination workshop in mid January. However, distribution of the report did not actually occur until early January 2004.

REFERENCES

Abbott, R. D., and Poulin, R. J. 1996. "The Future of ADMARC: A Policy Analysis." Agricultural Policy Analysis Project (APAP) Research Report 1012, USAID, Washington, DC.

ADMARC. 1990. ADMARC Annual Report and Accounts. Blantyre: ADMARC.

Benson T., J. Kaphuka, S. Kanyanda, and R. Chinula. 2002. *Malawi: An Atlas of Social Statistics.* National Statistical Office, Zomba, Malawi and International Food Policy Research Institute, Washington, DC, USA.

Binswanger, H., S. R. Khandakar, and M. Rosenzweig. 1993. "How Infrastructure and Financial Institutions Affect Agricultural Output and Investment in India." *Journal of Development Economics* 41: 337–66.

Chirwa, E. W. 1998. "Fostering Private Food Marketing and Food Policies after Liberalisation: The Case of Malawi." In *Liberalized and Neglected? Food Marketing Policies in Eastern Africa,* ed. P. Seppala, World Development Studies 12, Helsinki: United Nations University/WIDER.

Deaton, A. 1998. *The Analysis of Household Surveys.* Baltimore: Johns Hopkins Press for the World Bank.

Evans, H. 1990. "Rural-Urban Linkages and Structural Transformation." Discussion Paper INU 71, Infrastructure and Urban Development, World Bank, Washington, DC.

Fafchamps, M., and E. Gabre-Madhin. 2001. "Agricultural Markets in Benin and Malawi: Operation and Performance of Traders." Working Paper Series 2734, World Bank, Washington, DC.

Harrigan, J. 1991. "Malawi." In *Aid and Power: The World Bank and Policy Based Lending,* ed. P. Mosley, J. Harrigan, and J. Toye, Vol. 2: Case Studies, pp. 201–67. London: Routledge.

Kherallah M., N. Minot, R. Kachule, B. G. Soule, and P. Berry. 2001. *Impact of Agricultural Market Reforms on Smallholder Farmers in Benin and Malawi: Final Report*, 2 vols. Washington, DC: IFPRI.

Kydd, J., and R. Christiansen. 1982. "Structural Change in Malawi since Independence: Consequences of a Development Strategy based on Large-Scale Agriculture." *World Development* 10 (5): 355–75.

Lundberg, M. 2005. "Agricultural Market Reforms." In vol. 1 of *Analyzing the Distributional Impact of Selected Reforms.*, ed. A. Coudouel and S. Paternostro, 145–212. Washington, DC: World Bank.

National Statistical Office. 2000. *The Poverty Analysis of the Integrated Household Survey 1997–98: The State of Malawi's Poor: The Incidence, Depth, and Severity of Poverty.* http://www.nso.malawi.net.

Nthara, K. 2002. *What Needs to Be Done to Improve the Impact of ADMARC on the Poor, Phase II.* Final report prepared for the Joint Oxfam Program in Malawi, Blantyre.

O&M Associates. 1999. *Commercialization and Privatisation Programme for ADMARC.* Draft final report prepared for the Ministry of Finance, Lilongwe.

Rubey, L. 2003. "After the Food Crisis in Malawi: Finding a Way Forward." Mimeo. USAID, Lilongwe.

———. 2004. "Do No Harm: How Well-Intentioned (but Misguided) Government Actions Exacerbate Food Insecurity: Two Case Studies from Malawi." Mimeo. USAID, Lilongwe.

Scarborough, V. 1990. "Domestic Food Marketing Liberalization in Malawi: A Preliminary Assessment." ADU Occasional Paper 13, Wye College, University of London, London.

Sharma, M., M. Tsoka, E. Payongayong, and T. Benson. 2002. *Analysis of Poverty Dynamics in Malawi with an Assessment of the Impact of ADMARC on Household Welfare.* Draft report submitted to the World Bank.

World Bank. 2003. *A User's Guide to Poverty and Social Impact Analysis.* Washington, DC: World Bank, Poverty Reduction Group (PRMPR) and Social Development Department (SDV).

———. 2004. *Malawi Country Economic Memorandum: Policies for Accelerating Growth.* Report 25293-MAI. Africa Region, PREM 1. Washington, DC.

13

TAJIKISTAN
Cotton Farmland Privatization

SAROSH SATTAR AND SHABIH MOHIB

The objective of this Poverty and Social Impact Analysis (PSIA) was to analyze the poverty impact of cotton farmland privatization, which began in Tajikistan in 1998.[1] Understanding these changes to the structure of the farmland economy is important because of the predominance of the agricultural sector in the economy and its relationship to the population's welfare. Also agriculture plays a significant role in its ability to reduce the high level of poverty, especially among rural households, in Tajikistan. Unless land privatization—especially in cotton-growing areas—is carried out in such a way as to directly improve farmers' welfare, its benefits will translate into little real reduction in poverty.

The analysis focused primarily on the income implications of cotton farmland privatization. The privatization process for these lands has diverged the most from true land privatization, which is normally understood to be giving farmers title over a specific piece of land and authority to grow what they choose and sell their output where they choose. The three main questions that this report addressed were

- What has been the impact of cotton farmland privatization on poverty?
- Who currently benefits from cotton production and marketing?
- How can cotton production and marketing be improved to increase productivity and income?

The findings of the report suggest total estimated losses ranging from US$163 million to US$205 million annually, and are the result of the current structure of cotton farmland production, processing, and marketing. These losses (which translate into 10 to 13 percent of GDP) in potential income for farmers have a severe and negative impact on the welfare of farmers and their families, with consequences of high poverty rates and extensive deprivation.

The study's discussion of the impact of privatization focused primarily on income rather than more broadly on social consequences. The reason for this approach was that privatization did not have a sufficiently long enough track record in Tajikistan to allow for distinguishing the specific social impact of privatization from the other changes that were occurring throughout the country.

COTTON IN TAJIKISTAN: A BRIEF BACKGROUND

The agricultural sector plays a critical role in Tajikistan's economy even though 93 percent of the land is mountainous. Most of the arable land is concentrated in the Khatlon and Sugd provinces, with limited arable land in the *Rayon* province under Republican Supervision (RRS). Fifty-six percent of irrigated lands are under rotational cotton cultivation.[2] Cotton is the most important agricultural crop in Tajikistan in terms of employment and export earnings: the cotton sector employs more than half of the labor force and generates about 18 percent of the country's total export earnings.

Recent economic growth has resulted in poverty reduction but there has been concern about the concentration of poverty in rural areas, which are mostly cotton growing. Over the last five years the GDP growth rate has averaged about 8 percent, while poverty rates, measured at US$2.15 per day (at purchasing power parity), have fallen—from 81 percent in 1999 to 64 percent in 2003. However, Tajikistan remains the poorest country in the Central Asia, with a per capita GDP of US$191. Poverty is concentrated in rural areas, where 73 percent of the population resides. About 65 percent of the total population live in Khatlon and Sughd, the two main cotton-growing provinces. These two provinces account for 72 percent of the poor and 75 percent of the extremely poor, as shown in table 13.1. This is an interesting finding: since cotton accounts for about 11 percent of GDP and is the major cash crop, cotton-producing areas would not be expected to be the poorest regions of the country.

Significant liberalization and partial privatization have taken place in the cotton sector since independence, but there are problems with

Table 13.1 Regional Distribution of the Population, the Poor, and the Extremely Poor, 2003

Province	Population	Distribution of the poor		Percent of population living in poverty		
		All poor	Extreme poor	Urban	Rural	Total
Khatlon	33	40	51	78	78	78
Sugd	32	32	24	59	66	64
RSS	23	17	16	55	44	45
Dushanbe	9	7	3	49	. . .	49
GBAO	3	4	6	74	86	84
Tajikistan	100	100	100	59	65	64

Source: Tajikistan Poverty Assessment Update, World Bank (2004).
Note: The poverty lines have been adjusted for regional prices differences.

passing the proceeds through to the farmer. Price distortions as well as institutional setting issues hamper effective pass-through. The ginning subsector has been privatized, input prices have been liberalized, the financing and marketing of cotton have also been privatized, and most of the cotton farmlands have been restructured, but only a minority of them have been privatized.

Most cotton farms were "privatized" by giving *collective* land tenure rights to farmers. These collective rights have resulted in no significant increase in individual farmers' authority compared with their authority in Soviet times. State farm restructuring, the main restructuring method that the government has used to "privatize" collective farms, confers collective land tenure upon the group of farmers working on the land, but with little additional real change in terms of decision-making authority. Though farmers have the right to opt out of the collective farm, this could result in a farmer who declined to participate in the collective receiving land that is noncontiguous and possibly below average in quality; hence few—if any—farmers leave the collective. Farm management has remained in the hands of the same individuals who were managers prior to privatization. Though they are nominally elected by the farmers in the collectives, the key to their authority is the support of local governments.

Financing for the collective cotton farms is provided by loan brokers to farm managers primarily in the form of inputs in kind. The farm manager agrees to deliver a certain quantity of seed cotton in return for the financing. The ginning subsector is controlled principally by input financiers. This subsector acts as a de facto monopsony. The marketing of cotton is mainly carried out by input financiers, as they have the first claim on cotton produced by farms.

The World Bank has implemented a Farm Privatization Support Project (FPSP) whereby 10 collective farms (of which 8 are cotton) have been transformed into small family farms where the government has issued land use certificates to individual farmers along with seed capital grants.[3] Under this method farmers have direct control over crop choice and all financial appropriative decisions. Moreover, this project supported infrastructure rehabilitation, primarily of the water distribution network. Water user associations were formed, which ensured the payment of water user charges.

Lint cotton production has fallen from its 1990s level, although there has been some improvement since 1999. This is primarily because seed cotton production has fallen, and lint conversion rates have dropped. The area under cultivation has remained fairly constant, although seed cotton yields have fallen by 32 percent during 1990–2003, going from about 2.8 to about 1.9 tons per hectare, as shown in figure 13.1. The major reasons for this fall in yield are (1) the poor quality of inputs, which is a result of the lack of an efficient crop-financing mechanism; (2) inefficiencies in the ginning subsector; (3) problems with the marketing of cotton; and (4) the lack of effective privatization of the factors of production.

Twin issues of vital importance confronting policy makers are how to improve productivity in the cotton sector and how to pursue privatization of cotton farmlands. These are two key objectives stated in the Tajikistan Poverty Reduction Strategy Paper (PRSP).

FIGURE 13.1   **Seed Cotton Yields and Area Cultivated, 1990–2003**

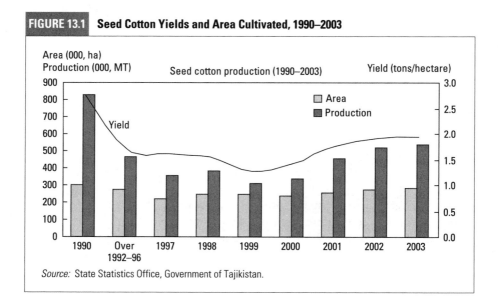

Source: State Statistics Office, Government of Tajikistan.

OBJECTIVE AND IMPLEMENTATION OF THE PSIA

The principal objective of this PSIA was to analyze the poverty impact of the privatization of cotton farmlands. The work sought to address three key questions:

- What was the impact of cotton farmland privatization on cotton production and marketing chains, in terms of prices and institutional arrangements and hence on poverty?
- Who benefited from cotton production and marketing?
- How can cotton production and marketing be improved to increase productivity and income?

The study endeavored to answer these questions by analyzing the poverty impact of cotton farmland privatization by different methods deployed in Tajikistan. The two methods were State Farm Restructuring (SFR) and the World Bank Farm Privatization Support Project (FPSP). In addition, the IFC had implemented the Farmers' Ownership Model (FOM), which provided financing to restructured and privatized farms. The main focus of the study was on access to land, crop choice, and the participation of farmers in the financial affairs of farms.

The study analyzed the cotton production and marketing chains and the distortions that existed within them. Where possible, these distortions were quantified. In addition, a stakeholder analysis was carried out to assess the incentives and relative importance of each stakeholder in the privatization process. Within this context, a gin zoning map was formulated for each cotton-producing *rayon,* showing the location of gins in the cotton-production areas along with the main loan brokers operating in that area.

Building on the discussion, we assessed the welfare impact of the inefficiencies in the cotton production and marketing chains. The analysis focused on the economy as a whole as well as on the welfare (as measured by income) of farmers.

The analysis provided some policy advice, with a rationale, for addressing the major issues with the aim of improving the welfare of the farmers and reducing poverty in Tajikistan.

It is important to state why the focus of this study was on only cotton farmlands. First, cotton farmlands make up three-fourths of total farmlands. Second, noncotton farmland privatization took place in a framework that provided farmers with full appropriative rights on lands. The Land Code was silent on the issue of renting and leasing of land; this practice was ongoing but informal for agricultural land. However, local governments were (and, as this chapter goes to print, they currently remain) at liberty to interpret the Land Code to determine whether land could be rented or not. There were no bottlenecks or impediments to the privatization of these lands. For most noncotton farms, the government gave inheritable but not tradable land use certificates to individual farmers. In addition, noncotton farms grow noncash crops and therefore have not attracted the rent-seeking vested interests that have affected the cotton sector.

METHODOLOGY OF THE ANALYSIS

The methodology adopted in this report included

- a partial equilibrium analysis on the impact of different farmland privatization methods on the incomes and welfare of farmers,
- a stakeholder analysis of the cotton sector in order to determine the incentive structures of various players and their control over the privatization process, and
- quantification of the costs of distortions and inefficiencies within the cotton production and marketing chains.

In deciding on the methodological approach for the PSIA, consideration was given to the following points:

- The importance of indirect impacts: The net effect of the privatization process would be transmitted mainly through two channels. The first channel would be the impact of privatization on farmers' incomes and welfare through asset endowments and changes in institutional arrangements. The second channel would be the overall impact on the economy of such privatization and the government's fiscal position that resulted from the change in cotton yields. In addition, the privatization process would alter the incentive structures of major stakeholders who control, either notionally or effectively, the different factors of production in the cotton sector.
- The availability of data: The primary source of data for quantitative analysis was the Tajikistan Living Standard Survey 2003. The problem here was that, from the dataset, it is not possible to distinguish clearly between cotton and noncotton farmers. There were only 79 households within the dataset that grew cotton, out of 1,572 rural agriculture households. These observations were insufficient for conducting robust quantitative analysis. However, significant statistical time-series data were available on seed cotton production and marketing by provinces. These data were supplemented by rich qualitative information that was available on the marketing and distribution chains.

■ Time and resource availability: Privatization of cotton-growing farmlands was ongoing at the time when this study was being conducted. There was no track record to make a comprehensive comparison of the differences in outcomes between state farms and restructured farms. Furthermore, an agricultural survey did not exist.

■ Local capacity: There were significant numbers of donors, civil society organizations, and international organizations involved in the cotton sector reform program in Tajikistan. These stakeholders also provided significant information for this study.

WHY PRIVATIZE FARMLANDS?

The primary reason for privatizing state and collective farms was to improve their productivity and to increase the incomes of farmers. Higher productivity (yields) would create a virtuous cycle of sustainable growth and poverty reduction.

Figure 13.2 shows that that most seed cotton cultivation takes place in the Khatlon and Sughd provinces, where 78 percent of the extremely

FIGURE 13.2 **Area Under Cultivation, by Province, 1997–2003**

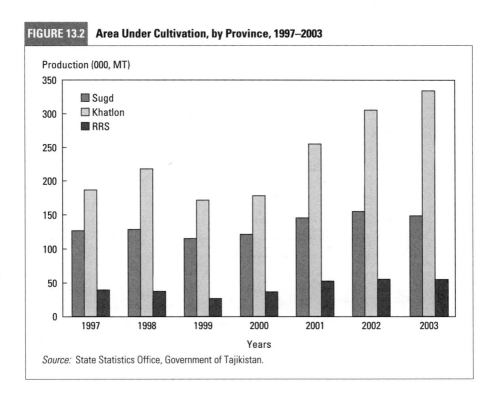

Source: State Statistics Office, Government of Tajikistan.

poor people live. Seed cotton yields have been increasing since 2000, but they remain significantly lower than their 1990 levels. In 2003 seed cotton yields were 1.9 tons per hectare, 32 percent lower than the 2.8 tons per hectare in 1990.

Lower yields represent direct losses to the country and to farmers in particular, in terms of income forgone. Analysis suggests that if seed cotton yields could be increased from 1.9 tons per hectare back up to 2.8 tons per hectare, Tajikistan would earn an additional US$100 million per year.

ALTERNATIVE FARM PRIVATIZATION METHODS

The process of privatizing cotton farmlands began in 1996. At that time there were 668 state and collective farms (*sovkhozes* and *kolkhozes*) and 168 seed and animal pedigree research farms. These farmlands were located primarily in the irrigated zone of Khatlon and Sughd and in RRS. After independence, Tajikistan opted to transform itself from a controlled economy to a market-based economy. Among other important areas of structural adjustments, farmland privatization became a key policy element of the move toward the market economy.

From 1997 onward the government implemented wide-ranging reforms in the cotton sector, including the deregulation of agricultural pricing, procurement, and trade policies. According to the government, almost 73 percent of all state and collective farms have to date been privatized. The majority of the remaining 27 percent of farmlands grow cotton; these remain state owned, collective farms. Privatization of cotton farmlands to date has used two methods: state farm restructuring (SFR) and the method used by the Bank's Farm Privatization Support Project (FPSP). These methods are described below. It is important to note that in Tajikistan the land is owned by the government, but its use right is vested with the Tajik citizen, family, individual, or group of individuals. The land use right is inheritable but this right cannot be rented, leased, transferred to nonfamily members, mortgaged, or sold. The land use right is registered and is backed by the government.

State Farm Restructuring

The process of state farm restructuring works along the following lines. The collective farm is broken down into its constituent brigades, and each brigade is transferred to an elected farm manager. The process of electing the farm manager is carried out at a farm meeting convened by the local government and the state land committee. At this meeting, farm members are informed of the government's decision to transform the collective farm into *dekhan* farms (in Tajik, the word *dekhan* literally means peasant or worker farms). The local government proposes a farm manager for each *dekhan* farm and asks for confirmation by the members by a show of hands. It is not clear what criteria are used to propose the farm manager, and the rules do not specify criteria. Generally the farm manager is the person who was previously the head of the respective brigade under the collective farm. The general meeting endorses the nominee for the post of farm manager. Once this endorsement is obtained, the nominee is officially made the farm manager, often for life, unless the farmers pass a motion of no confidence by a simple majority at the annual general meeting.

The newly established *dekhan* farm managers get together to form a *dekhan* farm association and elect a chairperson to head this association. Generally the former chairperson of the collective farm assumes this position. Any livestock on the farm is given to the *dekhan* farm under whose jurisdiction it is located. In addition, the local governments take into their direct control the uncultivated land area of farms as a "reserve fund" for providing lands to future generations. Once the collective farm is restructured in this manner, the state land committee issues a land use certificate to each *dekhan* farm in the name of the farm manager with a list of the names of members. The farm manager takes over all of the running decisions formerly vested with the collective farm chairperson, including the procurement of all crop inputs, marketing, and financial management.

Farms restructured in this way are typically large—the farm restructuring attended by the task team resulted in the creation of seven *dekhan* farms, each of approximately 110 hectares. Nearly all collective farms restructured to date have been transformed in this way. Effectively, restructuring does not change the incentive structures within farms. What does change is the responsibility for the delivery of social services. The restructuring process also means that the social services supported by the original state farm (for example, kindergartens, schools, and hospitals) are transferred to their parent ministries.

Farm Privatization Support Project

In 1998 the Government of Tajikistan, with the support of the World Bank, began the implementation of the Farm Privatization Support Project. Under this pilot project 10 farms covering an area of 17,000 hectares were privatized. Of these 10 farms, 8 were cotton farms. As was the case with state farm restructuring, the social services provided by these farms to members were transferred to their parent ministries. Then the FPSP used a four-step approach to privatization. First, farms were divided into their constituent brigades and per capita land was divided among farmers by lottery. Inheritable but not tradable land use certificates were provided by the state land committee to *individual farmers,* reflecting the allocation of lands. Second, water user associations were formed and intra-farm water distribution infrastructure was rehabilitated. This would ensure a community-managed water provision system, a water charge collection mechanism, and maintenance of the intra-farm water distribution system. Third, a grant of US$300 per hectare was provided by the project to farmers to obtain crop inputs or any farm needs to start farming as an independent family farmer. Fourth, technical assistance in growing cotton independently was provided to farmers by using demonstration plots. These were plots where local consultants, along with scientists from the local research institutions of the Tajikistan Academy of Agricultural Sciences (TAAS), showed farmers how to grow cotton independently. The reason for the fourth step was that during Soviet times farming was very specialized, with each farmer concentrating on a specific task. Training was considered important because after privatization the farmers would need to undertake all the tasks themselves. This approach resulted in the formation of small family farms with varying sizes of 2 to 20 hectares (an average area of about 15 hectares).

Cotton Financing and Marketing under the IFC FOM

The IFC has implemented the FOM for providing crop financing to restructured or privatized farms. Under this pilot project, a joint stock company, SugdAgroServe (SAS) was established. This company is owned by about 350 farmers. Membership in SAS is open to restructured farms and to those privatized under the FPSP. SAS does not deal with collective farms. Proof of restructuring or privatization by producing a land use certificate is required by the IFC.

SAS provides financing to members for crop inputs at commercial terms and uses future cotton crops as collateral. These loans can be repaid to SAS in cash or as raw cotton. In addition to providing crop financing, SAS provides technical assistance to farmers by imparting knowledge on effective crop growing practices, and also assists farmers in marketing their cotton and in marketing it on better terms. SAS does not interfere with intra-farm financial management issues, leaving that task to farm managers or to private farmers. Farms under SAS have shown increased productivity of seed cotton.

IMPACT ANALYSIS OF INDIVIDUAL AND COLLECTIVE LAND TENURE

We now compare incentive structures, land ownership, financial management, and income generation and sharing for farmers under each privatization method.

However, before conducting a comparative analysis it is important to point out the pivotal difference between each method—land tenure and usage right. In the case of the FPSP, land tenure rights are vested with the farmer; in case of SFR, land use rights are collective, with the farm manager making decisions on behalf of the members. The FOM is silent on this issue and supports both forms of land tenure and usage rights. This pivotal difference results in remarkably different intra-farm incentive structures, as can be seen in the comparison set out in table 13.2, which compares the differential impacts of individual land tenure and collective land tenure on the incentives for and incomes of farmers.

Table 13.2 Comparison of the Impacts of Individual and Collective Land Tenure

Impact on	FPSP—Individual land tenure	SFR—collective land tenure
Access to land and asset endowment	Individual inheritable and nontradable rights that can be revoked only by "irrational" use of land. The law does not define rational use.	The land is managed by farm managers. There is no clear demarcation of physical location of land for each farmer. The law is not clear on procedures on separation from collective. The farm manager has the latitude to exclude and include members.
Wealth	Positive impact on assets and hence on wealth, as farmer has clearly demarcated land which increases potential income as well as generating a positive net present value.	The farmer does not have clear title to demarcated land, hence any calculation of income or net worth is not possible.
Empowerment	Within boundaries of "rationality" the farmer can choose the crop—albeit tacit pressure from local governments remains on the farmer to grow cotton.	The farm manager makes all decisions on behalf of the farm and pays a wage to workers. Wage reflects employment rather than ownership.

(continued)

Table 13.2 Comparison of the Impacts of Individual and Collective Land Tenure *(Continued)*

Impact	FPSP—Individual land tenure	SFR—collective land tenure
Income generation and price changes	The farmer decides on input procurement and financial dealings of farmland. The farmer has full appropriative rights on the proceeds from cotton.	The farmer has no control over land input-output of the farm. It is the farm manager who decides on how profits will be shared within the farm.
Rotation of farm control	Since the farmland is individually owned, the issue of rotation of control does not arise.	Farm managers are nominated by local governments and confirmed by a show of hands at the general body meeting called at the time of restructuring. Farm managers are elected for life unless farm members pass a motion of no confidence with an absolute majority at the annual general meeting. The law does not fix any term or re-election rules.
Risk exposure and mitigation	The farmer has more control over cropping decisions.	Farms under *kolkhozes* tended to over grow cotton and not rotate adequately. As a result yields fell and farms had to cultivate yet more area under cotton to meet production targets. Restructuring does not change the way farms are managed or run from earlier times.
Cotton picking incentive and quality of cotton. The way cotton is picked, impacts on the length of the cotton fiber and whether it fetches a higher price.	Pass-through of cotton proceeds to the farmer is direct. He or she receives higher prices if cotton is of better quality, hence the incentive to pick with care is greater.	Farmers (pickers) are paid per kilogram irrespective of the quality of picked cotton, therefore the incentive to pick with care is not as direct.
Experience with dealing with all aspects of the production and marketing chains.	The farmer will require training, demonstration, and support to farm independently.	Production will continue as before and no additional training will be required.

Source: Based on stakeholder analysis by authors, and World Bank staff.

The comparison between individual and collective land tenure indicates that the farmer's land access, wealth, income, empowerment, and ability to mitigate risk are more favorable under individual land tenure. It is important to note that the social service delivery (education and health) deteriorated across the board in Tajikistan, both in farms that remained state-owned collective farms and in privatized and restructured farms. Consequently, the welfare of children in particular, but also workers, most likely has worsened. This is the result of general underfunding of social services by the state collective farms or the parent ministries, which is because of their respective weak financial and fiscal situations. Further research at the local level on access to key social services would shed further light on the extent of the deterioration of land access to these services.

COTTON PRODUCTION AND MARKETING, POST-1996

Post independence, the cotton sector production and marketing chain were transformed. Major changes have occurred in financing, in the privatization of gins, and in the liberalization of crop cultivation. These changes are discussed below.

The Financing Chain and "Future" Contracts

Prior to independence, crop financing was provided by the Soviet Union. Post-1996, the Government of Tajikistan did not have the resources to provide financing for cotton cultivation and needed to search for alternative sources. The government entered into discussion with Paul Reinhart SA, an international cotton trading firm, in this regard. This company proposed an arrangement whereby it would on-lend to the Government of Tajikistan US$138 million from Credit Suisse First Boston (CSFB), provided the government would give a sovereign guarantee to CSFB that it would repay the loan in U.S. dollars. This guarantee was given and financing was provided to the government via the National Bank of Tajikistan, at an interest rate of 10 percent per year. Over time, other foreign financiers entered the arena and some, including Paul Reinhart SA, provided financing directly to loan brokers. Foreign financiers have recently started to provide crop financing directly to local loan brokers. These loan brokers are, in practice, merely local agents for foreign financiers.

The government further determined that AgroInvest (the former AgroPromBank) would handle cotton-financing issues. AgroInvest remained a public financial institution. Based on this decision, the National Bank of Tajikistan transferred the finances to AgroInvest at a mark-up of 12 percent. AgroInvest resolved to engage a group of loan brokers that would deal with farms. This meant that farms were rationed to specific loan brokers. These loan brokers were sole credit providers and worked with the tacit support of local governments, cornering specific cotton-growing areas where farms could liaise only with that broker. The lending rate charged by loan brokers ranged between 19 percent and 25 percent in U.S. dollars. Higher lending rates resulted in higher input costs for the farmer, and hence lower profits. In addition, AgroInvest did not provide guidelines to brokers on interest rates they could charge on loans.

These loan brokers and restructured farms would enter into future contracts, which would be witnessed by the government at the *rayon* level. These future contracts stipulate that, in return for crop financing, farms would deliver a fixed amount of cotton to predetermined gins. Crop financing was provided in kind. Once the raw cotton was ginned and readied for export, the account of the farm would be credited with the price of lint cotton prevailing at the Liverpool Cotton Exchange, less transport costs. If a farm was not able to deliver the agreed amount of raw cotton to the gins, then the amount of shortfall would be treated as debt and interest would accrue on it. If the farm delivered more cotton than was stipulated under the contract, then the broker would credit the account of the farm accordingly.

Privatization of Cotton Gins

As part of the cotton sector reform, the government privatized all 23 state-owned gins in 2000. Privatization resulted in loan brokers' gaining control of 5 gins directly and having a majority shareholding in another 15. More gins have since been established, bringing the total number of gins currently operating in Tajikistan to 38. Other than the privatization drive, the government has made no change to the tax code that links the local governments' revenue collection mechanism to cotton processed in gins under their jurisdiction. Local governments derive an important share of their revenue from gins; hence they have an incentive to keep cotton ginning within their region. This aspect of the taxation code effectively zones cotton production to local gins.

Liberalization in Crop Cultivation and State Interference

Between 1996 and 2003, the government issued 71 decrees that provide the legal basis for the agricultural sector reform and the ensuing privatization and farm restructuring carried out to date. One of these decrees also eliminated local government interference in the agricultural sector, although the government maintains its policy of formulating national cotton targets, as was done by the Soviet Union in pre-independence times.

STAKEHOLDER ANALYSIS OF THE COTTON SECTOR

From the impact assessment of individual and collective land use tenure, it was concluded that privatization that results in the transfer of individual land tenure to farmers is the preferred alternative. A detailed stakeholder analysis was prepared based on interviews of farmers, input financiers, local government officials, and civil society organizations. The aim of this analysis was to determine

- the costs and benefits of privatization for each stakeholder,
- the importance of each stakeholder for the success of privatization, and
- the degree of influence of the stakeholder over the privatization process.

The stakeholder analysis shows that privatization resulting in the provision of land use tenure to individual farmers would be opposed by farm managers, loan brokers—both foreign and local—and gin owners. This opposition is primarily because these stakeholders are extracting rents from the cotton sector at the expense of farmers. These are the same groups that would favor preserving the status quo.

The stakeholder analysis also shows that the central government would, in principle, be in favor of privatization on all accounts except the issue of the loss of direct control over farms. The reason for this support stems from the need to increase the productivity of farmlands and thereby improve the fiscal and external positions of the country. In addition, the equitable privatization of farmlands is a stated objective of the government in the PRSP.

Local governments, on the other hand, benefit from the current organizational setup because they have control over farms and have an incentive to collude with rent-seeking stakeholders to maintain the status quo. However, once local authorities understand that privatization and liberalization would have a positive effect on yields and hence on revenues, they will no doubt support the process. The detailed stakeholder analysis matrix is presented here in table 13.3.

Table 13.3 Matrix of Identification of Stakeholder Groups, Their Interests, Importance, and Influence

Stakeholder groups	Interest(s) at stake in relation to privatization of cotton farmlands	Effect[a] + −	Importance[b]	Influence[c]
Central government	• Equitable land distribution • Increase export earnings • Control over farms • Increase in cotton yield • Higher tax revenue • Reduce poverty	+ + − + + +	5	5
Local governments (*hakumats*)	• Control over farms • Patronage of farm managers • Patronage of gins & loan brokers • Tax revenues	− − − +	4	4
Farm association chairperson / *dekhan* farm manager	• Control over farm • Patronage of gins & loan brokers • Status in community • Rents from production chain	− − − −	3	3
Farmers	• Increase in income and welfare • Increase in productivity • Crop choice freedom • Freedom to procure inputs • Improve gender balance • Social service previously provided by collective farms	+ + + + + −	5	1
AgroInvest shareholders	• Profits from financing cotton • Control over cotton sector	− −	3	3
Loan brokers (future contractors)	• Profits from input supply due to competition • Reduce farm debt stranglehold • Patronage of farm associations and farm managers	− − −	2	4
Ginnery owners	• Patronage with local government and loan brokers • Forced processing of raw cotton at specified gins	− −	3	4

Source: World Bank staff analysis/estimates.

a. Effect of privatization on interest(s).
b. Importance of stakeholder for success of privatization of cotton farmlands.
c. Influence of stakeholder over privatization of cotton farmlands.

1 = Little/No Importance
2 = Some Importance
3 = Moderate Importance
4 = Very Important
5 = Critical Importance

Following this stakeholder analysis, the PSIA aimed at quantifying the rents being extracted by different stakeholders, as discussed below.

QUANTIFYING RENTS AND COSTS OF INEFFICIENCIES

The cotton sector in Tajikistan is clearly in transition. Some aspects of it are controlled by a small group of private entrepreneurs, working like a cartel. Government is targeting of cotton production, and there are informal means of ensuring that targets are pursued. Such a hybrid system has the potential of creating lopsided incentive structures, because private stakeholders use their control over financial resources and ginning assets in order to maximize profits, and the government uses its formal and informal control mechanisms over farmlands and the general administrative network in order to maximize tax revenues and cotton production.

Future Contracts and Accumulation of Debts

Since private crop financing began in the form of future contracts, cotton farmlands have accumulated significant debts. According to a recent study by the Asian Development Bank (ADB), total external cotton farm debts stood at US$65 million on January 1, 2004. The principal and interest breakdown of these debts has not yet been established because of a poor data recording system. The process of future contracts and subsequent accumulation of debts is depicted in annex 13A, and is as follows.

■   **Over-invoicing of inputs by loan brokers:** Cotton inputs were provided by the loan broker in kind rather than seed capital in cash. The broker acted as an input procurer and supplier. These inputs were generally overpriced. Conservative estimates suggest that inputs were overinvoiced between 10 and 25 percent. Calculations suggest that if inputs were overinvoiced by 10 percent, a sum of US$9 million was extracted annually from the cotton sector. This figure increases to US$21 million per year if inputs were overinvoiced by 25 percent. Taking into account this resource appropriation, the question arises as to why the farm manager accepted overpriced inputs. The answer lies in two key areas:

  ■   A lack of alternative crop financing mechanisms along with pressure from the government to grow cotton meant that farms concluded future contracts with loan brokers, irrespective of the terms of the contract.

- The farm manager was elected with the support of local authorities but was not answerable to farmers in any effective sense on farm management issues. By law, the farm manager could borrow in the name of the farm but was not personally liable for repayment. This resulted in imprudent borrowing. In addition, the incentive of sharing "rents" from overinvoicing with brokers was strong.
- **Delay in input delivery by loan brokers:** The supply of cotton inputs was often significantly delayed, which meant that farms could not start cultivating their cotton on time. Again, the farm had to accept this suboptimal financing arrangement because it was the only source of financing available.
- **Poor quality and inadequate quantity of inputs:** Input overinvoicing was compounded by inputs of poor quality. The lack of financial disclosure requirements for farms meant that farmers did not know what the contracted quantity was and thus could not compare it to the delivered quantity.

These distortions notwithstanding, the seed cotton quantity that farms contracted to deliver in these future contracts was very optimistic. The optimistic targets were dictated by local authorities who were concerned with achieving their regional share of cotton production targets. Owing to the problems highlighted above, and to weather-related issues, crops failed in 1999 and 2001. In addition, during 2002 the world price of cotton fell by 50 percent. Farms could not deliver the contracted amount of cotton to loan brokers. This put farms in arrears on their debt service commitments. Over successive years farms could not meet their yearly contracted cotton production targets (which were optimistic to begin with), and previous arrears kept accruing interest. In this way, farms accumulated large debts. The result is that indebted farms became "captive" to the brokers, having to surrender their cotton to specific brokers with no possibility of marketing their cotton independently and then settling their debts. The government views these debts as private obligations because it recognizes restructured farms as private entities.

Increasing farm debts translated into nonperforming loans for AgroInvest Bank, and into higher external indebtedness of the country to international loan financiers. AgroInvest carried out a debt-equity swap with foreign financiers: in exchange for cotton debts, foreign financiers were given minority shareholding in AgroInvest. This move further consolidated the control of foreign financiers over the cotton sector, but the problem of nonperforming domestic loans remained an issue. On December 31, 2003, the government split AgroInvest into two financial entities: KreditInvest and AgroInvest. All nonperforming loans were transferred to KreditInvest, while AgroInvest recapitalized. The policy of how to deal with the past stock of debts, and how to ensure that further debts do not accumulate, is currently being discussed.

Effective Cost of Ginning in Tajikistan

The average nominal cost of ginning cotton in Tajikistan is about US$140 per ton. However, the effective cost of ginning is significantly higher because of higher accrued interest costs for the farm owing to ginning delays, lower ginned cotton outturns, and the deterioration in cotton quality because of gin delays.

Gins have a perverse incentive to delay cotton ginning, which emanates from the fact that gins are owned by loan brokers who charge farmers interest on input finance until the cotton has been ginned and is ready to be exported. The longer it takes to gin cotton, the longer the time for which interest is charged by the loan broker. Tajik gins take, on the average, 200 days to gin cotton, compared with 110 to 120 days for Western gins. This delay results in the following:

- **Higher accrued interest for the farm.** Typically, loan brokers provide inputs at interest rates in the range of 14–30 percent. Table 13.4 calculates the interest cost to the cotton sector of the additional days required for ginning in Tajikistan. The low-cost scenario is based on an interest rate of 14 percent; the high-cost scenario is based on an interest rate of 30 percent.
- **Reduction in working capital of farms.** In the regular cotton cultivation cycle, farmers plant cotton in April each year and pick the

Table 13.4 Additional Interest Cost Borne by Cotton Sector from Delays in Ginning

Category of expenses	Low	High
Input finance per hectare (US$)	300	300
Interest rate	14%	30%
Interest cost for 110–20 days (average 115 days)	13.2	28.4
Interest cost for 200 days	23.0	49.3
Excess interest cost from delays (200 days vs. 115 days)	9.8	21.0
Number of hectares cultivated in 2003	284,367	284,367
Total excess interest cost borne by the cotton sector (US$)	2,781,343	5,960,021

Source: World Bank staff estimates.

cotton by mid-November. The cotton is then sent for ginning. In other countries, gins process the cotton in 3 months. This would mean that by mid-February farms would be able to dispose of their ginned cotton and buy inputs in time for the next cultivation season. In Tajikistan ginning takes about 6.5 months. This means that by the time farmers want to plant the next crop they still have their working capital tied up in last year's crop and they need to borrow money from loan brokers again. This fact unnecessarily increases the stock of financial resources required for cotton cultivation. For an economy with limited capital, the opportunity cost of tying up financing in this way is immense.

- **Losses due to low gin outturns.** The ginned cotton outturns in Tajikistan range between 24 and 32 percent, compared with an average of 36 percent for Western gins—a difference of 4 to 12 percent. The reasons for the low outturns are many, and include old machinery that is not well maintained; a cotton supply that is captive because tax code provisions provide an incentive for local authorities to exert pressure on farms to have their cotton ginned in specific gins, providing little incentive for gins to compete and improve productivity; and a lack of accountability of the physical cotton received by gins, leading to the theft of cotton by unscrupulous workers. It is estimated that losses due to low cotton outturns, at different outturn levels, could range between US$51 million and US$77 million.

- **Inverse relationship between cotton quality and ginning delays.** Cotton is a delicate and easily degradable commodity. If raw cotton is not ginned within 90 days after being picked, its quality deteriorates. This is because cotton starts absorbing moisture, which adversely affects its quality and hence the price at which it sells. Gins in Tajikistan do not have adequate or proper storage facilities. According to agronomics, cotton quality can deteriorate 5–10 percent after the first 90 days, depending on specific storage conditions. It is difficult to calculate how much it deteriorates, but it is certain that Tajik cotton quality does deteriorate.

The main cause for these problems is the monopsonistic structure of the ginning subsector. Gins are owned by input suppliers, farms are forced to have their cotton ginned in specific gins, and primary cotton grading is done by gins. This report does not look into the opportunity cost of these losses in terms of tax revenue and export earnings forgone, but these indirect impacts are significant.

Interference in a Policy of No Interference

According to a presidential decree of 2000 the government is not supposed to interfere with the production decisions of farms. This decree is intended to free farms from the interventions of local authorities. However, the central government continues to set yearly cotton production targets. For 2004, the production target is 610,000 tons of raw cotton. These targets are passed through the bureaucratic chain just as in Soviet times, with local governments interfering in farm cultivation decisions. This propagates and strengthens the existing financing and ginning arrangements. It is fundamentally contrary to the stated policy of no interference, and creates gray areas for targeted state interventions.

A scenario analysis carried out by the ADB to assess cotton profitability in Tajikistan shows that Tajikistan would have a comparative advantage in cotton production under a fully liberalized and privatized environment (ADB 2002: 54). This means that, if left to their own devices, farmers are likely to choose to grow cotton under a liberalized environment. However, the research also points out that at present yield levels and distortions, it is not profitable for farmers to grow cotton. It is probably for this reason that the government is encouraging farms to grow cotton. The correct policy would be to address and solve these distortions so that yields can increase and the economy can enter the virtuous cycle stylized in figure 13.1. Keeping this in mind, the government should not fear that in the absence of state targets cotton production will fall. However, in the presence of distortions and the absence of planning and state interventions, there is a possibility that, given crop choice, farmers will choose to grow other crops.

Cotton Grading and Pricing System

A cotton grading system fulfills four criteria. It enables the quality of the product to be fully described, makes it possible to maintain a high level of integrity of standards that are recognized by the buyer and seller, provides transparency in the operation, and facilitates operation at a reasonable cost.

The international standard of cotton grading is, by default, the U.S. Department of Agriculture (USDA) standard, and is used by major cotton-exporting countries such as Australia. Tajikistan produces less than 1 percent of world cotton production, but it has its own classification system. For a foreign buyer, the Tajik grading system does not fulfill the above four criteria. This makes it risky for foreign buyers to buy Tajik cotton from overseas, thus impeding competition on the demand side. In addition, this parallel system adds unnecessary costs for the government and adds another layer of activity for buyers who need to link the Tajik standards to the default world standard.

Another area of concern is that in Tajikistan gins determine the quality of the cotton that is brought to them for processing. Because gins are owned by loan brokers, the owners have an incentive to tell farms that their cotton is of a lower quality (even if this is not true), so that they can buy it from them at a lower price and sell it for a higher price. Since farms have no choice but to use a specific gin, if the gin disputes the cotton quality it is easy for the gin to "de-grade" the cotton. This is possible because of the lack of an independent verification and certification system for cotton production by farms.

The cotton exchange fixes a minimum cotton price that is calculated using a formula based on the latest Liverpool Cotton Exchange price, adjusting it downward for costs incurred in transportation. A minimum price is fixed to ensure that buyers do not exploit farms by buying at low prices. The mechanism has its advantages and disadvantages. The advantages are that the price is calculated in a transparent manner and provides a benchmark for farms for selling their cotton. In a system where the majority of the farmers do not have a say in the financial affairs of the farm, a fixed minimum price provides a reference point for farmers to assess the possible profitability of the farm.

The disadvantage is that this system provides cotton at lower, rent-adjusted prices to loan brokers, because rents extracted from cotton production act as a de facto subsidy for the financiers. For agents who are not part of the rent-extraction chain, such as spinning mills or other buyers, the competition becomes unfair because the price paid by loan brokers and foreign financiers (including rents) is lower than the price paid by agents outside of the rent chain. This provides a disincentive to competition and further vertical integration in the cotton sector. It is difficult in this report to establish the level of subsidy thus provided, but the issue needs to be explored further in the context of the comprehensive a agricultural sector study.

Legislative Clarity on Farm Restructuring

From the time land reform started in Tajikistan until the first quarter of 2004, a total of 71 decrees and resolutions were passed by the government. There are three main issues regarding the numerous decrees and resolutions passed to date.

■ **The lack of clarity and depth of the laws.** The decrees and resolutions have been brief and often have not been adequately followed up by regulations. Some decrees lack specificity, some even contradict one another and are open to differing interpretations. For example, the Law on *Dekhan* Farms does not clearly lay down the modalities of restructuring, the responsibilities of farm management, the rights of farm workers, or the rules governing the conduct of business. Different local governments have implemented laws in the way in which they choose to interpret them.

■ **Lack of dissemination of the changes in the laws.** From field visits conducted at cotton-growing farms and in interviews with farmers, it is apparent that farmers are not aware of the changes in the laws and the decrees that are fundamental anchors of the reform process. This finding has been confirmed by civil society organizations working in the area of land reform in Tajikistan. Lack of knowledge of the laws leaves room for the exploitation of stakeholders by rent seekers.

■ **The cost of legal redress.** In far-flung cotton-growing areas there is a very limited presence of personnel from the Ministry of Economic Arbitration. If farmers have issues that require redress they have to travel to provincial capitals. The cost of the entire trip, along with court fees, deters farmers from using such services.

Analyzing the laws and decrees individually is outside of the scope of the PSIA. The issues highlighted above need to be looked into detail under the World Bank follow-up project on facilitating farm privatization further in Tajikistan.

Total Losses from Inefficiencies and Rent Seeking

The current distortions represent a cumulative loss to the economy of between US$63 and US$105 million annually. A breakdown of this loss by component is provided in table 13.5.

Inefficiencies in the ginning subsector (in the form of low gin out-turns and higher financial costs) account for the majority of direct losses of earnings in the cotton-growing subsector. However, rents from input finance also cause significant indirect losses. These indirect losses stem from cotton yields that are lower than they would otherwise be. Because of rent-seeking in input finance, seed cotton yields are at 1.9 tons of seed cotton per hectare. If input finance is provided competitively (as is the

Table 13.5 Losses from Inefficiencies and Rent Seeking

	Low	*High*
Cumulative loss as percent of GDP	**4.0**	**6.7**
Cumulative Loss	**62.9**	**104.7**
Low gin outturns *(low 32% to high 24%)*	51.6	77.4
Financial costs due to long gin processing time		
(low interest rate 14%, high interest rate 30%)	2.8	6.0
Rents from input finance (low 10% over invoicing higher 30%)	8.5	21.3

Source: World Bank staff estimates.
Note: Amounts are in millions of U.S. dollars.

case with IFC SAS), yields can be increased to 2.8 tons of seed cotton per hectare.

Losses in the cotton sector affect the government as well as farmers. On the government side, these losses translate into lower tax earnings from cotton taxation and lower foreign exchange earnings, which constrains the public sector resource envelope and hence limits the government's ability to spend on social and infrastructure needs. The poverty and social impact of this loss depends on the expenditure priorities of the government. Given the immense need for improving the social and productive infrastructure, the lack of resources translates into a lower quality of heath care, low investment in the educational system, and a lack of adequate upgrading of physical infrastructure. Together these gaps constrain economic growth and income generation for all sectors of the economy.

On the farmers' side, the impact of the loss of these resources means lower incomes and hence lower expenditures. The cotton-growing areas of Tajikistan are home to the highest prevalence of the extremely poor. With resource leakages from inefficiencies and rent-seeking, and the resultant lower yields, it is difficult for farmers to move out of poverty. In addition to forgone resources, the current cotton production and marketing chains do not provide farmers with a share of cotton proceeds.

"Pass-Through" of Cotton Proceeds

The current organizational setup of farms under the SFR and the distortions prevalent in the cotton production and marketing chains negatively affect the incomes of farmers. Figure 13.3 shows the distribution of cotton proceeds within the production and marketing chains. The notional pass-through bar shows the how proceeds would be distributed to each stakeholder if the system functioned in the way that it was designed to function. The effective pass-through bar shows how proceeds are actually being distributed in the current system. The main points to take note of between the notional and the effective pass-through are the following:

- Farmers are not receiving adequate wages. Farmers should notionally receive US$111 per month in terms of wages but effectively are receiving only payment in kind in terms of cotton stocks and limited cotton seed oil. When monetized, this in-kind payment is not even one-fourth of the wages the farmers should receive.
- Whereas farms should be making a profit, effectively they are making losses. These losses are adding to farm debts.

FIGURE 13.3 **Distribution of Cotton Proceeds within the Production and Marketing Chains**

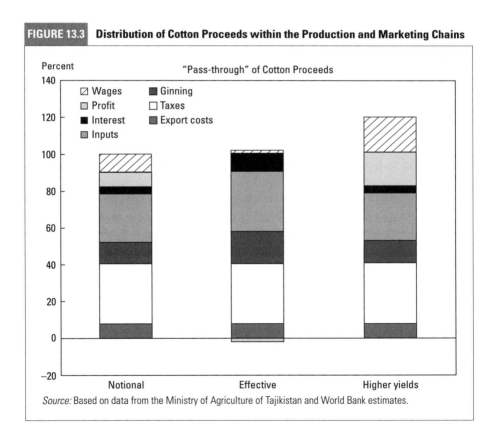

Source: Based on data from the Ministry of Agriculture of Tajikistan and World Bank estimates.

■ Proceeds that should be going toward wages and farm profits are being absorbed by loan financiers and in the cost of ginning. Effective costs are higher because of rent seeking and inefficient ginning processes.

The bar on the right labeled "higher yields" shows the projected impact of privatization and liberalization. With the same level of input financing in a competitive environment, yields will rise. Higher yields in an environment where notional pass-through prevails will result in the farmer and the farm making higher profits. The welfare analysis considers how the current effective pass-through affects the farmer.

IMPACT OF RESTRUCTURING ON POVERTY

The restructuring of farms has effectively resulted in farmers becoming wage laborers. Since wages are often in arrears, farmers' income and consumption are severely restricted. Even though Tajikistan is producing and exporting a lucrative crop, farmers are not adequately compensated for their work.

Labor Migration

The pass-through analysis shows that currently farmers are not adequately compensated for their labor and that farms are not making a profit. In Tajikistan, this situation has encouraged men from agricultural families to migrate to Russia as seasonal laborers. Their womenfolk are left behind to work on the cotton farms so that families can maintain their membership in farms, and hence their future claims on land.

From estimates carried out by the International Organization for Migration (IOM), Tajikistan officially has 600,000 migrants in Former Soviet Union (FSU) countries; 40.8 percent of them are from Khatlon (IOM 2003: 32). Migration has had both positive and negative effects on welfare. The positive impact has been on the incomes of families in the form of remittances. The negative impact has been on the dynamics of family lives: as men move out for extended time periods, there is a greater tendency for family cohesion to weaken. In addition, research carried out by the IOM shows that sexually transmitted diseases are on the increase in Tajikistan. Migration also puts a disproportionate burden of work on children in households. During cotton picking season children are mandated to pick cotton. During this time schools remain closed (schools in Tajikistan are closed for two months longer than those of other countries). The second-order impact of these issues need to be further studied.

Access to Education and Health Care

The farm restructuring process and the subsequent transfer of schools and kindergartens from the farm to the relevant ministry placed greater budgetary requirements on the government. Lack of financial resources meant that the government could not provide these services in adequate quantity or quality. This reduction in the quantity and quality of social services has had a significantly negative but unquantifiable impact on farmers. The resource wastage resulting from distortions translates into public social services forgone. Improved services could be provided by the government if the distortions are addressed, thereby providing more resources to the budget.

IMPACT OF PRIVATIZATION ON DISTORTIONS

Privatization in itself does not address the other distortions within the input finance and ginning subsector. It is thus important for the privatization to move hand in hand with the liberalization of the sector. The next section presents some options that can be taken by government. Privatization along with liberalization would allow farmers to choose what crop to plant and to control financial decisions pertaining to their lands. Liberalization measures dealing with problems in input finance and inefficiencies in the ginning sector would allow alternative crop financing mechanisms to develop and would improve gin efficiency by instilling competition within the subsector. These measures would lead to higher yields, higher incomes, and a reduction in poverty.

Based on the preceding analysis, two policy options, along with their costs and benefits, were presented. For each option, the feasibility and complementary policies that would be needed are discussed.

Option 1

Option 1 is to privatize all cotton farms on the lines of FPSP while leaving other aspects of the cotton production and marketing chains unaltered.

- **Impact.** Farmers would be assured land tenure and have appropriatory rights over their land, thereby improving farmer welfare and increasing incentives for farmers to enhance productivity. The control of farm managers would diminish. Cotton yields would improve, as farmers would be able to use seed capital provided as part of the FPSP privatization to buy inputs at competitive prices. However, because distortions and inefficiencies in the production and marketing chains would remain, the proceeds from cotton cultivation would continue to be lower because the quality of ginned cotton would be lower and marketing would be carried out monopsonistically.

■ **Beneficiaries:** The clear beneficiaries would be farmers, who would have higher incomes and access to land. The government would also benefit from enhanced revenue collection from cotton taxes and higher export earnings.

■ **Losers:** Farm managers would lose control of farms. Control of input financiers (loan brokers) over cotton production would weaken because farmers would have seed capital and thus would have a choice of input procurement. Hence the rent-seeking from an inefficient input supply would be significantly reduced, as would the collusion between input supplies and unscrupulous farm managers.

■ **Feasibility and complementary policies.** This option is preferred over maintaining status quo because it provides direct control of the land to the farmer, thereby making the farmer an active economic agent in cotton production. However, this option is not the best solution because (1) it does not address the distortions within the ginning and marketing chains that are vital elements of the cotton value chains, and (2) rent capture would only shift from input suppliers to gin owners and cotton marketers.

A complementary policy would need to ensure that land tenure is not revocable. This would assist in effective collateralization of land and development of the financial sector.[4] In the case of Option 1, the government would need to ensure that the social services previously provided by the collective farms and transferred to the state at privatization are run efficiently. Because higher yields would translate into enhanced revenue to government, there would be some fiscal space to increase spending on social services.

Option 2

Option 2 is to privatize all cotton farms on the lines of the FPSP and also to liberalize the production and marketing chains. The liberalization measures and their rationales are reviewed below.

Barring the Supply of Inputs in Kind and Developing Alternative Crop Financing Mechanisms

The practice of supplying inputs in kind should be stopped. Efforts should also be made to develop alternative crop financing mechanisms such as the SAS. It is still not clear why AgroInvest engaged loan brokers at a mark-up in the first place, nor is it clear why loan brokers were allowed to provide inputs in kind to farms. It is also not clear why the quoted prices of inputs were not scrutinized. It is possible that all these practices were established because the system of crop financing was in transition. It is clear and is accepted by farm managers, local governments, civil society, and farmers that inputs supplied in kind by loan brokers were generally overpriced, of inferior quality, and delivered late. This causes significant problems for farmers and is arguably responsible for lower yields and for deterioration in the terms of trade and hence debt accumulation.

The IFC SAS provides a very robust control check for the above assertion. As presented earlier, the FOM is a crop finance and market development model. SAS essentially provides input credit in a timely manner. The farmer can choose to take cash or ask for input from SAS. Inputs are provided at competitive rates, and interest on loans is 14 percent for members of SAS and 16 percent for nonmembers. SAS allows farmers to repay loans in cotton or cash and assists in marketing cotton at competitive prices. This is essentially what the loan brokers do for farms, except that the use of loan brokers is fraught with issues highlighted earlier. In Sughd Province, SAS farmers have registered average yields of 2.5 tons of raw cotton per hectare, while non-SAS restructured farms are registering yields of about 1.9 tons per hectare. The only perceptible difference in the two arrangements is the timely, competitive, and efficient delivery of inputs to farms. SAS farms are also repaying their debts.

It is thus important for government to bar the practice of input supply by loan brokers to farms, and to introduce transparency in the future contract—a template that clearly shows the amount of money borrowed. The nominal interest rate charged with the repayment terms would go a long way toward introducing transparency into the current system.

At the same time, the farm privatization effort should facilitate the formation of family farms that are large enough to be able to borrow resources from private sources effectively, provided that they are not taxed or overindebted. The study of the optimal size for a family farm and the development of alternative crop financing mechanisms needs to be further explored. The government decree of noninterference in farm cropping decisions should be enforced.

Scrutinizing Farm Debts

Farm debts need careful scrutiny and the issue should be addressed within a comprehensive cotton sector liberalization program. It is crucial that farm debts not recur.[5] The treatment of farm debts is important for the privatization process. Box 13.1 presents a discussion of how this issue can be resolved.

In both options presented, the government must play a key role in terms of the privatization and the liberalization of the cotton

---

BOX 13.1 Resolving Cotton Farm Debts in Privatization

According to work carried out by the Asian Development Bank, the total stock of farmland debts outstanding as of January 1, 2004, was US$65 million. There are various weaknesses with this data. These are that

- the principal and interest breakdown is not known,
- the data collection methodology is not clear, and
- discrepancies and inconsistencies exist among National Bank database, AgroInvest, and loan financiers.

The first step in devising a debt-resolution policy is to establish the magnitude of the debt. A committee comprising all stakeholders needs to be constituted. This committee should reconcile the figures and agree to a final set of numbers. The stakeholders involved include farms (borrowers), government (guarantor), and loan financiers.

The second step entails resolving the reasons that led to the accumulation of these debts. If these issues are not resolved, then the flow of debt accumulation will continue. The resolution of debts has to go hand in hand with the resolution of distortions in the cotton production and marketing chains.

Once the debt numbers have been established, the government has two main options:
1. The government can suspend further accumulation of debt on arrears outstanding and let farms pay down debts over a period of 5 years. However, the distortions highlighted herein have to be addressed in order for farms to increase their productivity and become able to repay their debts. Here it is crucial to know that even in the low distortions case, a total debt of US$65 million is lower than the amount lost each year due to inefficiencies.
2. The government can suspend further accumulation of debt on arrears outstanding, and can distribute the principal component of debt to farms and declare a moratorium on repayment of the principal for a fixed time period. The government would then privatize farms and build into the privatization process a clause saying that farmers have to repay principal amounts within 2 years of the end of the moratorium. Failure to pay would result in the accumulation of interest at market rates with the possibility of land tenure rights being revoked. The government, local loan brokers, and international financiers would each write off one-third of the amount of the interest incurred.

Source: Data from ADB report (listed in references), and World Bank staff analysis.

production and marketing chains as well as in settling the debt issue. It is equally important to note that farms that have had recourse to alternative financing (via SAS) have started paying off loans.

Severing the Link Between Cotton Taxation and Gin Location

The link between cotton taxation and gin location needs to be severed. The current taxation system is structured so that local governments collect taxes on cotton processed in ginneries located in their respective jurisdictions. Local governments try to maximize their collections by forcing farms to process cotton in gins located within their jurisdiction. These gins are generally controlled or owned by loan brokers who provide inputs to farms. Local government pressure on farms to process inputs in specific gins assures a gin of a "captive" cotton supply. To begin with, gins have an incentive not to increase efficiency as discussed earlier. By providing a captive cotton supply, local governments impede competition between gins and leave farmers with little or no room to bargain with gins to provide incentives to improve their efficiency. Instituting an alternative tax regime that ensures that local governments continue to receive their taxes from cotton grown by farms in their respective jurisdictions while changing the gin as the tax unit would go a long way toward instituting competition between gins.

The functioning of the current cotton taxation system needs to be reviewed systematically with respect to (1) revenue sharing between the central government and local governments, (2) the effective tax rate, and (3) the cost of the current system in terms of output forgone. An alternative system that would break up the status of gins as tax units needs to be designed in the context of scaling up farm privatization. The alternative tax collection mechanism would need to ensure local government tax receipts and effective and constant tax rates on cotton, and an efficient collection mechanism. At the same time, the central government should inform the farmers of the fact that they are not bound to have their cotton processed in a specific gin, thus preventing unscrupulous local government officials from taking advantage of uninformed farmers.

Phasing Out Cotton Crop Production Targets

Cotton crop production targets set by the government need to be phased out. By decree, the central government has stopped local governments from interfering in the crop production and marketing decisions of farms. However, the central government still devises tentative yearly cotton production targets (for 2004 the target was 610,000 tons of raw cotton). Central and local government budgets are based on this target, which is very optimistic. These indicative targets are distributed through the governance structures down to the local government level. Government officials, who have worked for the last 70 years under socialism, take these indicative targets as plans that need to be fulfilled and pressure farmers to grow cotton. The farm manager who retains his or her position with the tacit support of local authorities abandons strategic crop planning and merely goes for cotton cultivation, even though the inputs received are at inflated rates, are of poor quality, and are delivered late. Because current yields per hectare are lower than those required to fulfill the plan, the farm manager decides to plant more cotton than is feasible, thus ignoring the crop rotation requirement. This degrades the fertility of the land.

Implementing an Integrated Cotton Development Program

The government should implement an integrated cotton development program. In the current cotton marketing and distribution set-up, it is the gin that grades the quality of cotton that farms bring for processing. Because of the shortage of working capital and the long turnaround times in Tajik gins, farms often sell raw cotton to gins. This gives gins the incentive to undergrade the cotton; gins buy the undergraded cotton at low prices and sell it at higher prices. Farms do not have recourse to an independent grading agency. In addition, Tajikistan maintains its own rating standard for cotton, which does not conform to the USDA standard. The main issues involved in maintaining Tajik specific standards are that

■ foreign buyers will be unsure about the quality of Tajik cotton and will be deterred from buying cotton from Tajikistan; and
■ another layer of bureaucracy is added to the current system.

Exporting cotton entails a convoluted and cumbersome documentation process that requires a lot of knowledge and contacts in the cotton trade chain, and that costs time and commission charges. Export procedures need to be simplified. In addition, more competition in the cotton-buying arena has to be encouraged. Cotton auction centers should be set up in each cotton-growing district where buyers could bid for and buy raw cotton.

International donor agencies, including the Bank, have successfully established independent cotton-grading agencies in India, Pakistan, and Zimbabwe. The Government of Tajikistan needs to be made aware of the benefits of establishing an independent cotton-grading agency in the context of an integrated cotton-development program in the cotton sector. The feasibility of cotton price setting also needs to be considered along with the establishment of cotton auction centers. Currently, the Tajikistan cotton exchange determines a minimum price for cotton. However, buyers treat this price as a ceiling rather than a floor, and use "rents" as de facto subsidies to buy cotton at a lower effective price. Auction centers would increase competition, which would translate into higher prices for farms. This entire issue has to be holistically considered in the context of scaling up farm privatization in Tajikistan.

- **Impact:** Option 2 will increase seed cotton yields most and ensure that farmers receive an adequate share of cotton proceeds while other agents also receive adequate compensation for economic service provided. Higher yields and incomes for farmers will help stimulate the economy.
- **Beneficiaries:** The principle beneficiaries under Option 2 would be farmers. Second-order benefits from multiplier effects of higher spending would be spread across the economy. The government budget fiscal and external positions would improve as a result of higher yields and stimulus to the economy.
- **Losers:** Stakeholders who benefit from the current distortions and inefficiencies would lose their rents. The main losers are input financiers (foreign and domestic) and gin owners. The losers are few but well entrenched. These agents would oppose liberalization openly and tacitly.
- **Feasibility:** In terms of equity and efficiency, Option 2 is the most feasible for stimulating the agricultural sector and reducing poverty. Implementing policies that affect entrenched rent-seeking stakeholders would require significant determination by the government. However, there are clear and present benefits of privatization and liberalization of the cotton sector. In addition, partial privatization is no better than no privatization.

A QUESTION OF TRADEOFFS

This PSIA has provided an analysis of the income implications of cotton farmland privatization. The main issues impeding cotton sector development have been presented, along with two options for moving ahead with privatization. These two options would eachhave a different impact on cotton sector productivity and income distribution.

The government could choose to maintain the status quo. However, by maintaining the status quo, the government would implicitly decide to keep the vested interests intact, a decision that would continue to exploit the farmer. This decision would translate into low yields and incomes for farmers, low cotton tax revenues and low subsequent export earnings, and high rents for the vested interests. What is important is that the government clearly recognize that the status quo is a choice that would have significantly negative consequences for the entire economy.

Alternatively, the government could choose to adopt a comprehensive privatization and liberalization program that would improve productivity and incomes for farmers and the country as a whole (Option 2), while eliminating distortions and rent seekers from the sector. It could also choose to adopt a privatization program that would preserve the vested interests in the cotton production and marketing chains while providing greater control of land use rights to the farmer (Option 1). Both these options would be an improvement over the status quo. However, Option 2 would be most effective in alleviating the problems with the cotton sector while productivity remains low and farmers' poverty level remains high. The government needs to choose the option that is consistent with its implicit welfare function.

It is important that the government be fully supported by donors and civil society in its effort to privatize and liberalize the cotton sector. In addition, transparency and accountability needs to be increased by involving civil society organizations in developing support for change. Besides undertaking reforms within the marketing and production chains, it is crucial to develop support for reform and change from stakeholders outside of the entrenched system. To this end, active dissemination and information campaigns need to be carried out in collaboration with civil society organizations such as Action Against Hunger—an international NGO the purpose of which is to reduce hunger and malnutrition—to inform farmers of the costs of distortions. This would help generate a sustained demand for change from the majority of farmers and from agents that do not derive benefits from the status quo.

THE IMPACT OF THE PSIA

Though the PSIA was completed only recently and the full impact of the work cannot be determined at this early stage, some early and important contributions are already known. These are:

■ Identification of the main sources of distortions in the cotton production and marketing chains is essential. The PSIA identified the
main impediments to improving the welfare of cotton farmers. By
focusing on the multiple players and incentive structure, the report
identified which aspects of the sector would need to be reformed to
obtain the desired decline in poverty.

■ Quantification of losses is another essential step. Though it was
apparent even prior to the PSIA that the current set-up of the cotton
sector was distortionary, the magnitude of the losses resulting from
them were not apparent. The PSIA's major contribution was in identifying the main sources of distortion, quantifying the large losses in
this sector, estimating their impact on farmers' incomes, and highlighting the opportunity cost to Tajikistan.

■ Provision of policy alternatives for addressing the distortions is the
final major lesson from this PSIA. In addition to the quantification
of welfare losses, the PSIA has provided a menu of reform options
and identified the winners and losers among them. The PSIA estimated the impact of different reform measures, including the cost of
no reform. If the government decides to reform the cotton sector, the
findings of the PSIA provide advice on the key distortions that need
to be eliminated to obtain a supply response.

LESSONS LEARNED

Some of the key lessons learned from this work are:

■ A PSIA provides a unique vehicle for understanding *stakeholder
incentives* to raising barriers to welfare improvements—something
that poverty assessments and sector-level analyses rarely address or
capture well. Stakeholder analysis provides a good instrument for
structuring the multiple factors that lead to the observed outcome
(in our case, high poverty in cotton areas). It can also extend this
analysis further to determine the extent of profits (or rents) captured
by various groups, a determination that is useful for understanding
the degree of resistance that would exist to implement change.

■ The approach that is adopted to carry out the analysis is critical to its
success, especially in the manner the team is structured. Team composition and interaction with stakeholders is critical to understanding
the manifold facets of an issue that has its roots in both the political
and economic arenas. The team working on this PSIA benefited from

being multidisciplinary and having an in-depth knowledge of the culture, the political players, and the agricultural sector.

■ Consultation with civil society organizations throughout the process is necessary on two grounds: (1) these organizations are a source of information on on-the-ground realities, and (2) they can build a constituency for reforms. The most affected stakeholders in Tajikistan are the farmers. They are dispersed and do not have a unified bargaining platform. This role is, by proxy, played by civil society organizations such as Action Against Hunger, CARE International, and so on.

NOTES

1. Other team members included Bobojon Yatimov, Jeren Kabaeva, and Jossy Moeis.
2. Rotational crop production is necessary to restore the nitrogen balance of the land, which is depleted by cotton production. In practice, crop rotation is not carried out, so the land becomes depleted, leading to a fall in its productivity.
3. Other donors are involved in supporting the government in the rural sector, but not in the process of cotton farmland privatization.
4. In the present situation, land can be rented but cannot be traded or transferred to nonfamily members. This impedes the collateralization of land.
5. The Asian Development Bank's Farm Debt Resolution and Policy Reforms report (ADB 2004) endorsed this point.

REFERENCES

ADB (Asian Development Bank). 2002. *Cotton in Central Asia: A Review of Policy and Technology*. Manila, Philippines.

ADB (Asian Development Bank). 2004. Farm Debt Resolution and Policy Reforms. Manila, Philippines.

IOM (International Organization for Migration). 2003. *Labor Migration from Tajikistan*. Geneva.

World Bank. 2004. Tajikistan Poverty Assessment Update. Washington, DC.

Depiction of Debt Chain in Cotton Production in Tajikistan

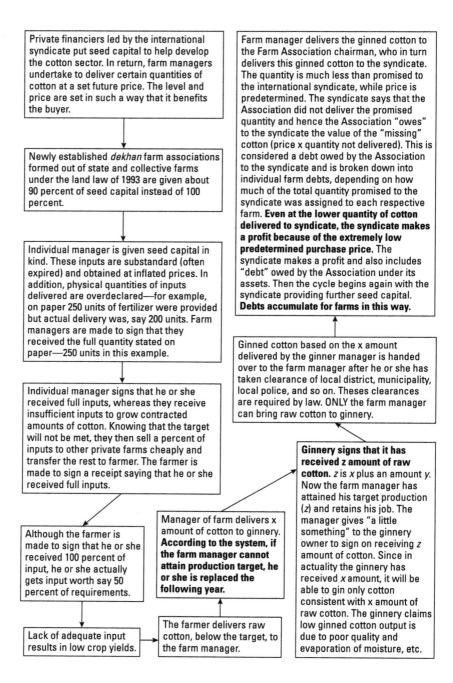

Private financiers led by the international syndicate put seed capital to help develop the cotton sector. In return, farm managers undertake to deliver certain quantities of cotton at a set future price. The level and price are set in such a way that it benefits the buyer.

Newly established *dekhan* farm associations formed out of state and collective farms under the land law of 1993 are given about 90 percent of seed capital instead of 100 percent.

Individual manager is given seed capital in kind. These inputs are substandard (often expired) and obtained at inflated prices. In addition, physical quantities of inputs delivered are overdeclared—for example, on paper 250 units of fertilizer were provided but actual delivery was, say 200 units. Farm managers are made to sign that they received the full quantity stated on paper—250 units in this example.

Individual manager signs that he or she received full inputs, whereas they receive insufficient inputs to grow contracted amounts of cotton. Knowing that the target will not be met, they then sell a percent of inputs to other private farms cheaply and transfer the rest to farmer. The farmer is made to sign a receipt saying that he or she received full inputs.

Although the farmer is made to sign that he or she received 100 percent of input, he or she actually gets input worth say 50 percent of requirements.

Lack of adequate input results in low crop yields.

Manager of farm delivers x amount of cotton to ginnery. **According to the system, if the farm manager cannot attain production target, he or she is replaced the following year.**

The farmer delivers raw cotton, below the target, to the farm manager.

Farm manager delivers the ginned cotton to the Farm Association chairman, who in turn delivers this ginned cotton to the syndicate. The quantity is much less than promised to the international syndicate, while price is predetermined. The syndicate says that the Association did not deliver the promised quantity and hence the Association "owes" to the syndicate the value of the "missing" cotton (price x quantity not delivered). This is considered a debt owed by the Association to the syndicate and is broken down into individual farm debts, depending on how much of the total quantity promised to the syndicate was assigned to each respective farm. **Even at the lower quantity of cotton delivered to syndicate, the syndicate makes a profit because of the extremely low predetermined purchase price.** The syndicate makes a profit and also includes "debt" owed by the Association under its assets. Then the cycle begins again with the syndicate providing further seed capital. **Debts accumulate for farms in this way.**

Ginned cotton based on the x amount delivered by the ginner manager is handed over to the farm manager after he or she has taken clearance of local district, municipality, local police, and so on. Theses clearances are required by law. ONLY the farm manager can bring raw cotton to ginnery.

Ginnery signs that it has received z amount of raw cotton. z is x plus an amount y. Now the farm manager has attained his target production (z) and retains his job. The manager gives "a little something" to the ginnery owner to sign on receiving z amount of cotton. Since in actuality the ginnery has received x amount, it will be able to gin only cotton consistent with x amount of raw cotton. The ginnery claims low ginned cotton output is due to poor quality and evaporation of moisture, etc.

14

TANZANIA
Crop Boards Reform

SABINE BEDDIES, MARIA CORREIA,
SHASHIDHARA KOLAVALLI, AND ROBERT TOWNSEND

This chapter illustrates parts of the process, analytical work, and impacts of a larger poverty and social impact study of Tanzania's crop boards, which was conducted jointly by the Government of Tanzania, the European Union (EU), and the World Bank between July 2003 and September 2004. The larger PSIA study analyzed the coffee, cotton, cashew, and tea industries. Because more information from household surveys, institutional mapping, and stakeholder dissemination is available for the coffee and cotton sectors, this chapter focuses only on these two crop industries.[1]

REFORM CONTEXT AND CHOICE

In Tanzania, agricultural growth is central to reducing poverty, which is highly concentrated in rural areas. Agriculture remains the dominant sector in Tanzania's economy, accounting for about half the country's GDP and employing about 70 percent of the country's labor force. Nearly 90 percent of the poor in Tanzania are in rural areas; the sale of food and cash crops and livestock products accounts for about 75 percent of rural household incomes. Over the 1990s agricultural growth averaged 3.6 percent, with growth rates increasing at the end of the period.

Crop boards play a significant role in determining the production and investment environment of Tanzania's agricultural export crops.

Crop boards exist for cashews, coffee, cotton, pyrethrum, sisal, sugar, tea, and tobacco. The government, in its Agricultural Sector Development Strategy, has set an ambitious target of sustained 5 percent annual growth in agriculture. Improving the performance of export crops is essential for growth, since domestic demand for food is not likely to grow enough to absorb incremental production of 5 percent annually. Improving the competitiveness of exports, in turn, will depend on continued advances in productivity and efficiency in marketing to lower costs. Structural changes currently taking place within the Tanzanian economy are welcome and positive, but these changes also create imperatives for adjustment within traditional sectors. This is particularly the case because the faster-growing sectors (such as mining) are not those on which the poor depend for livelihoods.

The value of Tanzania's agricultural exports increased rapidly from 1990 to 1999 but then decreased with declining world prices. By 2002, export values were 13.5 percent higher than they had been in 1990. This represents a better performance than Kenya but worse than Uganda over the same period. Alongside decreasing international prices, private and public interventions in export crop production and marketing have often constrained producer incentives.

The institutional structure for production and marketing affects the competitiveness of export crops, and crop boards are part of the present structure. These boards were formed in Tanzania after the liberalization of the early 1990s to replace their predecessors, the marketing boards. The crop boards were expected to continue many of the regulatory, reporting, and service activities of the former marketing boards, but were not expected to be directly involved in marketing or production. As a transitional arrangement, however, the minister of agriculture may authorize crop boards to perform limited responsibilities for marketing when the private sector is not active. The primary functions of the boards included improving quality, ensuring fair prices, and, in some cases, providing inputs.

The activities and performance of the crop boards have varied, raising concerns about their impact on industry performance.[2] Some boards facilitate the provision of inputs—an example is the cotton board, which supervises the operation of Crop Development Fund that is used to supply seeds and other inputs. Others, such as the coffee board, focus on licensing and quality control through regulation. Stakeholders have observed problems—such as inadequate accountability to traders and farmers, disruption of marketing and exports, and exclusion of the private sector from marketing—that are attributed to the boards. At the same time, the boards are perceived to benefit smallholders by improving access to inputs and dampening monopsonistic tendencies in marketing. The marketing liberalization of the early 1990s has witnessed a certain amount of re-regulation by some boards in 2000/1 in an effort to further address concerns about product quality, fair prices, and input supply.

Although the Government of Tanzania had taken steps to address perceived deficiencies of the boards, several issues remained to be addressed, thus justifying further analysis and action. Past government actions have included redefining crop industry legislation to incorporate provisions for increased stakeholder participation, managing crop development funds, and making information more readily available to farmers and other key stakeholders. The government has also introduced reforms to reduce or abolish taxes that were a burden to smallholder farmers, and reduced malpractices by private traders in the purchasing and selling of agricultural commodities.

Within government, there is also apprehension over the possible impacts of reforms, such as leaving smallholders without inputs if the boards withdraw, lack of sufficient private sector competition to offer "fair" prices to producers, and declining product quality. The government's recognition that further reforms are likely to be necessary is reflected in its prioritizing of a crop board analysis in Tanzania's Second Poverty Reduction Strategy Progress (PRSP) Report of 2001/2. This analysis was listed as a key action in the poverty reduction strategy policy matrix 2002/3–2004/5. The donor-supported Performance Assessment Framework (PAF) matrix that supported the implementation of the government's PRSP also had a further review of the roles and funding arrangements of the crop boards as a policy benchmark, with reforms to the corresponding legislation expected subsequent to the analysis. In addition, the government's Rural Development Strategy and its Agricultural Sector Development Strategy note the need for attention to the boards.

DESIGN OF THE PSIA

The Poverty and Social Impact Analysis was a response to government and development partner interest in examining the role and function of the crop boards as part of implementation of the PRSP. Earlier research had also highlighted the need for additional focus on the boards (Baffes 2002, 2003; Mitchell 2002). The current study reviews the role, performance, and funding of crop boards. It further examines reform options for the crop boards by reviewing existing institutional arrangements for these crops and evaluating the effectiveness of the boards' functions in relation to existing or potential alternative arrangements.

The objectives of the study were fourfold:

- to review the source and use of funds of the crop boards to determine who is paying for what services;
- to review the existing institutional environment and arrangements governing the production, processing, and marketing of coffee and cotton, and to review the regulatory, service, and revenue collection functions of these boards;
- to evaluate the impacts of reform options in the regulatory, service, and revenue collection functions of the crop boards, with a particular focus on smallholder farmers and vulnerable stakeholders; and
- to identify reform options.

Methodology

Crop boards were analyzed using a case study approach as parts of larger systems that encompass crop sectors (North 1990; Yin 1994). A systems perspective recognizes that changes in one aspect of the industry can have broad effects on other parts of the industry. The study employed a case study method to obtain the necessary insights into the dynamics of the formal and informal institutional arrangements in the individual crop industries and crop boards. These arrangements determine the transactions between the players within the different crop industries and their boards; they also determine their underlying incentives, and thus they shape the institutional environments or "systems" in which the crop industries operate. The study team chose this approach in order to add value to existing work by uncovering the institutional arrangements and dynamics within each crop industry and its board while, at the same time, pulling together findings by acknowledging the players and institutional environments to be part of a larger system. This chapter focuses on the methodology used for the analysis of the coffee and cotton industries.

A mixed methods and sequenced data collection approach was used for incremental in-depth insights. The study used both primary quantitative and qualitative data and secondary data. Identifying analytical gaps, the team conducted a literature review, which draws heavily on analytical work previously conducted by the Bank's Development Economics Department (DEC) on constraints to the development of Tanzania's main agricultural crops.[3] For the primary data collected for the different crop industries, work was carried out in a multistage process comprising a financial review of all eight crop boards, institutional mapping of four crop industries,[4] and—in the case of coffee and cotton only—a household survey of producers, an analysis of coffee auction data, and two stakeholder workshops.

- **Financial review of all crop boards.** The financial review, carried out as part of this study in 2003–4, examines the source and use of funds over the three preceding years, identifies services provided by the crop boards, and examines resources allocated by activity/service performed. The study is based on a review of reports and on interviews conducted with all the crop boards.
- **Institutional mapping of the coffee and cotton industries.** The mapping was designed to identify key agents and stakeholders and to develop hypotheses for carrying out the coffee and cotton household survey. Key-informant interviews and focus group discussions were designed to allow for a comprehensive and in-depth understanding of the dynamic relationships between various institutional arrangements. Stakeholder perceptions, interest, and degree of influence in the crop industries, along with stakeholder voice and political power—including avenues and measures of effectiveness— were also considered, as were the political economy within the coffee and cotton industries. Qualitative data were collected from about 20 focus groups and more than 45 in-depth key-informant interviews from September to October 2003. Samples were drawn from representatives of the crop boards, local governments, private buyers, exporters, processors, input supply agents, interest groups, NGOs, crop associations, primary societies, cooperative unions, and farmer group associations.[5] Data were collected in the northern, southern, and western coffee zones and the western cotton-growing area. Findings from institutional mapping in the coffee and cotton industries shaped the focus and generated the hypothesis of the subsequent household survey in these two sectors.[6] Information collected included data on the roles, functions, and financing of the boards. It further included information on the effects of board interventions on formal and informal institutional structures and dynamics within the crop industries in terms of quality, input supply and credit, competition, and fair trade (Kolavalli and Beddies 2004).
- **Household survey of coffee and cotton producers in the major crop producing areas.** Based on the institutional mapping of coffee and cotton, hypotheses were developed relating to institutional develop-

ments and the incidence of benefits for households from service functions of the boards. From these hypotheses, a household survey of coffee and cotton growers, nearly 1,600 each, was designed and carried out from December 2003 to January 2004. Coffee growers were sampled from the three growing zones: the north, including both high and low elevations; the south; and the west, covering both Arabica and Robusta growing areas. The survey of cotton growers was conducted in four districts in the western cotton-growing area. In two of the districts, passbooks, a forced saving scheme,[7] were piloted in the 2001–2 season. The information collected included production and marketing information for one year, socioeconomic aspects of households, and their understanding and awareness of board functions.

■ **Analysis of coffee auction data.** Auction data for this report, which were primarily used to determine changes in product quality, cover coffee sold at the Moshi Auction from 1991 to 1998 and the years 1999–2000, 2002–3, and 2003–4. The data for the first eight years include four years before and four years after the 1994 liberalization permitted private buyers to buy primary processed coffee from growers. The analysis of the data covers only mild arabicas for which classes are determined during liquoring, as the purpose was to examine the quality of coffee supplied to auction by different institutions. The information for the first eight years cover only northern coffee; the information for the three most recent years include both northern and southern coffees.

■ **Stakeholder workshop with coffee and cotton industry stakeholders.** In September 2004, two 1.5-day workshops were carried out with coffee and cotton stakeholders, the two crop boards, and World Bank and European Union (EU) representatives. The coffee stakeholder workshop was attended by 51 representatives of the coffee industry and the board in Moshi; 55 representatives of the cotton industry and the board attended the stakeholder workshop in Mwanza. Workshops aimed to validate key report findings, gain stakeholders' ownership of policy options, and come to a consensus among key stakeholders on viable changes to crop board acts, regulations, and activities of the coffee and cotton boards and their governance (including issues of finance and accountability). The workshops resulted in deliberations and presentations of individual working groups, which have contributed to the current national debate on policy reforms in the sector.

Mixed-method data was collected as follows (box 14.1). Topic guides and thematic sets of questions were used to collect qualitative data. For the

BOX 14.1   Data Collection Methods

The topic guides or thematic sets of questions were used for the key-informant interviews and focus group discussions to solicit information on

- government policies;
- rules and regulations of the boards and governments at various levels relating particularly to the operation of traders, the supply of services, and taxation;
- services provided by private, collective, and nonprofit organizations;
- crop processing and marketing channels;
- input supply and credit arrangements;
- activities of producer and other stakeholder organizations;
- political representation and voice of various stakeholders; and
- research and extension services.

The survey tested several hypotheses. For coffee, the hypotheses addressed

- the ability of and rationale behind a grower's choice of marketing channel and price—innovative channels include farmer groups and independent primary societies;
- the relation between quality, choice of marketing channel, and quality-enhancing practices;
- socioeconomic factors and quality enhancing practices; and
- coverage and welfare implications of the voucher scheme.

For cotton, the hypotheses addressed

- relations among socioeconomic factors, input supply, and access to market information and productivity;
- input supply related functions of the board; and
- the impact of the removal of uniform pricing offered by cooperative societies on the poor.

Within crop-growing areas, districts were selected on the following dimensions:

- agro-climatic and bio-physical factors: suitability of soil and climatic conditions, yields and unique crop husbandry requirements, pest incidence, the state of plantations, and produce quality;
- socioeconomic factors, such as land/asset holdings of growers, dependence on crop income, labor availability, gender relations, ethnic and cultural differences, employment opportunities, and characteristics of local trading communities;
- infrastructure factors: coverage and quality of roads, availability of public transport and communication, availability of public accommodation, density of buying posts, distance to processing facilities, and
- institutional factors: the level of taxation, licensing requirements and fees, and decision-making processes and constraints within the institutional environment.

Source: Authors' compilation.

institutional mapping, the team used open-ended data collection tools and methods to gather information on the institutional arrangements and environments in which the crop industries operate (Strauss and Corbin 1990; DFID and World Bank 2005). Structured questionnaires were used to collect quantitative data from crop-producing households. For the benefit incidence analysis, a structured questionnaire was developed and pre-tested by the Bank and a local consultant team in both coffee- and cotton-growing areas. Site selection within crop-growing areas was based on secondary spatial information that was obtained from the crop boards.

Institutional mapping was conducted for coffee in 11 districts and 5 regions in the north, south, and west, and for cotton in 9 districts in 3 regions in the west. Because the household survey complemented the coffee and cotton mapping, it was conducted in the respective coffee and cotton growing district and regions.

The Choice of Approach

The study employed institutional mapping for its stakeholder and institutional analyses. It also assessed implications and impacts using a benefit incidence analysis to obtain an "incentive-consistent" understanding of the crop industries as systems. Based on the institutional mapping, arrangements for an appropriate regulatory and service role for the crop boards were proposed. For the stakeholder and institutional analyses, the team identified the institutional structures and traced flows of funds, decisionmaking, and information within the coffee and cotton industries, including crop boards, and then surveyed households of producers (Bianchi and Kossoudji 2001; Brinkerhoff and Crosby 2002; North 1990). The objective was to uncover the various interests and incentives of the different actors, and to develop an incentive-consistent story of the relevant institutions, the nature of their influence on various aspects of production and marketing, the reason that outcomes (husbandry practices, processing, quality, prices received, industry development) are the way they are, and the influence of the crop boards. Mapping addressed the following questions:

- What are the institutional gaps in meeting producer needs, in order to generate incentives for technical change?
- How have the boards tried to fill this gap?
- What are the technical and institutional challenges faced by the industry, and are these challenges adequately met by existing institutional arrangements?

■ Do the prevailing institutions favor some groups of producers over others?

■ What are the interests that sustain the existing institutional environment?

The research team used the boards' regulatory and service provision functions as initial points of entry. The team then traced the activities of the boards down to the level of the producer, noting institutional arrangements that exist in the sector across different production regions. Subsequently, the team worked back to the crop boards and other agents at the top of the chains, tracing both these arrangements. Within each arrangement in the crop production and marketing chains, the study assessed

■ the type of information the agents have,

■ the existence and nature of complementary arrangements,

■ the outcomes of exchange for the agents involved, and

■ exposure to various forms of taxation (by boards and local governments) and industry or board regulations.

A household survey of coffee- and cotton-growing producers was conducted to determine the effectiveness and benefits incidence from coffee and cotton boards' services to their constituents. Prior to liberalization, government controlled production tightly, setting prices and supplying inputs. Since liberalization, individual growers and primary cooperative societies have more choice about what kinds of practices to follow or how to market their produce. Knowledge of production practices, the ability to raise resources, an understanding the working of markets, and the ability to take advantage of seasonal price variation all affect returns. Whether poorer households, which are characterized by limited access to resources and information and deficient human capital, do as well as less poor households under these conditions is an important consideration. For the coffee industry, additional hypotheses tested how new institutions that seem to have empowered individuals and groups are performing, particularly in terms of influencing practices adopted by members. The hypotheses to be tested for cotton relate largely to incidence of benefits from services performed by the board.

The Choice of Process

During the scoping mission and for the duration of the work, the World Bank and the EU representatives worked closely with the government task force, a group comprising representatives of the Ministry of Agriculture and Food Security and the Ministry of Cooperatives, which was set up to review the crop boards. The Bank team also established co-operation with the EU as financial partner in the study early on in the process. All three groups contributed to the preparation of the concept note. They defined the study objectives, scope, and methodology used to address local concerns with export crops and reflect local stakeholder inputs and demands. Based on national debate on the magnitude of reform impacts and poverty reduction effects, the Bank decided to change the initial in-depth focus of its concept note from the cashew to the cotton sector to reflect the higher number of smallholder producers in the latter sector. The government also needed to be assured that there was no pre-set agenda that might predetermine study findings. Hence, the government, Bank, and the EU jointly selected coffee and cotton for a detailed analysis based on producer numbers and poverty levels, as well as the urgency of perceived concerns about present board functions. This early and comprehensive stakeholder dialogue and collaboration, where considerable effort went into obtaining agreement on study objectives, scope, and methodology, is seen to have been crucial for the later development of in-country ownership of interim study findings. The government presented the study findings to stakeholders on its own and is advancing some of the proposed reform options.

As a joint government, Bank, and EU product, the study was characterized by extensive collaboration during its design, analysis, and dissemination phases. The inputs into the design provided by the government task force and the EU enabled the team to conduct the analysis per se, and to start building in-country ownership of subsequent study results. During the analysis, close cooperation was essential to gain access to often-sensitive data and to key stakeholders. The team collected and analyzed data in a transparent manner, and made available intermediate reports to all those who participated in the study. During the dissemination phase, close collaboration among the government, the EU, and coffee and cotton industry representatives was crucial for organizing and conducting the stakeholder workshops, encouraging an open policy dialogue, and promoting the implementation of the proposed reform options.

A multidisciplinary team of four local consultants from the University of Dar es Salaam and Sokoine University, along with two international Bank consultants, conducted the study using their expertise in local knowledge, agronomy, rural development, institutional economics, and social analysis. This approach was essential for drawing on local expertise, but also for building in-country ownership of results.

The team conducted the study in several phases, where secondary data analysis and review of key documents informed the design of the qualitative mapping, which in turn informed the quantitative household survey for the coffee and cotton industries. This approach was key to building up incremental knowledge of the different crop industries. At the same time it enabled the process to be flexible enough to adapt the process of data collection and analysis to new insights and implementation issues related to the work, such as delays with procurement of local consultant contracts, or delivery of interim outputs.

The study was conducted through multiple funding sources, comprising Bank budget, trust funds, and EU funds, with the latter covering all local consultant costs. The team completed the data collection and analysis after one fiscal year, in June 2004. This tight time frame proved challenging in view of the often unexpected lengthy EU procurement procedures of local consultant contracts. To accommodate stakeholder schedules, the policy dialogue took place in September 2005 through stakeholder workshops.

From the outset, a stakeholder dialogue for mere dissemination of results at the *end* of the study was not seen as a viable option. Instead, the policy dialogue was initiated during the study design and continued throughout its implementation. During the fieldwork, the study extensively consulted with industry stakeholders such as growers, exporters, local buyers, processors, district commissioners/licensing authorities, relevant board officials, NGOs, Cotton Development Fund (CDF) voucher administrators, and estate owners. This approach was chosen to raise stakeholder awareness of the entire study process including data collection, analysis, and discussion of findings in stakeholder workshops. The approach raised stakeholders' expectations and ensured their contribution to the study during the course of the fieldwork, because they saw potential benefits of reforms. It also ensured that the different stakeholder interests would be represented in the stakeholder workshops. Considerable attention went into preparing the materials for discussion in the workshops to structure the dialogue in such a way that all interests had a voice and could influence the outcomes, empowering stakeholders who are often reluctant to voice their opinions in stakeholder meetings organized by the government.

MAIN FINDINGS

As an upstream PSIA, the study findings have informed the national debate on crop board reforms. The government, the Ministry of Agriculture and Food Security, and the Ministry of Cooperatives are the main stakeholders that are taking forward some of the proposed reforms.[8]

Export Growth and Global Market Challenges

At the global level, the downward secular trend in real-world commodity prices is likely to continue, with continued cyclical volatility. Commodity prices have declined relative to manufacturing for more than a century. Factors contributing to this trend look set to continue, although a reduction in OECD farm subsidies is possible, which could raise commodity prices.

Tanzania's crop industries face the challenge of declining world market prices and changing market opportunities. Eighty-five percent of Tanzania's agricultural export revenues come from five crops: coffee, cashew nuts, cotton, tobacco, and tea. The country's agricultural exports increased rapidly from 1990 to 1997 but then weakened substantially, particularly for cotton and coffee. For instance, coffee contributes some US$115 million to the country's export earnings per year. It also provides income to some 400,000 smallholders who produce 95 percent of the coffee on average plot sizes of 1 to 2 hectares; estates grow the remaining 5 percent. Cotton contributes about US$90 million to export earnings annually and provides employment for approximately 400,000 families; these are mostly smallholders producing cotton on farms of 0.5 to 10 hectares, with the average holding being 1.5 hectares. As for future opportunities for growth in international markets, premiums are large for differentiated products and niche markets; however, these market shares are difficult to penetrate. Prospects also vary by crop. For coffee, the potential for increased demand exists among lower-quality and specialty coffees.

The Evolution of the Crop Boards

The Government of Tanzania has historically taken an active role in agricultural export crop markets. Marketing boards, which operated from the mid-1970s to mid-1980s and were the precursors to crop boards, were created as public agencies to fulfill a range of marketing activities. During marketing liberalization in the 1990s, the government replaced the monopoly marketing boards with crop boards. A first phase of reforms in the early 1990s saw cotton "marketing" functions transferred to cooperative unions. A second phase, which began in 1993–4, saw the government eliminate the monopoly held by the boards and unions for export crops, including coffee and cotton, allowing the private sector to compete with the unions in marketing.

Producer gain was offset after initial supply response. Although official statistics suggest a significant initial supply response after the reforms of the early 1990s, gains in the producer's share of the border price were offset in the late 1990s by an appreciation in the real exchange rate. In these years, coffee saw an overall decline in production but an increase in the supply for Robusta coffee.[9] Seed cotton output almost doubled the year following the reform, only to decline gradually to below pre-reform levels. As for prices, reforms increased the share of the export price received by producers. They also provided farmers with prompt cash payments. Producer price gains, however, have been largely offset by an appreciating exchange rate, which followed sectoral reforms.

Government introduced new regulations after several years of crop marketing in a more liberalized environment. The Coffee and Cotton Board Acts introduced new regulations in 2000–1. These Acts allow each board to carry out activities it deems necessary, advantageous, or proper to benefit the particular commodity industry. Under the legislation, crop boards have the power to inspect, monitor, register, regulate, and license crop varieties, production, marketing, grading, standards, trading, processing, storage, sale, and exporting.

Crop boards have used numerous instruments aimed at enhancing competition, value added, quality management, and credit and input supply. To this end, the boards applied buying rules, introduced a "one license rule" to maintain the integrity of the coffee auction, announced "indicative" prices in all crops (except coffee), and required that growers be registered. Recent exceptions to the one license rule in coffee were introduced.

A stronger role for quality control is also provided by the recently enacted Crop Board Acts (2001, 2003). Interventions for coffee and cotton have included enforcing grading at buying posts for most crops and monitoring the quality of seed cotton processed at ginneries, both of which have involved considerable enforcement. Recently introduced provisions for the direct export of higher-quality coffees—although intended to facilitate the export of estate production—have encouraged its production. Current interventions to improve credit and input supply on the part of boards include the provision in the Act to establish funds and input schemes; the coffee board is offering a repayment guarantee to groups of growers that bring coffee directly to the auction and, in collaboration with the Tanzania Coffee Association, is introducing a coffee voucher program. Boards have no credit programs per se in any of the sectors.

Crop boards are primarily accountable to the Ministry of Agriculture and Food Security rather than to industry stakeholders, but they are financed entirely by stakeholder contributions and income from properties. More than 75 percent of board revenues come from an export levy and from license fees (except in the case of cotton). Expenses are largely administrative.[10] Only the coffee board seemed to meet the requirement of the Act on stakeholder representation, and there is little representation of traders on any of the boards. Members of parliament have been included to represent growers. Crop Acts enable the ministry to exercise considerable control over the boards. And some of the discretionary power and actions of the boards do not necessarily lead to a stable and predictable environment for private sector development.

Institutional Development and Dynamics

A review of current crop industry dynamics revealed various institutional developments, including vertical integration, the emergence of producer organizations, and increased competition in crop buying. Firms that are integrated from crop buying to export have emerged following liberalization, which has led to important investments in crop processing. Crop buying as a sole activity is limited because of the price risks inherent in buying and the inability of firms to raise capital at low costs. The one license rule, which the coffee board introduced to maintain integrity of the coffee auction, has reduced competition in crop buying. Producer organizations have also emerged following government revision of cooperative policy and legislation in 2002. These organizations include farmer groups and cooperative societies that market coffee independently from unions.

Most important among the newly emerging groups are coffee farmer groups that were initiated by private companies and NGOs to bring together producers of good-quality coffee. Although these groups have increased competition and empowered producers, they continue to need technical and organizational support, which are likely to come from vertically integrated firms. Opening up markets benefited farmers because of an increase in private trader competition, which, in turn, raised relative farm-gate prices.[11] Direct sales of coffee to the auction by farmer groups yielded higher returns than other marketing channels. But the analysis also indicates that some farmers prefer selling their products to cooperative societies and unions, largely because these societies and unions stretch payments over two installments as opposed to private traders, who provide a one-off payment. A second installment acts as forced savings to be used later in the year, when income is needed.

Issues related to the decline in cotton quality, which probably started prior to liberalization, remain. The effects of production and processing practices on quality differ from one crop to another, as do overall conditions for quality. For cotton lint, for example, the decline in premiums for cleanliness likely began in the 1980s. According to auction information, coffee quality, however, does not appear to have declined after liberalization. An examination of the class of mild arabica coffees produced in the north zone sold at the Moshi auction for four years before and four years after liberalization suggests that coffee quality—in terms of class alone—has not been affected by liberalization, with estates producing higher-quality coffee than other growers. The quality profile brought to the auction by various institutions also shows that quality overall of coffee has not declined.

Crop-specific production and processing practices have an impact on quality. Agro-ecological and climatic conditions have an impact on all the crops, particularly on the inherent quality of coffee. The type of cotton variety sets an upper bound on quality that can be achieved. Disease control is also important for maintaining quality standards, particularly for cotton. For both coffee and cotton, producer practices largely determine quality; secondary processing has marginal impacts.

In the case of cotton, for example, current pricing does not seem to reward higher quality, with ginners making up in capacity utilization what is lost in quality premium. For coffee, firms trade in both bulk lower-quality coffee as well as lower volume of higher-quality coffee. In coffee, the extent of the adoption of improved grading practices is mixed. Exporters who had established large buying operations indicated that it was difficult to enforce grading because they bought coffee through agents. In sum, grading practices appear to have declined but practical difficulties suggest that enforcing grading is not the answer.

Credit and input use is low, but emerging schemes suggest the potential for improved access in the future. The level of input used is currently low. Coffee and cotton producer surveys indicate that only about 13 percent of the coffee growers used inorganic fertilizers. Application of nutrients for cotton was equally low. The level of use of pesticide on cotton, which is essential for improving yields and quality, is somewhat higher, reflecting its higher impact. Emerging input supply arrangements include guarantees linked to the sale of coffee through the auction; contract farming in cotton, which allows ginners to offer credit and extension services to individuals who can offer collateral; and the use of agents (including private buyers), who are familiar with borrowers and thus able to recover credit. Public programs—such as coffee vouchers and cotton passbooks that allow a portion of growers' sale proceeds to be retained for inputs the following seasons—have not proven to be effective.

Moving Forward: Reforming the Crop Boards

Clearly delineated board functions and accountability structures within the crop industries are crucial for the design of crop board reforms. Such reform is essential for the industries to become competitive in the global market.

The Role and Functions of Crop Boards

Crop boards undertake a mix of public and private activities. Crop boards in Tanzania are performing important public functions and providing some services that producers value and seek to continue. At the same time, the interventionist stance of the boards, particularly with the changes incorporated in the recently passed acts and amendments, often handicaps traders who try to respond as needed to rapid and profound changes in local and global markets. At present, crop boards have a mix of public and private (commercial) activities, including regulation, provision of service, and collection of revenue. The regulatory responsibilities of the crop board can be in conflict with their service functions—for example, regulation of the industry can conflict with the ability to engage in economic activities in competition with the private sector. Conflict of interest can also arise when boards compete in the industries they regulate (table 14.1).

Reforms of the crop boards should thus be designed to have clearly delineated functions and accountability structures within their respective crop industries. Specifically, reforms should be devised to (1) retain the functions and services that the industry stakeholders value, (2) improve accountability and management so that services are provided more cost effectively, and (3) bring about the withdrawal of the boards from interventionist activities that distort the needed institutional evolution of Tanzania's marketing structures.

Options for Reform

Stakeholders and observers consulted in the course of the study raise four concerns about the boards as they operate at present. The first concern is that the boards fulfill dual roles as regulators and participants in markets, and they are thus vulnerable to conflicts of interest. Second, the functions

Table 14.1 Delineation of Public/Private Functions

Public Functions	Associated Private Functions (trade associations, industry boards, producer associations, and so on)	Individual Private Functions (farmers, businesses, and so on)
• Regulation and enforcement (including of licenses) • Basic data collection, analysis, and market information • Contract enforcement • Law and order	• Advocacy for industry interests both domestically and internationally • Forum for problem solving and dispute settlement • Product promotion and quality (where country reputation matters, such as for cotton) • Research and extension (private delivery with public cost sharing) • Crop development (for example, the Cotton Development Fund)	• Production • Quality (such as coffee liquoring) • Marketing • Transportation • Storage • Processing • Input supply (for example, input passbook system, input voucher program)

Source: Authors' compilation.

of the boards currently mix public and private roles without adequate distinction between them. Third, boards are insufficiently accountable to stakeholders in terms of performance and funding. And fourth, present sources of funding are variable, which introduces an element of uncertainty in provision of key services. The persistence of problems that the boards were intended to address, together with the four general concerns noted above, motivate consideration of options for reform of the boards. The overall reform options for delineating private and public financing and management of the crop board functions, which are put forward for consideration, are based on the review of institutional developments in the four export crop industries.

Option 1: Boards Are Publicly Financed with a Mandate to Focus on Public Services

With this option, the source of financing would change from the export levy to the government budget. If the export levy were retained and converted into an export tax flowing into the general revenues, then the industry would not realize any savings. If the levy were dropped, then producers and traders of the studied export crops would save about US$2.5 million per year, which would be paid by other taxpayers. The shift to financing by the government budget would add some stability to the revenues of the boards. The functions of the board would be restricted to public functions (perhaps including other activities that meet the criteria for public goods) (see column 1 of table 14.1). The boards would not engage in associated private or individual private activities (table 14.1, columns 2 and 3). This option pursued alone would create a risk that the activities best undertaken jointly by private entities may not be undertaken at all, since it is not certain that the private entities would be able to overcome the barriers to coordination required for joint actions. Even under this option, the board may provide any coordination that the private entities may feel is necessary, utilizing funds from user contributions or other sources.

Option 2: Boards Are Privately Financed with a Mandate to Focus on Associated and Individual Private Services

Under this option, the respective industries would manage the boards, which would be financed through the export levy. This would require the Ministry of Agriculture and Food Security to relinquish control of the boards to the industry (farmers, traders, exporters). The board would in effect become an industry association. Public functions such as industry regulation and data collection would be transferred to government agencies such as the Ministry of Agriculture and Food Security and/or the Ministry of Cooperatives and Marketing and financed through the government budget. The ministry, however, would have the option of outsourcing provision of some of these functions to the industry organization. The boards would become more accountable to their constituents and financiers. The industry would determine the levy commensurate with the level of services desired. The risk associated with this option is that public functions passed to the government might not be accorded the budget required to fulfill them. Moreover, although the board would be accountable to constituents, not all of those constituents have the same interests, and the board would have to use a structure of governance that avoids capture by particular interests. This option would be suitable where there is considerable congruence of interests among stakeholders and where industry organizations have a balanced representation of stakeholders and the capability of taking on development activities.

Option 3: The Boards Are Jointly Financed, Providing Associated Private Services Financed by a Levy and Contracting for Public Services

Under this option, the boards would undertake a combination of public and associated private activities not dissimilar to some of the current board functions, but with a clearer delineation of the public and the private functions. Under this option, the boards would essentially become industry associations that meet the needs of their members and that also are contracted by the government, on a performance basis, to undertake certain public functions that are vitally important to their constituents and members. The levy would finance associated private activities (table 14.1, column 2), and public revenues from other sources would finance public functions (table 14.1, column 1) contracted to the boards for implementation. Boards would still experience variability in financing, but would have two flows of financing and hence greater flexibility to manage the variability. If the boards were contracted under competitive bidding to undertake public functions, they would have to meet agreed-upon standards of service in order to keep the contracts. The composition and internal rules of governance of the boards would be enhanced to increase oversight and accountability. This option offers compelling benefits. However, since it looks on the surface like a retention of the status quo, there is a risk that reforms would be taken forward in name only, and not in fact.

Option 4: The Boards Remain as They Are

There is also the option of "no change." This option would be based on a view that the costs of the boards are justified because there are no alternative ways to provide the benefits they deliver. This study has shown that alternative approaches to providing many of the present services offered by the boards are not only possible, but in fact they are already on the ground and competing with activities of the boards. If there is no change, then the problems highlighted above will continue to the detriment of the sectors. Hence, no change is not really an option but is presented here to provide a baseline.

Implications for Specific Boards

Based on the analysis above and the relative importance of the public, private, and associated private functions in the coffee and cotton subsectors, the study team recommended implementing Option 1 for the coffee industry and Option 3 for the cotton industry (table 14.2).[12]

Table 14.2 Activities, Revenue Sources, and Accountability Measures under Proposed Reforms

Board/Option	Activities	Sources of revenue	Accountability measure
Coffee: Option 1	• Public goods, including dissemination of price information • Management of auction • Liquoring service • Associated activities as PPPs	• Property income • Budget support • PPP supported by donors or budget	• Accountability to government and stakeholders • Strict accountability to stakeholders for PPPs
Cotton: Option 3	• Public goods, including dissemination of price information • Classing services • Quality pilots, through inspection at ginneries • Coordination of input supply	• Property income • Budget support • Levy • Budget/donor support for pilots	• Accountability to government and stakeholders • Stakeholder-controlled units under the board to manage industry development and input funds

Source: Authors' compilation
Note: PPPs = public-private partnerships.

Coffee Board Recommendations

The key reform recommendations for the coffee industry are concerned with market regulations and input supply. They include

■ making the coffee auction voluntary by removing the one license rule,
■ reducing all license fees to the cost of recovery by eliminating discretionary power of the boards to issue and revoke licenses, and
■ discontinuing the input voucher scheme.

Other recommended reforms include permitting those who have invested in common pulping units to purchase unprocessed coffee cherries from producers, removing the requirement of registering all growers, shifting from quality and grading inspection to ensuring accurate weights and measures, and ensuring an effective legal framework for branding and appellation.

Reform Option 1 appears suitable for coffee because institutional options for quality enhancement and input or credit are already available to growers, with the potential for innovative arrangements to emerge with fewer constraints on the scope of activities of private traders. Moreover, the developments already present in the sector— particularly the emergence of producer organizations—make it feasible to overcome free-rider problems in developing effective input supply systems and maintaining quality, thus reducing the need for public coordination.

Cotton Board Recommendations

Key recommendations for the cotton sector emphasize regulation, quality management, and input schemes. These recommendations include

- reducing license fees, ceasing setting indicative prices, and providing market information throughout the season;
- focusing on cotton inspection at ginneries rather than buying centers;
- introducing innovative pilot initiatives for quality enhancement; and
- reducing the role of the board in the management of the Cotton Development Fund (CDF) and input passbook scheme.

Another recommendation is to achieve greater producer representation in the Tanzania Cotton Association, which is primarily an interest group of cotton buyers, ginners, and exporters. Reform Option 3 appears suitable for cotton because of the need for coordination to overcome problems associated with quality and input or credit supply. Innovative pilots are needed to learn more about institutional arrangements conducive to managing quality. Seed supply continues to require public coordination. The forced savings programs that seem to be critical to making inputs available to producers (such as the passbook program) can be made more effective by enhancing stakeholder control over these programs.

The Debate of Stakeholder Workshops on Proposed Reform Options

In the coffee workshop, four working groups discussed the issues of

- regulation, licensing, and market functions;
- quality management;
- input supply and credit; and
- associated private activities and board governance.[13]

The coffee workshop came to a consensus on a limited role for the board as executor for a specific and defined function with associated standards for performance. Assigned by the public sector and the industry, the board would have a constructive role in enhancing the competitiveness of the coffee sector. This would imply that the board would be accountable to government and the industry, which includes smallholders. It would also imply that the deliverables are specified and budgeted, financial controls and reporting procedures are imposed, budget is modest and reflects lean staffing and defined scope, and that public financing for public functions is delegated to the board. Finally, it would imply that a cess or levy for functions is delegated by the industry, and that the size of the levy and the share that is contributed by industry is reduced, given the present incentive environment and importance of coffee to smallholders.

Based on the workshop consensus, the next steps suggested were a reconsideration of the content of the Acts; a review of the composition and membership of the board; a clarification of the specific work program of the board for the coming period, including deliverables and standards; a consideration of budget and source of funds; and a review of the level of cess and levies. The workshop did not reach consensus on the substance of the public functions. Specifically, the nature of the needed regulatory regime for the industry was seen as an issue for public policy rather than for the boards.

For the cotton workshop, five working groups discussed issues of

- achieving a robust industrial structure capable of meeting global challenges,
- regulating grading practices,
- improving cotton seed supplies,
- improving insecticide supply through CDF/passbook and facilitating contract farming, and
- activities, composition, finances, and accountability of the board.[14]

Stakeholders agreed on the need to rationalize licensing procedures, and to continue the public coordination of seed supply. Views were exchanged on regulating grading practices, rationalizing buying centers, and increasing market information through fortnightly price announcements. The workshop also discussed organizing farmer groups; managing and enhancing the quality and availability of cotton seed; finding sustainable funding for research and development; the status of the CDF; and cotton board functions, management, and financing.

IMPACT OF THE PSIA

The reform will have different impacts on the different industry stake-holders, in-country dialogue, and Bank operations.

Policy Dialogue and Public Debate In-Country

This study is expected to inform the future functions of the coffee and cotton boards. Using a process of active policy dialogue at the outset—with the preparation of the Concept Note in August 2003—and continuing this dialogue throughout the study implementation ensured a transparent approach and in-country ownership of results. For instance, the interim outputs and the final report were disseminated to industry stakeholders by government officials on behalf of the joint team of government, the EU, and the Bank. Presenting various reform options, the study contributed substantially to the upstream policy dialogue on the planned crop board reform in the country. The ongoing dialogue and close collaboration among study partners facilitated the process, and allowing for an open debate about different and challenging reform options.

The coffee and cotton stakeholder workshops resulted in a number of issues being tabled to ensure a clearer delineation of roles, functions, and funding of the boards. The government considered the proposed reform options and weighed their respective costs and benefits (see table 14.3). Current actions taken include a cabinet decision to

- abolish the levy that financed the running costs of the boards and replace it with budget financing;
- abolish the crop development funds;
- improve the quality of extension; and
- undertake further analysis on some specific elements of reform, such as a review of one license rule in coffee industry.

The government has developed a crop board action plan that, if implemented, would lead to substantial reforms.

Effects of the Reform on Industry Stakeholders

The lines that divide winners and losers, and therefore the interests that may come into conflict, are not always clear or consistent in all the reforms. As the choice of reform options is still subject to ongoing national debate,

Table 14.3 Options for the Reform of Tanzania's Crop Boards

Proposed Options	Benefits	Costs
Coffee: Publicly financed with a redefined mandate to focus on public services	• Saves the industries, and ultimately farmers about US$2.5 million annually which will be paid by other taxpayers. • Adds more stability to financing of boards.	• Possible lapse in provision of associated private support
Cotton: Jointly financed with the provision of associated private services and contracting for Public Services	• Burden of private financing for public service provision reduced • Provides accountability of the Boards to industry stakeholders • Provides more stable financing for public goods • Greater efficiency of resource use	• Possible retention of de facto status quo despite decision to change • Possible capture by particular interests within the Boards, as above
No change	• Avoid the risks of implementing inappropriate policies	• Present concerns remain unaddressed • Continued cost to the industry, including farmers of US$2.5 million with lack of accountability of the boards

Source: Authors' compilation.
Note: The larger study identifies options for reform for the cotton, cashew, coffee, and tea sectors.

specific impacts on different stakeholders cannot be delineated. Hence, overall impacts are presented below.

Impact of the Reform on the Producers

Any division between small and large producers would be of obvious interest. As the boards' direct participation in marketing has been excluded by earlier reforms, this round of reforms sought to change the regulatory environment for the private sector and to improve effectiveness of the boards' delivery of key services. Key outcomes of these reforms— improved access to market information, increased competition, and greater accountability of service providers—will potentially benefit smallholders as much as large producers. Nevertheless, a section of the stakeholders expressed concerns that some of the market reforms, such as the proposal to make the coffee auction voluntary, entailed risks of limiting access to markets for small producers under some conditions. The proposal to finance regulatory functions of the boards through budgets rather than through a cess on produce, however, elicits supports from all stakeholders, particularly the producers.

Impact of the Reform on the Private Traders, Cooperatives, and Processors

Another divide exists between cooperative societies and private traders. The cooperatives—many of which had scaled down or closed their operations after market deregulation—perceive that deregulation generally broadens opportunities for private traders. Policy makers are therefore mindful of the effects that proposed reforms are likely to have on the competitiveness of cooperative societies. Although most producers welcome increased competition for their produce and have demonstrated their capacity to select options that yield the highest returns, a significant section of producers remains loyal to cooperative societies. Apart from any nonpecuniary benefit that they may obtain from belonging to cooperatives, producers appreciate the "second payments"—a tradition they have become accustomed to that provides an income source later in year (a form of forced savings).

Having been used to stable prices offered by cooperatives, some producers also feel that traders are unscrupulous and indifferent to pursuing national interests, such as maintaining the quality of exports. Local coffee buyers who wish to export would benefit from the removal of the one license rule for coffee, allowing greater access to cheaper finance and that would enable them to reduce their exposure to price risks. Similarly, larger and more reputable cotton-processing firms look more favorably toward measures that seek to control the quality of seed cotton marketed in the country or measures that collect taxes more effectively from processors. Smaller, local firms often perceive a freer regulatory environment to favor global firms. These smaller firms harbor concerns that they would be overwhelmed by competition. However, the measures to reduce licensing fees and streamline procedures are likely also to reduce entry costs, which would enable many small local buyers to enter the market. Stakeholder views converge regarding poorly administered programs, such as the voucher scheme, which are uniformly disliked.

Effects of the Reform on Bank-Financed Operations

The study supports the PAF actions, as highlighted in the first section of this chapter. These actions in turn formed the benchmarks for the Poverty Reduction Support Credits. The government, building on the results of the larger study, committed to develop and implement a reform strategy. The strategy was to apply initially to two crop boards, consistent with Agricultural Sector Development Strategy. Following cabinet approval, implementation of crop board reforms are envisaged to be monitored in subsequent PRSCs. The study was conducted jointly with government, the European Union, and the Bank with participation from civil society and joint financing from the donor community.

LESSONS LEARNED

- **Multistakeholder participation requires a different way of doing business, with clients and donors seen as true partners.** A joint government-, Bank-, and donor-produced PSIA takes significant time, effort, and flexibility to accommodate the different perspectives, interests, and bureaucratic requirements of all partners. A new approach to working relations was necessary to allow for mutual understanding among stakeholders as partners at different governance levels. Throughout the process, decision making was subject to negotiation and intermediation; thus timeframes and resources for delivering outputs had to be stretched to accommodate multistakeholder participation. The coordination of multiple partners and the resulting procurement procedures caused delay in the fieldwork and data analysis, which made it challenging to work with the Bank's conventional fiscal-year delivery targets. The partnership, however, has vastly contributed to the ownership of interim results and to the future implementation of policy options.

- **Local capacity building is essential, but it can contribute to delays.** The team designed the PSIA to be conducted with a local research team, with the objective of contributing to capacity building in Tanzania. However, the level of effort and resources required to work with local researchers while ensuring quality control of their inputs was significant.

- **Good analytical work is complex and methodologically challenging.** Analytical work to support decision making that meets the information needs of various stakeholders is often complex and methodologically challenging, which can imply extra costs. A mix of methodologies may need to be used depending on the nature of information needed—for example, institutional mapping may be most appropriate to understand the potential for institutional development, economic models may be appropriate to quantify relationships and impacts on various stakeholders, and surveys may be appropriate to estimate benefit incidence. Substantial effort is needed to understand the information needs of various stakeholders, develop the information and help them make informed decisions.

- **The analysis phase of the PSIA is only the beginning. The real challenge lies in policy implementation.** A key stage of the PSIA—the implementation of the proposed reform options—actually begins after the report is completed. The required funding for implementation needs to be adequately budgeted, either through the government budget or through support from development partners. The implementation of policy options is also subject to frequently vested and often conflicting interests between the different stakeholder groups, even within one group, such as government (for example, different ministries can have different incentives). Hence, when designing PSIAs, greater attention to the process character of the PSIA is needed to plan for adequate resources and timeframes for dissemination, policy dialogue, and reform implementation. Given the often-limited budgets for analytical work in the World Bank's Africa region, mainstreaming the PSIA in operations is a challenge for country units.

- **Policy reforms are ultimately political, so working on PSIAs from a pure technical angle is often insufficient.** There has been a fairly long lag between the completion of the study and the recent cabinet decision and government action plan for implementation the reforms. It is important to try to understand and not underestimate the interests vested in maintaining the status quo of particular policies. Engaging these key stakeholders at the political level in the process could reduce delays in policy decision and implementation.

NOTES

1. The Bank team consisted of Maria Correia, Robert Townsend, Shashidhara Kolavalli, and Sabine Beddies. Local and international partners were the Government of Tanzania, the European Commission, the University of Dar es Salaam, and Sokoine University. Financial support from the World Bank, the Norwegian and Finnish–supported Trust Fund for Environmentally and Socially Sustainable Development (TFESSD), and the European Union are gratefully acknowledged.

2. Members and chairpersons of boards are appointed by and accountable to the Minister of Agriculture and Food Security. The members are usually selected from among those that are recommended by various stakeholder organizations.

3. The study builds on previous research carried out by the World Bank, including "Tanzanian Agricultural Exports: Challenges and Constraints in a Global Environment" by Don Mitchell and John Baffes.

4. *Institutional mapping* is defined as the identification of static structures and the tracing of dynamic flows of decision making, resources, and information.

5. Site selection within crop-growing areas was guided by secondary spatial information obtained from the boards and included the following dimensions: (1) agro-climatic and bio-physical factors, (2) socioeconomic factors, (3) infrastructure, and (4) institutional factors.

6. The methodology developed during the coffee and cotton mapping guided the mapping of the cashew and tea industries.

7. Passbooks are booklets to keep records of a farmer's cotton sales and the corresponding amount he or she could claim in inputs the following season. In 2003–4, the board issued passbooks to force the saving of a portion of the sale proceeds for the purchase of inputs the following season.

8. There have been several changes to the ministerial structures following the elections in December 2005.

9. There are three kinds of coffee (mild Arabica, hard Arabica, and Robusta) emerging from two types of coffee plants (Arabica and Robusta). About two thirds of Tanzania's total production is Arabica coffee grown in Arusha and Kilimanjaro regions in the north, and Mbeya and Ruvuma regions in the south. The remainder is Robusta coffee, which is grown in the lake region of Kagera, and Mbeya and Ruvuma regions in the south.

10. The larger study, which analyzed the coffee, cotton, cashew, and tea industries, found, that taken together, expenditures of the four boards amount to about US$5 million annually.

11. Farm-gate prices are the prices that farmers receive for the commodities they market without transportation or processing costs.

12. The larger study recommends Option 1 for the cashew industry and Option 2 for the tea industry.

13. In the coffee workshop, regulation, licensing, and market functions were discussed in view of compulsory and blind auctions, the one license rule, direct export for specialty coffee, licensing regulations, restrictions on cherry buying, and registration of coffee growers. Quality management was discussed in terms of inspections at buying posts, training in quality management, liquoring services, and indirect support to producer group formation. Input supply and credit were discussed in view of input supply, credit, vouchers, and payment through the board. Finally, associated private activities and board governance were discussed concerning the collection of a cess for research, promotion of coffee, extension, and supply of planting material.

14. In the cotton workshop, a robust industrial structure was discussed in terms of the reduction of licensing requirements and level of license fees, the effects of cess/taxes on industry structure, producer empowerment through access to improved information, and producer registration requirements. The regula-

tion of grading practices was discussed in view of rigorous seed-cotton quality checks at ginneries rather than inspections at both villages and ginneries, and efficient third-party quality inspections. Improving cotton seed supplies was debated in terms of the purity of available varieties, adequate and accountable varietal research, and limitations to seed production commercialization. Improving insecticide supply was debated in view of producer voice in CDF decision making and responsiveness to the needs of the fund, a reorganization of insecticide distribution and private sector delivery of pesticide, and limitations to coordination among seed-cotton buyers to prevent side selling and to facilitate contract farming. Activities, composition, finances, and accountability of the board were discussed regarding the role, organization, and funding of extension; stakeholder representation on the board and in the industry; and appropriate sources of finance and accountability.

REFERENCES

Baffes, J. 2001. Tanzania's Tea Sector: Constraints and Challenges in a Global Environment. The World Bank, Washington, DC.

———. 2002. "Tanzania's Cotton Sector: Constraints and Challenges in a Global Environment." Africa Region Working Paper Series 42, World Bank, Washington, DC.

———. 2003. "Tanzania's Coffee Sector: Constraints and Challenges in a Global Environment." Africa Region Working Paper Series 56, World Bank, Washington, DC.

Bianchi, R. R., and S. A. Kossoudji. 2001. "Interest Groups and Organizations as Stakeholders." Social Development Paper 36, World Bank, Washington, DC.

Brinkerhoff, D., and B. L. Crosby. 2002. *Managing Policy Reform: Concepts and Tools for Decision-Makers in Developing and Transition Countries.* Bloomfield, CT: Kumarian Press.

Carr, M. K. V. et al. 2003. *Tanzania Coffee Research Institute: Strategic Action Plan 2003–2008, Contributing Towards a Profitable and Sustainable Coffee Industry in Tanzania.* TaCRI and Cranfield University.

DFID (Department for International Development), and World Bank. 2005. *Tools for Institutional, Political and Social Analysis in PSIA: A Sourcebook.* Washington, DC: World Bank. http://web.worldbank.org/WBSITE/EXTERNAL/TOPICS/EXTSOCIALDEVELOPMENT/EXTTOPPSISOU/0,,menuPK:1424015~pagePK:64168427~piPK:64168435~theSitePK:1424003,00.html

European Union. 2003. *Draft Final Report: Appraisal Project Proposal of Seed Multiplication and Distribution in Western Cotton Growing Area.* Consultant report.

Gibbon, P. 1999. "Free Competition Without Sustainable Development? Tanzanian Cotton Sector Liberalization, 1994/95 to 1997/98." *The Journal of Development* Studies 36 (1): 128–50.

Kolavalli, S. and S. Beddies. 2004. *Report on Phase One: Institutional Mapping of Coffee and Cotton, Reform of the Tanzania Cotton, Coffee, Cashew and Tea Boards: Options and Implications for Other Crop Boards.* World Bank, Washington, DC.

Larsen, M. N. 2003a. "Re-Regulating a Failed Market: The Tanzanian Cotton Sector 1999–2002." IIS/GI. Kongevej Working Paper 03.2, Institute for International Studies, Copenhagen.

———. 2003b. Quality Standard setting in the Global Cotton Chain and Cotton Sector Reforms in Sub-Saharan Africa. IIS/GI. Kongevej Working paper 03.7, Institute for International Studies: Copenhagen.

Maro, W. E. 2003. "Tanzania Country Report: 2001/02. Competition and Coordination in Cotton Market System in Southern and Eastern Africa." Economic Research Bureau, University of Dar es Salaam.

Maro, W. E., and C. Poulten. 2002. "System Overview Report for Tanzania." Economic Research Bureau, University of Dar es Salaam and Imperial College at Wye, UK.

Mitchell, D. 2001. "The Tanzanian Cashew Market." Development Economics Vice Presidency, World Bank, Washington, DC.

Mitchell, D., and J. Baffes. 2002. "Tanzanian Agricultural Exports: Challenges and Constraints in a Global Environment." World Bank, Washington, DC.

North, D. 1990. *Institutions, Institutional Change and Economic Performance.* New York: Cambridge University Press.

Ponte, S. 2001. "Coffee Markets in East Africa: Local Responses to Global Challenges or Global Responses to Local Challenges?" CDR Working Paper 01.5, Centre for Development Research, Copenhagen.

———. 2002. "Standards. Trade and Equity: Lessons for the Specialty Coffee Industry." CDR Working Paper 01.13, Centre for Development Research, Copenhagen.

Ponte, S., and F. Kuwuma. 2003. "Coffee Certification in Uganda: A Feasibility Study (first draft)." Study commissioned by DFID and the Uganda Coffee Development Authority.

Poulten, C., P. Gibbon, B. Hanyani-Mlambo, J. Kydd, W. Maro, M. Nylandsted Larsen, A. Osorio, D. Tschirley, and B. Zulu. 2003. "Competition and Coordination in Liberalized African Cotton Market Systems." *World Development* 32 (3): 519–36.

Strauss, A., and J. Corbin. 1990. *Basics of Qualitative Research: Grounded Theory Procedures and Techniques.* Newbury Park, CA: Sage Publications.

TCB (Tanzania Coffee Board). 2001. *Coffee Sector Strategy.* Dar es Salaam, Tanzania: Business Care Services, Ltd.

———. 2002. *Action Plan on: The Implementation of the Coffee Sector Strategy 2002–2006.* Moshi: Tanzania Coffee Board

———. 2003. Coffee Industry Act (no. 23 of 2001). The Tanzania Coffee Industry Regulations, 2003.

Temu, A. A, A. Winter-Nelson, and P. Garcia. 2001. "Market Liberalisation, Vertical Integration and Price Behaviour in Tanzania's Coffee Auction." *Development Policy Review* 19 (2): 205–22.

Yin, R. K. 1994. *Case Study Research, Design and Methods,* Thousand Oaks, CA: Sage Publications.